PARLIAMENTARY HISTORY RECORD SERIES

Volume 1

TORY AND WHIG

The parliamentary papers of Edward Harley and William Hay offer a unique insight into the politics of the 1730s and 1740s. Their journals are two of the most important sources for the debates in the house of commons during the latter part of Sir Robert Walpole's premiership, and provide two contrasting perspectives. Harley was a leading figure in the tory party, and a fierce critic of the whig ministry; Hay was an independently-minded but committed ministerialist. Both journals extend beyond the fall of Walpole in 1742; Hay gives an account of events in the Commons, while Harley, who succeeded to the earldom of Oxford in 1741, has a rare insider's view into proceedings in the house of lords during the whig supremacy. Also presented in this edition are Harley and Hay's other known surviving parliamentary papers. The extended introduction places the texts in context, examining the careers of Harley and Hay.

Dr STEPHEN TAYLOR is lecturer in history, University of Reading; Dr CLYVE JONES is assistant librarian, Institute of Historical Research, University of London.

PARLIAMENTARY HISTORY RECORD SERIES

ISSN 1368–5375

General Editor: Mark Knights

This is an occasional series of primary documents relating to the parliamentary history of the British Isles. It aims to include material from all periods about the parliaments of England, Scotland and Ireland. The texts will be edited by both established and younger scholars, and will appear with full notes as well as detailed and discursive introductions. The series will be invaluable for anyone interested in political history, but will also have a wider appeal as a source for social, economic, religious and literary developments. Enquiries about the series are welcome and should be directed to the General Editor at the School of History, University of East Anglia, Norwich.

TORY AND WHIG

THE PARLIAMENTARY PAPERS OF
EDWARD HARLEY, 3rd EARL OF OXFORD, AND
WILLIAM HAY, M.P. FOR SEAFORD
1716–1753

Edited by

STEPHEN TAYLOR
University of Reading

and

CLYVE JONES
Institute of Historical Research
University of London

THE BOYDELL PRESS
THE PARLIAMENTARY HISTORY YEARBOOK TRUST

First published 1998

A publication of the Parliamentary History Yearbook Trust
published by The Boydell Press
an imprint of Boydell & Brewer Ltd
PO Box 9, Woodbridge, Suffolk IP12 3DF, UK
and of Boydell & Brewer Inc.
PO Box 41026, Rochester, NY 14604–4126, USA

ISBN 0 85115 589 8

A catalogue record for this book is available
from the British Library

Library of Congress Catalog Card Number: 97-15604

This publication is printed on acid-free paper

Printed in Great Britain by
St Edmundsbury Press Ltd, Bury St Edmunds, Suffolk

For
Bernard and Margaret Taylor

CONTENTS

LIST OF TABLES, MAPS AND ILLUSTRATIONS

This book is produced with the assistance of
a grant from Isobel Thornley's Bequest to
the University of London and a loan
from the Marc Fitch Fund.

ACKNOWLEDGMENTS

It is now ten years since we began work on this project. It was originally conceived much more narrowly, as an edition of the parliamentary journal of the tory, Edward Harley, third earl of Oxford. But it became apparent at an early stage that it would be attractive to publish together the two major unpublished parliamentary diaries for the 1730s, and thus we decided to include also the journal kept by William Hay, whig M.P. for Seaford. Inevitably, during such a long period of gestation, we have accumulated many debts. In the first place, we are grateful to Cambridge University Library, Northamptonshire Record Office, the British Library Board, Hereford Record Office, the Public Record Office and the Bodleian Library for permission to reproduce documents in their possession. Without their co-operation this edition would not have been possible. However, we owe a particular debt to the late Mr Christopher Harley for his hospitality and his generosity in allowing us to make use of the manuscripts which survive at Brampton Bryan. In addition, we have made use of various other collections in the course of our research, and we would like to thank Gloucester Public Library, Hereford City Library, the Huntington Library, the Lewis Walpole Library, Warwickshire County Record Office and especially East Sussex Record Office for their assistance. References to the Stuart Papers in the Royal Archives, Windsor Castle, are made by the gracious permission of Her Majesty The Queen. We are grateful too to the History of Parliament Trust for permission to make use of unpublished material in which it holds the copyright. Numerous scholars have helped us by providing references or answering queries, among whom Miss Melanie Barber, Professor Derek Beales, Dr Judith Curthoys, Dr Diana Greenway, Dr Stuart Handley, Dr Julian Hoppit, Dr John Jones, Dr Mark Knights, Dr Chris Kyle, Mr Peter Salt and Dr David Wykes merit special mention. Mr Christopher Whittick has not only provided invaluable help in our research into the Hay family, but he has also commented in detail on the notes to Hay's letters, saving us from many errors. We owe a particular debt to Andrew Hanham, David Hayton, Joanna Innes and John Walsh, who all undertook the burden of reading and commenting on part or all of the introduction. Liz Griffiths gave invaluable assistance in preparing the genealogical tables. We would like to thank Alasdair Hawkyard for compiling the index and Mrs Carol Mackay and Mrs Elizabeth Berry for typing it. It was possible for us to make use of papers at the Huntington Library, San Marino, California, and at the Lewis Walpole Library, Farmington, Connecticut, thanks to the award of Visiting Fellowships to Clyve Jones and Stephen Taylor respectively. In addition, Stephen Taylor would like to thank the Master and Fellows of Jesus College, Cambridge, and the Research Board of the University of Reading, who both contributed towards the costs of the research for the volume. He also owes a debt to the Humanities Research Board of the British Academy for granting him a period of research leave, during which the introduction was written.

October 1996   S.J.C.T.
                                                                                    C.J.

ABBREVIATIONS

B.I.H.R.	*Bulletin of the Institute of Historical Research*
B.L.	British Library
Bodl.	Bodleian Library, Oxford
Brent	Colin Brent, *Georgian Lewes, 1714–1830. The Heyday of a County Town* (Lewes, 1993)
brig.-gen.	brigadier-general
bt.	baronet
capt.	captain
c. in c.	commander in chief
Chandler	*The History and Proceedings of the House of Commons from the Restoration to the Present Time* (14 vols., 1742–4)
C.J.	*The Journals of the House of Commons*
Cobbett	*The Parliamentary History of England from the Earliest Period to the Year 1803* (36 vols., 1806–20)
col.	colonel
Colley	Linda Colley, *In Defiance of Oligarchy. The Tory Party, 1714–60* (Cambridge, 1982)
comm.	commissioner
Complete Peerage	G.E. C[okayne], *The Complete Peerage*, ed. Vicary Gibbs *et al.* (13 vols., 1910–40)
Dalton	*George the First's Army 1714–1727*, ed. Charles Dalton (2 vols., 1910–12)
D.N.B.	*Dictionary of National Biography*
EH	Edward Harley, 3rd earl of Oxford
E.S.T.C.	Eighteenth-Century Short Title Catalogue
gen.	general
H.J.	*Historical Journal*
H.M.C.	Historical Manuscripts Commission
H.L.R.O.	House of Lords Record Office
HoP	History of Parliament
Lambert	*The House of Commons Sessional Papers for the Eighteenth Century*, ed. Sheila Lambert (147 vols., Wilmington, Del., 1975)

[I]	Irish/Ireland
ld. lt.	lord lieutenant
lieut.	lieutenant
L.J.	*The Journals of the House of Lords*
lt.-gen.	lieutenant-general
lt.-gov.	lieutenant-governor
maj.-gen.	major-general
matric.	matriculated
Musgrave, *Obituary*	Sir William Musgrave, *Obituary Prior to 1800* (Harleian Soc. XLIV–XLIX, 6 vols., 1899–1901)
Namier and Brooke	*The House of Commons 1754–1790*, ed. Sir Lewis Namier and John Brooke (3 vols., 1964)
P.R.O.	Public Record Office
regt.	regiment
R.O.	Record Office
Sedgwick	*The House of Commons 1715–1754*, ed. Romney Sedgwick (2 vols., 1970)
Statutes of the Realm	*The Statutes of the Realm from Original Records* [ed. A. Ludders *et al.*] (11 vols., 1810–28)
Torrington	*House of Lords Sessional Papers*, ed. R.W. Torrington (60 vols., Dobbs Ferry, N.Y., 1971–7)
V.C.H.	Victoria County History
WH	William Hay

INTRODUCTION TO THE TEXTS

In some respects the reigns of George I and George II are well provided with accounts of parliamentary proceedings. This period saw the development of regular reporting of debates in the press, notably in the monthly periodicals *The Political State of Great Britain* (1711–37), *The Historical Register* (1716–38), *The Gentleman's Magazine* (1731–) and *The London Magazine* (1732–). These magazines, which tended to copy reports from each other, provided the basis for the collections of Richard Chandler and Ebenezer Timberland, published in 1741, and, ultimately, for Cobbett's *Parliamentary History* in the early nineteenth century.[1] However, this contemporary press reporting has numerous shortcomings. It should certainly not be regarded as an eighteenth-century *Hansard*. Above all, the reports are very incomplete. The editors of the magazines tended to concentrate on providing accounts of a relatively small number of often controversial debates. Thus, press reporting of parliament in the early eighteenth century is nowhere near as full and detailed as that of the *Parliamentary Register* in the 1780s and 1790s. Moreover, as Mary Ransome has pointed out, the published debates of the early eighteenth century are of variable quality and need to be used with care. Occasionally, M.P.s appear to have sent their own speeches for publication – Edward Harley's intervention in the debate on the motion for Walpole's removal in 1741 is a good example.[2] But generally the magazines were dependent on notes taken by people who gained admission to the galleries. Before 1738 their reports 'probably give a fair indication of the arguments used on both sides, though it would be unwise to assign any particular argument to any particular speaker'. But, after the resolution of the Commons against the reporting of debates in 1738, the magazines' sources of information dried up and it becomes difficult to judge when the reports 'are fictitious and when genuine', making it 'unwise to assume that they do more than show the prevailing political opinions of the time'.[3]

The limitations of the published sources mean that historians of the early eighteenth century are dependent on manuscript accounts not merely to provide the flavour of proceedings in parliament, but also for much of their information about what was said. Unfortunately, relatively little material of this kind has survived. The letters of M.P.s and peers and of visitors to parliament often contain good accounts of individual debates, as is revealed in Edward Harley's papers printed below. It would be easy to construct a lengthy list of such correspondence, but two of the richest sources are

---

[1] *The History and Proceedings of the House of Commons from the Restoration to the Present Time* (14 vols., 1742–4) [known as *Chandler's Debates*]; *The History and Proceedings of the House of Lords, from the Restoration in 1660, to the Present Time* (8 vols., 1742–3) [known as *Timberland's Debates*]; *The Parliamentary History of England from the Earliest Period to the Year 1803* (36 vols., 1806–20) [known as Cobbett].

[2] Cf. Cobbett, XI, 1268–9 with below pp. 50–1, 250–1. Another example is Sir John St Aubyn's speech on the Quakers Tithe Bill, first published in the *Gentleman's Magazine*, VI (1736), 365. See also B.L., Stowe MS 354, f. 240: J. Howe to ?, 31 July 1739.

[3] Mary Ransome, 'The Reliability of Contemporary Reporting of the Debates of the House of Commons, 1727–1741', *B.I.H.R.*, XIX (1942–3), 67–79 (quotation at p. 79). The magazine reports were still unreliable in 1748. Bishop Secker's speech during the committee on the Bill for Disarming the Scottish Highlands on 10 May 1748, for example, bears little resemblance to the report of it originally published in the *London Magazine*. Compare Cobbett, XIV, 269–76, with Lambeth Palace Library, MS 1349, pp. 159–66.

probably the French ambassador's reports in the 1730s and the Stuart papers at Windsor Castle.[4] However, the most important manuscript sources are the diaries and journals kept by members of parliament. These are often a little disappointing in comparison with those for other periods. None of those known to survive for the reigns of George I and George II provide the detailed reports of debates recorded in the diaries of Anchitell Grey (1667–92) and Sir Henry Cavendish (1768–74).[5] More significantly, perhaps, very few journals and diaries exist for the early Georgian period. For the Commons Sir Edward Knatchbull's diary covers the period from 1722 to 1730,[6] the years from 1730 to 1733 are covered in some detail by the earl of Egmont,[7] Philip Yorke's journal contains notes on the years 1743–8 and 1750,[8] and Richard Neville Aldworth provides very patchy, but occasionally detailed, accounts of 1747–66.[9] For the house of lords there are even fewer sources, Bishop Secker's journal, which covers the period from 1735 to 1743, providing the only detailed account of proceedings in the Lords during these two reigns.[10]

The journals of Edward Harley and William Hay are, therefore, of especial significance, because they fill the gap between the reports of Egmont and Yorke, thus providing a unique insight into the last years of Walpole's premiership. Harley's journal, moreover, is a valuable addition to Secker's journal for the study of the Lords and is the more interesting because it is the only known parliamentary journal to include accounts written by someone who was a member of both houses of parliament. In content, the two journals complement each other well. In both the sessions covered in greatest detail are those of 1735, 1736 and 1741–2. Some debates are reported by Hay but not by Harley, and vice-versa. But, in those cases where both discuss the same debate, comparison of their accounts reveals the differing perspectives of a tory and a whig.

The parliamentary journal of Edward Harley, 1735–1751

Edward Harley's parliamentary journal is now MS Add. 6851 in Cambridge University Library, having been presented by Sir Stephen Gaselee, fellow of Magdalene

---

4 On the reports of the French ambassador, see Paul Mantoux, *Notes sur les comptes rendus des séances du parlement anglais au XVIIIe. siècle conservés aux archives du Ministère des affaires étrangères* (Paris, 1906). Among printed sources one might note H.M.C., *15th Report, Appendix, Part VI* (manuscripts of the earl of Carlisle).

5 Anchitell Grey, *Debates of the House of Commons, from the Year 1667 to the Year 1692* (10 vols., 1773); *Sir Henry Cavendish's Debates of the House of Commons, during the Thirteenth Parliament of Great Britain*, ed. J. Wright (2 vols., 1841).

6 *The Parliamentary Diary of Sir Edward Knatchbull 1722–1730*, ed. A.N. Newman (Camden Soc., 3rd ser., XCIV, 1963).

7 H.M.C., *Diary of Viscount Percival, afterwards Earl of Egmont* (3 vols., 1920–3). Reports of parliamentary debates are less frequent for 1734, the last session in which Egmont sat in the Commons. They do continue to appear in his diary between 1735 and 1739, but they are more infrequent, less detailed and often based on information from others.

8 B.L., Add. MS 35337: the Commons journal of Philip Yorke. Parts of the Yorke journal were printed by Cobbett in his *Parliamentary History*. A new edition is being prepared by Richard Connors for the Parliamentary History Record Series.

9 Berkshire R.O., D/EN/O34/1–24. These notes, written almost entirely in pencil, would appear to have been made during the course of debates. The most detailed coverage is of the sessions of 1755–6 and 1756–7.

10 B.L., Add. MS 6043: 'Reports of the debates in the house of lords from 1735 to 1745 by Dr Secker, whilst bishop of Oxford'. Cobbett also printed extracts from Secker's journal. A scholarly edition is being prepared by Clyve Jones.

College, in 1935. Its earlier history is not clear, though it was acquired by Sir Thomas Phillipps and sold at the Puttick sale of his manuscripts in 1849.[11] The journal is a small volume, measuring 6½″ x 4½″, bound in calf by Brotherton in 1850, replacing an earlier binding of red russian. The condition of the manuscript, however, would suggest that it was first bound by Phillipps rather than Harley. The journal itself is divided into two volumes, and the fact that the first page of both is dirty and torn indicates that the two volumes were bound together sometime after they were written. Since the journal begins in 1735, and not when Harley entered the Commons in 1727, it is possible that there was another volume covering the parliament of 1727–34 which has been lost. The journal contains no explicit indication of the author, but there is no doubt that it was written by Edward Harley. Not merely is the handwriting the same as in Harley's letters, but internal evidence identifies him as the author. In the account of the debates on the motion for Walpole's dismissal on 13 February 1741, for example, Harley's speech contains references to the first earl of Oxford which could only have been made by his nephew.[12]

Both volumes of the journal were foliated by Harley himself. Volume 1 runs from folio 1 to 142, though folios 6–8 are missing. Volume 2 contains 136 folios. Harley wrote on the recto of each folio, leaving the verso blank for later additions and corrections, which are numerous. These additions might give the impression that he wrote up the journal on a regular basis, soon after the events he was describing, but this was probably not the case. On numerous occasions Harley followed a bill through all its parliamentary stages before moving on to a different subject or bill. Thus, in the entry beginning on 7 February 1735, when the engravers' petition was presented, Harley noted not only the introduction of the Copyright Bill on 4 March but also its receiving the royal assent on 15 May. Similarly, in the entry dated 16 February 1736 dealing with the Westminster Bridge Bill, he recorded the failure of the lottery after the end of the parliamentary session. It is probable, therefore, that Harley wrote up the journal after the end of each session, though doubtless he was working from papers and notes taken while parliament was sitting. A date of composition later than the end of the year in which the events took place, however, is unlikely. The further deliberations of parliament about Westminster Bridge in 1737 and 1738, for example, are noted not at the end of the entry of 16 February 1736, but on the facing verso page.[13]

It should be emphasized that Harley was not writing a daily record – he produced a journal, not a diary. Much of it is a basic account of proceedings in the Commons from 1734 to 1741 and, thereafter, in the Lords, though he continued to comment on events in the lower house even after his succession to the peerage. Many sessions, however, receive only cursory treatment, and that is increasingly the case after the fall of Walpole in 1742. Only two of the sessions between 1742–3 and 1751 have more space accorded to them than that of 1739, which is the shortest before 1742. But the basic format remains the same throughout. Harley recorded issues that were debated, resolutions that were made and divisions that occurred. His account is both less and more than a series of extracts from the *Journals* and *Votes*. It is less in the sense that

---

[11] Cambridge U.L., MS Add. 6851, f. 1. It was Phillipps MS 21888.

[12] The speech was also attributed to Harley in the printed account of the debate and in a manuscript version which appears to have circulated at the time. Below pp. 50–1, 250–1.

[13] Many of the comments added on the verso pages, however, further amplify or develop the main entries. These entries may be material which Harley later decided that he wished to include (see, e.g., the entry for 13 Feb. 1741) or related material that he overlooked when writing the main entry (see, e.g., the proceedings on the Yorkshire election petition, beginning 24 Feb. 1736).

Harley made no attempt to be comprehensive. It is more in that he appears to have been trying to construct a personal *aide memoire* to the issues and debates which interested him, an impression reinforced by the presence of an index of subjects at the end of volume 1.[14]

Detailed accounts of debates are rare. Harley's reports of proceedings in the Commons in February 1735 about the hearing of election petitions and of the second reading in the Lords of the Indemnity Bill in May 1742 are two examples of the infrequent occasions on which he identifies speakers and gives a summary of what they said. More often, he provides a commentary on debates, highlighting aspects of particular concern to him. Thus, his account of the 1736 Mortmain Bill focuses on the motives of the bill's promoters and the 'Agreement' by which the universities secured their exemption. Similarly, when describing the debate on the motion for Walpole's dismissal in February 1741, he concentrates on the behaviour of the tories, and especially of him and his brother, who refused to vote. Harley's journal is perhaps most valuable not for what it tells us about the content of the speeches made in the Commons and Lords, but for the insights he provides into the motives and prejudices underlying some debates and resolutions. Walpole inevitably figures prominently, as do the Patriots, of whom, as will be seen, Harley was very distrustful. His journal is, therefore, a very personal document, which reveals much more about its author than many superficially similar documents, such as the Knatchbull diary.

Harley's commentary on politics under George II provides a valuable insight into the tory mentality in this period, and much of this material is drawn on in this introduction. But it is important not to overlook the value of the journal in other ways and the significant contribution it makes to our knowledge of the political history of the period. Not least Harley records six division lists, one for the Commons and five for the Lords, none of which have survived in other sources.[15] The five Lords' lists represent nearly half the total number of division lists which have survived for the period covered by his Lords' journal. Moreover, time and again Harley provides brief but significant insights into what was happening in parliament. These are often most valuable when he is reporting some of the less high-profile debates. Thus, Harley reveals that the 1743 Rogues and Vagabonds Bill failed to reach the statute book because the Speaker objected to the Lords' amendments on the grounds that it was a money bill. This measure was accorded only brief entries, but the same point could be made about Harley's reports of debates on election petitions, which provide some of his longest entries. Harley's interest in this subject doubtless reflects the fact that he saw the ministry's treatment of election petitions as a striking example of Walpolean corruption. But, although petitions were often politically contentious, they rarely received much attention in the press. Thus, Harley's detailed accounts of the proceedings on the Marlborough petition in 1735 and the York and Scarborough petitions in 1736 help to illuminate an important but neglected part of the business of the Commons. Even more neglected in press reports were debates about parliamentary procedure, and here too Harley provides valuable new material – the debate on the

---

[14] This index has not been printed in this volume. It occupies ff. 139v–142r of volume 1 of the manuscript journal.

[15] The divisions concerned are those on the Westminster Bridge Bill (31 Mar. 1736), Hanoverian troops (1 Feb. 1743), the case of *Le Neve* v. *Norris* (16 Apr. 1744), the war in Flanders (2 May 1746), the Heritable Jurisdiction Bill (24 May 1747) and the Mutiny Bill (15 May 1749). In all these cases Harley recorded only the minority, and the list for 1 Feb. 1743 is only a partial list. The division on 16 Apr. 1744 was abandoned before telling.

Lisle privilege case in 1740 is accorded more space than any other debate for three sessions. Finally, it should be noted that Harley's journal is not a narrowly parliamentary one, but also includes references to events outside the palace of Westminster. Thus, he gives a brief account of the meeting at the Fountain Tavern in the aftermath of Walpole's fall in 1742 and some insight into the negotiations between the tories and the ministry in 1744–5.

The parliamentary journal of William Hay, 1734–1744

The parliamentary journal of William Hay is preserved among the Langham manuscripts at Northamptonshire Record Office (L(c)1732–1735), although there are no other Hay manuscripts with it. It almost certainly passed into the hands of the Langham family after the death of Francis Tutté, William Hay's nephew, in 1824 when the Glyndebourne estate was inherited by James Hay Langham.[16] The journal is contained in four volumes, each measuring 8" x 6½". The first volume begins with the entry for 17 January 1734 and finishes mid-way through the entry for 21 April 1735. Volume 2 covers the remainder of the 1735 session and the 1736 sessions. Volume 3 runs from 1737 to 1740, and volume 4 contains the entries for the session of 1741–2, 1742–3 and 1743–4, together with three additional papers at the end. A note at the beginning of the first volume, in a different hand from the rest of the journal, states that 'These notes were written by William Hay.' There is, however, no reason to doubt this attribution, as Hay's authorship is confirmed by his account of the Seaford by-election and by the use of the first person in his entry on the poor law report in 1735.[17]

Unfortunately, the text which we possess of Hay's journal is not the original, but a copy made, probably after his death, either by his son, Thomas, or by one of his daughters.[18] This clearly makes it more difficult to draw firm conclusions about how the document was composed, but some deductions can be made from the text itself. Like Harley, Hay composed the text for each session sometime after the end of that session. This is made clear by, for example, his entries for 5 and 30 April 1736 discussing the Mortmain and Quaker Tithe Bills. In both cases, once Hay had begun his accounts of these measures, he followed their progress through both Commons and Lords before moving on to other subjects. But, as with Harley, the suspicion must be that he relied upon notes which he had taken at the time and which he later worked up into a more coherent account. Some evidence for this practice is, perhaps, provided by the journal itself. Towards the end of the manuscript the copyist notes that 'What follows was not wrote into the book from whence the former part was transcribed, but was on loose pieces of paper.' What follows at this point are three separate pieces: first, a continuation of the account of the 1744 session; second, a 'paper without date', but in fact part of the proceedings in 1738; and, third, an account of the debate on the wool report in 1735. The format of the last of these, the debate on the wool report, is different from that of the rest of the journal and resembles the type of brief notes of

---

[16] The connexion between the Hays and Langhams was forged by WH's great-aunt Martha, who, in 1666, had become the third wife of Sir William Langham, 3rd bt.

[17] See below, pp. 91, 120–1.

[18] See the note before the entry for 18 Jan. 1744. Below p. 189. It is unlikely that Hay's second son, William, made the copy, as he was in India from 1752 until his death in 1763. In favour of Thomas as the copyist, it might be pointed out that his own membership of Commons, as M.P. for Lewes, gave him an interest in its proceedings. In favour of one of his daughters is the fact that they were responsible for the publication of their father's *Works* in the 1790s.

speakers and speeches which might have been made during a debate. It is possibly a small remnant of Hay's original notes.

Hay may have written up all the journal at one time, but this seems unlikely. The surviving manuscript varies quite markedly in character from session to session. The contrast is most striking if one compares the sessions of 1734 and 1735 with those of 1739–40 and 1741–2. Hay's accounts of the earlier sessions contain a large number of individual entries, most of which are quite short. His reports of individual debates tend to sum up the arguments used on either side, sometimes mentioning a few prominent speakers. These sections of the journal appear to have been intended as a personal record of proceedings, designed for Hay's own use, an impression reinforced by his inclusion of lists of accounts, petitions and other related matters at the end of the 1735 session. Hay's style when recording the events of the sessions of 1739–40 and 1740–1 is, by contrast, very different. The sections of the journal dealing with these two sessions do include dated accounts of debates, which still incorporate summaries of the arguments used by some of the speakers, but much more space than in earlier sessions is given over to commentary on the significance of the events being reported. Moreover, these later sessions were written up more in the form of a history of the period, intended to be read by a wider audience.[19] The opening of the session of 1739–40, for example, was clearly not written by Hay for himself alone:

> I come now to the sixth Session of this Parliament: which met the 15th. of November 1739. This was earlier than Parliaments had met for many years: and was Occasioned by the Declaration of a War against Spain. Before I take notice of the proceedings in this Session; it will be necessary to take Notice of one thing which was the principal Consideration of the last.

It would appear, therefore, that the purposes for which Hay kept his journal changed. Indeed, since we do not know whether the original manuscript was in one volume or several, the transcript may include two or more different documents, kept at different times for different purposes.

The most obvious contrast between the two journals is their length – Hay's, at over 58,000 words, is almost twice as long as Harley's. Moreover, Hay covers a shorter period (1734–44) than Harley (1735–51), and, within that period, he only records five sessions in any depth.[20] There are no entries for 1739 and 1740–1,[21] only one for 1737, while the sessions of 1738, 1742–3 and 1743–4 all receive rather cursory treatment. Hay's journal is, therefore, at least for those five sessions, much the more detailed of the documents. Like Harley, he shows a particular interest in the events surrounding the fall of Walpole, providing one of the fullest contemporary narratives of what happened in the Commons from the opening of the first session of George II's third parliament. To the narrative Hay added some distinctive insights, ascribing the principal cause of Walpole's fall to 'the hatred of the City of London'.[22] But the main value of the journal lies in Hay's accounts of the sessions of 1734–6. For these years he provides brief coverage of a large number of debates, many of which are not

---

[19] This is not to say that Hay intended his journal for publication; the wider audience may simply have been his descendants.

[20] 1734, 1735, 1736, 1739–40 and 1741–2.

[21] We know from other sources that WH was present during these sessions, so it is not clear why there are these lacunae. Either WH did not keep any record of debates, or his notes were lost before the transcript was made.

[22] Below p. 181.

covered in the printed accounts. Not only do these add significantly to our knowledge of some of the major parliamentary debates of the period, such as the attempt to repeal the Test Act and the Mortmain Bill of 1736, but Hay also often illuminates otherwise obscure issues, such as the Witchcraft Bill of 1736.

Like Harley's journal, Hay's also tells us a great deal about its author's own political views. Throughout the text he records his own opinions about issues debated and often on which side he voted, even if it is clear that he did not speak. But the most significant additions to our knowledge of Hay's politics are the five speeches of which he gives verbatim accounts. These are not the only occasions he spoke in the Commons, and they are, in some ways, a revealing selection. Three – those on the Quakers Tithe Bill in 1736, the army estimates in 1738 and the Place Bill in 1740 – address major issues. Of these, the 1736 speech on the Tithe Bill is the most interesting, revealing the idiosyncratic position which he adopted on this issue. All these will be discussed later. The other two, by contrast, were both delivered during debates about Commons' practice and procedure – the Lisle case in 1740 and the admission of strangers in 1741. They highlight the fact that, like Harley and so many other diarists, Hay had a great interest in procedural matters, which are a recurring subject of the journal. Some entries, like the account of the election of the Speaker in 1735, add colour to our knowledge of the proceedings of the House in the early eighteenth century,[23] while others confirm and extend our understanding of procedure.[24] Nonetheless, for all that the journal reveals about Hay, it is surprising that it does not reveal more. He was remarkably silent on the issues in which he was most deeply involved.[25] There is a brief, but only a brief, entry about the poor law committee in 1735, and Hay makes no reference to his failed legislation of 1736, or to his involvement in later bills on the subject of the poor laws and vagrants.

The correspondence of Edward Harley
The first earl of Oxford left one of the biggest archives available for any eighteenth-century politician. The papers of his nephew, while significant, are not nearly as extensive. This edition includes only the letters and papers – or the sections from letters – relating to parliamentary affairs.[26] Most of these are drawn from the papers kept by the third earl himself and the rest of the Harley family, though these are dispersed in three separate archives.[27] The largest single group comes from the section of the Portland collection in the British Library. Of the 85 items from the Portland manuscripts, 21, all letters to Abigail Harley, have already been printed, in

---

23 Below p. 102.

24 E.g., Sheila Lambert has shown that many bills *must* have been prepared before the appointment of a drafting committee. Hay confirms this, noting on 28 Feb. 1734 that the bill for the more easy redemption of mortgages had been drawn up before the appointment of the drafting committee on that day. Interestingly, however, it had been prepared not by Alington, the chairman of the drafting committee, but by Sir Joseph Jekyll, who was not even a member of the drafting committee. Sheila Lambert, *Bills and Acts. Legislative Procedure in Eighteenth-Century England* (Cambridge, 1971), p. 62; below, p. 98; *C.J.*, XXII, 263.

25 In a similar way, Knatchbull's diary tells us very little about his 1723 Workhouse Test Act.

26 In most cases only the sections of letters which relate to parliamentary affairs have been printed. However, the letters to Harley from Gwyn and Benson have all been printed in full, because they are less easily accessible to scholars and the non-parliamentary parts of them are only short.

27 On the Harley papers more generally and the relationship between the various collections, see Clyve Jones, 'The Harley Family and the Harley Papers', *British Library Journal*, XV (1989), 123–33.

whole or in part, in the reports of the Historical Manuscripts Commission. The British Library collection, however, includes not only Edward Harley's correspondence with his aunt Abigail and with the first and second earls, but also papers which are clearly part of the third earl's own archives, notably those in Add. MSS 70497–8. It is a little puzzling how these came to form part of the Portland collection, since the Harley papers passed to the Bentinck family through the second earl of Oxford's only surviving child, Margaret, on her marriage to the duke of Portland in 1734.

It is easier to explain the location of the other papers of Edward Harley. The second major group of documents printed in this edition (23 items) come from the Harley papers at Brampton Bryan, which descended, along with the estate, to the house's present owner, Christopher Harley.[28] Two further letters are to be found among the Rodney papers in the Public Record Office. These almost certainly came into the possession of that family as a result of the marriage of Anne Harley, one of the third earl's granddaughters, to George, second Baron Rodney in 1781. The remaining items printed below come from other collections. Three letters were found among the papers of one of Harley's Herefordshire neighbours, William Brydges, which are now in the Herefordshire Record Office, while a manuscript copy of his speech on the motion to remove Walpole in 1741 is preserved among the Ballard papers in the Bodleian Library. Seven more come from other collections in the British Library – three from the Hardwicke papers and four from the Newcastle papers.

Twenty-four different correspondents are included in this edition. Harley's most regular correspondents, at least among his surviving papers, were women, highlighting the political awareness and involvement of women within the family. His aunt Abigail is represented by 36 letters, while his wife, Martha, was the recipient of a further 17. The only other people to reach double figures are Edward Prideaux Gwyn, whose brother Francis was an contemporary of Harley's at Christ Church and who later served as a tory as M.P. for Christchurch and Wells, and James Brydges, marquess of Carnarvon. Gwyn was the author of 12 letters, while Carnarvon's correspondence with Oxford about his plan to stand for Radnorshire at the 1754 elections accounts for 11. Among the minor correspondents family members are prominent: the first earl of Oxford (4), the second earl (4), Auditor Harley (3), John Harley (2) and Lord Harley, later the fourth earl (1). Small groups of letters, mainly about Oxford's absence from the Lords during the trial of the rebel peers in 1746, were exchanged with the duke of Newcastle (4) and Lord Hardwicke (3). Most of the remaining correspondents were Herefordshire gentry, though of particular interest is the letter from Martin Benson, Harley's tutor at Christ Church, who later became a whig bishop of Gloucester and who wrote to his pupil about proceedings in the Commons on the Oxford University riots in 1716. In addition to the correspondence this edition includes five papers in Harley's hand. Three of these relate to his Jury Acts of 1730 and 1733, but the most important is the list (item 15) of those bishops voting for and against the rider offered by Lord Nottingham to the Bill for Strengthening the Protestant Interest in 1718.[29]

---

[28] There is a card catalogue for this collection at Herefordshire R.O., where there are also photocopies of some items. Regrettably, Christopher Harley died while this volume was in proof.

[29] There is no other known copy of the division on this issue. The two other division lists in this edition, however, those on the impeachment of Oxford (item 6) and the bishops for and against committing the Bill for Strengthening the Protestant Interest (item 15), also survive in other collections. *British Parliamentary Lists 1660–1800: A Register*, ed. G.M. Ditchfield, David Hayton and Clyve Jones (1995), pp. 44–5.

The papers printed below complement Harley's journal well. Over half of them come from the period before he entered parliament in 1727. This section includes reports of debates on issues such as the impeachment of the earl of Oxford (3–7), the repeal of the Occasional Conformity and Schism Acts (15–23), the Peerage Bill (25–32), the South Sea Bubble (38–9, 42–4, 46, 48–51, 53–6), the Westminster Dormitory case (43–6, 48), the Blasphemy Bill (47–50, 52) and the Atterbury plot (62–3, 65–6). In some cases, these reports were provided to Harley for people, such as Gwyn and Benson, who were present at the debates. But, more often, they are contained in letters written by Harley himself. It is possible that he was occasionally present in the Commons himself. Many of his letters, however, were written from Oxford, and it is clear that Harley was relying on, and probably often copying, reports received from friends in London. Indeed, for parts of the 1715–21 parliament he appears to have been receiving a regular stream of letters informing him of events at Westminster. The best example of this is the Gwyn correspondence. Thus, Gwyn's report of the Bill for Strengthening the Protestant Interest (16) was copied by Harley almost verbatim into his letter to his aunt (17). But Gwyn was not his only informant. The letter to Abigail includes material not found in Gwyn's report, most notably a list of bishops voting for and against the bill. Similarly, two weeks later, on 8 January 1719 Harley sent his aunt an account of the Commons debate on the bill (21). This was followed on the 11th by a second letter (22), in which Harley, having told her that he had received 'a further Account of the Debate', copied the substance of a letter from Gwyn, which he had received on 9 January (20). Unfortunately, it is not clear who Harley's other correspondents were. It is unlikely that Martin Benson, who had sent him details of the Commons' proceedings on the Oxford University riots of 1717, would have been a regular attender at parliamentary debates. Although there is little evidence, it is likely that Harley received much of his information from his father,[30] and another correspondent may have been Timothy Thomas, a student of Christ Church between 1712 and 1727 who was appointed in 1726 to the rectory of the Harley family living of Presteigne.[31]

Even the correspondence for the period after 1727 complements the journal. A group of letters contain reports of proceedings in the parliament of 1727–34, for which no journal survives. These include accounts of the debates on the employment of Hessian troops (70) and on Dunkirk (71), as well as material relating to the Jury Bills (72–7, 82). Thereafter, remarkably little correspondence has survived to illuminate events inside the Commons and Lords, except for papers on the motion for the dismissal of Walpole in 1741 (84–5) and the Mutiny Bill of 1750 (108). However, from 1721 onwards a fair amount of material has survived concerning Harley's activity in parliamentary elections. Every general election from 1722 to 1754, except 1734, is represented in his correspondence, though probably the most interesting letters shed light on the family's response to Robert Harley's defeat at Leominster in 1741. In addition, there are insights into the Herefordshire by-election of 1742 and the Oxford University election of 1751 and an account from Timothy Thomas of the bitterly contested Denbighshire election of 1741.

One group of letters in this edition, however, stands out above all the others in significance. The 13 written by Edward Prideaux Gwyn are of the first importance for the political and parliamentary history of the Sunderland-Stanhope ministry in

---

[30] See the letters of 25 Apr. and 2 May 1721, below pp. 231, 232.
[31] Below p. 203: EH to Abigail Harley, 6 Feb. 1718.

relation to its reform programme of 1718–19 and they merit more detailed consideration. This programme had three aims – reform of the universities;[32] relief for dissenters by the repeal of the Occasional Conformity and Schism Acts, and perhaps also of the Test Act; and reform of parliament by the repeal of the Septennial Act and the introduction of the Peerage Bill. The ministry faced strong opposition to these plans, especially in the Commons, not only from the tories, but also from the schismatic whigs under Walpole and Townshend and the friends and clients of the prince of Wales, who had quarrelled with his father in 1717. The reform of the universities, the repeal of the Test and the repeal of the Septennial Act were all abandoned before the introduction of legislation, and ultimately only the repeal of the Occasional Conformity and Schism Acts reached the statute book. The Church Bill, as this latter measure was called, is the subject of Gwyn's letters of 23 December 1718 and 8 January 1719.[33] It was controversial among many of the clergy and their tory supporters, and it has left a good deal of archival material to enable it to be studied in some detail.[34] Indeed, the bulk of Gwyn's reports is already available in print in letters from Harley to his aunt of 25 December and 11 January.[35]

The other major reform proposal, the Peerage Bill, was, if anything, more controversial. By limiting the size of the house of lords and thus restricting the prerogative of the king to create new peers, the bill sought to change the constitution and, had it come into force, it would have altered the balance of power between Lords and Commons in favour of the former. Paradoxically, however, relatively little archival material has survived, particularly for the debates in the upper house where the bill dominated business between 28 February and 6 March 1719, on its first, unsuccessful introduction, and in the first week of the new session in late November 1719, when it passed the upper house, only to be defeated in the Commons in December. The Gwyn–Harley correspondence thus helps to fill an important gap in our understanding of the politics of this period. In fact, only one other source deals directly with the Lords' debates on this measure, the letters from Lord Newburgh to his brother the earl of Cholmondeley.[36] Three of these describe, albeit cursorily, the passage of the bill in November, for which no Gwyn letters have survived. However, the seven letters written by Gwyn between 25 February and 26 March 1719 are the major source for the first attempt to pass the bill through parliament. For this earlier period, Gwyn's correspondence is much fuller than Newburgh's, containing detailed summaries of individual speeches, often with actual quotations.

---

[32] John Gascoigne, 'Church and State Allied: The Failure of Parliamentary Reform of the Universities, 1688–1800', in *The First Modern Society. Essays in English History in Honour of Lawrence Stone*, ed. A.L. Beier, David Cannadine and James M. Rosenheim (Cambridge, 1989), pp. 401–29.

[33] Below pp. 208–9 and 212–13.

[34] Graham Townend, 'Religious Radicalism and Conservatism in the Whig Party under George I: The Repeal of the Occasional Conformity and Schism Acts', *Parliamentary History*, VII (1988), 24–44; Stephen Taylor, ' "Dr Codex" and the Whig "Pope": Edmund Gibson, Bishop of Lincoln and London, 1716–48', in *Lords of Parliament: Studies, 1714–1914*, ed. R.W. Davis (Stanford, 1995), pp. 9–28, 183–91.

[35] Below pp. 209–10 and 214–15. EH's letters to Abigail have already been printed in H.M.C., *Portland MSS*, V, 574–6.

[36] Cheshire R.O., DCH/X/8 (Cholmondeley of Cholmondeley papers), printed in Clyve Jones, 'Parliament and the Peerage and Weaver Navigation Bills: The Correspondence of Lord Newburgh with the Earl of Cholmondeley, 1719–20', *Transactions of the Historic Society of Lancashire and Cheshire*, CXXXIX (1990), 31–61.

A recent study of the Peerage Bill has based a new interpretation of its origins and progress on Gwyn's letters.[37] His reports make it clear that the duke of Somerset did not spring the motion to consider the state of the peerage on an unsuspecting house of lords on 28 February.[38] More significantly, the detailed speeches recorded by Gwyn provide the historian with the only direct evidence of the motives of the ministers for bringing in the bill. Sunderland's speech on 3 March reveals the importance of the problem of trying to rectify the anomalous situation of the Scottish representative peers in the Lords in the genesis of the bill.[39] This aspect has largely been neglected by historians. More interestingly, Gwyn's record of the speech by Stanhope, who 'thirded' the bill on 4 March, highlights a hitherto unsuspected motive of the ministry – the attempt to end the fear of the English peerage of being swamped by socially unsuitable newcomers, a fear exaggerated by recent creations, but none the less real.[40]

The correspondence of William Hay

In marked contrast to Edward Harley, William Hay has left no collection of papers other than the journal. Indeed, the only correspondence of his known to have survived is to be found among the papers of the duke of Newcastle in the British Library. This collection contains 47 items connected with Hay. While most of these are letters to the duke, there is also one letter to Colonel James Pelham, one letter from James Hurdis, son of Thomas Hurdis, rector of Ringmer, two lists of Lewes voters in 1733 and an enclosure from one of Hay's letters, also about the Lewes election.

The subject matter of the correspondence varies considerably. There are letters about local government and justice in Sussex and requests for patronage at Charterhouse, alongside the 38 papers concerning parliamentary affairs which are included in this edition.[41] Among these, Hay's last surviving letter to Newcastle reveals some of the local negotiations which led to the presentation of a petition to the house of lords on 5 December 1753 for the improvement of the road from Uckfield to Langley. The bill which resulted from this petition eventually passed into law in March 1754, Hay having served as chairman of both the drafting committee and the select committee.[42] However, the main interest of Hay's parliamentary papers lies in the 36 items about the Sussex and Lewes elections of 1734, and particularly the detailed insight Hay provides into the canvassing between early August 1733 and the middle of January 1734. Hay's role as Newcastle's agent in Lewes during this period make this correspondence of particular interest, and both its value and Hay's role will be explored later in this introduction.[43]

---

37 Clyve Jones, ' "Venice Preserv'd; or A Plot Discovered": The Political and Social Context of the Peerage Bill of 1719', in *A Pillar of the Constitution: The House of Lords and British Politics, 1660–1784*, ed. Clyve Jones (1989), pp. 79–112.

38 Below pp. 216–17. Cf. Basil Williams, *Stanhope. A Study in Eighteenth-Century War and Diplomacy* (Oxford, 1932), p. 405.

39 Below p. 219. For the problem of the under-representation of the Scottish peerage in the Lords see also the speeches of Argyll on 28 Feb. and Archbishop Sharp on 3 Mar. Below pp. 217, 220.

40 Below p. 221.

41 The letters not included in this edition are B.L., Add. MS 32687, ff. 403–4, Add. MS 32689, ff. 393–4, 483–4, Add. MS 32691, ff. 370–1, Add. MS 32707, f. 347, Add. MS 32711, f. 226, Add. MS 32724, ff. 38–9, Add. MS 32728, ff. 321–2 (all to the duke of Newcastle) and Add. MS 32725, ff. 77–9 (to Colonel Pelham).

42 For the passage of this bill through the Commons, see *C.J.*, XXVI, 862–3, 873, 877, 940–1, 946, 962.

43 Below pp. lxxxii–lxxxvi.

THE HARLEY FAMILY

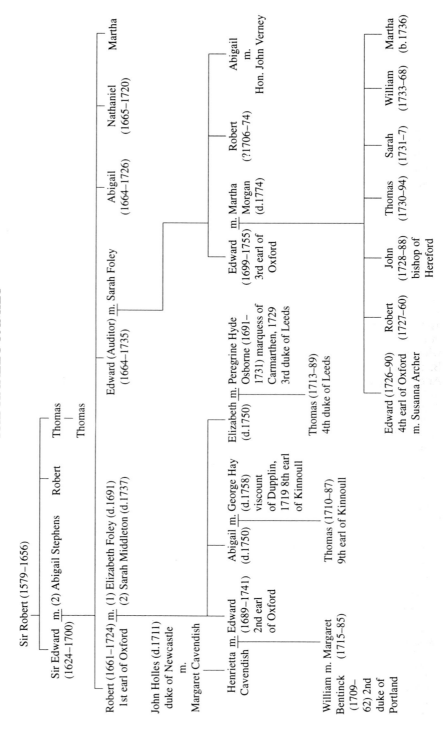

EDWARD HARLEY, 3rd EARL OF OXFORD
(1699–1755)

The early life of Edward Harley

The Harleys were descended from a long line of Herefordshire squires who had been in possession of the family home of Brampton Castle, Brampton Bryan, in the far north-western corner of the county, a mile or two from the Radnorshire border, since 1309.[1] In the early seventeenth century Sir Robert Harley had restored the family fortunes and fought on the parliamentary side in the Civil War, as did his son, Edward. Subsequently Edward Harley, who was knighted in 1661, had a long political career, sitting in ten parliaments for Herefordshire and New Radnor Boroughs between 1646 and 1698. Although he had no scruples about conforming to the Church of England at the Restoration, he inherited his father's presbyterian principles. His politics were 'country', then whig, supporting exclusion and the revolution of 1688. William III rewarded Sir Edward with a grant of lands in Radnorshire, which carried extensive electoral interests, to add to the influence which the family had in Herefordshire.[2] Sir Edward, in turn, passed on his political principles to his sons, Robert (1661–1724) and Edward (1664–1735). Both began their political lives as devout whigs. Edward, indeed, played an active role in the revolution, buying arms in London and meeting the prince of Orange at Salisbury.[3] It was, however, Robert who established the Harleys among the leading families in post-revolutionary Britain. He became one of the most important political figures of the reign of Queen Anne, rising to be speaker of the house of commons, secretary of state, and from 1711 to 1714 lord treasurer (effectively prime minister[4]). In May 1711 Robert was created first earl of Oxford and Earl Mortimer.

The Harleys' local influence was consolidated by two marriages. In 1685 Robert married Elizabeth Foley, one of the daughters of Thomas Foley, M.P., of Witley Court in Worcestershire. Elizabeth died six years later, but on 5 September 1698 Edward Harley married her sister, Sarah.[5] Thus both brothers were closely tied by marriage to an important family in a neighbouring county, while their uncle Paul Foley, speaker of the house of commons between 1695 and 1698, lived at Stoke Edith in Herefordshire. This alliance was of obvious importance in local politics, but it also had reverberations at Westminster as Robert Harley and Paul Foley emerged in the 1690s as the leaders of the 'New Country Party'. Thus, the Harleys were instrumental in bringing about the realignment of English politics in the decade after the revolution, as the adherents of the 'New Country Party' gradually came to be absorbed into the tory party. Edward Harley – or the 'Auditor', as he was often called, having been made joint auditor of the imprests for life in 1702 – was eclipsed by his brother, but always remained one of his closest political allies. He was classed as a tory as early as

---

[1] For a history of the Harley family to the early seventeenth century, see Jacqueline Eales, *Puritans and Roundheads. The Harleys of Brampton Bryan and the Outbreak of the English Civil War* (Cambridge, 1990), ch. 1. See also Clyve Jones, 'The Harley Family and the Harley Papers', *British Library Journal*, XV (1989), 123–33.

[2] *The House of Commons 1660–1690*, ed. B.D. Henning (3 vols., 1983), II, 494–7.

[3] HoP, draft biography, by David Hayton.

[4] See Geoffrey Holmes, *British Politics in the Age of Anne* (1967), Appendix C.

[5] B.L., Add. MS 70079: genealogical papers.

December 1701, and again in lists of 1708 and 1710. But the Auditor's toryism remained somewhat idiosyncratic. He had continued to frequent nonconformist conventicles in the 1690s, and even at the end of Anne's reign he retained some sympathy for dissent, voting against the Schism Bill in 1714.[6]

Edward Harley the younger, later third earl of Oxford, was therefore born in late August 1699 into a prominent and increasingly powerful family.[7] Known in the Harley family circle (and later by his friends at Oxford University) as Neddy, he was the Auditor's eldest child. He was followed by three others: Robert, who was baptized on 15 September 1700 but died less than a year later on 28 June;[8] a second Robert, probably born in 1706; and a daughter, given the family name of Abigail.[9]

Edward Harley's early life was to follow closely that of his cousin Edward (1689–1741), who, as the only surviving son of Robert, was known as Lord Harley from his father's elevation to the peerage in 1711 until he succeeded as second earl of Oxford in 1724. There was almost exactly ten years' difference in their ages and both attended Westminster School, progressing thence to Christ Church, Oxford, the future Lord Harley going up in 1707 and Edward in 1717. At Oxford, however, their careers began to diverge. Lord Harley left without a degree and was propelled into politics in 1711, having been elected for New Radnor Boroughs. He was quite active in support of the ministry in the Commons in 1711–15, but showed little interest in politics after his father's fall from power.[10] Edward, by contrast, remained at Oxford, where his tutors were Martin Benson, later bishop of Gloucester, Samuel Palmer and Timothy Thomas. He was awarded his M.A. in 1721, though there appears to have been some opposition in the university to the degree.[11] Thereafter his entry into politics was much more leisurely than his cousin's. He was not elected M.P. for Herefordshire until 1727, but he then became an active parliamentarian and rapidly emerged as one of the leading figures of the Hanoverian tory party.

As will be seen, Edward had a passion for politics from an early age. However, not all his interests were political, as the letters of Dr William Stratford, canon of Christ Church, reveal. Edward possessed the two saving family vices – books and drink.[12] Both vices were shared with the first and second earls of Oxford, though Edward did not pursue them to the excess of his cousin, whose bibliophilia led to his near bankruptcy just as surely as his drinking led to his early death. Indeed, his rather serious, even priggish, character, evident from much that he later wrote, was clear early on: 'his life is so much of a piece, so very regular and good, that it affords not any variety

6 HoP draft biography by David Hayton.

7 He was baptized on 27 August 1699. B.L., Add. MS 70079.

8 *Ibid.*

9 Besides his grandmother Abigail Stephens, Edward had an aunt Abigail, with whom he corresponded, particularly while attending Oxford University (see below, pp. 199–236), and a cousin Abigail, daughter of the first earl of Oxford, who in 1709 married Lord Dupplin (see genealogical table).

10 HoP, draft biography, by David Hayton; Sedgwick, II, 112.

11 For the identification of EH's tutors, see B.L., Add. MS 70373, ff. 78–9: Martin Benson to Lord Harley, 20 Feb. 1717; Add. MS 70498, ff. 53–4: Auditor Harley to EH, 21 Feb. 1721; Add. MS 70237: EH to Oxford, 16 Aug. 1720. On his honorary degree, see H.M.C., *Portland MSS*, VII, 296: Stratford to Lord Harley, 2 May 1721; B.L., Add. MS 70145: EH to Abigail, 2 May 1721; *Remarks and Collections of Thomas Hearne*, ed. C.E. Doble, D.W. Rannie *et al.* (11 vols., Oxford, 1884–1918), VII, 237–8. According to E.G.W. Bill, Edward was the first gentleman commoner to whom an honorary degree was awarded in the eighteenth century. *Education at Christ Church Oxford 1660–1800* (Oxford, 1988), p. 181.

12 H.M.C., *Portland MSS*, VII, 234–5; Hearne, *Remarks*, VI, 127, 155, 162, 339 (collected coins); VII, 91; IX, 222. Edward also indulged himself in grouse shooting (H.M.C., *Portland MSS*, VII, 239), and in 1719 his father recommended fencing to him for his health (Add. MS 70498, ff. 49–50: Auditor to EH, 19 Jan. 1719).

for a correspondence', wrote Stratford in 1718.[13] Two years later Stratford noted that Edward was becoming bored even with academic life at Oxford: 'the father begins to stir in him, and he is for somewhat a little more substantial than poetry'.[14]

The main characteristic which Edward shared with his father was his piety. The Auditor's religiosity was central to his life and gave him a significantly separate political identity from his elder brother. Edward's sober education had equipped him since childhood with a knowledge of scripture, which, as his father later reminded him, 'alone can direct us to the Path of Endless Bliss and Fortifie our minds to bear Up against the many temptations and Difficulties with which we are to Contend in this State of mortality'.[15] But Edward's christian education did not stop there. At university he moved from the study of mathematics to astronomy, which, as the Auditor pointed out, 'tends to give those great and Noble Ideas of the Divine Majesty which leads us to the Admiracon of his amazing Love to mankind in their redempcon'.[16]

Edward's religious opinions were strongly high church. Notwithstanding the Auditor's residual dissenting sympathies, the Harley family had come to be identified with the high church toryism which was the dominant intellectual force at Christ Church and Oxford.[17] In 1718 Edward was incensed by a university preacher who espoused the 'Bangorian' principles, which had been made famous the previous year in a sermon delivered by the radical whig latitudinarian, Benjamin Hoadly, entitled *The Nature of the Kingdom of Christ*.[18] In the same year he was appalled at reports about the Trinitarian controversy among the dissenters in Exeter, denouncing them as 'Ignorant, Fanatical Infidels'. This threat from arianism led directly to the attempt by his father, during the debates on the repeal of the Occasional Conformity and Schism Acts in January 1719, to add to the bill a clause requiring office holders to make a declaration affirming their belief in the Trinity. Two years later the Auditor was one of the leading figures behind the attempt to pass the Blasphemy Bill. Edward regarded the defeat of these measures as a betrayal of God and Christianity, and he condemned the bishops who opposed them as the defenders of 'blasphemy and Infidelity'.[19] Edward, however, was as distrustful of the extreme high flyers as his uncle had been. A sermon preached on Restoration Day in 1719 angered him almost as much as the Bangorian one of 1718, and he denounced the preacher as 'as great a coxcomb as ever Magdalen College bred though Sacheverell himself was one of her Fellows'.[20]

In one respect, however, Edward was to disappoint his father: he had little interest in the law. The Auditor had attended the Middle Temple, being called to the bar in 1688. In 1719 he tried to persuade Edward to take up lodgings in Lincoln's Inn, much against the young man's inclinations and Dr Stratford's wishes, who shared Edward's desire to see him continue his studies in Oxford.[21] Edward seems to have persuaded

---

[13] H.M.C., *Portland MSS*, VII, 232: Stratford to Lord Harley, 30 Jan. 1717/18. See also, B.L., Add. MS 70034: EH to Abigail, 13 Feb. 1717/18 (on Mr Bridgwater's son); *ibid.*, same to same, 27 Feb. 1717/18 and Add. MS 70145: same to same, 5 May 1720 (on his brother Robert).

[14] H.M.C., *Portland MSS*, VII, 270: Stratford to Lord Harley, 18 Feb. 1717/20.

[15] Brampton Bryan MSS, Bundle 117: Lord Harley to EH, 14 Dec. 1713; B.L., Add. MS 70498, ff. 53–4: Auditor Harley to EH, 21 Feb. 1721.

[16] B.L., Add. MS 70498, ff. 49–50: Auditor Harley to EH, 19 Jan. 1719.

[17] The most visual manifestation of the Harleys' transition from presbyterianism to high church anglican-ism is the lavish baroque chapel built by Lord Harley at Wimpole.

[18] H.M.C., *Portland MSS*, VII, 246: William Stratford to Lord Harley, 2 Dec. 1718.

[19] Below pp. 233, 209, 215: EH to Abigail, 4 May 1721, 25 Dec. 1718, 13 Jan. 1719.

[20] H.M.C., *Portland MSS*, V, 587: [EH] to Abigail Harley, 28 June 1719.

[21] *Ibid.*, VII, 250–1. He had, however, been formally admitted to Lincoln's Inn on 21 Jan. 1716. *The Records of the Honourable Society of Lincoln's Inn. Admissions* (2 vols., 1896), I, 378.

his father that the law was not for him, and the Auditor had to bide his time until he could push his second son Robert in that direction. Robert attended Lincoln's Inn in 1724 after leaving Christ Church without a degree and was called to the bar in 1730.

Edward's reluctance to pursue a legal career did not affect the closeness of father and son or his ability to act for his family.[22] Recent research has shown that the Auditor acted as his elder brother's 'man-of-business' for most of his political career.[23] This function, at least in part, appears to have been devolved upon Edward from around 1719, if not earlier. Edward dealt with some of Lord Oxford's business in London while the latter was in Herefordshire. He made an investment in African Company stock, negotiated about the purchase of an estate in Staffordshire and kept an eye on legal cases involving tenants of the Harley family.[24] Edward also appears to have acted as a man-of-business for Lord Harley.[25]

In December 1721 the Auditor seems to have been responsible for trying to arrange 'a very scandalous match' for Edward. The earl of Oxford, considered that 'it would have been the ruin of the family ... it was unmeet in all respects, but his dear brother happened to be entangled in it by prospects of a great fortune'. There is no evidence who the proposed wife was, but Edward 'had the utmost aversion' to the marriage and his uncle managed to 'put an end to it but with great difficulty, and that it required a good deal of management'.[26] There were also rumours of an impending marriage in 1723, but it was not until 16 March 1725 that Edward married Martha, daughter of John Morgan, M.P. of Tredegar, Monmouthshire.[27] In some ways this was a surprising alliance. The Morgans were the leading whig family in South Wales and two of Edward's brothers-in-law sat alongside him in the Commons as whigs.[28] However, this does not seem to have affected the marriage. Gawen Hamilton's charming portrait of Edward, Martha and their seven children, painted in 1736, was clearly more than a conventional work. The couple's devotion to each other, and to their family, is clear from their correspondence – even when he was piloting his favourite Jury Bill through the Commons, Edward was longing 'for the day to come when I may ... return to your Arms who I love beyond expression'.[29]

Upon the rumours of a marriage in 1723, Dr Stratford had lamented that the young Edward had not 'spent two or three years abroad, before he had been tied down to work for the continuation of the family'.[30] In 1725, with a new wife, this was precisely the situation in which he found himself. In 1724 the earl of Oxford, to whom Edward had been close, died. The succession of his unambitious son, coupled with the retirement of the Auditor from active politics, left Edward as the custodian of the Harleys' political interest. Then, in October 1725 the second earl's only son died within a few days of his premature birth, leaving Edward heir presumptive to the earldom by the special remainder granted in 1711 to the male heirs of Sir Robert Harley, the first earl's grandfather. Margaret, the second earl's daughter, would inherit the Harley-Cavendish

22 B.L., Add. MS 70034: EH to Abigail Harley, 4 Jan. 1719; Add. MS 70498, ff. 61–2: Auditor Harley to EH, 8 June 1733; Add. MS 70087: EH to ?, 13 Sept. 1735.

23 HoP draft biography.

24 B.L., Add. MS 70237: EH to Oxford, 16 May 1719, 5 Apr. 1720.

25 Brampton Bryan MSS, Bundle 6, Packet 7.

26 H.M.C., *Portland MSS*, VII, 308: Stratford to Lord Harley, 6 Dec. 1721.

27 *Ibid.*, p. 354: Stratford to Lord Harley, 2 Apr. 1723; *Complete Peerage*.

28 For John Morgan, and his sons Thomas and William, see Sedgwick, II, 275–7.

29 *Manners and Morals. Hogarth and British Painting 1700–1760* (1987), no. 64. See, e.g., B.L., Add. MS 70497: EH to Martha Harley, 20 Jan., 5, 21 Mar. 1729/30, 28 Mar., 2 Apr. 1730.

30 H.M.C., *Portland MSS*, VII, 354: Stratford to Lord Harley, 2 Apr. 1723.

estates in Cambridgeshire and London, but in 1740 Edward purchased from his cousin Brampton Bryan and other properties in Herefordshire, Shropshire and Radnorshire.[31] The birth of two sons, Edward in 1726 and Robert in 1727, ensured the continuation of the family name, and in the latter year Edward was elected to the Commons as M.P. for Herefordshire.

When Edward Harley entered parliament in 1727 at the age of 28, he was no novice in politics. On his arrival at Oxford it was assumed that he would become a 'hearty ... Tory'.[32] While at university he had been a keen observer of the political scene, receiving letters not only from his father and uncle but also from friends such as Edward Prideaux Gwyn (printed below, pp. 208–26). His enthusiasm for politics is manifested by his own letters, which relayed much of the political information he was receiving and not a few of his own judgments on affairs back to his aunt Abigail, who spent most of her time at the family home of Eywood, built by the Auditor in 1702. Prominent in this correspondence were events which directly affected the family, like Oxford's trial, and debates in which his father was particularly active, such as the repeal of the Occasional Conformity Acts and the Blasphemy Bill. But Edward's interests ranged wider, including the Peerage Bill, the Westminster Dormitory case and the South Sea crisis, and by the early 1720s there are tantalizing hints that he may have become involved in Westminster politics himself. According to his own testimony, in 1720 Edward assisted the Levant Company (or, as he called it, the Turkey Company) in a case before the house of commons and was assured that what he said 'had carried the Question in their Favour'.[33]

Edward had also become involved in local politics while still at Oxford. The Harley family's interest in Radnorshire had been virtually eliminated at the 1715 general election,[34] but it retained considerable influence in Herefordshire and at Leominster, the Auditor's constituency. In the summer vacations Edward often returned to the family home at Eywood, south-west of Brampton Bryan, and as early as 1718 he was entertaining the Leominster corporation in an attempt to shore up the family interest there.[35] At the 1722 general election the Auditor had wished to relinquish his seat, which he had held since 1698, because of his ill health. But, having received a 'kind invitation' from the town, he stood again, only to be heavily defeated.[36] Lord Harley's name was canvassed in relation to the county seat, but Lord Oxford was unable to secure his adoption, and he was eventually returned to the Commons on the family's interest in Cambridgeshire.[37] There appears to have been no suggestion that Edward should stand as a candidate in the 1722 elections. His role then seems to have been confined to supporting the efforts of his uncle and father, though there is some evidence that he was also involved as a burgess in the election at Ludlow.[38] However, in 1723, when Sir Edward Goodere's health declined, Edward was approached to stand for Herefordshire.[39] The offer appealed to him, and later in the year he was busy

[31] Brampton Bryan MSS, Bundle 7.

[32] H.M.C., *Portland MSS*, VII, 214: Stratford to Lord Harley, 6 Jan. 1715/16.

[33] Below p. 227: EH to Oxford, 5 Apr. 1720.

[34] Sedgwick, I, 380–1; H.M.C., *Portland MSS*, V, 663; Brampton Bryan MSS, Bundle 117: correspondence on Radnor election in 1715.

[35] B.L., Add. MS 70237: EH to Oxford, 12 Sept. 1718.

[36] Sedgwick, II, 110

[37] *Ibid.*, p. 111. See below, pp. lvi–lviii.

[38] Below p. 238: Frederick Cornwall to EH, 23 Mar. 1722.

[39] B.L., Add. MS 70085: Auditor Harley to ?, 9 Apr. 1723; below pp. 240–1: EH to Mr Brome, 18 Apr. 1723.

cultivating his interest.[40] However, the fears about Goodere's health proved unfounded and it was not until the general election of 1727 that Edward was returned as M.P. for Herefordshire along with Velters Cornewall.

Parliamentary activity of Edward Harley: house of commons

The destruction of the records of the house of commons in the 1834 fire has made it difficult to tell how active M.P.s were. The only remaining official record is the printed *Commons Journals*. This source does not record attendance, but it does list all M.P.s nominated to committees, the chairmen of committees of the whole house and, by implication, the chairmen of other committees,[41] and tellers in divisions. In theory, and usually in practice, an M.P. had to be present in the house to be nominated to a committee and, as not all M.P.s present were nominated (except for the committee of privileges, normally appointed on the first day of each session),[42] it may perhaps be assumed that nomination indicated interest by an M.P. in the subject of the committee, either personal or because the bill concerned the affairs of his constituents or locality. The mechanism for the choice of tellers in a division (two on each side) is not known, but acting as a teller clearly demonstrates interest in and commitment to the subject of the division. Bearing in mind the limitations of this evidence,[43] how active was Harley in the Commons?

He sat for 14 sessions from 1728 to 1741 and attended every session. During the first two years of George II's reign, as Linda Colley has shown, 'Disillusionment with the new King and depression at Walpole's effortless majorities led, inevitably, to parliamentary absenteeism.'[44] This may, in part, account for the fact that Harley was nominated to only three committees in his first session. However, his first nomination was to the second committee established in 1728, and he was the third named (and the second tory), possibly reflecting the prestige of the Harley name.[45] In the 1729 session Harley was nominated to 16 committees and acted as a teller once, for the minority on the Greenwich Hospital establishment.[46] The following year his tally of committees rose to 21. These included the chairmanship of one drafting committee,[47] for his own Jury Bill, and he subsequently acted as chairman of the committee of the whole house

---

[40] B.L., Add. MS 70237: EH to [Oxford], 6 Oct. 1723.

[41] The presenters of bill, first nominees to committees, reporters to the house from committees, and conveyors of bills to the Lords are almost always the same person and are usually the chairmen, though there are exceptions. This pattern can thus reveal the identity of the M.P. 'in charge' of particular pieces of legislation. Likewise, while every M.P. present was a member of a committee of the whole house, the chairman was often the M.P. who initiated the bill.

[42] If we take nomination to the committee of privileges as an indication of attendance on the first day of a session, Harley failed to attend on that day in the 1728, 1729, 1733, 1734, 1739–40 and 1740–1 sessions.

[43] Other indexes of parliamentary activity are even more problematic. Our knowledge of an M.P.'s speeches, for example, depends entirely on the vagaries of reporting in contemporary periodicals, letters and diaries.

[44] Colley, p. 209. A.A. Hanham concurs in this view. 'Significantly, there are almost no references to Tory speakers in the reports of parliamentary proceedings in 1728 and 1729 that were being compiled and sent to the Pretender's court, now preserved in the Stuart papers at Windsor.' 'Whig Opposition to Sir Robert Walpole in the House of Commons, 1727–1734', University of Leicester, Ph.D., 1992, p. 119.

[45] *C.J.*, XXI, 37, 67, 89.

[46] *Ibid.*, pp. 211–313 *passim* (tellership, p. 229).

[47] The 'drafting' committee, which drew up bills to be presented to the house. Membership of these committees can be taken to show a special interest in the subject of the proposed bill, since those named to 'draft' bills were usually those who spoke in favour of the motion for leave to introduce it – the first-named was invariably the M.P. who initiated the motion, the next was usually the seconder, and so on.

on the same bill.[48] Thereafter Harley was a regular committee man. For the ten years from 1731 to his succession to the peerage, his nominations to 342 committees ranged from a low of 18 in 1734 to a high of 48 in 1739. His increased activity may reflect renewed tory vigour as the parliamentary opposition to Walpole, in co-operation with dissident whigs, grew in strength. But it probably also reflects Harley's own growing prominence as a parliamentarian.

Harley was nominated to six 'drafting' committees while an M.P.: the Bribery Bill in 1729 (with four other M.P.s); the Jury Bill in 1730 (with three others); a bill to amend the 1730 July Act in 1731 in relation to Middlesex (with two others); a bill on the expiring laws in 1733, which included his own 1733 Jury Bill to extend the life of the 1730 act (with 16 others); a bill on the delay of legal causes after the issue had been joined (with three others); and he was added to the drafting committee on a bill to encourage iron making in England in 1738.[49] He was appointed as the chairman of six committees: on his Jury Bill in 1730, on four estate bills in 1733, 1739 and 1740–1, and on a bill concerned with a change of name in 1738.[50] He was also chairman of three committees of the whole house: again, on his own Jury Bill in 1730, on a divorce case in 1739, and on the delay of legal causes in 1740–1.[51]

Harley was clearly a conscientious committee man who was in demand for a wide variety of business. Overall, he averaged 24 committees per session between 1728 and 1741, and during the parliament of 1727–34 was among the 35 most frequently nominated M.P.s in the house. The subject of these committees ranged widely, but may be conveniently grouped into four: estate, economic, social, and miscellaneous, including legal affairs. Over the 14 sessions during which Harley sat in the Commons, estate bill committees accounted for just over 18 per cent of his nominations and the economic committees for a further 50 per cent. The latter included a great many bills on roads and highways, a high proportion of which were concerned with Hereford-shire and adjacent counties, enclosures and navigation. But there were also subjects of national importance, such as the importation of tobacco and iron, the manufacture and exportation of wool and woollens, the recovery of small debts, and fraud in gold and silver wares.

The miscellaneous group comprised nearly 30 per cent, with subjects ranging from bills on new churches and naturalizations, to the Cotton Library (reflecting his and his family's interest in book collecting) and the fees of officers of the Commons. A high proportion of this group concerned legal matters – the regulation of attorneys and solicitors, the language of legal proceedings, and the regulation of juries in Middlesex. Between 1727 and 1734, indeed, Harley was being named to most, if not all, Commons' committees on legal business, reflecting his interest in reforming certain areas of legal practice. The social group accounted for only 2 per cent of Harley's nominations, but it included two of the most contentious committees of the period: the enquiry into the state of gaols (1729) and the enquiry into the charitable corporations (1732, 1733).[52] While the gaols committee has been seen as a point of contact between the dissident whigs and the tories, it tended to be dominated by the whigs. Its active core of over 50 M.P.s included only six tories, of whom Harley was

---

[48] *Ibid.*, pp. 392–587 *passim* (Jury Bill, pp. 498, 522, 542, 551). It is possible that the Jury Bill drafting committee never met. See below, p. xlv, n. 119.

[49] *Ibid.*, XXI, 265, 498; XXII, 128; XXIII, 622, 187.

[50] *Ibid.*, XXI, 498; XXII, 159, 166; XXIII, 169, 280, 339, 347, 349, 692, 698.

[51] *Ibid.*, XXI, 542, 547, 666; XXIII, 147, 661, 663.

[52] *Ibid.*, XXI, 238; XXII, 14, 280.

not one.[53] Indeed, he saw it as giving birth to a distinct group of opposition, and often anti-clerical, whigs – 'the Spawn of the Goal [sic] Committee', as he referred to them in 1736.[54]

Harley was thus one of the most active tory 'reformers' in the house. As the 'spirit of reformation' grew in the 1730s and the tories shook off the lethargy of the late 1720s, Harley stands out as one of the five tories most committed to the attack on abuses in legal and related matters.[55] This is perhaps shown most clearly by his election by ballot to the committee of enquiry into the charitable corporation. In 1732 he polled 294 votes, coming equal seventh out of 21 M.P.s elected, and equal fourth of the tories. In 1733, when opposition voting was more 'cohesive and disciplined', he came equal second with 211 votes, another tory topping the poll with 212.[56] Harley's position as a leading tory activist on legal reform is underlined by his appearance as one of eight tories in the opposition list for the customs' fraud enquiry in 1733.[57]

Finally, he was a teller on 19 occasions: once each in 1729, 1731, 1732, 1736 and 1737; twice in 1734, 1735, 1739–40 and 1740–1; and three times in 1733 and 1739. In all but one case, the vote in 1740–1 over the recovery of small debts, Harley was with the minority. Some of these divisions took place on legal matters, such as the prevention of wrongful imprisonment in Scotland (1735) and justices of assize (1739), which reflect his personal interest and commitment to reform. Others, like the votes on the Place Bills of 1734 and 1740 and the 1736 Bill for regulating elections, were on legislation which, as we shall see, was close to Harley's heart as a 'country' tory. Others were on tactical and substantive motions intended by the opposition to condemn government policy – on policy towards Spain (1739–40), on supply and taxation (1733, 1734, 1737, 1739), on elections (1733), on a call of the house (1732), and on the address on the king's speech (1735).[58]

Parliamentary activity of Edward Harley: house of lords

The historian of the house of lords is better provided with sources which make possible an analysis of the parliamentary activities of peers and bishops. The printed *Journals* record attendance,[59] protests (with signatories), and chairmen of committees (those lords who reported from committees to the house).[60] Unlike the *Commons*

---

53 Hanham, 'Whig Opposition', pp. 119, 236–7, 242; Colley, p. 211. Harley was not one of the 88 nominated to the gaols committee in 1730. *C.J.*, XXI, 444–5.

54 Below p. 19.

55 Hanham, 'Whig Opposition', pp. 276–7, 280–1.

56 *Ibid.*, pp. 315–16, 336–7. In 1732 he was also nominated to the committee to manage the conference with the Lords over the charitable corporation. *C.J.*, XXI, 848.

57 H.M.C., *15th Report, Appendix, Part VI*, pp. 112–13: Charles Howard to Lord Carlisle, 24 Apr. 1733.

58 *C.J.*, XXI, 229, 635, 826; XXII, 115, 148, 201, 230, 258, 328, 484, 715, 834; XXIII, 236, 359, 361, 407, 438, 635, 692.

59 There are two problems with the printed attendance record, which is based on the manuscript minutes of the house: the latter is not infallible and the former sometimes differs from the minutes. For a discussion of this problem see *The London Diaries of William Nicolson, Bishop of Carlisle, 1702–1718*, ed. Clyve Jones and Geoffrey Holmes (Oxford, 1985), pp. 27–32.

60 They also record nominations to committees. But, as the practice of the house by the eighteenth century was that *all* members present in the house when the committee was established were automatically members of the committee, nomination is no guide to the interest or commitment of a peer or bishop. A.J. Rees, 'The Practice and Procedure of the House of Lords, 1714–1784', University of Wales (Aberystwyth), Ph.D., 1987, p. 463.

Journals, the *Lords Journals* do not record divisions and tellers. But these can be found in the manuscript minutes, which survived the 1834 fire.

Between the succession of Harley to the earldom of Oxford in 1741 and his death in 1755, he attended all 15 sessions of parliament. The level of his attendance varied from a high of 75 per cent in the 1743–4 session to a low of 20 per cent in the short five day session in the summer of 1754. His average attendance over the 15 sessions was 47 per cent. (See Fig. 1 below.) Insufficient work has been done on attendance in this period for a wide-ranging comparison to be drawn between Oxford and his fellow peers. However, his average attendance was better than that of all but 13 of the 56 bishops who sat in the Lords between 1741 and 1762. This fact is the more significant because the bishops were generally more diligent in parliamentary duties than the peers.[61] On the other hand, if we compare Oxford with four of the other leading tory peers in the 1741–2 session, we can see that he comes third after Bathurst, who had a staggering attendance record of 96 per cent, and Gower with 61 per cent. Thanet comes fourth with 54 per cent, while Lord Ailesbury, another leading tory, attended on 45 per cent of the days on which the house sat. In 1743–4 Oxford was the most frequent attender among the leading tory peers, present on 63 occasions (75 per cent), followed by Ailesbury (74 per cent), Gower (70 per cent), Bathurst (68 per cent), Beaufort (34 per cent) and Thanet (33 per cent).

Fig. 1. The attendance of the third earl of Oxford, 1741–1755

Date of Session	(a) No. of days the Lords sat	(b) No. of days Oxford sat	(b) as a percentage of (a)
1741–2	86	52[62]	60
1742–3	62	37	60
1743–4	85	63	75
1744–5	70	46	66
1745–61	26	46	37
1746–7	89	43	48
1747–8	77	40	52
1748–9	89	44	49
1749–50	64	14	22
1750–1	82	45	55
1751–2	67	19	28
1753	82	33	40
1753–4	68	26	38
1754	5	1	20
1754–5	75[63]	16	21
Total	1,126	524	47

Source: L.J., XVI–XXVIII, passim.

[61] Stephen Taylor, 'The Bishops at Westminster in the Mid-Eighteenth Century', in *A Pillar of the Constitution. The House of Lords in British Politics, 1640–1784*, ed. Clyve Jones (1989), pp. 139–40, 157–8.

[62] Oxford was introduced into the Lords on 14 Jan. 1742, and from this date he was present on 67 per cent of the days on which the house met.

[63] The Lords sat for 80 days in this session, but five of them occurred after Oxford had died.

One way of mitigating the effects of absence from the Lords was for a peer to leave a proxy with one of his colleagues to be cast, if called for, in divisions of the house (but not in committees). Oxford left his proxy only once during the 14 sessions which he attended, in his last session of 1754–5. On 26 February 1755 his proxy was registered as being held by Lord Foley, who continued to hold it until Oxford died. Oxford held another peer's proxy only twice: Lord Lichfield's from 14 February until the end of the session on 2 May 1745, and Lord Foley's from 10 April until 11 May 1748, this proxy being vacated by Foley's return to the house.[64] In none of these three periods did a division take place in which proxies were used. Indeed, in the 14 sessions attended by Oxford, proxies were used only six times, and only once after the 1743–4 session, reflecting the fall in the number of divisions in this period compared with previous decades. The infrequent use of proxies in the 1740s and early 1750s may account for Oxford's sparse record in his area, though it is also clear that the administration made more use of them than the opposition.

While Oxford was a diligent attender at debates, he never acted as a teller in the Lords' divisions. This fact, however, probably does not reflect any lack of interest in matters before the house. During the 1740s and early 1750s the number of divisions declined quite dramatically from the level of the previous three decades. There were 14 in 1741–2 and 11 in the following session, but only one other session in the period witnessed more than three.[65] More indicative of Oxford's political commitment is his record of protesting. By 1741 the great days of protesting were over, and during his time in the Lords there were only 15 protests.[66] Oxford signed all but two: those of 12 March 1742 on the Mutiny Bill, which was signed by Abingdon alone, and 9 December 1743 on pay for the Hanoverian forces, which was entered before Oxford had arrived in London. Oxford's record, indeed, was better than that of any other opposition peer. His closest rivals were Shaftesbury, a leading opposition whig, who signed 12, and three other leading tory peers – Lichfield (11), Beaufort (11) and Ailesbury (10). Protests provided those in opposition with an excellent opportunity for propaganda, especially when lords entered their reasons for protesting. It is hardly surprising, therefore, that most of Oxford's protests were on issues close to the heart of the opposition: Place and Pension Bills, the employment of Hessian and Hanoverian troops, the continuation of the war in Flanders (1746) and the Heritable Jurisdictions Act of 1747. Two protests, however, do not fall into this category: those on the bill for the more speedy trial of the rebels in 1746, which Oxford entered alone, and on the Worcester Roads Bill of 1749, which he signed along with Shaftesbury and Foley. But both of these protests reflect Oxford's continuing interest in the law, and particularly his concern at the erosion of English liberties. He claimed that the bills were pieces of retrospective legislation and thus, as he noted in his journal about the former, 'contrary to the Common Law of England'.[67]

64 H.L.R.O., Proxy Books, XVII–XXX (1741/2–1754/5).

65 There were eight divisions in the session of 1747–8. By contrast, there were none in the sessions of 1744–5 and 1754.

66 Two more were entered on 22 Dec. 1741, before Oxford was introduced into the house on 14 Jan. 1742. These were signed by Haversham alone. There were no protests between June 1749 and November 1755. The following is based on the protests in the *L.J.*, since not all are listed in J.E. Thorold Rogers, *A Complete Collection of the Protests of the Lords* (3 vols., Oxford, 1865). Those of 12 Mar., 26 Mar., 6 Apr. 1742 and 25 Feb. 1746 are missing, along with the second protest of 1 Feb. 1743.

67 *L.J.*, XXVI, 544; XXVII, 356–7; below p. 76. Oxford did not enter his reasons for protesting against the Bill for the more Speedy Trial of the Rebels. The point about retrospective legislation was one of four reasons for the protest against the Worcester Roads Bill.

An analysis of the chairmen of committees in the Lords has been undertaken by Sir John Sainty.[68] By the late 1710s the chairmanship of the committee of the whole house was usually carried out by one individual, who received remuneration in the form of a pension.[69] Chairmanship of 'select' committees (not a term used in the eighteenth century), however, remained open to any peer or bishop. Between 1741 and 1755 Oxford chaired 18 committees with a maximum of no more than four in any one session (1741–2 and 1748–9).[70] None of these was concerned with controversial legislation: 11 were estate bills, four were road bills (three of which concerned Herefordshire roads), two were naturalizations, and one was a local tithe bill.

Harley and toryism

Recent historians of early eighteenth-century toryism have identified Edward Harley as one of the party's leading figures.[71] This is not surprising. He came from a prominent tory family and, as we have seen, had tory principles instilled into him in his youth. Even after the '45 rebellion, when the tory party was beginning to lose a little of its distinctive identity, contemporaries still did not hesitate to call Harley a tory.[72] Moreover, an examination of the surviving parliamentary division lists for the period shows that Harley consistently voted against the administration, both in the Commons and in the Lords.[73] Here, however, one might raise questions about Harley's toryism. Some historians have argued that the whig–tory dichotomy of Anne's reign was replaced in the years after the Hanoverian succession by a court–country one, a country opposition to the whig regimes of George I's and George II's reigns supplanting former loyalties.[74] The evidence of division lists appears to support this interpretation. In all the lists Harley appears voting alongside whigs as well as tories, and whig names appear on all the protests which Harley signed while in the Lords.

Was there, therefore, anything distinctively tory about Harley's politics between 1727 and 1755, or should he be regarded simply as an adherent of an undifferentiated country opposition? It is difficult to believe that Harley himself would have spent long pondering these questions. It is clear from his journal and correspondence that, while he was prepared to act in concert with whigs on many issues, there was much that divided him from opposition whigs. Harley frequently attacked the behaviour of 'those who had given themselves the Name of Patriots'. Predictably, he was particularly scathing about the conduct of men who, in the aftermath of Walpole's fall, had been 'purchased by Places in the Treasury and Titles' and had 'betrayed' the 'Country Party'. But, even before 1742, he had been critical of the politicking of men with

---

[68] J.C. Sainty, *The Origin of the Office of Chairman of Committees in the House of Lords* (H.L.R.O. Memorandum No. 52, 1973).

[69] *Ibid.*, pp. 1–12. During the period Oxford was in the Lords, it was normally the earl of Warwick.

[70] In Sainty's ranking of members of the Lords by the number of 'select' committees they chaired, Oxford reached sixth position in 1741–2 and fourth in 1748–9. Only three other opposition peers chaired more committees in any one session: Sandwich in 1741–2, Folkestone in 1753 and Shaftesbury in 1744–5, 1746–7, 1748–9, 1751, 1751–2 and 1753. *Ibid.*, pp. 23–5.

[71] Sedgwick, I, 75–6; Eveline Cruickshanks, *Political Untouchables. The Tories and the '45* (1979), p. 76; Colley, pp. 68, 72–5.

[72] E.g., Horace Walpole, *Memoirs of King George II*, ed. John Brooke (3 vols., New Haven, 1985), I, 186.

[73] These comments are based on an analysis of the parliamentary lists recorded in *British Parliamentary Lists 1660–1800. A Register*, ed. G.M. Ditchfield, David Hayton and Clyve Jones (1995).

[74] For the best statement of this view, see W.A. Speck, 'Whigs and Tories Dim their Glories: English Political Parties under the First Two Georges', in *The Whig Ascendancy. Colloquies on Hanoverian England*, ed. John Cannon (1981), pp. 51–70.

whom he co-operated on occasions. Thus, the 1739 secession was denounced by Harley as 'An Idle Project, contrary to all the Rules and Being of Parliament'.[75]

However, the differences between Harley (and most tories) and the opposition whigs were highlighted most starkly by religion, and in particular the debates of the 1736 session, the high point of anti-clericalism in the 1730s.[76] Three measures came before the Commons during this session: the Mortmain Bill, which restricted the ability of charitable corporations to receive benefactions of land and estate from individuals; the Quakers Tithe Bill, an attempt to relieve Quakers of high costs when they were prosecuted for non-payment of tithes; and a motion for the repeal of the Test Act. All received support from both government and opposition whigs, and all were opposed by the tories. In Harley's opinion both the Mortmain Bill and the Quakers Tithe Bill were cloaks for more fundamental attacks on the Church and anglicanism. He believed that the aim of the latter was to exempt the Quakers 'from the payment' of tithes, while the former was an attempt to undermine corporate anglican philanthropy, its 'true Design' being 'against all publick Charitys'. Harley was active in the opposition to these measures, presenting the petition of the trustees of the charity schools against the Mortmain Bill,[77] and he was not slow to note the role of the opposition whigs in supporting them: 'None were more forward in those Invectives than Mr Sandys and the Patriots, (as they are termed) and those who by the Name of Georgians, (being Trustees for that Colony) as the Heathcotes, White, Hucks, Moore Laroche etc and were the Spawn of the Goal [sic] Committee.'[78] Tories like Harley were certainly prepared to work with dissident whigs when they shared common ground, but tory anglicanism inhibited the formation of a united country opposition.

It is always difficult to determine how far political opinions are influenced by religious belief. In Harley's case, however, it seems clear that his support for anglicanism and the Church was an expression of his own deep religious convictions. He came from a deeply religious family and had learnt his prayers well. Harley's more personal letters, especially those to his wife, are suffused with pious reflexions, which go far beyond what was merely conventional in the mid-eighteenth century. Central to his beliefs, moreover, was a providentialism which linked religion with public affairs. Thus, on the defeat of the Blasphemy Bill in 1721, he wrote to his aunt: 'I think since our Holy Religion and its Great Author is thus betrayed, We can expect nothing but Misery and Desolation.' Twenty years later he was writing to his wife in a similar vein: 'we have no reason to expect fruitful seasons while so much Corruption and vile Perjury prevails.'[79] In the light of the Auditor's early presbyterianism and his long and slow transformation into a high churchman, it is perhaps unsurprising that Edward's

---

[75] Below pp. 59, 56, 37. See also, e.g., his criticisms of the behaviour of the whigs during the Porteous debates. Below, p. 30.

[76] For the centrality of religion to tory identity in this period, see Colley, ch. 4.

[77] He was approached by the trustees partly because his father had been their chairman between 1725 and 1735. He had also defended them when they were attacked in parliament during the 1733 session. Church of England Record Centre, NS/SP/1/1: Minutes of the trustees of the charity schools, 6 Apr. 1736; *The Diaries of Thomas Wilson, D.D., 1731–7 and 1750*, ed. C.L.S. Linnell (1964), p. 95.

[78] Below pp. 21, 19. Of the Georgians named, Hucks, White, More, Laroche and John Heathcote were all generally supporters of the administration. George and William Heathcote were opposition whigs. Sedgwick, II, 121–5, 156–7, 198, 274–5, 533–4. The gaols committee 'was a fraternity of rank-and-file Whigs in which discontented and uncommitted independents tended to predominate'. Hanham, *Whig Opposition*, p. 242.

[79] Below pp. 233, 254: EH to Abigail Harley, 4 May 1721; EH to Martha Harley, 12 May 1741.

own anglicanism was tinged with a residue of what might be called puritanism, illustrated by his reluctance to travel on Sundays.[80]

Harley thus fits the profile of an early Hanoverian tory. Before moving on, however, a slight note of caution should be sounded. There is no doubt that Harley was perceived as a tory by contemporaries, and, on occasions, he was not only seen, but also acted, as a tory leader.[81] But, in neither his journal nor his correspondence did he ever describe himself simply as 'a tory'. On a number of occasions he came very close to so doing. Thus, in his comments on the Commons' debate of 13 February 1741 he described the behaviour of the 'Torys' in a context which clearly included him.[82] Nonetheless, Harley's reticence about explicitly calling himself a tory might indicate that he retained some aversion to 'party' as a form of political organization, inherited from his uncle and father. Indeed, as late as 1733 the Auditor can be found rejoicing in the fact that his son had never 'become a Prostitute to any Party'.[83] Whatever the case, Harley was never a 'high flying' tory. His early distrust of extremists like Sacheverell continued through his political career, as was recognized in 1745 by the earl of Chesterfield, who clearly distinguished between the 'cool good sense' of men like Oxford and 'the red hot absurd Tories' led by the duke of Beaufort.[84]

Harley and jacobitism

In recent years one of the major debates in the field of early eighteenth-century politics has been the identity of the tory party. Was it a predominantly jacobite party, the position enunciated in the History of Parliament's volumes for 1715–54 and developed by Eveline Cruickshanks in *Political Untouchables*? Or was it, as Linda Colley has argued, a party fundamentally loyal to the Hanoverian succession with a small jacobite wing?[85] Edward Harley has never been more than a bit player in this debate. However, he has been described as a jacobite – explicitly by the History of Parliament and implicitly in *Political Untouchables*.[86] Linda Colley, by contrast, has portrayed Harley as a committed Hanoverian tory in her article on the Cocoa Tree.[87] An examination of these claims will probably do little to settle the wider debate about the tory party, but the issue must be addressed as it is central to understanding the nature of Harley's toryism. There are five pieces of evidence which can be used to support the claim that Harley was a jacobite, two of which come from jacobite sources and three from whig sources. By examining each, it will become clear that the case is, at best, very weak.

The first piece of 'jacobite' evidence is the list of lords and gentlemen given to James Butler, an agent of Louis XV, in September 1743.[88] This has been described as

---

[80] B.L., Add. MS 70497: EH to Martha Harley, 3 May 1741.

[81] See below, pp. l–lii.

[82] Below p. 51.

[83] B.L., Add. MS 70498, ff. 61–2: Auditor Harley to EH, 8 June 1733.

[84] P.R.O., Granville Papers, 30/29/1/11: Chesterfield to Gower, 13 Apr. 1745 n.s.; *Private Correspondence of Chesterfield and Newcastle 1744–46*, ed. Sir Richard Lodge (Camden Society, 3rd ser., XLIV, 1930), p. 44: Chesterfield to Newcastle, 13 Apr. 1745 n.s.

[85] Sedgwick, I, 62–78; Cruickshanks, *Political Untouchables, passim*; Colley, ch. 2.

[86] Sedgwick, I, 76; Cruickshanks, *Political Untouchables*, pp. 75, 105.

[87] Linda Colley, 'The Loyal Brotherhood and the Cocoa Tree: The London Organization of the Tory Party, 1727–1760', *Historical Journal*, XX (1977), 77–95.

[88] The original is in Archives du Ministère des Affaires étrangères, Paris, Mémoires et Documents, Angleterre, 76, ff. 203–7. It is printed in Cruickshanks, *Political Untouchables*, pp. 115–38. A copy sent by Balhaldy to James, the Old Pretender, is in the Stuart Papers at Windsor Castle, Royal Archives, S.P. 253/51.

'a list of persons expected to declare for a restoration, or more probably to declare for a free Parliament (as in 1660) to effect a restoration, in the event of a successful attempt by the French to restore the Stuarts'.[89] There are, however, problems with this interpretation. First, although it is headed 'Etat des seigneurs ... sur lesquels on peut compter', the document in fact appears to be little more than a list of those in opposition to the ministry, including such stalwart whigs as the dukes of Bedford, Rutland and Somerset, the earls of Chesterfield, Stanhope, Rockingham, Shaftesbury and Carlisle, George Grenville and George Lyttelton. Second, the manner of composition of the list hardly inspires confidence in its accuracy and suggests that it was probably another product of the exaggerated and unrealistic optimism that distorted so much jacobite intelligence. While we know that Butler attended the Lichfield races, an annual social occasion which brought together the region's tories, Balhaldy's letter to the Old Pretender describing the way in which the list was drawn up makes it clear that, for the most part, it was reliant on information provided by a few committed jacobite agents in London – 'it was not possible to make [it] fuller or distincter, in the time, or the then season of the year, when every creature was in the countrey, who could best inform about any particular county'. In fact, Balhaldy does much to destroy the credibility of the document, claiming that it actually underestimates jacobite strength. Remarkably, he suggests 'that it is not to be doubted, but there are many of as great rank, interest, influence and attachment to the royal cause, if not greater, Omitted, then those who are named'. Indeed, in his opinion 'there was no period of time, since the revolution, but there were three fourths of the landed interest of England, and two thirds of the City of London, zealous for your Majestie's return'.[90]

Thomas Carte provides the second piece of evidence for Harley's jacobitism in a report sent to the Stuart court in exile in 1749. In it he wrote that 'There can't be 2 better men, nor are there any more universally esteemed than the D[uke] of B[eaufort] and E[arl] of O[xford] the chief of the Tories, but they are not active enough, the one by his gout, the other by his constitution.'[91] As with the Butler list, there are problems with the content of Carte's letter. He merely stated that Beaufort and Oxford were tory leaders, not jacobite ones. The claim that his statement shows that Harley was a jacobite thus rests on the contentious assumption that the tory party was a jacobite party, though, to be fair, this was probably an assumption shared by Carte himself. Moreover, Carte himself can hardly be described as a reliable witness. He was notorious for his gullibility – in 1739 he was persuaded that Walpole was inclining towards jacobitism and acted as an intermediary between him and the Pretender – and it is difficult to believe that tory M.P.s would have trusted much information to him.[92]

One piece of evidence from whig sources provides superficially strong evidence of Harley's sympathy for jacobitism. It comes from a letter from Alexander Hume Campbell, the opposition whig M.P. for Berwickshire, about the trial of the rebel peers in 1746. Hume Campbell reported that

the Chancellor some few days ago told Lord Oxford that he must stay in town for some time. The other said he would not. The Chancellor with some warmth

89 Cruickshanks, *Political Untouchables*, p. 115.

90 Royal Archives, S.P. 253/14: Balhaldy to James, 13 Nov. 1743; Colley, p. 71.

91 Royal Archives, S.P. Box 1/299: Thomas Carte to ?, n.d. [1749]. In Sedgwick, I, 76, this passage appears to be quoted as direct evidence that Harley was a jacobite. In Cruickshanks, *Political Untouchables*, p. 75, it is paraphrased thus: 'Carte who knew him describes him as being devoted to the Pretender's cause.'

92 G.H. Jones, *The Main Stream of Jacobitism* (Cambridge, Mass., 1954), pp. 205–6; Cruickshanks, *Political Untouchables*, pp. 23–4.

answered that the Lords would force him, and being [asked] how, said, By fine as they had done in the year one thousand seven hundred and fifteen and would be very severe. The other replied he would stand it all and go out of town...[93]

Hume Campbell told this story as a rumour, but Oxford did not attend the trial, excusing himself by the illness of his wife and son in letters to Newcastle and Hardwicke.[94] However, Hume Campbell also notes that the reason for Oxford's uneasiness related to a constitutional debate about whether it was necessary, by the terms of the Union, for all the Scots peers to be summoned to the trial. Indeed, he predicted that, to circumvent this problem, the rebel peers would be proceeded against by impeachment, and it was this device to which Oxford was objecting. Thus, even if we discount the corroborating evidence of John Harley and assume that Oxford's excuse was manufactured, he was just as likely to have absented himself from the trial because of constitutional scruples as jacobite ones. Indeed, the former are the more plausible if we bear in mind his concern for the liberties of Britons, manifested in his opposition to the government over the Porteous affair and in some of the protests which he entered as a peer.[95]

The second piece of whig evidence comes from Horace Walpole's account of the debates on the Scottish Forfeited Estates Bill of 1752 in his *Memoirs*. He notes that Oxford was one of 'six Tory lords' who voted against the Bill, while talking earlier of the opposition of 'half a dozen Jacobite lords'.[96] Walpole undoubtedly saw Oxford as a jacobite. However, Walpole's testimony must be approached with considerable caution. Even if he did not believe that all tories were jacobites, he certainly used the two terms interchangeably. To rely on Walpole's identification of jacobites thus involves the *assumption* that the tory party was a jacobite party.

Finally, there is Chesterfield's correspondence with Newcastle and Gower about the state of the tory party in 1745 after Gower's defection to the administration, which Cruickshanks uses to support her case that Oxford was a jacobite. The crux of what Chesterfield had to say about Oxford is contained in his statement that 'the small band of opposition which I find is forming itself under the Duke of Beaufort's banner, would I believe give neither of us much trouble were it not for two or three names that I see in that list, I mean Lord Oxford, Watkin and Cotton'.[97] It is clear at once that Chesterfield does not call Oxford a jacobite. Cruickshanks, however, glosses Chesterfield's letter by quoting R.J. Phillimore, the nineteenth-century biographer of George Lyttelton, who wrote of this episode that 'when it was discovered that Gower was really a friend to the Hanover succession, the Tories discarded him for being their leader, and adopted a determined Jacobite the Duke of Beaufort in his stead'.[98] Thus, by implication, Oxford too was a jacobite because he enlisted under 'Beaufort's banner'. There is little doubt about Beaufort's jacobitism. However, Chesterfield is very careful to distinguish between Oxford and Beaufort. Chesterfield was clearly surprised that Oxford was co-operating with Beaufort. As already noted, he believed that he could be separated from 'the red hot absurd Tories'. Indeed, Chesterfield had hopes that Gower would be able 'carry off the best' of the tories, including Oxford,

---

[93] H.M.C., *Polwarth MSS*, V, 179.

[94] Below pp. 258–9.

[95] Below p. 30; see above p. xxxvi. For John Harley's reference to the illnesses of his mother and brother see his letter of 29 July 1746, below p. 260.

[96] Walpole, *Memoirs*, I, 186, 179.

[97] P.R.O., Granville Papers, 30/29/1/11, ff. 290–1: Chesterfield to Gower, 13 Apr. 1745 n.s.

[98] Cruickshanks, *Political Untouchables*, p. 75, quoting *Memoirs and Correspondence of George Lord Lyttelton*, ed. R.J. Phillimore (2 vols., 1845), I, 238.

leaving 'only a marked avowed Jacobite faction behind him'.[99] Rather than hinting at Oxford's jacobitism, therefore, this letter can be interpreted as demonstrating that, in Chesterfield's opinion at least, Oxford was *not* a jacobite tory.

It is, of course, impossible ever to demonstrate conclusively that someone was not a jacobite. The nature of the movement demanded secrecy; sympathizers often destroyed compromising correspondence and were inclined to equivocate about their views even to friends and relations. However, it is clear that the evidence for Harley's jacobitism is, at best, very thin, if not virtually non-existent. The case against Harley being a jacobite becomes stronger if other evidence is examined. There are, for example, no letters from Harley to the Stuart court in exile, although such letters from other Englishmen can be found among the Stuart papers. Nor is there any evidence of Harley being involved in any of the many jacobite plots and conspiracies. He was certainly not involved in the planning for the invasion and rebellion in 1743–5. Indeed, with the exception of the Butler list discussed above, there is not even a mention of him in any of the letters and papers of that period in either the French archives or the Stuart Papers. On the other hand, Harley's willingness, in common with many other tories, to become involved in negotiations with both the ministry and Leicester House in the 1740s and 1750s would seem to indicate that he had some positive commitment to the Hanoverian regime.[100] So, if Edward Harley was not a jacobite tory, what kind of a tory was he?

Harley and 'country' toryism

In a typically self-conscious moment Harley wrote to his wife in 1731 saying 'one cannot bear too publick a testimony against Pensions and Corruption.'[101] Judging by the content of his 'Journal', he never forgot this early statement of his responsibilities as a member of parliament. It also neatly summarizes much that was central to Harley's political philosophy. In 1982, in a very apt phrase, Linda Colley described him as an exponent of 'Country toryism'. The pairing of these two concepts should not surprise us. As David Hayton has shown, as early as 'Anne's reign Country sentiment seems to have been largely absorbed into back-bench Toryism'.[102] Harley's 'country' toryism involved him subscribing to the 'country' platform of the 1730s, enunciated in the *Craftsman*, which brought together dissident whigs and tories in opposition to Walpole's administration. But, as we shall see, it also meant more.

Harley was a consistent and enthusiastic advocate of the 'country' programme of reforms which aimed at securing the independence of parliament and of its members from the corrupt influence of the ministry. Thus, he supported bills to prevent bribery at elections and for higher landed qualifications for M.P.s, as well as the place and pension bills that provided the main focus for 'country' attacks on the administration in session after session.[103] He had no problems acting with 'the Patriots' on measures such as these, and he was a teller alongside Samuel Sandys for the Place Bill in 1740.[104]

---

99 *Ibid.*; *Correspondence of Chesterfield and Newcastle*, p. 44.
100 These negotiations are discussed below, pp. lii–lv.
101 Below p. 248: EH to Martha Harley, 18 Feb. 1731.
102 Colley, p. 73; David Hayton, 'The "Country" Interest and the Party System, 1689–c.1720', in *Party and Management in Parliament, 1660–1784*, ed. Clyve Jones (Leicester, 1984), pp. 37–85, quotation at p. 65.
103 On the 1729 Bribery Bill, see below p. 243: EH to Auditor Harley, 11 May 1729. On the 1734 Landed Qualification Bill, see below p. 250: Auditor Harley to EH, 9 Feb. 1733/4. On pension bills, see below pp. 247–8: EH to Martha Harley, 18 Feb. 1731; *L.J.*, XXVI, 85. On place bills, see below pp. 41, 51, 58; *L.J.*, XXVI, 92.
104 Below p. 41.

He was also happy to join with dissident whigs in what he regularly called 'the Country party' on motions to reduce the size of the army, to give Vernon the credit for the capture of Porto Bello and, especially, in attacks on the employment of Hessian and Hanoverian troops.[105] Harley took particular pleasure in joining the popular cry against Hanoverian influence, determined to protest 'against making myself and those I represent tributary to any foreign power'. This should serve as a timely reminder that anti-Hanoverianism was not inconsistent with loyalty to the Hanoverian succession. Indeed, as Harley wryly noted in the debate on the employment of Hessian troops in 1730, had any tory been as 'free with his Majesty's dominions abroad, and talked so much of the Compact between King and People' as some of the 'old Whigs', 'He had been sent to the tower'.[106]

When the whigs fell away from true 'country' principles, however, Harley denounced them. Thus, William Pulteney's Place Bill, introduced after the fall of Walpole in 1742, was condemned as a 'sham Bill and of no use'.[107] But, even before the 'betrayal' of 1742, there were tensions between dissident whigs and tories even over 'country' issues. As early as March 1721, in one of his earliest recorded comments on a 'country' issue, Harley was expressing concern about the future of parliament itself in response to speculation that the whigs would introduce a bill to prolong still further the life of the 1715 parliament.[108] It was only natural, therefore, that in 1734 he was one of the speakers in support of a motion to repeal the Septennial Act. This was a classic country proposal, intended to make the Commons more responsive to those it represented by subjecting its members to more frequent elections. Even so, the motion, moved by the tory William Bromley, revealed tensions between opposition whigs and tories. Some whigs saw it as an attack on their electoral influence, while others continued to regard the Septennial Act as one of the pillars of the Hanoverian succession. The debate was dominated by the tories and it was only with reluctance that the Patriots supported the motion.[109]

Harley's concerns, however, were never limited to the programme of reform enunciated by the 'Country Party'. In his case, at least, country principles entailed a more general commitment to combat corruption and jobbery, which was directed in part, though never exclusively, against the ministry. One aspect of this was his intense interest in election petitions. There were occasional triumphs. In 1735 Harley was able to record the role of the independent whig Sir Joseph Jekyll in pointing out the 'injustice' of the Marlborough petition, as a result of which Walpole was not able to 'Spirit up his Fools'. But more often he is found expressing a widespread opposition complaint, that the ministry used its majority in the committee of elections in a partial way to unseat opposition M.P.s and replace them with its own supporters. The Wells election petition of 1735 was particularly galling as it resulted in the return of William Piers who, Harley noted, 'was never chose by this City, yet had been twice voted duly elected by the House of Commons'.[110] Harley's personal campaign against corruption, however, is revealed more clearly in the list of bills which he denounced as 'jobs', such as the Westminster Bridge Bill (1736), the Derwentwater Estate Bill (1738), the

---

[105] Below pp. 36, 45; B.L., Add. MS 51396, f. 27: Winnington to Fox, [5 Feb. 1730]; H.M.C., *Egmont Diary*, I, 315; Cobbett, XII, 1186–9.

[106] Below p. 244: EH to Martha Harley, 5 Feb. 1730.

[107] Below p. 58.

[108] B.L., Add. MS 70145: EH to Abigail Harley, 12 Mar. 1720/1, 20 June 1721.

[109] *The Political State of Great Britain*, XLVIII (1734), 547; Hanham, 'Whig Opposition', pp. 389–93; Colley, p. 216.

[110] Below, p. 6. Piers unseated Harley's old friend and correspondent, Edward Prideaux Gwyn.

bill for registering deeds (1740), the grants made in 1741 to pay Henry Popple's debt and the Buckingham Assizes Bill (1748). Unfortunately, his 'Journal' does not record enough details to reveal the reasons why Harley objected to these bills, but it is clear that he felt that most, if not all, involved sacrificing the national interest to sectional or individual interests. Moreover, these were not necessarily party issues. On the Westminster Bridge Bill, for example, Harley found himself as one of a small minority of 12, among whom M.P.s with City links were prominent.[111]

It is tempting to see country ideology as essentially backward-looking, even negative, a reaction to the growth of government which had taken place so rapidly as a consequence of Britain's emergence as a major European power after 1688. This was certainly an important stimulus to country politics, but so too was a more positive commitment to the preservation of the rights and liberties of Englishmen. These two strands, of course, often converged, as in the opposition to the 1741 Seamen's Bill, when it was the state, justifying itself by the needs of defence in time of war, which was threatening to impose measures 'destructive of the Liberty and Rights of the Subjects'.[112] Moreover, there was also an active, reformist strand to 'country' toryism. As Linda Colley has shown, this found particular expression among the members of the Harley Board, the tory club established by Edward Harley in the autumn of 1727.[113] Its members were the moving force behind a number of pieces of reformist legislation in the parliament of 1727–34. Board members brought in the 1727 bill to prevent irregularity in the delivery of election writs and a 1734 'bill that would have shifted responsibility for road maintenance from the poorer to the more affluent inhabitants of each parish'. More significantly, in 1732 Thomas Bramston secured an act to regulate the qualifications of J.P.s, while in 1730 Edward Harley piloted through parliament his own Jury Bill. All these measures reflected the concerns of the 'country' programme by seeking, at least in part, to combat the corrupt exercise of money and power. But, conversely, and more positively, they sought also to buttress the influence of the landed gentry in the administration of local government and justice.

As we have already seen, Harley was one of the most active tory 'reformers' in the Commons. But it is worth looking in some detail at the Jury Bill, in part because it was Harley's major legislative achievement and in part because it was one of the major achievements of 'country' toryism. It should be noted, however, that the tory reformism exemplified by the Harley Board only provides part of the context for the passage of the Jury Bill. A recent study of the opposition in the Commons between 1727 and 1734 has pointed out that this was a time of particularly acute criticism of the workings of the civil law, so that by '1730 the impetus to eliminate corruption of one kind or another had become almost an obsession with MPs'.[114] One ministerial commentator wrote that 'there are but too many young Gentlemen of the House, who think themselves not only empower'd, but also qualified to compose, and digest a new Corpus juris for the use and government of this nation'.[115] The list of 'law reform activists' includes not only tories and opposition whigs, but a fair number of government supporters. Their interests ranged from attacks on the fees of court officials, through attempts to reform the practices of the ecclesiastical courts and small debts bills, to

111 Below pp. 13, 34, 48, 53, 82.
112 Below p. 52.
113 The remainder of this paragraph is based on Colley, 'The Loyal Brotherhood and the Cocoa Tree', pp. 82–3.
114 Hanham, 'Whig Opposition', pp. 257–8.
115 B.L., Althorp MS, E4: Robert Taylor to S. Poyntz [26 Feb. 1730], quoted in *ibid.*, p. 258.

the activities of the gaols committee.[116] Harley's bill of 1730 can be seen as but one manifestation of their grievances, as the preamble to the bill makes clear:

> Whereas many Evil Practices have been used in corrupting of Jurors returned for the Tryal of Issues joined to be tryed before Justices of Assize or *Nisi prius*, and many Neglects or Abuses have happened in making up the Lists of Free-holders who ought to serve in such Tryals to the great Injury of many Persons in their Properties and Estates. In order to prevent the like Practices, Neglects and Abuses, Be it Enacted...[117]

On 13 March 1730 Harley was given leave by the Commons to bring in a bill for the better regulation of juries and was ordered to prepare the bill along with William Lacon Childe, Thomas Bramston and Sir William Yonge. The first two were tories, members of the Harley Board and active reformers.[118] Yonge, however, was a Walpolean whig, although Hanham does list him among the law reform activists.[119] Thirteen days later, on 26 March, Harley presented the bill to the house; it received its first reading and was ordered to be printed. In order to combat what were described as the 'many Evil Practices ... used in corrupting of Jurors', the bill aimed to establish new procedures for their selection.[120] On 11 April it was taken into consideration by a committee of the whole house with Harley in the chair. At this stage several amendments were made, and there is evidence that at least one – that on special juries – was a ministerial amendment brought forward by the attorney-general Philip Yorke and the solicitor general Charles Talbot.[121] Four days later Harley reported the amendments to the house, they were accepted and the bill was ordered to be engrossed. On 20 April it passed its third reading and Harley was ordered to carry it up to the Lords, which he did on the following day.[122]

The role of Yorke, Talbot and possibly Yonge in the bill's passage through the Commons is significant. The 'countenance', if not of the ministry then at least of some of its members, was clearly crucial to the success of a measure like the Jury Bill.[123] In this case the distinction between ministers and the ministry is an important one, because it is far from clear that the ministry had a clear collective position on the bill.

[116] Hanham, 'Whig Opposition', pp. 276–7.

[117] Lambert, VII, 28.

[118] Childe was one of the Shropshire M.P.s who, in 1727, had brought in a bill to prevent irregularity in the delivery of election writs. *C.J.*, XXI, 159; Sedgwick, I, 550. For Bramston, see above p. xliv.

[119] Sedgwick, II, 567; Hanham, 'Whig Opposition', p. 277. Drafting committees may not always have sat. (Hanham, 'Whig Opposition', pp. 275–7. Cf. Sheila Lambert, *Bills and Acts. Legislative Procedure in Eighteenth-Century England* (Cambridge, 1971), p. 62.) In some cases bills were already drafted and perhaps in their final form when the motion for leave to bring in a bill was debated. This may have happened with the 1730 Jury Bill (see below, 'Harley's parliamentary papers', item 76, which may be part of an early draft drawn up before the committee was appointed), and Harley may have discussed it informally with his backers (i.e., those named as fellow 'drafters'), though possibly not with Yonge. Had the full drafting committee met and worked out a text, the contribution of the government member, Yonge, would perhaps not have made it necessary for the government to amend it so heavily later on. Another possibility is that Yonge's being named one of the drafters meant that he had a right to inspect it on behalf of the government before it was brought in. We owe these suggestions to Andrew Hanham.

[120] Lambert, VII, 21–8; *C.J.*, XXI, 542.

[121] *C.J.*, XXI, 542, 547 (which lists some, but not all, of the amendments, and not the one on special juries); B.L., Add. MS 33052, ff. 69–71: 'Observations on the Jury Bill'; below p. 245: EH to Martha Harley, 11 Apr. 1730. It is not, perhaps, insignificant that, on the act's expiry in 1733, *The Craftsman* published an article praising the act in general, but taking exception to the clause on special juries. *The Craftsman*, No. 344, 3 Feb. 1733.

[122] *C.J.*, XXI, 547, 551; *L.J.*, XXIII, 543.

[123] Below p. 245: EH to Martha Harley, 11 Apr. 1730.

Some 'Observations' on the bill, prepared for the ministry just before it was considered by the Lords, confirm that the government had played no part in initiating the legislation: the 'King's Servants had no other hand in it, but to add those Clauses about special Juries'. The same paper concluded that the bill did not affect the crown's authority very much, and that in some instances it might actually be increased.[124] However, 20 years later George II was reported as thinking that 'the Crown has lost a great deal' by the act. Townshend, the senior secretary of state and 'leader' of the house of lords, was also 'much against it', but he was reported to have said that he would not oppose it as he was about to leave the government.[125] Ministers may, therefore, have had reservations about the bill and may have tried to make it more acceptable by amending it in the Lords. This suggestion is given some credence by the bill's slower progress through the upper house, where it was closely scrutinized. Most of the Lords' amendments were made at the instigation of the judges, particularly Sir Robert Raymond, chief justice of the king's bench, and Sir John Comyns and Sir William Thompson, barons of the exchequer, all of whom had been whig or whig-convert M.P.s. These amendments were concerned mainly with clarifying the text, adding clauses to cover the City of London and the county palatines of Cheshire and Lancashire, dropping one clause and, perhaps most significantly, reducing the value of the estate which a juryman must have from £300 to £100.[126] The bill had its third reading on 12 May and then returned to the Commons, which agreed to the Lords' amendments on 13 May. Two days later, at the prorogation of the parliament, it received the royal assent to become 3 Geo. II, c. 25.[127]

Edward Harley's two other personal legislative achievements form an epilogue to the 1730 Jury Act. The following year a bill was introduced into the Commons to amend the act in relation to Middlesex. The drafting committee, established on 12 March 1731, consisted of Thomas Bramston, Harley and Yonge. Bramston was chairman of the select committee (Harley was the second named), and he reported the bill, with amendments, on the 16th. It subsequently had a trouble-free passage through the Lords and received the royal assent on 9 April.[128] Two years later Harley proposed a bill to make perpetual the 1730 Act, which was due to expire in 1734. This bill was subsumed into a general bill for the continuation of seven acts and passed both houses, receiving the royal assent on 13 June 1733.[129]

Harley's satisfaction in passing the 1730 Jury Bill into law was doubtless increased by the knowledge that he was completing a work undertaken by his father 20 years earlier. The 'Observations on the Jury Bill' of 1730 noted that 'That part of the Bill which concerns the Freeholders Book and the Ballot, did pass the House of

---

124 B.L., Add. MS 33052, ff. 69–71. The 'Observations' are in the papers of the duke of Newcastle, but copies may have been distributed to other ministers, particularly Townshend, the senior secretary and 'leader' of the house of lords. The final paragraph notes that the bill 'is proper for Consideration of the Judges', which was ordered on 21 Apr., so the document cannot have been written after that. Nor was it written before 15 Apr., when the clause about special juries must have been added.

125 B.L., Add. MS 35412, ff. 205–6: Newcastle to Hardwicke, 2 Aug. 1752, quoted in Jeremy Black, 'George II and the Juries Act: Royal Concern about the Control of the Press', *Historical Research*, LXI (1988), 60. As attorney-general Hardwicke had helped to amend the bill in the Commons.

126 These amendments were made in the committee of the whole house on 29 Apr. Further sittings of the committee on 1, 4 and 9 May made further amendments, focusing mainly on the technical issue of the oaths to be taken by under sheriffs. H.L.R.O., Manuscript Minutes, 29 Apr., 1, 4, 9 May 1730. Sedgwick, I, 569; II, 379–80, 467–8.

127 *L.J.*, XXIII, 572, 578; *C.J.*, XXI, 586–7

128 *C.J.*, XXI, 666, 676, 685, 700, 704, 719, 724.

129 Below p. 249.

Commons in the Year 1719, and was now again brought in and met with a generall concurrence in the House of Commons'. This clause was part of the Bill for preventing the corrupting of juries prepared and brought into the Commons on 8 February 1720 by four M.P.s including Auditor Harley. Although the bill passed the Commons on 8 March, it was lost in the Lords at the end of the session.[130] A second attempt was made by the Auditor in 1721, but this too failed in the Lords having passed the Commons.[131] The Jury Act was Harley's greatest, and only major, legislative achievement. He himself commemorated it in a portrait which still hangs over the staircase at Brampton Bryan, in which he is portrayed, along with two of his children, holding a copy of the act. On the table by him lies a 'Draught of a Bill for preventing Bribery and Corruption in Elections of Members to Serve in Parliament 1729'. The presence of this bill is more puzzling. It is generally recognized to have been the handiwork of Sir Watkin Williams Wynn and, while Harley was a member of the drafting committee and its passage gave him the 'greatest Satisfaction', he was not even present in the Commons for the crucial final votes.[132] Nonetheless, his depiction with the 1729 Bribery Bill and the 1730 Jury Act is an eloquent testimony to his commitment to the principles of 'country' toryism.

Harley and the family tradition

To describe Harley as a 'country' tory, even a reformist 'country' tory, goes a long way towards defining his political ideas. But it is not altogether sufficient. He was very conscious of being a Harley and of the political legacy bequeathed to him by his father and, above all, by his uncle. In the mind of Edward Harley the Harley legacy exercised a much greater influence than normal family piety; it deeply affected his political principles and behaviour. To understand how and why this was the case, we need to look back at the career of Robert Harley, first earl of Oxford.

Two events in the first earl's life were to figure large in the political tradition and family mythology that he handed on to his descendants and successors. The first was the unsuccessful assassination attempt in March 1711, while the second was his impeachment for high treason and misdemeanours and his imprisonment in the Tower of London from 1715 to his release on 1 July 1717. Oxford's nephew Edward, who was later to emerge as his true political heir, was only eleven at the time of the assassination attempt, but neither the event nor the significance attached to it within the family could have escaped his notice – to this day the knife, along with the coat and waistcoat worn by Oxford, are preserved at Brampton Bryan. However, the latter ordeal, which probably shortened Oxford's life, was the more important to the family, who represented it as the great man being threatened with martyrdom for his political principles and for his service to queen and country. Edward Harley grew to manhood in a household overshadowed by his uncle's imprisonment. One of his earliest surviving letters is a report to his aunt Abigail about the adjournment of the impeachment in June 1715.[133] At the same time Abigail was writing frequently to him on the

---

130 B.L., Add. MS 33038, f. 71; *C.J.*, XIX, 256, 262, 271, 280, 285, 288, 293, 296; *L.J.*, XXI, 275, 286, 300, 307, 317, 326, 329, 348–9, 360.
131 Below p. 228.
132 Hanham, 'Whig Opposition', pp. 170–1; *C.J.*, XXI, 265; below p. 243: EH to Auditor Harley, 11 May 1729.
133 B.L., Add. MS 70145: EH to Abigail Harley, 18 June 1715. See also H.M.C., *Portland MSS*, V, 512: same to same, 23 June 1715.

same subject.[134] This correspondence itself is significant, but its language, suffused with providentialism, is even more so. Edward himself had no doubts 'but what the Almighty who has often delivered our Dear Freind from his most inveterate Enemies, will deliver his Servant still'.[135] Towards the end of Oxford's imprisonment Edward became more intimately involved in events, writing a 'Memorandum about Lord O[xford's] Tryall. 1717', which covers the final week before his release. On 25 June 1717, the day after the crucial division in the Lords which virtually guaranteed the earl's freedom,[136] Oxford went to Westminster Hall from the Tower accompanied not only by his son, Lord Harley, and his cousin Thomas, but also by his nephew Edward. On 1 July, the day Oxford was finally released from the Tower, he went to the Auditor's house in Lincoln's Inn Fields and Edward was there to record that 'there has not been known so universal a Joy and such great rejoycing throuout England since the Restoration as was upon the Earl of Oxfords being acquitted'.[137]

The memory of Oxford's ordeal was consciously preserved within the family and incorporated in a tradition which stretched back to the 1640s and the sufferings of Edward's grandfather and great-grandfather in the civil war. On Edward's election to the Commons in 1727, his father wrote to the second earl that the event recalled to him

> the Providence and mercy of the Allmighty to the Family. After the burning of the Castle at Brampton and the great depredations that were made upon the Estate, Lingen Croft and Conningsby said that the nest was burnt and that there should be no more of the Family in this Country; the same was repeated by Conningsby and his Emissories at the time of the infamous Impeachment of your Father. I will add no more upon this subject but only desire your Lordship to read the 37th Psalm [Fret not thyself because of evil doers].[138]

A few years later he was instructing his great-nephew, Lord Dupplin (then aged 24), on the vicissitudes of the family's history.[139] The date of 1 July, however, seems to have assumed particular importance as an anniversary within the family, the second earl writing that 'this most memorable day ought not to be passed by as a common day'. His uncle the Auditor replied that it did indeed demand 'from us the most thankful and most humble acknowledgement of the Divine Goodness in the Deliverance of your most dear Father, who was not only rescued from the rage of his Enemies who cruelly sought after his Life, but his Honor and Reputation were cleared from their malicious and wicked expressions'.[140]

Edward Harley observed the anniversaries as religiously as any member of the family. On 8 March 1717, in his first year at Christ Church, he wrote to the earl of Oxford, still imprisoned in the Tower, congratulating him on his providential escape from the assassin's knife and suggesting that the day 'must ever be commemorated by us and Posterity as an annual Festival'.[141] The following year he arranged a celebration

---

134 B.L., Add. MS 70088.

135 B.L., Add. MS 70145: EH to Abigail Harley, 18 June 1715.

136 See Clyve Jones, 'The Impeachment of the Earl of Oxford and the Whig Schism of 1717: Four New Lists', *B.I.H.R.*, LV (1982), 66–87.

137 Below pp. 202–3.

138 B.L., Add. MS 70381: Auditor Harley to Oxford, 8 Sept. 1727.

139 *Ibid.*: same to same, 10 Apr. 1734.

140 B.L., Add. MS 70140: Oxford to Auditor Harley, 1 July 1733; Add. MS 70381: Auditor to Oxford, 3 July 1733 (draft in EH's hand).

141 Brampton Bryan MSS, Bundle 117: EH to Oxford, 8 Mar. 1716–17. Oxford himself certainly celebrated the day. See Jonathan Swift, *Journal to Stella*, ed. H. Williams (2 vols., Oxford, 1974), II, 508, 634–5.

in college and another later in the year to mark the first anniversary of Oxford's release from the Tower.[142] Harley also became some kind of unofficial keeper of the family records. He organized, annotated and copied many of the documents now preserved at Brampton Bryan, including a copy of the list of the division in the house of lords on 24 June 1717.[143] In 1733 he even sent to the second earl some of the papers he had copied, telling his cousin that one of his uncle's letters was 'more valuable ... than any acquisition of wealth which might have been heaped up by the Methods so much practised in his prostitute Age'.[144]

Moreover, in the case of Edward Harley, at least, the memories of Lord Oxford extended well beyond family piety into politics. From an early age he was eager to defend the family's reputation. It appeared only justice to him that some of his uncle's impeachers fell as 'the first Sacrifices to the Rage of their own Party' during the South Sea crisis. Indeed, he took such delight in the fate of John Aislabie, who had played a leading role in Oxford's impeachment and whom he considered 'a family enemy', that William Stratford had to remind him of christian teaching.[145] It is hardly surprising, therefore, that within three years of his election, Harley was on his feet in the Commons 'publickly justifying my Lord Oxfords Memory and Administration'. The occasion was the debate in February 1730 on the restoration of the harbour at Dunkirk contrary to the Treaty of Utrecht, when Walpole had attacked the policies of the Oxford ministry in an attempt to deflect criticism.[146]

But the influence of Oxford's legacy on Edward Harley's political principles revealed itself most clearly during the debate of 13 February 1741 on Samuel Sandys's motion for an address to the king to dismiss Walpole. In his speech Harley, referring explicitly to his uncle's impeachment, stated that he would not censure anyone without 'Facts and Evidence'. He then walked out of the chamber and refused to vote, a course of action in which he was joined by many tories, including his brother Robert.[147] By his own account his speech to the house was short and to the point, though he could not resist reminding Walpole that he was doing 'that Honourable Gentleman and his Family that Justice which He denyed to Mine'. However, in his journal Harley elaborated a little on his behaviour. He explained that the accusation was founded only 'on Common fame', that 'no particular facts were stated nor any Evidence produced either viva voce or Written to support the Charge'. Those who withdrew, he wrote to Brydges, 'think we have acted consistent with our own Principles which so much abhor Bills of Pains and Penalties, that we avoided even the shadow of one'.[148] In 1742 Harley, now sitting in the Lords as the third earl of Oxford, was an enthusiastic supporter of the enquiries into Walpole's conduct as prime minister, entering his protest on the defeat of the Indemnity Bill which effectively put a stop to proceedings

---

[142] H.M.C., *Portland MSS*, VII, 236: Stratford to Lord Harley, 8 Mar. 1718.

[143] Below pp. 200–2. See Jones, 'Impeachment of the Earl of Oxford', pp. 79–87. Two other copies of the list in other hands can be found in B.L., Add. MS 70088.

[144] B.L., Add. MS 70381: EH to Oxford, 14 Dec. 1733.

[145] B.L., Add. MS 70145: EH to Abigail Harley, 12 Mar. 1721; H.M.C., *Portland MSS*, VII, 291: Stratford to Lord Harley, 2 Mar. 1721.

[146] Below p. 244: EH to Martha Harley, 28 Feb. 1730; Cobbett, VIII, 798–800; H.M.C., *Egmont Diary*, I, 74.

[147] Colley, p. 228. Harley's fellow M.P. for Herefordshire, Velters Cornewall, however, voted for the motion, explaining that he had 'been longer in Parliament and had been a eye witness to more of his iniquitous doings'. Herefordshire R.O., Brydges Papers, A81/IV/William Brydges 1714–40: Cornewall to Brydges, 20 Feb. 1741. In the Lords the earl of Oxford did not abstain, but voted against the motion to remove Walpole. B.L., Add. MS 47000, ff. 111–12.

[148] Below pp. 50–1; below p. 252: EH to William Brydges, 21 Feb. 1741.

in parliament. But even in 1741 he was clear that that was a different case. Indeed, he had then looked forward to the time 'when a proper legal, Parliamentary Enquiry may be made, and when clear facts and full Evidence will plainly discover who are the Enemies of their Country'.[149] One might claim that the Harley legacy gave a distinctive tinge to Edward Harley's toryism – at the very least, it undoubtedly made him a fierce opponent of impeachments. This principle, indeed, found expression on other occasions. In 1737, for example, one of the reasons Harley opposed the government's proceedings against the city of Edinburgh after the Porteous riots was that they established 'another Precedent for this arbitrary Method of Proceeding by Bills in Parliament'.[150]

Harley and the leadership of the tory party

Before leaving the subject of Harley and toryism, one theme remains to be discussed: Harley's role as a tory leader. Two preliminary points need to be borne in mind. First, there was no such thing in the early eighteenth century as *the* leader of the tory party (nor, indeed, was there ever a single leader of the whigs). William Wyndham perhaps came as close as any individual to exercising leadership of the party, at least in the Commons, in the years before his death in June 1740. Chesterfield noted that he commanded broader support than any other opposition leader, but, as Harley's journal reveals, some tories were distrustful of his links with the Patriots and were reluctant to follow wherever he led.[151] During the late 1730s Gower was the leading tory in the Lords, but he failed to build on this foundation after Wyndham's death and his place was taken by Beaufort in 1745. However, while Beaufort may have emerged as the leading tory, he never exercised any form of ascendancy over the party as a whole. Second, Edward Harley possessed an eminent name, one which was perhaps even more identified with toryism after Oxford's imprisonment. Yet the name itself brought little influence in tory circles. Edward's cousin, the second earl, had never emerged as a leading tory, his lack of interest in politics and his poor attendance in parliament disqualifying him from such a role. Edward, by contrast, as has been seen, was a committed and effective parliamentarian, and it is hardly surprising that he emerged as one of a group of tory leaders in both the Commons and the Lords.

Indeed, he began to play a significant role in tory organization as early as the year of his election, when he founded a Board of like-minded, country tory M.P.s, which met at the Cocoa Tree coffee house in Pall Mall. Initially, there were only six members of the Harley Board, but the Board's, and by implication Harley's, significance increased markedly in 1734 when a further nine members were admitted. The Board met every Thursday during the parliamentary session, and it developed into 'a vital and durable component of tory organization'.[152] By the end of the 1735–41 parliament Harley was widely recognized as one of the leaders of the parliamentary party. In a letter of June 1741 George Bubb Dodington listed the leaders of the opposition. The peers named by him were Oxford (Harley had just succeeded his cousin as third earl) first, and then Thanet, Gower, Bathurst, Cobham and Chesterfield, the first four of whom were tories. In the Commons Dodington singled out Lord Noel Somerset (who became fourth duke of Beaufort in 1745), Sir John Hynde Cotton, Sir Watkin

---

149 *L.J.*, XXVI, 130–2; below p. 50.
150 Below p. 30.
151 Colley, pp. 226–7 and n. 70; below p. 37. Cf. the comments of William Hay in Nov. 1739, below pp. 154–5.
152 Colley, 'The Loyal Brotherhood and the Cocoa Tree', pp. 82–3, 86, 95.

Williams Wynn and Nicholas Fazakerley, all of whom were tories, alongside the whigs, Pulteney, Sandys and Thomas Pitt, and the independent Sir John Barnard.[153] Thus, Harley was not only one of the four leading tories in the Lords, but, before his succession to the peerage, he had clearly also been among the five most important tories in the Commons.

Some evidence of the extent, but also the limitations, of Harley's position as a tory leader in the latter years of the Walpole ministry is provided by the motion of 13 February 1741 for Walpole's dismissal. By Harley's own account he and his brother Robert 'were the *first* who refused to Vote in this Question and publickly left the House'.[154] In all 37 M.P.s withdrew and a further 16 voted against the motion.[155] Those who withdrew might be regarded as following Harley's lead and thus be seen as the nucleus of the Harleyite group within the party. However, only four of this group were members of the Harley board – Bacon, Mordaunt, Prowse and Harley himself – and it is clear that some of the others could not be described as Harleyites. They included, for example, the veteran William Shippen, widely seen as a leading tory himself and one of the jacobite fringe of the party. Thus, while Harley was undoubtedly an influential figure within the tory parliamentary party, there was probably no more than a handful of M.P.s who might in any sense be regarded as his followers.

Through the 1740s and early 1750s Oxford's name occurs consistently in discussions of leading tories. He was singled out by the earl of Chesterfield as a leading and influential figure in 1745.[156] Subsequently, he was involved in drawing up the answer of 'the Lords and Gentlemen in the Oposition' to the prince of Wales's Carlton House declaration.[157] The following year he played a prominent role at the meeting held at the St Albans Tavern on 1 May 1749 to concert opposition to the ministry's threat of a visitation of Oxford University.[158] Equally significant, perhaps, was the respect accorded to Oxford by tories in the country. In particular, he was clearly highly regarded in that bastion of high church toryism, Oxford University. In 1732 Harley had been chosen to succeed William Bromley as one of Dr Radcliffe's Trustees. Just over a decade later his name was being mentioned in university circles as a possible successor to Lord Arran as chancellor of the university, rumours which were circulating again in 1751.[159]

However, it is worth recalling the remarks of Thomas Carte in his report to the Pretender in 1749: 'There can't be 2 better men, nor are there any more universally esteemed than the D[uke] of B[eaufort] and E[arl] of O[xford] the chief of the Tories, but they are not active enough, the one by his gout, the other by his constitution.'[160]

---

153 William Coxe, *Memoirs of the Life and Administration of Sir Robert Walpole, Earl of Orford* (3 vols., 1798), III, 575: Dodington to Argyle, 18 June 1741. The identification of the Oxford mentioned in this letter as the 3rd earl is slightly problematic. Dodington was writing from Eastbury in Dorset on 18 June, and it seems unlikely that news would have reached him of the 2nd earl's death just two days earlier. However, the letter has a postscript dated 3 July, so it is possible that Oxford's name was a later emendation or that that section of the letter was written after 18 June. Certainly, what is known of the 2nd earl makes it highly unlikely that Dodington was referring to him.

154 Below p. 50. Our emphasis.

155 Colley, p. 349 n. 73.

156 P.R.O., Granville Papers, 30/29/1/11, ff. 290–1: Chesterfield to Gower, 13 Apr. 1745 n.s.

157 Below p. 82. Theophilus Leigh's account of the letter singles out 'the D[uke] of B[eaufor]t and Ld. O[xfor]d'. Balliol College, Oxford, MS 403, ff. 58–9: Leigh to the duchess of Chandos, 19 Feb. 1748.

158 *The Yale Edition of Horace Walpole's Correspondence*, ed. W.S. Lewis (48 vols., New Haven, 1937–83), XX, 50–1: Walpole to Mann, 3 May 1749.

159 Hearne, *Remarks*, XI, 37; Bodl., MS Ballard 2, ff. 134–5: R. Rawlinson[?] to Thomas Rawlins, 12 July 1743; below p. 268: Oxford to Mr Aubrey, 21 Feb. 1750/1.

160 Royal Archives, S.P. Box 1/299: Thomas Carte to ?, n.d. [1749].

Carte's point here is far from clear. Oxford was plainly not inactive. As we have seen, having thrown himself into his work as an M.P., he was subsequently one of the most active of the tories in the Lords and signed more protests than any other peer during his time there. It is possible that Carte was criticizing Oxford for his lack of commitment to the jacobite cause. But perhaps more plausible is the suggestion that he was reluctant to take on the role of tory leader. Oxford, it should be remembered, was first and foremost a country politician. During the 1741 elections he prided himself on his 'plain Frock', in contrast to the 'fine Laced Cloaths' of the 'Courtiers'.[161] He had a profound distaste for London. It was a 'filthy town', which he could not wait to leave to return to his family in Herefordshire.[162] Oxford demonstrated little love for politicking; rather, it appeared to be an activity to which he committed himself from a sense of duty. If he never emerged as a dominant influence within the tory party, it may well have been because he was temperamentally unsuited to such a role.

Leicester House and the ministry

The 1730s had seen considerable co-operation between tories and dissident whigs, particularly on 'country' issues. In the years after Walpole's fall, however, the picture becomes more complex. While the tory party demonstrated a predictable suspicion of those whigs, such as Bath and Granville, who had betrayed them in 1742, whigs in the Leicester House circle around the prince of Wales continued to provide useful allies on occasions. Moreover, there were also intermittent negotiations between tory leaders and the administration. As Linda Colley has shown, the party's solidarity inhibited any real progress towards the ending of tory proscription, the ministry being prepared to do no more than employ a few tories 'only upon a personal foot, and ... without their followers'.[163] Nonetheless, these high political manoeuvrings provide some indication of the ways in which the ties which had underpinned party alignments in the 1730s had begun to weaken by the mid 1750s. As we have seen, the earl of Oxford was one of the most prominent and consistent tory critics of the administration during this period, and he co-operated closely at times with opposition whigs. But, like many of his colleagues, he also became drawn into negotiations with the ministry.

Oxford appears to have played little, if any, part in the abortive negotiations for the inclusion of tories in the ministry immediately after Walpole's fall. This is perhaps the less surprising given his obvious distrust of the motives of the Patriots even in the 1730s. However, he was more active in 1744–5, when the Pelhams were showing some interest in the creation of a broad-bottom administration. In December 1744 Gower, Philipps, Cotton and John Pitt were all given office, and Chesterfield hoped that Oxford and others would be persuaded to come over with Gower, thereby leaving only a jacobite rump behind them.[164] In the ensuing parliamentary session of 1744–5, as Oxford recorded, the tories 'acquiesced' in the ministry's measures on the assurance from 'their Freinds who had joined the Pelham Party that they would in return consent to the passing Constitutional Bills'.[165] It soon emerged that one of the most important issues was the remodelling of the commissions of the peace to include more tories.

161 Below p. 255: EH to Martha Harley, 17 May 1741.
162 B.L., Add. MS 70497: EH to Martha Harley, 2 Apr. 1730.
163 Colley, ch. 9, quotation at p. 240.
164 *Ibid.*, p. 244; *Private Correspondence of Chesterfield and Newcastle*, p. 44: Chesterfield to Newcastle, 13 Apr. 1745 n.s.
165 Below p. 73.

Oxford corresponded with Hardwicke, the lord chancellor, about the Herefordshire list, and a new commission for the county was issued in August. However, none of the other tory demands were met, and the ministry's response was inadequate even on the issue of J.P.s. As Oxford complained, 'a new Commission [was] granted to some few Counties, but not to those where the Greivance was most Complained of.'[166]

By 1746 Oxford was once again clearly in opposition, protesting against both the Bill for the more easy trial of the jacobite rebels and the continuation of the war in Flanders. He continued to be a leading opposition peer to the end of his life, opposing the Heritable Jurisdictions Bill in 1747, the Mutiny Bill in 1749, the Regency Bill in 1751 and the Forfeited Estates Bill in 1752.[167] During this period, like many tories, he was prepared to act in concert with Leicester House, most notably in 1749 in response to the threatened visitation of Oxford University. However, even though Oxford appeared as lord privy seal and his son, Lord Harley, as a commissioner of the treasury in a prospective Leicester House ministry drawn up in 1750, he kept the prince of Wales at a distance. The response of 'the Lords and Gentlemen in the Oposition' to Frederick's Carlton House declaration, which Oxford helped to draft, was 'cautious and non-committal'.[168] His 'Journal', indeed, suggests a certain suspicion of the prince's motives. Although he was making entries ever more infrequently, he still took care to note occasions on which 'the Princes party' were on the wrong side of a question.[169] Among all the whig peers in opposition, Oxford was perhaps closest to Anthony Ashley Cooper, fourth earl of Shaftesbury. Not only was Shaftesbury one of the most active opposition peers in the Lords, but he had also, along with the earl of Lichfield, introduced Oxford into the house in 1742.[170] In 1751 Oxford and Shaftesbury were both involved in an attempt 'to form a regular Party' to maintain the momentum of opposition after the prince of Wales's death.[171] Westmorland, Stanhope, Dodington and Dashwood were also involved, and there were plans to fund James Ralph's journal the *Remembrancer*. On 15 April Shaftesbury reported that 'the project of union went on very successfully', and in May he voted in the minority against the Regency Bill along with Oxford and Stanhope. But, by then, hopes for a united opposition were all but dead. Stanhope's manifesto had failed to provide a basis for joint action, and Ralph was reduced to writing begging letters to Oxford, lamenting the fact that 'there seems to be neither concert, nor Inclination to oppose'.[172]

On the basis of the available evidence, however, it is very difficult to be certain what were Oxford's political aims and motives during the last decade of his life. His record of opposition to the ministry in the Lords and his links with Shaftesbury and Leicester House are only part of the story. In January 1751, for example, only weeks

[166] B.L., Add. MS 35602, ff. 97–102, 114–15: Oxford to Hardwicke, 9 July, 13 Aug. 1745; P.R.O., C234/15; below p. 73. Oxford lists the nine 'proposals' delivered to Gower by Beaufort and Wynn, below p. 73.

[167] *L.J.*, XXVII, 118–19; below pp. 81, 84; Walpole, *Memoirs*, I, 78, 186.

[168] Walpole, *Correspondence*, XX, 50–1; 'Leicester House Politics, 1750–60, from the Papers of John, Second Earl of Egmont', ed. Aubrey Newman, in *Camden Miscellany Vol. XXIII* (Camden, 4th ser., VII, 1969), p. 116; below p. 82; Betty Kemp, *Sir Francis Dashwood. An Eighteenth-Century Independent* (1967), pp. 30–1.

[169] Below pp. 82, 84.

[170] *L.J.*, XXVI, 32. Shaftesbury was a diligent attender in the Lords and between 1742 and 1755 he entered his protest on 12 occasions, only once less than Oxford.

[171] *The Political Journal of George Bubb Dodington*, ed. John Carswell and Lewis Arnold Dralle (Oxford, 1965), pp. 110–11 (7 Apr. 1751).

[172] *Ibid.*, pp. 113, 114 (15, 23 Apr. 1751); Walpole, *Memoirs*, I, 78–9; Bodl., MS D.D. Dashwood I. 1/2/3: James Ralph to Oxford, 10 May 1751. For the failings of Stanhope's manifesto, cf. Kemp, *Dashwood*, pp. 33–4; Colley, pp. 260–1.

before the negotiations described above, Oxford's second son, Robert Harley, was a candidate at the by-election for Oxford University. Harley was defeated by another tory, Sir Roger Newdigate, with a third tory, Sir Edward Turner, finishing at the bottom of the poll. What was surprising about the result was that most of Harley's support came from the whigs in the University, and he gained almost all the votes cast in the whig strongholds of Christ Church, Exeter and Merton.[173] The whigs may have rallied to Harley because he was a Christ Church man and because he was the least unattractive of the candidates – Newdigate, in particular, was seen as an extremist. However, it is also possible that Westminster politics impinged on the election. Horace Walpole claimed that at the time of the election Oxford was being 'courted' by Henry Pelham. If Walpole was right, it might account for Harley receiving such solid support from the whigs, particularly since Turner, though a tory, had whig connexions and was to stand on the 'New Interest' for Oxfordshire in 1754. Oxford's reaction to Pelham's approaches is even less clear. He categorically denied that his son had been 'set ... up' by Christ Church, yet his behaviour was certainly open to misinterpretation. Having instructed his son not to stand, in order to avoid a contested election, Oxford then changed his mind, 'permitting his Son to be proposed afresh'.[174] Later, in the aftermath of the election, Robert's brother, Thomas, commented on the foolishness of the university in electing 'a man who is altogether obnoxious to the Court'. Robert Harley was undoubtedly presented as a tory – his 'party' was 'not so violent, though altogether founded on the same principles of Honesty' as Newdigate's. However, he was clearly portrayed as the candidate who would have the greatest credit and respect with the ministry.[175]

Whatever was taking place behind the scenes at the time of the university election, Oxford was certainly maintaining some contacts with the ministry, particularly with Lord Hardwicke. In February 1748 he wrote to the lord chancellor pleading the case of Herefordshire landowners for some relaxation of the orders relating to infected cattle. Later the same year he successfully applied to Hardwicke for the rectory of Corwen in Merionethshire for Samuel Palmer, and the following year, on his death, he asked that it be granted to Palmer's cousin.[176] It is important not to make too much of these contacts. Writing to a Herefordshire neighbour in 1748, Oxford admitted to an 'acquaintance' with the chancellor, but denied any 'Interest with Him', adding that 'the Proscription laid on my Family above 30 years ago does not seem to be yet taken of'.[177] Nonetheless, even these limited contacts were not typical of a leading tory. It is, therefore, hardly surprising that there were rumours in 1754 that Oxford 'has long

---

[173] A True Copy of the Poll taken at Oxford January 31, 1750 [1751]. See also, W.R. Ward, Georgian Politics. University Politics in the Eighteenth Century (Oxford, 1958), pp. 188–91; Paul Langford, 'Tories and Jacobites 1714–1751', in The History of Oxford University. Vol. V. The Eighteenth Century, ed. L.S. Sutherland and L.G. Mitchell (Oxford, 1986), pp. 125–6.

[174] Walpole, Memoirs, I, 33; Langford, 'Tories and Jacobites', p. 125; below p. 268: Oxford to Aubrey, 21 Feb. 1751; Warwickshire R.O., Newdigate Papers, CR136/B1482: William Blackstone to Newdigate, 13 Jan 1750/1; P.R.O., 30/20/24/2, pp. 69–70: Thomas Harley to [Robert Harley], 7 Feb. 1750/1. The news that Oxford received from his son John, that the 'Heads ... are determined to sett up some other person' if Robert did not stand, may have persuaded him that a contest was inevitable and thus that Robert should become a candidate. Below p. 267: John Harley to Oxford, 11 Jan. 1750/1.

[175] P.R.O., 30/20/24/2, pp. 69–72: Thomas Harley to [Robert Harley], 7 Feb. 1751.

[176] B.L., Add. MS 35590, ff. 12–13, 46–7, 425–6: Oxford to Hardwicke, 10 Feb., 13 Apr. 1748, 31 Oct. 1749. Palmer was Oxford's former tutor at Christ Church.

[177] Herefordshire R.O., Brydges Papers, A/81/IV/ William Brydges 1741–61: Oxford to William Brydges, 21 Aug. 1748. There are hints that the Yorke family had held Harley in respect ever since the 1730s. See the report by Hardwicke's eldest son of Harley's 'generosity' in the debate on the removal of Walpole in

been making court to the Chancellor'.[178] And there may have been some substance to the rumours. In 1754 or 1755 Oxford was once again recommending names to Hardwicke for inclusion in the Herefordshire and Radnorshire commissions of the peace. But, even more significantly, in March 1754, on the death of Henry Pelham, the earls of Oxford and Shaftesbury assured the duke of Newcastle 'That they were determined to support, by themselves and the friends they could have any Influence over, his Grace of Newcastle in whatever Measures he should think proper to take on this unfortunate Juncture for supplying the Place of his deceased Brother'.[179] Oxford died in 1755, so it is impossible to say where these overtures may have led. Even so, it is clear that the process was beginning which facilitated the return of the Harley family, along with many other old tory families, to court at the accession of George III.[180]

Harley and local politics

The first general election in which Edward Harley played a role, albeit a very minor one, was that of 1722. By this time the Harley interest in the border counties of England and Wales had already been severely weakened. During the reigns of William and Anne the family's real stronghold was not its native county, but Radnorshire. Edward's uncle, Robert Harley, himself represented New Radnor Boroughs from 1690 until his elevation to the Lords in 1711, when he was succeeded as M.P. by his son Lord Harley, while from 1698 he secured the county seat for his cousin Thomas. But the family did, in addition, exert considerable influence in Herefordshire. The county itself was only represented by a Harley – Sir Edward – for five years during the two reigns, but Auditor Edward Harley was one of the M.P.s for Leominster, the Herefordshire borough closest to the family homes of Eywood and Brampton Bryan, in every parliament from 1698.[181] However, Harley power was severely curtailed in the aftermath of the Hanoverian succession. The family's great local rival, Thomas, Lord Coningsby, was not only appointed to the lord lieutenancies of Herefordshire and Radnorshire, but, perhaps more importantly, he also replaced the earl of Oxford as steward of the king's manors in Radnorshire, an office which carried with it a great deal of electoral influence in both the county and the boroughs. Coningsby was bent on the destruction of the Harleys at both local and national level – in 1715 he moved Oxford's impeachment – and he used his new power to bring Harley dominance of Radnorshire to an end. Both Thomas Harley and Lord Harley were defeated at the 1715 elections, leaving the Auditor, who survived a contested election at Leominster, as the family's only representative in the Commons.[182]

After 1715 the electoral influence of the Harley family was thus largely confined to Herefordshire. There were a number of powerful interests in the county. Alongside the Harleys were the Foleys and the Scudamores. James, Viscount Scudamore, had been

February 1741. Philip Yorke, *The Life and Correspondence of Philip Yorke, Earl of Hardwicke* (3 vols., Cambridge, 1913), I, 252.

[178] National Library of Wales, Harpton Court MSS, C/34: T. Lewis to H. Lewis, 12 Mar. 1754, quoted in J.C.D. Clark, *The Dynamics of Change. The Crisis of the 1750s and English Party Systems* (Cambridge, 1982), p. 52.

[179] B.L., Add. MS 32734, f. 179: Memorandum of Lord Halifax, 7 Mar. 1754; Add. MS 35604, ff. 361–2.

[180] On George III's accession the fourth earl of Oxford was appointed a lord of the bedchamber.

[181] Edward Harley was not returned at the general election of January 1701, but was seated on petition in April. HoP, draft article, 'Leominster', by David Hayton.

[182] D.R.Ll. Adams, 'The Parliamentary Representation of Radnorshire 1536–1832', University of Wales (Aberystwyth), M.A., 1969, pp. 210–15. Sedgwick, II, 380–1, 570–1, 259.

one of the county's M.P.s during the latter half of Anne's reign, but, on his death without male heir in 1716, the interest went into eclipse. But, by the early 1720s the Cornewalls of Moccas Court were emerging as a major force in county politics and, with the Harleys and Foleys, were virtually to monopolize the parliamentary representation for the rest of the eighteenth century. Many other families, however, were also important enough to exercise a voice in county politics, notably the Morgans of Kinnersley and, particularly early in the period, the duke of Chandos and the earl of Coningsby. In the reigns of George I and George II, as in those of William and Anne, great emphasis was placed on the unity of the county. To some extent this rhetoric was disingenuous, being employed by the leading families to secure approval for their candidates at county meetings. It is clear that the earl of Oxford was irked by his failure to obtain a county meeting in 1721–2 to nominate his son.[183] But, significantly, 1722 witnessed the only contested election between 1710 and 1754. County unity was more than mere rhetoric, though it was undoubtedly facilitated by the fact that the Herefordshire gentry were overwhelmingly tory. In this period the county was only represented briefly by a whig between 1717 and 1722. Political agreement in the face of whig oligarchy was essential; divisions could only offer opportunities which the whigs might exploit.[184]

Many of the same families had influence in the boroughs of Hereford and Leominster. The Harley interest at Hereford was limited, though at times their exercise of it could be significant because of the interaction of borough and county politics. But in Leominster they played a much more significant role, along with the Coningsbys. Indeed, in 1745 Velters Cornewall reported that 'Lady Coningsby, Lord Oxford, and Sir Robert Cornwall ... have the love and almost all the votes of that town.'[185] This statement is somewhat misleading, as the borough was, in fact, fairly open and none of the local families was able to establish a predominant influence. It witnessed contests at all but two of the elections held between 1715 and 1754 and was represented by 12 different M.P.s. Moreover, the constituency also had a reputation for corruption, Auditor Harley complaining in 1721 that 'the Best Bidder will have the Best Interest to be returned'.[186] However, the complaints of the Harleys and others about venality must be placed in context. Leominster tended to prefer to be represented by local men. Of the 12 M.P.s returned between 1715 and 1754, only one did not have estates in or near the borough, and only two did not come from long established local families.[187]

The second general election of the Hanoverian period, held in 1722, brought no improvement in the Harleys' situation. On the contrary, in many respects 1722 marked the nadir of their electoral fortunes. Lord Harley was elected for Cambridgeshire, where his marriage to Lady Henrietta Cavendish Holles had made him an influential landowner, but in the aftermath of the elections there was no member of the family representing any of its traditional interests in the west country. At Leominster the Auditor, having originally decided not to stand for re-election, was persuaded to change his mind by a letter of invitation from some of the electors. At the poll he was decisively defeated. Within the family it was viewed as an honourable defeat, Harley having stood firm against the corruption of the other candidates, especially of Sir George Caswall who was reported as saying that he would 'spend thousands'.[188]

---

[183] B.L., Add. MS 70383, ff. 80–1: Oxford to Lord Harley, 19 Jan. 1722.

[184] HoP, draft article, 'Herefordshire', by David Hayton; Sedgwick, I, 257–8; Namier and Brooke, I, 303.

[185] Quoted in Sedgwick, I, 259.

[186] B.L., Add. MS 70140: Auditor Harley to Chandos, 21 Dec. 1721 (not sent).

[187] Sedgwick, I, 259; Namier and Brooke, I, 304–5.

[188] B.L., Add. MS 70383, ff. 94, 95: Oxford to Lord Harley, 9 Mar., 18 Mar. 1722; below p. 238: EH to Oxford, 27 Mar. 1722.

What happened in the county is both more complex and more obscure. It is clear that Oxford wanted Lord Harley to stand, and he presented his son as a focus for the unity of the county following the 'Civil and Military oppressions' inflicted on it by Coningsby. Predictably, he made the conventional appeal to the decision of a county meeting, offering to defer to the opinion of the gentry if they should choose to unite behind two other candidates.[189] However, this strategy failed badly. One problem was that the county meeting never took place. There was opposition to it from some of the gentry, which might suggest that they had reservations about a Harley candidature.[190] Moreover, one of the opponents appears to have been Thomas Foley, referred to in some of the Harleys' correspondence as 'Fituan'. Foley was trying to negotiate a compromise with, among others, the duke of Chandos which would secure his son's return for Hereford. These negotiations impinged on the county election because Chandos's nephew by marriage, Sir Hungerford Hoskyns, was standing for the county with his uncle's support. A county meeting resulting in two agreed candidates, however, would inevitably have occurred at the expense of Hoskyns, a whig, who had aroused considerable local hostility by his support for the repeal of the Occasional Conformity and Schism Acts. Foley's negotiations undermined Oxford's plans, not least because the earl wanted to make use of Foley, one of his old allies, as an intermediary with the county gentry. Not only did Foley refuse to act in this way, but he also appears to have spread stories that Lord Harley would not be a candidate.[191]

A second problem was confusion and misunderstanding within the family. Oxford endorsed one of the many letters about the election 'Herefordshire Mistake &c.', and not without reason.[192] On successive days in late January 1722, well over two months after the likelihood of a Harley candidature was first being publicly discussed in Herefordshire, Lord Harley and his father wrote to each other. The former was under the impression that 'it was designed that not one of the family should come in next parliament'. The latter, by contrast, was still pressing his son to consider standing for the county, assuring him that 'you may easy carry it stil: but then you must come down without delay'.[193] Oxford and Lord Harley were simply unable to communicate effectively. What eventually occurred was a three-way contest between Velters Cornewall, Sir Edward Goodere and Sir Hungerford Hoskyns. None of these had the formal backing of the Harley interest, but privately the Harleys favoured Cornewall and Goodere, despite his connexions with Coningsby, over the whig Hoskyns, and in spite of the fact that Oxford thought both Hoskyns and Goodere were 'very dishonourable'.[194]

Thus, Brampton Bryan and Eywood were marginalized during the elections. In the aftermath even friends, like William Stratford, canon of Christ Church, were lamenting the damage done to the Harley interest in Herefordshire and ridiculing the official

---

[189] B.L., Add. MS 70085: undated paper about Herefordshire election (probably Oct./Nov. 1721).

[190] B.L., Add. MS 70383, ff. 80–1: Oxford to Lord Harley, 19 Jan. 1722.

[191] *Ibid.*, ff. 80–1, 91–2: same to same, 19 Jan., 20 Feb. 1722; B.L., Add. MS 70237: Lord Harley to Oxford, 3 Feb. 1722; below p. 237: EH to Lord Harley, 9 Feb. 1722; Herefordshire R.O., Brydges Papers, A81/IV/Francis Brydges 1721–3: William Brydges to Francis Brydges, 23 Jan. 1722; Sedgwick, II, 151. Foley's machinations backfired. The local gentry reacted against the attempt to compromise the city election, a new candidate appeared and Foley withdrew from the contest before the poll. Sedgwick, I, 258.

[192] B.L., Add. MS 70237: Lord Harley to Oxford, 24 Jan. 1722.

[193] *Ibid.*: same to same, 27 Jan. 1722 (this letter is also endorsed 'Mistakes'); Add. MS 70383, ff. 83–4: Oxford to Lord Harley, 28 Jan. 1722.

[194] B.L., Add. MS 70383, f. 82: Oxford to Lord Harley, 26 Jan. 1722. There were in fact some rumours that Oxford was supporting Goodere. Add. MS 70237: Lord Harley to Oxford, 3 Feb. 1722.

family line, propagated in this case by Edward Harley, that it had emerged intact.[195] The 1722 elections were clearly a blow for the Harleys. Not only were they left representing none of the constituencies in Herefordshire or Radnorshire, but their management of the county contest was widely seen as 'very odd'.[196] But there was probably something to be said for the analysis of Oxford, the Auditor and Edward Harley. They were able to celebrate the defeat of Hoskyns, yet they had not had to compromise their position by supporting any of the candidates. Indeed, as Oxford reported to his son, 'Not one of this family appeard personally', nor had they canvassed votes before the poll. Indeed, if Oxford was correct in believing that up to a third of the electors abstained, then there may be evidence to suggest that others followed the Harley line.[197] There can be no doubt that family interest was much weakened in the aftermath of the Hanoverian succession, and its weakness was revealed starkly in 1722. Both the earl of Oxford and his brother were in poor health, while Lord Harley was neither present in the county nor much interested in politics. But the residual strength of the interest was demonstrated by the approaches to Edward Harley in 1723, when Sir Edward Goodere was rumoured to be ill. Long before the vacancy finally occurred when Goodere stepped down at the general election of 1727, Harley had established himself as his successor.[198]

Harley's election, alongside Velters Cornewall, as M.P. for Herefordshire in 1727 was seen as a providential triumph within the family. He thus reasserted their political prominence in the county. Lacking the power in London enjoyed by his uncle and father, Harley was unable to do anything to restore their local influence to the heights it had reached under William and Anne. From 1727, however, his own position as knight of the shire was unchallenged. There was some talk about an opposition to Cornewall in 1727, but Harley was not threatened. Indeed, Chandos, who was attempting to set up his son as a candidate, specifically denied that he would 'join in any Opposition' to him. Further vague rumours of an opposition circulated in 1741, but these too proved unfounded.[199] Harley's local preeminence was based on an appeal to 'country' principles and the interest of the county, to independence and freedom from corruption, which was perhaps less of a rhetorical device than it had been when employed by Robert Harley. He certainly portrayed himself as sharing the prejudices of the country gentry, assuring them in 1741 that he 'would not so much as ask a Vote, but would leave myself to their free choice which was not to be corrupted like the Voters of Leominster and Hereford'.[200]

However secure Harley's own position may have been, he was still aware of the need for co-operation with the other leading families in the county. To some extent Harley influence depended on the maintenance of good relations. Thus, when Edward Harley succeeded to the peerage on the death of his cousin shortly after the 1741

---

[195] H.M.C., *Portland MSS*, VII, 319–20, 322: Stratford to Lord Harley, 2, 21 Apr. 1722.

[196] Herefordshire R.O., Brydges Papers, A81/IV/Francis Brydges 1721–3: William Brydges to Francis Brydges, 14 Dec. 1721.

[197] B.L., Add. MS 70383, ff. 98–9: Oxford to Lord Harley, 3 Apr. 1722; Add. MS 70219: Oxford to Velters Cornewall, 3 Feb. 1722. No Harleys are recorded as voting in the poll book. *A Copy of the Poll for the County of Hereford taken at the County-Court, held at the City of Hereford, on Wednesday the Twenty-Eighth Day of March, Anno Domini 1722...* (n.p., n.d.).

[198] B.L., Add. MS 70085: Auditor Harley to ?, Apr. 1723; below pp. 240–1: EH to Mr Brome, 18 Apr. 1723; Add. MS 70237: EH to Oxford, 6 Oct. 1723.

[199] Herefordshire R.O., Brydges Papers, A81/IV/William Brydges 1714–40: Chandos to William Brydges, 14 July 1727, Cornewall to William Brydges, 5 Oct. 1740, 20 Feb. 1741, EH to William Brydges, 21 Feb. 1741.

[200] Below p. 253: EH to Martha Harley, 12 May 1741.

election, his brother, Robert, declined to stand for election in his place 'in order to preserve the friendship between the familys and the Unity of the County'. Instead, Thomas Foley of Stoke Edith, a long-time ally of the Harleys who had been unsuccessful at Hereford in 1721, was the candidate with the full support of Brampton Bryan.[201] Doubtless some wider agreement was reached, because, in 1747, Foley stood down to be replaced by the third earl's eldest son, Edward. Remarkably, Lord Harley even had the support of Sir Hungerford Hoskyns, the defeated whig candidate in 1721, and he continued to represent the county until his father's death in 1755.[202]

As has been seen, the Harleys were not without influence in other constituencies, but it was not great. Edward Harley continued to take an interest in electoral politics in Hereford and Radnorshire, where he was prepared to support Lord Carnarvon in 1754.[203] In 1751 he tried to secure his son's election as M.P. for Oxford University, in a contest which has already been described.[204] But the family was most successful in Leominster, where Edward's brother, Robert, had succeeded their father as recorder. Here Robert was returned as one of the borough's representatives in both 1734 and 1742, coming top of the poll on both occasions. In the interim, however, he was defeated at the general election in 1741. As in 1722 defeat was attributed to the power of money, and the two brothers came away from the poll 'in more spirits than if we had a Victory'. Edward Harley claimed that Robert had had the support of 'the united Voice of the County and the Substantial Inhabitants', and he planned to print the poll, doubtless hoping it would reinforce the identification of the Harley family with the interest of the county on the basis of country principles.[205] But even at Leominster, the Harleys' success was only limited. In 1747, for reasons which remain obscure, they retreated from the borough, and in 1754 Robert Harley was returned to parliament, on the interest of his cousin, Lord Foley, as M.P. for Droitwich, for which he served until his death in 1774.[206]

The third earl of Oxford thus revived and consolidated the position the Harleys had enjoyed in Herefordshire since the early seventeenth century, as one of the county's leading families. He ensured, moreover, that this local power base was passed on intact to his son, and his descendants continued to share the county representation with the Foleys and Cornewalls through the rest of the eighteenth century. However, despite his efforts and the limited success of his brother at Leominster, Edward Harley was unable to re-establish the family's electoral power, even in constituencies like Leominster, Radnorshire and New Radnor, where it had been dominant in Anne's reign. Robert Harley's candidature for Oxford University in 1751 was revealing. It demonstrated that the third earl had developed into one of the tory party's leading politicians, worthy of contesting the most prestigious tory constituency in the country. But precisely because he was a prominent tory, proscription under George I and George II ensured that, in local politics as in national politics, Edward Harley could never hope to emulate the uncle he so admired.

---

[201] Brampton Bryan MSS, Bundle 117: Robert Harley to Thomas Foley, 3 Sept. 1741.
[202] Below p. 263: Hoskyns to Oxford, 26 June 1747. The county was contested in 1754, but little material seems to have survived from this election and it is difficult to discover the nature of the divisions.
[203] Adams, 'Parliamentary Representation of Radnorshire', pp. 247–8, 251, 257, 280–1, 288–94; below pp. 269–77.
[204] See above, p. liv.
[205] Below pp. 252–3: EH to Martha Harley, 7, 10 May 1741.
[206] Sedgwick, II, 112. The Harley family did, however, retain a considerable interest at Leominster for some years. See Lewis Walpole Library, Farmington, Connecticut, Hanbury Williams Papers, CHW 67, ff. 66–7: Capel Hanbury to Charles Hanbury Williams, 26 Aug. 1752.

WILLIAM HAY AND THE PELHAM FAMILY

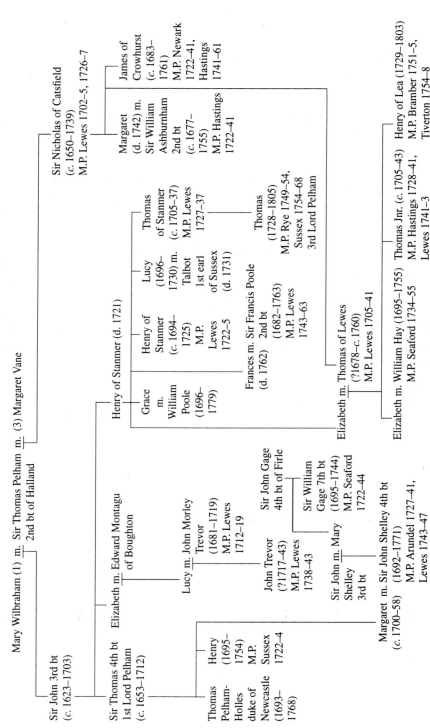

WILLIAM HAY, M.P. FOR SEAFORD
(1695–1755)

The early life of William Hay

Born at Glyndebourne, Sussex, on 21 August 1695, and dying on 22 June 1755, William Hay was a near contemporary of Edward Harley. However, we know much less about Hay than about Harley. Some financial and estate papers, including a few letters to William Hay, are preserved among the Glyndebourne papers at East Sussex Record Office[1] and in the files of the *Morrice* v. *Langham* case in the chancery papers at the Public Record Office.[2] But there is no collection of personal family papers apart from the parliamentary journal printed below, and only the correspondence with the duke of Newcastle seems to have been preserved elsewhere. Thus, for our information about Hay's early life – and, indeed, most of the rest of his life outside parliament – we are almost entirely reliant on the memoir written by his nephew the Rev. Francis Tutté, which is prefixed to the collection of his works published in 1794.[3]

According to Tutté, the Hays were an ancient Sussex family who settled at Glynde-bourne in the early seventeenth century. Like Sir Robert Harley, William Hay's great-grandfather, Herbert Hay, M.P. for Arundel, took the parliamentary side during the civil war, but he was secluded by the army in 1648. His maternal grandfather, Sir John Stapeley, represented Lewes in the Cavalier Parliament, but neither his grandfather, John Hay, nor his father William appear to have served in parliament.[4] Hay's early life was certainly unsettled, and probably unhappy. His father died in 1697, and about a month later his mother married Merrick Jenkins, one of the executors of his father's will.[5] A son, Charles, was born in April 1699.[6] But within two years Hay's mother was also dead,[7] and his grandfather, Sir John Stapeley, became his guardian. Stapeley then died on 22 August 1701, followed by his wife Mary on 20 March 1709. At that point

---

[1] East Sussex R.O., GBN.

[2] We would like to thank Christopher Whittick of the East Sussex R.O. for making available his notes and preliminary listing of P.R.O., C109/15–18.

[3] Unless otherwise indicated, this section is based on Tutté's biography in *The Works of William Hay* (2 vols., 1794). Reprinted *Literary Anecdotes of the Eighteenth Century*, ed. John Nichols (9 vols., 1812–16), VI, 346–58.

[4] Tutté claimed that John Hay served as M.P. for Rye and Sussex, but he confused John Hay with his uncle William, who represented Rye in the Long Parliament and again in the parliaments of 1656, 1659 and 1660, and Sussex in the parliament of 1654. Tutté is also incorrect in his claim that WH's father served as M.P. for Seaford in 1692.

[5] Tutté's account of WH's early life is not very reliable. In addition to the errors already noted, Tutté states that William Hay the elder died in 1695. In fact, his will is dated 14 Oct. 1697, and probate was granted to Barbara Jenkins, otherwise Hay, on 15 Nov. 1698. P.R.O., PCC 233 Lort (we would like to thank Stuart Handley for this reference); P.R.O., C109/15–18. However, he had clearly died shortly after making this will, as his wife married Jenkins on 16 Nov. 1697 in London at Holy Trinity Minories. Guildhall Library, MS 10091/32: marriage allegations, Apr. 1695 – Dec. 1697; MS 9243, p. 154: marriage register of Holy Trinity Minories.

[6] *The Parish Register of Glynde Sussex 1558–1812*, ed. L.F. Salzman (Sussex Record Society, XXX, 1924), p. 31.

[7] Her will, dated 13 Nov. 1700, was proved 10 Feb. 1701. East Sussex R.O., SM/D3, p. 167. Tutté states that she died in 1700.

Hay's maternal aunt, Mary Dobell, became his guardian.[8] In 1705 Hay himself was sent to school in the village of Newick and then in 1710 to the grammar school at Lewes.[9] On 20 March 1712 he matriculated at Christ Church, but in 1715 he left Oxford without taking a degree and was admitted first to Lincoln's Inn and then to the Middle Temple.[10] During the next few years he travelled extensively, touring England and Scotland in 1718 and then going on the Grand Tour, to France, Germany and Holland, in 1720.

There is no evidence that Hay was called to the bar, nor that he worked as a lawyer.[11] He was still at the Middle Temple in March 1717,[12] but Tutté records that his legal studies were cut short, sometime between 1715 and 1720, by an attack of smallpox which damaged his eye-sight. This was Hay's second physical affliction, as he had been born a hunchback dwarf. We know almost nothing about Hay's activities between this time and his entry into parliament in 1734. According to Tutté, 'he for some years resided at his house in the country', and he certainly did extensive work on the gardens at Glyndebourne in 1722–4.[13] He became an active justice of the peace, first appearing on the surviving fiats in 1727, and he was appointed as chairman of quarter sessions for the eastern division of Sussex in 1733.[14] He also embarked on a career as a minor 'man of letters'. His first publication, *An Essay on Civil Government*, appeared anonymously in 1728 and revealed his whig principles.[15] He followed this in 1732 with a defence of the reimposition of the salt tax,[16] a proposal for the reform of the poor laws in 1735, which was reprinted in 1751,[17] and a discussion of the principles of morality and religion in 1753.[18] But Hay did not write only on public affairs. In 1730 he published *Mount Caburn*, a poem dedicated to the duchess of Newcastle,[19] and towards the end of his life he translated Browne's poem *De Animi Immortalitate* and a selection of the epigrams of Martial.[20] His most popular, and possibly his most interesting, work, however, was his discussion of his own physical disabilities, published in 1754 under the title *Deformity: An Essay*. It went through

---

8 P.R.O., C109/15–18: Administration of the will of William Hay granted to Mary Dobell, widow, 27 Aug. 1709; G.E. Cokayne, *Complete Baronetage* (6 vols., 1900–9), III, 97–8.

9 Brent, p. 94.

10 *D.N.B.* Admitted to Lincoln's Inn, 22 Jan. 1714; to Middle Temple, 24 May 1715. *Records of the Honourable Society of Lincoln's Inn* (2 vols., 1896), I, 375; *Register of Admissions to the Honourable Society of the Middle Temple* (3 vols., 1949), I, 275.

11 Cf., *D.N.B.* with John Hutchinson, *A Catalogue of Notable Middle Templars, with Brief Biographical Notes* (1902), pp. 115–16.

12 P.R.O., C109/15–18: conveyance from John Read to WH, 14 and 15 Mar. 1717.

13 *Ibid.*: accounts for work on gardens.

14 P.R.O., C234/37. WH was not named on the fiat issued on 22 July 1723. His charge to the grand jury in 1733 is printed in Hay, *Works*, I, 303–16.

15 [William Hay], *An Essay on Civil Government* (1728). For a discussion of this pamphlet, see below pp. lxv–lxix.

16 Below p. lxix. This pamphlet was not included in WH's *Works*. It may be one of two works, both printed for J. Roberts: *A Letter to a Country Gentleman on the Revival of the Salt Duty* (1732), or *The Case of the Salt-Duty and Land-Tax, Offered to the Consideration of Every Freeholder* (1732). On the basis of internal evidence the latter is more likely to be WH's work.

17 [William Hay], *Remarks on the Laws Relating to the Poor. With Proposals for their Better Relief and Employment. By a Member of Parliament* [1735]; *Remarks on the Laws Relating to the Poor... First Published in 1735; and now again Submitted to Consideration. With an Appendix* (1751).

18 William Hay, *Religio Philosophi: Or, the Principles of Morality and Christianity, Illustrated from a View of the Universe, and of Man's Situation in it* (1753; 2nd edn., 1754; 3rd edn., 1760).

19 William Hay, *Mount Caburn. A Poem. Humbly Inscribed to Her Grace the Dutchess of Newcastle* (1730).

20 *The Immortality of the Soul. A Poem. Translated from the Latin of Isaac Hawkins Browne, Esq; by William Hay, Esq.* (1754); *Select Epigrams of Martial. Translated and Imitated by William Hay* (1755).

three editions in London within two years, while in addition there were at least two Dublin editions.[21] It attracted some critical acclaim, one contemporary describing the work as 'a master-piece of humour, wit, ingenuity, elegant style, fancy, and good sense. But, above all, it has the simplicity of Montaigne without his vanity.'[22]

In 1731 Hay married Elizabeth Pelham, the second daughter of Thomas Pelham of Catsfield Place, Sussex, and a cousin of the duke of Newcastle. Thus was forged the personal connexion with Newcastle, on whose interest he was returned as M.P. for Seaford at a by-election in January 1734. It was doubtless partly through the Pelham interest that he was appointed a commissioner of the victualling office in May 1738. In 1747, however, he had to resign the office when it became incompatible with a seat in the Commons under the terms of the Place Act of 1742. Instead, he was granted a secret service pension of £500 per annum, which he retained until his appointment as keeper of the records in the Tower in 1754.[23] Hay's eldest son, Thomas, a lieutenant-colonel in the dragoons, followed his father into parliament, serving as M.P. for Lewes between 1768 and 1780, while his second son, William, became a member of the supreme council at Calcutta. However, none of his five children produced an heir and on the death of his younger daughter, Frances, Glyndebourne passed to Francis Tutté.

Parliamentary career of William Hay

Hay's nephew recorded that 'he was one of "the first in, and the last out of, the House of Commons" '.[24] This statement was not mere family piety; it is clear that William Hay was an active parliamentarian. In contrast to Edward Harley, he took an active part in legislative work from his first session in 1734, being nominated to 24 committees, including his first drafting committee on a bill concerning the redemption of mortgages,[25] and acting twice as a teller. Indeed, judging by the evidence of committee nominations, Hay was even more active in the Commons than Harley. He was nominated to 302 committees in the 11 sessions between 1734 and 1744 (the period covered by the journal), with a high of 45 in 1736 and a low of 11 in 1741–2. This was an average of just over 27 committees per session, compared with Harley's 24 during his time in the Commons. Fifteen of these were drafting committees, and Hay acted as chairman of nine committees and four committees of the whole house. However, he was a teller on only seven occasions, far less frequently than Harley. He told for the majority twice – in 1739 on Westminster Bridge and in 1740–1 on supply. But, surprisingly perhaps for a ministerialist, on the other occasions he was with the minority – on an estate bill and on the bill for regulating elections in Scotland in 1734, on the Quakers Tithe Bill in 1736, and on the Rogues and Vagabonds Bill and County Elections Bill in 1743. On some of these occasions he was clearly voting against the government. On the Scottish Elections Bill Hay seems to have been supporting the Speaker on a procedural question, while in 1736 he found himself telling with the

---

[21] William Hay, *Deformity: An Essay* (1754; 2nd edn., 1754; 3rd edn., 1755; Dublin, 1754; '4th edn.', Dublin, 1754). This work was also reprinted in *Fugitive Pieces on Various Subjects by Several Authors* (1761; 2nd edn., 1765; 3rd edn., 1771; Dublin edn., 1762).

[22] Nichols, *Literary Anecdotes*, VIII, 520.

[23] Sedgwick, II, 119.

[24] Nichols, *Literary Anecdotes*, VI, 350.

[25] WH showed a particular interest in this measure, seconding the motion to bring in the bill. But the drafting committee never met, the bill having already been drawn up by the master of the rolls. See below p. 98.

tory, Sir John St Aubyn, after a debate in which they were the only two members to speak against the Quakers Tithe Bill.[26]

Analysis of Hay's nominations to committees by the four broad subject categories reveals a pattern broadly similar to Harley's. During the 11 sessions covered by his journal, estate bill committees accounted for 14 per cent of Hay's nominations, economic committees for 45 per cent, miscellaneous affairs for 34 per cent and social affairs for about 6 per cent. The final figure is worth highlighting, because it suggests that Hay was nominated to more than twice as many committees on social issues as Harley. One might question the statistical significance of the numbers, but an analysis of Hay's nominations to drafting committees and of his chairmanship of committees confirms the inference that he had a special interest in social matters. Moreover, many of the economic committees to which he was nominated also had a strong social element. In 1736 and 1737 he was nominated to drafting committees on the poor laws and in 1737 also to one on insolvent debtors;[27] in 1738 to one on the relief of prisoners in King's Bench; in 1739 to bills on rogues and vagabonds and the relief of insolvent debtors;[28] in 1740–1 to a Bill on the Recovery of Small Debts; and in 1743 again to a Rogues and Vagabonds Bill. His chairmanship of committees included a select committee on the poor law in 1735, and second reading committees on insolvent debtors and poor relief in 1737, and on rogues and vagabonds in both 1739 and 1744.

Hay, therefore, like Harley was a reformer committed to the improvement of local administration and justice. The emphasis of his interests, however, was different from Harley's, and he concentrated his efforts on issues of social welfare. This impression, derived from examining his committee work in the 1730s and 1740s, is reinforced by recent research on the period between 1746 and 1754. By the late 1740s he was often one of the first nominated to committees on social topics, revealing not only that he was a regular attender of the house, but also that he was known to be interested and knowledgeable in the field. His particular enthusiasm was for the reform of the poor law. As Richard Connors observes, 'on the subject of poverty and poor law policy Hay was something of an expert', and in the Commons he became 'a well-known advocate of proposals which sought to reform the poor laws and the structures of local government'.[29] However, this cause features so large in Hay's career that it merits separate treatment later.

Hay was clearly a diligent M.P. In addition, he was a keen parliamentarian. Like many parliamentary diarists, including Harley, he demonstrated a close interest in Commons' procedure. But Hay was also a strong advocate of the rights and privileges of the house. In 1736, for example, Hay voted with the minority against accepting the Lords' amendments to the Westminster Bridge Bill. He accepted the Speaker's argument that 'the Honour and Priviledges of the Commons' were at stake. In Hay's opinion, the bill was a money bill, and he saw himself as defending the right of the Commons alone to dispose of money which 'came out of the Subjects Pocket'.[30] It was also, in part, a concern to assert the privileges of the lower house against the upper

---

26 For the Scottish Elections Bill see *C.J.*, XXII, 304, and below pp. 98–9. For the Quakers Tithe Bill see below pp. 140–4.

27 *C.J.*, XXII, 607, 746–7, 782.

28 WH was the only person named to the drafting committee on the bill for the relief of insolvent debtors. However, he does not appear to have been the chairman of the subsequent second reading committee, even though he was ordered to carry the bill to the Lords on 10 April. *C.J.*, XXIII, 246, 288, 323.

29 R.T. Connors, 'Pelham, Parliament and Public Policy, 1746–1754', University of Cambridge, Ph.D., 1993, pp. 181–2, 230–2.

30 Below p. 145.

that led Hay, at the beginning of the session of 1741–2, to urge the enforcement of the standing order against the presence of strangers. The Lords were enforcing their order, turning away even members of the Commons. Therefore, urged Hay, the Commons should do the same. But Hay was also anxious to assert the dignity of the house and ensure the privacy of debate. He claimed that the Commons had become a 'Common House', a 'Coffee House' and a 'Play-House', from which 'ignorant or Malicious People' carried away 'false or partial representations of Debates'.[31] However, while Hay was always ready to assert the privileges of the Commons against the Lords and outsiders, he had little sympathy for those who abused those privileges. In 1740 Hay argued forcefully in favour of a resolution that privilege from prosecution should not be allowed to M.P.s absent abroad. Indeed, he believed that it was desirable to extend the resolution to include all members absent from the house without leave. In Hay's view, there was a real danger that privilege would become an abuse, allowing M.P.s to obstruct justice, thereby bringing the Commons itself into disrepute.[32]

Hay and whiggery

As has been noted, the fact that Hay's papers have not survived means that we know less about his career than Harley's. In some respects, however, Hay's political principles are better documented than Harley's. In the first place, Hay's 'Journal' reveals more about his ideas, not least because he used it to record some of his own speeches in full. Secondly, as already mentioned, a few years before his entry into parliament, Hay wrote a short theoretical treatise expounding his beliefs about the origin and nature of government. His *Essay on Civil Government* probably grew out of reflections on his duties as a magistrate. He set out to establish clearly the 'Civil Obligations' of both magistrates and people. In particular, he sought to establish government's 'Right to Authority', the knowledge of which was essential for subjects required 'to swear that a Government is Rightful'.[33] The only book Hay admitted to consulting was William Temple's *Essay on Government*. Indeed, he claimed that what he wrote was simply the product of his own thoughts on the subject, 'guided by Reason' and 'formed on Recollection and Consideration of what he had read or heard'.[34] His treatise, however, is not particularly original or profound. Nonetheless, it provides a valuable insight into the political principles of a rank-and-file court whig.

Having established the necessity of government – to provide for the security of men's 'Temporal Blessings' – Hay focused on its origins. Surprisingly perhaps for a whig, Hay believed that the most plausible origin of civil government was 'Paternal Authority'. However, he found it 'scarce credible' that any government still subsisted on its original foundations and went on to argue, in more characteristically whig fashion, that

> it is Contract alone that is the only just Foundation of it, and the Cement by which the constituent Parts of it are united. For though Paternity or Conquest may in Fact have given Occasion and Opportunity to exercise a Civil Authority, yet they are far from giving a Right to it: That can be derived only from the Consent of the Party governed; for no Man can claim either a Divine or Natural

---

[31] Below pp. 167–8.
[32] Below pp. 159–60.
[33] *On Civil Government*, p. iv.
[34] *Ibid.*, pp. v–vi.

Right to controul another; since God hath neither expressly declared by Revelation, or by any other means marked out or designed any particular Persons for Governours, but hath made all Men by Nature Equal.

Hay readily admitted that in many cases no express, still less written, contract existed. But such a contract was not necessary, because 'a Tacit Deference to Authority for any length of time may be construed to amount to a Consent'. Moreover, this contract, even when established by such 'Tacit Deference', bound not only those who made it but also their posterity.[35]

The notion of a contract, of course, implied a right of resistance. Predictably, Hay had no time for those who propagated ideas of non-resistance and passive obedience. On the contrary, he pointed out that even the biblical texts on which such ideas were based commanded submission only to 'good Magistrates'. However, he was careful to limit the right of resistance. The people could not be justified in resisting in 'all Cases of Mismanagement'. Indeed, sometimes the state would be damaged more by attempts to redress grievances than by the grievances themselves. In such circumstances, 'the Publick Good of Society' outweighed the complaints of individual subjects. Thus, resistance was only justified when the people's 'Lives', 'Liberty', 'Possessions' or 'Religion' were 'notoriously invaded'. The 'whole Body of the People' had to be aware of the magistrate's misgovernment. The grounds for resistance could not, therefore, be defined in advance, but they would 'sufficiently discover themselves' if the occasion arose.[36]

Hay discussed these issues in a general, abstract manner, and he made no reference to the British constitution. However, it is clear that he was providing a defence of the British monarchy and of the Hanoverian succession in particular. James II, he argued, had possessed no divine right to the English throne, and thus the revolution of 1688 was justified because James had broken his contract with the English people by invading their property and undermining their religion. A new contract, symbolized perhaps by the Bill of Rights, had then been agreed by William and the people. But Hay was addressing himself not merely to those who were convinced about the legitimacy of the revolution. In his view, even those who denied that resistance had been justified in 1688 were obliged now to give their allegiance to the Hanoverian monarchy because it had now survived for long enough to have established consent by 'Tacit Deference'.

Hay's discussion of the forms of government was also couched in general terms. He accepted that government in general was 'the Ordinance of God', though he did not discuss this point beyond making a reference to the Bible. The particular form of government in any state, however, was not prescribed by God, but rather left to the decision of the people. Hay then described the various forms of government in conventional terms, dividing them into monarchy, aristocracy and democracy, and he followed Temple in emphasizing that all had their strengths and weaknesses.[37] But whatever form of government existed in a state, it possessed 'absolute Authority', which, within its 'proper Sphere of Human Jurisdiction', was 'Unaccountable and Uncontroulable'. Such an authority was necessary to secure the public good, but it did not mean that a prince had the power 'to do whatever he pleases'. On the contrary, he was bound to rule according to the laws of God and nature, which included, in Hay's

---

[35] *Ibid.*, pp. 1, 3, 8–9, 10–11.
[36] *Ibid.*, pp. 13, 16–17.
[37] *Ibid.*, pp. 20–1.

opinion, respecting the 'Natural Rights' of the subject. Any prince who invaded those rights was guilty of breaking his contract with the people; his government became a 'Tyranny'.[38]

At this point in the pamphlet, Hay expressed no preference for any one form of government. On the contrary, he believed that 'there is scarce any Constitution so ill contrived, but the People may live easily under it, if it be duly observed', and he argued that 'every Private Man ought to be contented with that established in his own Country, and to contribute his utmost Endeavours to support it'.[39] However, by the end of the *Essay* it is clear that Hay thought that the British constitution shared the characteristics of the ideal form of government. He argued that there were several powers in the state – of making laws, of executing them, of conducting foreign policy, and so on – but that it was

> not necessary that they should be all vested in the same Person, for Experience evinces the contrary: And it has been the Practice of all the wisest Nations to divide them, esteeming it as the best Security of their Liberty, to have one part of the Supreme Authority a Cheque upon the other.

Such a division of powers had disadvantages. Lack of unanimity could prevent that state from acting with 'Vigour and Steadiness', while conflicts between the powers could lead to 'Civil Dissension'. But, in Hay's view, these disadvantages were more than outweighed by the advantages, which he saw as lying primarily in the preservation of the liberty of the subject.[40]

In the *Essay on Civil Government*, therefore, Hay showed himself to be a whig committed to the maintenance of the revolutionary settlement. But, more than that, he outlined some of the principles which were to govern his behaviour in parliament. Throughout his parliamentary career, for example, he consistently opposed place bills. In 1740 Hay was the first to speak against the motion for a bill, and he tackled head-on the opposition argument that the crown, through its distribution of places to M.P.s, was exercising an 'unjust Influence' over the parliament. The independence of M.P.s was guaranteed because they were all men of property, while the rights of the electors were maintained by the requirement that any M.P. appointed to office had to submit himself to re-election. Indeed, Hay believed that a place bill, rather than preserving the constitution, would be 'injurious' to it. It would infringe the rights of electors, by limiting their choice of representatives and perhaps preventing them from choosing the person they thought most capable. It would also be an infringement of the natural rights of every office holder, 'by depriving him of that Capacity to which he was born: a Capacity of Advising in the making the Laws of his Country'. Moreover, a place bill directly threatened the balance of the constitution in two ways. First, it would throw 'more power into the hands of the Lords ... for if the favours of the Crown are excluded this House, they will flow in larger Streams to the Other'. Second, there would be a danger that office holders, excluded from parliament, would come to form 'a distinct Interest; which in the end may be distructive to the Parliament itself: As the Power of the Army was in the last Century'.[41]

---

[38] *Ibid.*, pp. 29–31.
[39] *Ibid.*, p. 24.
[40] *Ibid.*, pp. 60–1.
[41] Below pp. 156–9. In 1734 Hay had also been the first to speak against the Place Bill, but then he had concentrated more on the 'Injury' to the rights of electors and M.P.s. Below p. 97; Cobbett, IX, 367.

Similar concerns for the balance of the constitution are revealed in Hay's contributions to debates about the army. He consistently opposed opposition attempts to reduce the size of the army, but it is only in 1738 that his journal contains a full account of his reasons for supporting the maintenance of a standing army even in peacetime. Hay explicitly addressed the opposition objections to a standing army on the grounds of expense and the threat it posed to the constitution. He denied categorically that the army posed any threat to the constitution. He pointed out that the British army was

> composed of our own People; and voted Annualy by Parliament, directed by his Majesty; commanded by Officers who are Men of Honour; Many of them of great Fortune, Birth, and Alliance ... who must be blind to their own Interest and that of their Posterity, before they can entertain a thought of invading the Rights of their Country.

Indeed, far from threatening the constitution, the 'Army has for some years preserved' it. It was the guarantor of the protestant succession, and Hay predicted that, if it were disbanded, within a year the king would be driven out of the kingdom, to be replaced by 'a Popish Prince and no Parliament'. Hay admitted the opposition's second argument, that the army was expensive. In his view, however, the question was not its expense, but its necessity. He reminded the Commons not only of the threat from France, Britain's 'natural Ennemy',[42] but also of the need for the army at home to support the rule of law. Indeed, so prevalent was the 'licentiousness' of the press that 'all legal Authority' was being undermined, 'a Spirit of Opposition, of Disobedience and Disloyalty' was spreading, and the country was being threatened by the rule of the 'Mob'. In such circumstances, Hay warned, 'to weaken and disarm the Government ... is to distroy it'.[43]

Hay was particularly sensitive to the constitutional position of the army. During his first session in the Commons, he showed especial interest in an opposition motion that army officers should not be removed without a court martial. The dissident whigs were attempting to embarrass the ministry over the dismissal of the duke of Bolton and Lord Cobham for their part in leading opposition to Walpole's Tobacco Excise Bill. Hay, however, found it 'extraordinary, that Persons who had always been against any Forces, should now be for making the Army more Independent'. He saw the issue in primarily constitutional terms, claiming that the true aim of the opposition 'was to weaken the power of the Crown and to encrease that of the two Houses; which might be a prelude to future Innovations, and was not unlike the Attempt of Wresting the power of the Militia from Charles the first'. The motion was an attack on the royal prerogative and, if it succeeded, it would, in his opinion, 'distroy the ballance in the Constitution, and might prove the subversion of it'.[44]

The *Essay on Civil Government* thus provides a guide to the principles underlying Hay's behaviour in debates which raised constitutional issues. But it also touched on other matters which later came before Hay as an M.P. One of the most important of these was taxation, a subject on which Hay had firm views. He accepted the necessity of taxation, but argued that the state had a duty to levy taxes equally – all subjects benefited from government, so all 'should contribute his Proportion towards it'. In his

---

[42] Hay also revealed his concern about French power in the navy debate of 1735. Below p. 105.

[43] Below pp. 149–51. The printed version of WH's speech lays particular emphasis on Hay's fears about growth of licentiousness and the threat of mob rule. Cobbett, X, 375–9.

[44] Below pp. 95–6.

view, the most equitable taxes were 'sumptuary' ones, 'since they not only serve to restrain Luxury, but fall on those who may well afford to contribute largely to the Publick, when they can throw away so much on their own Vanity and Folly'.[45] Consequently, Hay was an enthusiastic supporter of Walpole's attempts gradually to shift the burden of taxation away from the land tax to indirect taxation. In 1734 he voted for the continuation of the salt tax. His motives might appear selfish – he recorded in his journal that 'I should have thought I acted against the Interest of every Landholder, if I had Voted against it.' But two years earlier he had written a pamphlet defending the revival of the salt tax. That pamphlet was probably *The Case of the Salt-Duty and Land-Tax*, and assuming his authorship it makes clear the grounds of Hay's support for the salt tax. The land tax, the pamphlet claimed, was a 'grievous' tax, because it was paid by only a part, 'perhaps not a twentieth Part', of the population, while 'the moneyed Men are excused from their share of the Burthen'. Moreover, the injustice of the tax itself was exacerbated because the system of assessment meant that it was levied unequally.[46] The salt tax, by contrast, was 'a Tax which is laid on the People in general, where every one pays in proportion to what he consumes; where generally every one's Consumption is in proportion to his Circumstances'.[47] It was a more equal and more just tax.

In general, therefore, Hay emerges from his pamphlets and journal not merely as a whig, but as a committed ministerial whig. Time and again in his journal, from the petition of the tea dealers in 1734 to the debates on Hanoverian troops in 1742 and 1744, Hay simply echoed the ministerial line. Within the whig party his allegiance clearly lay with the Old Corps, led first by Walpole and then by the Pelhams. In the debate on the motion for Walpole's removal in February 1741 he intervened twice in defence of the prime minister.[48] His distaste for the antics of the Patriots is clear from his account of the Westminster election petition in December 1741. Hay complained repeatedly about the Commons ignoring the evidence before it, which, he believed, showed that 'the Injury was done by the Party that complained'. When the sitting members were unseated, he concluded his account gloomily that it had been the 'most violent proceeding I remember'.[49] Even after Walpole's fall, he can be found condemning as 'unparliamentary' Pulteney's efforts to create a secret committee to investigate the last ten years of the Walpole ministry.[50]

On Hay's death in 1755 Newcastle lamented the loss of 'a very faithful, and useful Servant in the House of Commons; Who, in Two and Twenty Years Attendance there, was scarce ever absent at one single Question; and never gave a wrong Vote, to the best of my Remembrance'.[51] While the duke's tribute to Hay's loyalty was clearly well deserved, it should be recognized that he was quite capable of demonstrating a certain independence of thought and action. Indeed, Hay was not beyond criticizing Walpole himself, condemning the grants he obtained just before his resignation as 'an Abuse of the Kings favour'.[52] But, given what has already been said about the nature of his whiggery, it should come as no surprise that Hay was particularly concerned

[45] *On Civil Government*, p. 58.
[46] Below p. 97; *The Case of the Salt-Duty and Land-Tax*, pp. 8–9, 15–17.
[47] *The Case of the Salt-Duty and Land-Tax*, pp. 10–11.
[48] I.G. Doolittle, 'A First-Hand Account of the Commons Debate on the Removal of Sir Robert Walpole, 13 February 1741', *B.I.H.R.*, LIII (1980), 125–40.
[49] Below pp. 171–3.
[50] Below p. 181.
[51] B.L., Add. MS 32856, ff. 167–8: Newcastle to Holdernesse, 24 June 1755.
[52] Below p. 176.

with issues where he believed the balance of the constitution to be affected. In 1736 William Pitt was dismissed from his cornetcy 'for having voted and spoke in Parliament contrary to [the King's] approbation'. In Hay's view this action was designed to ensure office holders' support for the ministry, and he condemned it as a 'Measure, which if successfully pursued, undermined the Freedom of Parliament'.[53] Nor was Hay's criticism of the ministry confined to the pages of his journal. Although he consistently supported the administration in all recorded divisions, his journal reveals that on occasions he did vote against the ministry in the Commons. Thus, he joined with the opposition in a debate on the Scarborough election petition when he felt that justice was not being done.[54] But the strength of his convictions was perhaps demonstrated most clearly by his support for election bills in 1735 and 1736. The 1735 bill prevented the quartering of soldiers in parliamentary boroughs during elections. The popularity of the measure prevented ministerial opposition, but it would have been lost in a surprise division on the third reading had Hay not supported it, along with Winnington, Hanbury Williams and Selwyn, 'against our Friends'. The 1736 bill, stating that borough electors had to be qualified to vote for twelve months before an election, was more controversial and was opposed by the ministry. It was finally defeated in committee, but Hay, believing it to be a 'very reasonable' bill, voted with the minority and 'gained much ill Will by it'.[55]

Hay thus provides a useful reminder of how different eighteenth-century parties were from their modern counterparts. Hay was regarded as a reliable ministerialist; he was an office holder and an pensioner. Yet, admittedly only on rare occasions, he can be found in opposition to the administration. Hay exercised independent judgment as an M.P. To gain the support of men like him, the ministry had to appeal to principle and conviction at least as much as it relied on the imposition of discipline. Having said this, however, it is important to emphasize that a chasm divided a ministerial whig like Hay from a tory like Harley. The 1735 debate on the Wells election petition, though a minor issue, illustrates well their different perspectives. As has been seen, Harley found it incredible that the Commons, for the second time, voted that William Piers had been elected. Hay, on the contrary, believed that the petitioners' case was 'so clear' that he was surprised they won the division by only 14 votes.[56]

Hay, whiggery and religion

It has long been recognized that religion, especially high anglicanism, was a crucial component of post-revolutionary toryism. Recently, historians have also become increasingly aware that religion, whether anti-clericalism, latitudinarianism or dissent, played an important part in the formation of whig identity.[57] Remarkably little work has been done, however, on the period after the Hanoverian succession. Linda Colley has anatomized the nature of tory anglicanism in the early Hanoverian

---

53 H.M.C., *15th Report, Appendix, Part VI*, p. 172: Lady Irwin to Carlisle, 20 May [1736]; below p. 146.
54 Below p. 140. See also his concerns about the resolution passed on the Southwark election petition in February 1736. Below p. 130.
55 Below pp. 122, 135.
56 Compare the accounts of Harley and Hay, below pp. 5–6, 113–14.
57 Geoffrey Holmes, *British Politics in the Age of Anne* (1967); G.V. Bennett, *The Tory Crisis in Church and State 1688–1730. The Career of Francis Atterbury, Bishop of Rochester* (Oxford, 1975); Mark Goldie, 'Priestcraft and the Birth of Whiggism', in *Political Discourse in Early Modern Britain*, ed. Nicholas Phillipson and Quentin Skinner (Cambridge, 1993), pp. 209–31; Justin Champion, *Pillars of Priestcraft Shaken. The Church of England and its Enemies, 1660–1730* (Cambridge, 1992).

period,[58] but work on the whigs has tended to concentrate on 'country' ideology and religion has rarely been discussed.[59] However, as will be seen, it was an important element in the political ideology of William Hay – latitudinarianism, anti-clericalism and erastianism combined to give his whiggery a distinctive edge.

The importance of religion for Hay is highlighted by the fact that, towards the end of his life, he wrote a tract on religion entitled *Religio Philosophi: Or, the Principles of Morality and Christianity, Illustrated from a View of the Universe, and of Man's Situation in It*. His purpose in writing this tract was to provide a defence of religion, and, more specifically, christianity. By 'rectifying Mens Ideas, and by removing Vulgar Prejudices', he aimed 'to fix RELIGION on a FIRM BASIS'. Like the *Origin of Civil Government*, this was very much a personal statement – Hay had 'scrupulously avoided reading any thing new' on the subject, so that his opinions would be 'in the strictest Sense, his OWN'.[60] Much of what Hay said was commonplace, though, as will be seen, in some respects he was idiosyncratic. However, it is equally clear that his views were those of a whig – it is significant that the work was dedicated to Arthur Onslow, the Speaker of the house of commons. The tract ranged more widely than its sub-title might suggest and, to clarify the relationship between Hay's religion and his whiggery, discussion of Hay's opinions will be divided into three parts: his religious beliefs, his thoughts on the relationship between church and state, and his anti-clericalism.

Hay's religious beliefs may be described as latitudinarian. Above all, he emphasized that, in matters of religion, men should not be 'led by AUTHORITY or CUSTOM', but should 'follow NATURE and REASON; Guides, who afford the best Lights in every Search after Truth; and Interpreters of Scripture, who are the least fallible'.[61] By considering the nature of the world and man's position in it, Hay argued that it was 'rational to believe' that God had provided man with some guide 'to enlighten his Understanding, fortify his Reason, incline his Will, and moderate his Passions'. He further demonstrated that only christianity had 'the Characteristicks of a true Religion'.[62] Christianity was above all a reasonable religion. It was 'the most perfect System of Morality that ever was proposed to Man'. It required no 'vain Ceremonies ... but only a right Disposition of the Mind, and a reasonable Employment of it's Faculties'. The doctrines of christianity were few and simple, while its ceremonies – baptism and the Lord's supper – were 'easy' and 'in their own Nature indifferent'.[63] Hay was aware of the limits of reason. He reminded his readers of the 'Weakness' of their own 'Understanding', and urged them not immediately to reject the scriptures merely because they did not understand them. However, he had no doubt that reason was the best guide in the interpretation of the Bible. Ultimately, free enquiry would support the truth of christianity. Predictably, therefore, Hay was hostile to tradition,

---

[58] Colley, ch. 4.

[59] See, e.g., H.T. Dickinson, *Liberty and Property. Political Ideology in Eighteenth-Century Britain* (1977); J.G.A. Pocock, 'The Varieties of Whiggism from Exclusion to Reform', in *Virtue, Commerce and History* (Cambridge, 1985). Reed Browning, *Political and Constitutional Ideas of the Court Whigs* (Baton Rouge, 1982), however, does contain some discussion of religion in a chapter on Archbishop Herring, and Marie P. McMahon, *The Radical Whigs, John Trenchard and Thomas Gordon. Libertarian Loyalists to the New House of Hanover* (Lanham, Md., 1990), has some useful comments on whig anti-clericalism in the period 1714–22.

[60] *Religio Philosophi*, Preface.

[61] *Ibid.*

[62] *Ibid.*, pp. 43, 47.

[63] *Ibid.*, pp. 117–20.

which he portrayed as the imposition of a merely human authority. He condemned the Athanasian Creed, and, by implication, other creeds, 'for setting up a human Composition, as the Standard of Salvation'. Similarly, no forms of worship were prescribed in scripture and they were therefore 'indifferent'.[64]

At this point Hay's argument impinged on the subject of church–state relations. While forms of public worship were 'indifferent', Hay insisted that there 'must be some. Men cannot assemble to serve GOD, without some Time or Place appointed for their Meeting: without observing some Form, when met: and without having some Persons among them to officiate.'[65] As long as the forms of worship were decent and intelligible and 'agreeable to Reason and Scripture', every people was 'at Liberty to chuse their own Form'. Hay, however, elaborated on this point by stating that every government ought to 'establish' some form for the use of their people *for the Sake of Order*.[66] Governments, indeed, had a 'Right to inform the Opinions of their Subjects'. This right derived not from any responsibility for their subjects' spiritual welfare, still less from a duty to educate them in the principles of true religion, but rather from their concern with the temporal welfare of the state. Religion, Hay argued, teaches virtue and morality, which are enforced by the promise of 'future Rewards and Punishments'. Thus, it exercises a powerful and important influence over men's behaviour in society. Moreover, since men are guided by their beliefs, 'Error may be succeeded by Sedition, and false Imaginations by real Disorders.' Only one church should be established, however, in order to unite the people as much as possible and to prevent 'Animosity and Dissension; for no Disputes can rise so high as those on' religion.[67]

Hay's views were, therefore, decidedly erastian. Governments had a right, if not a duty, to establish religious forms and ceremonies, while the people had an obligation to conform to those forms as long as they contained nothing 'sinful'.[68] Indeed, even when abroad a traveller ought to attend the services of the church established there, 'for where-ever a Man is, he owes Obedience to the Civil Authority'.[69] As has been shown, Hay thought that the essential doctrines of christianity were few and simple, and he seems to have believed that these could be found in every christian church, whether that of England, Scotland, Sweden, France, Geneva or Rome. Some forms of worship were preferable to others – the 'most rational Forms are those which have the fewest Ceremonies'. But, in the final analysis, 'Forms and Ceremonies are not of the Essence of Religion', and dissent from the established church could not be justified in matters which were 'in their own Nature indifferent'.[70] Even so, as one might expect given Hay's views on the exercise of reason in matters of religion, he was a supporter of the principle of toleration. Governments should not impose forms and ceremonies, 'but should leave to every Man the Christian Liberty of worshipping GOD in any other Way he likes better, provided he disturbs not the Peace of the Society'. Indeed, the imposition of uniformity was counterproductive, since it led only to dissension and conflict. By contrast, however paradoxical it seemed, 'PERMITTING A LATITUDE IN OPINION BEGETS UNITY.'[71] But Hay's support for toleration, at least as explained in *On*

---

64 *Ibid.*, pp. 219–20, 210, 227–8, 136, 181–2.
65 *Ibid.*, p. 173.
66 *Ibid.*, p. 182. Our emphasis.
67 *On Civil Government*, pp. 38–40.
68 *Religio Philosophi*, p. 183.
69 *On Civil Government*, pp. 41–2.
70 *Religio Philosophi*, pp. 182–4; *On Civil Government*, p. 41.
71 *Religio Philosophi*, pp. 182, 222.

Civil Government, was limited and circumscribed. He certainly believed that a man's belief was a matter for him and God alone, as long as it continued 'locked up in his own Breast ... But if he offers to persuade or force others into his Opinion, he justly incurs the Penalty of the Law for acting in contempt of Human Authority: or if the Law excuses him, I should think his own Conscience would not.'[72]

Hay was, therefore, firmly committed to the idea of a national, established church, albeit on erastian principles. He also supported the principle of toleration, though it is clear that he did not feel that the dissenters, who differed from the Church of England over matters of worship and discipline, were justified in their separation. This hint of a lack of sympathy for dissent was apparent in the debate over the repeal of the Test Act in 1736. The motion was easily defeated, but the fact that only 123 M.P.s voted for it understates support for the dissenters among the whigs. Many whigs were 'in their Hearts for' the motion, but opposed it merely on the grounds that the time was not right, 'the meaning of which', as Harley noted sardonically, 'was that it might distress Sir Roberts administration'.[73] Hay, however, 'both spoke and voted against' repeal, and in his account of the debate there is no evidence that he had any sympathy for the claims of the dissenters, either then or in the future, to have public office opened up to them.[74]

As might be expected of someone with such erastian views, Hay was fiercely anti-clerical. He accepted the need for clergy as educators, to instruct the people and lead them in worship.[75] But their role was very limited. They were 'to leave the Gospel ... the sole Standard of Faith and Practice; to deliver it without Mystery to all the ignorant; and to encourage and invite all, that are capable, to examine and judge of it by their own Reason'.[76] Moreover the clergy were appointed, just as the church was established, primarily 'for the Sake of Order'. Hay admitted that, before the establishment of christianity, the clergy were not appointed by the state. But he argued that, before that time, they possessed no temporal power, which only came to the church later, 'either by a Grant from the State, or by Usurpation; the Pretence of a Divine Right to Power or Possessions being as scandalous as groundless'.[77] Hay, indeed, went further, and poured scorn on the idea of an apostolic succession. He denied that the clergy derived either their existence or any of their power from the institution of Christ or of his apostles as commanded in the Bible, arguing instead that 'all Persons of equal Capacity were equally capable to instruct both themselves and others'. Thus, the appointment of ministers was merely a matter of convenience.[78] A large part of *Religio Philosophi* is devoted to attacking the disputes and usurped powers of the clergy, as recorded in ecclesiastical history, which, in Hay's opinion, was no more than a 'Collection of the Ignorance, Folly, Credulity and Superstition of weak Men; of the Knavery, Forgery, and Imposition, of the Pride, Avarice, and Ambition, of the Tyranny, Persecution, and Cruelty, of worldly Men! and the greatest Reproach to Christianity!'[79] At the end of the tract Hay claimed that his attacks on 'the false Pretensions and Usurpations of the Clergy' did not refer to the anglican clergy in 'an Age so enlightened

---

[72] *On Civil Government*, pp. 40–1.
[73] Below p. 21; N.C. Hunt, *Two Early Political Associations. The Quakers and the Dissenting Deputies in the Age of Sir Robert Walpole* (Oxford, 1961), ch. 8.
[74] Below pp. 133–4.
[75] *Religio Philosophi*, p. 185; *On Civil Government*, p. 40.
[76] *Religio Philosophi*, p. 209.
[77] *Ibid.*, pp. 185–7.
[78] *Ibid.*, pp. 186, 189–90.
[79] *Ibid.*, p. 208.

as this'.[80] But this profession should be treated cautiously. No doubt there were some clergy who fitted Hay's portrait. Others, however, believed that they had a commission from Christ, they believed in the apostolic succession and they saw themselves as more than mere teachers of the gospel. They would have seen, and they would have been right to have seen, Hay's writings as an attack on much of what they believed.

In the 1730s Hay's fierce anti-clericalism found expression in a number of parliamentary debates. Indeed, in contrast to his position on the repeal of the Test Act, Hay was often more radical than many of his whig colleagues when the rights and privileges of the clergy were being discussed. In his first session in parliament, for example, he voted with the minority in favour of the Ecclesiastical Courts Bill, which would have curtailed their jurisdiction, and he believed that its defeat stemmed from 'a fear of disobligeing some of the Clergy, just before the Elections'.[81] More revealing, perhaps, was Hay's behaviour during the debates on the Mortmain Bill in 1736, the purpose of which was to prevent all gifts of land or money to charitable corporations, unless made at least a year before the grantor's death. This measure was widely seen as an attack on high church anglican philanthropy, and as such met with fierce opposition from the tories and many of the bishops. During its passage through parliament Hay consistently supported making the bill as rigorous and effective as possible. His views were expressed most clearly when the Commons debated the Lords' amendments to the bill, which included a clause stating that it should not extend to purchases of lands made by corporations. By his own account, Hay was alone in opposing this amendment, which he believed 'in great measure frustrated the Intention of the Bill'.[82] His support for the more extreme anti-clerical position was also manifested in the discussions about the universities. Hay voted with the minority in the debate on the clause to limit the right of Oxford and Cambridge colleges to purchase advowsons, the right of presentation to church livings, supporting an amendment proposed by Samuel Sandys that they should be prohibited from purchasing any more. This clause had in fact been offered by the universities themselves in return for their exemption from the provisions of the bill. Hay clearly also disapproved of this exemption, though he did not vote against it. He not only argued that the universities were sufficiently well endowed already and that they had done nothing to merit special favour from the government. But he also believed that the Church was 'over stocked' with clergy, 'and many had been better bred to some other calling, more usefull to their Country, and beneficial to themselves'.[83]

Hay should not be seen as untypical – Sir Richard Cocks, for example, expressed similar views.[84] Indeed, erastianism and anti-clericalism were common among whigs in the early eighteenth century, and it is hardly surprising to find them combined with a latitudinarian theology.[85] However, even if Hay's religious ideas were similar to those of many fellow whigs, he combined the elements of latitudinarianism, erastianism and anti-clericalism in an idiosyncratic way to give his whiggery a distinctive

[80] *Ibid.*, pp. 229–30.

[81] Below p. 101.

[82] Hay also stated that others agreed with him, and it is possible that many, like Winnington, were reluctant to vote against the amendment for fear of losing the whole bill.

[83] Below pp. 137–8. In fact, Hay made these comments about 'the learned Professions', but at this time many, if not most university graduates entered the Church.

[84] Cocks, however, was far more sympathetic to dissenters than Hay. See *The Parliamentary Diary of Sir Richard Cocks, 1698–1702*, ed. D.W. Hayton (Oxford, 1996), pp. xxii–xxv.

[85] T.F.J. Kendrick, 'Sir Robert Walpole, the Old Whigs and the Bishops, 1733–36: A Study in Eighteenth-Century Parliamentary Politics', *Historical Journal*, XI (1968), 421–45.

tinge. This was first revealed in 1735 during the debates on the Scottish Church Patronage Bill when Hay found himself voting, admittedly with the majority, along-side the tories. But their reasons for opposing the bill were very different. The tories opposed it because it aimed to repeal the Patronage Act of 1712, passed by the tory ministry of Queen Anne's last years in an attempt to curtail the democratic tendencies in Scottish presbyterianism. This act was seen, with some justification, as an anglican attack on the Church of Scotland. Hay, on the other hand, was as opposed to clerical-ism in Scotland as in England, and he voted against the bill because he thought it 'might encrease the temporal Power of the Clergy' there.[86]

Even more striking was Hay's attitude towards the Quakers Tithe Bill of 1736. As has been seen, this was a measure which divided whigs from tories, and opposition to the bill was almost exclusively a tory cause. At the report stage, however, Hay was one of only two M.P.s to speak against the bill. The other was a tory, Sir John St Aubyn, and together they acted as tellers for the minority. Hay's grounds for oppos-ing the bill were highly idiosyncratic, simultaneously revealing both his anti-clericalism and his suspicion of dissent. He had no sympathy for the argument that the clergy had a right to tithes by divine right; they were rather property allotted to them by the laws of the land. As such, he supported the clergy in their defence of their claim to receive tithes from Quakers. However, Hay did share the Quakers' belief that the ecclesiastical courts were 'a Greivance'. But, in his view, they were a grievance not only to the Quakers but also to the rest of the king's subjects. He found it 'extra-ordinary' that in tithe disputes the clergy were 'Judges in their own Cause', and he believed that the Church had established jurisdiction over marriage, wills and moral offences merely to gain monetary profit. Ideally, Hay would have liked to see the courts' abolition and he pressed the Commons again to consider an ecclesiastical courts bill. On the one hand, therefore, Hay objected to the Quakers Tithe Bill because it was not anti-clerical enough. On the other hand, he opposed it because it upset the balance established between Church and dissent by the revolution settlement. Hay argued that it was essential that parliament reaffirm its commitment to that settle-ment, that it made it clear 'that Churchmen and Dissenters now stand on the foot on which they are to remain'. To do otherwise would encourage further demands from both sides and 'open a door to all those religious (rather let me call them those idle those irreligious Disputes) which once threw this Nation into confusion'. The bill, indeed, not merely proposed extending the toleration as it affected Quakers, it also accorded them privileges which were not enjoyed by anyone else. 'It takes away the Prosecution against him in the Spiritual Court, whilst it leaves it in full force against Others; and I will never consent to leave him a remedy against me, which I have not against him; or to exempt him from a Process to which I and all the rest of the Kings subjects are liable.' Such partiality to the Quakers was not only unjust, but it also broke through the principle that governments should encourage men to conform to the established church. Thus, the bill was dangerous because it actually encouraged people 'to turn Quakers'.[87]

Hay and the reform of the poor laws
If Hay's religious beliefs added a distinctive tinge to his whiggery, his commitment to poor law reform further differentiated him from many other court whigs. During his years in the Commons poor law reform was a recurrent subject of debate, which to

[86] Below p. 121.
[87] Below pp. 141–4.

some extent, like Edward Harley's Jury Bill, cut across party alignments.[88] For the best part of 20 years Hay was a leading figure in this debate, both inside parliament and without.[89] He was not only the driving force behind a number of the legislative proposals of the period, but he was also the author of a major pamphlet on the subject, *Remarks on the Laws Relating to the Poor*, which was first published in 1735 and then reprinted, with some additions, in 1751.[90] Hay, however, was less successful than Harley in piloting legislation through the Commons and on to the statute book. Harley's Jury Bill became law; Hay's proposals, by contrast, were repeatedly rejected. He did, indeed, play a major part in securing the passage of the Rogues and Vagabonds Act of 1744, but, as we shall see, that measure fell far short of the type of reform he was advocating.

The *Remarks*, advocating an ambitious reform of the poor law on the basis of the 'union' of parishes, appeared at around the time that the newly elected parliament of 1735 began to take the poor law into consideration. It is not clear why Hay became an advocate of poor law reform, though it is evident that he was drawing on his experiences, and his frustrations, as a justice of the peace in Sussex. His interest in the subject, however, needs to be seen in the context of recent developments in local government and parliament. In the 1690s and early 1700s parliament had considered various proposals to reform the system of poor relief along the lines of the corporations of the poor which had been established in Bristol and other towns.[91] These attempts failed, but the 1720s and early 1730s witnessed the rapid expansion of parish workhouses, and this movement may have convinced advocates of 'union' schemes that the time was ripe for another attempt.[92] Certainly, in the early 1730s there was renewed parliamentary interest in the poor laws, manifested in the introduction of a number of local bills and two more general measures.[93]

As Joanna Innes has pointed out, Hay was primarily concerned with 'enhancing public management of welfare provision'.[94] In common with many, though by no means all, commentators,[95] he emphasized the failings of the statutory system of poor relief, based on the parish rate, but he did not draw the conclusion that the principle of statutory provision of poor relief was flawed. Rather, he sought to create new public bodies which would meet the needs of the poor more effectively. The root of the problem, according to Hay when he published the second edition of his pamphlet,

[88] Connors, 'Pelham, Parliament and Public Policy', p. 238.

[89] For an account of the wider debate about poor law reform, see Joanna Innes, 'The "Mixed Economy of Welfare" in Early Modern England: Assessments of the Options from Hale to Malthus (1683–1803)', in *Charity, Self-Interest and Welfare in the English Past*, ed. M. Daunton (1996), pp. 139–80. We are very grateful to Joanna Innes for allowing us to see her paper before publication, and the following paragraphs owe much to her discussion. For a general account of the poor law see Paul Slack, *The English Poor Law 1531–1782* (1990).

[90] [William Hay], *Remarks on the Laws Relating to the Poor. With Proposals for their Better Relief and Employment. By a Member of Parliament* ([1735]; 2nd edn., 1751).

[91] Innes, '"Mixed Economy"'; Sidney and Beatrice Webb, *English Poor Law History. Part 1: The Old Poor Law* (1927), pp. 116–20.

[92] Timothy Hitchcock, 'The English Workhouse. A Study in Institutional Poor Relief in Selected Counties, 1696–1750', University of Oxford, D.Phil., 1985, ch. 8.

[93] *Failed Legislation, 1680–1800. Extracted from the Commons and Lords Journals*, ed. Julian Hoppit (forthcoming). We are grateful to Julian Hoppit and Joanna Innes for making this material available to us in advance of publication.

[94] Innes, '"Mixed Economy"'.

[95] Some continued to defend the system of parochial relief. See, e.g., [Charles Gray], *Considerations on Several Proposals, Lately Made for the Better Maintenance of the Poor* (1751). Gray is discussed by Innes, '"Mixed Economy"' and by Connors, 'Pelham, Parliament and Public Policy', pp. 252–3.

was 'the obligation on each Parish to maintain its own Poor'. As a result, 'Every Parish is in a State of expensive War with all the rest of the Nation; regards the poor of all other Places as Aliens; and cares not what becomes of them if it can but banish them from its own Society.'[96] In the first place, therefore, he argued for the effective abolition of the law of settlement, giving to 'every Man' the 'Right to reside in any Place where he can best provide for himself and his Family', with legal settlement in that place following after a period of residence.[97]

Hay then proceeded to consider how to provide for the poor in their place of settlement. Drawing on the work of three seventeenth-century writers – Sir Matthew Hale, Sir Josiah Child and John Cary – he argued that the parishes should be replaced by larger districts. The parish poor rates should be united in a common fund which, in each district, should be entrusted to the management of a corporation established for the care of the poor. Each corporation would then be responsible for providing 'proper Buildings' for the poor. Thus far, Hay suggested, all these writers were agreed, and the remainder of the pamphlet was taken up with his gloss on 'these fundamental Points'.[98] In the first place, he believed that the districts should be as large as possible. Within each district three buildings should be erected: a hospital 'for the Impotent'; a house of correction for criminals, including 'all Rogues, Vaga- bonds, and Beggars'; and a workhouse 'where all the honest and industrious Poor are to find Employment'.[99] He went on to argue that the money needed by the new corpor- ation should 'be raised by an equal Rate throughout the District'. In Hay's view this was crucial to avoid conflict between parishes, though he did, at the same time, hold out the hope that his reforms would lead to the reduction, and even the disappearance, of the poor rate.[100] Finally, Hay suggested that the members of the corporations should only be subject to the qualification of 'having such an Estate'. This, too, was an important part of his scheme, as he thought it essential to remove the management of the poor from the hands of the overseers into those of 'Persons wiser and more disinterested'.[101]

It is clear that Hay was the leading influence in the committee of 57 M.P.s appointed by the Commons on 27 March 1735 'to consider the Laws in being relating to the Maintenance and Settlement of the Poor'.[102] He acted as chairman of the committee, drafted its resolutions and then reported them to the house on 2 May. Not merely did the committee agree that 'the Laws in being relating to the Maintenance of the Poor of this Kingdom are defective', but it went on to recommend that they be reformed along the lines laid down in Hay's pamphlet. In one respect it was more pre- cise than Hay had been, suggesting that the counties be made the unit of administration for the new poor law. But it was more vague than Hay had been in its resolution that the members of the new corporations should merely be 'proper Persons'.[103] Action on the report was postponed until 1736, when Hay was one of three M.P.s appointed to draft a bill on the basis of the previous year's resolutions. Opposition, however, led to the watering down of the proposals. As a result, in Hay's opinion, the 1736 bill set the qualification of the guardians too low and failed to establish an equal county rate, thus

96 *Remarks* (2nd edn.), p. ix.
97 *Remarks* (1735), pp. 10–11.
98 *Ibid.*, pp. 36–7.
99 *Ibid.*, pp. 37, 39–43.
100 *Ibid.*, pp. 46–8; *Remarks* (1751), pp. x–xi.
101 *Remarks* (1735), pp. 50–1; *Remarks* (1751), pp. ix–x.
102 *C.J.*, XXII, 434.
103 *Ibid.*, 483–4; below pp. 120–1.

retaining 'some of the old Leaven of Settlements and distinct Parochial Interest'.[104] Despite these concessions a combination of apathy and support for the old system of parochial rates, which Hay portrayed as fundamentally self-interested, ensured that the bill had a very slow progress through the Commons. Edward Harley thought it 'a chimerical Scheme' and recorded that 'the blanks were filled up by the Gentlemen who brought in the Bill few others giving any attention to it'. Eventually, the bill was killed off at the report stage, though the house did allow copies with the amendments to be printed in order to allow further discussion of the subject.[105] Harley's views are, perhaps, suggestive of some of the underlying reasons for the bill's failure. While poor law reform did attract cross-party interest, ambitious 'union schemes', such as those advocated by Hay, tended to be associated with whigs, perhaps because of their implicit challenge to the parish. We lack the evidence to explain fully the motives of the bill's opponents, but it is possible that hostility to the destruction of the old paro- chial system may have been, at least in part, an expression of support for the con- tinuing involvement of the Church in the organization of charity.[106]

The Commons returned to the subject in the following session, when Hay was again appointed to a drafting committee charged with preparing 'a Bill or Bills for the better Relief and Employment of the Poor; and for the more effectual punishing Rogues and Vagabonds'.[107] Under the influence of Sir Joseph Jekyll, who had praised Hay's ideas in 1735, the committee agreed to divide the proposals of 1736 into two, a Rogues and Vagabonds Bill and a separate Poor Bill. Hay played a leading part in the debates on both measures, bringing in the Rogues and Vagabonds Bill and serving as chairman of the select committee on the Poor Bill.[108] However, despite his prominent role, he was unhappy with the legislation which further diluted the original proposals of 1735. The Rogues and Vagabonds Bill omitted all reference to 'passing the Vagrant', while the Poor Bill significantly reduced the size of the new districts. Hay later admitted that he was 'not sorry' that the bills failed to reach the statute book.[109]

Hay later claimed that, 'Finding all his Endeavours ineffectual, he was discouraged for some Years from any new Attempt.'[110] His account, however, is somewhat mislead- ing. It is true that he played little part in further attempts by members of the Commons to reform the poor laws in 1740, 1742 and 1746.[111] But he was an important figure behind the ultimately successful attempts to reform and strengthen the laws against rogues and vagabonds along the lines of the failed bill of 1737, though with the clauses relating to the passing of vagrants being restored. The issue next came before the Commons in 1739, when Hay was a member of the drafting committee, presented the bill to the Commons and then chaired the select committee. On this occasion the bill

---

[104] *C.J.*, XXII, 607; *Remarks* (1751), pp. iii–iv. The bill is printed in Lambert, VII, 199–225. A summary of its main provisions is given in *Remarks* (1751), pp. 60–9.

[105] Below, p. 18; *Remarks* (1751), p. iv. For the bill's progress see *C.J.*, XXII, 626, 676, 685, 695, 702, 706, 708, 713–17. The amended bill is printed in Lambert, VII, 227–54.

[106] We owe this point to discussions with Joanna Innes.

[107] *C.J.*, XXII, 746–7.

[108] *Ibid.*, 786, 895; below p. 121. Hay's recollection in 1751 that he had presented the Poor Bill is mistaken. It was brought into the house by John Pollen, who had also served with Hay on the drafting committee of the 1736 Poor Bill. *Remarks* (1751), p. vii; *C.J.*, XXII, 810.

[109] *Remarks* (1751), pp. v–vii. The two bills are printed in Lambert, VII, 283–94, 295–313.

[110] *Remarks* (1751), p. vii.

[111] Hay was a member of the drafting committee for the 1740 Poor Bill, but, according to the *Journals*, he played no part in framing the other legislation. *C.J.*, XXIII, 485. The 1740 bill was lost through the repeated postponement of the committee of the whole house. It is unclear what the bill aimed to do. It was printed, but no copy survives in Lambert, VIII.

was lost in the Lords, but in the next session it reached the statute book, with Hay again serving as a member of both the drafting committee and the select committee.[112] This was not the end of the matter, however, as the 1740 act was soon found to be in need of amendment, and between 1742 and 1744 parliament again batted around ideas for the reform of the vagrancy laws. A bill in 1742, in which Hay played no obvious part, was defeated on its third reading in the Commons.[113] But in the following session Hay was a member of a committee set up by the Commons to consider both the 1740 act and the settlement laws. He appears to have been unhappy with some of the committee's recommendations about settlement, but he was one of 11 M.P.s responsible for bringing in a Rogues and Vagabonds Bill based on its report. This attempt to revise the legislation of 1740 passed the Commons, but failed in the Lords.[114] Finally, in 1744, a new Rogues and Vagabonds Bill did pass into law, strengthening the punishments laid down in the 1740 act. Once more, Hay played an important part in piloting the bill through the Commons, sitting on the drafting committee, presenting the bill to the house and then acting as chairman of the select committee.[115] Between 1737 and 1744 Hay had been more active than any other M.P. in the efforts to reform the vagrancy laws. Even so, he was never entirely happy with the legislative initiatives of the period, and in 1751 he claimed that the acts of both 1740 and 1744 were defective. Hay continued to believe that it had been a mistake to separate consideration of the vagrancy laws from that of the poor law more generally. He remained opposed to the passing of vagrants, arguing that it would be less trouble and expense to keep them 'employed' in the counties where they were found. Moreover, he was still urging that houses of correction should be put under the management of guardians of the poor who would ensure that they were workhouses where criminals would 'acquire a habit of industry'.[116]

In the session of 1747–8 Hay returned to the subject which he had 'warmly at Heart', the reform of the poor law.[117] Inspired by the success of voluntary charities in establishing hospitals and infirmaries, Hay brought in a bill 'for the better Relief of the Poor by voluntary Charities'.[118] This bill aimed to establish a corporation in every county, composed of the 'Persons the most eminent for Quality, Dignity, Office, and Estate', which would be empowered to receive gifts and bequests and to use them for the relief and employment of the poor. Hay attempted to make his proposals more acceptable to the Commons by leaving the existing laws unaltered; the new corporations would supplement existing provision, not replace it. However, there are hints that Hay saw his proposals, if passed into law, as providing some kind of blueprint for the further reform of the poor law. He certainly raised the possibility that, at some time in the future, the corporations might be enabled to raise money by a county rate. Moreover, he sought to ensure that the guardians would be disinterested people, thus

---

[112] *C.J.*, XXIII, 232, 237, 341, 449, 477. The act was 13 Geo. II, c. 24.

[113] *C.J.*, XXIV, 288.

[114] *Ibid.*, 354, 395, 402–3; *L.J.*, XXVI, 252–3. The earl of Oxford claimed that the reason for the bill's failure was the Speaker's insistence that it was a money bill, resulting in the rejection by the Commons of some of the Lords' amendments. Below p. 64. The bill was returned to the Lords and a conference took place between the two houses, but the Lords then put off further consideration of the bill until after the end of the session. *C.J.*, XXIV, 476–8; *L.J.*, XXVI, 252–3.

[115] *C.J.*, XXIV, 492, 494, 517. The act was 17 Geo. II, c. 5.

[116] *Remarks* (1751), p. vi.

[117] *Ibid.*, p. vii.

[118] *C.J.*, XXV, 465; *Remarks* (1751), pp. vii–viii. The bill is not printed in Lambert, IX, nor in Torrington, vol. 1747–8 to 1753, but its main provisions are summarized in *Remarks* (1751), pp. 70–4. The best modern discussion of the measure is in Innes, '"Mixed Economy"'.

correcting what he saw as one of the failings of existing poor law.[119] The Voluntary Charities Bill passed the Commons, but disappeared during the committee stage in the Lords.[120] One of the reasons for its failure may have been that, like the 1736 Mortmain Act, which Hay had supported, it could be portrayed as an attack on anglican philanthropy – by placing the management of charities in a body of laymen, it threatened the influence of the Church and its clergy. Three years later, in 1751, Hay was again a prominent figure in an attempt to reform the laws relating to the poor, bringing in a Poor Marriage Bill.[121] According to the preamble, this bill was intended to contribute to the growth of the population, 'the Strength and Security of a Nation', by encouraging the poor to marry.[122] Despite this rather innocuous title, however, this bill was, according to Richard Connors, 'innovative and radical'.[123] Most notably, perhaps, in the context of the present discussion, it proposed exempting married persons from the settlement laws. But this attempt to enact some part of Hay's 1735 proposals also failed when the committee of the whole house was adjourned without date on 26 March 1751.[124]

In retrospect both the Voluntary Charities Bill and the Poor Marriage Bill appear as part of a revival of interest in poor law reform, which gathered pace as parliament responded to growing concern about crime and poverty in the wake of the War of the Austrian Succession.[125] The highpoint of parliamentary interest came on 1 February 1751 with the appointment of a committee to consider the laws relating to felonies. Hay was added to the committee 12 days later, and the following month the house instructed it also to consider the related issue of the poor laws.[126] It was the appointment of this committee which prompted Hay to reprint his *Remarks* of 1735, in the hope that they would influence the new debate.[127] Perhaps they did, since the conclusions reached by the committee in many ways echoed Hay's arguments of the 1730s. In particular, it recommended the abolition of the settlement laws, the replacement of the parish by the county as the basic unit of administration and that more attention be paid to the employment of the poor. In the following session these resolutions gave rise to two bills, one introduced by Sir Richard Lloyd, the other by Lord Hillsborough. Hillsborough's bill was the more radical, advocating the abolition of the Elizabethan poor law. In its place, it proposed the creation of corporations of guardians of the poor, funded by a county rate, which were to establish hospitals for children, the sick and the aged. Meanwhile, the relief of the able poor was to be coordinated at a parish level

---

119 *Remarks* (1751), pp. vii–ix. The corporation would be composed of all local peers, the lord lieutenant, custos rotulorum, high sheriff, knights of the shire, bishops, deans, archdeacons and every person who possessed an estate worth £300 per annum, who chose to act. In addition, anyone who gave £100 would be entitled to become a guardian for a year. *Ibid.*, pp. 71–3.

120 For its passage, see *C.J.*, XXV, 464–5, 476, 494, 496, 498; *L.J.*, XXVII, 166–7, 170.

121 *C.J.*, XXVI, 61. The drafting committee was composed of Hay and Robert Nugent, while the committee of the whole house on the bill was chaired by William Thornton. *Ibid.*, pp. 41, 152. For an account of the bill, see Connors, 'Pelham, Parliament and Public Policy', pp. 230–2.

122 The bill is printed in Lambert, IX, 237–40.

123 Connors, 'Pelham, Parliament and Public Policy', p. 231.

124 *C.J.*, XXVI, 152.

125 On this period, in addition to Innes, '"Mixed Economy"', and Connors, 'Pelham, Parliament and Public Policy', ch. 5, see Nicholas Rogers, 'Confronting the Crime Wave: The Debate over Social Reform and Regulation, 1749–1753', in *Stilling the Grumbling Hive. The Responses to Social and Economic Problems in England, 1689–1750*, ed. L. Davison, T. Hitchcock, T. Keirn and R.B. Shoemaker (Stroud, 1992), pp. 77–98.

126 *C.J.*, XXVI, 27, 39, 123.

127 *Remarks* (1751), pp. xi–xii.

by overseers who were accountable to the county corporations.[128] Hay, however, played little part in the parliamentary process. He did attend a dinner at Lord Hillsborough's on 27 February 1752 held to discuss the drafting of the Poor Relief Bill, but he was not himself a member of the drafting committee for either that bill or Lloyd's.[129]

Once again, both bills failed to pass the Commons and parliament did not return to the reform of the poor law again before Hay's death in 1755. His record as a reformer was, therefore, very different from Edward Harley's. Unlike Harley he left no legislative achievements behind him, apart from the 1744 Rogues and Vagabonds Act, which he believed to be seriously flawed. In the final analysis, it proved impossible in the mid-eighteenth century to mobilize sufficient parliamentary support behind the kind of general legislation to which Hay was committed. On the other hand, perhaps more than any other single person, he helped to determine the framework for the debate on the poor laws, both in parliament and in the press, between the 1730s and the mid-1750s.

Hay and Sussex politics

In the field of local politics there was a stark contrast between William Hay and Edward Harley. Even while he was a member of the house of commons, Harley was the leading representative of one of the most important aristocratic families in Herefordshire, whose political and social influence stretched into neighbouring counties. The family's position owed much to the career of Robert Harley and their landholdings never rivalled those of the great noble families, but Brampton Bryan exercised a powerful voice in county affairs. Hay's estates at Glyndebourne, by contrast, simply made him a member of the county gentry in Sussex. Within the county – or, at least, within the eastern part of the county – the family was far from insignificant. Hay's grandfather and son, as well as Hay himself, served as M.P.s for Sussex constituencies, and he was also appointed as chairman of quarter sessions. But the most important landowner in Hay's part of Sussex was Thomas Pelham-Holles, duke of Newcastle, whose houses at Halland and Bishopstone were near Lewes. Indeed, the combination of Newcastle's extensive Sussex properties and his position as secretary of state made him the dominant figure in county politics during the reigns of George I and George II. Hay's political career undoubtedly owed much to his ties with the Newcastle interest in Sussex. He linked himself with Newcastle partly through choice and a recognition that Newcastle was the county's leading representative of the whiggery which he held so dear. But Hay was also tied to Newcastle by marriage. His wife, Elizabeth, was Newcastle's second cousin, and through her Hay became a part of the extensive and powerful Pelhamite interest in Sussex. His father-in-law, Thomas Pelham of Lewes,[130] his uncles by marriage, Thomas Pelham of Stanmer, Sir Francis Poole, James Pelham of Crowhurst, and Sir William Ashburnham, and his brothers-in-law, Thomas Pelham of Lewes and Henry Pelham of Lee, all owned property in the county and all sat alongside Hay as M.P.s for Sussex constituencies at some point in the period 1734–55.[131]

---

[128] Lambert, IX, 405–44. For a discussion of this bill and Lloyd's, see Innes, '"Mixed Economy"', and Connors, 'Pelham, Parliament and Public Policy', pp. 235–40.

[129] Connors, 'Pelham, Parliament and Public Policy', p. 238; *C.J.*, XXVI, 331, 413–14.

[130] Also known as Thomas Pelham of Catsfield.

[131] The Pelham interest was much more extensive than this. See genealogical table, p. lx.

Unfortunately, with the exception of the 1734 elections, little evidence remains of Hay's involvement in Sussex politics. He was first elected as M.P. for Seaford at a by-election in January 1734, caused by Philip Yorke's elevation to the Lords as Baron Hardwicke. It is clear that Hay was Newcastle's candidate. The duke sent a letter recommending Hay to the town and he paid the expenses of the election entertainments – 'a dinner to the Gentlemen, a double fee to the Ringers, and a double portion of Beer to the Populace', together with the promise of half a guinea for 'the common Voters'. Despite rumours of an opposition, Hay 'had the promise of every Voter: every thing passed as well as could be wished'.[132] This was hardly surprising as the combination of the influence of the Bishopstone estate, which adjoined the town, and treasury patronage, which was of considerable importance in a Cinque port, effectively gave Newcastle the nomination of the borough's two M.P.s. At the general election later that year Seaford merited only the briefest mention in the correspondence between Hay and the duke, and the Newcastle interest ensured that Hay continued to be returned without opposition until his death in 1755. The only exception to this pattern occurred in 1747, when Newcastle refused to recommend William Gage, who had succeeded his cousin as Hay's colleague in 1744. After entering the Commons Gage had gone into opposition with the prince of Wales, and at the general election Newcastle replaced him with William Pitt. Gage, however, forced a contested election, standing with Lord Middlesex against Hay and Pitt. But Newcastle acted decisively to maintain his interest in the town, personally canvassing the voters and 'sitting next to the returning officer at the poll', and his candidates were returned with a comfortable majority.[133] One Sussex observer loyal to the Pelhamite interest dismissed events in Seaford as 'a ridiculous opposition' entered into by Gage merely 'that he might have something to talk of at Leicester House'.[134]

Hay's involvement in the 1734 elections for Sussex and Lewes is much more fully documented than his own election for Seaford. The general election was dominated by the issue of the excise crisis, with the opposition hoping to drive home its advantage against Walpole's ministry, and two of the most keenly fought contests were those in Sussex for the county and Lewes.[135] In the county Newcastle's brother, Henry Pelham, and James Butler were challenged by a combination of an opposition whig and a tory, Sir Cecil Bishopp and John Fuller. A similar alliance was forged in Lewes, between Nathaniel Garland, 'a "Rigid Dissenter"', and Thomas Sergison, a high churchman, to oppose the sitting members, Thomas Pelham of Stanmer and Thomas Pelham of Lewes, both of whom had supported the Tobacco Excise Bill.[136] Newcastle preserved much of his correspondence about these elections, and it is clear that the whole of his network was mobilized to fight the challenge from the opposition in the family's electoral heartlands. Besides the candidates, other members of the family and many of the Pelhams' friends and clients from across the social spectrum joined in the canvassing. The most energetic of them, and Newcastle's most prolific correspondent, was Robert Burnett, the duke's agent for the county election in Lewes and the surrounding area. But Hay was also particularly active, writing to Newcastle

---

[132] Letters 19 and 20 below pp. 305–6; B.L., Add. MS 32688, ff. 592–3: Newcastle to the bailiff, jurats freemen and inhabitants of Seaford, Oct. 1733; ff. 353–4: Hurdis to Newcastle, 20 Sept. 1733.
[133] Sedgwick, I, 369–70.
[134] H.M.C., *10th Report, Appendix, Part I*, p. 297: Bishop Richard Trevor to Edward Weston, 4 July 1747.
[135] Paul Langford, *The Excise Crisis. Society and Politics in the Age of Walpole* (Oxford, 1975), chs. 8–9; Basil Williams, 'The Duke of Newcastle and the Election of 1734', *E.H.R.*, XII (1897), 448–88; Brent, pp. 172–7.
[136] Brent, p. 173; Cobbett, VIII, 1311.

more frequently than anyone except Burnett.[137] Indeed, despite his gentry status, Hay was effectively Newcastle's agent in Lewes, at least until the opening of the parliamentary session in January 1734 when he left the county for London.[138]

Hay's early letters, between August and the beginning of October 1733, are primarily concerned with the county election. He canvassed the freeholders in the region around Glyndebourne, particularly in his parish of Ringmer and in the Cliff area to the east of Lewes. Fears about the excise were common and it was widely rumoured that there had been an intention to tax food.[139] But by the beginning of September Hay believed that the duke's supporters were having some success in countering the opposition's propaganda, reporting that 'the Country People' were beginning to treat their 'Stories ... with contempt and ridicule'.[140] Meanwhile, Hay was spreading his own propaganda, reminding dissenters who might be tempted to support the opposition of the Schism Act passed by the tories in the last year of Queen Anne's reign, a tactic which had 'an admirable Effect'.[141]

But perhaps the most interesting aspect of Hay's electioneering was the stream of canvassing lists which he sent to Newcastle. Indeed, he provided the duke with many more of these lists than any other correspondent, though sometimes he had not compiled them himself.[142] Three of the lists relate to the Sussex election – those accompanying Letters 1, 6 and 7 – and the survival of the poll book makes it possible to assess the accuracy of Hay's information. The first accompanied his letter of 9 August 1733 and was an analysis of the freeholders of the Cliff who were eligible to vote in the election. A major problem for Hay in his attempts to calculate the strength of the Pelham interest was the high proportion of 'no shows'. In fact, 41 per cent of the 39 freeholders named in this list did not vote on 9 May 1734. Of the remainder Hay forecast 51.6 per cent accurately. This was a low percentage, but it was still nine months before the election and Hay was rather more accurate with his next two Sussex lists, both of which concerned his own parish of Ringmer. The first, in his letter of 24 August, gave the names of 21 voters, and the second, sent six days later, listed 24 voters. Hay's predictions of voters' intentions were correct in 88.5 per cent and 73.3 per cent of cases respectively. In both lists, however, 'no shows' were again a problem, accounting for 38 per cent and 33.3 per cent of those listed. The number of Ringmer freeholders who did not vote is surprising, but so too was the support for the opposition on polling day, when 12 freeholders from Ringmer cast their votes for Pelham and Butler, 12 for Bishopp and Fuller, and one split his votes between Pelham and Bishopp. Not only was Glyndebourne in the parish, but Pelham and Butler had the active support of the rector, Thomas Hurdis, and then, after his death, of the curate who was appointed by the new rector at Hay's nomination. One can only assume that Hay was less successful than he had thought at dispelling fears of the excise.

It may also be the case that Ringmer suffered from neglect, as from the middle of October Hay appears to have been drawn increasingly into events at Lewes. Gradually, Newcastle and his correspondents became more confident about the outcome of the

---

[137] Williams's article is primarily concerned with Sussex and makes extensive use of Newcastle's correspondence.

[138] On the role of the election agent more generally, see E.A. Smith, 'The Election Agent in English Politics, 1734–1832', *E.H.R.*, LXXXIV (1969), 12–35.

[139] See below pp. 285, 286.

[140] Below p. 293.

[141] Below pp. 282–3, 286.

[142] The list enclosed in Hay's letter of 15 Nov. 1733, for example, was compiled by Stonestreet and Earle. See below p. 311.

Sussex election. By the end of September Henry Pelham was reporting his belief that 'We shall carry it, I verily beleive by a great majority, but it is more up hill work than ever I expected to see in this country.'[143] The Lewes election, however, was more of a problem. As in the county, the excise crisis had done much to alienate the voters from the ministry and the opposition was considerably strengthened by the compromise reached between 'the Dissenters and the Tories'.[144] But the biggest problem was the two candidates. On the one hand, Thomas Pelham of Lewes, Hay's father-in-law, could hardly be persuaded to canvass, not thinking it 'proper to go round himself to the People'. On the other hand, Thomas Pelham of Stanmer 'never comes to Lewes but he gets drunk' and did more damage to the cause by his presence than by his absence.[145] When the election finally took place on 27 April 1734, the vote was very close, only eight votes separating Nathaniel Garland from Thomas Pelham of Lewes.[146] Ultimately, the election turned on the election of the high constables in October 1733 and the meeting of the Quarter Sessions on the day before the poll. In October the Pelhams, largely by bribing the steward, managed to secure the election of two Pelhamite supporters, Thomas Friend and James Reeves, as high constables, the borough's returning officers. Then, on 26 April 1734 a Pelhamite majority on the bench upheld appeals against the poor books of the parishes of All Saints, St Anne's and St John's. Since the franchise in Lewes lay in the inhabitants paying scot and lot, this manoeuvre gave the constables considerable scope to refuse disputed votes at the poll.[147]

In the absence of a lead from the candidates, it was Hay who took responsibility for co-ordinating the Pelhams' campaign in Lewes between mid-October and early January, though he received considerable help from Sir William Gage, his fellow member at Seaford, and from Burnett. Clubs for Pelhamite supporters were organized. Tradesmen met at the White Hart, while 'the inferiour Voters' were encouraged to attend the Black Lion and White Lion, where the jockey William Lawrence organized proceedings.[148] Orders from, and work at, the local whig houses – Glyndebourne, Firle, Stanmer, Bishopstone, Halland and Glynde – were used to reward loyal Pelhamite

[143] B.L., Add. MS 32688, ff. 421–4: Pelham to Newcastle, 29 Sept. 1733, quoted in Sedgwick, I, 332.

[144] B.L., Add. MS 33073, f. 80: Newcastle to duchess of Newcastle [Aug. 1733]; below p. 295.

[145] Below pp. 300, 298, 307.

[146] The result was: Thomas Pelham of Stanmer 84; Thomas Pelham of Lewes 83; Nathaniel Garland 75; Thomas Sergison 70.

[147] Brent, pp. 175–6. The behaviour of the constables in allowing and disallowing votes led to a bitter pamphlet controversy, in which three versions of the poll were published. 1. *A Poll Taken by Tho. Friend and James Reeve, Constables of the Burrough of Lewes. On the 27th of April 1734. For the Election of Members to Serve in this Present Parliament for the Said Burrough* (London: W. Russ, 1734). The poll is followed by details of the twenty-four disputed voters on each side. It was clearly published at the instigation of the opposition. 2. *An Exact State of the Poll Taken by Tho. Friend, and James Reeve, Constables of the Borough of Lewes, on the 27th Day of April, 1734. For the Election of Members to Serve in this Present Parliament. In Answer to a Pamphlet Lately Published Relating to the said Election* (London: J. Wilford, 1734). Following the poll this pamphlet repeats the information of (1), but gives further material justifying the decision of the constables. It was clearly published by the constables at the instigation of the Pelhamite side. 3. A third poll book with no title page. East Sussex R.O., LEW/C5/3/5b (the only known copy). This claimed to be an impartial assessment of the conduct of the constables in allowing and disallowing the queried votes for both sides. It contains a great deal of information about the voters, their rights and their residence qualifications, supported by a lot of documentation. The conclusions which it draws are almost invariably against the decisions of the constables, whom it blames, though not in so many words, for partiality towards the Pelhams. It was probably another opposition publication. Certainly it advertized the originals of the documents it printed as being available for inspection at Lidgitter's coffee house, which had probably been one of the opposition's meeting places during the election.

[148] Below p. 300.

supporters and to attract floating voters. Tenants who were threatening to vote for the opposition were given notice to quit, while properties had to be found for supporters 'warned out' by the opposition. At least one voter, William Ashby, was secured by the payment of debts due to him.[149] Then towards the end of December, Hay devoted more and more attention to the drawing up of the parish poor books, which were so important in establishing an individual's right to vote.

At one point Hay noted that 'this is a Year when worthless fellows are to be valued', and, indeed, Hay's attention to detail is remarkable. Through the election campaign he supplied Newcastle with a series of very detailed canvassing lists, which together suggest that Hay was both an informed and an astute agent. The first of Hay's Lewes lists accompanied his letter to Newcastle of 25 October. At this time Hay was quite optimistic, thinking that there was 'a Majority of about twenty', and he sent with his letter a list of 54 voters who met at the White Hart.[150] Thirty-nine of these were marked with a tick, as certain supporters, of whom 35 (90 per cent) voted for the Pelhams, while 2 voted against and 2 did not vote.[151] Just two days later Hay sent to the duke a much more sophisticated analysis, which included the names of 162 voters divided into seven classes. This list, compiled, it should be noted, five and a half months before the election, was remarkably accurate. Only 22 of the 162 voters listed (13.6 per cent) did not vote. Of the 147 whom Hay claimed to be either certain or probable in their classification, 129 actually voted, and of these 108 (83.7 per cent) voted as Hay had predicted.[152]

By this time Hay was less sanguine about the situation in Lewes, and he was warning the duke that the opposition 'gain ground every day'.[153] The next list which survives was that compiled by Stonestreet and Earle, which was sent to Newcastle on 15 November. It revealed that the gap between the sitting members and their opponents was as little as 3 votes – the Pelhams were estimated to have 87 and 89 votes, Sergison 84 and Garland 74. When compared with the final result, the canvassers had clearly exaggerated Sergison's support. Even so, the list was remarkably accurate. Twenty-four of those listed (14.4 per cent) did not vote.[154] But, of the 143 who did, 120 (83.9 per cent) voted as forecast (61 pro, 53 con and 6 split votes). Hay's last attempt to forecast the poll was enclosed in his letter to Newcastle of 27 December. It consisted of a list of most of the voters for Lewes and was described by Hay as 'the most Complete that I have been Yet able to compose'.[155] It did not, however, contain the names of all the Lewes voters, having 149 names, whereas 156 voters were allowed in April 1734. At the next election, in 1741, it is interesting to note that as many as 214 voted.[156] Initially Hay calculated that there were '69 Friends, 67 Enemies, and 13 One

---

[149] Below p. 309.

[150] Below pp. 301–2.

[151] Four were marked with an 'x' (possible opponents?) but voted for the Pelhams, six were marked with a 'Q' (one voted pro, three con and two did not vote), and five were left unmarked (four pro and one did not vote).

[152] Fifteen were listed as entirely doubtful, of whom seven voted for Garland and Sergison, three for the Pelhams, one split his votes and three did not vote.

[153] Below p. 306.

[154] Or, more correctly, they are not shown as voting in the poll book. The opposition version of the poll book (item 1 in n. 147 above) gives a list of disallowed votes, and seven of these 24 did vote for Sergison and Garland, but their votes were disallowed by the constables.

[155] Below p. 318.

[156] The higher number of electors in 1741 was probably the result of Newcastle and Sergison cramming the available properties with 'pliable tenants'. Brent, pp. 177–8. In 1722 144 had voted. Sedgwick, I, 335–6.

and One' (i.e., split votes), but later in the same paragraph he revised his calculations
to '71 for us, 63 against us; and 14 One and One'. Compared with the election itself,
these figures are impressively accurate: 78 voted for the Pelhams, 67 for the opposition, and 11 split their votes. Moreover, Hay had not only formed a good impression
of the general picture, but he also had a very clear idea of individual voting intentions.
Of the 69 'Friends', only seven (10.1 per cent) did not vote for the Pelhams – four
voted for the opposition and three did not vote. Of the 67 'Enemies', again seven
(10.4 per cent) did not vote for Sergison and Garland – four voted for the Pelhams and
one split his vote, while two voted for the opposition but their votes were
disallowed.[157] Hay's predictions about the 13 split voters was less accurate, four (30.8
per cent) voting for the Pelhams or the opposition.

It is striking that the lists were so accurate in their predictions of voters' allegiance
in such a bitterly-contested election which finally took place four months after the
compilation of the last list. They would suggest, therefore, that the majority of voters
were fixed in their intentions and that there were few floating voters. However, as has
been seen, the early lists contained a fairly high proportion of no shows. This number
had declined by the time of Hay's last list, but even that did not contain the names of
all those eligible to vote in Lewes. Clearly, one of the most serious problems facing
not only Hay and the Pelhamites but also the opposition was to appeal to these
undecided voters. In an election as close as that of Lewes in 1734 their behaviour
could be crucial, and the Pelhams' victory was certainly made more secure by the fact
that, in the months from January to April, their supporters were marginally more
successful in winning them over.

Hay's abilities as an election agent contrast vividly with John Harley's sanguine
and inaccurate reports to his father at the time of the Oxford University by-election in
1751.[158] Many other Pelhamite supporters contributed to Hay's calculations. But it is
Hay who emerges from the correspondence, much of it admittedly written by him, as
the central figure in co-ordinating the campaign in Lewes until January 1734. As the
constituency has sometimes been seen as one of the most 'troublesome' in Sussex,[159]
Newcastle and the candidates were fortunate to have a member of the family prepared
to work so hard to ensure success, and whose predictions were so reliable.

It is important to remember, however, that Hay's gentry status meant that he was
never simply Newcastle's agent. There is no evidence that he played a similar role
when Lewes was contested again in 1741;[160] certainly no correspondence between
Hay and Newcastle has survived. Yet Hay's property at Glyndebourne gave him a
certain influence of his own in the borough. This was made clear when Hay's son,
Thomas, was elected as M.P. for Lewes in 1768, not on the Newcastle interest but in
opposition to it. The duke's original candidate for the town was William Plumer and,
when he withdrew, Newcastle initially gave his support to Thomas Hay. But he
rapidly withdrew that support, apparently fearing that the junior branches of the family
might be attempting to establish an independent interest to the exclusion of the Pelham

---

[157] If one includes the disallowed votes, Hay's accuracy rises to 93.3 per cent.

[158] Below pp. 265–7. John Harley's belief that his brother would win the election was, nevertheless, shared
by some outside observers. See Lewis Walpole Library, CHW 52, ff. 97–8: Henry Fox to Hanbury
Williams, 15 Jan. 1751.

[159] Sedgwick, I, 336.

[160] On the management of the Pelham interest in Lewes in 1739–41 by William Poole and Thomas
Stonestreet, see Judith Brent, 'The Pooles of Chailey and Lewes: The Establishment and Influence of a
Gentry Family, 1732–1779', *Sussex Archaeological Collections*, CXIV (1976), 71–2.

name. Hay, however, was persuaded to remain in the contest as an 'independent' and had support from a number of neighbouring gentlemen, some of whom, like Henry Shelley, had previously supported Newcastle. In the confusion some of Newcastle's tenants voted for Hay, either because they had already promised him their votes or because they still believed he had the duke's support, and Hay was able to defeat Newcastle's new candidate, Sir Thomas Miller.[161] Newcastle's grip on Sussex politics may well have been failing in the year of his death. Nonetheless, the election highlighted the dangers of ignoring the local influence even of someone as closely linked with the family as Thomas Hay.

[161] Brent, 181–2; Namier and Brooke, I, 394–5.

EDITORIAL CONVENTIONS

The aim in preparing this edition has been to make the text clear and readable without losing the character of the originals. The spelling, capitalization and punctuation of the original documents have been retained, except where it has been necessary to modernize punctuation and capitalization for the sake of clarity. As in most eighteenth-century texts, spelling is often idiosyncratic. Harley regularly used 'ei' rather than 'ie' and spelt Tuesday 'Teusday'. Hay's journal contains even more variant spellings, and in many cases 'c' is used rather than 's' (e.g., cencure) and 'i' rather than 'e'. Moreover, spellings in Hay's journal are often inconsistent, probably reflecting the different practice of William Hay himself and the son who copied the text. Abbreviations and contractions have been silently expanded, though where there might be some doubt the inserted letters have been included within angle brackets < >. However, 'con' has been retained in words like 'relacon' and 'educacon', and 'm̄' (which is not used consistently by either Hay or Harley) has been printed as 'm' rather than 'mm'. Abbreviations for pounds – li., ll., and l. – have all been modernized as £ and placed before the figures to which they relate. Words and passages which are underlined in the original texts are printed as italic in this edition. A few obvious errors in the originals, such as the repetition of a word, have also been corrected silently. Round brackets ( ) and square brackets [ ] are printed as used in the original texts; angle brackets < > are reserved for editorial matter. Where the manuscript has been damaged or is illegible, editorial suppositions about the missing words are supplied in angle brackets. No attempt has been made to reproduce exactly the visual appearance of the various lists included in the edition, but their layout generally reflects that of the originals.

The layout of Hay's journal broadly reflects the original, with the dates of entries appearing flush centre as they do in the original. However, the three groups of entries transcribed by the copyist from 'loose pieces of paper' (see above pp. xviii–xix) have been inserted at the appropriate points in the main text. Their location in the original manuscript is noted in the footnotes. A few notes written on the usually blank verso sides of the folios in Hay's journal are printed in this edition as footnotes, identified with the letters a–k.

The layout of Harley's journal has been altered rather more. For the sense of clarity and ease of reference, the dates of his entries have been put into italics. In addition, where Harley immediately goes on to record further proceedings on a bill or other matter, his subsequent entries on that subject have been indented. The journal then reverts to the left margin when he begins the entry for a new subject. As has been noted, Harley wrote the main journal on the recto of each folio, leaving the verso blank for later additions. There are too many of these additions, and they contain too much information that is central to the concerns of the journal, to print them as notes. The additions made by Harley on the versos have, therefore, been inserted at the most appropriate point in the main text, but they are distinguished from the rest of the text by being printed within curly brackets { }.

In both journals running heads give the year of the session.

In the correspondence, information about the place and date on which the letter was written is recorded in the heading. Where only a section of a letter has been printed, missing text is denoted by .... .

An Appendix, printed at the end of the volume, contains brief biographical details of all those M.P.s, peers and bishops who were sitting in parliament at the time they are mentioned in the text, or, in the case of M.P.s, were about to be elected.

LIST OF HARLEY'S
PARLIAMENTARY PAPERS

No.	Correspondent	Date	Location
1	To Lord Harley	31 Jan. 1716	B.L., Add. MS 70381, ff. 164–5
2	From Martin Benson	4 Apr. [1717]	Brampton Bryan MSS, Bundle X
3	From Abigail Harley	28 May 1717	B.L., Add. MS 70088
4	From Abigail Harley	12 June 1717	B.L., Add. MS 70088
5	To Abigail Harley	18 June 1717	B.L., Add. MS 70145
6	Lords' division list	24 June 1717	Brampton Bryan MSS, Bundle 117
7	Memorandums about Oxford's trial	1717	B.L., Add. MS 70088
8	To Abigail Harley	6 Feb. 1718	B.L., Add. MS 70034
9	To Abigail Harley	18 Feb. 1718	B.L., Add. MS 70034
10	To Abigail Harley	27 Feb. 1718	B.L., Add. MS 70034
11	To Abigail Harley	9 Mar. 1718	B.L., Add. MS 70034
12	To Abigail Harley	18 Mar. 1718	B.L., Add. MS 70034
13	To Abigail Harley	2 Dec. 1718	B.L., Add. MS 70034
14	To Abigail Harley	7 Dec. 1718	B.L., Add. MS 70034
15	Lord Nottingham's clause	22 Dec. 1718	Brampton Bryan MSS, Bundle 117
16	From E.P. Gwyn	23 Dec. 1718	Brampton Bryan MSS, Bundle X
17	To Abigail Harley	25 Dec. 1718	B.L., Add. MS 70034
18	From E.P. Gwyn	27 Dec. 1718	Brampton Bryan MSS, Bundle X
19	To Abigail Harley	4 Jan. 1719	B.L., Add. MS 70034
20	From E.P. Gwyn	8 Jan. 1719	Brampton Bryan MSS, Bundle X
21	To Abigail Harley	8 Jan. 1719	B.L., Add. MS 70034
22	To Abigail Harley	11 Jan. 1719	B.L., Add. MS 70034
23	To Abigail Harley	13 Jan. 1719	B.L., Add. MS 70034
24	To Abigail Harley	18 Jan. 1719	B.L., Add. MS 70034
25	From E.P. Gwyn	25 Feb. 1719	Brampton Bryan MSS, Bundle X
26	From E.P. Gwyn	28 Feb. 1719	Brampton Bryan MSS, Bundle X
27	To Abigail Harley	1 Mar. 1719	B.L., Add. MS 70034
28	From E.P. Gwyn	4 Mar. 1719	Brampton Bryan MSS, Bundle X
29	From E.P. Gwyn	5 Mar. 1719	Brampton Bryan MSS, Bundle X
30	From E.P. Gwyn	5 Mar. 1719	Brampton Bryan MSS, Bundle X
31	From E.P. Gwyn	7 Mar. 1719	Brampton Bryan MSS, Bundle X
32	From E.P. Gwyn	26 Mar. 1719	Brampton Bryan MSS, Bundle X
33	From E.P. Gwyn	16 Apr. 1719	Brampton Bryan MSS, Bundle X
34	To Abigail Harley	17 Dec. 1719	B.L., Add. MS 70145
35	From E.P. Gwyn	14 Jan. 1720	Brampton Bryan MSS, Bundle 102
36	To Abigail Harley	17 Jan. 1720	B.L., Add. MS 70034
37	To Abigail Harley	3 Mar. 1720	B.L., Add. MS 70145
38	To earl of Oxford	5 Apr. 1720	B.L., Add. MS 70237
39	To Abigail Harley	7 Apr. 1720	B.L., Add. MS 70145
40	To Abigail Harley	2 Aug. 1720	B.L., Add. MS 70145
41	To Abigail Harley	23 Feb. 1721	B.L., Add. MS 70145

No.	Correspondent	Date	Location
42	To Abigail Harley	12 Mar. 1721	B.L., Add. MS 70145
43	To Abigail Harley	19 Mar. 1721	B.L., Add. MS 70034
44	To Abigail Harley	28 Mar. 1721	B.L., Add. MS 70034
45	To earl of Oxford	4 Apr. 1721	B.L., Add. MS 70237
46	To Abigail Harley	8 Apr. 1721	B.L., Add. MS 70145
47	To earl of Oxford	25 Apr. 1721	B.L., Add. MS 70237
48	To Abigail Harley	2 May 1721	B.L., Add. MS 70145
49	From Auditor Harley	2 May 1721	B.L., Add. MS 70498, ff. 55–6
50	To Abigail Harley	4 May 1721	B.L., Add. MS 70034
51	To Abigail Harley	9 May 1721	B.L., Add. MS 70034
52	To Abigail Harley	21 May 1721	B.L., Add. MS 70145
53	To Abigail Harley	27 May 1721	B.L., Add. MS 70145
54	To Abigail Harley	30 May 1721	B.L., Add. MS 70034
55	To Abigail Harley	13 June 1721	B.L., Add. MS 70145
56	To Abigail Harley	18 June 1721	B.L., Add. MS 70034
57	To Abigail Harley	22 June 1721	B.L., Add. MS 70145
58	To Lord Harley	28 Jan. 1722	B.L., Add. MS 70381, f. 169
59	To Lord Harley	9 Feb. 1722	B.L., Add. MS 70381, ff. 170–1
60	From Frederick Cornwall	23 Mar. 1722	B.L., Add. MS 70085
61	To earl of Oxford	27 Mar. 1722	B.L., Add. MS 70237
62	Account of Layer's trial	Jan. 1723	Brampton Bryan MSS, Bundle 117
63	Memorandums about the Atterbury plot	1722–3	Brampton Bryan MSS, Bundle 117
64	To Mr Brome	18 Apr. 1723	B.L., Add. MS 70086
65	To anon	14 May 1723	Brampton Bryan MSS, Bundle 117
66	List of speakers for and against Atterbury	16 May 1723	Brampton Bryan MSS, Bundle 117
67	From earl of Oxford	4 July 1727	B.L., Add. MS 70498, ff. 68–9
68	To William Brydges	4 July 1727	Hereford R.O., A81/IV
69	To Auditor Harley	11 May 1729	B.L., Add. MS 70140
70	To Martha Harley	5 Feb. 1730	B.L., Add. MS 70497
71	To Martha Harley	28 Feb. 1730	B.L., Add. MS 70497
72	To Martha Harley	26 Mar. 1730	B.L., Add. MS 70497
73	To Martha Harley	28 Mar. 1730	B.L., Add. MS 70497
74	To Martha Harley	2 Apr. 1730	B.L., Add. MS 70497
75	To Martha Harley	11 Apr. 1730	B.L., Add. MS 70497
76	Clause of Jury Bill	1730	Brampton Bryan MSS, Bundle 117
77	Paper on Jury Act	1730	Brampton Bryan MSS, Bundle 117
78	To Martha Harley	11 Feb. 1731	B.L., Add. MS 70497
79	To Martha Harley	18 Feb. 1731	B.L., Add. MS 70497
80	To Martha Harley	23 Feb. 1731	B.L., Add. MS 70497
81	To Herbert Aubrey	22 Jan. 1732	Hereford R.O., A81/IV
82	Draft of Jury Bill	1733	Brampton Bryan MSS, Bundle X
83	From Auditor Harley	9 Feb. 1734	B.L., Add. MS 70498, ff. 63–4
84	Speech on motion to remove Walpole	13 Feb. 1741	Bodl., MS Ballard 29, f. 130
85	To William Brydges	21 Feb. 1741	Hereford R.O., A81/IV
86	To Martha Harley	7 May 1741	B.L., Add. MS 70497
87	To Martha Harley	10 May 1741	B.L., Add. MS 70497
88	To Martha Harley	12 May 1741	B.L., Add. MS 70497
89	To Martha Harley	15 May 1741	B.L., Add. MS 70497
90	To Martha Harley	17 May 1741	B.L., Add. MS 70497
91	To Martha Harley	22 May 1741	B.L., Add. MS 70497

No.	Correspondent	Date	Location
92	To Martha Harley	26 May 1741	B.L., Add. MS 70497
93	To Martha Harley	29 May 1741	B.L., Add. MS 70497
94	From Timothy Thomas	5 June 1741	B.L., Add. MS 70085
95	To Lord Hardwicke	26 June 1741	B.L., Add. MS 35586, ff. 368–9
96	To Thomas Foley	26 June 1741	Brampton Bryan MSS, Bundle 117
97	To Lord Hardwicke	22 July 1746	B.L., Add. MS 35588, ff. 264–5
98	To duke of Newcastle	22 July 1746	B.L., Add. MS 32707, ff. 486–7
99	From duke of Newcastle	26 July 1746	B.L., Add. MS 32707, ff. 482–3
100	To duke of Newcastle	29 July 1746	B.L., Add. MS 32707, ff. 499–500
101	To Lord Hardwicke	29 July 1746	B.L., Add. MS 35588, f. 284
102	From John Harley	29 July 1746	P.R.O., 30/20/24/2, pp. 101–4.
103	To duke of Newcastle	8 Aug. 1746	B.L., Add. MS 32708, ff. 39–40
104	From Robert Gwillym	19 June 1747	B.L., Add. MS 70085
105	From Lord Foley	25 June 1747	B.L., Add. MS 70498, ff. 37–8
106	From Sir H. Hoskyns	26 June 1747	B.L., Add. MS 70085
107	From Wallwyn Shepheard	12 July 1747	B.L., Add. MS 70085
108	From Lord Harley	23 Jan. 1750	P.R.O., 30/20/24/2, pp. 97–100
109	From John Harley	11 Jan. 1751	B.L., Add. MS 70498, ff. 75–6
110	To [Herbert] Aubrey	21 Feb. 1751	B.L., Add. MS 70085
111	From Lord Carnarvon	27 May 1753	B.L., Add. MS 70498, ff. 5–6
112	From Lord Carnarvon	9 June 1753	B.L., Add. MS 70498, ff. 7–8
113	To Lord Carnarvon	16 June 1753	B.L., Add. MS 70498, f. 9
114	From Lord Carnarvon	28 June 1753	B.L., Add. MS 70498, ff. 10–11
115	To Lord Carnarvon	13 July 1753	B.L., Add. MS 70498, ff. 14–15
116	From Lord Carnarvon	19 July 1753	B.L., Add. MS 70498, ff. 16–17
117	To Lord Carnarvon	27 July 1753	B.L., Add. MS 70498, ff. 18–19
118	From Lord Carnarvon	6 Aug. 1753	B.L., Add. MS 70498, ff. 20–2
119	To Lord Carnarvon	10 Aug. 1753	B.L., Add. MS 70498, f. 23
120	From Lord Carnarvon	18 Aug. 1753	B.L., Add. MS 70498, ff. 24–5
121	From Lord Carnarvon	23 Aug. 1753	B.L., Add. MS 70498, ff. 26–7

LIST OF HAY'S
PARLIAMENTARY PAPERS

No.	Correspondent	Date	Location
1	To duke of Newcastle	9 Aug. 1733	B.L., Add. MS 32688, ff. 56–7
2	To duke of Newcastle	11 Aug. 1733	B.L., Add. MS 32688, ff. 72–3
3	To duke of Newcastle	14 Aug. 1733	B.L., Add. MS 32688, ff. 98–9
4	To duke of Newcastle	16 Aug. 1733	B.L., Add. MS 32688, ff. 121–2
5	To duke of Newcastle	21 Aug. 1733	B.L., Add. MS 32688, ff. 161–2
6	To duke of Newcastle	24 Aug. 1733	B.L., Add. MS 32688, ff. 175–6
7	To duke of Newcastle	30 Aug. 1733	B.L., Add. MS 32688, ff. 228–9
8	To duke of Newcastle	6 Sept. 1733	B.L., Add. MS 32688, ff. 273–4
9	To duke of Newcastle	12 Sept. 1733	B.L., Add. MS 32688, ff. 325–6
10	To duke of Newcastle	24 Sept. 1733	B.L., Add. MS 32688, ff. 379–80
11	To duke of Newcastle	9 Oct. 1733	B.L., Add. MS 32688, ff. 480–1
12	To duke of Newcastle	11 Oct. 1733	B.L., Add. MS 32688, ff. 482–3
13	From J. Hurdis	11 Oct. 1733	B.L., Add. MS 32688, ff. 490–1
14	To duke of Newcastle	15 Oct. 1733	B.L., Add. MS 32688, ff. 504–5
15	To duke of Newcastle	19 Oct. 1733	B.L., Add. MS 32688, ff. 526–7
16	To duke of Newcastle	25 Oct. 1733	B.L., Add. MS 32688, ff. 584–9
17	To duke of Newcastle	27 Oct. 1733	B.L., Add. MS 32688, ff. 599–600
18	List of Lewes voters	27 Oct. 1733	B.L., Add. MS 32688, ff. 603–4
19	To duke of Newcastle	27 Oct. 1733	B.L., Add. MS 32688, ff. 601–2
20	To duke of Newcastle	31 Oct. 1733	B.L., Add. MS 32688, ff. 616–17
21	To duke of Newcastle	3 Nov. 1733	B.L., Add. MS 32689, ff. 7–8
22	To duke of Newcastle	8 Nov. 1733	B.L., Add. MS 32689, ff. 13–14
23	To duke of Newcastle	10 Nov. 1733	B.L., Add. MS 32689, ff. 15–16
24	To duke of Newcastle	12 Nov. 1733	B.L., Add. MS 32689, ff. 19–20
25	To duke of Newcastle	15 Nov. 1733	B.L., Add. MS 32689, ff. 24–5
26	List of voters	15 Nov. 1733	B.L., Add. MS 32689. ff. 26–7
27	To duke of Newcastle	18 Dec. 1733	B.L., Add. MS 32689, ff. 86–7
28	To duke of Newcastle	22 Dec. 1733	B.L., Add. MS 32689, ff. 90–1
29	To duke of Newcastle	27 Dec. 1733	B.L., Add. MS 32689, ff. 106–7
30	List of voters	27 Dec. 1733	B.L., Add. MS 32689, ff. 108–9
31	To duke of Newcastle	29 Dec. 1733	B.L., Add. MS 32689, ff. 110–11
32	To duke of Newcastle	3 Jan. 1734	B.L., Add. MS 32689, ff. 128–9
33	To duke of Newcastle	7 Jan. 1734	B.L., Add. MS 32689, ff. 134–5
34	To duke of Newcastle	19 Jan. 1734	B.L., Add. MS 32689, ff. 144–5
35	Enclosure in no. 34	17 Jan. 1734	B.L., Add. MS 32689, ff. 146–7
36	To duke of Newcastle	6 June 1734	B.L., Add. MS 32689, f. 263
37	To duke of Newcastle	7 Sept. 1734	B.L., Add. MS 32689, ff. 375–6
38	To duke of Newcastle	20 Sept. 1753	B.L., Add. MS 32732, ff. 692–3

THE PARLIAMENTARY JOURNAL OF
EDWARD HARLEY,
3rd EARL OF OXFORD,
1734–1751

The first Parliament of King George the 2d which had sat 7 Sessions was prorogued April 16, 1734 and was dissolved the next Day, when the Writs for a New Parliament bore Teste, and were made returnable June 13, 1734.

May 8, 1734. E. Harley and Velters Cornewall Esqs were chose Knights of the Shire for the County of Hereford without Opposition.

January 14, 1734/35. The Parliament met, and the House of Commons chose Arthur Onslow Esqe (who had been Speaker in the last Parliament) Speaker without Opposition. He was presented and approved of by the King January 23, when the King made a Speech to both Houses. The 23rd, 24th, and 25th were employed in the Members taking the Oaths.

On Monday January 27, 1734/35, The House sat to do Business, when an Address of Thanks to the King was moved by Mr Hedges and Seconded by *Mr John Campbell* Knight of the Shire for Pembrokeshire. {Mr Campbell was also chose for the shires of Cromartie and Nairn in Scotland, (the first Instance of any ones being chosen a Member of Parliament in Scotland and England). He made his Election for the County of Pembroke.}

In the last Paragraph of the Motion this amendment was proposed by Sir William Windham.

To assure his Majesty that [as soon as the proper information of the state of Publick Affairs is laid before this House] They would chearfully and effectually raise such Supplys, as shall be necessary for the Honour and Security of his Majesty and his Kingdoms [and in Proportion to such Efforts as shall be made by our Allies who are under the same Engagements with us and who are not involved in the War.]

The amendment was Debated, and the House Divided whether The Amendment stand part of the Question.

	Ayes			Noes	
Tellers	Sir J. Cotton	185	Tellers	Sir W. Yonge	265
	E. Harley			Mr Henry Bromley	

January 28. A Petition of Bussy Mansel Esqe complaining of an undue Election and Return for the County of Glamorgan was presented. [Mr Talbot eldest Son to the Lord Chancellor the sitting Member.] Such arbitrary and illegal Proceedings in the Sheriff were complained of, that a Motion was made for Hearing the Petition at the Bar. House Divided.

	Ayes			Noes	
Tellers	Sir E. Deering	} 153		Sir William Gage	} 235
	Mr Bramston			Mr Brereton	

February 6. A standing Order made relating to the Qualification of Members. That upon the Petition of any Electors complaining of an undue Election and alledging that some other Person was duely elected, the sitting Member may Demand and examine into the Qualification of such Person so alledged to be duely elected in the same manner as if such Person had himself petitioned. A standing order. {This Order was made upon the Petition of the Voters of Cricklade in Com. Wilts against Mr Gore sitting Member in behalf of Lord Tullimore, who declined petitioning in his own name, being not qualifyed.[1]}

---

[1] Charles Moore (1712–64), 2nd Baron Moore of Tullamore [I]; succ. 1725. As the franchise of Cricklade lay only with the freemen of the borough, Tullamore may not have been qualified to petition as a voter. The petition was that unfair and illegal practices had been used in Gore's favour; the petition was withdrawn on 7 Mar. *C.J.*, XXII, 333, 406.

February 7. A Petition from the Engravers presented. Upon which a Bill was brought in to Encourage the Arts of Designing Engraving and Etching Historical and other Prints by vesting the Properties thereof in the Inventors and Engravers for a Limited Time March 4, which had the Royal Assent May 15, 1735.

February 7. In the Committee of Supply 30000 Seamen were proposed for the Year 1735. Which was opposed because of the great Debt on the Nation, and our yearly Expence being between 3 and 4 Millions which is as great as was in the late War, and now we are in peace with all Europe. A lesser number proposed 20000, which after a long Debate was put to the Question.

           Ayes   183   Noes   256.[2]

Then the Question for the 30000 was voted.

A Division upon the Sea Service has not been known many yeares before.

February 14. Debate in the Committee of Supply upon the Army. 25744 Men proposed by the Ministry, 17000 by the Country Party which was the Question put.

           Ayes   208.   Noes   261.

February 18. Shaftsbury Election heard at Bar. Sitting Member Mr Bennet. Petitioner Mr Stephen Fox. The Last Determination of the House concerning the right of Election read. Note this was the first Election tryed after the passing the Act against Bribery. February 20 Mr Fox voted duely elected Ayes 203 Noes 88.

March 10. Mr Gybbons Motion was taken into Consideration relating to the Clause in the Act against Bribery 2d Geo. 2di That the last Determination of the House touching the Right of Election should be final and conclusive as to the House. {Precedents for this Motion see the Journals of October 25, 1690, December 5, 1691, December 14, 1697, March 17, 1713/14, April 2, 1714.[3]}

Sir W. Yonge agreed to the Motion in general but desired to be satisfyed whether it was to extend to those Entries in the Journals (particularly ancient ones) where it was inserted That the Right of Election *Is* in such or such, without the Word *Resolved.* Whether to those where it was only said the Right of Election is *Agreed* to be.

Sir Joseph Jekyll Master of the Rolls: A Vote is a legal Right. Where the Entry in the Journal is *Resolved* it is absolute and can admit of no Dispute.

Where it is that the Right of Election *Is* in such and such is the Determination of the House, and the Word *Resolved* being Omitted makes no alteration.

Agreement is the Act of the Parties and no Declaration of the House, but a very strong Evidence of Right.

Mr Fazakerley: This is a beneficial Law and reduces things to a Certainty and lays down a Rule by which the House may guide themselves, therefore ought to be extended as far as the Reason of it will admit, therefore in many Cases to agreements.

Mr Winington: Agreements cannot be allowed for there are many contrary to Resolutions of the House.

Sir W. Windham: Where the Agreement and the Resolution differ, The Resolution must be your guide to Determine. But where an Agreement appears in an Old Journal and which has been acquiessed in many years, and never disputed, It is the strongest Evidence of Right and equal to a Resolution.

---

[2] This vote was in the committee of supply (see Hay journal, pp.104–5), and so is not recorded in *C.J.*
[3] See *C.J.*, X, 451–3, 573–4; XII, 6–8; XVII, 499–500, 529–36.

Speaker: Agreed, of late is the Word and Act of the Parties, but there are Instances in old Journals where the Words *Agreed* and *Allowed* seem to be a Resolution. The Entry in the Journal will speak itself.

After Several Amendments to the Question it was Ordered.

That the Counsel at the Bar of this House, or before the Committee of Privileges and Elections be restrained from offering Evidence touching the Legality of Votes for Members to serve in Parliament, for any County, Shire, City, Borough, Cinque Port or Place, contrary to the last Determination of the House of Commons; which Determination by an Act passed in the 2d year of his Present Majesty's Reign, intituled an Act for the more effectual preventing Bribery and Corruption in the Elections of Members to serve in Parliament, is made final to all Intents and Purposes whatsoever, any usage to the contrary notwithstanding. {In the next Session January 16, 1735/36 This Order was made a Standing Order of the House.}

The next Day March 11. The Wells Election was heard at the Bar of the House. When this Order was Read and the last Determination of the House made 18 of April 1729 concerning the Right of Election for the City of Wells.

{*March 19.* In the Committee upon Hearing the Southampton Election this Order was Read before the Councel proceded.}

March 11. Wells Election heard at Bar on the Petition of Mr Speke and Mr Piers against Mr Hamilton and Mr Edwards sitting Members.

Counsel for the Petitioners offering to produce Evidence in Order to disqualify Persons upon account of their not being legal Burgesses.

Counsel for the Sitting Members object to the said Evidence being produced.

Question That the Counsel for the sitting Members be directed to proceed in their Objection. House Divided. Ayes go forth.

Ayes   144.   Noes   141.

After Hearing the Counsel on both sides to the objection. The House after Debate and on a Division Came to this Resolution.

That the Counsel for the Petitioners be restrained from giving Evidence that it is a necessary Qualification of a Burgess of the City of Wells, that such Person, previous to his being made a Burgess, was a Freeman of the said City, admitted to his Freedom in one of the Seven Companies within the said City, intituled to such Freedom by Birth, Servitude, or Marriage.

Yeas   125.   Noes   112.

This Resolution establishes the Honorary Burgesses of Wells. For by the last Resolution the Qualification relates to the Freemen only.

See the Resolution on the right of Election, 18 February 1695, 30 May 1716, 11 April 1717, May 2, 1723 and April 18, 1729.

Further Hearing March 13.

Further hearing March 18.

When John Joyce a Freeman of the City of Wells being called to give Evidence as to the Right of the Eldest Sons of Freemen there to be admitted to the Freedom of the said City.

The Counsell for the sitting Members objected to the admitting this Person to be an Evidence. For this Right ought not to be proved by a Witness who is a Freeman himself and of consequence has an Interest in it. Where the Evidence is to create any priviledge to Himself, by encreasing his own right or taking from others. He ought not to be admitted.

The House were of a different opinion and Resolved that John Joyce be admitted to give Evidence etc.

Yeas   115.   Noes   113.

Further hearing March 20.

Further Hearing Wells Election March 25.

When the Question was first put That Mr George Hamilton is duly elected. Yeas 175. Noes 193.

The same Question on Mr Edwards passed in the Negative without a Division.

Mr Speke and Mr Piers voted duly elected.

The Court were so angry at the other Divisions and particularly that which related to the Burgesses, That they summoned their whole force and all their troops being resolved to carry their Members tho' they had lost the City.

Note Mr Piers was never chose by this City, yet had been twice voted duly elected by the House of Commons.

March 12, 1734/35. A Petition from Scotland presented complaining That Andrew Fletcher of Miltoun[4] one of the Judges had imprisoned 40 Burgesses of the Burgh of Haddingtoun whereof seventeen were acting Magistrates without any Evidence laid before Him, for committing them without Bail, and directing His Warrant to all officers Civil and *Military*.

The Question was That this Petition be referred to the Committee of the whole House. After a long Debate the House divided. Yeas 155. Noes 197.

This Petition gave occasion to a Motion March 14 That Leave be given to bring in a Bill *For the better Security of the Liberty of the Subject in that part of Great Britain called Scotland and* for explaining and amending an act passed in the Parliament of Scotland in 1701 Intituled an Act for preventing wrongous Imprisonment and against undue Delays in Tryals.

After Debate the Question was put That the Words under which the Line is drawn stand part of the Question. Yeas 147. Noes 215.

March 28. This Bill ordered to be printed.

May 2. Upon the 3d reading of the Bill an amendment was proposed, a Debate arising. It was moved that the Debate be adjourned till Monday. This was with an Intention to fling out the Bill. House Divided.

Yeas   131.   Noes   124.

On Monday May 5. The Debate was resumed. And upon the Question for passing the Bill. House Divided.

Yeas   139.   Noes   131.

This Bill was afterwards flung out by the Lords upon the Question for Committing the Bill. Contents 28. Not Contents 68. Upon which 17 Lords protested.[5] See the Protest in my Votes for this year.[6]

{*February 26.* In the *Mutiny Bill* passed this Session, A Clause was inserted for the *Relief of Persons hastily listing themselves.*}

---

4 Andrew Fletcher (1692–1766), Lord Milton; lord justice clerk in Scotland, 1735–48.

5 The Lords' vote and protest were on 9 May. *L.J.*, XXIV, 548–9.

6 The *Votes* were the published daily proceedings of the house of commons, begun in 1679. Harley's copy has not been found. His copy of the protest must have been a manuscript one for it does not appear to have been printed.

March 18, 1734/35. £26000 granted towards settling and securing the Colony of Georgia in America.

March 19. Report from the Wool Committee.

March 21. Northampton Election heard at the Bar. A Compromise between Lord Halifaxs and Lord Northamptons Family. The Freemen excluded a right of Voting and Mr George Compton declared duly elected.[7]

March 28. Marlborough Election heard at Bar. Petitioners Mr Newnham and Mr Hayes. Sitting Members, Mr Lisle, Mr Seymour.[8]

 The Right of Election is in the Mayor and Burgesses only. And the Merits of the Petitioners Election depended upon the disqualifying 11 Burgesses, by controverting the Election of Edward Bell one of the Common Council, on which the Right of Election of those Burgesses depended.

 The Council for the Sitting Members objected that such Evidence should not be given at the Bar of the House, where the Witnesses are not examined upon Oath, and when Bells Election was confirmed by a Verdict in Kings Bench by 12 Men upon Oath, and by Witnesses proving the same upon Oath. Yet the House came to the Resolution that Evidence to disqualify those Burgesses by controverting Bells Election should be admitted. Yeas 176. Noes 172.

 The next Day Witnesses were examined who confirmed Bells Election to have been good. Sir R. Walpole in a long Speech laboured to show the contrary and to work up his Creatures to a Division, but the Master of the Rolls (Sir Joseph Jekyll) had spoke so very strong on the other side and shewed the injustice of setting Bells Election aside, and the bad consequences of hearing Evidence at the Bar contrary to a Verdict. That Sir Robert finding He could not Spirit up his Tools, He gave up the Question. And It was resolved that Bell was duly elected a Common Council Man, without any Division, The Sitting Members were afterwards Voted duly elected.

 This was a great blow upon the Court, and especially on Lord Hertfords Interest in this Burrough. For this Verdict being confirmed and the 11 Burgesses established, Lord Bruce has obtained the Borough.

 Mem. Winingtons scandalous Assertion relating to Mr Northey one of the Jury Men.

March 31, 1735. Petition of the Innholders and Alehousekeepers of York complaining of Soldiers being quartered upon them by the procurement of the Mayor and Mr Thomson their Members, because they would not vote for Thomson and Sir W. Milner at the last Election, was heard according to Order by a Committee of the whole House.

 The Witnesses were examined on Oath.

April 2. The Petition voted frivolous and vexatious.

Yeas 231.   Noes 124.

 The Hearing took up three days, and though it was late at night when the Hearing was over the 3d day, yet the Report was immediately made.

---

[7] See Sedgwick, I, 293; Hay journal, p. 112; and *C.J.* XXI, 354, 426 for the background.

[8] Thomas Newnham (later M.P. for Queensborough) and Benjamin Hayes were favoured by Walpole, who wished to overturn the verdict of a trial at the assizes in order to return his candidates. This was strongly opposed by Sir Joseph Jekyll (see below) and William Pulteney. H.M.C., *Egmont Diary*, II, 167.

April 3, 1735. Report of the Southampton Election.

Resolved. That the Mayor and Bailiffs of the Town and County of the Town of Southampton, are the Returning Officers for the said Town and County.

April 11. Bill for the Encouragement of the Arts of Designing and Engraving Historical and other Prints by vesting the Properties thereof in the Inventors and Engravers during the Time mentioned in the Bill Passed.

April 14. Resolved. That the Rents and Profits of the forfeited Estate of the late Earl of Derwentwater[9] be applied towards the finishing the Building of Greenwich Hospital.

April 15, 1735. Merits of the Election for the City of Bristol heard at Bar against Mr Coster the sitting Member. When upon opening the Case and Examining Witnesses on the Petitioners side (which was on behalf of Mr Scrope though He did not petition himself) they found so much difficulty to proceed themselves in proving what they aimed at, which was to confine the Election for the future to the Corporate Body exclusive of the Freemen, and which to others appeared so contrary to usage, That the further Hearing was adjourned to the 17th and from thence to the 23d. But on the 22d the Petitions were withdrawn, and the order for hearing discharged.

April 16. Report from the Committee relating to Franking of Letters. See the Resolutions.[10] Upon the 3d Resolution a Debate arising. The Debate was adjourned to the 22th from thence to the 25th when the Resolution being amended was agreed to.

April 17. Report of the Wendover Election. The Merits were that the sitting Member Mr Boteler was not qualifyed. Resolved a Void Election.

April 21. Report from the Wool Committee. See the Resolutions upon which a Bill was ordered to be brought in but afterwards laid aside.[11]

April 22. Bill for amendment of the Law relating to Actions on the Statute of Hue and Cry passed.[12]

April 22. Bill for limiting the number of officers in the House of Commons read a 2d time. At Question for Commitment passed in the Negative Yeas 190. Noes 214. The Debate was begun and cheifly carried on by young Gentlemen who were chose this Parliament and had never spoke before.

For the Bill	Against the Bill
Mr Granville	Mr Whitmore
Mr Delme	Mr Herbert of Oakley
Mr Pit	Mr Hanbury Williams
Mr Berkley	
Mr Boone	
Mr Littleton	
Mr Hume Campbell	
Lord Polwarth	

9 James Radclyffe (1689–1716), 3rd earl of Derwentwater; executed for his part in the 1715 Jacobite rebellion.
10 *C.J.*, XXII, 462–5.
11 *Ibid.*, pp. 470–1. The bill was defeated on its 2nd reading on 25 Apr. *Ibid.*, p. 476.
12 The bill received the royal assent on 15 May.

Tellers

Yeas		Noes	
Lord Morpeth	190	Mr Pelham	214
Mr Granville		Mr Whitmore	

April 30. Bill for regulating the Play Houses flung out by appointing a long day for going into the Committee to consider further on the Bill. The opposition was by the young people of the House, and by Lord Baltimore and other freinds to Sir William Lemmon[13] who was the Ground Land-Lord of Goodmans feilds playhouse.[14] The other Play Houses were for the Bill that They only might be established by Law. See the coming in of the Bill <on 3 April>[15] and the Progress of it and the Several Petitions for and against it.[16]

May 1. Bill for inclosing and adorning Lincolns Inn feilds passed.[17]

May 1, 1735. Report relating to the York buildings Company taken into Consideration. When the House voted that several frauds had been committed by the Company but would not name any particular person to be Guilty of doing them, this was to Screen the Governour Mr Solomon Ashley who was a member of the House, and who by his behaviour made it a doubt whether He most Fool or Knave.

May 2. Mr Hay reports several Resolutions relating to the Maintenance and Settlement of the Poor. The House agree to the Resolutions with an alteration to one which see May 7. [No Bill ordered this Session.] See Resolution relating to the Poor March 1, 1698.[18] See page 54.[19]

May 2. Bill relating to Scotch Patronage. Rejected upon the Question for a 2d reading. Yeas 62. Noes 109.

May 5. Bill for vesting the Copies of Printed Books in the Authors or Purchasers of such Copies during the Times limited by the Bill. Passed. Flung out by the Lords by appointing a long day for the 2d reading.[20]

May 6. Bill for applying the Rents and Profits of the forfeited Estate of the Earl of Derwentwater towards the finishing of Greenwich Hospital.[21] Note in the Bill there is a Clause for the payment of £2000 to Lord Gage for his Services in recovering the

---

[13] Sir William Leman (1685–1741), 3rd bt.

[14] Goodman's Fields (east of the Minories) had been built over by 1720, and one of the resulting streets was Leman St., on which a shop was converted into a theatre in 1729. In 1733 the actor Henry Gifford built another theatre on Ayliffe St., known as the Goodman's Fields Theatre, which was closed in 1751, becoming a warehouse.

[15] Here EH left a gap.

[16] See *C.J.*, XXII, 444, 453, 455–6, 459, 469–70, 477–8. See also V.J. Liesenfeld, *The Licensing Act of 1737* (Madison, 1984), ch. 2; and Hay journal, p. 120 below.

[17] The bill is printed in Lambert, VII, 175–81. See also *C.J.*, XXII, 481; Cobbett, IX, 944–9.

[18] The resolution was on 3 Mar. 1698 (*C.J.*, XII, 140–1). See Hay's account of this day, pp. 120–1.

[19] I.e. folio 54. See entry for 3 Mar. 1736, p. 18 below.

[20] The bill was read for the 1st time in the Lords on 6 May; the 2nd reading was finally postponed on the 12th for two weeks, but parliament was prorogued on the 15th. *L.J.*, XXIV, 544, 548, 550, 559.

[21] This was the 3rd reading of the bill, which received the royal assent on 15 May. *C.J.*, XXII, 486, 493.

Estate to the publick. For He was the principal person concerned in detecting the Frauds of Birch, and Eyles and Bond as Commissioners of the forfeited Estate and made the Complaint to the House.[22] Lord Gage had his Information from <blank>[23]

May 8. A Bill from the Lords Intituled an Act for regulating the Quartering of Soldiers during the Time of the Elections of Members to serve in Parliament was passed with some amendments. See the Lords Protest upon some amendments made to this Bill when it was in the Committee of the Lords House.[24]

May 15. The Session Ended by Prorogation.

[22] John Birch, John Eyles (see Appendix) and Denis Bond (1676–1747), M.P. for Dorchester 1704–10, Corfe Castle 1715–27, Poole 1727–30 Mar. 1732, as commissioners for the forfeited estates of the 1715 rebels, were involved in the fraudulent sale of the Derwentwater estates. In 1731 the fraud was exposed by a parliamentary enquiry. See Sedgwick, I, 462, 470–1; II, 21.

[23] Here EH left a gap.

[24] There were two protests on 16 Apr. *L.J.*, XXIV, 519–20.

Second Session

Parliament met January 15, 1735/36. No opposition to the Address.

January 16. Order of last Sessions which Declared the last Determination of the House as to the Right of Election to be final. Made a Standing Order.
　　Order. That the Petitioner and Sitting Member upon controverted Elections for Counties to be heard at the Bar or before the Committee do deliver Lists to each other of the Persons objected to by them and the Several Heads of Objections distinguishing the same against the names of the Voters excepted to. {See November 29, 1699 when this Method was found Inconvenient and Ordered to be laid aside.}[25]
　　This order made for the sake of the Yorkshire Election where it was first Practised. The same order for the County of Norfolk January 19.

January 22. Mr Conduit moved to repeal the Statute of King James the first. Intituled an Act against Conjuration and Witchcraft. Which was ordered, and He accordingly brought in a Bill, which passed few or none giving themselves any Concern about it.[26]

January 27. 15000 Men voted for Sea Service for the year 1736.

January 28. Motion that the Ordinary Estimate of the Navy for 1736 be referred to the Consideration of a Select Committee. Passed in the Negative. Yeas 155. Noes 256. [See page 6 the same Question proposed last Session][27]

January 29. 17704 Men voted for Guards and Garrisons, to which number there was little or no opposition, the King having made a Reduction of <8000> Men.[28]
　　But as soon as the House had agreed to the several Resolutions of the Committee Lord Cornbury moved and was seconded by Mr George Littleton to Address his Majesty to make a further Reduction and that of Corps. {Difference between reducing Corps and Private Men. By the Establishment a Marching Regiment which consists of *815* Men costs the Publick about *£15,217* yearly; so that if a whole Regiment should be reduced there would be a Saving of *£15217* a year to the Publick, whereas if an equal Number of Private Men only should be reduced, there would be a saving of the Pay of so many Private Men only, which in a year amounts to but £7427. So that the Saving to the Publick by reducing a whole Regiment of 815 will be *£7790* more than by reducing 815 Private men only. If a reduction of 8000 Men should be made by reducing of whole Regiments. There would be a saving of *£149,369* yearly whereas by a reduction of 8000 private men only, the Saving would be but *£73,000* yearly. So that the Difference to the Publick would be a Saving of £76,369 yearly in the one case more than in the other.} See the Motion which was finely drawn up by Sir William Windham.[29] This occasioned a long Debate. It passed in the Negative. Yeas 139. Noes 205.

February 2. Motion by <Samuel Sandys>[30] That the Supplies necessary for the service of the ensuing year be raised within the year. It passed in the Negative without a Division.[31]

---

[25] See *C.J.*, XIII, 9.
[26] It received the royal assent on 24 Mar.
[27] I.e., folio 6, missing in the ms.
[28] Here EH left a gap. See also Hay journal, pp. 128–9 below.

[29] See Cobbett, IX, 1016, for the motion.
[30] Here EH left a gap. For Sandys see *ibid.*
[31] For the debate see *ibid.*, 1016–32.

February 9. Petition of the Manufacturers of Fustian in the Town of Manchester, complaining that Prosecutions have been carryed on against Persons using or wearing the said Manufactures, when printed or painted under pretence that they are liable to the Penalties of the Act for prohibiting the use and Wear of Callicoes made in the 7th year of King George the first, and desiring that the said act might be explained.

The Prosecution against these Fustians was begun and carried at Norwich by Alderman Vere who is Member for Norwich, and as these Fustians hindred the Sale of the Norwich stuffs.

At the Committee The Dealers in Fustians proved the benefit of this Manufacture.[32]

That the Prime Costs of the Materials were 6 shillings 4s Cotton and 2s Flax to make a Peice. That when a Peice was fully manufactured and had gone through the several Hands of Picking, Cleansing, Carding, Spining, Winding, Warping, Weaving, Whitening, Printing and Duty, it sold for 40s.

And as the encrease from 6s was to 40s.

So where the prime Cost was 36s the encrease was to £6.

The Value of these Goods at Liverpoole only when manufactured <£>400,000.

February 16. Report from the Committee made. And a Bill ordered to be brought in. And the Bill passed.[33]

February 10. Election for the Borough of Southwark heard at Bar. Petitioner Mr Sheppard. Sitting Member Mr Heathcote.

Standing Order of the House made the 16th of January last relating to the last Determination read.[34]

The Resolution of the House of the 10th of November 1702 whereby the Right of Election was resolved to be only in the Inhabitants thereof paying Scot and Lot was read.[35]

Objection made to One *Antrobus* that He does not pay Scot and Lot. To prove it, The Rates were produced, and a Witness called to prove that He had looked over the Rate and Antrobus his name is not there.

Allowed. That if a Person was rated for a Warehouse a Shed etc. and is no House-keeper but only a Lodger, He is a good Vote.

To prove Non payment of any Rate, the Mark or Cross against the Name in the Parish book is not sufficient Evidence. The Demand must be proved.

Voters not allowed to prove, That *They* voted other wise than they were set down on the Bailiffs Poll.

Other Evidence of it might and ought to be admitted, otherwise it would place great power in the Hands of the Returning officer. And This seemed to be the Sense of the House notwithstanding the Case of the County of Bedford was read 14 July 1715.[36]

The Bailiff of Southwark gave Evidence That no objection was made of this kind at the time of the Poll. That the Books were signed by the Inspectors, and that He took the utmost care to prevent or rectify Mistakes in taking the Poll.

---

[32] The committee met at 5.00 p.m. that afternoon; Harley was a member. *C.J.*, XXII, 551–2.

[33] The bill received the royal assent on 24 Mar.

[34] *C.J.*, XXII, 498, that a counsel should refrain from offering evidence contrary to the last determination of the house.

[35] *C.J.*, XIV, 24–5.

[36] See *ibid.*, XVIII, 224.

February 12. Further Hearing.

A Person who had taken *the Oath*, appointed by the act against Bribery, at the time of the Election, *not* admitted to be examined, in order to prove *his* having received a Bribe to give his Vote.

Other Witnesses were called and allowed to prove it.

February 17. Further Hearing.

The Evidence for the Petitioner having proved scarce any of the Allegations of the Petition. The sitting Member produced no Evidence, but rested his Cause upon what was said against Him. And it was resolved that He was duly elected Nemine Contradicente.

The Petitioner had most wretched freinds Charles Eversfeild being the cheif Manager; and his Case most simply managed. For it was notorious to the whole Town that some 1000 pounds had been spent *on both sides at this* Election.

February 16. Report from the Committee relating to the Building a Bridge at Westminster.

The Evidence before the Committee and the Report set forth that the Horse Ferry was the most convenient place. But on the opinion of General Wade The Resolution of the Committee and the House is that New Palace Yard is the most convenient place for the building the Bridge. And a Bill in pursuance of the Resolutions was ordered to be brought in.

A Motion that the Report should be printed rejected. The Bill passed.

{*March 31, 1736.* Upon the Question for passing the Westminster Bridge Bill the House divided.

	Yeas	117.	Noes	12.
Tellers	Sir G. Oxenden		Sir J. Barnard	
	Mr Conduit		Mr Alderman Heathcote	

The 12 that gave their negative were. *Mr Conyers*, *Mr Trefusio*, *Mr Archer* of Berkshire, Sir C. *Mordaunt*, Mr *E. Harley*, Mr *Marshall*, Mr *Erskine*, Sir F. *Childe*, Mr *Watts*, Mr Alderman *Perry*, Mr Alderman *Willimot*, Sir G. *Caswall.*}

And the Bridge was to be built with Stone from New pallace yard to the Lambeth side and made a free Bridge. The Method to raise the Money for it was to be by way of Lottery. But this affair being looked upon as a job and the City of London being averse to it. The Lottery never filled. {The next Session a Bill was brought in and passed to amend the former in which the Scheme of the Lottery was altered and in the Months of November and December 1737 the Lottery was drawn. When the Commissioners met they disagreed as to the Place where the Bridge should be built whether at the Palace yard or the Horse Ferry, upon which a new bill was passed 1738 to fix it at Palace yard.}[37]

February 20, 1735/36. Bill for further regulating Elections presented by Sir John Rushout to the House. This Bill went as far as a Committee and there dropped. There being so many various opinions of Gentlemen for the sake of their particular Interests in their Boroughs. This Bill was again attempted by Sir J. Rushout the next Session but it did not pass.

[37] See also pp. 23, 39 below.

February 24. Report from the Committee of the whole House upon the Petition of the Justices of the Peace of Midlesex relating to Spirituous Liquors.[38] See the Resolutions;[39] the Report referred to the Committee of Supply. Upon which Resolution A Bill was brought in[40] and passed by which it was enacted That no Person after the 29th of September 1736 should retail Spirituous Liquors of any sort in less quantity than two Gallons without paying £50 for a Licence. In this Act is inserted a Form of Conviction for selling Ale etc. without Licence.

This was the famous Gin Act, of which Sir Joseph Jekyll Master of the Rolls was the great promoter. The Drinking Gin and other spirituous Liquors was come to so great an exess and occasioned so many villanies and enormities among the Common people, that it was of publick service to suppress these liquors, but the Method of doing it wrong.

February 24. Election for the County of York at Bar.

| Sir Rowland Wynne | Petitioner |
| Sir Miles Staplyton | Sitting Member |

Mr Strange Counsel for the sitting Member states the Poll.[41]

Sir Miles Stapylton	7896
Sir Rowland Wynne	7699
Majority	197

He objects to 1609 of those who Voted for Sir Miles and proposes to leave a Majority for Sir Rowland of 1412.

Fifteen Heads of Objections.

1st. 589. Have no Freeholds for which they were assessed.
2d. 229. No Freeholds in the place for which they polled.
3d. 488. Have not 40s per annum.
4th. 98. Not assessed for 40s per annum.
5th. 19. Minors.
6th. 12. Purchasers within a year before the Election.
7th. 14. Not having 40s per annum exclusive of Purchases within the year.
8th. 17. Prevailed on by Threats to give their Votes.
9th. One that polled twice.
10th. Three that polled twice. The first time for the Petitioner, afterwards for the sitting Member.
11th. 97. That have no Freeholds within the County of York.
12th. One a Lunatick.
13th. One an alien.
14th. 39. Not to be found, no such Persons.
15th. One not present at the Election.

The objection of not being rated in Proportion waved.

---

[38] The petition has not survived, but in Jan. 1736 the Middlesex quarter sessions did publish a report made by a committee of J.P.s into the number of gin shops and 'the Mischiefs occasioned thereby'. *Political State of Great Britain*, LI (1736), 168–74.

[39] *C.J.*, XXII, 586–7.

[40] The bill was brought in on 29 Mar., passed the Commons on 20 Apr., and received the royal assent on 5 May. *C.J.*, XXII, 658, 690, 704.

[41] For John Strange see Appendix. The full poll, on 15 May 1734, is printed in Sedgwick, I, 357. This is clearly a slip of the pen and Strange must have been the counsel for the petitioner Wynne.

Several Books being produced as the Original Poll. It was objected by Mr Pauncefort and Mr Murray Counsel for Sir Miles, That the said Books ought not to be admitted as Evidence, the same having not been delivered over upon Oath and not within the Time limited by Law, and no Proof having been given that no alterations had been made therein after the Election and before the Delivery.

The Counsel on both sides were heard to the objection.

The Act of the 10th of Queen Anne read.[42]

Report of the 12 of March 1727[43] on the Election for the County of Bucks read. (A Case in point, and though a Precedent made by Sir William Yonge yet He debated and Voted against it in this Question, it not being for his purpose now, though it was then.)

Whether those Books should be brought up, occasioned a long debate.

Those who were against bring them up, argued, That the Sheriff had not complyed with the Act, the Poll was no Record though put among the Records of Sessions. For it was not properly authenticated by being delivered to the Clerk of the Peace within 20 days after the Election by the Sheriff on Oath made before the two next Justices, and unless this was done the Quarter Session had nothing to do with the Poll, for as a Court they have no power whatsoever to have the Poll laid before them or to take any Cognizance of it.

It was answered, That it would be very hard that the Omission or ill Practice of a sheriff should affect the sitting Member who was not privy to it, who would be entirely nonsuited and stopped from proceeding if the Poll was not admitted, which though not sworn to was lodged among the Records of the Sessions. That the House were not to guide themselves by the Letter of the Law, but the Intention of the Legislature, who never intended to tye up its self from proceeding to hear an Election because a Sheriff failed in his Duty.

It was replyed. That nothing was more common in the Courts below That a nonsuit would be directed where the Regular forms were not observed. That an Affidavit though never so necessary and material to the Merits of the Cause could not be read, if it was not upon Stamp Paper. That if the Legislature itself did not regard its own acts but thought fit to construe them as it best served present purposes, How could it be expected That they would be obeyed and observed without Doors; That the producing the Clerk of the Peace to prove those books, was not the best Evidence the Matter in dispute would admit of. The Sheriff might be here himself to give an Account relating to the Books and some Members were for adjourning the further Consideration till the Sheriff could attend. But the Majority would not hear of this.

When it seemed to be the Sense of many Gentlemen and particularly Sir Joseph Jekyll Master of the Rolls that the House was not to judge according to the Letter but the construction of the Act.

Sir Miles Staplyton acquainted Them That He had Witnesses ready at the Door to prove that the Poll was taken from the Sheriff after the Election, and that it was altered before it was returned to Him, and upon that Account He refused to swear to the Truth of it. But those Witnesses were not permitted to appear, the Master of the Rolls debated warmly that they should be heard and upon this Evidence being refused to be admitted He altered His Vote.

At first it seemed to be determined that the House should not guide themselves by the Letter of the Law, and Now they were to judge equitably without being fully informed by Evidence.

---

[42] See p. 16, n. 46 below.
[43] I.e., 12 Mar. 1728. *C.J.*, XXI, 80.

The Question for admitting those Books called the Original Poll was proposed. (See the Question at large.)

But the Previous Question being put. It was resolved in the Affirmative. Yeas 201. Noes 164. Then the main Question was carried without a Division.

February 26. Further Hearing. When it was proposed by the Petitioners Counsel in order to disqualify *John Maken* to prove by parole Evidence that He had no Freehold at the Time of the said Election in the Place where He then *Swore* that his Freehold did lye.

Journals of the 17th of April 4th Charles the first touching the Election for the County of York.[44] {April 17: 4 Charles. At the County Election of York Several Voters refused to tell their Names, but it appearing that they answered to these 3 Questions, That they had 40s Freehold per annum, That they were Resiants in the County at the date of the Writ, and That they were not polled before. Resolved. That if an Elector a Freeholder being by the Sheriff demanded His name shall refuse it, He is not disabled to be an Elector.}

Of the 16th of January 1710. County of Rutland. {Case of Rutland is, Parole Evidence was admitted against a Deed not produced.

Case of Bedford determined in a very thin House, and in a Parliament when Party rage was supported and carried on with the greatest injustice.}

17th of April 1735. Borough of Wendover in Com. Bucks. which states the parol Evidence given against the Sitting Members Qualification in contradiction to his Oath taken at the Election (A Case not to the purpose) {No Qualification required in a Freeholder but that He should have 40s per annum and be resiant in the County till the Resolution. (See the Acts of Parliament since) If Parole Evidence is admitted against the Freeholders Oath, the Sitting Members Seat is affected by Evidence He cannot contradict. For there is no Method to compel Persons to produce the Titles to their Estates, Speakers Warrant cannot be extended to this. The Statute of 7 & 8 Will. III, cap. 25[45] and 10 Anne[46] by requiring the Oath of a Freeholder at the Election seems to make this final and has enacted a punishment for a false Oath. (See the Journals of the Progress of those Bills. January 17, 20, February 1, March 2, 20, 24, 1695.[47]) The House was of this opionion in the Resolution they came to the same day January 16, 1695 in the Case of the Counties of Hertford and Surry when they refused to admit Parole Evidence against the Freeholders Oath. No usage to the Contrary till the Case of Bedford in 1715 as mentioned before.

By Parole Evidence Freeholder is Accused of Perjury who is not present to defend himself. Contra in the Qualification of a Member, His Rentroll being in his own power.}

After Debate it was Resolved That Parol Evidence be admitted as to a Person being no Freeholder at the Time of the Election who Swore Himself then to be a Freeholder. Yeas 206. Noes 152.

44 *C.J.*, I, 884 (17 Apr. 1628).

45 Act for Further Regulating Elections of Members to Serve in Parliament. *Statutes of the Realm*, VII, 109–11.

46 10 Anne c. 31: 1711 Act for the More Effectual Preventing Fraudulent Conveyances in order to Multiply Votes for Electing Knights of the Shire to Serve in Parliament. *Ibid.*, IX, 698–700. This act repealed the oath required by 7 & 8 Will. III, c. 25 and replaced it with a new one.

47 I.e., 1696. *C.J.*, XI, 394, 398, 424, 481, 525, 529.

March 2. Further Hearing.

John Machen objected to as having no Freehold in the Place He polled for. The Witness proceeded to give Evidence of that Disqualification by relating the Confession of the said J. Machen. Which Evidence was objected to.

Journal of 16th of April 1724 in relation to part of the Report of the Election of the County of Northumberland touching the Evidence produced to disqualify several Voters by the Confession of the Parties was read.[48]

[Note at this Election for the County of Northumberland the Freeholders were not sworn.]

The Resolution of the House of the 12th of February last in the Election of Southwark against admitting the Counsel to examine Thomas Gaman in contra-diction to his Oath was read.[49]

Quere? Where a Person himself cannot be a Witness, can what He says to another be admitted as good Evidence?

The House determined it might and Resolved.

That Evidence be admitted as to what a Voter *Confessed* of his having no Freehold who at the Time of the Election swore He had. Yeas 181. Noes 132.

Counsel proceeded to examine Witnesses.

When an objection was made to the Evidence of a Witness which tended to prove that the Person to be disqualifed had *no Freehold* at all in the Place for which He polled, when in the List of Objections delivered in pursuance of the Order of the House of January 16 last the objection to this Person was That He was not assessed, nor Had 40s per annum in the Place. That this Evidence would be contrary to the Order. In the Debate it was said

That the objections were very different. Having no Freehold relates to the Tenure.

Objection not Having 40s per annum admits the Tenure but disputes the Value.

Title Deeds necessary to prove the Freehold.

Assessments to prove the Value.

Where Deeds are mentioned they must be produced.

Where you would show that a Person is not rated in Proportion, the Assessment itself must be the Evidence.

It is usual to produce Poor rates and Church Assessments, Land Tax and Constables Rates.

Resolved.

That Evidence be admitted as to a Persons having no *Freehold at all* to whom the Petitioners objected in their List of Objections, that such Person had not a Freehold of 40s per Annum.

No Division on this Question.

March 4. Further Hearing.

March 9. Resolved. That Persons whose Freeholds lye within that Part of the County of the City of York, which is commonly called the Aynsty, have a Right to Vote for Knights of the Shire for the County of York.

The Petitioner objected to those Votes at first but gave them up afterwards, and there was no Debate nor Division.

---

[48] See *ibid.*, XX, 324–5.
[49] See *ibid.*, XXII, 558–9, 604; above p. 13.

April 22. The Councel for the Petitioners concluded their Evidence after 18 days Hearing, and pretended to disqualify 712 only out of 1619 to which they at first objected, and left a Majority of 515 for the Petitioner though they proposed at their opening to leave a Majority of 1412. See the particular objections to those disqualifyed in the Vote of this day (April 22).

{*May 4, 1736.* Further Hearing, When Mr Pauncefort and Mr Murray opened on the Side of the Sitting Member by observing upon the Evidence of the Petitioner. But before They entered into the Examination of any Witness. Mr Winnington by the consent of the Petitioner and his Freinds and by Direction of Sir R. Walpole moved to adjourn the further Hearing to this Day Sevennight. By which this tedious, perplexed, and most expensive Hearing was Dropped. The Manner in which this was ended showed the Folly of the Petitioner and his Freinds as much as the begining of it did their Conceit and Obstinacy. For had it been given up a Day or even two Hours sooner before the Sitting Members Council opened, they had prevented all the just reflections which the Council cast upon their Cause, their Evidence, and themselves.}

February 27, 1735/36. In the Committee of Ways and Means. Sir Robert Walpole acquainted the Committee That to make good the Supply granted for the year and the Deficiences of the last year there would be wanted £2,300,000 and proposed to raise it in this manner

2s on Land	<£>1,000,000
Malt	<£>750,000
From the sinking Fund	<£>600,000
	£2,350,000

Sir J. Barnard proposed to Mortgage the sinking Fund for the <£>600,000: at 3 per Cent. Sir Robert readily complyed with this proposition, it being part of his scheme and which He was affraid and unwilling to propose himself least He should disoblige the Moneyed Men, in the City.

March 3, 1735/36. The Resolutions of the House of last Session relating to the Laws for the Maintenance and Settlement of the Poor were read.[50] And a Bill ordered to be brought in for reducing the Laws relating to the Poor into one Law. Mr Hay, Mr Hooper and Mr Pollen ordered to prepare the same. The Bill was brought in and read a 1st and 2d time and committed and in the Committee the blanks were filled up by the Gentlemen who brought in the Bill few others giving any attention to it, the Bill thus filled was ordered to be printed for the use of the Members that it might be considered against another Session, and nothing more done in it this.[51] This Bill of Mr Hays a chimerical Scheme not possible to be put in Practice. The Laws in being much better and sufficient if put in due execution.

March 8, 1735/36. Report from the Committee of Elections touching the Matter of the Election of the Borough of Stamford in Com. Lincoln.

[50] See *ibid*, XXII, 483–4, 487–8 (2 and 7 May 1735).
[51] This took place on 11 Mar. *Ibid.*, XVII, 626.

John Proby Esqe   Sitting Member
Savill Cust Esqe   Petitioner[52]

The Cheif Question in the Committee was as to the Right of Election, There being no Resolution of Parliament relating to this Borough.

The Petitioner insisted that the Right of Election was in the Inhabitants *being Householders* paying Scot and Lot and not receiving Alms.

Sitting Members Counsel That the Right was in the Inhabitants at large.

Question that those Words [being Householders] stand part of the Question. Yeas 121. Noes 126. The Noes were 146: but 20 were lost by the mistake of Mr Henry Bathurst the Teller. It being the first time of his telling.

After this Question was carried. The next night Mr Cust gave up. And Mr Proby was voted duly elected by the Committee. And to those Resolutions the House agreed. And settled the Right of Election in the Borough of Stamford *to be in the Inhabitants paying Scot and Lot, and not receiving Alms or Publick Charities.*

The Same Day was the Report of the Election for Lewes in the County of Sussex.

Resolved. That the Right of Election is in the Inhabitants being Householders paying Scot and Lot.

This was heard and agreed by Consent of the Petitioners Mr Sergisson and Mr Garland. And the sitting Members Mr Pelham of Stanmer and Mr Pelham of Lewes who were voted duly elected.[53]

Mortmain Bill

March 10, 1735/36. Sir Joseph Jekyll presented to the House a Bill to restrain the Dispositions of Lands whereby the same become Unalienable.

March 11. The Bill was ordered to be printed.[54]

April 15. The Bill passed. Yeas 176. Noes 72.

This Bill was drove on by the intemperate Zeal of Sir Joseph Jekyll Master of the Rolls. The Specious Pretence for it was to prevent dying Persons depriving their Heirs of their Estates by leaving them in Charity. The Extravagant Will of Norton[55] who had made the Parliament his Executors first gave the Handle. But the true Design of many of the House was against all publick Charitys which appeared by the Warmth and Bitterness of their Speeches against the two Universities, the Charity Schools, Queen Annes Bounty to the poor Clergy, and to the Clergy in General. None more forward in those Invectives than Mr Sandys and the Patriots,[56] (as they are termed) and those who by the Name of the Georgians, (being Trustees for that Colony) as the Heathcotes,[57] White, Hucks,[58] Moore, Laroche etc. and were the Spawn of the Goal Committee.[59] The Governours of Queen Annes Bounty

---

52 Cust's challenge to the interest of the earls of Exeter and Gainsborough had caused a riot at the election. Sedgwick, I, 279.

53 See *ibid.*, pp. 335–6.

54 Printed in Lambert, VII, 255–8. As an act it was 9 Geo. II, c. 36.

55 Richard Norton of Southwick, near Portsmouth, died on 10 Dec. 1732, leaving his estate to parliament and various charities. Musgrave, *Obituary*, IV, 307; *Gentleman's Magazine*, III (1733), 57–62, prints the will.

56 Dissident whigs who in the late 1720s and 1730s joined with the tories to oppose the Walpole ministry.

57 Two nephews and a son of the former M.P. Sir Gilbert Heathcote. See Appendix.

58 Robert, not William, Hucks. Sedgwick, II, 156–7.

59 Appointed 25 Feb. 1729, and revived in 1730, the parliamentary gaols committee brought together independent and dissident whigs – giving rise to a distinct group of whigs – and tories. See Colley, p. 211.

petitioned against this Bill. But the Petition was not allowed to be referred to the Committee. Yeas 95. Noes 143.[60] This determined the fate of other Petitions against the Bill as that from the Trustees of the Charity Schools presented by E. Harley.[61]

When this Bill was in the Committee April 5. Mr Sandys moved a Clause to restrain the Colledges from purchasing any Livings for the future, and to take of the obligation from the fellows of taking Orders. He was seconded by Dr Lee the Civilian.[62] This was rejected upon the Question. Yeas 130. Noes 227.

The Clause in the Bill for exempting the two Universities,[63] was inserted upon an Agreement made with those Heads of House who had been sent up with the Petitions from the Universitys, and were drawn into this out of fear of having some hardships imposed upon and which terrors were flung out on purpose, therefore they consented to have the number of *Livings* in the disposal of the Several Coledges limited to half the number of Fellows or students. {See a List of the number and value of Livings belonging to each Colledge in Oxford in my large Book.}[64] Cambridge was first drawn into this agreement by Harding the Clerk of the House and one of the fellows of Kings.[65] And Cambridge afterwards prevailed with Oxford by refusing to join with them in any opposition. Whereas if neither had complied but had been resolute in their opposition, they would have had better terms. As appeared by what Sir R. Walpole said in the Debate, who was so pleased with this concession, that though in private He had pretended to be their Freind, yet as He too frequently shews his Wantonness in Power, so in this Debate He could not help sneering these Delegates, by saying That He never hoped to see the Universitys come to such a temper as to offer to limit the number of their Livings, but since they had done it they ought to be complyed with, when it can be done by their own Consent and free from clamour.

Those who spoke for the Bill were	Against the Bill
Sir Joseph Jekyll	Lord Noel Somerset
Mr Sandys	Mr Watkin Williams
Mr Glanville	Mr Shippen
Mr Heathcote	Mr Bird
Mr Moore	Mr Digby
Mr Giles Earle	E. Harley
Mr Orde	Sir John Barnard
Mr Fazakerly	

Test Act.

{Note this Affair had been long in the thoughts and under the Consideration of the Dissenters, and they once had determined to have the Motion for the Repeal of the Test Act made in the last Session of the late Parliament, in hope that the ensuing Elections might have influenced several Members to have been for Repeal in hopes of gaining the Dissenters Votes in their Elections. But from this Attempt the Heads of the Party were disswaded or either bribed by the first Minister Sir R. Walpole.

[60] The vote, not to allow the petition to go to the committee of the whole house but to let it lie on the table, was on 2 Apr. *C.J.*, XXII, 669–70.

[61] The charity schools petition was presented on 8 Apr., and ordered to lie on the table. *Ibid.*, p. 678.

[62] I.e., a doctor of civil law. See Appendix.

[63] The debate on this clause took place on 5 Apr. 1736. H.M.C., *Egmont Diary*, II, 255.

[64] Not found.

[65] Nicholas Hardinge (1699–1758), fellow of King's College, Cambridge; clerk of the Commons 1732–48; M.P. for Eye 1748–58. Sedgwick, II, 108–9.

In the first Session of this Parliament it being Uncertain whether Peace or War was to be the fate of England, they again declined this proposal. But this Session the face of things being altered, there being the appearance of Peace, the Dissenters had several Meetings to consult Methods to persue to it. The Select Committee of Dissenters appointed by the General Meeting who were made tractable to Sir Robert's Commands were for dropping it, But the General Meeting determined to the Contrary.[66]}

March 12. Mr Walter Plumer moved for the repeal of the Test Act and was Seconded by Sir Wilfrid Lawson. Sir Robert Walpole giving an opposition to it, most of his Creatures though in their Hearts for it voted against the repeal, arguing that this was not a proper time (the meaning of which was that it might distress Sir Roberts administration) and many of them in their speeches reflected on the Church Establishment. It was said that the Dissenters were encouraged to this by a promise from Sir Robert by which He engaged them in his Intrest in the Elections, and now failed to serve them. On the Division it was carried.

	Yeas	123.	Noes	251.
Tellers	Sir Wilfrid Lawson		Sir J. Cotton	
	Mr Walter Plumer		Mr Watkin Williams	

Quakers Tyth Bill

March 17. Mr Glanville presented a Bill for the more easy recovery of Small Tythes etc. from the people called Quakers.[67] Though this was the Specious Title yet the Intent of the Bill was to exempt them from the payment by putting the Recovery of Tyths under the Jurisdiction of the Justices of Peace and taking them out of the Power of the Ecc<l>esiastical Courts.

See the Several Petitions of the Clergy against it.[68]

The Province of Canterbury and York heard by their Council against the Bill.[69]

Law of Tyths before the Conquest. See Bracton.[70]

Tyths paid in England several hundred years before their were any Quakers.

Statutes since the Reformation relating to Tythes 27: H<en>. 8: and Edw. 6:

1: of William and Mary confirm Ecclesiastical Jurisdiction. By this Bill Tyth<es> in kind are taken away. The Justice of Peace is <to> set the Price, the Clergy are to take at one price and to buy the same at another. Evidence taken away. The Courts can compel Persons to give Evidence the Justices cannot. When New Rights are created they may be subjected to New Laws. It is contrary to Liberty to subject ancient property to New Jurisdiction. See the Act of Toleration[71] relating to Tyths that they

---

[66] On 26 Mar. 1735 a meeting of the Dissenting Deputies resolved to push for the repeal of the Test and Corporation Acts in the next session of parliament. There followed various meetings of both the Deputies and a committee chaired by Samuel Holden. On 14 Jan. 1736 Holden and the committee warned the Deputies that Walpole was opposed to the attempt and advised them not to press the issue. Nonetheless, the Deputies resolved to make an 'early and vigorous application to Parliament', a decision they re-iterated at another meeting on 25 Feb. N.C. Hunt, *Two Early Political Associations. The Quakers and the Dissenting Deputies in the Age of Sir Robert Walpole* (Oxford, 1961), pp. 146–52.

[67] Printed in Lambert, VII, 259–66.

[68] *C.J.*, XXII, 655 (26 Mar.), 657, 659 (29 Mar.), 660 (30 Mar.), 666 (31 Mar.), 670 (2 Apr.), 671 (5 Apr.), 673 (6 Apr.), 700 (3 May).

[69] On 12 Apr., the day of the 2nd reading. *Ibid.*, p. 683.

[70] *De Legibus et Consuetudinibus Angliae.*

[71] Toleration Act (1 Will. & Mar., c. 18), clause 4 referred to tithes. *Statutes of the Realm*, VI, 74.

may be recovered in the Ecclesiastical Courts. Bill for recovery of Small Tyth 3 years before the Legislature.[72]

April 12. Division on the Committment of the Bill.

> Yes   221.   Noes   84.

April 21. Division in the Committee to leave the Chair. (Colonel Bladen Chairman)

> Yeas   88.   Noes   194.

April 30. The Bill reported, which was entirely altered from that brought in. Objection to its being Engrossed it being a New bill. Let the Report lye to be considered as the Bill for the Recovery of Small Debts in the City of London did,[73] or let it be printed that the Clergy may see it and be heard by Council if they think fit. Neither of these granted.

Sir John St Aubin spoke very strongly against the Bill. See his Speech in the Gent<leman's> Magazine.[74]

That the Bill be engrossed.

> Yeas   160.   Noes   60.
>
>   Tellers
> Sir Thomas Aston   Sir J. St Aubin
> Mr Tracey   Mr Hay

May 3. That the Bill do Pass.

> Yeas   164.   Noes   48.

Note all the discontented Whigs joined with the Court and the Promoters of this Bill.

When the Bill came into the House of Lords[75] the Clergy were again heard by their Council against it. And Lord Chancellor Talbot and Lord Hardwick both spoke against the Bill with great Strentgh of reason.

Question for Committment. May 12, 1736.

> Contents   35
> Not Contents   54

The Bill was rejected.

March 31. Debate on the Place Bill.

>   Question for Committment
> Yeas   177.   Noes   224.

29 March. Sir Joseph Jekyll Master of the Rolls presented a Bill for laying a Duty upon the Retailers of Spirituous Liquors (commonly called the Gin Bill). The practice of drinking this pernicious Liquor was got to so great an excess among the common People, that it occasioned the greatest vilanies and immorlaties, and destroyed their

---

[72] Act for the More Easy Recovery of Small Tithes of 1695. 7 & 8 Will. III, c. 6.
[73] See Hay journal, p. 140.
[74] *Gentleman's Magazine*, VI (July 1736), 365–7. Hay also spoke against it, see journal pp. 141–4.
[75] Printed in Torrington, vol. 1734–8, pp. 187–94.

Health. This made Gentlemen concur in the passing of this Bill though there were several hard and wrong things in it. The Court came into it as it greatly encreased the Civil List. By this Act 20s per Gallon is laid on all Spirituous Liquors sold by Retail, and £50 for a Licence. The Penalties levived by the Middlesex Justices on those who sold in less quantities than <two>[76] Gallons came to a vast Sum of Money.

Scarborough Election.

April 21. Scarborough Election heard. Lord Dupplin voted not duly Elected. Mr Osbaldeston duly elected. Right of Election determined to be in the Common Council consisting of two Bailiffs, two Coroners, four Chamberlains and 36 Burgesses *only.* The ancient Right was in the Commonalty at large.

Return in primo Edw 6th Intra facta in plenam Car inter Ballios Burgenses et Communitatem Villae de Scarborough.

The same 7 Edw 6ti.

The same 1mo et 2da Phil et Mariae. 14o Eliz et 28: Eliz:

It is uncertain whether this Borough is by Grant or Prescription, but supposed to be by Charter of Henry 1st. The Constitution of it is very extraordinary For the Common Council being the Capital Body dissolves itself every Michelmas and then re<e>lects itself.

29 April. Address to congratulate the Prince of Wales Marriage.[77] The same Day A Bill to *exhibit* a Bill for Naturalizing the Princess of Wales presented read a first and 2d time, ordered to be Ingrossed, without being Committed, read a 3d time and passed.[78]

May 5. Commons agree to the Lords Amendments to the Bridge Bill, in which it was argued that the Privilege of the House was concerned. See the Journal and Votes.[79] This Bridge was so favourite a job that it must pass notwithstanding any reasons to the Contrary.

11 May. A Petition of Mr Halsey was presented Complaining of an undue Election for the County of Hertford. Note this was presented upon a Certificate from the Crown office That Mr Caesar was returned and before Mr Caesar was sworn or took his Place.[80]

20 May. King came to the House and Prorogued the Parliament. Sessions ended.

---

[76] Here EH left a gap. See 24 Feb. 1736, p. 14.

[77] See *C.J.*, XXII, 697.

[78] It received the royal assent on 5 May.

[79] See *C.J.*, XXII, 705–6, and *Votes* (1735–6), p. 339, which refer back to the Journals for 19 May 1662 on proceedings upon a conference on the amendments made by the Lords to a Bill for Highways. See also p. 145 below.

[80] See *C.J.*, XXII, 712; Sedgwick, I, 260–1.

Third Session.

The Parliament did not meet till the first of February 1736/37 for the King had staid late in the year at Hannover, and lay Wind bound at Helveotslyoys 5 weeks, and in attempting to come over had like to have been cast away. He did not land till January 14 and not being well afterwards the Parliament was opened February 1 by Commission, when Lord Chancellor Talbot delivered the Speech.

The Address was moved by Mr Tracey member for Tewksbury and 2d by Mr Henry Fox, passed without a Division though not Nem. Con. Mem. This Address was not presented by the whole House but by such Members as were Privy Counsellors.

10 February. 10000 Men voted for Sea Service.[81]
    £219201: 06: 05: voted for the Ordinary of the Navy.

21 February. 17704 Land Forces Votes.
    £647549: 11: 03: ½ voted to difray the Charges of the Land Forces.

Motion for a Settlement on the Prince of Wales

{When this Motion came on Sir R. Walpole told Mr Watkin Williams that if He or Mr Shippen would vote against it and bring over some of the Torys to do the same, He would get £20000 to be given to Lady Derwentwater[82] which He refused to do, and told Sir R. Walpole that though He should be very glad that poor Lady might have something out of Her Husbands forfeited Estate, yet He could neither apply for Her or anyone else in so mean a manner.}

February 22, 1736/37. Mr Pulteney moved an Address to the King to settle <£>100000 per annum out of the Civil List on the Prince of Wales. In his argument for it He insisted That it was the Right and Power of Parliament to Grant, to Appropriate and to Resume Money even from the Throne.

Renumerated the Settlements made upon the Several Princes of Wales from Edward Black Prince, who had Acquitan and Cornwall besides.

Henry the 4th Settlement on Henry the 5th. See Cooks Report the Princes Case.[83]

Henry the 7th a Prince Covetous and jealous of his Son yet settled <£>5000 per annum as a jointure on the Princess.

Prince Charles, Duke of York who had granted to Him by King Charles 2d <£>100000. Settlement on the Prince and Princess of Denmark. On the Present King when Prince.

He mentioned the several Civil List Revenues.

Produced an Original Paper in Lord Chancellor Clarendons Hand by which it appeared that the Publick Revenue Civil and Military in King Charles the 2ds reign was but <£>850000 per annum.

King James the 2d Revenue and the Oeconomy of his Reign may be seen in the Journals 1688.

---

81 For detailed accounts see *C.J.*, XXII, 732–7.
82 There was no such person in 1737. The wife of the last earl of Derwentwater (attainted and executed in 1716) had died in 1723. Derwentwater's brother, Charles Radclyffe, who illegally styled himself earl of Derwentwater, was married to a Scottish peeress in her own right, the countess of Newburgh (d. 1755).
83 The 8th part of the *Reports* of Sir Edward Coke.

King William had no Established Civil List till 1698: at first it was only granted from year to year was afterwards (in 1698) made up <£>600000. Out of which was the Settlement on the Prince and Princess of Denmark; also £100000 to Duke of Schombergh, which was afterwards changed to <£>5000 per annum to the Post office, also <£>15000 to the French Protestants.

The whole Civil List Revenue of Queen Anne though granted for £600000 did not produce communibus Annis <£>590000 at a Medium. Out of which she gave above <£>700000 at different times.

The late King had £800000 per annum.

The Present King has £800000 clear and the Parliament to make good Deficiences, upon which pretence in the year <1729>[84] the Parliament granted Him <£>115000. The Parliament also gave £80000 on the Princess of Oranges Marriage, and it is reckoned that £70000 per annum will be an addition to the Revenue by the Gin Act. He then mentioned the Sums that have been lavished away, and a List that was laid before the House of 2 Millions given for Secret Service to unknown persons from March 1721 to March 1725.

That in the whole reign of Queen Anne there were but two Sums but what were publickly accounted for. And these were well known. The One Sum <£>1500 was to entertain Prince Eugene, the other <£>1000 given to Prince George of Denmark.

Sir John Barnard One of the Members for the City of London Seconded the Question.

Sir Robert Walpole spoke against it.

The Power of the House is only at the *time* of Appropriation.

No Grant of Money appropriated without a recommendation from the King. This would be a Grant in despight of the King.

He made a long Pathetick Speech to move the Passions upon what might be the consequences of an entire Breach between Father and Son. It is a Wound but hoped not immedicable Vulnus esse irecidendam. (He pretended almost to shed tears though as soon as He had carried his Question and the whole was over He turned the Affair into ridicule.)

Sir R. Walpole enumerated the present Expence of the Kings Family

	<£>150000 per annum
To the Prince of Wales	<£>50000
To the Duke of Cumberland	<£>8000
To the Princess of Orange	<£>5000
To the 2 eldest Princesses	<£>5300
To the two youngest	<£>2000

Medium of the Kings Household Expenses

In Queen Annes Reign	<£>83000
In King George the first	<£>86000
In the present Kings	<£>121000

The Expence of the Prince of Oranges Wedding was <£>50000. The same will be for the Prince of Wales.

Dutchy of Cornwall brings in	<£>60000 per annum
Principality of Wales but	£1100 per annum.

---

[84] Here EH left a gap. See J.H. Plumb, *Sir Robert Walpole* (2 vols., 1956–60), I, 201.

Sir Robert then delivered a Message to the House from the King in the Middle of his Speech, which was thought to be very unparliamentary but more so that this Message was printed in the Votes. See the Votes February 22.

Mr Hedges Treasurer to the Prince said That from what his Highness had informed Him, the Answer of the Prince was different from what was inserted in the Message. That the Prince upon recollection had reduced the Message and his Answer into Writing that it was something to this effect (as far as I remember or could take Mr Hedges Words) The King will settle <£>50000 per annum on his Highness provided He will hinder any undutifull application to Parliament. That the Prince answered. After expressing Duty etc. to the King. He was sorry He could not obey his Majestys Commands since his Servants were not to move the Address, that if the same allowance was settled on him, as his Majesty enjoyed when Prince of Wales it might prevent any application to Parliament. The Affair is in other Hands I am sorry for it. Mr Hedges also mentioned that the Prince said to the Lord Chancellor That He had formerly given his Lordship a Letter to deliver to the Queen to desire she would interceed with the King for a Settlement, but receiving no answer to that Letter it deterred Him from making any further application.

Mr Hedges said the Princes yearly Expenses were £63000 per annum.

Those who spoke For the Question were

    Mr Pulteney
    Sir J. Barnard
    Lord Baltimore Lord of the Bed Chamber to the Prince
    Mr Herbert of Oakley Park. Treasurer to the Prince.
    Mr John Pit
    Sir William Windham

Mr Philips Gybbon	Sir John Rushout
Mr Littleton	Mr Harry Bathurst
Mr Walter Plumer	Mr Noel
Sir Wilfrid Lawson	Sir Thomas Saunderson
Mr Grenville	Mr Frederick
Mr Bootle	Mr Hedges

Those who spoke Against the Question
    Master of the Rolls Sir Joseph Jekyll
    Sir Robert Walpole first Minister
    Mr Pelham Paymaster of the Army
    Mr Strange Sollicitor General
    Sir W. Yonge Secretary at War
    Mr Joseph Danvers a dull Joker.

	Yeas	204.	Noes	234.
Tellers	Mr Pulteney		Mr Horace Walpole	
	Sir J. Rushout		Mr Edgecumbe	

When this Question was Debated in the House of Lords the Division was.

	Contents		Not Contents	
	28		79	
Proxies	12	Proxies	24	
	40		103	

See the Lords Protest.[85]

---

[85] The division was on 25 Feb. 1737. *L.J.*, XXV, 31–2.

It is to be remarked that when the Duke of Newcastle delivered the same Message to the Lords which Sir Robert Walpole had done in the House of Commons, no Notice whatsoever was taken of the difference between the Princes answer as Mr Hedges had reported it and the Message, nor did any of the Princes freinds in the House of Lords offer any thing in contradiction to the Message and Answer as delivered by the Duke of Newcastle.

{Note the Princess of Wales was brought to Bed of a Princess August 1, 1737. September 10: the King sends a Message to the Prince to leave St James. See all the Letters and Messages on this Occasion at the end of my Volume of Votes for the year 1737.}

Weobley Election.

3 March 1736. Report from the Committee touching the Election of Weobley. Right of Election resolved to be in the Inhabitants of the ancient Vote-Houses of 20s per annum Value and upwards residing in the said Houses 40 Days before the Election and paying Scot and Lot and also in the Owners of such Ancient Vote-Houses paying Scot and Lot, who shall be resident in such Houses at the time of the Election. Serjeant Birch Resolved not to be duly elected and Captain Cornewall to be duly elected.[86] Note Birch was dead when this Matter came to be heard, and therefore no one defended his Right, and Cornewall made a Compromise with Mansel Powell who had bought Several Houses in this Borough with old Barneslys Money,[87] to agree to this Right of Election which would fix the Borough for the future in the Interest of Powell, if Powell would not defend Birchs right, who could have been proved to have been duly elected, Had a Defense been made for Him.

4 March 1736. Petition of the Iron Masters against the slitting Mills and Manufacturing of Iron in the Plantations.

March 7. Petition in defense of the Plantations.
See the Several Accounts and Papers relating to Iron laid before the house. 25 March etc. and 25 April 1737.[88]

15 March 1736. A Petition of Richard Aston Esqe presented to the House the purport and design of which was to oblige Oriel College in Oxford to renew their Lease with Him. The Motion for referring it to a Committee passed in the Negative. Yeas 101. Noes 119. See the Journal or Votes where Petitions of the like unreasonable nature are inserted.[89]

---

[86] The election had been on 30 Apr. 1734, when Cornewall had come bottom of the poll with 37 votes. John Birch had died on 6 Oct. 1735. Sedgwick, I, 259–60, 462.

[87] William Barnsley of Eardisley Park, Herefordshire, had died at the end of Mar. 1736. Mansel Powell (latter M.P. for Weobley, see Appendix), his attorney, acquired Barnsley's property in 1738 by a forged will disinheriting the only son. See *ibid.*, II, 364; and for the details of the 1749 case by which the property was restored to the son, see the *Gentleman's Magazine*, XX (1750), 364–8. If Harley wrote this section of his journal at the time of the events described, Powell must have been fraudulently purchasing houses at Weobley before Barnsley's death or before he acquired the property. According to the *Gentleman's Magazine*, p. 365, Powell had 'been concerned for the old gentleman in many purchases, mortgages, &c'.

[88] *C.J.*, XXII, 824, 862.

[89] *Ibid.*, pp. 801–2; *Votes* (vol. for 3rd session of 8th parliament of George II), pp. 121–4.

17 March. A Bill to make perpetual an act made in the 7th year of George 2di to prevent the Infamous Practice of Stockjobbing passed Nem: Con:

24 March. Flint Election heard at Bar. Several Witnesses having proved illegal Practices of the Returning officer at the Time and taking and closing the Poll A Motion was made that the Counsel for the sitting Member be directed to proceed in order to justify the Return before the Merits of the Election are proceeded upon. But as the Returning officer could not be justifyed, the Court resolving to skreen would involve the Return with the Merits and therefore put an negative on the Question.

{In a Committee of the whole House March 28 to consider of the National Debt Sir John Barnard proposed reducing <24>[90] Millions of the National Debt on the South Sea Annuities to 3 per Cent. (See Sir J. Barnards printed Reasons which He gave to the Members.[91]) After a Long Debate, Sir R. Walpole finding fault with Barnards Scheme proposed the Resolutions as they stand in the Votes March 30 of reducing *All* the Funds carrying 4 per cent to 3.

Yet when these Resolutions were reported March 30 Sir Robert proposed the adjournment of the Report for a fortnight, and when a Bill was ordered to be brought in Sir Robert desired the Speaker that neither He nor any of his Freinds might be named to bring it in.}

30 March 1737. Sir John Barnards proposal of reducing the Debts to 3 per Cent which Sir R. Walpole agreed to in the Committee, but when this Resolution came to be reported to the House, Sir Robert being affraid of his Freinds in the City appeared against it and Voted for an adjournment of the Report. Which was carried against Him. Yeas 157. Noes 220. Soon after a Motion was made That this House as soon as the Debt is reduced to 3 per Cent will take off some of the Heavy Taxes which oppress the Poor and the Manufactures. It passed in the Negative.

Tellers	Lord Morpeth	Yeas	Lord Vere Beauclerk	Noes
	Mr E. Harley	142	Mr Edgecumbe	200

When the Bill for 3 per Cent was ordered in Sir R. Walpole would not let any of his Freinds be named to bring it in. And 29 April when the Question was put for the Commitment of the Bill it passed in the Negative.

Yeas 134. Noes 249.

Affair of Captain Porteous.

In April 1736 One Andrew Wilson was executed at Edinburgh. Captain John Porteous commanded the City Guard, and there being a Crowd to see the Execution Porteous ordered the Guard to fire upon the People, which they did but over their Heads so that no one was hurt. This angered Porteous upon which He fired his own peice and killed a man. For this He was tried the July following and condemned. But was more than once repreived by Queen Caroline who was then Regent. The People being enraged by this Repreive and imagining that a Pardon was to be sent, A great

---

[90] Here EH left a gap. The figure is from Barnard's speech in Cobbett, X, 74–93 (figure in col. 86). For the full debate see *ibid.*, 73–154.

[91] *A Proposal Towards Lowering the Interest of all the Redeemable National Debts, to 3 per cent per annum. And Thereby to Enable the Parliament to give Immediate Ease to His Majesty's Subjects, by Taking off some of the Taxes which are most Burthensome to the Poor, and Especially to the Manufactures* (1737).

number of them forced open the Prison doors took Porteous out and hanged Him on a Sign Post near the place where He shot the Man. This extraordinary affair was conducted in such a regular manner that though the Mob had secured the Guard and were Masters of the City yet no manner of Hurt was done to any other person, and as soon as they had hanged Porteous the whole Body was dispersed and the City was as quiet as if nothing had happned. And none of the persons concerned were discovered.

Notice was taken of this Riot and Murder by many Lords in their Speeches the first day of the Session. And they ordered the Provost of Edingburgh Mr Andrew Wilson to attend whom they committed, and *ordered in a Bill* to disable the said Andrew Wilson from holding or enjoying any office in Great Britain and for imprisoning Him, and for abolishing the City Guard, and for taking away the Gates of the Netherbow port, and keeping open the same. {It is unusual for a Bill of this kind to begin with the Lords. They by the Constitution are the Judges the Supreme Court of Judicature, the Commons are the Grand Inquest.} The Provost petitioned to be heard by Council against the Bill, before this came on. There was a Debate in the House of Lords in a Motion for Declaring Porteous Trial erroneous, but at lentgh the Motion was dropped without a Question.

The Lords having ordered the Scotch Judges to attend to be examined, when they came a Debate arose whether they should be examined at the Bar or on the Wool-Sacks. And for the greater Freedom of Debate and to Search Precedents on this Subject, the Lords resolved themselves into a Committee where it was carried that the Scotch Judges should be examined at the Bar 48: to 37: When this Resolution was reported after some little Debate it was carried in the Affirmative.[92]

Contents		Not Contents	
In the House	47	In the House	36
Proxies	16	Proxies	15
	63		51

After this the Scotch Judges were called in and appeared at the Bar in their Robes.

The Provost and City of Edingburgh were heard by their Council against the Bill upon the 2d reading.

May 13. It was read a 3d time and passed on a Division 54 Contents 22 Not Contents.

May 16. The Bill was sent to the Commons where after some Debate it was read a first time, and ordered to be read a 2d.

A Conference desired with the Lords that the Grounds upon which the said Bill proceeded in the House of Lords may be communicated to the House. See these proceedings at the Conference.[93]

The Provost and City petition to be heard by Council against the Bill at the 2d reading

June 1. Council was heard for and against the Bill which Hearing and Examination of the Witnesses held a Week.

The Question for Commitment June 9 Occasioned a very long Debate. Which was agreed to on a Division. Yeas 124. Noes 118.

---

[92] On 2 May 1737.
[93] The conference was held on 17 and 18 May. *C.J.*, XXII, 885, 887; *L.J.*, XXV, 121, 123.

June 13. The House resolved itself into a Committee upon the Bill, where the Preamble and every Clause was opposed and Debated with so much strentgh, that the Bill not only changed its name, but its form, as may be seen by comparing the Bill sent from the Lords and that which passed.[94]

In the Committee the Bill was near being quite lost, for after all the Amendments were made, the Bill appeared so very different from that which came from the Lords, that the Question for reporting the Bill with the Amendments was very strenuously opposed, and after a long Debate, the Division was 130 for Reporting 130 against it, when Colonel Bladen the Chairman gave the Casting Vote in favour of the Bill, though it has been generally observed that in such Cases, the Chairman has given his Vote for that side of the Question which <is> against any Alteration of our Laws or in favour of any Person that is to suffer by a new Law.

The Report made the next Day. A Debate upon the clause for imposing a Fine on the City of Edingburgh. Motion to recommit the Amendment Yeas 123. No 144.

June 15. The Bill read a 3d time and many amendments made to the Title. That the Bill do pass.

       Yeas   128.   Noes   101.

{An Act likewise passed for the more effectual bringing to Justice the Persons concerned in the Murther of Captain Porteous and punishing such as shall knowingly conceal any of the said offenders.}

The Fine laid on the City of Edingburgh was £2000, which was applied to Porteous Widow. [Note she was a low mean Woman had formerly been a Cook, and had as it was said behaved so ill to Her Husband that they had been for some time parted.]

The Riot at Edingburgh and the Murder of Porteous happening during the Regency of the Queen who had sent the Repreive to Scotland. Lord Hardwick the Chancellor to make his Complement to the Queen first stirred up this Publick Inquiry, and was the Occasion of his exerting himself so warmly for the Bill against the Provost and City of Edingburgh. Those who are called the Patriots in both Houses espoused the Bill, not only that they might gain another Precedent for this arbitrary Method of Proceeding by Bills in Parliament, but in hopes to ruin Sir R. Walpole with the Scotch.

The Ministry at first neglected it, but afterwards joined in it to keep the Parliament sitting to prevent the King from going abroad again. Though the Bill which came from the Lords was entirely altered by the Commons, yet those very Lords who had been concerned in drawing and carrying this Bill through their House, agreed quietly to all the Amendments made by the Commons.

May 20. A Bill brought in which subjected all Plays to be acted on the Stage to the Examination of the Lord Chamberlain. By this means several good plays were suppressed and dull ones Licensed. Passed June 1.[95]

---

[94] The Lords' bill is printed in Torrington, vol. 1734–8, pp. 209–12; the act (10 Geo. II, c. 34) can be found in *Statutes at Large from 9th to 15th Year of King George II* [vol. xvii], ed. D. Pickering (1765), pp. 166–7. The differences were that the bill imprisoned Wilson, while the act did not; the bill abolished the Edinburgh Town Guard and took away the gates of the Nether-Bow Port, while the act did not; and the act imposed a fine on the city, while the bill had not.

[95] Received the royal assent, 21 June.

May 24. A Bill ordered to enable the King to settle £50,000 per annum on the Princess of Wales as a jointure during the *Term of Her Life*. Passed June 2.[96]

June 10. A Report was made from the Committee to whom the Petition of the Inhabitants of Several Parishes in Middlesex was referred, which Petition complained of abuses and frauds in levying and collecting the County Rates. Upon the Examination before the Committee it appeared that the Petition was malicious and had been contrived and carried on by Thomas Robe a Middlesex Justice against his Brethren out of picque because they had opposed his being chose Clerk of some of the Markets. The House voted the Petition vexatious Scandalous and malicious and ordered Robe and one Stephen Lebas into Custody. The Report printed. See the same.[97]

June 21, 1737. The Session Ended.

[96] Also received the royal assent, 21 June.
[97] Printed in Lambert, XIV, 171–322.

Fourth Session.

January 24, 1737/8. The Parliament met.

February 3. Debate on the Army in the Committee. 18000 Men proposed. Lesser number of 1200<0> moved for. Upon this Question the Committee divided.

	Yeas	166.	Noes	249.
Tellers	Mr William Pit		Colonel Mordaunt	

18000 Men Voted.

February 16. £4000 voted for the Repairs of Westminster Abbey. Yeas 174. Noes 61.

February 17. Committee of Ways and Means

Supply voted for 1738	<£>2,222 000

Means	
Land Tax at 2s	<£>1,000,000
Malt	<£>750 000
Sinking Fund	<£>500 000
	<£>2 250 000

Sir R. Walpole. One Million of Debt to be paid off to the Bank.

Sinking Fund yeilded last Year	<£>1,300 000
Bounty on Corn last year	<£>132 000
Duty on Tea encreased since the Smugglers	
Act passed which is about 18 months	<£>80 000

69000 pound weight of Tea condemned since the Act. And 4890 Houses for Tea entered.

February 20. The Speaker ill House adjourned to Thursday.

Thursday February 23. House met, The Speaker continuing ill adjourned to March 1.

March 1. Speaker attended, the House sat to do business.

March 3. A Petition of the Merchants complaining of the Spanish Depredations[98] presented desiring to be heard by themselves *and* Council. [And] being contrary to the Forms of the House, was altered to *Or* in the Motion for Hearing the Merchants, which was appointed for Thursday the 16th.

Motion for the Memorials etc. sent to the Court of Spain with the *Answers* thereto. Sir R. Walpole said the last answer from Spain came on Saturday and was unsatisfactory, yet not proper to lay it at this time before the House, because it might irritate and put things past retreive.

The Question was whether these Words *and of the answers which have been given or received to the Memorials Representations and Letters* stand part of the Question.

---

[98] Since the granting of restricted British trade with the Spanish colonies in 1713 (see below, p. 36, n. 118), there had been a growing illicit trade, which the Spanish tried to curb by increasing their coastguards. After a lull in such Spanish activities in the early 1730s, these 'depredations' on British trade had been renewed in 1737.

	Yeas	99.	Noes	164.
Tellers	Mr Sandys		Mr Winnington	
	Mr Littleton		Mr Tracey	

Note This last answer of Spain with a Draft of a Letter from Mr Keene the Minister at Madrid[99] given in answer to it was laid before the house March 24.[100]

March 7. Petition for <£>2000 for the further repair of St Margarets Church rejected.

| | Yeas | 131. | Noes | 141. |

March 8. Petition from the Earl of Kintore for the Securing the Succession of his Honours and Estate in case He and his Brother die without Issue; Earl Marshall being in the Remainder who was attainted.[101] A Motion was made that a Bill be brought in according to the Prayer of the Petition, This the Court opposed under pretence that it was giving too much encouragement to those who had been in the Rebellion in 1715. But the true reason was, in Case of Lord Kintores and his Brothers Death the Honour and Estate might descend to General Keith Earl Marshalls Brother who was not attainted, and who is in the Service and in great Esteem at the Court of Russia[102] and who had not asked the favour of the Ministry, and to bring Him to sollicite it of them and thereby lay an obligation on Him. Sir R. Walpole divided for the Bill because He pretended it might be limited afterwards. His Creatures voted against it. Yeas 158. Noes 155.

March 13, 1737/38. An Ingrossed Bill from the Lords. Entituled an Act for exemplifying the last Will of Arthur Earl of Anglesey and making the same Evidence in all Courts of Law and Equity in Great Britain and Ireland was read a 2d time and Council heard against it. The Intent of the Bill was not to establish or make good the Will or to preclude any person instersted <sic> from contesting the validity of it, but as part of the Estate lay in Ireland to make the Exemplification Evidence, it being hazardous to carry the Original Backward and Forward cross the Sea. No opposition was made to it in the House of Lords and Lord Chancellor was so clear in his opinion that no one could be hurt or prejudiced by it That the Lords rejected Lord Angleseys Petition which was afterwards received by the Commons,[103] where a party opposition was stirred up out of private picque of some Persons to Frank Annesley to whom my Lord had given his Estate. Therefore on the Question for Passing the Bill The House divided Yeas 101. Noes 140.[104]

March 16. Standing Order relating to Keeping Places in the House renewed.[105]
    Clause in the Land Tax Bill to exempt the Parish of St Marys in Oxford from paying that part of the Tax chargeable on the Houses pulled Down for the Building Dr Radcliffes Library. Opposed by Hucks, White, Laroche and the Georgians.[106]

---

[99] Benjamin Keene (1697–1757), minister plenipotentiary to Spain 1727–34, envoy extraordinary 1734–9.
[100] For the list of correspondence, though the contents are not given, see *C.J.*, XXII, 125.
[101] For details see *ibid.*, pp. 70–1.
[102] James Francis Edward Keith (1696–1758), lt.-gen. of the Empress Anna's bodyguard.
[103] *C.J.*, XXII, 87.
[104] On 27 Apr. 1738. *Ibid.*, pp. 165–6.
[105] See *ibid.*, p. 97.
[106] See p. 19 above.

March 27. Double Return for New Windsor Heard at Bar when Lord Vere Beauclerk was voted duly returned Yeas 240. Noes 160. The other Gentleman returned was Mr Oldfeild. At the Election upon closing the Poll they had each an equall Number though the Mayor was Lord Veres freind and had struck of many Votes of Oldfeild for whom an undoubted Majority appeared upon the Hearing.[107]

Upon the Division the *Yeas went forth*, for as it was a double Return they are both Esteemed as Petitioners and withdraw after taking the Oaths and therefore the *Yeas* are to go out to bring the Member in.

See the same in Mr Bromleys Parliament, 16 December 1710: Borough of Devizes.[108]

March 28. The Hearing of the West India Merchants which had been several Days before the House Ended. When Mr Murray[109] the only Counsel had summed up the Evidence, Mr Pulteney offered Several Resolutions asserting our particular rights by Treaties and stating the Facts and cruelties exercised by the Spaniards to the Merchants Ships and Sailors. Sir Robert Walpole against particularising our rights and moved a more general Question.

The Question on which the Committee divided was whether part of Mr Pulteneys first Resolution should stand. (See these Resolutions among my Votes)[110] Yeas 209. Noes 256. Afterwards Sir R. Walpole moved his Question as it is printed in the Votes.

Report of the Affair of the West India Merchants.[111] Motion for Recommitment of the Resolutions.

Tellers	Yeas		Tellers	Noes
Sir W. Wyndham			Mr Pelham	
Mr Sandys	163		Mr Edgecumb	224

April 12. Complaint that several Members Hands were forged in the Franks on several Letters. Several persons taken in Custody others sent to Newgate.

April 14. Debate in the Committee of the whole House upon the Bill for explaining an Act for the Application of the Rents and Profitts of Lord Derwentwaters Estate.[112] The outward Pretence for this Bill was to sell part of the Estate to clear off the Mortgage upon it. The private Intent was a Job for Colonel Lyddell[113] for it was intended to sell that part of the Estate upon which were Mines and Woods and Lands capable of great Improvement, and not that part which was fully improved. The Debate run upon this and the Right that Mr Radcliffes[114] two Children had to the Estate this last was argued and insisted upon very strongly by Mr Fazakerley. Division in the Committee.

Yeas   97.   Noes   42.

---

[107] Beauclerk and Richard Oldfield, who had been supported by the duke and dowager duchess of Marlborough, had each polled 133 votes. Sedgwick, I, 193.

[108] *C.J.*, XVI, 436.

[109] William Murray. See Appendix.

[110] *Votes* (of 4th session of 8th parliament), no. 42, pp. 196–7, gives a long resolution on the rights of the British to sail in South American waters, which was reported to the House on 30 Mar. *C.J.*, XXIII, 133–4.

[111] On 30 Mar. *C.J.*, XXIII, 133–4.

[112] Bill printed in Lambert, VII, 359–66; it received the royal assent, 20 May. The act referred to was 8 Geo. II, c. 29.

[113] George Liddell. See Appendix and Sedgwick, II, 216.

[114] Probably Charles Radclyffe (1693–1746). Brother of the last earl of Derwentwater, he had illegally assumed the title in 1731, and was executed for his part in the '45 Rebellion.

April 17. For Ingrossing the Bill 131. Noes 85.

April 18. A Petition complaining of a Combination in raising the Price of Coals. Debate whether a Bill should be brought in, or the Petition be referred to a Committee to examine the allegations of it.

Question to refer the Petition Yeas 158. Noes 134.[115]

April 20. House adjourned to Monday the Speaker being ill.

April 26. Bill for explaining the Gin Act reported.[116] An objection was made to a Clause after one of the amendments was agreed to. A Debate arose upon the Point of Order, whether a Clause could be disagreed to upon the Report when the House had agreed to the Amendments made by the Committee to that Clause. It was agreed by the Speaker and the House that it was contrary to all former Proceedings to do it.

The right Method is to disagree to all the Amendments and then leave out the Clause, or *otherwise* to leave out the Clause on the 3d reading. If the House agree to the amendments of the Committee on the Report, and then reject the Clause; They would agree and disagree to the same thing in the same debate.

Preamble to a Clause in this Bill transposed.

April 27. Dartford Turnpike Bill reported in which was a Money Qualification for the Commissioners. Yeas 46. Noes 40.

May 2. Resolutions relating to the Iron Manufactory. The Contest between the Iron Masters in England and those in the Plantations.

May 15. A Bill for the more effectual securing and Encouraging the Trade to America brought in by Mr Pulteney read a 3d time. Question That it pass

Tellers	Yeas	Tellers	Noes
Sir W. Wyndham Mr Littleton }	73	Mr Pelham Mr Stephen Fox }	143

The Purport of the Bill was for Encouraging the Sailors by giving them the Prizes they should take if there should be a War with Spain.

May 20. The Session Ended by Prorogation.

---

[115] A bill did emerge from the committee, and it received the royal assent on 20 May.
[116] It also received the royal assent on 20 May.

Fifth Session.

February 1, 1738/39. The Parliament Met.

The Address moved by Mr Hanbury Williams and 2ded by Mr Francis Fane (who was this Session made Chairman of the Committee of Supply and Ways and Means). A Warm Debate against the Address as it approved of the Convention Treaty with Spain.[117]

Yeas   230.   Noes   141.

February 6. Motion for an Address that the Instructions given to the Governours of the Plantations in America, or any Commanders of Ships or Minister in Spain and Consuls since the Treaty of Seville[118] relating to the Spanish Depredations be laid before the House.

Yeas   113.   Noes   183.

February 6. Motion for Copies or Extracts of Memorials or Representations made to the King of Spain or his Ministers relating to the Spanish Depredations.

Yeas   120.   Noes   200.

February 14. Debate on the Army in the Committee of Supply. 18000 Men moved for. Amendment proposed 12000. The Question for the lesser Number put. Yeas 153. Noes 238.

Then the Question for 18000 Men was voted.

February 15. Report of the Army. Question to agree with the Committee.

	Yeas		Noes	
Tellers	Mr Whitworth	129	Mr Bramston	73
	Mr Owen		E. Harley	

February 23. Petition of the City of London against the Convention presented.

Petition of the London Merchants trading to the West Indies against the same.

Motion that they be heard by themselves *or Council* (according to the Prayer of their Petition) That these Words *Or Council* stand part of the Question. House divided. Yeas go out. Yeas 207. Noes 242.

Same Question the same Day on the Petition from the Bristol Merchants. Yeas 208. Noes 237.

February 26. Petition of the Owners of the Ship Sarah Captain Vaughan Master presented against the Spanish Depredations. Question That they be heard by their Council. Yeas 162. Noes 175.

March 1. Debate of the Lords upon the Convention Treaty. An Address of Approbation moved by Lord Cholmondeley. {Note the Prince of Wales Voted against this Address and was the first Vote He ever gave.}

---

[117] The convention of El Pardo, which settled the terms for compensation, sought to end the growing clamour, begun in 1737, for reprisals against Spanish interference with British trade to the Spanish colonies.

[118] Of 1729, when the restricted British trade with the Spanish colonies granted by the 1713 treaty of Utrecht was confirmed.

Contents	71	Not Contents	58
Proxies	24	Proxies	16
	95		74

See the Lords Protest and the List of those who Voted For and Against the Question.[119]

March 8. Debate in the House of Commons in a Committee of the whole House upon the Convention. The fullest House and the longest sitting that has been known of many years. I was in the House 17 hours.

Yeas	260.	Noes	232.

See the printed List.[120]

March 9. The Convention Treaty again debated on the Report. Question to agree to the Report. Yeas go forth.

Yeas	244.	Noes	214.

Mem: Mr Pulteney, Mr Sandys and Sir W. Wyndham declaring in their Speeches that they would withdraw from Parliament, which they and several other Members of the Country Party to the number of <160>[121] and it was styled The Secession,[122] They did not attend Parliament that Session; Many not all, some few for Private buisness of their Boroughs etc. An Idle Project, contrary to all the Rules and Being of Parliament, and not approved of without Doors and in the Country. Which brought these Absenters to Parliament again the next Session.

March 20. Resolutions relating to the Wollen Manufactury reported. And a Bill ordered upon them in which Bill was inserted a Registry of Wool all over the Kingdom within 10 miles of the Sea or Navigable River, this the few Country Gentlemen who continued their Duty in Parliament objected to and threatning to write into their Several Countries for Petitions against it, this part of the Bill was consented to be dropped by those who brought it in.

March 23. An Ingrossed Bill to enable the Inhabitants of St Nicholas in Worcester to raise Money for rebuilding their Parish Church, was read a third time. Resolved. That the Bill do pass Yeas 88. Noes 77. This Bill met with no opposition through the whole Progress of it till the Question for passing was put.[123] When Mr Henry Fox, 2ded by Mr Hanbury Williams, who were supported by Sir William Yonge and Mr Henry Pelham moved to reject the Bill without making any one Objection to the Merits of the Bill, but avowed that they did it out of personall anger to Mr Sandys (who brought

---

[119] Various versions of this division list exist, and some were printed, along with the protests. See Clyve Jones and Frances Harris, '"A Question ... Carried by Bishops, Pensioners, Place-men, Idiots": Sarah, Duchess of Marlborough, and the Lords' Division over the Spanish Convention, 1 March 1739', *Parliamentary History*, XI (1992), 254–77. For the protests see *L.J.*, XXV, 308–9.

[120] This also appeared in several versions. See, e.g., Chandler, XII, Appendix. See also Sedgwick, I, 129–30.

[121] Here EH left a gap. The figure is from H.M.C., *Egmont Diary*, III, 33: 13 Mar. 1739.

[122] See Colley, pp. 224–5.

[123] It received the royal assent, 19 Apr.

this Bill in) as He was one of the Members who had withdrawn their attendance from the House since the Convention, and who had appeared only in the House upon Account of this Worcester Bill. Had They prevailed in their Violence and rejected the Bill, the Innocent and the Constituents would have suffered for a supposed fault of their Member. So Unparliamentary and violent attempt has scarce been known, and Had it succeded nothing could have justify an absense from Parliament so much as this.

March 26. A Petition of Mrs Stephens for a Reward to discover Her Medecine for the Cure of the Stone. Question to refer the Petition to the Committee of Supply Yeas 105. Noes 62. Where £5000 was voted for Mrs Stephens and a Bill was ordered accordingly and passed both Houses.[124]
This Sum would have better become the great Civil List.

March 29. Division on the Commitment of the Carriers Bill. Yeas 48. Noes 22. This was a Contest between the Shoemakers and Carriers who spent a great Sum of Money in it. April 27. That the Bill pass Yeas 78. Noes 58.[125]

March 30. Motion by Mr White a Fanatick[126] and Sir Joseph Eyles to repeal the Test Act. Sir R. Walpole spoke and voted against it. Motion for bringing in the Bill rejected. Yeas 89. Noes 188. Mem: Sir Roberts Speech upon the High Churchmen who were absent at this Question upon account of the Secession.

April 3. A Bill for registring Deeds brought in by Mr Winnington. In the Committee The Person to be appointed Register was to be the Clerk of the Peace. It was proposed He should be choose by Freeholders of £100 per annum. For the Clerk of the Peace. Yeas 65. Noes 40. A bad bill. Passed the House of Commons. Not passed by the Lords who ordered the Judges to prepare a Bill against next Sessions.[127]

May 3. A Message from the King to desire the Parliament would enable Him to grant an Annuity of £15000 per annum to His Son the Duke of Cumberland, and an Annuity of £24000 per annum to the four Princesses to take effect after his Demise. A Bill ordered accordingly.[128]

May 10. A Message from the King for more Money to enable Him to augment his Forces by Sea and Land. Referred to a Committee of Supply where £500000 was voted though no Services were specifyed. This Resolution was reported May 14, when E. Harley divided the House against the Question that it might hereafter be seen on the Journal in how thin a House so great a Sum was voted.

Yeas	141.	Noes	20.

---

[124] See *C.J.*, XXII, 302. The 1st reading of the bill was on 26 Apr. (*ibid.*, p. 340), and it received the royal assent on 14 June.
[125] It received the royal assent, 14 June.
[126] For John White, described as 'a professed Dissenter' and 'no friend to church establishment', see Appendix and Sedgwick, II, 533–4.
[127] See *L.J.*, XXV, 393, 398, 400, 408, 413, 416. In 1740 a bill was brought in and 1st read on 1 Apr., was committed on 16, 21 and 24th, but no further progress made.
[128] It received the royal assent, 14 June.

May 11. Question to recommit the Westminster Bridge Bill so far as it related to the Lottery which Sir J. Barnard shewed to be a Job.

	Yeas	59.[129]	Noes	158.

May 14. Question for passing a Bill for explaining and amending the Ancient Acts of the 8th of Richard the 2d and 33d of Henry act that none shall be Justice of Asize in his own Country.[130] This Bill was brought in by Winnington to enable the Judges to sit on the Crown Side in their own Countys. It was said this was the desire of Chief Justice Willes.[131]

	Yeas	118	Noes	<42>[132]
Tellers	Lord Sidney Beauclerk		Mr John Talbot	
	Dr Lee		Mr E. Harley	

June 14. Sessions Ended. The Parliament prorogued.

---

[129] *C.J.*, XXIII, 359, gives the figure 52.
[130] The statutes were 8 Ric. II, c. 2 and 33 Hen. VIII, c. 24.
[131] Sir John Willes (1685–1761), lord chief justice of the common pleas 1737–61.
[132] Here EH left a gap. The figure is from *C.J.*, XXIII, 361.

Sixth Session.

November 15, 1739. The Parliament met.

War having been proclaimed with Spain,[133] which the Nation expressed so great a desire of and even forced the Ministry into it who would rather have gone on in their old method of making Treaty upon Treaty. No opposition was given to the Address nor to any of the Supplys.

November 21. An Address moved by Mr Pulteney, Sir W. Windham and Mr Sandys etc. to desire his Majesty not to enter into any Treaty with Spain, unless Spain acknowledged our Right to navigate in the American Seas without being searched. This Adddress communicated to the Lords and those called the Patriots of both Houses attended it to Court. See the Kings Answer November 26.[134]

November 26. 35000 Men voted for Sea Service for 1740 at £4 per Man per Month.
28850 Men for Guards and Garrisons.
Charge of the Same £860150: 10s: 4d: ½.
Charge of 6 Regiments of Marines for 1740 comes to <£>118214. 01s: 00:
Besides these and other Expenses. February 7: there was voted £22880: 19s: 2d for defraying the Charge of General and Staff Officers for 1740.
And £34587 on account of reduced officers of Land Forces and Marines.

November 27. A Motion for an Address to his Majesty that He would be pleased to give Directions, that the Body of Marines intended to be raised may be done in the most frugal Manner, by having as many private Men and as few officers as the Nature of the Service will admit etc. Yeas 95. Noes 177.

November 29. Motion for Copies of the Instructions and Letters sent to Mr Keene authorizing Him to conclude the Convention. Passed in the Negative. Yeas 98. Noes 171.

December 18. Motion made for a Call. A Negative put upon it by the Direction of Sir R. Walpole without any Persons speaking against the Question. House Divided Yeas go out.

	Yeas	61	Noes	136
Tellers	Mr Harley		Mr Edgcumbe[135]	
	Mr Carew		Mr Laroche	

The private reason given was to retaliate the affair of the Secession. Which was rather confirming that wrong step than disapproving it, and was saying upon the Journals that the Members should not attend.

The first Instance of a Negative given to a Call. Afterwards <31 January 1740>[136] when Another Call was moved the Question was agreed to, Horace Walpole said in his Speech the first Negative was given out of Joke.

---

133 The famous war of Jenkins's Ear.
134 *C.J.*, XXIII, 390.
135 *Ibid.*, p. 407, gives Mr Treby, i.e. George Treby (?1684–1742), M.P. for Dartmouth 1727–42. Sedgwick, II, 476–7.
136 Here EH left a gap. For the date see *C.J.*, XXIII, 440. The call agreed to was for 21 Feb., when it was then adjourned for a month. *Ibid.*, p. 475.

January 15, 17, 1739/40. Hearing of the Plymouth Election at Bar when by the Resolution of the House the *Freeholders* were excluded from voting contrary to charter and usage, and the Resolution of the House 9th June 1660 explained away by making the Word *Commonalty* extend to Freemen only.[137] Yeas 180. Noes 119. This flings the Borough into the power of the Dock and Navy.

January 29. Motion to bring in a Bill to limit the Number of Officers in the House of Commons moved by Mr Sandys 2ded by Mr Watkin Williams. The Bill was not to exclude all Place men but inferior ones only. Passed in the Negative.

	Yeas		Noes	
Tellers	Mr Sandys }	206.	Mr Winnington }	222.
	Mr E. Harley		Mr Speke	

February 4. Sir R. Walpole proposed in the Committee of Ways and Means to raise £1,200,000 out of the sinking Fund, which was £200,000 more than had been voted in the Committee of Supply. Objections were made to This as being unparliamentary, without precedent and overturning all the Methods of granting Money, for the Services ought first to be voted, and then the Means equall to those Services. Those who objected being unwilling to give a Negative to the Main Question as we are now in War, proposed the Question for leaving the Chair that some expedient might be found. Sir Robert unwilling to consent to this; but just before the Question for leaving the Chair was going to be put, Mr Pulteney proposed it as a point of order and desired that the Speakers opinion whether Money could be granted without a Demand or being asked by the Crown. Sir Robert rather than have the Speaker declare his opinion which must and would have been in this point against Him, said He would only move the Million at this time, if it was understood to grant the £200,000 if the King sent a Message. February 12. The Message was delivered by Sir R. Walpole and referred to the Committee of Supply where the Sum was voted.

February 13. A Report from the Committee who were to consider how far the Privilege of the House ought to be allowed to Members absent in Forreign parts during the sitting of Parliament. This arose upon a Motion of Lord Baltimores and occasioned by Mr Lisle Member for the County of Southampton having as it was suggested withdrawn out of the Kingdom to defraud his Creditors.[138] The Committee sat and after searching the Journals finding no precedent in point came to no Resolution the first day. On the 2d other Members attending than were present at the first they came to a *Resolution* That Privilege should not extend to any Member in forreign parts except those employed by the King.

{The Resolution the Committee came to was this

Resolved

That it is the Opinion of this Committee that such Members of this House who do Absent themselves in Forreign Parts during the sitting of Parliament, save such as shall be employed in his Majestys Service abroad are no ways entitled to the Privilege of this House so as to obstruct any Actions, Suits, Process or Proceedings in any of his Majestys Courts of Justice.

---

[137] *Ibid.*, p. 59.
[138] See Sedgwick, II, 218–19. In 1739 Caecilius Calvert exhibited a bill in chancery claiming Lisle's estate for a debt of £400. Lisle fled to Montpellier. On 28 Feb. 1740 Calvert petitioned the Commons stating that he could not proceed with his bill because of Lisle's parliamentary privilege. Lisle was ordered to attend the house on 13 Mar. when, in his absence, his privileges were suspended until he attended.

Strictly speaking a Member cannot claim Privilege but only during his actual attendance. Therefore if it was taken from those in Forreign parts, the same reason might take it from those who were absent in the Country or else where.}

Upon the Report this Resolution was not read that it might not appear in the Votes till it had passed the Determination of the House. And therefore was ordered to be taken into Consideration on the Fryday following, which was accordingly done. Upon which was a Debate, Sir W. Wyndham, Gybbons, Sandys, Sir William Yonge Winington and the Men of Order were against it, as being too General, and as there was no Precedent, That no particular charge was made against Mr Lisle, nor no proof made of what what <sic> suggested, that if it was true, yet for his fault, innocent person who might be abroad for their Healths, might be deprived of their Privilege. That the most proper way was to have a complaint made against Mr Lisle by Petition from his Creditors. To appoint Him a day to appear in his Place, and if He did not attend, to Suspend Him from Privilege during the time He should absent Himself. (In support of this Mr Cullifords Case as nearest in point was quoted.) {Mr Culliford[139] was a Member of the Irish as well as English Parliament and between the Privilege of both defrauded his Creditors. He being accused of several Misdemeanors was ordered to attend in his Place, and having neglected the same (for He was then in Ireland) is suspended from the Benefit of Privilege till He shall attend in his Place. See March 8 1692. He attended March 13[140] and had leave to wave his Privilege. The same March 8: was a Report from the Committee to search Precedents what the House hath done in Cases, where any of their Members have been imployed in Forreign Service beyond the Sea or where any Member hath been otherwise absent. This Consideration of this Report referred to the Committee of Privileges and Elections who did nothing upon it.}

To avoid a Negative on the Main Question, and also that the Resolution should not appear on the Votes, the Question was that the Report be Recommitted. Yeas go out

	Yeas		Noes	
Tellers	Mr Gybbons	77	Mr Plumtree	73
	Mr Sandys		Mr Erle	

February 28. A Petition of Mr Calverts was presented against Mr Lisle but He not being in the House, the Petition was ordered to lye upon the Table, and Mr Lisle Ordered to attend in his Place that Day fortnight.

March 13. Mr Lisle not attending, Mr Calverts Petition was read. And it was then resolved Nem. Con.

That Edward Lisle Esq be suspended from the Benefit of the Privilege of this House (except as to his Person) until He shall attend this House in his Place.[141]

---

[139] William Culliford (d. 1724), M.P. for Corfe Castle 1690–9, was never an Irish M.P., but was commissioner for revenues [I] 1684–8, 1690–2, and was accused of malpractice in the Commons and dismissed the service. He defended himself on 23 Feb. 1692, and was summoned to appear before the Irish Commons in Oct. 1692, but pleaded his privilege as an English M.P. The Commons renewed its investigation in Feb. 1693, and as Culliford was absent during the debates, there was a move to expel him. On 8 Mar. he still had not appeared so a motion was carried to withdraw his privileges, which continued despite his attempt on 13 Mar. to vindicate himself. HoP, draft biography.

[140] I.e., 8 and 13 Mar. 1693. *C.J.*, X, 846, 850.

[141] For details see *C.J.*, XXIII, 499; Sedgwick, II, 218–19.

February 18. A Petition from the Justices of Westminster in answer to the Commons Address to the King, setting forth that by reason of the present great frost and the impressing Seamen out of the Colliers in the Summer *there were not Coals in the River or on shore sufficient to supply the Town for a fortnight.* Petition referred to a Committee.

February 19. Bill for registring Seamen read a 2d time. The Question for the Committment passed in the Negative without a Division, for the Bill was to compel all persons employed on the Water in all navigable Rivers etc. to Register and deprived this Sort of them of their Liberties in the most arbitrary Manner, that the Bill could not be defended.

It was afterwards proposed to appoint a Committee of the whole House to prepare Heads of a bill for the better Encouragement of the Seamen. This was objected to and a private Committee was desired to examine the abuses relating to the Seamen. Upon the Question for a Committee of the whole House, the House divided.

| Yeas | <71> | Noes | <63>[142] |

February 20. Motion by Lord Polwarth to vacate Mr Corbetts Seat for accepting a Salary of £200 per annum as Secreary to the Court of Assistants for releif of Sea officers widows it being insisted upon to be a new created office and appeared to be so from the Accounts and papers laid before the House. Yet voted otherwise.

| Yeas | 182.[143] | Noes | 223. |

Immediately after Mr Sandys moved for a Committee to inquire what new offices have been created since the 25th of October 1705 etc. It passed in the Negative. Yeas 154. Noes 196.

<Volume 2 of Edward Harley's journal.>

Mem. The Conference between the Lords and Commons upon the Recoinage 1695. The reasons offered by the Commons were Reported by Mr Montague[144] Chancellor of the Exchequer but they are not entered in the Journals.

Sheriffs to be chose by the County see 28 Edw. 1 cap 8.
Sheriffs shall be affirmed by the Chancellor Treasurer Barons of the Exchequer etc. See 9 Edw II: Stat 2 cap 1: No Man to be Sheriff <illegible>. See also 14 Edw 3: <illegible> 43 Edw. 3 c 95. 23 Hen 6: cap 8 <illegible>. 1 Ric: 2 cap. 11. 12 Ric: 2: cap.2.

Continuation of the Sixth Session.

February 21, 1739/40. Mr Pulteney moved for an Address to the King that He would give Directions to the proper Officers to lay before the House, all the Powers Instructions, Memorials, Letters and Papers relating to the Convention between Great Britain and Spain concluded at the Pardo, January 14, 1739 NS.

---

[142] Here EH left gaps. The figures come from *C.J.*, XXIII, 468.
[143] *Ibid.*, p. 473, gives a figure of 132.
[144] Charles Montagu (1661–1717), baron (1700) and earl of Halifax (1714); chancellor of the exchequer 1694–9; first lord of the treasury 1697–9, 1714–15; one of the five whig junto lords.

In his opening of this Motion He acquainted the House, that His Intention was to follow the Precedent in 1715 made by Sir R. Walpole when He joined with Him in Impeaching Queen Annes Ministry,[145] and therefore if He succeded in his Question of having those Papers laid before the House, should afterwards move for a Select Committee of 21 to whom these Papers might be referred.

The Motion was Seconded by Sir William Windham. This ocasioned a very long and warm Debate. Sir R. Walpole to avoid the strentgh of the Question, and not knowing how far an Enquiry into the Convention which was become so odious to the whole Nation might affect even his own Creatures. That to Divert the attention of the House from the Question, He applyed it personally to Himself, Called upon those who were his Freinds to stand by Him. Said He was now upon his Tryal; and desired either Acquittal or Judgment. That in his ludicrous Hours He had drawn Articles against Himself, and could not find any but what there was some Resolution or Vote of Parliament for. That the only use of this Question was to see who should be uppermost. By this personal Harangue He kept his Mercenaries together.

Sir W. Wyndham was very severe in his Reply to Him. That He could not apply this Question solely to himself without assuming the Supremacy of Power, and owning that He did every thing in the Ministry. That if He was in earnest to be acquitted or condemned and to be impartially heard, He should join in the Question to lay the Papers before the House. But instead of That, He cryes out Let me stand upon my Tryal – but you shall not examine you shall be denyed the means of Evidence etc.

Yeas 196.		Noes 247.
Sir W. Wyndham ⎱	Tellers	Mr Henry Pelham ⎱
Mr Sandys ⎰		Mr Winnington ⎰

When the Affair was over Sir Robert thanked many of the Members for their attendance and accepted of their congratulations, as if he had been really tryed and acquitted.

February 25. The House in the Committee of Supply voted the Ordinary Estimate of the Navy, to which Lord Polwarth made great objection, and had called for several papers to shew the abuses and mismanagement of the Navy. (See the Several Papers and Accounts referred to this Committee in the Vote of this Day relating to the Navy.)

The next day February 26. When the Report from the Committee was made Lord Polwarth moved a Question that to apply towards defraying the Ordinary charge of the Navy, or to any Head contained in the ordinary Estimate thereof, any Sum of Publick Money exceeding the Sum granted by Parliament for that purpose, is a Misapplication, and ought to be prevented. It passed in the Negative.

March 4. Upon the Report of the Mutiny Bill Sir William Yonge Secretary <at> War offered some Words to explain the clause relating to the Justices settling the Prices of Provisions in their Quarter Session so as to oblige the Innkeepers to provide Victuals for the Soldiers as well as Quarters. He quoted the Attorney Generals[146] Opinion that they are now obliged, This occasioned a Debate in the House Many Gentlemen being of a different Opinion, and all seemed to agree that it was a very difficult point to determine, and at last it was agreed not to insert the Words but to leave the Law as it

[145] The ministers impeached were Lords Oxford (Harley's uncle), Bolingbroke, Strafford and the duke of Ormonde.

[146] Sir Dudley Ryder. See Appendix.

now stands unexplained. In the next Session this was made part of the Mutiny Bill. See the Act 1741.

March 6. A Message from the King That He had received Proposals for a Marriage between his Daughter the Princess of Mary and Prince Frederick of Hesse and hoped the House would enable Him to give her a Portion. The next day the House in a Committee of Supply Voted £40000 for the Portion. Which was agreed to by the House March 10.

March 11. A Bill to restrain Horse Races passed and sent to the Lords.[147]

March 13. A Bill for amending and enforcing the Laws relating to Rogues and Vagabonds etc. passed and sent to the Lords.[148]

March 13. Several Resolutions reported from the Committee who were appointed to Consider of Heads of a Bill for the better Encouragement of Seamen to enter voluntarily into his Majestys Service.
    To the First and 2d Resolution the House agreed.
    The Third passed in the Negative Yeas <55> Noes <78>.[149]
    The Consideration of the rest were adjourned till that day sen'night, and then was dropped.

March 17. An Instruction to the Committee to whom the Bill for remedying some Defects in the Act of the 43 of Eliz: for the releif of the Poor, to receive a Clause to direct the Inhabitants of Every Parish to elect annually double the number of Persons necessary to be appointed Overseers of the Poor, and to direct the Justices to nominate one half of the Persons so returned.

March 17. The Lords send a Message to the Commons to desire their Concurrence to an Address of Congratulation on the taking of Porto Bello.[150] To which the House agreed with An Amendment which was *with Six Ships of War only* Yeas 36 Noes 31. These Words were rejected upon a Division by the Lords[151] before the Address was sent to the Commons. But afterwards they agreed to them. This Address was proposed by the Country Party.

March 20. Standing Order of the House against Written Protections of the 31st of January 1718[152] read and ordered to be Reprinted and published and to be set up at Westminster Hall Gate and other publick Places in London and Westminster, and on the Wall with in the New Session House at Edingburgh, and a Copy of the said Order to be sent to the Clerk of the Peace for Every County, City etc. in England, and to the Principal Clerks of the Session in Edingburgh, with Directions to them to deliver a true Copy thereof to the Sheriffs yearly. And all Sheriffs etc. are prohibited to enter in their Books any Protection or Written Certificate signed by any Member, but upon

---

[147] It received the royal assent on 29 Apr.
[148] It also received the royal assent on 29 Apr.
[149] Here EH left gaps. The figures are from *C.J.*, XXIII, 499.
[150] The text of the address is in *L.J.*, XXV, 484.
[151] There is no record of a division on these words, either in the Journal or the Manuscript Minutes; they may have been rejected (in the committee of the whole house) without a formal vote.
[152] I.e., 1719. See *C.J.*, XIX, 82.

such Protection or Written Certificate being given to them forthwith to return the
same to the Clerk of the House.

Ordered

That the Clerk do fortwith acquaint the House with such Protections or Written
Certificates, as shall be so returned to Him, if the Parliament be then sitting, if not,
within 3 days after their next Meeting.

March 21. A Motion was made that the Commissioners of the Admiralty do lay before
the House a List of the ships of War as have been employed as Cruisers for the Protection of Trade on this side Cape Finistre since the 10th of July last etc. Passed in the
Negative Yeas 97. Noes 145.

This Motion arose from the Spaniards having taken 5 Merchant Ships in the Chops
of the Channel. This was a usual Question in Queen Annes War with France and
always granted when asked, though it was now denied. The reason was plain that it
might not appear that the Ministry had been neglegigent in appointing proper Cruisers,
and that many ships were continue to lye idle at Spitehead with their complement of
men, who might have been much better employed in this Service.

The Account of Repairs of the Ships in Ordinary for the year 1739	<£>20,326: 07: 04: ½
The Account of What Money has been applied on Account of Mooring Chains etc.	<£>1058: 14: 00
Estimate of the Building Rebuildings and Repairs of ships for the year 1740	£119,394:
{Estimate of the Charge of General and Staff Officers for 1740	<£>22880. 19. 02.}

March 28. A Petition of the Merchants presented by Sir J. Barnard complaining of the
Embargo laid on, and that the Admiralty would not grant Protections unless each
Merchant ship provided a certain Number of Mariners in Proportion to what they
carry for the Use of the Ships of War, that the Petitioners were unacquainted with
such severe Terms etc. See the Petition.[153] Motion to refer the Petition to a Committee
and the Petitioners to be heard by themselves before the said Committee. Passed in
the Negative. Yeas 95. Noes 166.

See the Orders of Council in 1692 and 1702 relating to Embargos.

Embargo are laid on by Prerogative.

Pressing is against Law.

Grants of Parliament for The Year 1740.

1739	Men	Money
November 26. For the Sea Service from the 1st of January next	35000	<£>1820000: 00: 00:
<*November*> 30. For the Land Service (Guards and Garrisons) including 2141 Invalids and 815 Highland Regiment for Great Britain, Guernsey, and Jersey	28852	<£>860150: 10: 04: ¼

---

153 *Ibid.*, XXIII, 513–14.

Six Regiments of Marines for 14 Months from October 25 1739.	4890	<£>118214: 01: 00:
January 17, 1739/40. For Gibraltar, Minorca and the Plantations	11607	<£>266203: 02: 01: ½
January 28. Additional Men to the 6 Regiments of Marines	2040	<£>33429: 00: 00:
Twenty Men to each of the 4 Companys of Invalids and one New Company to be raised	181	<£>2450: 13: 6:
For Officers Widows		<£>3998: 00: 00:
For the office of Ordinance for Land Service		<£>94071: 11: 03:
Extraordinaries for Ditto		<£>46362: 13: 05
Sums replaced to the Sinking Fund		<£>25865: 18: 09:
		Money
Subsidy to the King of Denmark		<£>58333: 06: 08:
For the out Pensioners of Chelsea Hospital		<£>10347: 06: 00
February 4. For Greenwich Hospital		<£>10000: 00: 00
For Westminster Abbey		<£>4000: 00: 00
For the Affrican Company		<£>10000: 00: 00
February 7. For General and Staff officers		<£>22880: 19: 02
For Half pay officers		<£>34587: 00: 00
For Georgia		<£>4000: 00: 00
February 14. By a Vote of Credit to his Majesty on Account		<£>200000: 00: 00
For Extraordinaries incurred and not provided for		<£>9477: 00: 00
February 26. For the Ordinary Estimate of the Navy		<£>199704: 08: 03
March 10. For a Marriage Portion to Princess Mary		<£>40000: 00: 00
Totall of Grants		<£>3874076: 03: 7: ¾

Money raised for the Year 1740

	£	s	d
November 29, 1739. By the Malt Tax	750,000:	00:	00:
December 4. By 4s Land Tax	2,000,000:	00:	00:
January 22, 1739/40. By the Surplus of Grants in the Exchequer for 1739.	88722:	07:	10: ¼
February 5. By the Sinking Fund	1,000,000:	00:	00:
February 18. More Ditto on the Kings Message to the House of Commons	200,000:	00:	00:
March 11. By Money in the Exchequer for Lands in Christophers	21000:	01:	08: ½
Totall Money raised	4059722:	09:	06: ¾
Deduct Totall of Grants	3874076:	03:	07: ¾
To Ballance	185646:	05:	11:

April 16. An Ingrossed Bill from the Lords entitled An Act for the Publick Registering Deeds, Conveyances and Incumbrances etc. Resolved to be Committed. Yeas 124
Noes 80: --- April 21. The Question in the Committee of the whole House was
Whether the Clerks of the Peace should be the Registers in the several Counties Yeas
91. Noes 122. As this Question was carried in the Negative, the Bill was dropped by
the great Favorites of it, it being a Job only.

April 23, 1740. The House was informed that the Writ and Indenture of Return
annexed to the Writ for a Member to serve for Leskard in Cornwall was after the
Election sent up by the Post that the Western Mail was Robbed and the Writ and
Return were taken away with other Letters. As this was an entire New Case the House
were at a loss How to proceed. Some Members proposed to hear viva voce Evidence
of the Election and Return and upon this to admit Mr Trelawny who was the Gentleman elected, but this proposal of admitting Viva Voce Evidence to supply a Record
would not be listened to. Then it was proposed That the Lord Chancellor should make
a Fac Simile, but this was not approved. The House not knowing what to do
adjourned the Consideration to a day when the Session would be over.

{See the next Sessions 19 November 1740. This Matter was again heard and
several Persons examined in relation to it, when it was Ordered Nemine Contradicente.[154]

That the Deputy Clerk of the Crown do file among the Returns of Members to serve
in his present Parliament for the County of Cornwall, *the Counterpart* of the Indenture, executed by the Sheriff of Cornwall, of the Return of Charles Trelawny Esqe to
serve as a Burgess for the Borough of Leskeard as the Return of the said C. Trelawny
Esqe to Parliament, it appearing to this House, that the Writ and the Principal Part of
the aforesaid Indenture were taken away, in coming up to the Clerk of the Crown, by
Highwaymen, who destroyed the same by burning them.}

April 22, 1740. A Free Conference with the Lords on the Bill to prohibit Trade with
Spain being appointed, the Managers for the Commons went up to the Painted
Chamber[155] at the time appointed by the Lords, where they waited above ½ an hour,
the Lords not coming the Managers returned to their own House, and Mr Horace
Walpole reported what had Happned, upon which a Debate arose; It was said that
though it was not imagined that the Lords not coming to the Conference at the time
appointed was done with an Intent to put any affront or show a slight to the Commons,
yet as such an affair had happned, the House ought to take some notice of it, as well
to vindicate their own Rights as to justify the Proceeding of the Managers. And that
the most proper and gentlest Method of taking Notice of it would be to appoint a
Committee to Search Precedents of what had been done in the like Cases, that if the
Lords should send a Message and give reasons for their not appearing which should
be Satisfactory to the Commons, that Committee need not make any Report, if the
Lords should send no Message, the House would then have time to consider what was
proper to do. – Other Members said That as the Lords did not mean any affront or
slight, the Managers retiring from the Place of Conference was taking sufficient Notice

154 See *ibid.*, pp. 535–6.
155 The regular venue for joint conferences between the Lords and the Commons, it was situated between
the court of requests and the house of lords. See *The London Diaries of William Nicolson, Bishop of
Carlisle, 1702–1718*, ed. Clyve Jones and Geoffrey Holmes (Oxford, 1985), pp. 70, 75–6, for its location
and a brief description of the procedures used at such conferences.

and they moved the Orders of the Day to be read. This was objected to as doing Nothing, and it was moved to Adjourn, which was complyed with. The Occasion of the Lords not coming at the time appointed was That they were debating among themselves in what Manner to meet the Commons whether with their Hats On or off. When the Lords heard that the Commons were adjourned, They Ordered the Council which were attending upon a Cause to be called in without taking any Notice of what had passed.[156]

The next Day April 23 The Lords resumed their Debate about the Manner of Meeting the Commons, when the Duke of Argyle moved *That the Lords who shall go to the Free Conference with the Commons do proceed into the Painted Chamber to the said Conference covered.* After Debate The Previous Question was put whether that Question shall be now put. It was resolved in the Negative.

Earl of Abingdon afterwards desired that the Clerks should not enter either of the Questions upon the Journals which the Lords agreed to without coming to any Question upon it, but the Clerks were to observe it to be the tacit consent of the House. The Lords then sent a Message to the House of Commons to Acquaint them That their Lordships were prevented by extraordinary Business from Meeting the Commons yesterday at a Free Conference on the Subject Matter of the last Conference as was desired by them, and that the Lords do appoint the said Free Conference presently in the painted Chamber.

The Managers for the Commons attend at the Free Conference. The Lords came in according to Rank, the Duke of Bedford who was the cheif Manager first, then the other Dukes, then the Earls Bishops and Barons, they came to the End of the Table covered, then uncovered then sat down and put on their Hats. When any Lord spoke He was uncovered. Those who spoke were the Dukes of Bedford and Newcastle, and Earl of Cholmondely. For the Commons Mr Horace Walpole Sir John Barnard and Mr Sandys. [See the Proceeding at a Conference 1728 entered in my folio Volume 1st, p. 42.][157]

April 29, 1740. The Sessions ended.

---

[156] The counsel was William Murray and the case *Viscount of Arbuthnot* v. *Spotswood.*
[157] I.e., 19 and 24 Mar. 1729. *C.J.*, XXI, 272, 289–90. The folio volume has not been found.

The Seventh Session of this Parliament began the 18th of November 1740.

25 November. Thanks of the House given to Vice Admiral Vernon for his Services in the West Indies, and the Speaker ordered to signify the same to Him.

27 November. Forty Thousand Men voted for Sea-Service for the year 1741.

2 December. Proceedings against the author Printer and Publishers of a Paper Intituled *Considerations upon the Embargo on Provision of Victual* which was voted a Libel etc. See December 3, 12, 15.[158]

11 December, 1740. Resolved. That the Number of Land Forces for Guards and Garrisons etc. for 1741 be Twenty nine Thousand and Thirty Three Men, officers included.
   That a Sum not exceeding £883,189: 02: 06: be granted for defraying the said Charge.
   That 6930 Marines be continued for 1741.
   That £124052: 05: 00: be granted for defraying the said Charge.
   That 5705 additional Land Forces be raised for the year 1741.
   That £116322: 04s 02d be granted for maintaining the said additional Forces.
   That 4620 additional Marines be raised.
   That £90201: 10: be granted for maintaining the said Marines.

Fryday February 13, 1740/41. A Motion was made by Mr Sandys 2ded by Lord Limerick for an Address to remove Sir R. Walpole from the Kings Presence and Councils for Ever.
   {My Brother and I were the first who refused to Vote in this Question and publickly left the House between 12 and one in the Morning after I had delivered my Sentiments which as far <as> I could recollect were as follows[159]
   Mr Speaker
   I do not stand up at this late time of Night either to Accuse or to flatter any Man. Since I have had the Honour to sit in this House my only Motive for opposing the Measures of the Administration was, because I thought them Wrong; and as long as they are so, I shall continue to give as Constant an Opposition to them. The State of the Nation by their Conduct is deplorable, a War is destroying us abroad, and Poverty and Corruption are devouring us at Home.
   But whatever I may think of Men, God forbid, that my private Opinion, should be the only Rule of my Judgment, I should desire to have an Exterior Conviction from Facts and Evidence, and without These, I am so far from condemning that I would not censure any Man; I am fully satisfied in my own Mind that there are those who give pernicious and destructive Councils, and I hope a Time will come, when a proper legal, Parliamentary Enquiry may be made, and when clear facts and full Evidence will plainly discover who are the Enemies of their Country.
   A Noble Lord to whom I have the Honour to be related, has been mentioned in this Debate; He was Impeached and Imprisoned, and by that Imprisonment his years were shortned, and the Prosecution was carried on by the Honourable Person who is now

---

[158] The author and publisher was William Cooley and the printer was John Hughes. *C.J.*, XXIII, 545–7, 560–1, 563. The embargo was on Irish trade.
[159] Another, slightly variant text of this speech, can be found in Bodl., MS Ballard 29, f. 130, printed below, pp. 250–1.

the Subject of your Question, though He knew at the Same time, that there was no Evidence to Support it.

I am Now Sir glad of this opportunity to return Good for Evil, and do that Honourable Gentleman and his Family that Justice which He denyed to Mine.}

The Charge was General being an Account of his Administration as to our affairs at Home and Abroad, no particular facts were stated nor any Evidence produced either viva voce or Written to support the Charge, or to bring it Home particularly to Sir R. Walpole so as to distinguish Him from any of the rest of the Administration or Privy Council. As the Accusation was founded on Common fame and every Member was to judge by his own private Opinion, Many of the Torys whose Principles abhor even the shadow of Bills of Pains and Penalties, or to censure anyone without Evidence refused to Vote in the Question and withdrew. Some few of them divided against it. Several of the Torys for it as thinking it matter of Advice only to the King to remove a Minister whom all were satisfyed was a very ill one. The whole Affair was brought on and managed (in a very weak manner) by the Patriots who were set to work by the Duke of Argyle. It was said that Mr Pulteney in their Private Meetings had endeavoured to diswade the bring<ing> it on. He spoke in publick for it but in a more disconcerted manner than ever He was known.

Numbers on the Division Yeas 106. Noes 290. It was reckoned that there was that day in the House near 500 members so that the rest withdrew.

The same Question was moved in the House of Lords the very same Day by Lord Carteret and 2ded by Lord Abingdon.

Contents   47 ⎫
Proxies   12 ⎬ 59
                  ⎭

Not Contents 89 ⎫
Proxies   19 ⎬ 108
                  ⎭

It was afterwards moved, That any attempt to inflict any kind of Punishment on any Person without allowing Him an opportunity to make his Defense or without Proof of any Crime or Misdemeanor committed by Him is contrary to Natural Justice, the fundamental Laws of this Realm and the Ancient established usage of Parliament and is a High Infringment of the Liberty of the Subject.

As no Lord could give an Negative to this Proposition the only Debate was whether it should be now put. And the Previous Question being put Whether that Question shall be now put, the House Divided.

Contents   81.
Not Contents   54.

Then the main Question passed in the Affirmative.

February 12. The Place Bill passed the House of Commons having met with no Opposition in the Progress of it. The Courtiers being affraid to oppose it this Session, it being so near a new General Election. The Bill was flung out in the House of Lords upon the Question for Commitment.

Contents   44
Not Contents   63

See the Protest upon it which is excellent well drawn.[160]

160 The vote was on 26 Feb. A summary of the debate is in Cobbett, XII, 1–2. For the protest see *L.J.*, XXV, 611–12.

March 4, 6, 9, 10. A Bill for the Encouragement of Increase of Seamen and for the better and Speedier manning His Majestys Fleet, was under the Consideration of the Committee of the whole House.

This Bill was of two parts. The one to Encourage Seamen to inlist, The other compulsory. The first might have been done by Proclamation, but was inserted in the Bill to sweeten the other compulsory Clauses which were taken from an Act of the 4th and 5th of Queen Anne which Law was never put in practice and found to be against Liberty.

The Encouragement £5 to every able Seamen and £3 to every ordinary.

Compulsory Clauses

Justices of the Peace are required to cause a search to be made for all Seamen as *lie hid, withdraw* or conceal themselves.

It was moved that after the Word Seamen to insert who are not Freeholders *or have a right to Vote for Members in Parliament.*

An Amendment proposed after the Word Freeholders to insert of 40s per annum in order to leave out the Words under which the Line is drawn.

Question that the Words or have a right to Vote for Members in Parliament stand part of the Clause.

Yeas   111.   Noes   151.

Privy Search to be made either by Day or Night. Power to enter any House and if Entrance be not readily admitted then to force open the Door etc. in order to make such Search.

Division on this Clause. Yeas 156. Noes 122.

Another Clause to impower the Justices to examine the Constables etc. upon Oath concerning their Execution of the Warrants and to impose a fine of five pounds upon them for any Neglect Connivance or other offence. By this a Man was to accuse Himself.

Yeas   154.   Noes   115.

All these Clauses were so warmly and thoroughly debated in the Committee and as they were so destructive of the Liberty and the Rights of the Subjects and therefore raised so great a clamour without Doors. And though Sir Robert Walpole and his Attorney General Sir Dudley Ryder laboured very hard in defense of them, yet all these vile compulsory Clauses were given up upon the Report March 13.

A Clause was offered in the Committee to limit the Wages of Seamen in the Merchant Service to 35s per month.

Question for bringing up the Clause. Yeas 143. Noes 92.

Question on the whole Clause. Yeas 143. Noes 118.

March 13. A Petition of the London Merchants against this Clause. And upon the Report of the Bill (this Day) Sir J. Barnard moved that this Clause might be adjourned in order that the Merchants might be heard against it. Which the Court would not admit of. Yeas 142. Noes 196.

Afterwards Sir J. Barnard exposed the whole Clause and shewed it was absurd and impracticable and would be destructive of Trade. For the Clause 183. Against 127.

March 23. Seamens bill read a 3d time. That the Bill Pass.[161]

	Yeas	153	Noes	79
Tellers	Sir W. Yonge		Mr Bathurst	
	Mr Arundel		Mr Harley	

---

[161] It received the royal assent on 25 Apr.

April 14. £300000 granted to enable the King to support the Queen of Hungary, for preventing the Subversion of the House of Austria, and maintaining the Pragmatick Sanction.[162] See the Kings Speech and the Address[163] to which Mr Pulteney and Sandys were the most forward to concur. Mr Shippen spoke against the Resolution but no Division.

April 14. £7066. 13. 08. granted to pay Henry Popples Debt as agent of one of the Independent Companies.[164] A Job.

£650 granted to Receiver General of Scotland said to be a Loss by the failure of Popple. An arrant dirty Job. Yeas 67. Noes 37.

April 25, 1741. Session ended by Prorogation.

April 27, 1741. Parliament Dissolved. Writs bore Teste for a New one April 28 and made Returnable 28 of June.

May 27, 1741. Election for the County of Hereford when E. Harley and Velters Cornwall were again choose without opposition.

June 16. Lord Oxford died. January 6, 1741/42 Mr Foley of Stoke chose Knight of the Shire in the room of E. Harley.

---

162 The Habsburg family law promulgated by the Emperor Charles VI in 1713 to ensure the undivided succession of his own heirs male or female throughout the Habsburg lands. During the 1720s and 1730s the estates of the Holy Roman Empire and the major European powers (including Britain in 1731) agreed to uphold the Sanction. On the emperor's death in 1740, his eldest daughter, Maria Theresa, succeeded to her father's lands and titles (queen of Hungary and Bohemia), except the Empire. However, Frederick II of Prussia repudiated his father's agreement to the Sanction, invaded Silesia, and inaugurated the war of the Austrian succession (1740–8).

163 *C.J.*, XXIII, 702–3.

164 Henry Popple was the king's agent for the independent companies of foot in the islands of Jamaica and New Providence. See *ibid.*, p. 706.

<First Session.>

Decmeber 1, 1741. The New Parliament met when Mr Onslow who had been Speaker of the two former Parliaments was again chosen without Opposition. 489 Members were sworn the first day.

December 16. Question in the Committee of Elections who should take the Chair. Mr Giles Earle Chairman in the former Parliament who was set up by the Minister and so zealously supported by Him that to keep his troops together Sir R. Walpole dined with them at a Tavern in Kingstreet and came with them to the Committee. Dr Lee was set up by the Country Party.

>   For Mr Earle   238
>   For Dr Lee   242
>   ————
>   4   Majority

December 22. House of Commons sat till 5 in the morning declared the Westminster Election void. Lord Sundon voted not duly elected by a Majority of 5. Sir Charles Wager by 4.[165] The High Bailiff[166] taken into Custody for illegal and arbitrary proceedings. See the Censure of the House upon Soldiers being brought to the Election.[167] Blackerby and other Westminster Justices Reprimanded by the Speaker for sending the Soldiers. 23 January.[168]

January 21. A Motion made by Mr Pulteney that the several Papers presented to this House on Monday last and the Papers presented yesterday be referred to a Select Committee, and that they do examine the same and report to the House what they find Material in them.

Passed in the Negative Yeas 250. Noes 253.

>   { Yeas   250
>   Noes   253
>   Tellers   4
>   Speaker   1
>   ————

508 Members present the fullest House ever known. Upon the Question on the Convention March 8, 1738/39 there were present including the Tellers and the Speaker 497 Members. [See p. 46: when 518 voted.]}[169]

Had this Question been carried the Committee were to be 21 to be chosen by Ballot and be a Secret one the Minister fearing this, had mustered all his troops. This Question being lost Mr Pulteny moved for an Address that the Letters to and From the King of Prussia and his Ministers to his Majesty and his Ministers relating to the State of the War in the Empire be laid before this House.

Sir Robert fearing to lose this Question his Majority being so small on the other gave it up. And it was left to the King to give an answer to the Address. See the answer January 25.

---

165 Sundon's majority was 4 (216 to 220), while Wager's was 5 (215 to 220). *C.J.*, XXIV, 37.
166 John Lever, high bailiff of Westminster.
167 *C.J.*, XXIV, 37.
168 See *ibid.*, p. 54.
169 I.e., folio 46. See p. 58 below.

January 14, 1741/42. I took my seat in the House of Peers being introduced by the Earl of Litchfeild and the Earl of Shaftsbury.[170]

January 19. Question to proceed on the state of the Nation that day sen'night.

    Contents   53.
    Not Contents 77.

Proceed on Thursday.

January 27 and 28. Debate on the List of the officers belonging to the Establishment of Minorca laid before the House of Lords, by which it appeared that out of 19 officers, only 5 were attending their Duty. Debate adjourned to the next day January 28: when Major General Anstruther[171] attended according to order and being Lieutenant Governour of Minorca was examined as to the List and the state of the Island, Question stating the Fact and containing a Censure of this Neglect.

    Contents   57.
    Not Contents 69.

See the Protest, which fully states the whole Debate in a most strong and fine manner.[172] Question put afterwards and carried, was the stating the same fact but no Censure and concluding only with an Address to the King that He would give Orders that the officers should repair to their Posts etc. Which the King had done before the consideration of this List, and the Debate.

Sir R. Walpole having lost several Questions in the House of Commons as the Westminster Election, the Chairman of the Committee of Elections, and having prevented the Papers laid before the House being referred to a Select Committee determined to try his Strentgh on the Chippenham election which was heard at Bar January 28, 1741/42. The Right of Election was then carried against Him by a Majority of one only. 236 and 235. This Question He endeavoured to get explained the next day of Hearing February 2d. and accordingly rallied his troops but He found they deserted, for this Motion He lost by 16: 241 and 225. Perceiving that His Power was now gone in the House of Commons, soon after the loss of this Question He left the House that Evening with an Intention to come there no more, but to make his retreat into the upper. And accordingly the next Day February 3, The King came to the House passed the Malt Bill and then ordered the Chancellor that both Houses should adjourn themselves to the 18th.

During this Adjournment Sir Robert Walpole was created Baron of Houghton, Viscount Walpole and Earl of Orford. And He likewise prevails on the King to send a Warrant to the Deputy Earl Marshall That *Miss Maria Walpole* (his natural Daughter by Mrs Skerret) shall have and enjoy the same Place, Preeminence and Pecedence in all Assemblies and Meetings whatsoever as the Daughter of an Earl of the Kingdom of Great Britain. {This Girl is about 19 and is rather supposed to be the Daughter of Phil<ip> Floyd[173] than Sir Roberts. Sir Robert was so fond of Mrs Skerret that He married Her in 1737: a few months after the Death of Lady Walpole. Mrs Skerret lived with Sir Robert not above a year if so long. She died in 1738.}

---

[170] See *L.J.*, XXVI, 32.
[171] See Appendix.
[172] Forty-one lords protested, including Oxford. *L.J.*, XXVI, 47–8.
[173] Philip Lloyd (d. 1735), M.P. for Saltash, Aylesbury, Christchurch and Lostwithiel, 1723–35. Sedgwick, II, 220.

Thursday February 11, 1741/42. Sir Robert (now Earl of Orford) resigned his Places as Chancellor of the Exchequer and first Commissioner of the Treasury. Having first disposed of all the Places within his Gift and left an Empty Exchequer.

Mr Sandys accepted of the Chancellor of the Exchequers Place without the Knowledge of the Prince and his other Freinds except Mr Pulteney, Sir J. Rushout etc. Mr Waller was offered to come into the Treasury, William Chetwynd into the Admiralty which they refused as there was not an entire change of the Ministry.

Fryday February 12. A Meeting at the Fountain Tavern of 220 Members of the House of Commons and 35 Lords.[174] Duke of Argyles Declaration for a Coalition of Partys for altering Measures for bringing in the Tories as well as Patriots into Place without distinction of Party called the Broad bottom. The next Day the Treasury altered, the New Commissioners who were made Lord Wilmington, Mr Sandys, Sir J. Rushout, Mr Gybbon, Mr George Compton.

{Mem: Pulteneys and Sandys Speech<es> and Declarations at this Meeting to act with those they had done in the Intrest of the Country Party though they had then betrayed them.

See Two Pamphlets published in 1743 The one Entitled Faction detected wrote in defense of These Nominal Patriots. The other Entitled: The Defense of the People which is an answer to it.[175]}

February 16. Mr Pulteney brings a Letter from the King to the Prince. Debated at Charlton House. Lord Gower, Lord Bathurst, Lord Chesterfeild present, Duke of Argyle sent for, declares his former Resolutions That all or none should come in. Goes Home. It was afterwards agreed That the Prince should go the next Day to Court and That the Duke of Argyle should be desired to accept of his old Places.

February 17. Prince goes to Court. That night a Meeting at Mr Doddingtons, where the Tories present agreed to desire the Duke of Argyle to accept, and a Deputation appointed to acquaint Him with it. The next day He goes to Court and the Tories present as Sir Watkin Williams Wynne, Sir J. Cotton, etc. and Several Tory Lords go to Court with the Duke.[176]

Lord Carteret made Secretary of State in the room of Lord Harrington who was made President of the Council.

March 9, 1741/42. Motion by Lord Limerick seconded by Sir J. St Aubin That a Committee be appointed to enquire into the State of our Affairs both at Home and abroad for the last 20 years. Yeas 242. Noes 244. Earl of Orfords Money and Carterets management is supposed to have baffled this Enquiry.

{This Motion being baffled it occasioned so much Clamour on the new Administration, that Mr Pulteney who had been absent on <two words crossed out> by reason

174 See Colley, pp. 240–1.

175 The anonymously published *Faction Detected, by the Evidence of Facts* (1743), of 170 pages, which was a defence of William Pulteney, earl of Bath, was written by the earl of Egmont, though it is sometimes erroneously attributed to Pulteney and to Zachary Pearce. The answer, *A Defence of the People: or, Full Confutation of the Pretended Facts, Advanc'd in a Late Huge, Angry Pamphlet; Call'd Faction Detected. In a Letter to the Author of that Weighty Performance*, at 150 pages was not published until 1744. B.L., *E.S.T.C.* database.

176 Argyll had been offered, in the words of the duke of Beaufort, 'the Government of the Army' (i.e. master general of the ordnance). See Bodl., MS Ballard 29, f. 75: Beaufort to Paston, 18 Feb. 1742. See also Colley, p. 241. For Argyll's resignation of the post in Mar., see below, p. 58.

of his Daughters Death and Mr Sandys on his reelection at Worcester advised the renewal of it in another shape. And on March 23d Lord Limerick and Sir J. St Aubin moved That a Committee be appointed to enquire into the Conduct of Robert Earl of Orford during the last 10 years of his being First Commissioner of the Treasury and Chancellor and under Treasury of the Exchequer. Which was carried Yeas 252. Noes 245. To be a Secret Committee and to be chose by Ballot,[177] The Committee appointed to examine the Lists sat from Fryday Evening 6 of the Clock till 4 a clock Saturday noon. Lord Hartington in the Chair.

List of the Secret Committee chose by Ballot

Sir John St Aubin	518:	On both Lists
Samuel Sandys	516:	On Both Lists
Sir John Rushout	516:	On Both Lists
George Compton	515:	On Both
Lord Quarendon	512:	On Both
William Noel	512:	On Both
Sir J. Barnard	268:	Country List
Lord Limerick	266:	Country List
Edward Hooper	265:	Country List
Lord Cornbury	262:	Court List
Nicholas Fazakerly	262:	Country List
Henry Furnese	262:	Country List
Earl of Granard	259:	Country List
William Pitt	259	Country List
Thomas Prowse	259	Country List
Edmund Waller	259	Country List
William Bowles	259	Court List
Sir J. Strange Solicitor General	259	Court List
Colmondley Turner	259	Court List
Sir Henry Liddell	258	Court List
J. Talbot	258	Court List
William Finch	258	Court List
Hume Campbell	258	Country List

These four Last having an Equality of Voices it was determined by the Speaker who gave his Voice for Sir Henry Liddel and Mr Talbot. See the Votes 29 March 1742. Both these Gentlemen had voted against any Enquiry.

Note Sir John St Aubyn had every Vote that Balloted which was never known before.

Names on the Country List who lost it on the Ballot	On the Court who lost it on the Ballot
George Bubb Doddington	Lord Fitzwilliams
George Lyttleton	Sir Charles Gilmour
John Philips	Charles Gore
Sir Watkin Williams	Henry Arthur Herbert
Sir John Cotton	John Plumtree
	Sir John Ramsden
	George Wade
	James West

[177] The ballot took place on 29 Mar. *C.J.*, XXIV, 153–4.

Members who voted on the Ballot	518
Defaulters	31
Vacancies	8
Speaker	1
	558 }

March 10. Duke of Argyle went to Court and gave up all his Employments.[178]

March 26, 1742. Pension Bill read a 2d time in the House of Lords. Question that the Bill be Committed. Passed in the Negative Though no one spoke against the Bill but the Duke of Devon\<shire> who only said That He had formerly voted against Bills of this kind and would do so now, but offered no one argument or Reason against it. Lord Sandwick and Lord Rumney spoke for the Bill.

Contents	39	} 46
Proxies	7	
Not Contents	65	} 76
Proxies	11	

Lord Carteret the Head of the new Administration voted against the Bill, as did his freind Lord Berkley of Stratton.

April 6, 1742. Place Bill read a 2d time in the House of Lords. That the Bill be Committed

Contents	52.
Not Contents	81.

Bill rejected[179]
Lord Carteret voted against the Bill though He had always spoke for it when He was out of Place.

April 15. Mr Pulteney presented a bill to exclude certain officers from being Members of the House of Commons. A sham Bill and of no use.[180]

April 13. Nicholas Paxton[181] refusing to answer what was demanded of Him by the Secret Committee was Committed to the Serjeant at Arms. Yeas 197. No 136.

April 15. Paxton persisting in his refusal to answer was committed Close Prisoner to Newgate. Yeas 180. Noes 128.

Paxton had been employed by Sir R. Walpole in corrupting Burroughs with publick Money. He was to have been examined in relation to the Wendover Election where He carried down £500 to engage Votes for Mr Boteler[182] against Lord Limerick.

---

[178] As master general of the ordnance, to which he had been appointed in February. See above, p. 56.

[179] Twenty-six peers entered a dissent, including Oxford. *L.J.*, XXVI, 87. The bill was printed; see Torrington, vol. 1739–43/4, pp. 407–10.

[180] It received the royal assent on 16 June.

[181] Secretary to the treasury, 1730–27 July 1742; previously assistant solicitor, 1722–30. He accepted imprisonment rather than incriminate Walpole.

[182] John Botelor (1684–1774), M.P. for Wendover 1734–5. The election referred to was a by-election on 22 Apr. 1735. Sedgwick, I, 199–200, 477–8.

Note. This day April 15. Mr Edgcombe the Borough-Broker in Cornewall was made a Peer which prevented his Examination before the Committee. {Ille crucem Sceleris pretium tulit, Hic Diadema.}[183]

April 27. William Duke of Cumberland 2d Son to King George (being of Age the 15th) was introduced into the House of Peers by the Duke of Grafton and Duke of Dorset and was placed in the chair on the left Hand the Throne.

The same day Earl Fitzwilliams of the Kingdom of Ireland, having been created the 15th Instant Baron of Milton in England, was introduced by Lord Delawar and Lord Lovell.

Richard Edgcumbe created Baron Edgcumbe was introduced at the same time by Lord Delawar and Lord Lovell.

By the Accounts delivered into the Secret Committee it appears that the Secret Service Money from 1707 to 1720 amounted at a Medium to £44000. From 1731 to 1741 to £150000.

Grants for 1742.

Land Tax	<£>2,000,000
Sinking Fund	<£>1,000,000
Malt	<£>750,000
Bank Contract	<£>1,600,000
	<£>5,350,000

February 23. Hearing of the Election for the County of Denbigh began. Sir Watkin Williams Wynne Petitioner. Mr Midleton of Chirk Castle Sitting Member. Sir Watkin voted duly elected, and the Sheriff of Denbighshire sent to Newgate for male Practices. See the Votes.

Dr Lee who had been chosen Chairman of the Committee of Elections by the Country party now accepts the place of one of the Lords of the Admiralty and lists Him self with Sandys and Pulteney etc. who had deserted their Freinds. Duke of Bridgwater who had the commanding Intrest at Brackley refuses to let Dr Lee be rechose, and was therefore some Months out of Parliament, till the Ministry gave Eyles who served for the Devizes a place, and then got Dr Lee chose in his stead.

15 March. The Committee of Elections is closed by the contrivance of Sandys and the old Ministry to prevent the Hearing of several Petitions of the Country Party as that for the town of Denbigh etc.

The Enquiry of the Secret Committee was put an End to by the Prorogation of the Parliament July 15, 1742. After they had sat several Months and though they had made two Reports, neither of which were taken into Consideration, though they contained several strong facts as to the Conduct of Sir Robert Walpole in the Disposal and corrupt usage of Public Money. The Endeavours and good Intention of those who wished well to their Country were eluded by the corrupt influence of Sir R. Walpole and the mean complyances and base behaviour of those who had given themselves the Name of Patriots and had opposed his Measures, as Sandys, Gybbons, Pulteney, Carteret and their Tools who were now quietted and made the means to Screen Him by being purchased by Places in the Treasury and Titles. {Mr Edgcumbe (a member

---

[183] 'ille crucem sceleris, pretium tulit, hic diadema', from Juvenal, *Satires*, XIII, 105.

of Parliament) who was to be examined before the Secret Committee in relation to the Bribing the Cornish Borroughs was the Day before made a Lord. Paxton being sent to Newgate this Motto was given for Edgcumbe.

Ille crucem Sceleris Pretium tulit, Hic Diadema.}

Mr Pulteney created Earl of Bath July 13, 1742.

Note: The Day Mr Scroop[184] Secretary of the Treasury was to be examined before the Secret Committee Lord Limerick Chairman of the Committee was sent for to Court and had the Reversion of <remembrancer of the Exchequer>[185] in Ireland given to Him.

Paxton etc. refused to be examined before the Committee, was committed to Newgate. Bill to indemnify Him rejected by the House of Lords see the Protest.[186]

Lord Gower made Privy Seal.

Lord Bathurst Captain of the Band of Pensioners.

May 25, 1742. Debate in the House of Lords on the Indemnifying Bill.[187]

Lord Carteret: No Precedent for this Bill.

Contrary to Natural Justice, to the Equity of the Civil Law, to the Law of England, to the Rule of Parliament.

Contrary to Natural Justice–To Name a Person as Criminal and no Crime ascertained.

By the Civil Law there must be a Fact Certain, a Discovery Certain, a Reward Certain.

Illegal in a Private Person to publish an Advertisement to encourage Evidence. It would be criminal in a Minister to advice the Crown to publish a Proclamation to encourage Evidence against any one.

Great Difference between Jus and Lex.

You may make a Law but not Right.

Law of England very tender in Matter of Evidence. Swearing to Beleif not allowed by the Law of England. Probable Evidence sufficient before the House of Commons as they are the Grand Inquest.

House of Commons cannot examine on Oath, though it may be proper to connive at their Method of a Justice of Peace administring an Oath at their Door.

I am for Parliamentary Enquirys. Let the Rectum be done Recte.

It is an Anticipation of your Judicature.

Bill of Imprisonment for not speaking, Torture.

Lord Talbot: It was laid down as a Maxim in the Bishop of Rochesters Tryal[188] that what tended to discover Truth in a Parliamentary Manner, was Legal.

Sir Thomas Cokes[189] desired the Bill to indemnify Him against Scan<dulum> Mag<natum>.

Case of Porteous, a Reward was given to Indemnify those who would give Evidence.

[184] John Scrope (d. 1752), senior secretary to the treasury 1724–52.

[185] EH left a blank here.

[186] See p. 61 below.

[187] Bill for indemnifying such persons as shall, upon examination, make discoveries touching the disposition of publick money, or concerning the disposition of offices, or any payments or agreements in respect thereof; or concerning other matter relating to the conduct of Robert, earl of Orford, printed in Torrington, vol. 1734–43/4, pp. 411–14. For a slightly different account of the debate see the diary of Bishop Secker, printed in Cobbett, XII, 643–714.

[188] In 1723.

[189] This refers to the case of Sir Thomas Cooke (?c. 1648–1709), M.P. for Colchester 1694–5, 1698–1705, who was accused of corruption and of bribing M.P.s and peers to further his campaign of protecting the old East India Company (of which he was governor four times between 1692 and 1709) against

Lord Hervey: The Bill contrary to the Humanity of Mankind. It offers an Indignity to the House of Lords. I wish a Mark was put upon it. – It is a Proscriptive Table.

Civil List is not Public Money it is appropriated to the King and his Family and is not to be publickly accounted for.

Duke of Argyle: Lords in Power are fond of Modern Precedents, see The Case of the Masters in Chancery.

Tompson in the Charitable Corporation.[190]

Indemnity to discover frauds in the Customs and Excise and in the S<outh> Sea and East India Companies.

The Publick has a right to the Evidence of the Subject, and no man is to accuse Himself. This Bill provides for both.

Bill against Porteous a Man was forced at your Bar to give Evidence.

This Bill only puts the Commons in a Method to give Evidence at your Bar, you are afterwards a judge of it. If the Civil List should ever be declared by Parliament not to be Publick Money and not Subject to Enquiry, there is an End of your Constitution.

A Person was pardoned to Accuse me [the Duke of Argyle]. I gave my Vote for his Pardon.[191]

Bribery Act[192] indemnifys on Discovery.

Lord Cholmondeley: Against

Lord Berkley of Stratton: Against

Lord Chesterfield: I hoped an End of his Power would have been the End of his Measures.

The Aspersion is laid and admitted by the endeavour to fling out the Bill.

Articles of Impeachment when laid do not then come up proved. That is left to the Tryal.

The Nation expect an Enquiry from the other House. Justice from This.

The Bill facilitates your Judicature, if flung out, no Evidence can ever come before you for the future.

The Indemnity must be extended to the Extent of the Inquiry.

Civil List Bill *without Account* relates only to the Receipts but not to the Disburstments. It is given for the Support and Honour of the Crown, if misapplyed shall not the Parliament who are to make good the Deficiencys enquire into the misapplications.

Lord Chancellor: Against

Quotation from Lord Hales Pleas of the Crown Vol 2d title Approver.[193]

Civil List without Account relates to the Expences as well as Receipts.

Duke of Newcastle: Against

Lord Bathurst: For

Lord Islay: Against.

Contents 47. Not Contents 92.

See the Lords Protest on Rejecting the Bill.[194]

---

interlopers. He was imprisoned in the Tower from Mar. 1695 until the end of the session in Apr. 1696. For details see H.M.C., *Lords MSS*, new ser., I, 548–73; Cobbett, V, 911–27.

190 A scandal was exposed in 1731–2 when it was discovered that the Charitable Corporation, established to assist the poor by lending small sums of money on pledges, was being exploited to enrich its projectors, who charged a high interest rate. See Sedgwick, II, 457–8.

191 See Cobbett, XII, 649, for further details.

192 2 Geo. II, c. 24. See *ibid.*

193 For the quotation, see *ibid.*, p. 653.

194 The vote was Contents 47 + 10 proxies = 57; Not Contents 92 + 17 proxies = 109, and 32 (including Oxford) signed the protest. *L.J.*, XXVI, 131–2.

May 26. A Motion was made in the House of Commons to appoint a Committee to inspect the Lords Journals to see what they have done with the Indemnification Bill which was carried by 5. Yeas 164. Noes 159.

It is remarkable that this Question was carried against both the Old and New Ministry who opposed it.

See the Votes on the Report of this Committee.[195]

July 15, 1742. The Parliament was Prorogued.

Charge of the Train of Artillery sent to the Austrian Netherlands 1742 – <£>60,000

Exceedings on the Ordnance not provided for by Parliament 1742 – <£>98,048. 13. 05.

[195] See *C.J.*, XXIV, 259–60, for the report on 27 May.

<Second Session.>

November 16, 1742. The Parliament Met.
Division on the Address in the House of Commons.
Yeas   259.   Noes   150.

December 1. Motion to Enquire into the Conduct of the Earl of Orford. Yeas 186. Noes 253.
Note Sandys, Rushout, Gybbons who had been for the Motion and Enquiry and had constantly opposed Sir R. Walpole Measures when out of Place now voted for Him and against this Enquiry.
Debate in the House of Commons upon taking 16000 Hannoverian troops into English pay.
Yeas   260.   Noes   193.

February 1, 1742/43. Debate in the House of Lords upon the Hannover Troops.[196]
The Question was to Address the King that considering the excessive and greivous Expences incurred by the great Number of foreign Troops now in the Pay of Great Britain (Expences so increased by the extraordinary Manner of making the Estimates relating thereunto and which do not appear to us conducive to the Ends proposed) His Majesty will be graciously pleased, in Compassion to his People, loaded already with such numerous and heavy Taxes, such large and growing Debts, and greater annual Expences that this Nation at any time ever before sustained, to exonerate his Subjects of the Charge and Burden of those Mercenaries, who were taken into our Service last year, without the Advice or Consent of Parliament.

Contents 35.	Not Contents 90.
Lords who spoke	
For	Against
Earl Stanhope	Lord Carteret
who moved the Question	
Earl of Sandwich	Lord Bathurst
Duke of Bedford	Earl of Cholmondley
Lord Hervey	Earl of Bath
Earl of Chesterfield	Duke of Newcastle
Lord Lonsdale	Lord Chancellor

Afterwards Earl of Scarborough moved a Vote of Approbation of the Measure which was opposed by Earl of Oxford and Earl of Chesterfield.
Contents   78.   Not Contents   35.
See the Protest.[197]
Lords who voted For the first Question and Against the Second who did not Protest were

Duke of Montrose	Lord Romney
Earl of Suffolk	Lord Bristol
Earl of Halifax	Lord Hervey
Lord Lonsdale	Lord Brooke
Lord Masham	

---

[196] See also Cobbett, XII, 1058–1189.
[197] There were two protests that day, and Oxford signed both. *L.J.*, XXVI, 196–7.

The Prince staid during the greatest part of the Debate but went away before the Division. The Duke of Cumberland Divided in both Questions. Against the first and For the 2d.

Neither the Earl of Orford nor his Son Lord Walpole were present but purposely staid away, as they would not oppose so favorite a point as Hannover troops, nor would they Countenance a Scheme of Carterets.

25 February, 1742/43. Gin Bill passed.

Contents	59	⎫	82
Proxies	23	⎬	
Not Contents	38	⎫	55
Proxies	17	⎬	

All the Bishops present voted against this Bill and entered their Dissent. See the Protest of other lay Lords.[198]

February 11.[199] Question to Commit the Bill (brought in by Lord Rumney) for the farther Quieting and Establishing Corporations was opposed by Lord Chancellor.

      Contents   24.   Not Contents   63.

Bill rejected.

Vagrant Bill lost by the Commons disagreeing to the Lords Amendments which the Speaker took into his Head to be such as encroached upon the Privileges of the Commons in granting Money. Though the Commons disagreed as appears by the Votes Nemine Contradicente (which was done in flattery to the Speaker), yet most of them in Conversation in private ridiculed the Speakers Notions and thought the Amendments right. – A Conference was had upon this Bill, and Reasons given by the Commons. The Lords put off the consideration of those Reasons to such a day that the Parliament was prorogued, and thus a necessary Bill dropped.[200] [Note This Bill with the Lords Amendments passed the Commons the next Session February 1743/4 and was agreed to by the Lords and had the Royal Assent.][201]

Bill for rendring the Laws more effectual as to County Elections, (which was designed to curb the Power of Sheriffs and which had passed the House of Commons) was in a Committee of the House of Lords, where the Chancellor and the Earl of Bath by his amendments drew out the Sting of the Bill. When the Report was to be made the Court Lords who were against any Bill of this Kind moved to put of the Report to a long day, in which those who were for the Bill as sent up by the Commons agreed, as thinking the Bill as amended not sufficient to cure the Evil.[202]

---

198 Ten bishops and five peers entered a dissent, while ten further peers signed a protest, three of whom (including Oxford) did not subscribe to the second of the four reasons. *Ibid.*, pp. 218–19.

199 This should read March 11. Rumney was introduced on that day. *Ibid.*, p. 232.

200 The conference was held on 15 Apr. and the parliament was prorogued on the 21st. *Ibid.*, p. 240. The bill was printed. See Torrington, vol. 1739–43/4, pp. 445–68.

201 The Vagabonds, etc. and Houses of Correction Bill received the royal assent on 2 Mar. 1744. This bill was also printed, see Torrington, vol. 1739–43/4, pp. 487–510.

202 The bill was committed in the Lords on 15 Apr., and the report was put off until the 19th and then until 3 May. The parliament was prorogued on 21 Apr. *L.J.*, XXVI, 253, 255, 258.

April 21, 1743. The Parliament was prorogued after granting near 7 Millions and not passing one Publick Act for the Good of the People.

April 27. The King went on board the Yatchs for Holland in his Way to Hannover.

June 16. O.S. Battle of Dettingen.

Third Sessions.

December 1. The Parliament met.

December 7. Motion for an Address to Disband the Hannover Troops. Yeas <181>. Noes <231>.[203]

December 9. Motion for the Same Address in the House of Lords. Contents 36. Not Contents 71. See the Protest.[204]
    Mem: Lord Hervey took his Seat in the House of Lords as succeeding his Father who had been called up by Writ to his Fathers Barony, a Precedent for this in the Case of <Lord Clifford>.[205]

December 22, 1743. Mr Sandys created a Peer took his place in the House (being introduced by Lord Carteret and Lord Berkley) as Lord Sandys Baron of Ombersley. The Patent to his Heirs Male only.
    {*1743.* Mr Pelham made Chancellor of the Exchequer in the room of Sandys and first Commissioner of the Treasury in the room of Lord Wilmington deceased.
    Mr Winington Paymaster of the Army in the Room of Pelham.
    Mr Sandys Cofferer in the Room of Winington.
    Sir J. Rushout Treasury of the Navy in the room of Sir C. Wager deceased.
    Lord Midlesex a Commissioner of the Treasury in the room of Lord Wilmington.
    Mr Henry Fox a Commissioner of the Treasury in the room of Sir John Rushout.
    Lord Cholmondeley made Privy Seal in the Room of Lord Gower who resigned.}
    Also Mr Herbert of Oakley Park created a Peer took his seat (being introduced by Lord Monson and Lord Edgcumbe) as Lord Herbert Baron of Cherbury. The Patent to his Heirs Male only.

January 10. A Bill of Divorce between the Duke of Beaufort and Frances Scudamore Daughter of Lord Scudamore of Hom Lacy in Herefordshire for Her Adultery with Lord Talbot and to baztardise Her Daughter by Lord Talbot, read a 2d time in the House of Lords,[206] Council heard and Witnesses examined to prove the Allegations of the Bill,[207] none were produced against it.
    The next Day in the Committee Lord Ilchester Brother in Law to Mr Digby attempted to get a Clause inserted in the Bill to prevent the Dutchess from Marrying again as Mr Digby was in the Remainder. Bishop of Worcester (Maddox) spoke for it, and would have had the House resumed that it might have been further Considered. But it was opposed by Lord Gower and Lord Chancellor and the Clause dropped.

---

[203] Here EH left gaps. Figures from *C.J.*, XXIV, 487.

[204] Twenty-five (including Oxford) signed the protest. *L.J.*, XXVI, 276–7.

[205] Here EH left a gap. Charles Boyle succeeded his father (who had been called to the Lords in *his* father's barony) as Baron Clifford of Lanesborough in 1694, and succeeded his grandfather as 2nd earl of Burlington in 1698. *Complete Peerage*, II, 432.

[206] *L.J.*, XXVI, 287–8, 290.

[207] 'John Pargiter of Wardington in the County of Northampton, Farmer [told the Lords that] he lived near Chipping Warden and on the 2d June 1741 as the Duchess was walking alone in the Fields she was met by a man whom he did not know but described him and afterwards found it was the Lord Talbot that he saw the Duchess lie down on her Back with her Cloathes up and his Lordship upon her with his Breeches down the Exammont being within ten yards Distance from them.' H.L.R.O., Manuscript Minutes, 10 Jan. 1743/4. This case is discussed in Lawrence Stone, *Broken Lives. Separation and Divorce in England, 1660–1857* (Oxford, 1993), pp. 117–38.

January 13. The Bill passed the Lords.

When the Bill came to the Commons a Petition in behalf of Mr Digby was presented by Mr Henry Fox, but being exploded it was droped and no Amendment made but as to the Commencement of the Bill, which was agreed to by the Lords. The Bill had the Royal Assent March 2d.

January 11. Debate in the House of Commons on the English Forces. Question to leave the Chair. Yeas 165. Noes 277. Majority 112.

January 18. Debate in the House of Commons on Granting the Hannover troops. Yeas 271. Noes 226. Majority 45. – The next Day upon the Report the Question was again fully debated. And Mr William Pit offering to prove several facts (which He asserted) relating to the Misbehaviour of the Hannover troops in the last Campaign. Moved that the Debate might be adjourned to Monday, in order to introduce a 2d Question for such an Enquiry. Yeas 178. Noes 266. Upon which the Minority left the House for that night without staying till the main Question to agree with the Report was put. {Note. The Question for the Hanover troops was carried in both Houses by the influence and management of Sir Robert Walpole now Earl of Orford.}

January 31, 1743/4. Debate in the House of Lords on the Hannover troops. Motion against them moved by Lord Sandwich 2ded by the Duke of Marlborough who had been at the Battle of Dettingen and saw the Scandalous Behaviour of the Hannoverians and acknowledged the Facts asserted by Lord Sandwich.

      Contents   41.   Not Contents   86.

A Protest Entered the next day by <25>.[208]

A State of the National Debt as it stood on the 31 December 1742 and 31 December 1743.

Amount of the National Debt December 31, 1742.	<£>48,915,047: 16: 9
Increased between December 31, 1742 and December 31, 1743.	<£>2,318,600: 00: 00
Paid off within that time	<£>190,300: 00: 00
Amount of the Debt December 31, 1743.	<£>51,043,347: 16: 9

February 15. The Kings Message to both Houses relating to the French Invasion. See the Message and the Addresses of both House.[209]

February 24. Duke of Newcastle by the Kings Order lays before the House of Lords His Letter to Mr Thompson[210] resident at Paris to complain to the French Court that the Pretenders Son was in France and countenanced by the Court contrary to Treaties, and the French Minister Monsieur Amelots[211] answer that He had laid the same before his Master and that his Majestys Answer was That when the King of Great Britain gave a Satisfaction for his infraction of Treaties, He would then give an answer to the Complaint. Also the Deposition of the Master of the Dover Packet boat who saw the

---

[208] Here EH left a gap. Oxford was one of the protesters. *L.J.*, XXVI, 299–300.

[209] See *ibid.*, p. 311, and *C.J.*, XXIV, 568.

[210] Rev. Anthony Thompson, in charge of affairs in Paris 1740–4, formerly secretary and chaplain to the ambassador, the Earl Waldegrave, 1730–40. He was afterwards dean of Raphoe.

[211] Jean Jacques Amelot de Chaillou (1689–1749), minister of foreign affairs under Fleury, 1737–44.

Pretenders Son at Calais and the preparation the French were making for an Embarkation to invade England.

Duke of Newcastle concluded with no Motion as reasonably thinking that the late Address was sufficient and that there was no need of repeating it. But Lord Orford (who for the first time of speaking in the House since He was made a Peer) spoke for a new Address expressing great fears and Great Zeal. To this the Duke of Newcastle agreed and after some time the Chancellor penned a Question for an Address which was agreed to.

February 27. Colonel Cecil[212] committed to the Tower. The same Day at 6 in the Morning the Earl of Barrimore was taken into Custody and confined at his own House in Henrietta Street Cavendish Square being guarded by a file of Musqueteers. {*March 31, 1744.* Lord Barrimore was discharged upon Bail.}

March 2. The King came to the House and among other Bills passed one for suspending the Habeas Corpus Act for two Months to April 29.

March 15. N.S. War Proclaimed in France against England.

March 31. War Proclaimed in London against France.

In the Malt Act this year there is a Clause to exempt the first Buyer of Cyder for his own use only from the 4s Duty.

April 10. A Censure was moved on the Ministry for giving £40000 to the Duke D'Arembergh[213] to put the Austrian Troops in Motion as being a Misapplication of Publick Money and destructive of the Priviledges of the House. Yeas 145. Noes 259. {Question was. That the Issuing and Paying the Sum of £40000 to the Duke of Arembergh to put the Austrian Troops in Motion in 1742 was a Dangerous Misapplication of Publick Money and Destructive of the Rights of Parliament.} This was afterwards turned into a Vote of Approbation by an Amendment moved by Mr Winington. See the Votes.[214]

April 16. The Cause between Le Neve Appellant and Norris Respondent was determined in the House of Lords after three long days hearing.[215] This was the first Appeal against any of the Present Lord Chancellors (Lord Hardwick) Decrees. He took no part in the Hearing or Debate. Lord Orford (lately Sir Robert Walpole) strongly and scandalously sollicited it, and spoke an Hour in behalf of the Appellant. There was no one else spoke on the same side but his Son in law Lord Cholmondely, who rather read Notes that had been given Him, than spoke his own Sentiments. They were answered by Lord Bathurst and the Earl of Warwick. Upon the Question put for Reversing the Decree Lord Willoughby de Broke who had not attended till that Evening divided the House at the desire of Lord Orford, who vainly imagined A Majority of the Lords would follow Him as there used to do upon all his Jobs in the

212 Probably Lt.-Col. William Cecil (*c.* 1679–1745), equerry to George I and chief jacobite agent in London 1731–44. See Dalton, II, 35–8.
213 Leopold Philippe (1690–1754), duc d'Arenberg.
214 See *C.J.*, XXIV, 650.
215 See *L.J.*, XXVI, 366–8.

House of Commons. But the Honour of the Lords and the Justice of the Cause was too strong for Him. And though there was the greatest attendance of Temporal and Spiritual Lords during the whole Hearing and at giving Judgment that has been known, Yet upon the Division there were but nine who were for a Reversal.

Lord Orford
Lord Cholmondeley
Lord Walpole
Lord Ilchester (Fox)
Lord Fitzwilliams
Lord Ducie Morton
Lord Willoughby de Broke
Bishop of Exeter (Dr Clagget)
Bishop of Worcester (Madox)

Upon seeing the Numbers so few the Question was given up without telling.

April 27, 1744. The House was to be put into a Committee on the Bill to make it High Treason to hold Correspondence with the Sons of the Pretender which had been sent up by the Commons.[216]

Lord Chancellor moved an Instruction That the Committee do receive a Clause to suspend and Postpone the operation and Effect of the 10th Section of the Act of the 7th of Queen Anne[217] till after the Death of the Sons of the Pretender. [The Clause referred to provides, That after the Decease of the Pretender etc. no Attainder for Treason shall disinherit any Heir, nor prejudice the Right of any Person other than the Right of the Offender during his Natural Life.] Upon this Motion there was a long Debate. Those who spoke were as follows.

For the Clause	Against the Clause
Lord Chancellor	Duke of Bedford
Lord Ilchester	Lord Hervey
Lord Cholmondley	Lord Talbot
Lord Carteret	Lord Chesterfield
Bishop of Oxford	
Marquis of Tweedale	
Duke of Newcastle	

There was no Division which was occasioned by an ill timed Complement to Lord Halifax That it might not be seen that He voted for the Clause which He would have done had the House Divided. But however a Protest was entered by 19 Lords.[218]

The Bill itself to make it Treason to Correspond with the Pretenders Sons took its rise from Mr Hume Campbell Solicitor to the Prince, who this Session had come back to his old Freinds and had voted and spoke warmly and well against the Hannover troops. But to keep in the good favour of his Master moved this Bill and drew in some of the Tories to join Him as a means to take of the odium the Court cast on them as being Jacobites. To Keep up this Name and distinction was the private view of the Court in making this addition to the Bill in the House of Lords.

---

216 Printed in Torrington, vol. 1739–43/4, pp. 531–8.
217 7 Anne, c. 21: 1708 Act for Improving the Union of the Two Kingdoms. The 10th section referred to the treason law in Scotland. *Statutes of the Realm*, IX, 94.
218 Including Oxford. *L.J.*, XXVI, 380–1.

May 3. These amendments were debated in the House of Commons till between 12 and one in the morning. Division to agree with the Lords.

> Yeas   185.   Noes   106.

May 7, 1744. Debate on the Bill from the Commons intituled an Act for Enlarging and regulating the Trade to the Levant Seas. The intent was to lay open the Turkey Trade. Councel was heard for and against the Bill for 4 days and Sir Everard Fawkener[219] and the Turkey Merchants examined at the Bar. The cheif Defenders of the Bill were Lord Sandys, and Lord Warwick. Against it Duke of Bedford and Lord Sandwich. The Question was That the Debate be adjourned to this day Month in order to avoid the main Question of Commitment.

	Contents	Not Contents
	30	25
Proxies	5	8
	35	33

It was not usuall to call for Proxies where there had been an Examination of Witnesses upon Oath at the Bar.

Lord Chancellor voted against the Bill, who had two Proxies.[220]

Account delivered to the House of Commons March 13, 1743/4 of the Horses lost at the Battle of Dettingen.

Horse	99	valued at £20 each	£1980
Dragoons	232	at £15 each	<£>3480
	331		<£>5460

In the Value is included the Accoutrements as well as the Horse.

May 12, 1744. Parliament prorogued. In the Speakers Speech to the King He said £6,500,000 had been voted this year, and 10 Millions would be the Expence on the Nation. That it was therefore time for Publick Oeconomy etc.

---

[219] Sir Everard Fawkener (1684–1758), merchant and ambassador to Constantinople 1735–46, joint postmaster general 1745–58.

[220] Those of the earls of Breadalbane and Grantham. H.L.R.O., Proxy book, XIX.

<Fourth Session.>

November 24. Lord Carteret now Earl Granville by descent from his Mother quitted the Seals as Secretary of State, the Duke of Newcastle, Hardwicke Lord Chancellor, Mr Pelham Chancellor of the Exchequer and Several Lords their Dependents remonstrating to the King that his Measures were so violent that they could not act with Him. And though the King consented it was against his own pleasure and opinion.

{Mem: Lord Carteret sent for Lord Orford to town and offered Him the Treasurers Staff to join with Him against the Pelhams.

Mem: Some time before Lord Carteret was out He sent a Message by Lord Bath to Lord Chesterfield, Lord Gower and Lord Cobham with Authority from the King and Prince to confirm it That He would give them Chart Blanche and bring in all their freinds if they the Country Party would join Him, and as a proof of his Intentions would turn out the Pelhams the next day. Which they refused.

Soon after the Pelhams and Lord Chancellor negotiated with them upon which the changes were afterwards made. Note this Negotiation began in May 1743. Set on foot by Lord Bolingbroke[221] and transacted with Lord Chesterfield etc.

In this Change all Lord Baths freinds who were called the Deserters were turned out, few of Lord Carterets He having still the Kings Ear, and none of the Pelham or Walpole party except Jennison.}

November 27. The Parliament met.

December 22. Changes made in the Ministry.

The Inns		The outs
Waller	Cofferer in the place of	Lord Sandys
Dodington	Treasurer of the Navy	Sir J. Rushout
Arundel ⎫ Littleton ⎬	In the Treasury	⎧ Compton ⎨ Gybbons
William Chetwynd	Master of the Mint	Arundel
Sir J. Cotton	Treasurer of the Chamber	Lord Hobart
Lord Hobart	Captain of the Band of Pensioners	Lord Bathurst
Sir John Philips ⎫ John Pitt ⎬	Board of Trade	⎧ Sir Charles Gilmour ⎨ Benjamin Keen

{Note. Sir John Philips resigned his Place in the middle of the Session not approving of the Court Measures. This Place was afterwards given to Mr Baptist Leveson Gower younger Brother to Lord Gower Member for New Castle under Lime and the Writ was moved for the last day of the Session May 2d.}

Benjamin Keen	Paymaster of the Pensions	Ned Hooper
Duke of Bedford ⎫		⎧ Lord Winchelsea
Lord Sandwich ⎪		⎪ Sir C. Hardy dead
George Grenville ⎬	Admiralty	⎨ Dr Lee
Lord Vere Beauclerk ⎪		⎪ Philipson
Admiral Anson ⎭		⎩ Coburn
Lord Hallifax	BuckHounds	Jennison

---

[221] Henry St John (1678–1751), created Viscount Bolingbroke 1712, was attainted for treason in 1715, and restored in 1725 except for his seat in the house of lords.

Lord Gower	Privy Seal	Lord Cholmondeley
Lord Cholmondley	Vice Treasurer of Ireland	Harry Vane
Lord Chesterfield	Lord Lieutenant of Ireland	Duke of Devon<shire>
Duke of Devon<shire>	Lord Steward	Duke of Dorset
Duke of Dorset	President of the Council	Lord Harrington
Lord Harrington	Secretary of State	Lord Carteret,
		Earl of Granville

When Lord Hallifax who was Lord of the Bedchamber to the Prince, and Mr Lyttleton who was his Secretary came to Kiss his Hand upon their Preferment. He turned them both out of the Places they held under Him. For Lord Carteret had got so much the ascendant over Him that He was most highly displeased at his being turned out from being Secretary of State.

December 27. Lord Baltimore who was one of the Admiralty and also Lord of the Bed Chamber to the Prince resigns his Place at the Admiralty Board. Lord Archibald Hamilton stays in.

January 25. An Express brought the News of the Emperors Death.

March 18. Sir Robert Walpole Earl of Orford died.
Places held by the Walpole Family when Lord Orford asked and accepted a Pension of £4000 per annum out of the Excise.

	Per Annum £
Lord Walpole Auditor of the Exchequer	10000
Edward Walpole 2d Son of Lord Orford Clerk of the Pells	5000
Ditto Master of the Exchequer office	800
Horace Walpole 3d Son usher of the Exchequer	2000
Ditto a place in the Custom House	1000
Lord Orfords Pension	4000
	<£>22800 per annum
Horace Walpole Brother to Lord Orford	
Teller of the Exchequer	4000
Ditto Auditor of the Plantations besides	
Perquisites and Secret Services	2000
Brought over	22800
Totall held by the Walpole Family from the Publick per Annum	28800

The Fourth Sessions.

Parliament met November 27, 1745.[222]
This Session was remarkable for the Quiet of it. There being no Debate or Division on any Publick Matter in the House of Lords, and Few in the House of Commons.[223] The Court was divided into two Factions, The Carteret and the Pelham, and as they both strugled for Power, they both joined in all Votes for the supplies of the year, and

[222] EH wrote 1745 instead of 1744.
[223] There were 26 divisions. See *C.J.*, XXIV, 689–892 *passim*.

the Demands of the Court, and the Country party acquiessed in many of these (except the Vote of Credit) as they were assured by their Freinds who had joined the Pelham Party that they would in return consent to the passing Constitutional Bills. And the following proposals were delivered by the Duke of Beaufort and Sir W. Williams to Lord Gower.

1st. That there shall be new Commissions of the Peace for Every County, and that all Gentlemen of Fortune be admitted without Distinction.

2. That the Bill for the Qualification of Justices of the Peace be explained and made effectual.

3. That no Custom and Excise officers be allowed to Vote at Elections of Members to serve in Parliament and that a Bill be passed for that purpose.

4. That a Place Bill with restrictions be passed.

5. That there be an Enquiry into the State and Management of the Navy.

6. That when the Circumstances of Affairs will permit, such a Reduction of the Army be made, as shall be consistent with the Liberties of a Free People.

7. That there be as great Savings as possible in all Parliamentary Grants, and that a Spirit of Oeconomy be preserved.

8. That the 16000 Hannoverians shall not be continued in English Pay, but that other troops if necessary be provided in their Stead.

9. That such Measures only be persued as shall be consistent with the Interest of Great Brittain.

Of These Proposals None were complyed with but the Discharging the Hannoverians out of English Pay (See the Sum given for their Discharge).[224]

A Bill to regulate Elections of the Knights of the Shire.

A Bill to Secure the Qualification of the Justices of the Peace.

And a New Commission granted to some few Counties, but not to those where the Greivance was most Complained of.

But for a full and clear Account of this Session See a Pamphlet Entituled The Case fairly stated in a Letter from a Member of Parliament in the Country Intrest to one of his Constituents. 1745.[225]

Parliament prorogued May 2, 1745.

The King went abroad May <10>.

The King returned to England <31 August>.[226]

---

[224] The sum was £57,965 9s. 2½d, consisting of eight weeks pay for them to return home. *Ibid.*, pp. 762–3.

[225] Attributed to Thomas Carte. See Robert Harris, *A Patriot Press: National Politics and the London Press in the 1740s* (1993), pp. 72–4, 180–1, 188–9, 264.

[226] EH did not supply the dates here. They are taken from *Handbook of British Chronology*, ed. E.B. Fryde, D.E. Greenway, S. Porter and I. Roy (3rd edn., 1986), p. 46.

Fifth Sessions.

{The Pretenders Eldest Son landed in Scotland only with some Persons in <July>.[227]
Rebellion broke out in Scotland. 1745.
Rebells take Edingburgh.
Battle of Preston Pans. Cope[228] defeated.
Rebells take Carlisle.
Raise Contributions at Manchester and other places, march into Derby. Retreat from Derby the same way they came into Scotland leaving about 400 behind in Carlisle to secure their retreat.
Duke of Cumberland beseiges Carlisle which surrendered.
January 17, 1745/6. Battle near Falkirk General Hawley[229] defeated.
Duke of Cumberland goes to Scotland. Rebels retire from Stirling and the Seige of the Castle raised.
April 25, 1746. Rebells defeated near Inverness at the Battle of Culloden.
July 30. Mr Townley, David Morgan etc. were executed at Kennington Common.[230]
August 18. Lord Kilmarnock and Lord Balmerino beheaded on Tower Hill.
December 8. Charles Ratcliffe Esqe Brother to the late Earl of Derwentwater beheaded on Tower Hill.
Note Lord Kilmarnock, Lord Cromartie and Lord Balmerino were tryed by the Lords in Westminster Hall upon an Indictment when the two first pleaded Guilty. Lord Balmerino put himself on his Tryal and was found Guilty. See the printed Tryals.}[231]

Parliament Met October 17, 1745.

October 21. Habeas Corpus Suspended for six Months.

October 28. Question that a Committee be *Now* appointed to enquire into the Causes of the Progress of the Rebellion in Scotland. Yeas 112. Noes 194.

November 4. Report from the Committee of Supply upon the Estimate of two Regiments of Horse and 13 of Foot under the Command of Several Noblemen. This Estimate was very warmly debated both in the Committee and on the Report, and though it was brought in for 12 Months, yet upon the amendment for 4 Months the Court complyed without a Division. This was looked upon and debated as an arrant job on the Question for an Address to his Majesty, that the officers in these Regiments may not be allowed any Rank from their Commissions in the said Regiments; after those Regiments are broke.
It passed in the Negative. Yeas 132. Noes 155.
Same Question in the Committee. Yeas 124. Noes 126.

---

227 Here EH left a gap.
228 Sir John Cope (d. 1760), c. in c. in Scotland in 1745. The battle of Prestonpans was on 21 Sept. 1745.
229 Henry Hawley (?1679–1759), lt.-gen.
230 Francis Towneley (1709–46), captured at Carlisle. David Morgan was a barrister who acted for the duke of Beaufort, and a leading member of the Association of Independent Electors at Westminster.
231 *The Speeches of the Earls of Kilmarnock and Cromarty at their Trial before the House of Lords; with the Speech of the Lord High-Chancellor, ... as also the Sentence Pronounced against them and Lord Balmerino* (1746). B.L., *E.S.T.C.* database.

List of the Noblemen who were Commanders of these Regiments.

Horse	Numbers
Duke of Montagues	273
Duke of Kingstons	273
	546

Foot	
Duke of Boltons	814
Duke of Bedfords	814
Duke of Montagues	814
Duke of Ancasters	814
Marquis of Granby	814
Earl of Barkleys	814
Earl of Cholmondleys	814
Earl of Hallifax	814
Lord Viscount Falmouth	814
Lord Viscount Harcourts	814
Lord Gowers	814
Lord Herberts	814
Lord Edgecumbes	814
Numbers	10582

Pay of the Foot for 4 Months	£64360: 13: ½
Horse	<£>13176: 10:
Totall Expences for 4 Months	<£>77537: 03: ½

December 20, 1745. Message from the King to both Houses that He had sent for 6000 Hessians to be brought into Scotland. No Debate upon it in the House of Lords.

An amendment to the Address in the House of Commons made by Lord Cornbury (See the Votes of December 20 in which I have inserted the Amendment)[232] on which was a long debate. For the amendment 44. Against 190. Division on the main Question. For the Address 180. Against 32.

February 10. Duke of Newcastle and Lord Harrington resign the Seals of Secretary of State; which are both given to Lord Granville till a proper Partner could be found, who was to be (as said) Lord Cholmondeley.

February 11. Lord Gower resigns the Privy Seal. Lord Pembroke the Gold Key as Groom of the Stole. Duke of Bedford as first Commissioner of the Admiralty, the rest of the Board do the same (except Lord Archibald Hamilton). Mr Pelham resigns as Chancellor the Exchequer and first Commissioner of the Treasury and the rest of the Board (except Lord Middlesex do the same).

The Days following Lord Chancellor (Hardwick) and all the Pelham party intending to do the same, the Weight being so great, and the Supplys not being raised and the Moneyed Contractors, Gore, Vanneck and Gideon[233] the Jew in the City who had

---

232 For the amendment see *C.J.*, XXV, 25.

233 John Gore (*c.*1689–1763), leading government financier, and later M.P. for Great Grimsby 1747–61. Gerard van Neck. Samson Gideon (1699–1762), Jewish financier.

agreed with Pelham declaring they would be off their Bargain if He was out, and Granville not having formed a Party in the House of Commons. Lord Granville on the 14th resigned the Seals again and all the Old Ministry were restored to their Places. Winnington was the Negotiator. – The Blame was laid on the Earl of Baths rashness in going to the King to irritate Him against Mr Pitts being Secretary at War. If a New Ministry had succeeded Bath was to have been Chancellor of the Exchequer and first Commissioner of the Treasury, and Lord Carlisle to be Privy Seal. And Chief Justice Wills to be Chancellor. Within a few days after Lord *Berkley* of Stratton Captain of the Yeomen of the Guard and the Duke of Bolton freinds to Lord Granville resigned. {When Lord Berkley resigned his Staff to the Kings Hands, The King said He hoped his Lordship would not think it was his Act or Inclination, but He must Submit to the violence of the Times.}

Lord Torrington one of the Vice Treasurers of Ireland succeeded Lord Berkly to make room for Mr William Pit to be in his Place instead of Secretary of War about which place was the Contention. Lord Archibald Hamilton made Governour of Greenwich Hospital, and Lord Barrington succeeded Him in the Admiralty.

Mr George Grenville in the Board of Trade in the room of Colonel Bladen deceased. Mr Thomas Gore made Commissary General in the place of Mr Boone turned out.

April 23, 1746. Mr Winnington Pay-Master of the Army died and the Place is given to Mr William Pit. Sir William Yonge succeeds Mr Pit as joint Treasurer of Ireland. And Mr Henry Fox succeeds Sir William Yonge as Secretary at War.

February <10,> 1745/6. Brussels surrendred to the French on Capitulation after <three>[234] weeks seige.

February 25. Bill for the more speedy Tryal of the Rebells read a 3d time and passed the Lords. To which I was the only Negative, as I thought it a law ex post facto, and contrary to the Common Law of England. And I entered my Dissent to the Bill in the Journals the next Day.[235]

Number of Cattle which died in Middlesex from November 25, 1745 to 17 January 1745/6:

> Cows and Bulls   2266.   Calves   301.

{It appears from the Account of the Nett Produce of the Customs presented to Parliament, that the *Revenue* since the year *1724* (at which Time, Tea, Coffee and Chocolate began to be excised) has by Smuggling been defrauded of above 7 Millions Sterling.}

March 10. Debate in the House of Commons on Sir J. Barnards Proposal which was rejected though He offerred to save £400000 to the Nation by it,[236] and desired only till the day after to produce a List of Subscribers to raise the Money wanting which was

---

[234] EH left blanks here. Maurice of Saxony's troops had surrounded Brussels by 30 Jan. 1746 n.s. and the city capitulated on 21 Feb. 1746 n.s. Reed Browning, *The War of the Austrian Succession* (Stroud, 1993), p. 259; Heinrich Benedikt, *Als Belgien Österreichisch War* (Vienna, 1965), p. 95.

[235] Oxford was the only dissenter, and no reasons were given. *L.J.*, XXVI, 544. The bill received the royal assent, 19 Mar.

[236] Barnard's remedy for what he saw as corrupt and inefficient public finance was to raise subscriptions directly from the public cutting out the middlemen. For its rejection on 10 Mar., see Sedgwick, I, 436. This system was adopted in 1747–8. See P.G.M. Dickson, *The Financial Revolution in England. A Study in the Development of Public Credit, 1688–1756* (1967), pp. 226–7, 285–90

3 Millions and offered a Security of <£250,000>[237] for the payment of it. But Mr Pelhams Bargain with Gideon the Jew, Vanneck a Dutch man and others was accepted. Yeas 231. Noes 132.

National Debt 1746.

At Christmas 1745 as given into Parliament	<£>56,525,447

To which may be added

Civil List of King George 1st commonly called the 6d Act	<£>1,000,000
By the Duty on Glass	<£>3,000,000
Annuitys 1745 for Lives valued at 12 years purchase 22500	<£>270,000
Ditto 1746 45,000 at 12 years purchase	<£>540,000
Navy Debt at Christmas 1745 unprovided for by Parliament	<£>3,871,095
Totall of the National Debt at Lady day 1746	<£>65,206,542

April 11. Debate in the Committee of Supply to take 18000 Hannoverians into British Pay to serve in Flanders. Yeas 255. Noes 122. Mr Pit who had been so warm against the Hannoverian Troops before spoke as Warm now for this Measure.

April 14. Debated again upon the Report Yeas 199. Noes 83.

See the Elector of Hannovers Proposals delivered to the House in relation to these Troops.

Lord Harringtons Letter to the Dutch – and the answer of the Dutch Ministers.

April 19, 1746. The King came to the House and passed the Bill for suspending the Habeas Corpus Act for 6 Months longer.

May 2. Debate in the House of Lords upon carrying on the War in Flanders. Question moved by Lord Oxford seconded by the Duke of Beaufort.[238] Other Lords who spoke for the Question were Lord Talbot, Earl of Westmorland, Lord Lonsdale. Against it Lord Hallifax, Lord Sandwich, Duke of Newcastle, Lord Chancellor, Lord Harrington.

Contents 26. Not Contents 81.

Lords who voted for the Question.

Beaufort	Northampton	Thanet	Shaftsbury
Suffolk	Westmorland	Aylesbury	Litchfeild
Abingdon	Oxford	Ferrers	Aylsford
Stanhope	Hereford	Lonsdale	Wentworth
Maynard	Ward	Boyle	Montjoy
Craven	St John of Bletscoe	Mansel	Foley
Romney	Talbot		

See the Protest signed by the following Lords.[239] Beaufort, Montjoy, Suffolk and Berkshire, Northampton, Westmorland, Ferrers, Oxford and Mortimer, Abingdon, Aylesford, Hereford, Craven, Shaftesbury, Litchfeild, Stanhope, St John de Bletsoe, Ward, Maynard, Boyle, Foley, Talbot.

---

[237] Here EH left a blank. The figure of £250,000 for the deposit, to be paid in government securities, is obtained from Sir John Barnard, *A Defence of Several Proposals for Raising of Three Millions for the Service of the Government, for the Year 1746* (1746), p. 25.

[238] The motion was for an address to the king against carrying on the war in Flanders. *L.J.*, XXVI, 575.

[239] *Ibid.*, pp. 575–6.

April 28, 29, 30. Complements made by both Houses of Parliament to the Duke of Cumberland.

May 13, 15. Commons vote £25000 per annum out of the Aggregate Fund to the Duke of Cumberland and a Bill ordered accordingly which had the Royal Assent June 4.

June 3. Bill to prevent Smugling put off from time to time. See July 9.

June 6. The Report relating to the Army, see the Printed Report,[240] relating to Mastering, Recruiting and Cloathing.

June 16. Report relating to the Fees of the Serjeant at Arms.[241] See also June 19.

{*June 23.* Report from the Committee to enquire into the Causes of the Infamous Practice of Smugling. The Consideration adjourned from time to time and nothing done upon it. See July 9.[242]

June 27. A Bill brought in by the Attorney General for the further Punishment of Persons going around in defiance of the Laws of Customs or Excise passed. Royal Assent August 12.}

July 2. The Commons put of the Consideration of the *Amendments* made by the Lords to the Bill for the better Securing Prizes etc. for two months, looking upon it as a Money Bill.[243] And The Journals of the 3d of May 1699, 8th of April 1700 and 26th of March 1719 being Reasons for disagreeing with the Lords on several Bills. See the Votes and Journal of this Day.[244]

July 2. Bill from the Lords for Building a Chapel in Wolverhampton rejected and the Journal of 19 May 1662 in relation to the Reason of the Dissent of this House to some amendments of the Lords to the Bill for Highways read.[245]

August 5. Sir John Douglas a Member committed for High Treason to the Tower.[246]

August 12. The King came to the House and passed Several Bills among others
An Act to prevent Ministers officiating in Episcopal Meeting Houses in Scotland etc. An extraordinary Bill. See p. 126.[247]
An Act for disarming the Highlands in Scotland.
Parliament Prorogued.
{£500,000 granted for suppressing the Rebellion.
Lord Traquair committed to the Tower for High Treason. He was bailed February <9>,[248] 1747/8.}

---

240 For the report see Lambert, XVI, 143–377.
241 *C.J.*, XXV, 170–1, 173.
242 *Ibid.*, pp. 174, 180.
243 The bill was printed. See Torrington, vol. 1744/5–46/7, pp. 111–26.
244 *C.J.*, XXV, 178–9; and XII, 681–3 (1699); XIII, 317–19 (1700); XIX, 142–4 (1719), all disagreements over supply bills.
245 *Ibid.*, VIII, 435.
246 He was released in Mar. 1748 due to insufficient evidence. Sedgwick, I, 618.
247 I.e., folio 126. See entry for 10 May 1748, p. 83 below.
248 Here EH left a gap. The date comes from *Complete Peerage*, XII, pt. 2, 12.

Sixth Session.

Parliament Met November 18, 1746.

November 18. Lords pass the An <sic> Act for Suspending the Habeas Corpus passed by the Commons November 20.

Royal Assent November 21.

December 11. Lord Lovat Impeached and the Message carried to the Lords by Sir W. Yonge.

December 17. Articles carryed to the Lords.

January 14. Lord Lovats Answer.

January 16. Commons Replication carryed to the Lords.

March 9. Lord Lovats Trial began in Westminster Hall and continued the 10th, 11th, 13th, 16th, 18th, 19th when Judgment was given.

{When the Lords sent a Message to the House of Commons March 18, 1746/7 That they would proceed the next day to give Judgment against Lord Lovat.

They Resolved Nemine Contradicente That the Committee appoint to manage the Impeachment, be impowered, in case the House of Lords shall proceed to give Judgment before the same is demanded by this House, *to insist upon it* that it is not parliamentary for their Lordships to give Judgment, until the same be first demanded by this House.

The next day the Speaker with the Mace came to the Bar of the House of Lords and demanded Judgment.}[249]

April 9, 1747. Lord Lovat beheaded on Tower Hill.

December 15. <£>456733. 16. 03. granted to make good the Deficiency of the Civil List. See the other Grants this day as £500,000.

January 21. Resolutions in the Committee on extending the Window Tax. See the Act which had the Royal Assent February 5.

{*January 29, 1746/7.* Divisions upon the Window Tax.

Against the Limitation of the Number of Windows	152
For it	123
For the Clause in favour of the Universitys	124
Against it	39}

January 27. Resolution in the Committee on the Tax upon Coaches. See the Act which had the R<oyal> A<ssent> 24 March.

The same day £433,333. 06s. 8d. granted to the Queen of Hungary to maintain 60000 Men in the Low Countries for the year 1747.

£300,000 to the King of Sardinia.

<£>400,000 for 18000 Hannoverians.

<£>10000 for a Train of Artillery.

[249] See *C.J.*, XXV, 320–1.

February 9. Grants £24299. 01. 04. to the Elector of Cologne.

<£>8600 to the Elector of Mentz.

<£>26846: 11: 9: to the Elector of Bavaria.

<£>166198. 18. 4. ¼ for defraying the extraordinary Expences of the Rebellion 1746.

<£>161607: 17: 01: ½ for Hessian Troops.

£6120 for 408 Horses lost in Flanders and at the Battles of Falkirk and Culloden 1746.

£30000 to Westminster Bridge.

March 24. There was granted £500,000 to carry on the War with Vigour.

March 24. The Managers of the Impeachment against Lord Lovat appointed as a Committee to enquire into a Complaint made that John W<illia>ms Keeper of an Inn in Piccadilly had been beat at the Meeting of the Independent Electors of Westminster. This turned out so ridiculous a Enquiry that most of the Managers declined attending at Sir W. Yonges House where the Committee was held. No Report was made, and Sir William Yonge and Lord Coke who had promoted it laughed at.

April <17>.[250] The French enter Dutch Flanders and take Sluys, the Zealanders declare the Prince of Orange Stadtholder, the other Provinces afterwards do the same the States being overawed by the Populace.

Debt of the Navy 31 December 1746. <£>5,233,746. 19. 06. ¼.

State of the National Debt 31 <December>[251] 1746 as by the Account delivered to the House of Lords. <£>59,356,497. 16. 09. ¼

May 14, 1747. The Bill to take away the Heritable Jurisdictions etc. in Scotland passed the House of Commons. Yeas 137. Noes 53.

May 21. Debate in the House of Lords on the Commitment of this bill. Contents 79. Not Contents 16. Of which were only 3 of the Scotch Peers. Councel were heard on the 2d reading of the Bill in support of the Duke of Queensburys and Lord Egletouns Petitions against it.[252]

{Claims for the Hereditable Jurisdictions as printed in the publick Papers December 1747

For Hereditable Jurisdictions	<£>589081. 00. 00.
For Hereditable Clerkships	<£>9446. 13. 04.
Totall	<£>598,527. 13. 04.

I have heard that the Revenue of Scotland at the time of the Union was

£	
24000	Capital
5000	Current Cash
64000	Military and Civil Service
£93,000	

---

[250] Here EH left a gap. The date comes from the *Gentleman's Magazine*, XVII (1747), 177, 202.
[251] Here EH left a gap.
[252] The 2nd reading was on 20 May. *L.J.*, XXVII, 117. For the petitions see *ibid.*, pp. 114–15.

By the Resolution of the Court of Session in Scotland March 8, 1747/8 concerning the Values of the Heretable Jurisdictions

  Totall   <£>164232. 60. 00}

The Lords who voted against it were. Duke of Beaufort, Earls of Denbigh, Westmoreland, Doncaster, Shaftsbury, Litchfeild, *Murray, Sutherland, Moreton* These 3 were Scotch,[253] Oxford, Ferrers, Stanhope, Viscount Say and Sele, Lords Ward, Craven, Talbot. See the Protest[254] Subscribed by

Duke of Beaufort	Ferrers
Denbigh	Stanhope
Westmoreland	Ward
Shaftsbury	Talbot
Litchfeild	
Oxford	

June 18. Parliament prorogued.

June 19. Parliament Dissolved notwithstanding there was another Session remaining.

June 22. The Writs bore Teste and were made returnable August 13th.

July 15. Lord Harley and Mr Cornewall were chose for the County of Hereford without Opposition.[255]

---

[253] The duke of Buccleuch (who sat in the Lords by reason of his English title of earl of Doncaster, to which he had recently been restored) was also Scottish.
[254] For the protest see *L.J.*, XXVII, 118–19.
[255] See Sedgwick, I, 257–8.

<First Session.>

November 10. The Parliament met.
Mr Onslow was again chosen Speaker.

November 23. Lord Dupplin chose Chairman of the Committee of Privileges and Elections.

Estimate of the Charge of Guards and Garrisons and other Land Forces for the year 1748.[256]

Horse	1250
Dragons	6489
Foot	42200[257]
Total Number of Men	49,939
Totall of Pay for the Men and Contingencies	£1,267,376. 15s. 09d.
Victualling the Forces 1747	<£>43937. 11. 03.

Plantation Service 1748.

Number of Men	15027
Pay	<£>350034: 14: 01:

February 6, 1747/8. Lord Chesterfeild resigned the Seals of Secretary of State which were given to the Duke of Bedford February 13.
Mem: The Propositions sent by the Prince to the Lords and Gentlemen in the Oposition by Lord Talbot and Sir Francis Dashwood Dated June 4, 1747. The answer agreed to February 6, 1747/8 at the Duke of Beauforts present Duke of Beaufort, Lord Westmoreland, Lord Litchfeild, Lord Shaftsbury, Lord Oxford, Sir Walter Bagot, Sir John Cotton, Mr Prowse, which was presented to the Prince by Sir Francis Dashwood February 8. [See a Copy of the Proposals and the Answer among my Papers.][258]

March 23, 1747/8. Debate in the House of Lords on the bill for fixing the Summer Assizes for the County of Bucks at the Town of Buckingham. For Committing the Bill 56. Against it 40.

April 4. Bill read a 3d time and passed. Contents 29. Not Contents 54.
This Bill a job on the Court side to promote the Interest of the Greenvilles in the town of Buckingham, and on the Princes<?> as Court to support Chief Justice Willes for the Town of Aylesbury, who had removed the Assizes from Buckingham to Aylesbury the Summer Assizes during the Election year.

April <19,> 1748.[259] Preliminaries of Peace signed at Aix by the English French and Dutch Ministers, Queen of Hungary protests against it.

---

256 For details see *C.J.*, XXV, 440–1.

257 Figure should be £42,190. *Ibid.*

258 The proposals (or Carlton House declaration) are printed in *The Eighteenth-Century Constitution, 1688–1815*, ed. E.N. Williams (Cambridge, 1960), pp. 180–1. The answer, which was 'respectful but cold', is in B.L., Add. MS 35337, f. 116. See also, Colley, p. 254.

259 Here EH left a gap. The date 19th o.s./30th n.s. comes from the *Gentleman's Magazine*, XVIII (1748), 222.

October 11 N.S.[260] The Definitive Treaty of Peace signed at Aix la Chapelle by the Ministers of England, France and Holland.

February 2, 1748/9. The Peace proclaimed in London

Money Voted 1748.

To make good Deficiencys	<£>2,858,629
Forreign Subsidies	<£>1,743,313
Navy	<£>2,308,827
Army	<£>2,240,534
Grants	<£>1,533,783
	<£>10,689,086
National Debt at Christmas 1748	<£>78,341,736

May 10. Debate in the House of Lords in the Committee upon the Clause (in the Bill for inforcing the Act of the 19th of Geo. 2di for disarming the Highlands etc.) relating to the Episcopal Clergy in Scotland.[261] On the Division whether this Clause should stand part of the Bill. Contents 28. Not Contents 32.

Note 20 Bishops were present who unanimously voted against the Clause.

The next day the Court summoned their troops when the Clause was replaced by 37 against 32.

The Chancellor the great stickler for the Clause.

May 12. Lord Herbert of Chirbury created Baron Powis, Viscount Ludlow and Earl of Powis.

Fryday May 13. The King came to the House and prorogued the Parliament and at four a Clock the Same day He set out for Gravesend to go abroad the Yatch and lying Windbound at Harwich did not land in Holland till Sunday May 22. The King returned to England the middle of November 1748.

Gibson Bishop of London died, Sherlock Bishop of Salisbury translated to London and Gilbert Bishop of Landaff to Salisbury. Cresset Dean.

Dean of Hereford Dr Cresset made Bishop of Landaff.

---

[260] The date should be 18 Oct. n.s. (7 Oct. o.s.). The correct date comes from *ibid.*, p. 497.

[261] The clause prohibited all episcopal ministers in Scotland who had not received their orders from an English or Irish bishop from officiating in any meeting house. It was an amendment to a statute of 1746 (13 Geo. II, c. 38) which had enacted that the orders of all episcopal ministers had to be registered by 1 Sept. 1746, and that after that date only orders conferred by English or Irish bishops could be registered. See Stephen Taylor, 'The Bishops and the Government in the Mid-Eighteenth Century', in *A Pillar of the Constitution: The House of Lords in British Politics, 1640–1784*, ed. Clyve Jones (1989), pp. 153–6.

<Second Session.>

November 29, 1748. 2d Session The Parliament met.

26 January, 1748/9. Debate in the House of Lords on the Act declaring the Authority of the Commissioners appointed by his Majesty under the Great Seal of Great Britain for determining Appeals in Cases of Prizes.

The Doubt of the legality of this Commission arose from the Judges who were appointed Commissioners to act with the Privy Council, and were equally divided in their opinion, and when called upon by the Lords gave their several reasons for their opinion.

{*January 26, 1748/9.* The Judges were directed to deliver their opinion Seriatim whether the Commission be legal or not.

Legal	Illegal
Mr Baron Legge	Mr Justice Birch
Mr Baron Clive	Mr Justice Dennsion not a proper Commission
Mr Baron Clarke	Mr Justice Foster
Mr Justice Burnet	Mr Justice Abney
Lord Cheif Baron Parker	Mr Justice Wright
Lord Cheif Justice of the	Lord Cheif Justice of the
Kings Bench Lee	Common Pleas Willes}

March 15, 1748/9. Debate in the House of Lords on the 2d reading the Mutiny Bill. Motion by Lord Bath that it be an Instruction to the Committee, That they do provide that no Punishment shall be inflicted at any Court Martial which shall extend to Life or Limb. It was resolved in the Negative.

Contents   16.   Not Contents   88.

Note Lord Granville and his particular freinds were absent, and all the Princes party voted against the Instruction. As did the Duke of Cumberland. The Prince was present but did not Vote.

The 16 Lords who voted for the Instruction were

Dukes of	Beaufort
	Ancaster
	Rutland
Earls of	Westmoreland*
	Litchfeild
	Shaftsbury
	Chesterfeild
	Oxford*
	Bath*
Viscount	Folkstone
Lords	Ward
	Maynard
	Craven
	Rumney
	Talbot
	Ravensworth*

The Lords marked thus * spoke.

March 17. The House being in a Committee on the Mutiny Bill.

The following Question was put to the Judges – Whether the Half pay officers would by virtue of the first enacting Clause be Subject to Martial Law?

There were only the 3 Cheifs present. The Lord Chief Baron Parker of opinion That the Half pay officers were included. Lord Chief Justice Willes That the Clause did not extend to them. Lord Chief Justice Lee declared himself doubtfull for Want of due Information.

The Clause was afterwards agreed to.

March 18. The House again in the Committee on the Mutiny.

It was proposed to leave out those Words relating to the Half pay officers. After Debate

Contents   15.   Not Contents   72.

A Proviso was offered, That every Peer in the Army should by tryed by his Peers only in all capital Cases mentioned in the Bill and not by a Court Martial unless out of the Kingdom.

Contents   12.   Not Contents   73.

Note. Few of the 16 Lords who voted for the Instruction March 15 were pesent or voted either of these last Days.

May 26, 1749. The King not coming to the House. The Acts ready for the Royal Assent were passed by Commission to the ArchBishop of Canterbury, Lord Chancellor etc. The Commissioners Sat on a Bench below the Steps of the Throne in their Robes, the rest of the Lords were unrobed. The Speaker of the House of Commons was in his Black Gown, and when He brought up the Money Bill He only delivered it to the Clerk without any Speech.

In the Commission all the Acts to be passed were recited.

13 June 1749. Parliament prorogued.

3d Sessions.

16 November 1749. Parliament met.

{*16 November 1749.* A New Writ order'd for Westminster in the room of Lord Trentham on his being made one of the Commissioners of the Admiralty. Election began and Continued.

   The Scrutiny began 23 of February. High Bailiff call'd upon for the return of his Writ, who upon his Examination acquainted the House he was now in the Execution of it, That he avoided all unnecessary delay etc. Speaker directed to Recommend to him to Expedite the Election.}

29 November. See the Resolutions[262] for reducing the 4 per cent annuities to 3. – A Bill ordered upon them which passed the Royal Assent December 20. The great Companies refuse to Subscribe. – Afterwards agree and <£38,806,976>[263] Millions are Subscribed before the 28 of February the day fixed by Parliament.

   Land Tax 3s in the pound.

February 6. Bill ordered for the taking of the Duties on Pig and Bar Iron made in and imported from his Majestys Colonies in America.

Parliament prorogued.[264]

---

[262] *C.J.*, XXV, 903–4.
[263] Here EH left a gap. The figure comes from Dickson, *Financial Revolution*, p. 239.
[264] On 12 Apr. 1750.

<Fourth Session.>

January 17, 1750/1. Parliament Met.

January 22. The two Houses ordered a Paper entitled Constitutional Queries[265] reflecting on the Duke of Cumberland to be burnt by the Hangman in Palace yard January 25. – A Proclamation of a Reward of £500 to discover the author.

---

[265] See *C.J.*, XXVI, 9; XXVII, 478–9. The paper was called 'Constitutional Queries, Earnestly Recommended to the Serious Consideration of every True Briton'.

THE PARLIAMENTARY JOURNAL OF
WILLIAM HAY,
M.P. FOR SEAFORD,
1734–1744

These notes were written by William Hay. Born 1695. M.P. for Seaford from 1733 till his death in 1755 at Glynbourne Sussex.

In 1738 he was appointed a Commissioner of the Victualling Office and in 1753 he was made Keeper of the Tower Records.[1]

---

[1] WH was made keeper of the records in the Tower of London in 1754. See above, p. xviii, for a discussion of the identity of the copyist of the journal.

January 17. 1733/4.

The House ordered the Speaker[2] to issue his Warrant to the Clerk of the Crown to make out a new Writt for Electing a Baron for the Town and Port of Seaford in the Room of Lord Hardwick.[3]

January 20.

The Warden of the Cinque Ports's Praecept to the Bailiff of Seaford was delivered to the Bailiff: by the Favour of the Wardens Deputy, who has six Days allowed him by the Statute after the Receipt of the Writt to make out his Precept: and it was brought directly from his Office in Town, and not from Dover, where he resides, and whence I suppose the Writ ought regularly to be sent.

January 21.

The Bailiff gave Notice of Election on the 25th. The Duke of Newcastle told me it might have been on the 24th, but I doubt it, and think the Day of Notice and Election should not be both inclusive, the Statute requiring four day's Notice at Least.

January 25.

The Bailiff called a Comon Hall, where the Names of the Freemen were called over; then he nominated me as a Freeman, which was agreed to, and I took an Oath to be faithfull to the King and the Rights of the Corporation.

Then the Precept was read, and the Bailiff proposed me as their Member, which was unanimously agreed to. Then I executed one Part of an Indenture and the Bailiff set the Corporation Seal to the Other: Witnessing that they had elected me a Baron in the room of Lord Hardwicke to consent for them to such things as should be debated in Parliament.

January 28.

The Indentures with the Precept were returned to the Warden's Deputy's Office (or supposed so to be) and from thence with the Writt to the Clerk of the Crown; and a Certificate made out by him in this Form.

This is to certify that W<illiam> H<ay> Esquire is returned by Indenture a Baron for the Town and Port of Seaford to serve in this Present Parliament:

Witness our hands _____ } Clerks of the Crown.
                            _____

January 29.

I delivered this Certificate to Mr. Hamlin[4] who administered the Oaths of Allegance and Supremacy to me in the presence of Mr. Pelham, one amongst others appointed a Comissioner by the Lord Steward for that purpose: I paid Mr. Hamlin a Fee of £2 12s. 8d; and he gave me a new Certificate that I had taken the said Oaths before him; which I carried into the House, when I was introduced, and delivered in at the Table to the Clerk; who administered the same Oaths to me again, and then I made and subscribed the Declaration, and took and subscribed the Abjuration. And I paid a Fee of a Shilling to the Clerk.

---

[2] Arthur Onslow. See Appendix.

[3] Philip Yorke had been created Baron Hardwicke on 23 Nov. 1733.

[4] Zachary Hamlyn, first appointed clerk to Paul Jodrell, clerk of the Commons 1683–1727, became the unofficial clerk of the papers. O.C. Williams, *The Clerical Organization of the House of Commons, 1661–1850* (Oxford, 1954), pp. 40, 45, 52, 131 n. 2, 192, 194, 292, 307.

February 4.

The Petition of the Dealers in Tea was presented to the House, complaining of the Hardship of their being subject to the Excise Laws, that the Inland Duty of 4s. per Pound on Tea besides the Subsidies on Importation (about 9d) was more than twice the Value of it in Foreign markets, which had encouraged the Smugling it, to the carrying great Sums out of the Kingdom, the Diminution of the Revenue, the Prejudice of the East India Company, and the ruin of the fair Trader.

The Question was, whether it should be referred to a Committee.

In this Debate, It was agreed by all that great Quantities of Teas were run, Berry <sic – Perry?> said to the value of £500,000, Plumer £200,000, But I am informed by Mr. Walker, late Comissioner of the Customs, that 'tis about £100,000.

The Seisures last year Sir R. Walpole said amounted to £34000 in the whole.

It was said that the India Company have 3,000,000 pounds of Tea by them, which they would not sell at under value.

It was Agreed, that the Height of the Duty in Proportion to the Price of the Comodity was the occasion of running it (as it is in all Comodities).

Mr. Walker tells me the Prime Cost in the Country is about 6d. per Pound. Perry said in the Debate, it now sold in Holland for 2s and in 1730 for 7s. (which I suppose was occasion'd by the Dutch and French having each 4 Ships sent to China in 1729, as Sir R. Walpole said they had.)

Various methods were proposed to prevent the running. Some were for lowering the Duty (which had that effect as Sandys said on Chocolate and some other commodities, and had raised the Revenue into the bargain.)

Barnard was for proportioning the Duty to Value of the Tea, viz. each species of it.

The India Company to discourage Running propose to set up 1,000,000 of Tea at no Price, but sell it for what they can get, as Go<u>ld and Drummond informed the House.

Some said the returning the Duties to the Customs might prevent it, but without reason. Sir R. W<alpole> said that annihalating the Duty might prevent it, but removing it from one method to another would not alter the Case. And Bernard allowed, that as the excise Laws did not prevent Running so they were not the occasion of it.

The other Point debated was whether the Duty should be any longer collected by way of Excise.

Some said that Way was very burthensome and no Advantage to the Revenue; for if the Duty had produced more, it was not owing to that method of collecting, but to a greater consumption of the Commodity. Sir R. W<alpole> said that the run Tea more than answered the excess of the Consumption. That the lowest year of the Excise (which I think was £113,000, and including forfeitures 134,000) was more than the highest of the Customs, which amounted but to £110,000; – that comparing the seven last years of the Customs with the 7 first of the Excise, the latter had brought in £860,000 more to the Publick. – And that the Duty of Tea now in possession of the Company must be looked upon (unless exported) as so much Revenue in hand.

On the Division 233 were against referring the Petition to a Comittee, and 155 for it:

I voted with the Majority. For I thought the Petition ill timed. And thought it might be very reasonable to examine into Facts concerning the Running of Tea (which occasions so much Money to be yearly carried out of the Nation), yet I thought it more prudent to waive the Consideration of it now, than revive the unjust Clamour of the Excise, for which the Petition seemed calculated. – Besides, I thought it dangerous to try experiments, which might lessen the Revenue, at a time when it might be wanted for a War.

February 6.

In the Comittee of Supply, in considering the Estimate of the Charge of Guards and Garrisons and other Land Forces in Great Britain for 1734, the Question was whether in the 17,704 men (which all agreed was necessary this year, and was the same number as was voted last) three Regiments amounting to 1800 men sent to Gibraltar two years ago should be included.

Those who were against the Augmentation allowed that in our present State of uncertainty with regard to foreign affairs, it was necessary to secure Gibraltar, and put the Nation in a posture of Defence; they were willing to allow the same number as last year; but were against this Augmentation, unless they were informed from whence our danger was apprehended.

The Ministry kept a prudent reserve on that head, I suppose, for fear what they should say might be reported abroad and give umbrage to any foreign power.

The Master of the Rolls[5] voted against it for a very weak reason, which was, lest this Augmentation might be construed by foreign Powers, to be taking a Part in their Quarrels, when I believe he consented before to the Augmentation of Sea Men, which might more justly be called taking a Part, since they were an Offensive Force to be sent Abroad, and this only a defensive one, to be kept within the Kingdom.

On a Division 162 Voted against the Augmentation, and 262 for it.

I Voted for it; for since Gibraltar was to be secured, and such a Number of men were sent for that Purpose; and since the Nation was to be put in a posture of defence, I thought it very reasonable to put it in the same Posture of Defence it was in, before those Forces were sent to Gibraltar: especialy since it was to be done the cheapest way, by only adding private men to each Company. Besides, I thought that the Parliaments' concurrence with the King in this request (which was a very moderate one) would give his Majesty a greater influence in Foreign Courts.

February 7.

A Petition was presented by Sir John Barnard from the City of London for a Bill for the more easy and speedy Recovery of small Debts within the City and Liberties.

Mr. Earl moved that the Bill might be general for the whole Kingdom, and I seconded the Motion; for I know no greater Grievance than the difficulty of recovering small Debts; and where the Evil is General the remedy ought not to be particular.

It was ordered Nem. con. and Barnard was so out of humour, that the bill was not for the City, fearing that a general one might be lost, as it was once before, that he refused to be one of the Persons to bring it in.[6]

February 8.

I attended the Comittee of Elections, which met now for the first time. After eight nominated of the Comittee were assembled in the Speaker's Chamber, we adjourned into the House; and Mr. Earl was called on to take the Chair. Two Complaints refferred to the Comittee were read, and days were moved for and appointed to hear them.

---

[5] Sir Joseph Jekyll. See Appendix.
[6] The bill (printed in Lambert, VII, 159–70) was introduced by Sir William Yonge on 22 Mar.

Then the Comittee adjourned; and the Chairman signed Warrants[a] to bring up the Persons complained of, and orders for the Complainants Witnesses to appear. The orders were left with Blanks, for the Complainant to insert what Names of Witnesses he pleased, which the Chairman told me was the usual Method.

February 11.

In the Comittee on the Bill to oblige Possessors of Lands, adjoining to Highways to cut and keep low their Hedges; I took Notice of the Exception of Timber Trees, and desired, that as they were frequently an Annoyance to narrow Roads, that there might be some Provision for that Evil, that so the Remedy intended by the Bill might be rendered compleat: I therefore proposed, that if Timber Trees stood within such a distance of a Road not exceeding such a breadth, and were presented on Oath by the Surveyors as a Nusance at the Special Sessions, the Owner on Notice should be obliged to cut them down, or on his neglect for so many days after Notice, the Surveyors by order of the special Sessions might do it.

Or else a small Penalty should be imposed on the Owner and applied to the repair of the Road in that Place.

I was told such Amendments could not be proposed in the Comittee but must be proposed on reading the Bill.

February 12.

The House went into a Committee on the Petition of the Woollen Manufactures.

'Twas agreed on all hands, that the Prejudice to the Woollen Manufactury here was principally the Exportation of Wool and Woollen Cloths from Ireland. And that the methods hitherto taken to prevent it had proved ineffectual.

One method is guarding the Coast: and Ships for some years have been Stationed round Ireland and have been kept there (as Thomson[8] said) at £25000 per Annum expence. But notwithstanding this precaution, Mr. Walpole said, 14000 peices of Manufactured Cloth had been this year sent from Ireland to Lisbon only, and he had a list of the Ships in which they were sent: and Mr. Earl said, it was notorious that 90 ships had loaded with Wool from one Port in Ireland; paying ½ per Cent for doing it.

Another method proposed, was by inflicting severer Penalties for exporting Wool: but this I think would be very ineffectual. Severe Laws are seldom put in execution. And as Mr. Earl observed the offenders must be tried by an Irish Jury, who look upon the Cause as their own.

A third Way, which was proposed by Mr. Danvers, was to restrain the growth of Wool in Ireland, by obliging the Irish to turn the Course of their husbandry another Way: But this is a scheme only in Theory, and not to be put in practice: they will make

---

[a] the Warrants of the Chairman only. But when the house on the Report orders a person into Custody the Speaker signs a Warrant to apprehend him. As Mr. Spence[7] the sergeant informed.

Lord Wilmington told me, that formerly if a Person ordered into Custody could not be taken during the Sessions, nothing could be done against him afterwards, because all proceedings end with the Sessions, so that the Sergeant was punished more than the Party, being at Expence in sending after him to no purpose. But he obtained a standing order: that where the Party could not be taken through his own default, that the order for taking him might be revived the next Sessions; I supose on Motion for that purpose. The Case is the same if he refuses to pay his Fees. – And the present Speaker told me, the Order might be revived the next Sessions, though it was a new Parliament.

[7] Thomas Spence, sergeant at arms for the Commons 1717–37. P. Thorne, *Sergeants for the Commons* (1986), p. 30.

[8] Edward Thompson, commissioner of the Irish revenue. See Appendix.

the best Advantage of their land, and it is just they should. And we might as well think of hindering the Grass to grow in Ireland as the growth of Wool there, which is a gift God and Nature has bestowed on them.

In my Opinion, the only proper and effectual Remedy is to give the Irish encouragement to bring their Wool here, by giving them a better price than they can have elsewhere. Or to allow them some share in the Manufacture: which would be an encouragement to Industry there and employ their Poor. And I think the best of all would be to let them spin it, and send the Yarn to England, and the Manufacture compleated here; and this would be a great Advantage to both Kingdoms: since (as Mr. Thomson said) 288 persons are employed the thorough manufacturing one pack of Wool; and when thoroughly manufactured 'tis by all allowed worth six times the Value. He said the Irish would be content with the Spinning; and then would not think of Running their Wool. And that £35000 would purchas all the Yarn now spun in a year in Ireland.

Tis objected, the Spinning the Wool in Ireland would deprive us of that benefit. We should loose nothing; we have not at present that benefit. Tis now spun in Ireland or France and we are deprived of the benefit we should gain of compleating the Manufacture.

Another Objection is, that the Importation of Irish Wool, may lower the price of the English. Not at all: since there is demand, and a great demand for the Cloths made, at Foreign Markets. And Whether the Irish Wool is Manufactured in England or elsewhere it will make no difference in the Demand. But the Working it in England may raise the Price of some English Wool. For part of the Irish Wool being now Workt in France with their Wool encreases the Quantity of some species of Cloth which they could not make without it. If it was workt in England that species of Cloth would be less, consequently the Value of it would rise, and the Wool of which it is composed would yeild a better Price.

To prevent the Exportation of Wool from both Kingdoms Sir J: Rushout proposed; that all Wool should be packed in Linnen or Woollen only; great Frauds having been committed by screwing it into Barrels. – As also to prevent it being exported under pretence of being Manfactured, when but just worked up in the Gross together. – Which in my opinion were good Proposals.

February 13.

A Bill was moved for by Lord Morpeth that Officers of the Army should not be deprived of their Comissions but by a Court Martial, or an Address of either House of Parliament. At first the Motion was for all Officers in general; though it was afterwards softened by adding the words (not above the Rank of Colonels). This was seconded by Sandys.

It was somewhat extraordinary, that Persons who had always been against any Forces, should now be for making the Army more Independent.

What gave rise to this Motion was the removing the Duke of Bolton and the Lord Cobham last summer, as it was generaly thought by the power of the prime Minister, on declaring a dislike of the Excise Scheme: for vote against it they did not since it never came before the House of Lords.[9]

This was given as a reason in the Debate; and the other reasons given were, that Officers who had served faithfully might not be whispered out of their Employments by a first Minister. And that no officer might be removed for his Vote in either House; and consequently the freedom of Parliament be better secured. And Mr. Poulteney

---

[9] Bolton and Cobham were dismissed from their regiments in 1733.

declared, that to his Knowledge, the late Lord Stanhope[10] intended to have proposed such a Bill; and that the late King approved of it.

But in my Opinion the real Motives for this Motion were these:

It was intended as a Compliment to the Persons removed, particularly the Lord Cobham, who had been a Gallant Officer; for as to the other he had never served Abroad, and nobody regarded him. But it was remarkable that the Lord Cobham had been before removed in the Queens time, when Sir W. Wyndham was secretary of War,[11] who was now very Zealous for this Motion. It was likewise intended to ingratiate themselves with the Officers and to try the temper of the Army. But twas far from succeeding. General Wade spoke against it. He said, it would distroy all Subordination and Discipline in the Army: he declared his Vote was never influenced by his Post, and if he lost his Post by his Vote, he should esteem it an Honour. All the Officers voted against it, but the Lord Cathelough, who being Advanced by these removes declared he would not vote in his own Case, and so out of decency withdrew.

The Principal reason for the motion was to weaken the power of the Crown and to encrease that of the two Houses; which might be a prelude to future Innovations, and was not unlike the Attempt of Wresting the power of the Militia from Charles the first.

I was against the Question and never shall vote more sincerely in any case. For I thought it a direct invasion of the Prerogative. And that the erecting a new power either in the Army or the Parliament would distroy the ballance in the Constitution, and might prove the subversion of it.

The House shewed a great dislike to the Motion, and therefore they did not think proper to divide: and 'tis thought, if they had many Tories would have voted against it.

But they divided on a Motion which was made immediately after by Sandys, and seconded by Poulteney; and was to terrify the prime Minister. This was for an Address to the King to know by whose Advice he removed the Persons above mentioned, and what Crimes were alledged against them. 151 were for the Question, and 252 Against it.

February 19.

The Bill for better Qualifying Members was read the second time: and the Question being put for committing it 227 was against it and 128 for it.[12]

The substance of it was, that Leaseholders for 60 years Absolute; or determinable on their own lives should be qualified. That every Member should swear to his Qualification at the Table, and deliver in a particular of it.

I was against it, because I thought it was intended as a reflection on the present Parliament, and an Insinuation that several Members of the House were not qualified: Whereas in Fact there never was so many Gentlemen of fair and ample Fortunes within those Walls, as in this present Parliament.

February 20.

In the Committee of Ways and Means; Sir R. Walpole observed, that a Supply of £2,569,000 had been Voted for the Land and Sea service.

That there would be a Deficiency of near £100,000 on the Salt Duty at the end of 3 years, in the <£>500,000 for which it was given.

---

[10] James, 1st Earl Stanhope had died in 1721.

[11] Sir Richard Temple (cr. Baron Cobham in 1714) was col. of the 4th dragoons 1710–13. Sir William Wyndham was secretary at war 1712–13.

[12] C.J., XXII, 245 has the figures 208 to 127.

That there was a Deficiency of £30,000, on the Land Tax, of £43,000 on the General Fund, of £10000 on the Money granted to the African Company; which with some other deficiencies, which I have forgot, makes the whole supply for the current Service of the year amount to £2,707,000.

The Cause of the Deficency of the Salt Duty was the great Stock in hand, which the Dealers got, just before the Duty was revived. The Duty the first Quarter brought in but £3000, in the next it brought in 11000, in the next 24000, in the next 27000, in next 50000. And in the last 7 Weeks about £31000. So it had been gradualy increasing as the Stock in hand diminished and now on the best calculation on a Medium may be reckoned £184,000 per Annum.

In raising the £2,707,000 Sir R<obert> said the Malt would raise £750,000. One £1,000,000 might be raised by 2s on Land, and another 1,000,000 he proposed to raise by continuing the Salt Duty for 7 years longer. Or else there would be occasion for 4s. on Land.

The Question for continuing the Salt Duty bore some Debate, and the Arguments urged on both sides such as were used 2 years ago. On a Division 219 were for it, 121 Against it.

I was for it, and for the same reasons I gave in a Pamphlet I wrote two years ago on the Subject.[13] And I should have thought I acted against the Interest of every Landholder, if I had Voted against it.

February 26.

On the Question for Comitting the Bill for securing the Freedom of Parliaments by limiting the Number of Officers in the House of Commons; I was the first who spoke Against it. I called it a publick Proscription of some of my Countrymen, who were to be marked out for the Sacrifice: and banishing them from the Senate for no other Crime but because they were servants to their Prince. That the Committee would never Agree what Species of Men to exclude, or what to admit. If it were limited to such a number of each Species; and the Country not regarding the regulation should choose a greater, what was to be done on their being returned to Parliament? That such a scheme was not only Absurd and impracticable, but also very unreasonable. It is an Injury to the Persons excluded, by depriving them of a right they were born to, without any Crime proved or so much as suggested against them. It is an Injury to the Country by confining them in the choice of their Representatives: an Injury to the Crown in confining its Choice of Officers: And to the Parliament in depriving it of some of its Ablest Members. This Bill would reflect on the honour of those who at present enjoy Offices, as if they were influenced by them: on the honour of his present Majesty, as if he required of them things inconsistent with the service of their Country. And on the honour of the present Parliament as if its Members were corrupted, and there were Persons in it unworthy of their Seats. Besides that this Bill (if a remedy) was but a partial Remedy, since it extended but to one branch of the Legislature.

For the Comittment 191. Against it 230.

February 27.

The Comittee appointed to inspect what Laws were expired or near expiring, and what fit to be revived and continued, reported it their Opinion, that an Act of the 2nd. of his present Majesty for relief of Debtors with respect to the Imprisonment of their

---

[13] This may be one of two pamphlets: *A Letter to a Country Gentleman on the Revival of the Salt Duty* (1732), or *The Case of the Salt-Duty and Land-Tax, Offered to the Consideration of Every Freeholder* (1732). On the basis of internal evidence the latter seems more likely to be by Hay.

Persons, explained and amended by an other 3. Geo. 2. was near expiring, and fit to be continued.[14]

The House disagreed with the Comittee, because it Appeared by inspecting the Act it did not expire till the end of the next Sessions of Parliament.

On Debate on this Act, Mr. Palmer and Earl and others were against continuing it. They said it was a hardship on the Sheriff, who was answerable for the Escape of a Prisoner in execution, since the first 24 hours (by this Act) the Prisoner was to be carried where He pleased, and so might often get himself rescued. They said it was destructive of low Credit. And an encouragement to Knaves to run in Debt, when the terror of a Goal was removed, and they could insult their Creditor.

Barnard was not for laying aside the Act, but amending it. He thought it a defect, that, though the Debtor might deliver up his All yet he was not obliged to do it.

Sir W. Young was for reconsidering the Act; thought it in the main a good Law: and that every body must allow one Part of it very Valuable: which gives a liberty of pleading one Debt in Bar of another.

Every body agreed with the Comittee that the Law for the free Importation of Cochineal should be continued, and indeed made perpetual: since it was so necessary for dying our Cloaths. And Barnard desired the like Law for Indigo. That it might be imported directly from France, where is the greatest Plenty; and not, as at present, sent from thence to Spain, and from Spain to England; by which the Merchant pays double Freight.

February 28.

Allington moved for leave to bring in a Bill for the more easy compelling the Redemption of Mortgages:[15] for as the Law now stands, though the Mortgagor in possession is willing to redeem, yet before he does redeem, the Mortgagee may bring an Ejectment; this Bill was to provide that if he did bring an Ejectment, on the Mortgagors paying Principal and Interest into Court, that proceedings might stay, and the Court oblige the Mortgagee to recover.

I seconded the Motion: which I observed was generous from a Gentleman of the Long Robe; since 'twas to ease his fellow Subjects of Suits in Chancery. And I hoped that all Points of Equity which were well known and established might be made parts of the Comon Law: that Law and Equity might be not longer at Variance; and people carried from one side of Westminster Hall to the Other. What I said on that head met with Approbation, and I was named as one to bring in the Bill.

Allington shewed me the Bill ready drawn and he said, it was drawn by the Master of the Rolls.

March 8.

On reading the Bill for regulating Elections in Scotland a second time,[16] Objection was made to committing it, because there was a Clause in it to incapacitate several Persons from being Elected; which was irregularly inserted; because it did not fall properly under the title of the Bill, nor was it mentioned in opening the Motion for the Bill. Mr. Speaker expressed some resentment on the first reading of the Bill: and when the Objection was now started, said the Bill should be withdrawn, and a new one prepared not liable to Exception: he remembered an hundred Instances of Bills withdrawn on this account, but knew but one or two that were suffered to proceed.

[14] The acts were 2 Geo. II, c. 22 and 3 Geo. II, c. 27.
[15] Hay was nominated to the drafting committee with five others. *C.J.*, XXII, 263. The bill is printed in Lambert, VII, 155–8, and Torrington, vol. 1734–8, pp. 27–30.
[16] The bill is printed in Lambert, VII, 135–54, and Torrington, vol. 1734–8, pp. 15–26.

It was answered that this objection should have been made on the first reading, and could not properly be made after the House had so far approved of it, as to Order a second reading; So the Bill was committed. – But Objections are not easily made on the first reading of a Bill, since so little attention is generally given to it: which makes it very expedient to print Bills of a publick concern.

March 11.

In the Committee of Ways and Means, it was resolved without a Division, that £1,200,000 should be granted out of the sinking Fund towards the supply of the year. – For so much of the Navy Debt was intended to be paid off this year: the whole Amounting to upwards of 1,700,000, being the Deficiencies of the sums granted for the current service from 1721 to 1733. – And which were left on the Navy, rather than any other part of the service for each year, because the Navy Bills, 'till very lately, were in high Credit; and though they carried 5 per Cent Interest, yet they bore no Interest for the first half year.

It was objected; that the sinking Fund was appropriated to the payment of Debts before 1716: that the Creditors of the Nation took it to be so, or would not have consented to the lowering of their Interest; by which it was created: And that if it was applied to the Service of the year, the Debts would never be paid off.

It was Answered that the Creditors of the Nation had Option, either to take a lower Interest, or to be paid off: that they had no title to the sinking Fund, nor was there any Appropriation of it by Law: that they were only entitled to a perpetual Annuity redeemable by Parliament, and that the Parliament might take their own time to redeem it. That the Sinking Fund should always be applied that Way unless on emergent occasions; but on those occasions it was better to apply it to the current service than lay any new burthens on the People. And though the payment of the Debts might by that means be deferred, yet the Creditors were far from being uneasy, and liked it better than if they were paid.

– That in the present Case it was good Husbandry to proceed this Way: for the Navy Bills which were at 5 per Cent, were also at present at 5 per Cent discount: that the £1,200,000 of them to be paid off, might be paid by Money raised immediately at 3 or 3½ per Cent. on the Land and Malt Tax; which were paid quarterly into the Exchequer: which was better than paying it by the sinking Fund, which would not be in the Exchequer sufficient, nor the Account of it made up for the last half year till Michaelmas: but that would be time enough for the Applying to the other Services of the year.

March 13.

The Bill for the more effectual punishing assaults with an intent to rob was read a second time. – The punishment proposed was Transportation.

I spoke against committing it.

I thought there was a sufficient punishment already, and a better than was proposed by the Bill: for if the Offendor was too poor to be fined, yet he might be imprisoned, and the Imprisonment proportioned to the circumstances of the Offence: and as the Offendors had generaly nothing to loose but their Liberty, Imprisonment was a greater terror to them than Transportation: which it were to be wished were less common, and that Malefactors were employed at home.

It would be difficult to prove the Intent: the Assault was no proof of it, since it might be with a different intent; and therefore it could not be known but by the declaration of the Offendor, or unless he was actualy rifling the person Assaulted. If a Person was acquitted on this Law for want of proving the Intent, he may escape without any

Punishment for the Assualt, though guilty of it, since he cannot be tried twice for the same Fact.

It might occasion Malicious Prosecutions: and People who bore ill Will to others, would prosecute them on any Assualt on this Law: and, as they may be Evidence themselves on the Indictment, would go great lengths to prove it, in order to send them out of the Way.

This Bill would breed an impropriety in the Law: for it would inflict a higher Punishment on this sort of assault, which is of the lowest Class; and leave Assaults with an intent to Maim, ravish, murder etc. as they were; though in their Nature much more criminal: therefore the Bill had been more rational, had it extended to all Assaults with intent to commit Felony; though that were improper.

This Offence was no new one: Our Ancestors thought best to leave it to the Discretion of the Court; and if we alter the Law, I fear instead of mending it, we should introduce some inconveniences.

A Motion was made by Mr. Bromley and seconded by Sir J. St. Aubin, for a Bill to repeal the Septennial Act, and the more frequent calling of Parliaments.

It was said for the Bill.

1. That frequent Elections were agreeable to our old Constitution.
2. That Members chosen Annually or triennially would be less liable to be influenced by the Court, for there would not be time to get acquainted with them.
3. It would lessen the Expence of Elections; for nobody would be at a great Expence to be elected for a short time.
4. It would lessen the Heats of Elections: for Men would not be so eager after a Seat for a short time: since those elected must soon resign: and those disapointed would soon have another opportunity of standing.
   It was answered.
1. Nothing was more uncertain than our old Constitution, and there is no Period of time to which you can fix it: That the Statute of Edward 3[17] which requires Parliaments to be holden every year, does not require them to be so chosen. That nothing was more uncertain than the antient Practice: sometimes Elections were Annual: Sometimes the same Parliament sate many years: Sometimes there was a long interruption of Parliaments: Nothing fixed, as to the Places that should send Members: Nothing, as to the number to be chosen, And very often the King ordered who should be chosen. And indeed our Constitution did not gain a perfect Settlement 'till the Revolution; and there is no mention than <sic then?> of frequent Elections, in the Petition of Right, which there certainly would have been, had it been part of our old Constitution; especialy since King James held no Parliament in the three last years of his Reign.
2. Members chosen for a short time would be more complying with the Court, than those who depended on holding their Seats longer; and experience shews it to be so.
3. The Expence if Annual or triennial, would be more burthensome than once in seven years; and the Courtiers would tire out the Country Gentlemen.
4. If Elections were more frequent, the feuds occasioned by them would never ceace, for People would have no time to cool.

Besides: frequent Elections debauch the Lives and corrupt the Morals of the People: habituate the lower Sort to Idleness; ruin their Families; and are very prejudicial to the business and trade of the Nation.

247 voted against the Question, 184 for it. I voted against it.

---

[17] 36 Edw. III, c. 10 of 1382. *Statutes of the Realm*, I, 374.

March 18.

Mr. Poulteney moved for a Bill to exhibit a Bill for naturalizing the Prince of Orange.[18]

This was to pay a Compliment; and save time; because as the Law stands, no Naturalization Act can be brought in, 'till after the Party to be naturalized has taken the Oaths and received the Sacrament.

March 19.

It was read twice, ordered to be engrossed, ingrossed, read a third time, and sent to the Lords, the same Day.

It was not Ordered to be committed, because there were no Blanks in it. And a Bill need not be committed in which there are no Blanks.

March 21.

The Naturalization Bill came from the Lords, was read thrice, and ordered back to the Lords.

March 22.

Being ordered to carry a Naturalization Act to the Lords, I took it from the Table to go with: On holding it up (according to the usual Form) the Speaker called me to know if the Bill was signed by the Clerk,[b] and on my opening it he found it was not. On which he cautioned me never to carry a Bill without first looking into it to see if it was signed: for it might occasion the loss of it in the House of Lords.

N.B. The Breviate must always too be carried with the Bill.

On reading the order of the Day for going into a Comittee on the Bill for regulating Proceedings in Ecclesiastical Courts, Sir R. Walpole opposed, and proposed it might be put off for a month. – On a Division, Ayes 42. No's 39. – I voted with the minority: I thought the Bill a good one: it was to limit the time of Prosecutions Pro Salute Animae and Reformatione Morum; to oblige Prosecutor to give security to prosecute with effect; and to give Commutation money to the Poor. – I know not the Reasons why it was opposed; unless a dislike to the Person who brought it in:[19] and a fear of disobligeing some of the Clergy, just before the Elections.

March 28.

A Message came from the Crown to the House, and was brought up by Sir R. Walpole, who moved that it might be taken into Consideration the next day: which he said had been the usual Course.

This was opposed by Sir W. Windham and others, who were for deferring the Consideration, till the Members were sent for out of the Country that the House might be full. – On a Division 211 were for taking it into consideration the next day, and 121 against it.

The Speaker ordered all the Members to be uncovered whilst the Message was read.[20] —

---

[b] N.B. The signing by the Clerk is on the top of the Bill, in these words, Soit baillie aux Seigneurs.

N.B. There must be eight Members to present it at the Lords Bar. Where the Lord Chancellour comes to receive it.

[18] Prior to his marriage to the princess royal.

[19] Wyndham on 12 Mar. C.J., XXII, 277.

[20] The session continued until 16 Apr. Ibid., p. 316.

1734/5   The first Session of the Second Parliament of his present Majesty.

January 14.

The Parliament after several Prorogations met this day. The Duke of Devonshire, Lord Steward, came in Person about ten to the Court of Wards, to administer the Oaths of Allegiance and Supremacy to the Members, who after taking them went into the House.

About 460 were sworn by two o'Clock: when the King sent the Black Rod to command their attendance in the House of Lords where he ordered them to proceed to the choice of a Speaker, and to present him on the 23.

The House being returned, Mr. Herbert reminded them of the Kings order, and moved that Mr. Onslow the last Speaker might be reelected, he was seconded by Colonel Cholmondeley, and the Motion met with no Opposition. Mr. Onslow made a disqualifying Speech in his Place: after which the two members who moved conducted him from the bottom of the House with the usual reverences to the Chair. He stopped on the first Step, and again desired leave to return to his Place. Which being denied he took the Chair, and said he must then implore his Majesty to excuse him. After this Ceremony was over, Sir R. Walpole moved to adjourn to the day when the Speaker was to be presented: Which was done without Opposition. This Adjournment (as was universaly believed) was owing to Mr. Walpoles[21] Absence, who was sent Ambassadour to the Hague to mediate a Peace in conjunction with the Dutch, between the contending Powers of Europe: the King being unwilling to open the Parliament 'till the Ambassadour's arrival, who might lay the full state of affairs before them.

January 23.

The Parliament met: and the King commanding the House to attend him in the House of Lords, Mr Onslow was conducted thither and presented by Mr. Herbert and Mr. Cholmondeley, and after a disabling speech was confirmed and Complimented by the Lord Chancellor;[22] and his Petition on behalf of the Commons allowed. And then the Kings Speech was delivered.

The Speaker, being returned, reported to the House that his Majesty had been pleased to confirm him Speaker; and had granted them all their Priviledges in as Ample a manner as they were ever at any time enjoyed; particularly freedom from Arrest for themselves, Servants, and Estates; free Access to his Majesty; and freedom of Speech. Then he thanked the House for the Honour of his Post; promised to behave with the Impartiality and Modesty as the House had a right to expect and demand. Recommended to them the Observance of the orders of the House, those Wise Institutions left them by their Ancestors; particularly to avoid Altercations and Personal Reflections in debate and to come early to the House, the morning being the properest Season for business.

He then called for the Book, and first by himself took and subscribed the Oaths and Declaration. Then the Counties were called over in Alphabetical order, and as many as could conveniently stand on the Floor within hearing of the Clerk were sworn together, and subscribed the Roll in the Order they were called; the Clerk since the new regulation of Fees, demanding but a Shilling for his Fee; though most members gave him the old Fee of two Shillings.

---

[21] Horatio Walpole. See Appendix.
[22] Lord Talbot. See Appendix.

They proceeded to the letter E. the first day; and it was three days before the whole List was gone through.

January 27.

After the Members were sworn, the Speaker said it was usual to open the Sessions with reading a Bill, and ordered the Bill for preventing Outlawries clandestine to be read.[23] He then read the common Orders out of the Journal of the last Parliament, and put the Question on each. He then reported the Kings speech, of which he said to prevent mistakes he had obtained a Copy.

Mr. Hedges moved, and was seconded by Mr. Cambell, for an Address of thanks to his Majesty for his Speech, and to assure him of such supplies as should be necessary to enable him to Act that Part which Honour, Justice and the Interest of his People should require.

All agreed to return thanks; but Lord Morpeth and others desired the assurance of supplies might be left out. They said such assurances were often used as Arguments for granting whatever was demanded during a whole Sessions. It was answered the Words being general obliged to nothing in particular; nor was the freedom of any subsequent Debate ever restrained by such a promise.

Sir W Windam moved to add an Amendment viz: to assure the King of Supplies on laying proper information before the House of their Necessity, and in proportion to our Allies not involved in the War. – The first part of the Amendment was unnecessary, because implied in the Expression of granting necessary Supplies, which could not be judged so but on necessary Information: the other part was imprudent in declaring our Resolutions before hand, to all Europe and inglorious in putting ourselves under the direction of the Dutch. I voted against the Amendment for those Reasons. And on a Division 185 were for it, 265 against it.

January 29.

The House by Instructions to the Committee ordered them to hear some Elections on certain Days: which is not usual; and is done only on some extraordinary Allegations; and on Motion.

January 31.

It being observed the Sheriff of the County of the Town of Southampton had not returned his Precept (which was to the Mayor and Bailliffs of the said Town jointly and severally) with the Writ to the Clerks of the Crown: It was said that though by Act of Parliament he is to return the Writ he is not obliged to return his own Precept. And the Precept being to the Mayor and Bailiffs jointly and severally, and the Mayor and one Bailiff return one Person, and one of the Bailiffs Another, both returns are good.

---

[23] This was one of several such bills (others were the payment of tithes, the regulation of seamen's wages, the prevention of the stealing of cattle, the preservation of game, the regulating of scavengers, and the prevention of frivolous and vexatious arrests), which were heard at the opening of each session (immediately after the taking of oaths), and may have been designed to assert the right of parliament to deal with grievances before supply. Usually the bills proceeded only to first reading, though occasionally they got further (this was more common under Anne than under the Hanoverians), such as the bill to transport felons which passed the Commons in Mar. 1727. Though the bill for preventing clandestine outlawries appeared in this role as early as 1713, it only became the regular first bill of a session from 1727.

February 3.

The Committee[24] met the first time: and the Names of the Committees being called over and eight<?> answering, Mr. Earl was called unanimously to the Chair.

They first read the double Returns and Petitions on them in pursuance of the order of the House and Appointed days for them: and then the other Petitions in the order they were delivered.

February 5.

Guilford Petition was again delivered; which was ordered to be withdrawn and amended the day before, because one of the Allegations was against the returning Officer for admitting Persons to Poll for one of the sitting Members who was under age:[25] The House Agreed it would have been a Crime to have refused them, since the House alone are to judge of the Qualifications of their Members: and a Case was read in the journal January 11 1694 where the Mayor of Liverpool was censured and taken into custody for taking upon him to judge that the Coroner was incapable of being elected.

February 6.

It has long been a standing Order, that a Sitting Member might examine into the Qualification of the Person petitioning against him: and now on Mr. Gybbons Motion, it was likewise made a standing Order, that he might do it, on the Petition of the Electors, affirming another to be elected.

February 7.

In the Committee of Supply (which is always a Committee of the Whole House) Sir C. Wager moved that 30,000 Seamen should be allowed for the year 1735. (And this Motion was made before the Estimate of the Expence was delivered in, which is not very usual.) Before this Motion was seconded, Sandys moved that they might be only 20000, the Number voted last year, which Question being first seconded was first put.

Against allowing 30000, it was said we had not occasion for more than last year.

It was answered, though 20000 were only voted last year, yet more had been Employed by virtue of the vote of Confidence that past after. 23000 at a Medium the whole year, and now actualy 27000.

It was said allowing 20000 was in effect allowing 30000 when occasion required, since the whole number would not be employed the whole year.

It was answered, when they once took Men into pay they were obliged to keep them so, for if they were once dismissed, and there was afterwards occasion for them, they could not find them again.

It was said employing so many Seamen in the Fleet, made their Wages dearer to the Marchant, and was a prejudice to Trade: and had it not been for that more Corn might have been Exported last year.

It was allowed to be an Inconvenience, but such a one as must be submitted to for the publick Good: and it was said, that if the Merchants wanted men at home, it must not be wholy imputed to the Fleet, but also to great numbers of Seamen being employed Abroad, no less than 11000 in Merchant Ships being employed last year in the Mediterranean in Foreign service.

It was said we should not Augment our Fleet unless the Dutch did the same.

---

[24] The committee of privileges and elections.
[25] Richard Onslow (1713–76), son of Thomas, 2nd Baron Onslow, was elected at Guildford on 29 Apr. 1734.

It was answered the Dutch Marine was in so bad a state they were not in a Capacity of doing it: that they were most liable to be attacked by Land, and that since 1726 they had made two Augmentations of their Forces of 10000 Men each; so that whereas their usual standing force was 32000, they had now actually 52000 men.

It was objected, that our Arming would give Jealousie to the French and Spaniards and make them do the same.

It was answered, they set the Example; and when the French had 40 men of War and the Spaniards 30 of 50 Guns and upwards, and most of them in the Ports opposite to us, it would be the greatest Imprudence in us, not to be prepared with an equal Strength.

It was said, since the Powers at War had accepted his Majesty's good offices, and that his Majesty had prepared a Plan of Accommodation, our Arming would raise a suspicion against his Majesty's Impartiality.

It was answered, strengthening his Majesty's hands would inforce his Plan, and make them more likely to submit to an Accommodation.

On a Division 183 voted against 30000 Seamen, 256 for them. I voted with the Majority for the Reasons above mentioned.

February 13.
Mr. Waller moved to address the King to lay some Accounts before the House, which the House had actualy before them; this motion being seconded; and it being apprehended that if a Question was put it would have an ill appearence in the Votes; if it passed in the affirmative as if the Parliament suspected the account to be unfair; if in the Negative, that they justified it if it was so; it was moved to adjourn before the Question was put, which was done. And the Speaker said, though it was agreeable to Order for the House to determine on every Question in Agitation yet it was not necessary after the Hour of Adjournment, which is four of Clock, but then on motion the House might adjourn without coming to the Question; which Gybbon agreed to be Order.

February 14.
In the Committee of Supply the Question was whether there should be 17700 Land Forces (the number unanimously agreed to last year) for the service of the year 1735 or 25700, which Augmentation would occasion an additional expence of £147,000.

Those who argued against it said, that our Fleet was sufficient to defend us, and the Affections of the People our best security. That as we were told we were in a better state there was no necessity for the Augmentation. That the Dutch who are nearer the Danger make none. That we are not able to maintain the Ballance of Power without them, therefore should not advance before them. That they will be backward to assist when they see us so ready to take the whole Expence on ourselves. That if the Plan of Peace succeedes there is no occasion to Arm; if it does not this augmentation is not sufficient; nor can any one tell how these forces are to be employed.

That the Augmentation will be an Expence; which now we are so much in Debt, aught to be avoided: and being unnecessary will encrease the disaffection of the People.

That the Army is in itself a bad thing, dangerous to the King and to the liberties of the People; not to be kept up much less augmented, but on the greatest Exigency.

That this Augmentation may give Jealousy Abroad and frustrate the Mediation.

It was answered, that though we were at present in Peace, yet we knew not how soon we might be involved in a War; and though it was not yet convenient to declare; yet we should be in a Capacity for doing it; that on this Account the Dutch had not made the Reduction they otherwise intended. That Arming was the most likely way to inforce our Mediation, and secure a Peace; since it would make his Majesty speak with more weight, when the stronger Party should see, if they were unreasonable they would not be safe. That the last years Confidence had made our good offices accepted, the Augmentating our Forces might make them effectual, the not doing it might casue them to be rejected. In case of War this would enable us to perform our Treaty with the Dutch in 1713 of sending 10000 to assist in defending their Barrier, which would otherwise be ill defended by their Treaty of Neutrality.

As to the Expence it was said, that an ill-timed Frugality had occasioned our Debts at first, and might now encrease them; That there was all the Oeconomy possible in making the Augmentation, by bringing eight Regiments from Ireland, which might be again sent back, and by filling up them and the other Regiments before in England with private Men. That the expence was not great, and by procuring a Peace might save millions.

That his Majesty's past Conduct assures us he will make no ill use of these forces. That they had not been desired if not necessary; and when unnecessary will be reduced. That the People had no reason to be uneasy, if they were so it was from misrepresentation. 264 voted for the Augmentation, 208 Against it.[26] I voted with the Majority.

February 20.

The Petition for Shaftsbury was determined after 3 days hearing. The Right of Election by the last Determination in 1695 is in the Inhabitants paying Scot and Lot. And the Poor Books for each Parish for the year 1733 which were the last before the Election were produced and laid on the Table.

By the Mayors Poll after his scrutiny the Numbers were for Mr. Bennet Sitting Member 163. For Mr. Fox the Petitioner 159.[27]

Mr. Fox fairly disqualified 24 of the sitting Members Votes. And qualified 9 which were refused for him. So that there remained an incontestable Majority for him of 29. So that on the Question whether Mr. Bennet was Elected it passed in the Negative almost unanimously and without a division.

On the Question whether Mr. Fox was Elected on a Division it was carried in the Affirmative 203 to 88.

This Division was on the Evidence concerning Bribery which was produced on both sides; though no money was proved to be taken but by two of Mr. Bennets Voters. What cheifly affected Mr. Fox, was his saying to two Voters, who told him they were threatened to be Arrested, if they Voted for him, that if they were he would bear them harmless. Gybbon said this was within 7 & 8 Will. 3.[28] I think it was not, for it was only telling them they should not suffer by serving him, and removing the unjust Influence put on them by others. Besides I give little credit to Persons who Vote against a Gentleman, who appear as Witnesses, and not upon Oath.

February 24.

A Motion was made by Sir W. Wyndham and seconded by Sandys to refer the Estimate of the Ordinary of the Navy to a Select Committee before it came before the Committee of Supply. It was observed to be but £3000 less than the last year, though 10000 more men were voted, consequently more Ships would be in pay, and fewer

[26] Harley has 261 to 208. See above, p. 4.
[27] The figures given in Sedgwick (I, 236) are 168 and 174.
[28] 7 & 8 Will. III, c. 7, Parliamentary Elections Act.

remain in Ordinary, and that it was but £12000 less last year than the year before when there was but 8000 men. And it appeared on the Journals such Committees were not unprecedented.

It was allowed to be true, the more Ships were employed the less the Ordinary Expence should be. But Sir C. Wager said as there were about 80 Ships now in Ordinary (and which you must keep in repair if you will have a good Fleet, and which is now as good as any two Nations else have) the Money granted has not been sufficient, but he had a Bill to demand, when the Parliament would receive it. – It was said this Estimate was very particular, more so than any other, and that it was extraordinary to single it out. That every article was specified, and if the Vouchers were required, they might be produced at the Bar, in a Comittee of the whole House; which by Antient Order was the Committee where all things relating to the publick Money should be examined. Select Committees had sometimes been Appointed, but never produced any Good, but by few Mens getting the Management had served private Jobs. That though all that come are to have Voices, yet the Speakers Chamber[29] would hold but few Members, and few had convenience to hear. – On a Division 160 were for it, 198 aginst it. I was against it.

February 25.

On hearing the Warwick Petition at the Bar, the last Resolution in 1732[30] was read, settling the Right of Election in the Inhabitants paying Scot and bearing Lot. Attested copies of the Poor Books, as likewise of the Poll, were produced and laid on the Table. The Petitioners Councel delivered in a List of 104 Persons who Polled for the Sitting Members whose Names were not in the poor Books and were refused to vote for the Petitioners: which being admitted by the Councel for the sitting Members, and by Mr. Bromley one of the sitting Members, there remained above 60 Majority for the Petitioners and they were Voted duly elected.[31]

February 26.

Sir Walter Bagot offered a Clause to be added to the Mutiny Bill, to oblige Officers to carry Persons, who took Money to inlist, within 4 days before a Justice of Peace, either to inlist, or dissent, and on returning the money and 20s for charges to be discharged. – This was Occasioned by an Officer's detaining a Fellow, who received the Money, a Month to oblige him to inlist. – This met with no Opposition – no more than another, offered by General Wade and seconded by Sandys, That Fellows, who received the Money, and ran away before they went before a Justice, should be treated as Deserters.

In the Committee on Southampton Election it appeared, Mr. Henly was returned by the Mayor and one Bailiff, Mr. Conduit by the other Bailiff.[32] All the Returns the last 30 years had been made by the Mayor and both Bailiffs, by Indenture annexed to the Writ, without the Precept: but the Precept was now (as I suppose it always had been) to the Mayor and Bailiffs jointly and seperately. And the Instruction of the House to the Committee was to hear the Election and Return.

---

[29] The normal venue for select committees.
[30] The resolution was actually on 31 Jan. 1722. *C.J.*, XX, 113–14; XXII, 391; Sedgwick, I, 341.
[31] The new members were the brothers Henry Archer (1700–68), M.P. for Warwick 1735–68, and Thomas Archer (1695–1768), M.P. for Warwick 1735–41, Bramber 1741–7.
[32] For the background see Sedgwick, I, 253–4.

It was agreed by all to consider the Return first. It was urged to report the Return, before the Merits of the Election were considered. This was disallowed as contrary to the Instruction of the House, which was to hear both. And I think it tended to nothing; for it is evident, that the Returns are either both Good in point of Form or both bad. Indeed if one only could have been adjudged good, the Report might have served this End, that the Member so returned might have taken his Place, and the hearing the Petition against him might have been delayed.

The Committee resolved that the Mayor and Bailiffs of Southampton are the Returning Officer. – The Consequence of which I take to be that both Returns are bad, and after hearing the Merits of the Election one must be amended. Which I don't understand for the Precept being directed to Mayor and Bailiffs jointly and severally, both seem to me in point of form to be good.[33]

February 28.

In the Comittee of Supply £56000 was asked for a years Subsidy to the King of Denmark, persuant to a Treaty concluded with him for 3 years, which was referred to the Committee.[34]

In Opposition to this demand it was said. That though the Crown had a Power to make Treaties, yet this House alone has Power to support them; and consiquently had a right to examine and cencure them. That this demand came with an ill Grace after Augmenting our Fleet and Army: That it would be good to deny it, to discourage Ministers from making unnecessary Treaties. This Treaty was unnecessary, because we are not the first concerned in the Ballance of Europe. It was bad on Account of the Expence, and the putting ourselves in a condition of War when there is no occasion, will put us out of a condition when there is. It was bad because it would put Denmark out of a capacity of performing a Treaty with the Emperor, by which she engaged to assist him totis Viribus. It was a bad Treaty considered in itself, because we are to assist Denmark gratis, but Denmark is to be paid. It is bad compared with our former Treaty with Denmark in 1701[35] because here we pay the Subsidy and Forces at the same time; pay more Levy Money; and pay half of it down, though the forces are never employed.

That if forreign forces are necessary, the Prussians might have been more serviceable, since the Danes are pent up by their situation, and may not be able to come to our assistance. But foreign Troops are worse than our own because the Money goes out of the Nation. But they are not at all necessary, since by our late Augmentation we have forces enough in Great Britain and Ireland to satisfy all our Engagements.

It was Answered. No Argument was to be drawn from comparing this Treaty with that in 1701 because made in different Circumstances. This was not more expensive; the Subsidy was the same: and though the Levy Money is more yet by that Treaty the forces were taken into pay immediately, by this not 'till they are wanted. That the Treaty was necessary to give us Authority in making Peace; and to strengthen us in case of War. It was necessary to keep the Northern Crowns from engagements with the contending Powers, which would have made the breach wider and more difficult to be composed: and France had offered greater sums to Denmark to treat with them. That the Treaty was necessary, to enable us in case of a War to perform our engagements of

---

[33] Conduit was declared elected on 3 Apr. See below p. 114.

[34] Treaty of Westminster, 30 Sept. 1734.

[35] There were two treaties with Denmark (and the United Provinces) in 1701, signed at Odensee and Copenhagen.

take 10 per Cent from the most ignorant of the People; that it was better to take 20 per Cent in a Lottery where the rich only could venture. – That the stock jobbing Bill had sent people from the Alley[43] to their employments, but a Lottery would bring them back – The proposal of a Lottery met a general dislike.

Mr. Pulteney said, there were other means besides a Lottery within the reach of the Publick, and mentioned Nortons and Lord Derwentwaters Estates, which might be applied to this, and to building an Hospital for Foundlings.

Sir W. Young said the Exchequer received the Rents of Lord Derwentwaters Estate, and he believed there was 10000 or £12000 in hand: and he and Mr. Clayton moved to Address the King to apply it to this use; and Sandys seconded it. Sir R. Walpole said the Estate was vested in the Crown for the use of the Publick, and therefore could not be Applied without an Act of Parliament. Another Question was whether the Committe of Supply (that was closed) must be opened on this Occasion. The Speaker thought it very dangerous, especially in great Sums: it might be done; but if it was, it should be confined to that particular purpose. – Sir R. Walpole said a Committee of the Whole House may dispose of Money out of the Committee of Supply – And Sir J. Barnard said the Princesses Fortune out of the St. Christophers Money went not through the Committee of Supply.[44] – Though Sir R<obert> observed that the St. Christophers money was in the Crown, and made publick Money by Address only, and not as this by Act of Parliament.

March 24.

The House agreed to the report, that Sir W. Irby was duly elected for Launceston: He petitioned against the Lord King, who since his Election succeeded his Father in his Peerage: and made no defence. He had on the Poll 30 Votes and Sir W. Irby 29: and the right of Election was in the Mayor, Aldermen, and Freemen being Inhabitants at the time of their being made Free: and Sir <W. Irby> disqualified 4 or 5 of Lord Kings Votes, by proving them not inhabitants at that time.

March 25.

The Wells Election after many days hearing at the Bar was determined in favour of Piers and Speke Petitioners against Hamilton and Edwards.

The Right by the last resolution, is in Mayor, Masters, Burgesses and Freemen, admitted to their Fredom in any of the seven Companies, being thereunto intitled by Birth, Servitude or Marriage.

The Petitioners contended that the Qualification of Birth Servitude or Marriage should extend to Burgesses as Well as Freemen: but on a Question the first day in a thin House it was carried that they should be restrained from giving such Evidence (Which was thought a great point gained by Sir W. Windham in his favour, since it seems to imply the right of honourary Burgesses; and the Mayor and Masters who make them are in his Interest).

But notwithstanding that the Petitioners appear to have a clear Majority of near 40, though the Mayor who was partial to the sitting Members had given 10 or 12 Majority

---

[43] Exchange Alley, off Lombard Street, scene of the gambling fever in the South Sea Bubble in 1720.

[44] The French lands on the West Indian island of St Christopher were ceded to the British crown by the 1713 treaty of Utrecht. In 1717 the Commons' committee of supply voted to sell the lands and to use the proceeds for public use. In May 1733 Walpole proposed that £80,000 be paid for the marriage portion of the princess royal out of the St Christopher proceeds, and this was embodied in the Supply Act of that year (6 Geo. II, c. 25). *C.J.*, XVIII, 600; XXII, 146, 151–2; *Calendar of Treasury Books and Papers, 1731–4*, p. 393; H.M.C., *Egmont Diary*, I, 372.

on the Poll. The Case was so clear that Gibbons, Sir J. Barnard (and I think Sandys) Voted for the Petitioners: but Hamilton made so good Interest that it was carried but by 14.

March 28.

The Marlborough Election was determined at the Bar in favour of Lisle and Seymour against Newnham and Hays the Petitioners without a Division: The right of Election is in the Mayor and Burgesses: and the Petitioners endeavoured to disqualify Eleven Burgesses, whose election depended on that of one Bell a Common Council Man, who they said was not duly Elected; though on a Quo Warranto brought Against him in 1730 Bell had a Verdict in his favour and Judgement last Month entered upon it.

Though the House in this Case did not determine contrary to the Verdict and Judgement, yet on a Division the Day before they resolved, that the Petitioners should be admitted to give Evidence to contravert it: in which they were not only Warranted by the Precedents of Bewdley February 7. 1708 and of Queensborough April 17. 1729, but more so by Reason, for the sole right of judging and determining their own Elections is one of their most esential priviledges, and it would be highly imprudent to suffer themselves to be precluded from examining the Merits of Elections by Verdicts and Judgements in inferior Courts, which may be obtained by Collusion of the Parties, and are in the last resort to be decided by the House of Lords.

The ill consequence of a Determination against the Verdict would have been a distinction of Burgesses in the Corporation: for the New Burgesses disqualified from <voting> would have remained Burgesses to all other Intents and Purposes: but as they were not Capable of Voting they could not have communicated that right to others: and the old Burgesses could not do a corporate act without them: consequently when the old Burgesses were all dead there would be no Electors left; and the Priviledge of sending Members to Parliament would have been lost to that Corporation.

April 3.

The double return for Southampton was reported in favour of Mr. Conduit against Mr. Henly, and the Report agreed to by the House.

Mr. Henly had a Majority of one on the Poll.[45] He objected to 18 of Conduit's Voters as Aliens, who (all but two) produced Certificates of their takeing the Oaths on the general Act of Naturalization in Queen Anns Reign, or else exemplifications of particular Acts by which they were Naturalized. He likewise objected to ten as either not rated or not Housekeepers: but they were all clearly established. – Mr. Conduit added six to his Poll who all paid the Poor's Rates either before or after the Election; – the first purposely omitted, and the last coming into Houses after the Rates by which they polled were made, but long before the Election. He likewise objected to 22 Freemen who polled for Henly, because (as appeared by the Books of the Corporation) the Majority were not present when they were made; and such a power among others being given to the Mayor and Common Council generally without expressing any number of them to be a Quorum it was insisted on that a Majority of the whole Body ought to be present. – But it was said on the other side that the power of the Absent devolved on those that were present, and that a Majority of them was sufficient.

---

[45] Two polls were taken at this election: according to the one taken by the mayor Henley had 213 votes to Conduitt's 212; but the senior bailiff gave the vote as Conduitt 257, Henley 217. Sedgwick, I, 253–4.

April 14. 15.

On a Message from the Lords desiring the House to give leave to John Selwyn Esquire a Member to attend their Lordships to be examined as a Witness,[46] the House resolved, 1. that they would send an Answer by Messangers of their own; 2. that he have leave to go if he thinks fit.

April 16.

The House took into consideration the Report from the Committee, to whom the Kings Warrant permitting Letters to pass free from Postage was referred.

This Committee was Appointed at the Instance of Mr. Walter Plummer, who complained that the Post Office had charged a Letter which he had Franked, and when he inquired the reason of it there, he was Answered it was because the Letter did not relate to his own business; from which he inferred they had either opened or looked into his letter: but it appeared there was no occasion for that, since the Letter was marked with the Post Mark of Woobourn at a time when he was known to be at another Place. He said the design of the Motion was to inquire into the right the Members had to Franking; and if it was a Priviledge; that on the one hand they might not be interrupted in the injoyment of it, and on the other that the Revenue might not suffer by the Abuse of it.

The Committee after a strict examination into the Behaviour and Practice, of the Officers of the Post House, to find if they could fix any mismanagement either on them or their Superiors, (and perhaps to terrify both) came to several resolutions which were agreed to by the House.

1. They resolved that their Priviledge of Franking Letters began with the errecting the Post Office. – The Post Office was errected in 1660 by Act of Parliament;[47] and in that Act a Clause was prepared to be inserted to exempt the Members from paying for their Letters, which Clause was found among the Papers of that year: but it was omitted (as they were assured from certain Tradition) on the then Secretary of State[48] assuring the House in the Kings Name that their Letters should pass free, but desiring them to take it as a favour from the Crown: and the Kings Warrant has ever since been directed to the Post Masters for that purpose. And it appears by the Journals (I think in 1666) that they Voted a Person guilty of breach of Priviledge for charging a Members Letter.

Another Resolution was proposed in the Committee that this Priviledge was founded on a Right and not on a Favour, but it was rejected: and I divided against it in the Committee, for I think the Kings Warrant for the Constant enjoyment of it plainly shews the contrary. As to the Objection, that there could be no breach of Priviledge in a thing to which you had not a Right, it was well answered, that there might be a breach of Priviledge concerning a thing which you held only by favour of Another during the time you injoyed it: which I think may be illustrated by this Instance, that a Tresspass on Land which a Member holds as Tenant at Will is as much a Breach of Priviledge, as a Tresspass on his Inheritance.

2. They Resolved their Leters (not exceeding two Ounces) should go free 40 days before and after every Summons or Prorogation.

---

[46] Two John Selwyns, father and son, sat for Gloucester and Whitchurch at this time. One was a witness in the Hillsborough divorce case. See *L.J.*, XXIV, 514.

[47] 12 Cha. II, c. 35.

[48] Either Sir William Morrice, secretary for the north (1660–8), or Sir Edward Nicholas, secretary for the south (1660–2).

3. That 'twas a Breach of Priviledge for any Post Officer to detain, delay, open or look into their Letters without a Warrant in Writing from the Secretary of State for every such purpose.

4. For any Person to counterfeit the Hand or put the Name of any Member on a Letter.

It was a Question whether the Revenue lost more by the Franks than it gained by the Stamps on Newes Papers sent into the Country by virtue of the Franks, which would not otherwise be sent. – In 1716 the Franks amounted to about £17000 in 1733 to £38000. – The Method of computing them was sometimes of an Ordinary Post Night to Weigh all the Letters in the Office, and comparing the Weight of the Franked Letters with the weight of those not Franked. – But notwithstanding this encrease of franking the Revenue was not diminished in proportion, for in 1716 the Nett produce of the Post Office was £93367 in 1733 it was £91701. – In the years 1720 and 1721 it was at the highest on account of the South Sea, and in the last of those years in which it produced most it was £100979. – From 1716 to 1733 inclusive which is eighteen years the Total of the Nett produce was £1,755,720, at a Medium about £97500 per Annum. The total of the 700 per Week paid into the Exchequer £658,000 or £36400 per Annum. The total of the Pensions £445,098, at a Medium about £24700 per Annum. The Total of the Nett Revenue £652,621, at a Medium about £36200 per Annum.

Q. if more Letters are not franked by Clerks in Offices than by Members of Parliament.

April 17.

The Report from the Committee concerning Wendover Election was Agreed to by the House vacating the Election of John Boteler Esquire for Want of a Qualification.

The Statute[49] requires an Estate Of £300 per Annum, for a Mans own life or a greater Estate to his own use, above what will satisfy all Incumbrances, either in Law or Equity.

The Question was whether Mr. Boteler had not an equitable Qualification. He had an Estate left him for his own life and Afterwards to his Children of upwards of £2000 per Annum but first charged with the payment of his Debts, of which there remained about £8000 unpaid. About £1000 per Annum was in Jointure to his Widow: About £800 per Annum in Trustees for the Payment of the Debts: and a House and Park of 400 Acres and a Mill in Mr. Botelers Possession.

The Mill was let for £37 per Annum, the House had been let for £80 and the Park as a Farm (as appeared by Evidence) was worth at least £300 per Annum. But the House and Park were now let together at £200 per Annum.

The Committee did not think the House, Park, and Mill a Qualification, because it was to be valued only at the Rent it was then Let at. They did not esteem the Jointure or what was in Trustees to be so, because he could not receive the Profits of the first to his own use 'till after the Widows death, nor of the last 'till after the Debts were paid.[50]

April 21.

A Report was made from the Committee of the whole House, to whom it was refered to consider of Heads for a Bill for the more effectual preventing the Exportation of

[49] 9 Anne, c. 5 (1710), clause 1.
[50] For the background see Sedgwick, I, 477–8; *C.J.*, XXII, 466–8; and *Mr. Boteler's Case, as to his Qualification* (1735).

Wool run from Great Britain, and of Wool, and Wool manufactured from Ireland to foreign Parts.[51]

To this Committee was refferred the Report from the Committee to whom were refferred the several Petitions complaining of the same, made to the House March 19.[52]

And also an Account presented to the House March 25. 1731. of Woolen and Bag Yarn imported into England from Ireland from Xmas 1715 to Xmas 1729.[53]

And also an Account, then presented, of the duty paid for the same and how Appropriated.

And also an Account, then presented, of what Wool had been imported from thence in those Years.

The Committee came to six Resolutions which were agreed to by the House.

1. To take off the Duty on Bag yarn and Woollen Yarn imported from Ireland.

2. To extend the liberty of Exportation from Ireland to England to the Ports of Limerick, Galway, and Dundalk.

3. To carry no Wool etc. but between Sun rising and Setting.

4. To pack None but in Leather, Woolen, or Linnen.

5. To export none but so far Manufactured as to be incapable of being reduced again to Wool etc.

6. To carry none coast-wise, without first giving Notice to the cheif officer of the Port to which it is intended to be brought.

The first of these Resolutions was likewise a Resolution of the Committee to whom the Petitions were referred. But there were two other Resolutions of that Committee, which the Committee of the Whole House came to no determination on. One was to give further encouragement to Informers against Running, the Other to extend the Register in Kent and Sussex to all parts of Great Britain within 10 miles of the Sea.

As to the taking off the Duty from Irish Yarn the Committee was divided upon it, and I voted with the Majority (which was very great) for the Affirmative: for I think it the Interest of this Kingdom by all possible means to try to get Possession of the Irish Wool, and not to suffer it to go to France; which can only be done by making it more worth their while to bring it to us than to carry it thither. And the<re>fore every proposition that tends to promote it should meet with encouragement. – It were best of all for us to have their Wool unmanufactured, but if that cannot be, it is better to take it in Yarn than not at all; and Sir William Young Observed the French thought so; for a Bill had no sooner past the House of Commons a few years ago to take off the Duty on Irish Yarn, but it was taken off in France. And Mr. Stert shewed me a Letter from a corrispondent at Rouen, with a peice of Irish yarn enclosed, which sold there for 45 sous per pound, Irish combed Wool was sold there for 40 and 42. And Wool unmanufactured for 28. The English Wool and Yarn bore the same Price, but was not publickly entered as the Irish was. N.B. 92 pounds of Rouen are equal to 112 of ours. And I conclude unless we gave the Irish near the same price as the French do, the taking off the duty alone would not be a sufficient encouragement to them to bring it hither: and perhaps it might not be improper for Government to give them such a Premium on Importation as to make it come too dear to the French to employ in their Manufacture. Or if Nothing else will prevent it, it is better to let the Irish Manufacture it entirely than to let it be manufactured in France; since they are a dependent Nation from whose riches we may reap some advantage. And I believe it will be very difficult for the

---

[51] The bill was rejected on its 2nd reading on 25 Apr. *C.J.*, XXII, 496.

[52] See *ibid.*, pp. 422–3, and also above.

[53] See *ibid.*, XXI, 697 (account not printed). The date was 29 Mar. 1731/2.

future to prevent them, since they have lately tasted the sweets of it: for by being able to sell 10 per Cent cheaper they have intirely got the Trade from the English for Camlets and Stuffs at Lisbon: And it appeared by Certificate from the Vice-Consul there on the Oaths of the respective Masters of Ships, that from May 1733 to May 1734 there had been imported from Cork to Lisbon, 7 Bundles and 4 Packs of Goods, 119 dozens of Stockings, 44 peices of Stuffs, 4931 pieces of Camlets, 31 pieces of Frizes and Ratteens. Which by an Account of Mr. Sterts were computed at above £30000. Which Exportation from Ireland, Alderman Vere said, had reduced that from Norwich from £100,000 to £10,000.

The principal Objection to taking off the Duty from Irish Yarn was the Apprehension that the great Importation of it, would lower the price of our Wool, and consequently our Rents.

It was Answerd that Experience shewed the contrary: for Vere said when the Duty on Irish Wool was taken off it did not lower ours. And Sir W. Young said our Wool was dearest when there was most imported: and during the Plague at Marseilles. And I think it reasonable to suppose our Wool would not fall: for the Price of Wool depends on the price of commodities made of it; and their Price on the demand for them. But the Demand will be the same wherever the Wool is Manufactured; the only difference will be, that we shall have the Profit of the Manufacture, and of sending it to market, instead of the French. And sure they who are against Importing Irish Yarn for fear of lowering the Price of our Wool, must be as much against bringing in Irish Wool, since that Imported in the same Quantity must have the same Effect: which is consenting it should be Manufactured either by the Irish or French, for what else can become of it, unless it is bought up by Government and burnt as some have proposed.

Some who were against taking off the Duty likewise said, that Stopping the Irish Wool from going to France, would not hinder the French Manufactures; for in their best Cloths they did not use it; in several sorts of Stuffs they did; but if they could have Irish Wool no longer, it would force them to supply themselves with Wool from other Countries, which would serve their turn as well: which would be more prejudice than Advantage to us: It was allowed that the French could make their best cloths without English or Irish Wool, and it was said our own was made of Spanish only, (which I have since heard confirmed by a great Dealer in Cloth and Wool; who said the finest of our Wool without mixing would not make a Cloth of above 12s per yard). And Sir W. Young observed that the French out did us in Turkey by their Dye. But he said Stuffs exported are five times the Value of Cloth; and the French could not make them without mixing one third of fine[54] long Wool with their own; that ours and the Irish were the finest and longest from the Climate. It is certain that the French use great quantities of the last; and it is much to be doubted whether they could shift without it, though Drummond said great Quanties of Wool from Poland and Germany passed by the Way of Amsterdam to France: Which are Facts worth inquiring into: as likewise what Quantity is run from England; which some said was very little, and Sir J. Rushout affirmed to be three eights.

Sir T. Saunderson, who was against taking off the Duty said, that it would encourage a greater groth of Wool in Ireland; which many observed had prodigiously encreased since the Prohibition of Irish Cattle here; which had obliged the Irish to keep more Sheep: and therefore it should again be considered whether it should not again be taken off, since it has been such a Prejudice to the Woollen Manufacture here, which some foretold at that time.

---

[54] End of vol. L(c)1732.

The second Resolution for liberty to export Wool from Gallway and other Western Ports of Ireland to England, was thought very necessary for as only some Eastern Ports are now open the People in the West of Ireland can't send their Wool thither without great expence (viz: 6 per Cent, from some Parts as Vere told me) which puts them under a necessity of running what they don't use.

In the Debate many other Proposals were mentioned to prevent the Irish from running their Wool and Cloth. One was that they should not have Warehouses near the Sea, as they now have, from whence they run their Goods in Boats to Ships after they are cleared and out at Sea: and the Guard Ships have done so little to prevent it, that it was said they never made but one Seisure. – Another was a Register in Ireland. – Another was, to make the Consuls Account at Lisbon Evidence, and Affidavids sent over to convict the Offenders, for Sir T. Saunderson said all these Goods came to the Port of Lisbon, and all the Ships visited by the Custom House Officers: though prehaps, as Willimot said, that might occasion the running in Portugal.

It was observed too, that there were other causes of the decay of our Woolen Manufacture besides running: one great one was new Manufactures set up in France, Flanders, Germany, and Denmark. – Another Our Folly and Luxury in wearing Silks, which lessen our home Consumption, and Danvers mentioned the Neglect of burying in Wool, which he would extend to the Plantations.

April 22.
The Place Bill was read a second time, and on the Question for committment was rejected by about 30 Majority:[55] I voted with the Majority for the same reasons as I did last Parliament, and which I have before given: The Arguments were the same on both sides: but the Debate was carried on now on both sides only by the young Gentlemen of Great Estates, who had no Places or dependence on the Court.

April 24.
In the Committee of the House for Applying the late Earl of Derwentwater's Estate to Greenwich Hospital, Mr. Clayton offered a Clause to Empower the Lords of the Treasury to issue the sum of £700 to be paid Lord Gage to reimburse the Expense he had been at in detecting the Frauds relating to the Purchas of that Estate, and recovering it to the use of the Publick; the House thought he deserved so well in that Affair that they unanimously Agreed to make the sum £2000.

April 25.
The Bill for preventing the running Wool was read once, and on the Question for a second reading was thrown out by surprise in a very thin House;[56] which was very unparliamentary in a Bill of that Publick Nature.

April 28.
In a Committee of the House to Explain and Amend the Insolvent Debtor's Act[57] which was expiring, Mr. Sandys spoke against continuing any more of it than what related to setting one Debt against another, the rest (he said) was either useless, or distructive of small Credit. Sir John Barnard Mr. Oglethorp and my self spoke for

---

[55] Harley gives a majority of 24 (see above pp. 8–9) which is confirmed by *C.J.*, XXII, 472, with a division of 190 to 214.

[56] The voting figures were 42 to 65 on the bill's 1st reading. *Ibid.*, p. 476.

[57] 2 Geo. II, c. 20 of 1728. The amendment bill gained the royal assent on 15 May. *C.J.*, XXII, 493–4.

continuing the whole. I said it was a most excellent Law, and every part built on the generous principle of relieving the oppressed: One Part concerned the good treatment of Debtors on the Arrest, and if some Prisoners might sometimes escape by reason of it, that was not so great an inconvenience as the Oppression they underwent before that Act. Another Part concerned the hanging up tables of Fees, and though that had been generaly complied with; Yet if it had any where been omitted or should be for the future, if the Law should cease, there would be no compelling the doing it, or punishing the neglect. A third Part, was for discharging Prisoners for Debts under £100, on dilivering up their All: this was in favour of liberty; Agreeable to the Law of Nature which requires no impossibility; Agreeable to the intention of the common Law, which intends the Imprisonment only as a means to compel the Payment, if a Man was able: Such Imprisonment was cruel to the Debtor and no benefit to the Creditor, but put a man out of a capacity of gaining any thing to pay with, and robbed the Publick of his Labour: that the Law was no hindrance to Credit, for persons of good Charracters would still find it, and it was the Interest of Creditors to trust only such: And I questioned whether Credit was an Advantage to the inferior Sort; it might make them less Industrious; and if it was for necessaries they bought them dearer; and if for superfluities, it aught not to be encouraged; and as Sir J: Barnard observed it was a good Law lately made in one of our Plantations, that Alehouse Keepers should have no Action for Liquor sold.

The Committee divided upon this Part of the Act, and it was carried but by a small Majority for the continuance of it.

Every body was for continuing that Part of the Law, which was for setting one Debt against Another; which I said nobody could be against, unless those who wished for two Actions where there was occasion for none. But the Judges of the Comon Pleas had rendered it in a great measure ineffectual by determining it did not extend to Debts of different Natures: Lord Hardwick therefore added a Clause for that Purpose in the House of Lords, and was seconded in it by the Chancellor.

April 30.

The Playhouse Bill, which was looked upon as the Master of the Rolls's bill, was put off to a long Day in a thin House: I voted with the Minority for the Bill,[58] for I think those diversions are run into excess. This was no small displeasure to the Master of the Rolls and Sir J. Bernard, who first made the Motion on Account of the Playhouse in the City.[59]

May 2.

I reported from the Committee, which had been appointed on my Motion to consider the Laws relating to the Poor, ten Resolutions which they had come to on that Subject. These were drawn up by my self, and proposed to the Committee by Sir J. <sic> Beaumont, and were agreeable to a Scheme I had Published in a Pamphlet at the beginning of the Session,[60] which was got into most of the Members hands and had

---

[58] There were two motions on 30 Apr. The first, to postpone the committee of the whole house until 1 May, was defeated by 90 votes against 74. The second, to postpone the committee until 14 May, the day before parliament was prorogued, was agreed without a division. See V.J. Liesenfeld, *The Licensing Act of 1737* (Madison, 1984), p. 52, and Harley Journal, above p. 9.

[59] Either the theatre at Goodman's Fields, or possibly the proposal to build a new one at St Martin's-le-Grand. On the bill see Liesenfeld, *Licensing Act*, ch. 2.

[60] *Remarks on the Laws Relating to the Poor. With Proposals for Their Better Relief and Employment. By a Member of Parliament.* Printed for J. Stagg.

met with general Aprobation: The Principal Point was errecting publick Workhouses Hospitals and Houses of Correction in each County.

When I moved for a Day to take the Report into consideration Mr. Earle was for putting it off to a long day; which I opposed; for I said it would imply a dislike of the Propositions; and that the intention of making the Report was that it might be debated. That Gentlemen might know the Sense of the House and afterwards consult their Neighbours in the Country in order for a Bill another Sessions; and I was supported by Mr. Hooper Mr. Sandys and Mr. Gibbon; so Wednesday was appointed, when I gave the Reasons that induced the Committee to come to each Resolution: which were many of them unanimously, all of them generally agreed to by the House: There was but one which bore much debate, which was making the Governors of the Houses a Body Politick in Law, which the Master of the Rolls often insisted in the Debate was absolutely necessary to carry on any scheme of that Nature. He was very zealous for it, and paid me great Compliments on my Pamphlet and the Share I had borne in this Affair, as every one did that spoke on the occasion.

The same day a Bill brought in by Ereskine to repeal an Act of 10 Anne for restoring Patrons to the right of Presentation in Scotland[61] was put off for a Month on the Question for the Second reading. He said in favour of the Bill that it was to restore things to the State they were in at the time of the Union, which the Act of Queen Anne had altered, contrary to one Article of it, by which the Church Discipline was not to be altered in either Kingdom. It was said by some Scotch Members, that the People in many Places would not submit to the Act of Queen Anne, and that there was sometimes as much contest about introducing a Minister into a Parish, as electing a Member of Parliament. On a Division it was carried by a considerable Majority[62] for putting it off: the Minority did not appear in it; the Scotch were pretty equarly divided: Sir W. Windham and most of the Tories Voted for putting it off: because the Act of Queen Anne passed in their favorite Administration, and was to please the Church Party: I voted the same way, because I thought the Bill might encrease the temporal Power of the Clergy in Scotland, which I am against in any Nation.

May 5.

The Bill to explain an Act in Scotland for Preventing Wrongous Imprisonment there (which Bill was brought in in consequence of the Haddington Petition) was debated on the third reading.[63]

I was the first who spoke in the Debate. I said, I was prejudiced in favour of the Bill, because the Bill was in favour of Liberty: But that I must be satisfied in some particulars before I could give my consent to it.

As whether such a bill was wanted in Scotland: Whether it was consistent with the general System of their Laws, or would introduce any inconvenience and whether the People were now in a temper to receive it, for a good Law was not always expedient and the Habeas Corpus had sometimes been suspended in times of danger.

This bill was ill framed; One great objection to it was that the Name of the Informer was to be in every Warrant; this was not required by our Law; it was sufficient to specify the Cause only: in Treason it might be of dangerous Consequence to the State; it might prevent discoveries, Informers often making it a Condition, to have their Names kept a Secret; and it might be a Notice to Accomplices to make their Escape.

---

61 The Patronage Act of 1712.
62 The voting was 62 to 109. *C.J.*, XXII, 484.
63 See above, p. 110.

Another objection was, that it gave a Power to the Justice of Peace if he judged the Accusation to be groundless to discharge the Prisoner: this was not agreeable to the Common Law; for the Information being on Oath the Justice should either bail or commit in order to bring the Prisoner to his Tryal; but this was impowering him to try him himself; which might be of dangerous consequence in Cases of Treason. And I said that in consulting the liberty of the subject I would not do any thing to endanger the security of my Prince.

These objections were principaly insisted on by others that spoke after; and allowed to be good by those who were for the Bill: but Sir W. Wyndham and Master of the Rolls said it was unparliamentary to object to a Bill on the third reading; and that it might be Amended in the House of Lords: but sure trusting to that was much more unparliamentary.

On a Division the Bill was carried (against the Ministry) by a Majority of 8. 139 voting for it, and 131 against it. But it was rejected in the House of Lords.[64]

May 8.

The Bill for regulating the Quartering Soldiers during Elections was read a third time. By this the removing them from Borough Towns at that time was made Law; which had constantly been done before by Orders from the War Office. The Ministry disliked the Bill, because they would still have had it taken as a favour from the Crown: but it was too popular for them to oppose: so it mett with no Opposition: But on the third reading in a very thin House of under 70 Members, on the Question for passing, when Nobody expected it, Breerton divided the House, and it was carried but by 7 Votes:[65] and if Winnington, Sir H. Williams, Selwyn, and I, had not voted for the Bill against our Friends the bill had been lost. And Hampden went behind the Chair and did not Vote. And Breerton had no thanks from any body.

Accounts delivered in last Session.

1734.

Jan. 28. Prohibited East India Goods in the Warehouses at Michaelmas 1733. What since brought in, what exported, and what remained at Michaelmas 1734. Ditto in his Majesty's Warehouses in the Port of London. Ditto in the Warehouses of out Ports. Naval Stores imported from Russia into the Port of London from Michaelmas 1733 to Michalemas 1734. Ditto into the Out Ports.

Feb. 5. Number of Seamen at a Medium employed from January 1. 1733 to December 31. 1734.[d]

6. Money granted last Session to Greenwich now disposed of.[e]

7. Money ordered by the Lords of the Treasury, and received by the Treasurer of the Navy, for the service of it, from December 31. 1733 to December 31. 1734. Services not provided for in 1734.

[d] Number of Seamen employed 1734 was about 23,000 at a Medium.

[e] Yearly Expence of Greenwich estimated at £22,567 10s.

[64] The bill was not formally rejected by the Lords, but was lost by the ending of the session in the Lords on 15 May.

[65] The figures were in fact 47 to 38. C.J., XXII, 488.

10.   Services incurred by Augmenting Forces, and for Exigency of Affairs, pursuant to the Vote of Confidence.[f]

Money given for 1734. How disposed of till February 10. 1734.[g]

Money received for Greenwich for 1734. How applied.

Feb. 17. Arrears of Land Tax, due at Xmas 1734.[h]

Ditto on Houses.[i]

18.   Treaty with Denmark.

19.   Surplusses stated at Lady Day 1734.

Ditto at Michaelmas 1734.

His Majesties Warrant permitting Letters to pass free.

Feb. 24. Corn Exported from Xmas 1733 to Xmas 1734.[j]

25.   Money granted last Session to Westminster, how applied.

Mar. 7. Money received from Scotland from Xmas 1731 to 1732.

11.   Money expended in Georgia from June 9. 1732 to September 9. 1734.

20.   Corn exported from Scotland from Xmas 1733 to Xmas 1734.

24.   Earl of Derwentwaters Estate.

Estimates.

Feb. 5. Debt of the Navy at December 31. 1734.

The Ordinary of the Navy for 1735.

The Office of Ordinance for 1735.

10.   Guards, Garrisons etc. for 1735.

Forces in Plantations, Minorca and Gibraltar for 1735.

Out Pensioners of Chelsea for 1735.

Mar. 3. Forts etc. of Afracan Company for 1735.

4   List of half Pay Officers, and charge for 1735.

Officers Widdows ditto.

6.   Expence Necessary to compleat Greenwich and Plan.

---

[f] Services on the Vote of Confidence £81,568 5s. 11d.
£39,937 paid to the King of Denmark, the rest for bringing Forces from Ireland.

[g] Money given for 1734. How disposed of, see hereafter.

[h] Arrears of Land Tax due at Xmas 1734. For Sussex only £16,958.

[i] Ditto on Houses, <£>3,468.

[j] Corn exported. Barley 70,000 Quarters. Malt 223,124. Oatmeal 3,038. Rye 10,735. Wheat 498,196.
Bounty on it £163,476. Viz on Barley £8,778. Malt £27,890. Oatmeal £379. Rye £1,878. Wheat £124,549.
Of which from London. Barley 17,469. Malt 2,211. Oatmeal 484. Rye 1,478. Wheat 239,399.

Corn exported from Xmas 1731 to Xmas 1732.

Barley 13,874 Quarters	Bounty	£1,734	6s. 10½d.
Malt 161,075.		£19,236	13s. 8½d.
Oatmeal 1,274		£159	7s. 2¼d.
Rye 15,535		£2,718	14s. 8¼d.
Wheat 202,058		£50,514	12s. 6d.
	Total	£74,363	14s. 11½d

Corn exported from Xmas 1732 to Xmas 1733.

Barley 37,598 Quarters		£4,699	15s. 0d.
Malt 203,115		£25,389	7s. 6d.
Oatmeal 1,487		£185	18s. 9d.
Rye 28,155		£4,927	2s. 11¼d.
Wheat 427,199		£106,001	19s. 6d.
	Total	£142,001	19s. 6d.

	£
Supplies voted for 1735.	
For 30000 Seamen	1,560,000
25700 Land Forces	794,529
Forces in Plantations, Minorca, Gibraltar	215,710
Extraordinary Expences in 1734, not provided for	10,273
Chelsea Hospital	18,850
Denmark Treaty	56,250
Extra Expence of the Vote of Confidence	81,568
To compleat the last Sum	10,393
Reduced Officers for 1735	49,834
Officers Widdows Pensions	3,780
Ordinance	79,760
Extraordinary Expenses of the Ordinary unprovided for	24,693
Deficiency of Grants in 1734	36,406
Ordinary of the Navy	198,914
Greenwich Hospital	10,000
Afracan Company	10,000
Georgia	26,000
Westminster Abby	4,000
St. Margarets	3,500
	3,232,017

	£
Ways and Means	
Malt	750,000
Sinking Fund	1,000,000
Salt four years 'till 1746	500,000
Land Tax 2s.	1,000,000
	3,250,000
	3,232,017
	17,983

Petitions.

69 presented.

5 heard at the Bar. viz. Shaftsbury, Warwick, Wells, Northampton, Marlborough.

4 before the Committee viz. Southampton, Wendover, Canterbury, Launceston.

9 Withdrawn viz. St. Albans, Wallingford, Peebles, Ludgarshal, Forfar, Bristol, Crickdale, Dumfrees.

51 undisposed of.

An Account of how the Money granted in 1734 was disposed of.

	£
Navy (including 1,200,000 debt)	2,390,670
Greenwich	10,000
Ordinance	138,813
Forces	980,886
Deficiences	499,232
Westminster	4,000
Afracan Company	10,000
Augmenting forces	31,237
Denmark	39,937
	£4,014,768 6s. 2d.

Ways and Means 1734.

Malt	750,000
Salt	1,000,000
Sinking Fund	1,200,000
Land Tax 2s.	1,000,000
Arrears of Land Taxes	20,578
Arrears of Malt 1732	7,783

£3,978,362 10s. 10½d.

Deficency of Ways and Means   £36,405 15s.   4¼d.

	£	s	d
Ordinary of the Navy for 1734	202,670	5.	9.
		viz.	
The Execution of the Office[k]	28,062.	14.	1.
Captains Superannuated, Shipwrights, Masters, Caulkers, Surgeons, Punes, Boatswains, Gunners, Carpenters, Cooks	4,152.	9.	8.
Pensions to Flag and other Sea Officers, Widdows of Comissioners and Relations of Sea Officers	3,864.	0.	0.
Chatham Yard	3,507.	7.	2.
Deptford Yard	3,082.	11.	4.
Woolwich Yard	2,517.	8.	8.
Portsmouth Yard	4,164.	14.	6.
Sheerness Yard	1,808.	4.	6.
Plymouth Yard	2,503.	5.	6.
Officers of out Ports, viz. Deal, Harwich, Kinsale Yard, Port Mahon, Gibraltar, Antegua, New England, Nova Scotia	2,992.	9.	7.
Wages to Officers and Shipkeepers, of Ships lying in Ordinary	2,992.	9.	7.
Hulks and Small Vessels	4,070.	17.	1.
Rates £42,701. 18s. 3d. whence abating for ships at Sea £12,432. 2s. 6d. remains	30,269.	15.	9.
Harbour Victuals for 1428 Men per Annum	13,030.	10.	9.
Harbour Moorings, viz Cables Rigging	17,357.	10.	9.
Graving and ordinary Repairs of Ships, Yards, Docks, Warfs, Buildings, etc. in the several Yards and offices, viz. the Materials	59,289.	0.	0.
Sick and hurt Seamen	1,068.	15.	0.
Half Pay Officers	25,000.	0.	0.

[k] Of the <£>28,062. 14. 1. for the Execution of the Office Lords Commissioners £7000. Treasurer £2,000. Comptroller of the Treasurers Accounts £500. Of the Victualling Accounts £500. The Storekeepers Accounts £500. One Comissioner more £500. Of Chatham, Portsmouth, Plymouth £500 each. Secretary to the Lords of the Admiralty £800.

Land Forces in Great Britain 1734.

	£	s	d
Horse 2161	176,124.	13.	4.
Dragoons 2952	139,308.	6.	8.
Foot 10,221	228,657.	5.	10.
Invalids 1815	32,492.	1.	8.
6 Independent Companies in Scotland of 15651	9,115.	11.	6.
Staff Officers	10,880.	19.	2.
Garrisons with Fire and Candle	38,887.	7.	0½
Contingencies upon Account	15,000.	0.	0.
Total	647,429.	11.	3½

Forces in Plantations, Gibraltar and Minorca, 1734.

	£	s	d
Plantations 1780	36,943.	7.	6.
Garrisons at Anopolis Royal, Canso and Placentio	2,539.	1.	8.
Minorca 2460	51,136.	10.	0.
Officers of the Garrison etc.	6,200.	8.	9.
Gibraltar 3690	78,869.	0.	0.
Officers of the Garrison etc.	3,749.	12.	3½
Provisions for the Regiment at Anopolis, Canso etc.	1,558.	17.	1.
Provisions for the Regiments at Gibraltar	25,000.	0.	0.
Total	203,996.	17.	3½

January 15. 1736.

The Parliament met and the King in his Speech congratulated them on the happy Turn affairs abroad had taken, and informing them that Preliminaries of Peace were agreed to,[66] the Articles of which did not esentialy vary from the Plan proposed to him and the States; and left them to judge whether the influence of Great Britain had not a share in composing the Troubles and whether the continuance of some extraordinary Expence would not be necessary to perfect the Reconciliation.

Mr. Fox moved a Question ready prepared for an Address of thanks, and was by agreement seconded by Mr. Williams of Monmouthshire.

The Assurance of Peace was so generally agreeable that there was a long Silence several times on putting the Question, nobody taking exception to it: only at last Walter Plumer said, that he believed our extraordinary Armament last year had no influence in composing the Troubles, and it would have been the same if we had had but 5000 Men. And Shippen said he would not return thanks for a Peace before the Articles were communicated to us. Nobody else said any thing against the Question, and it passed without a Division.

January 16.

On presenting the Yorkshire Petition Sir W. Young moved that the Petitioner and sitting Member should before the hearing the Petition by such a Day diliver lists to each other of the Voters they object to: and after Debate an Order was made that it should be done on all Petitions concerning Counties.

The Journal of 1699 was produced to shew that an Order of that Nature had been reversed on Account of Inconvenience. The Journal of 1710 was produced to shew that such an Order was agreed to by the Parties, and Acquiesced in by the House, in the Case of Rutland.[67]

The Reasons urged for the Order were, the Expediting Justice, and giving the Parties time to prepare for their Defence; Against it, that by confining the Evidence to the Lists only, you might be deprived of some that might be necessary to come at the Merits of the Case.

It was doubted in the Debate whether a Sheriff should grant a Scrutiny in a County Election. Poulteney said, he had seen Counsel's Opinion that he should not, because the Voters took an Oath at Polling. But it was said that the Oath was imperfect, a Man might take it and yet be no Voter, for many Qualifications required by Law were omitted in it, as being of Age, in Possession a twelvemonth, and being Taxed.

On bringing in the Address, Sandy's said the Committee who were appointed to draw it up had exceeded their Authority for there were things in it not warranted by the Resolution, particularly the intimating that our Preparations last year had contributed to the Peace (which Shippen said he was informed the Ministry were very much allarmed at, when they first heard it, not knowing what it contained, though now they would assume to themselves the honour of it). It was said if the House believed that part of the Address to be true, they might agree to it, though it was not in the Resolution; and it was agreed to without a Division.

January 16.

The House went to St. James's with the Address.

---

[66] Between Great Britain and the United Provinces.
[67] See Harley journal, above p. 11, and below p. 129.

January 22.

Mr. Conduit moved for leave to bring in a Bill to repeal an Act made in the Reign of King James the first against Witchcraft;[68] he said it was made in the times of ignorance, and in compliment to the King who had writ a Book called Daemonologia: he said 123 persons had lost their lives by it. It was read, and was so very ridiculous that the most serious could not forbear laughing: and the Motion was agreed to without contradiction.

January 26.

In the Committee of Supply Sir C. Wager moved for 15000 Seamen for the Service of the ensuing year. Which was agreed to Nemine contradicente. A rare instance of Unanimity!

January 28.

Mr. Sandys moved to refer the Estimate of the Ordinary of the Navy to a select Committee to examine, and said if that Motion was approved of he would propose the same with relation to the other Estimate.

This was last year proposed by Sir W. Windham, and the Arguments used on each side were the same. On a Division 155 were for it 256 against it. I voted against it.

In the Debate Sandys said, there had been such a Committee in 1713.[69] And Gibbon, another in 1697. – Winnington said it was extraordinary to desire such an examination now, when £200,000 of the Navy Debt had this year been paid off.

In the Debate (though it was foreign to the Question) there was as much notice taken of the Estimate for Guards and Garrisons, as of the Ordinary of the Navy. Mr. Poulteney observed, several Articles of it were considerably encreased, as the Staff, Contingencies, Candles, and particularly that were last year £35000, whereas in 1719, it was but £29000. Mr. Pelham said be believed that might be accounted for by the increase of the Garrison Companies for securing the Peace of the Highlands: and he knew of no encrease of the Staff but what was given to the General there (meaning Wade) who he thought well deserved it.

In the Committee of Supply 17700 Men were voted for Guards and Garrisons in Great Britain. This passed without Opposition: Mr. Poulteney declared the Reduction greater than he expected; but said in times of full Peace he thought 12000 would be sufficient: Watkin Williams and Shippen said they did not oppose the number proposed this year, but hoped that Number was not always to be kept up, and declared against any certain Number of standing Forces to be established as part of our Constitution.

January 29.

It was reported, and agreed to unanimously by the House.

Immediately afterwards Lord Cornbury moved an Address (which he had ready prepared) to the King, to reduce his Forces as soon as possible, and in such a way as to give the greater Ease to his People; which was explained to be by the reduction of Corps as well as private Men:

This was seconded by Littleton in a long elaborate Speech. His Arguments for it turned on the good Oeconomy in doing it; and from the danger that might arise to the Constitution from such Numbers of Officers.

---

[68] The 1603 statute on witchcraft was 1 Jam. I, c. 12; and the 1735 bill became 9 Geo. II, c. 5.
[69] For the 1713 committee appointed on 29 Apr., see *C.J.*, XVII, 305.

It was answered, that it would be strange and inconsistent on the same day that we had Voted a Number of Forces to Vote an Address to his Majesty to reduce them; it would imply a diffidence in his Majesty, who had intimated in his Speech that he intended a farther Reduction. That it was not so decent to prescribe the Manner of doing it, and that the Manner proposed, though cheapest, might not be the most expedient, for by keeping a good Number of Officers an Army would be more easily formed in Case of Troubles Abroad or at home. That nothing was to be apprehended from the Officers; Men of Honour, Fortune, Family, and great Alliances, and whose Interest was firmly united with that of the Nation. Nor was it to be supposed they would be tempted to do wrong.

On a Division 139 were for it, 205 Against it. I both Spoke and voted against it.

February 6.

Sir John Rushout moved for leave to bring in a Bill for the further regulation of Elections.

He said he was far from proposing to alter the Right of any Persons in Elections, he only proposed to confirm them. He observed the imperfection of the Freeholders Oath in County Elections, and proposed to mend it by inserting all the Qualifications required in the Voters. Mr. Harley said, when it was mended he thought it should be final, and the Sheriff not permitted to go into a Scrutiny: I agreed with him, but added, that there should be a severe penalty in the Bill in case of Wilfull Perjury; for I believed a Man was not at present indictable, but was left to his own Conscience and the Justice of the House. Conduit said, he believed the right Voters in a County would never be known 'till there was a general Register, which he thought would be of great benefit; and wondered how Landed Gentlemen could sit year after year without proposing it.

As to Borough Elections Sir J. Rushout complained of Peoples getting into Houses just before an Election to Vote, and proposed that they should be Housekeepers a year before. – I observed, that as the last Resolution, was to be our Rule, it was necessary perfectly to understand it, before we could adhere to it. That in many Resolutions there were expressions, which though common in every mans mouth were understood by very few; and therefore aught to be better defined; As who should be deemed a Housekeeper: who Inhabitants, whether Residants in general, or only Persons legally Settled: Who paying Scot and Lot, an Expression used before the 43 of Queen Elizabeth,[70] and therefore a Poors Rate was not a full proof of it: It certainly meant in general Persons of Ability, on which their right of Voting should depend, and not on the Pleasure of Parish Officers and Justices of Peace in putting them in or leaving them out of a Poor Book; which had occasioned many unfair Practices.

February 10.

On hearing the Petition for Southwark, it was Resolved Nem. Con. No Voter shall be admitted to prove that he Voted otherwise than appears by the Poll: persuant to the Resolution of January 20, 1710 in the case of Rutland:[71] and the Journal of July 14, 1715 was read where another Person was not admitted to prove it, in the case of Bedfordshire.[72]

[70] This is probably a reference to 43 Eliz., c. 2, Act for the Relief of the Poor.
[71] See above, p. 127.
[72] See Harley journal, above p. 12.

February 12.

On the further hearing of Southwark Petition, it was Resolved without a Division, that a Person that had taken the Oath against bribery at the time of Election should not be admitted to give Evidence of his being bribed. Q. if this Resolution does not frustrate the Intention of the Act made in the second year of this King,[73] which was to make the criminal capable of being an Evidence in this Case.

February 24.

The Resolutions of the Committee of the whole House, to whom the Petition of the Middlesex Justices complaining of the excessive and pernicious use of Spiritous Liquors was referred, were reported and Agreed to: viz. that it was owing to the Low Price of them: that to discourage it an high Duty should be laid on the Retailers: that the Retailing should be only in such and such Places: and that none should Retail them without a licence with a Duty payable on it.

It was Objected that the putting down the Distillery would ruin Numbers of Families employed in it: that it would prejudice the Landed Interest, great quantities of Corn being employed in it: And that it was apparrent it had prejudiced the Brewery, the Duties on which had rather encreased since the encrease of the Distillery: and that the Revenue would suffer by putting it down since the Duties on all Spirituous liquors at a Medium for the last three years had been near £300,000 per Annum.

It was answered, that nothing was to be put in competition with the health and morals of the People; that if it was a prejudice to some Persons to put it down, it was a Charity to thousands: It would not prejudice the Landed Interest, people would eat and drink more, which would cause a greater consumption of Corn, Meat, and Beer: that the Duty lost by the Distillery would be replaced by that gained on Beer, Hops (and Malt for the current service) but if those did not rise in proportion, the Parliament would make good any deficiency.[74]

The Resolutions were agreed to without a Division.

On hearing the Petition for Yorkshire a Question was started, whether the Poll should be Admitted as Evidence, because it was not delivered in by the Sheriff on Oath by the Clerk of the Peace within twenty days as directed by 10 Anne.[75]

It was answered, that the Statute, though a direction to the Sheriff, was not intended to restrain the proceedings of the House: that the Sheriff, not having complied with the Act, the House was to consider how it stood before the making of it, when such Poll was always admitted as Evidence: that the House was to proceed by the best Evidence that could be got: this Poll was so: and if the House did not admitt it as Evidence there would be a total failure of Justice. 201 for 165 against the Evidence.[76]

February 25.

The Petitioners for Lewes having agreed to such right of Election as the sitting Members approved of; and to make no further Opposition. On the evening the Committee met: the Petitioners Council called for an Old Journal in 1628 in which was an

---

[73] Probably 2 Geo. II, c. 24: Act on Corrupt Practices in Parliamentary Elections.

[74] See Harley journal, above p. 14. For the background see L. Davison, 'Experiments in the Social Regulation of Industry: Gin Legislation, 1729–1751', in *Stilling the Grumbling Hive: The Response to Social and Economic Problems in England, 1689–1750*, ed. L. Davison, T. Hitchcock, T. Keirn and R.B. Shoemaker (Stroud, 1992), pp. 25–48.

[75] See Harley journal, pp. 15–16 above.

[76] The figure is 164 in *C.J.*, XXII, 588.

obscure entry of a Report from the Committee, viz. Agreed the Election in the Inhabitants, but there is no Resolution of the House on it, the only Resolution was, that
Mr. Stapley[77] was duly Elected. – The sitting Members produced three Witnesses to
prove, that the Custom and Common Opinion shewed it to be in the Inhabitants being
Householders paying Scot and Lot: And the Comittee resolved it to be so: and that the
sitting Members were duly elected.

I learnt one Point from Earl the Chairman, that he had no power to send for any
Papers of a Private Nature: and he was a little doubtfull whether the Minutes of a
Court Leet were not so: but he was afterwards satisfied they were not. – Mr. Strange
told me, that Householders of the Place might give evidence that the Right of Election
was in the Inhabitants at Large; but not that it was in the Inhabitants being
Householders, because it was narrowing the right to their own Advantage.

February 26.
On the further hearing of the Yorkshire Petition; A Question was put, whether Parole
Evidence should be admitted as to a Persons being no Freeholder who swore himself
to be a Freeholder at the time of Election; This was disallowed in the case of
Hertfordshire in 1695, and allowed in the Case of Bedfordshire in 1715.[78]

It was Objected that Parole Evidence was not of so high a nature: that the Statute
by prescribing the Oath intended it should be final: that it was unjust to Accuse a Man
of Perjury, or question his right behind his Back: that if it could be known whether a
Man was a Freeholder without seeing the Writings of his Estate, which the House had
no power to send for: and that such Enquiries were too Expensive for Gentlemen to
support: Sandys said, false Voters might be indicted, and if convicted, the records of
their conviction might be brought into the House, and would then be proper Evidence;
and Howe, in order to have proper Evidence proposed to examine the Witnesses in a
Solemn manner.

It was Answered that if Voters forswore themselves the House had a Right to inquire into it and to do Justice, or else Knights of the Shire might be chosen by Knights
of the Post. That Parole Evidence was (last Sessions in the Case of Wendover)[79]
Admitted to disqualify a Member, who had sworn to his Qualification, a fortiori ought
it to be admitted against the Oath of a Voter: that the Voters Oath was properly no
Evidence, since a man could not be evidence for himself. That the Statute intended
the Oath to be a restraint on the Voter, and prehaps on the Sheriff from entering into a
Scrutiny, but not to restrain the House from examining into Elections, which I said
was a fundamental right, Coeval with the Constitution, and which the Legislature
itself could not take away: and that the Justice of the House was not to wait 'till the
Voter was convicted, but might proceed on Parole evidence which was the comon and
usual Evidence before that House. – 212 for 159 against the Question.[80]

Vid. the Case of Rutland January 16, 1710 allowing Parole Evidence to be given of
a Mortgage. And the Case of Wendover April 17, 1735 allowing it against a Members
Oath of his Qualifications.

---

[77] Anthony Stapley (1590–1655) was resolved by the Commons to have been elected M.P. for Lewes on
   3 Apr. 1628. *C.J.*, I, 878. He was also elected for New Shoreham in 1624 and 1625, and for Sussex in
   1640, 1653 and 1654; and he was a regicide.
[78] See Harley journal, above p. 16.
[79] See *ibid.*
[80] The vote was 206 to 152. *C.J.*, XXII, 594.

March 2.

In the Committee of Ways and Means Sir R. Walpole proposed to pay £600,000 out of the Sinking Fund towards the current service of the Year: Instead of which Sir J. Barnard proposed to borrow that sum at 3 per Cent on the sinking Fund, and with the sinking Fund to pay off so much of the old Debt carrying 4 per Cent by which means he said the National Debt might gradually be reduced to 3 per Cent.[81]

On the Report, I returned my thanks to him for the proposal which I thought the best I had heard in Parliament. I thought I foresaw many great and good Consequences from it: by reducing the Interest of the Debt the National Interest of Money must abate: on that the Price of Land must rise; and Trade would advance in proportion. Those who wanted money might borrow it on easier terms to trade with; those who had Money could no longer live on Usury, but must employ it in Trade, or in the improvement of their Estates; for when they could no longer prey on their fellow Subjects they must seek for riches either out of the Ground or out of Foreign Nations, on which Account the Jewish Law which forbids Usury was the wisest Maxim any Nation could pursue. Another good Consequence from the Proposal, was encreasing the sinking Fund by degrees, to half as much again as at present, consequently the Debt may be paid off half as soon Again (or prehaps as soon again) as it could otherwise have been: therefore next to the Parent of the Sinking Fund, I thought our thanks were due to the Gentleman who made this proposal, who on the Ruins of one Sinking Fund had taught us to erect another more Ample and more beneficial.

On the further hearing of the Yorkshire Petition, it was resolved, to admit evidence of the Confession of the Voter that he had no Freehold, who swore at the Election that he had. Agreeable to the Case of Northumberland April 16. 1735.[82]

March 3.

I moved for leave to bring in a Bill for the better relief and imployment of the Poor etc and opened the Nature and Substance of the Bill to the House; and it was ordered Nem. Con.[83]

March 10.

On the Order for the Instruction to the Committee of Priviledges and Elections not to proceed on any Petitions after those mentioned in the order: I said I had no regard to any Election in particular but was in general against closing the Committee; and though it had been the Practice, it was a Practice I could not reconcile to Reason and Justice; if there was time for hearing more Petitions than those appointed we ought to proceed; Gentlemen had Petitioned long enough and there was no reason to put them off for a year longer, I thought the doing so was in a great measure a denial of Justice. But though I was in general Against closing the Committee, (which seemed to be the sense of the whole House) since they were resolved to close it, it was indifferent to me where they Stopped: and therefore on an Amendment proposed to the Question for Hearing the Petition concerning the Nairn Election I voted against it.[84]

---

[81] The committee of ways and means discussed this issue on 27 Feb. and reported on 2 Mar. *C.J.*, XII, 598, 604. According to Chandler (IX, 149–51), however, Barnard's motion was a ministerial motion.

[82] The date should be 1724. See Harley journal, above p. 17.

[83] The original bill, which was introduced on 11 Mar., is printed in Lambert, VII, 199–226, while the amended bill of 20 May is at *ibid.*, pp. 227–54. It was lost by the ending of the session.

[84] The voting was 106 to 137. *C.J.*, XXII, 625.

March 12.

Plummer moved to repeal the Test Act, so far as it obliges Persons admitted to Offices to receive the Sacrament: it was carried in the Negative 251, against 123.[85] I both spoke and voted against it. The Question was cheifly supported by Plummer and the Master of the Rolls. The Arguments for it were, that it was a prostitution of the Sacrement, which was instituted for religious purposes. That it was a just offence to many of the Clergy of the Church of England by obliging them to Administer the Sacrament to Persons unworthy to receive it. That it was no security to the Church, since Persons for the sake of Advantage might receive it insincerly. That it was not necessary for the exclusion of Papists, who might as effectualy be excluded from Offices by Refusal of the Oaths as they are from their Seats in Parliament. That no other Nation had such a Test. It was not required in Scotland of the Members of the Church of England. 'Twas a hardship on the Dissenters not to be capable of Offices, since they had always been friends to Government: they could not have profitable Employments and yet were subject to penalties for not undertaking the troublesome ones. That it was injurious to his Majesty to deprive him of the service of some of his faithfullest subjects: that the Law was to prevent Dangers from Papists and not intended against Dissenters, who concurred in it for the general Good though to their own prejudice, And that it would be hard now to turn it against them: that they were promised redress, that Bills had since been brought in several times in their Favour; and that King William had recommended their Cause in his first Parliament from the Throne.

It was Answered, that the Dissenters must think the communion with the Church of England sinfull or not sinfull; if they thought it not sinfull they might comply, and there was no occasion to repeal the Law; for so doing would Open the Door of Power to them; and if they should get into power, they would make it matter of Concience to employ it to distroy a form of Worship which they thought sinfull. As to Places and Preferments, if they were incapable of them, it was their own fault; the Law did not make them so, they brought the Incapacity on themselves. They were matters of favour and not of right; no Man had a Natural right to a Place, nor was it any persecution to be without one. As to any Promises formerly made them, they were not binding to the Legislature: that no further Promises were ever made them, nor did any of the Bills brought in in their favour ever intend them any thing more than the Toleration which they now enjoyed, and which every Body wished they might always enjoy. To demand more savoured of Ambition; to grant it would be dangerous to the Publick tranquillity and to their own Safety: instead of mending their Condition it might bring them under persecution: it might revive old heats and Animosities, and expose them to the fury of the Multitude; and if their Ill-wishers should at any time be in Power even this Application to repeal the Law might be remembered to their Costs.

The Prime Minister made a very artfull speech Against the Question: saying the Toleration was all that was ever promised the Dissenters, or they had reason to expect: expressing great kindness for them at the same time; and lamenting their Indiscretion in making this Application, contrary to their own Interest and the Perswasion of their best Friends.

It was confidently reported that he had promised them to repeal the Test, for their good Services in the last Elections: but I heard him say that he had always discouraged them when they applied to him on that head, and represented to them the folly of bringing it into Parliament, and impossibility of Success; but he said it was pressed on

---

[85] The Test Act of 1672 (25 Cha. II, c. 2). See *ibid.*, p. 629.

by Doctor Avery[86] and some more warm Men against the Opinion of the generality of the Dissenters.

They were earnest to divide the House that they might know their Friends: Not one Tory voted for them; and Sandy's, Barnard and most of the Patriots were against them.[87] This did not abate their Zeal; but Foster[88] and some of their Leaders, who attended, as soon as the House rose, were heard to say, they would renew their Application every year. But I should imagine with little prospect of Success, even in the last Session of a Parliament, which Plumer in the debate intimated he thought the best time to apply: especialy the last Session of last Parliament on the Clamour of the Excise.

March 16.

A Bill to amend an Act of the 7th. of the last King to encourage the Woollen and Silk Manufactures by prohibiting the use of printed Callicoes was passed.[89] This was clearly to except printed Cottons out of the Act. Which Washing well were become a general Wear for Women of the lower rank: and were made so beautifull as to vie with the Indian Callicoes; not be distinguished by the eye; but might by unravelling the Warp being Linnen, and the shoot Cotton, whereas the Indian are all Cotton.

The Doubt on this Act was raised by the Manufacturers of Norwich; who imputed the decay of their business very much to the wearing these Cottons, and they Published Advertisements to inform the World they were prohibited, and threatning to put the Act in Execution against the Persons who wore them. This put a great Check on the Manufacture in Lancashire, where it was solely carried on, and occasioned their application to Parliament to amend the Act.

And the Question was whether it was in general for the Advantage of the Nation to encourage this Manufacture or No.

It was said against it, that it lessened the wear and consumption of our Woollen Goods, which aught in the first place to be encouraged, since the Growth as well as the Manufacture were our own.

It was answered that the Decay of the Woollen Manufacture in general was to be imputed to other Causes, principally to all other Nations falling into it. All the Cotton imported was worked in Lancashire, and they knew it was not much encreased; little more being imported at London or Bristol, though there was more at Liverpool; last year there being imported there 4518 bags: that they had rather changed than encreased their Cotton Manufacture; employing the Cotton now in this Species of Goods, which formerly they worked into Fustian Frocks, which are now out of Fashion, and Cloth worn in their stead. That the Woollen Manufacture increased in Lancashire as well as the Cotton; that they had 1000 Looms now employed where 20 years ago they had none; and that in 1719 they began to Manufacture Shalloons and Camlets, and had got great part of the Norwich Trade, the People living and working cheaper with them. That the Materials of these Goods were, one third Linnen, and two thirds Cotton the Growth of our own Plantations. That the Manufacture employed Hands from 5 years old to 70, the Value of the Goods arising from Labour, for 6 Shillings worth of Materials would make a Peice of 24 yards, worth when plain about 27s., and

---

[86] Benjamin Avery (d. 1764), a physician and former presbyterian minister.

[87] For the vote see Harley journal, above p. 21.

[88] Probably James Foster (1697–1753), minister at the Barbican Chapel, and one of the leading figures behind the publication of *The Old Whig*.

[89] The amended act was 7 Geo. I, c. 12. The new bill passed the Lords without amendment on 23 Mar., was so reported to the Commons on the 24th, and became 9 Geo. II, c. 4. *L.J.*, XXIV, 620–1; *C.J.*, XXII, 650.

when Printed about 40: the Progress being, Picking, Carding, Spinning, Winding, Warping, Weaving, Whiting, and Printing. That it did not interfere with the Woollen, which would not supply the Place of these Goods, if they were put down; but German Linnens would be printed in their Stead, not Scotch, or Irish, few of which were printed, for the Scotch and Irish Manufacture was not yet sufficient to supply above an 18th. part of the demand in England. And a Linnen Draper gave Evidence that in 1724 he printed 3953 peices of German Cloth and no Fustians, in 1735 1801 Fustians and but 54 German Cloths, the last gradualy abating as the first increased. That the Importation of Cotton supported the Woollen Manufacture; for half the Exports to Africa were Coarse Woollen Cloths (that consumed 10 times the Quantity of Wooll as Norwich Stuffs) these were changed for Negroes, and the Negroes for Cotton in the West Indies; which paid 5 farthings per pound freight from thence; and that if it was not for the freight of Cotton, they could not trade thither nor bring their Sugars from thence so cheap. That the prohibition of Cotton would ruin two thirds of the Whites in the Sugar Islands, who were Cotton Planters, not rich enough to have Sugar Plantations. And it would beggar 100,000 people in Lancashire employed in the Manufacture. One Man said he and his Brother employed 6000, and 100 Horses to carry Goods to London and bring Cotton back; but since this Damp put on the Trade he could not employ them, not sell his Goods to the Drapers in London, but on Condition to take them back if the Act was not explained in their favour.

Notwithstanding Counsel was heard against this Bill, and Mr. Walpole spoke against it, it passed without a Division.

March 22.

Due one of the Sheriffs of London presented two Petitions, from the Lord Mayor Aldermen and Common Council of the City, at the Bar with his own Hand,[90] which is an Antient and immemorial Priviledge of the City of London; the other Sheriff being a Member of the House[91] did not for that reason joyn in presenting either of the Petitions.

March 24.

The House went into a Committee on the Bill for the further Regulating Elections: it related only to Boroughs and Cities: and the general purport was that by whatever right a Man Voted he should be in possession of it a Twelvemonth. And there was an Oath in the Bill which the Voter was to take to that effect: (but that was agreed to be left out, because of the Dispute there had been in the Yorkshire Election, whether the Freeholders Oath should not be final, and prevent an examination into his Qualification afterwards) the Design of the Bill was very good; it was to prevent the scandalous practice of making Burgage Freeholders, Honorary Freemen, and Scot and Lot men, Householders, and Potwallers, just before an Election. Though the Bill was ordered to be brought in Nem: Con: yet People were jealous how it might affect their Elections. The Persons chosen by Burgage Tenure first took the Alarm, so their Case was to be excepted. And the Ministry disliked the whole. So in the Committee many amendments were offered, and difficulties started to obstruct it, on which the Question was put for leaving the Chair, and carried on a Division, by a considerable Majority; I both spoke and voted against it, for I thought the Bill very reasonable. But I soon found I gained much ill Will by it.

---

[90] Sir Robert Godschall, sheriff of London 1735–6, and alderman. *C.J.*, XXII, 642.
[91] Sir John Barnard, sheriff 1735–6. See Appendix.

Sir J. Rushout finding the Bill not like to succeed afterwards moved Himself to put it off.

April 2.

A Petition was presented from several Parishes in the County of Middlesex complaining that the Money raised on them for the repair of Goals and Bridges, relieving maimed Soldiers and Marines, passing Vagrants etc. had been misaplied and embeze<ll>ed:

The Patriots were for refering it to a Committee in hopes on an examination of discovering some abuses in the Justices of Peace.

But it was carried in the Negative without a Division, for it was said, that if the Constables or the Treasurer of the County, into whose hands the money was paid, had embezled it, they should apply to the Quarter Sessions for redress; if the Justices of Peace had shared in the Fraud, they should apply to the Court of Kings Bench to punish them; or to the Lord Chancellor to turn them out. And there should be no Application to Parliament but on a failure of Justice in the ordinary Course.

April 5.

The House went into a Comittee on the Bill to restrain the Disposition of Lands, whereby the same became unalienable.[92]

It was brought in by the Master of the Rolls, and cheifly supported by him.

The Purport of it was to make Void all Grants of Lands, or Money to be laid out in Lands, to Corporations, or to Persons in Trust for charitable uses, unless given by Deed executed a year before the Death of the Grantor, and to be inrolled in 6 Months, and to take effect in Possession immediately without the Power of Revocation.

Against this Bill it was said, that the inconveniences intended to be prevented by Magna Charta and other Statutes of Mortmain were Donations to Monastaries, by which the Lands given were exempted from bearing their share of the Charges of the Publick; but Lands given to Corporations now were not intitled to Such an Exemption. That Charity ought not to be discouraged; that many would give Charities by Will who could not afford them during their Life. That many Publick Charities, and very necessary ones, were still wanting: and the only secure way of perpetuating them was by settling Lands upon them; And that there was no danger that Grants to Corporations would be exorbitant, since they could not be made without the Kings Licence.

It was answered; that, though Lands could not be granted immediately to a Corporation without Licence, yet the Statu<t>es of Mortmain were eluded, by vesting Lands in Trustees to such uses as a Court of Equity calls charitable within the intention of the 43 Eliz. c. 4.[93] That that Statute had opened a door to infinite Donations. That they were often given by dying Persons, who falsely believe such a weak Stratagem will atone for a Life ill spent, though they disinherit their own blood to whom they ought in the first Place to be charitable. That such Donations were in effect given to the Rich, who by Law are obliged to maintain the Poor, if they were not given. And that they were frequently abused and diverted from the Original Intention: it was therefore better for Persons to see to the distribution of their own Charities in their lives, and to give the whole at once, than to leave the Interest or Rent in perpetuity, which was subject to Misaplication. That much Money was spent in

[92] The bill is printed in Lambert, VII, 255–8. It gained the royal assent on 20 May.
[93] The act of 1601 concerning charitable gifts.

disputes about such Charities: they cannot be established at first, nor their Abuses be afterwards corrected without applying to a Court of Equity.

The Bill was carried by a great Majority, and I voted for it. It came back from the Lords with an Amendment made by Lord Hardwick; which was, that it should not extend to Purchases made by Corporations Bonâ fide.[94] I was the only Person, who objected to the Amendment, which I thought in a great measure frustrated the Intention of the Bill, which was to prevent Lands being unalienable; which were as much so when purchased by Corporations, as when given to them. Which every body allowed; but Winnington said we must be glad to get what we could and to pass the Bill in any Shape.

Petitions were presented by the Universities, the Sons of the Clergy, and the Governours for Queen Anne's bounty, to be excepted out of the Bill.[95] The two last were not referred to the Committee but were ordered to lie on the Table. As to Queen Anne's Bounty it was urged as a very good and necessary Charity by the Attorney General[96] who presented the Petition; and that £400, the sum usually employed in the Augmentation, would purchas but a smal Value in Land: But I observed that as there were several thousands to be augmented, the whole Purchas would be a very great Landed Property: for there were about 6000 Livings under £50 per Annum as the Attorney general himself had stated the Case: of which (as Murray[97] afterwards affirmed at the Bar) 1000 were under £10 and 1500 under £20. – When this Matter came afterwards under Debate before the Lords, it was complained of as an Abuse, that the Corporation to encourage Charities, ordered those livings to be first augmented, to which any thing was given, without regarding whether they were the smallest, which in reason ought first to be augmented. And it was said they had then £152000 South Sea Annuity to be laid out in Land, for which they allowed 3¼ per Cent and £4800 not Applied.

As to the Universities, the Ministry, designing to ingratiate themselves with them, consented to except them out of the Bill.[98] When the Clause was offered by my Lord Cornbury in the Committee, it was not oposed, though against the Opinion of many Gentlemen, who thought, that before such exemption was granted, there should have been some account of their present Possessions, and how they were Applied: for they were probably sufficient to answer the ends of their Institution; since no Endowments were necessary for the Rich, who could maintain themselves; and as to the Poor the learned Professions were over stocked, and many had been better bred to some other calling, more usefull to their Country, and beneficial to themselves. Many thought they did not deserve such Exemption, on Account of the little Zeal they had always shewn to the Family on the Throne. And indeed such large Societies with a great Property are a sort of Imperium in Imperio. And when disgusted may distress a Government.

A Clause was offered by Mr. Walpole on the Report to exempt Eaton, Westminster and Winchester: which met with little or no Oposition.[99]

The universities to obtain this Exemption offered to be confined as to their purchasing Advowsons (which Sandys on the first Motion for the Bill complained of, and said in time there would be none of any Value left for the Nobility and Gentry to

---

[94] The vote, on 15 Apr., was 176 to 72. It was returned from the Lords on 14 May. *C.J.*, XXII, 686, 714–15.
[95] The petitions had been presented on 25 and 26 Mar. *Ibid.*, pp. 653–5
[96] Sir John Willes. See Appendix.
[97] William Murray, later Lord Mansfield. See Appendix and Sedgwick, II, 285.
[98] The debate on this clause took place on 5 Apr. H.M.C., *Egmont Diary*, II, 255.
[99] The report took place on 8 Apr. *C.J.*, XXII, 680.

dispose of, but the Clergy would depend intirely on the universities). What they proposed was to limit the Number of their Livings to half the Number of their Fellows: Lord Cornbury (who offered this restriction, with the Clause of Exemption) said both universities had then about 600 livings; and Sir W. Wyndham said, that this would add but 48 livings to Oxford and 40 to Cambridge: But whilest this was debating, Sandys proposed the Question, that they should be restrained from purchasing any more than they now had: this was carried in the Negative 227 Against 130: I Voted with the Minority. It was afterwards proposed, that, though they were confined to such a Number of Livings, they should have liberty for changing them for better, for it was said they were generaly too small to tempt the Fellows to quit their Fellowships: for Sir W. Wyndham said Oxford had about 290 Livings; about 140 of them under £100 and about 90 under £50 and that Christ Church in particular had 86 Livings and not above 10 of them £100. But this Question was carried in the Negative; 152 against 128: for it was thought to little purpose to confine them in the Number of Livings, if they were left at liberty to augment them in Value. I voted with the Majority.

April 6.

On a Petition from the Marchants and Planters concerned in the Sugar Colonies against the Bill for granting his Majesty a Duty of 2s. per Gallon on Spirituous Liquors sold by Retale etc. as far as the same affected them, the Question was whether they should be heard by Counsel according to the Prayer of the Petition; which passed in the Negative: it being laid down as a Rule that Counsel should never be heard against a Money Bill. – Though Sandys called for several Journals to prove the contrary: though it was thought that none of them came up to the Point. Indeed I think if it ever had been allowed it might have been in the Case: for though the Bill by its Title was for granting a Duty to the Crown; yet it was not expected that any Money would be raised by it, but that the Revenue would decrease, for the Duty was laid so high on Retalers, with Intent to prohibit retaling.

April 7.

On the Question for ingrossing the Bill for preventing Clandestine Marriages,[100] it passed in the Negative without a Division.

It was brought in by Lord Gage; and the Intent of it was to prevent young Persons of Family and Fortune from Marrying beneath themselves.

The Purport of it was, that if a Man under 21 having £300 per Annum or Heir to the same, or a Woman under 18 having £5000 should Marry without consent of Parents or Guardians, such Marriage should be Void, provided the Parents or Guardians signified their dissent in 6 Months after Notice of the Marriage. Winnington added a Clause to vacate the Marriage of Idiots and Lunaticks.

On the Question this was spoke against by Mr. Gibbons and the younger Bathurst, but cheifly by myself.

I said the Bill went beyond its Title: that it was a restraint upon Marriage itself, and in some Cases a Dissolution of it after it was contracted. That such a Restraint was injurious to the Publick, by preventing the encrease of the People: and injurious to the Persons restrained by taking away their Natural Rights. That our Law encouraged Marriage; and had wisely fixed the Age of Consent of a Man at 14 and of a Woman at 12, the earliest Age in which they were supposed to be capable of preforming the first Command given to Mankind: and when they were capable of attaining the end of

---

[100] Printed in Lambert, VII, 195–8.

Marriage, no Law ought to deprive them of the means. That such a Restraint would force young Persons into a vicious course, which would tend more to the dishonour and ruin of Families than the meanest Match. Some Statutes indeed had laid a restraint on Marriage; the Statute of Merton[101] made the Heir by Knights service above 14 and under 21 forfeit the Value of his Marriage if he Married without the Guardians Consent, if the Guardian had tendered him a convenient Match and he had refused it. So the Statute of Philip and Mary[102] made a Woman under 16 marrying without Consent of her Parents or Guardians to forfeit her Fortune during life, and the Man to suffer two years Imprisonment: but those Statutes though they imposed Penalties went not so far as this Bill to disolve the Marriage, which is against the Law of God. That the Bill gave a sort of Papal Authority to Parents and Guardians, who for 6 months had it in their Choice either to confirm or dissolve the Marriage: and if they should dissolve it after consummation, a child might be born a Bastard, and the Woman be for ever disgraced. That I disliked the Bill too as it was a Law for the Rich and not for the Poor, and tended to create an invidious distinction in a free People like that of Patricians and Plebeians amongst the Romans, the last of whom were never at ease till they were suffered to marry with the Patricians. That such a Bill would often bring the Validity of Marriages into Contest on these Questions, whether the Persons married had such Fortunes, were of such an age, had their Parents or Guardians Consent etc; and that it was not reasonable the Validity of Marriages should stand on so precarious a foundation; since on the Validity of a Marriage depends a Persons Legitimacy, and on his legitimacy his Title to his Estate.

April 8.

The Report from the Committee to whom the Bill for the more easy and speedy recovery of smal Debts[103] was referred was taken into Consideration. This Report had lain a considerable time on the Table, because the Bill had been very much altered in the Committee; scarce a Clause in the Bill remaining as it was first brought in: This Sandys observed when the Report was first made: and both he and the Speaker informed this House, that it was agreeable to order and practice in such a Case, either to withdraw the Bill, and bring in a new one, to be read a first and second time in the regular Course; or to satisfy that defect, to let the Report (as it did in this case) lie the longer on the Table to be perused by the Members.

April 21.

On the Report of the Scarborough Election, the Resolutions were agreed to by the House; and Lord Dupplin voted out, who had stood on the Duke of Leeds's Interest, and been returned on a Pretence of a right of Voting in the Freemen, which was contrary to the usuage of the Place.

The Orders of the Day being immediately called for, before the Question was put, Sir Wilfrid Lawson got up, and said he had a right to be first heard, because he spoke to the last Matter, (which the Speaker said was agreeable to Order, unless where a Censure was proposed) and he moved that part of the Report might be read, where it appeared that one of the Bailiffs had declared that he would return Lord Dupplin right or wrong: the Ministry (who intended to compliment the Duke of Leeds) opposed

---

[101] Of 1236 (20 Hen. III). This is probably a reference to c. 6 and c. 7 on wardship. See M. Powicke, *The Thirteenth Century* (Oxford, 1962), pp. 69–71.
[102] Possibly a reference to 4 & 5 Phil. & Mar., c. 8 on abduction (1557).
[103] This bill was printed on 14 Apr., but there is no further mention of it in *C.J.*

this, and insisted on reading the orders of the Day: and Mr. Pelham said, it was known that Persons censured in such Cases commonly were not the real Sufferers; but Mr. Plumer rightly observed that the Punishment would fall in the right Place: if they were not set to work, they would bear it themselves, if they were, it was proper their Principals should suffer. – On division above 200 were for reading the Orders of the Day, and 81 against it. – I voted with the minority.[104]

April 30.

The Question was put for ingrossing the Bill for the more easy Recovery of Quakers Tythes.[105]

The Bill was brought in by Mr. Glanville,[106] and introduced by a very ingenious Speech, setting forth the Merits of the Quakers; representing them as a people as plain in their Manners as they were in their Dress: so quiet that none were ever found in any Riot or Rebellion; so innocent, that none were ever convicted of a Capital Offence: so charitable that they maintained their own Poor; constant friends to the Government: not like other dissenters aiming at Preferments; but desiring only to be eased in Concience: that it was against their Concience to pay Tythes or defend any Suit in the Spiritual Court: that above 1100 of them had been sued there and in the Exchequer for demands, recoverable before a Justice of Peace by 7 & <8> Will. 3.[107] and many of them had lain in Goal several years rather than pay very small Sums awarded against them: That they did not expect to be discharged of Tythes; they only desired they might be taken from them in the easiest and cheapest Way; which was best for the Proprietors as well as them: and were ready to practice passive Obedience, which others only pretended to.

The Purport of the Bill was, that Quakers should be sued for Tythes etc. under £20 before the Justices of Peace only, pursuant to 7 & 8 Will. 3.

On the first Opening of the Bill Shippen declamed against it, as if the Church were in danger, by taking away the Suit in the Spiritual Court. – Sir W. Wyndham was not against that (though he changed his opinion in the Committee) but thought there should be a liberty left of suing in the Superior Courts, or at least an Appeal to them from the Justices.

The Clergy took the Alarm; and the Bishops sent Petitions ready drawn into their Dioceses, which came up, signed by the Clergy from all parts of the Kingdom against the Bill. This Conduct of the Bishops and Clergy gave great offence to the Ministry, who looked on so many Petitions as a sort of Insult on them, by dictating to them in what manner to proceed: and therefore though the Bill came in against their Inclination, in the House of Comons they let Sir William Young assist in carrying it through, and though they kept Silence, yet on every division they Voted for it, that the Clergy might understand they were not to be forced into any measures: but when it came into the House of Lords, where it was thrown out, the Lord Chancellor and Lord Hardwick spoke against it; and the Lords in the Ministry (not to disoblige the Clergy too far) Voted Against it.[108]

---

[104] The vote was 211 to 81. *C.J.*, XXII, 695.
[105] For the Tithes Bill as ordered to be printed by the Commons on 17 Mar. 1736, see Lambert, VII, 259–65. For the bill as ordered to be printed by the Lords on 4 May 1736, see Torrington, vol. 1734–8, pp. 187–94.
[106] On 17 Mar. See Harley journal, above p. 21.
[107] See *ibid.*, above, p. 22, n. 72.
[108] It was rejected on 12 May by 35 to 54. See Stephen Taylor, 'Sir Robert Walpole, the Church of England and the Quakers Bill of 1736', *Historical Journal*, XXVIII (1985), 72.

May 5.

The House took into consideration the Amendments made by the Lords to the Bill for building a Bridge at Westminster. The Principal of which were, their adding the Names of Commissioners, their Striking out the Power given to 5 or more Commissioners to receive the Money: and their directing more particularly how the money given to the Archbishop for his Ferry should be applied.

Those who were for agreeing with the Alterations said, that it was no Money Bill: that it passed neither the Committee of Supply, or of Ways and Means: that it was no Tax publick or Private, but only a Voluntary Contribution: and that the Bill was of a Private nature. That the Lords had made alterations in the Bill for Relief of the charitable Corporation, in the Bribery Bill by altering the Penalty from 50 to £500, and in several other Bills: and that if we disagreed with them now the Bill would probably be lost, and so necessary a Work obstructed.

Those who were against agreeing to the Amendment said; that the Lords could make no alterations at all in Money Bills: nor in such parts of other Bills as concerned the Grant or Application of Money; that those Bills were to be looked on as the outworks to the other; and therefore ought to be carefully guarded. That the Question was not whether the Bill were publick or Private; whether the Money was raised by Tax or Voluntary Contribution; but whether it came out of the Subjects Pocket: and if it did, the Right of disposing of it belonged solely to this House, who represented the Commons, in whom the great Property of the Nation was vested. If the Lords had at any time made Alterations in such Bills it was time to put a stop to the Practice. But the Precedents were much Stronger the other Way; and several Journals were read to shew where the Commons had disagreed to their Amendments in Bills for Workhouses, Warehouses, Lighthouses, Highways, etc.[116]

Of this last opinion was the Speaker, who thought the Honour and Priviledges of the Commons were concerned in the Question: and was extremly mortified when he saw it would be carried against his Opinion. He had collected all the Precedents on the Subject, which he shewed me at his House; and desired me and several others to Speak and vote against it. Which I did.

On the Division it was carried by a great Majority to agree with the Amendments,[117] for the Ministry were unwilling to have a dispute with the Lords; or to loose so favorite a Bill, which was designed to oblige Westminster and Mortify the City.

The same Day.

The Bill for Naturalizing the Princess of Wales was passed.[118] No such Bill had been passed for Naturalizing the Queen when she was Princess. But the Ministry thought proper to pay this Compliment to the Prince by Ordering the Attorney General to move for the Bill very early, for fear any body else should propose it before them. It occurred to me at the time, that this might be unnecessary; and I was in Doubt whether they did not in some measure wound the Prerogative by this Compliment, by giving the Princess that by Act of Parliament, which Prehaps she might be intitled to by her Dignity: for she may well be taken to be within the Intention, if not within the Letter of 25 Ed. 3. St. 2.[119] which makes the Kings Children born beyond Sea capable

---

[116] See Harley journal, above p. 23.

[117] The figures were 160 to 106. *C.J.*, XXII, 705–6.

[118] Augusta (1719–72), daughter of Frederick II, duke of Saxe-Gotha, married Frederick, prince of Wales, in 1736.

[119] Here Hay mistakes Statute 2 of 1351 on labourers and artificers, for Statute 1 of 1350 on the status of children born abroad.

of inheriting. And the Statute of Treasons the same year,[120] makes it Treason, to violate the Wife of the Kings son, an Heir, and it is extraordinary unless she had the Priviledges of a Natural Born Subject. – I mentioned this Doubt to Sir R. Walpole, who said it had been considered, and My Lord Chancellor and Lord Hardwick were of another Opinion.

On the Motions for Congratulatory Addresses to the King and Queen, Prince and Princess on the Marriage three Speeeches were made by Pit, Lyttleton, and Greenville,[121] which were much taken notice of; and the more because they were known to be young Gentlemen very intimate with his Royal Highness, and 'twas thought that what they said was not without his privity. They said that a Marriage had been long desired and sollicited by the Prince; and that it was owing to the King and not to the Ministry; who, as they intimated, had always endeavoured to keep the Prince low, because he was not so complaisant to them as they expected; they ascribed many amiable Qualities to him particularly Generosity (which was not thought to shine in full lustre from the Throne) and said, that he had just Notions of Publick Liberty, and was a Friend to the Independency of Parliaments.

It is very certain that his Royal Highness was very uneasy, that the King did not allow him more for the support of his Household, which was (as I have heard) fixed on his Marriage at £50,000 per Annum. And he took it very ill, that from his coming into England he had not been allowed the Nomination of his own Servants, who all even to the meanest were placed about him by the Ministry.

These Speeches were soon carried to Court, and in a few Days Pitt, who was a Cornet in the Earl of Pembrokes Troop of Guards,[122] received a Message by that Lord at the Door of the House of Commons, that the King had no further Occasion for his Service. This was done to make all Persons who had the least dependance on the Court understand, that if they presumed to say any thing disagreeable in the House they must expect to be the worse for it. A Measure, which if succesfully pursued, undermined the Freedom of Parliament; if without success, may turn fatally on a Prince and Ministry.[123]

---

[120] I.e., 1351: 25 Edw. III, c. 2, on treason.

[121] These three were the nucleus of 'Cobham's cubs': Grenville and Lyttelton were Lord Cobham's nephews, and Pitt was their friend. Grenville was a favourite of the prince of Wales. Cobham had broken with Walpole and the three cubs delivered a series of speeches against the ministry. See Sedgwick, II, 84, 233, 355. For another account of the speeches see John, Lord Hervey, *Some Materials Towards Memoirs of the Reign of King George II*, ed. Romney Sedgwick (3 vols., 1931), II, 553.

[122] Pitt had been a cornet of Cobham's horse (2nd King's Own Regiment of Horse) 1731–6, which became Pembroke's regiment when Cobham was deprived of it in 1733. See above, p. 95.

[123] End of MS L(c) 1733.

February 1. 1736/7.

The Parliament met, and the King being indisposed the Session was Opened by Commission; which it had not been since the Reign of Queen Anne. – The Commission was to the Prince of Wales and several Lords (great Officers of State) Authorising them to do every <thing> in the Name of his Majesty, which Ought to be done on his Part in the present Parliament – during his Absence.

Sessions the fourth, beginning January 24. 1737/8.

Since the last recess two memorable things had happened at Court: the one the Death of the Queen; the other the Kings Order to the Prince to withdraw from St. James's: this happened before the Queens Death; and was carried so far as not to suffer the Prince to see the Queen even on her death-bed. It was imagined at first that the Queens Death would have weakened the Prime Ministers Credit at Court, and consequently his Influence in Parliament. But he was soon observed to be as much in the Kings Confidence as before, if not more firmly established in it. So that the Queens Death produced no other alteration in the temper of Parliament, than rendring the Prime Ministers friends more zealously attached to him, and his Enemies more violent in their Opposition.

The Kings Speech was very short and general, taking no notice of the State of our Affairs either at Home or abroad: in order to avoid giving a handle to any Cavil or Debate.

The Adress of Thanks was also an Adress of Condolence, and (but for Mr. Shippens Negative) was unanimously agreed to. Fox who moved it enlarged Copiously on the Character of the Queen, and great part of his Speech was afterwards inserted in the Adress: which by many was thought beneath the dignity of the House; both as being too long and too stiff and poetical in the Style; as well as ascribing such Virtues and perfections to the Queen as fall not to the share of any mortal.

Immediately after this Adress was reported and agreed to, Mr. Talbot moved a Congratulatory address on the Birth of the Princess, which was unanimously agreed to.

Lord Sidney Beauclerk immediately after moved a Congratulatory Message to the Prince and Princess on the same Occasion; which was also unanimously agreed to: the Ministry prudently forestalling the Patriots in it: who intended to have assumed the Merit of that Compliment to themselves, Lord Morpeth who spoke immediatly after saying, if he had not been prevented he intended to have moved it himself.

February 3.

In the Committee of Supply Sir W. Young moved the same number of Forces for the ensuing year, which were 17,704 Men. Lord Noel Somerset moved an Amendment by changing the number to 12,000 and was seconded by Mr. Berkley.[124]

This brought on the ann<u>al Debate; in which, those for the Amendment insisted on the Expence of the greater Number and the Danger to the Constitution: That it was now a time of profound Peace, and that if they were not reduced, they must conclude, the same Number was always intended to be kept up, and to be made part of our Constitution. If that was the Case, Mr. Berkley said it was a Constitution not worth preserving, and the sooner we fell into confusion the better, for out of Confusion might arise some Order. Mr. Plumer said, if the same Number was to be always Voted he desired not to live to the end of the Year. And Mr. Pulteney said, if he was to be a Slave, he cared not what was the Kings Christian Name, but thought if we once fell into confusion it would not be George: that he was zealous for the present Royal Family only for the sake of the Constitution: which is not the first time he has given them publick Notice to be on their good behaviour.

On the Division 165 voted for and 249 against the Amendment.[125] I both voted and spoke against it, and because what I said was generally approved by my Friends, and

---

[124] There were two Berkeleys sitting at this time. See Appendix.
[125] Harley has the figures 166 to 249. See above, p. 32.

I think contained almost all the Arguments made use of against the Amenendment, I will set it down word for word as near as I can recollect it.[126]

Sir

Whenever this Question has come before this Committee I have always declared my Sentiments against a Reduction of the present Number of Forces; because I have always thought such a Reduction against the Interest of the Publick. I still am of the same opinion; notwithstanding we are now in a State of Peace: for I think that Peace would be of short duration, should we leave ourselves unguarded at Home. I never think on this subject but I consider this Island as situated in the neighbourhood of France. I consider France as its natural Ennemy, and at the same time as the most powerfull of all Nations, and as the power of France is great, our jealousies and apprehensions ought to be great in proportion. And If we should weaken ourselves by a Reduction and consequently be left at the mercy of a more powerfull neighbour, what have we to expect but to be insulted and distressed. It may be thought, and I have often heard it said, that our Fleet will protect us: but our Fleet is not always sure of meeting an Ennemy; and if that expectation should fail what reserve have we then left but our Land Forces? and the present Number is so far from being too many, that I believe every Gentleman who now hears me must think them too few for such an Occasion. As to Affairs at home: I think the present Number of Forces far from too many, to withstand that unruly Temper which appears in the Multitude; and is ready to break forth on every occasion in Opposition to Authority. There is scarce a Law made but the People are told it is unreasonable, and immediatly prepare to resist it. So that it is now become a Question whether this Nation is for the future to be governed by a Mob, or by the Legislature. It is almost become a Question, whether his Majesty is any longer to enjoy his Prerogative of executing the Law. Nay, I am inclined to think, there could be no execution of Law in this Kingdom, if there were not an Armed Force in readiness to assist the Civil Majestrate. Is there a Ship stranded on the Coast? A Mob rises and plunders it. Is a Farmer going to transport his Corn? A Mob rises and stops him on the Road. Mobs not to be quelled but by an Armed Force. I am sure the Laws against Running of Goods, however necessary cannot be executed without it. I believe it requires an Armed Force to execute the late salutary Law against retailing Spirituous Liquors, and that the Majestrates have not strength to do it of themselves. If they have, I must then ask the Majestrates of this Great City, why they suffer such disorders daily in the Streets, why they do not apprehend the Roiters and bring them to Justice? 'tis a great Neglect of Duty; I must wonder at such Neglect, when they have before their Eyes so late an Instance of the Resentment of the Legislature against the Majestrates of Edinburgh,[127] for a Neglect of the like Nature. But I believe the Majestrates have not streng<t>h of themselves to execute that Law and indeed a Spirit of Opposition, of Disobedence and Disloyalty hath passed through this Land, and seized on the minds of the Vulgar; and it requires a very strong hand to curb and restrain it: therefore to weaken and disarm the Government, in my Opinion, is to distroy it. But let me now ask the same Question with the Gentleman who spoke last but one: from whence do these discontents proceed? Not from any Misconduct in the Majestrates: I know of none; I hear of none. Not from any Irregularities of the Soldiers, I don't hear but they behave themselves peacably in their Quarters. Nor do I think, as that Gentleman and some others do, that the Number of Forces is the very Cause of the

---

[126] A rather different version of WH's speech appears in Cobbett, X, 376–9.
[127] The Porteous Riots.

discontents. Reduce, say they, the Forces and the discontents will subside; reduce the Forces and his Majesty will regain the Affections of the People. If a strict adherence to Law and Justice have not secured him those Affections, I fear this expedient would prove ineffectual. The experiment is too dangerous, and I am moraly assured would not answer the end: for the Army is not the Cause of the discontents, but the discontents are one great Cause that make the Army Necessary. The Discontents in my Opinion flow from Another Cause; they are caused by that infinite Number of infamous and seditious Libels, that are weekly and daily published throughout the Kingdom: In which every act of State is censured and condemned: the Charracters of his Majesty and those in Authority under him are traduced: (even the Dead are not spared) their Persons vilified: their Actions misrepresented. This it is that poisons the Minds of the People. This it is that undermines all legal Authority. What Pity is it, that we cannot enjoy the liberty of the Press without this licentiousness! would to God that nothing but truth would flow from thence, and then we should be free from these disorders! But the Blessing and the Curse are inseparably annexed; and we must be content to take the one with the other. Since then we are under some sort of Necessity of indulging the People in their darling and with them inestimable Priviledge of abusing their Superiors, it is but common Justice to arm their Superiors with power to guard themselves against the Ill Effects of such Abuse. Will any Man say that the Law guards them? Far from it. Thousands of Invectives may be published in an hour, and from a thousand different Quarters. These are arrows that fly in the Dark, and it is difficult to discover the Hand that sends them. But supose the Author by chance detected, what is the Redress? You must pursue your Remedy for a Year or two, for an Injury committed in one Moment, and which may be repeated in the Next. And the Author convicted? Is he Pillored? Is that a Satisfaction to any particular Person for loss of Charracter? Is it a satisfaction to the Publick for the Disorder? Is the licence at all Repress'd? No: it breaks out with more fury. A convicted Author is commonly tryumphant: his Case is thought hard: he is pitied: he is Applauded; Nay we are come to that degree of degeneracy, that we generaly give more Credit to an Infamous Libeller than to the legal proceedings of a Court of Justice. Pardon this digression. Another Argument that weighs with me against the Amendment proposed, is the experience of past times: for when the Army has been reduced very low, it has proved very unfortunate to the Kingdom. When after King Williams War, the Forces were reduced very low, what followed? Another War more bloody and expensive: one Cause prehaps of which might be, the little Confidence which foreign Nations saw we reposed in our Princes. When after the Peace of Utrict the Forces were again reduced very low, what followed? A Rebellion, which endangered the Protestant Succession, and which might have been nipped in the Bud, had there been Forces Sufficient then in the Kingdom. I would not willingly tread in the same Steps for fear they should lead to the same Conclusions. I have heard but two Objections and I think there can be no more, that seem to carry any weight against the present number of Forces: that they are expensive: and that they may endanger the Constitution. That they are expensive I own. I wish the Expense less. I feel it sensibly. And prehaps contribute as much to it in proportion to my Circumstances, as any man in the Kingdom. But when we talk of Expense, the Question is, Is it necessary? If it is, I submit to it without repining: for I think too much frugality in a necessary expence may prove extreme Prodigality. And I had much rather undergo an expense, which I know I can bear, than bring upon myself and the Nation those Evils which were insuportable to our Forefathers, and which we should not be able to bear. As to the danger to the Constitution from the present Number of Soldiers I am under no Apprehensions of it. I consider them as an Army composed of our own People; and voted Annualy by Parliament, directed by his Majesty; commanded by Officers who are Men of Honour; Many of them of great Fortune, Birth, and Alliance; who have as much to lose as any Men in the Kingdom; and who must be blind to their own Interest and that of their Posterity, before they can entertain a thought of invading the Rights of their Country. Have armies in foreign Countries sometimes overturned their Constitutions? Give me leave to say that our Army has for some years preserved ours: So far from the Subverters, that I sincerely think they have for some years been the Guardians of our Liberty. I will put one Case, and then I have done. I will suppose that this Committee should now come to a Resolution to vote no Forces for the ensuing year, and the whole Army was to morrow disbanded. What think you Sir would be the Consequence? In my Opinion this would be the Consequence. Before the end of the year, his Majesty and the Royal Family would be libelled and mobbed out of the Kingdom and we should never meet again in this Place. What Government we might have in exchange I know not. None perhaps for some time. None I am sure that we should like. Most probably at last a Popish Prince and no Parliament. These are my real sentiments; and as they are such, I should not discharge the part of an honest man, and a good Subject, if I did not give my Negative to the Amendment.

The Prince who had ten Servants in the House of Commons, to shew his Indifference, and Impartiality, took four of them that day with him to Kew: the other six he suffered to follow their own Inclinations: and two of them viz: Littleton and Pitt voted for and the other four against the Amendment.

February 15.

A Doubt which was mention'd last year by Mr. More was proposed by him Again; which was, Whether Persons Offending any of the Mutiny Acts could be justly proceeded against after the End of the Year. It was the Opinion of Law<y>ers that they strictly could not, and that such Proceedings, though they were very common, were illegal; because those Acts being Annual, the Powers given by them expired with them. Therefore on the Report of the Mutiny Bill, a new Clause was now added to indemnify all Persons for what was past and to justify such proceedings for the future.

February 17.

In the Committee of Ways and Means Sir R. Walpole said, that since the last Act to prevent smugling, the Duty on Tea only had encreased £80000 per Annum, that 4890 more Houses had been entered for retailing it, and that in the last year 79000[128] pound wheight of it had been seised.

The Debt of the Navy at Xmas 1737 was £507,554.

The Estimate of the Ordinary of the Navy for 1738.

Lords of the Admiralty, Secretaries Clerks etc.	<£>28,062
Superannuated Officers	<£>5913
Pensions and other Allowances	<£>3378
Yards	<£>17733
Muster Masters and Other Officers of Out Ports	<£>3378
Wages to Vessels and Ships in Ordinary	<£>33653
Victuals to Men in them	<£>14694

---

[128] Harley has 69,000. See above, p. 32.

Harbour Moarings	<£>21481
Ordinary Repairs of Ships in Harbour, Docks, Wharfs, Buildings etc.	<£>63457
Sick and hurt Seamen	<£>1136
Half Pay Sea Officers	<£>30000
Total	<£>222885

Number of Ships belonging to the Navy.

Rates	1st.	7	Fire ships	3	
	2.	13	Yatchs	6	
	3.	40	Sloops	18	in all – 225.
	4.	64	Store Ships	1	
	5.	22	Hulks and small Vessels	24	
	6.	27			

This paper without date.[129]

The most important affair of the Session was the consideration of the merchants Petition complaining of the depredations of the Spaniards in America. This came on to be heard on Thursday the 16th. of February and then Mr. Murray their Council opened their Case in a very elegant Speech:[130] in which he advanced and established three Propositions.

1. That by the Law of Nations we had a Right to sail in those Seas, and to the Hospitality of their Shores. – Which is undeniable.

2. That it is not taken away by Treaty.

By the Treaty in 1667[131] Commerce was to be free through all the Dominions of the two Crowns, where it had formerly been carried on, either by Right, Connivance, or Indulgence.

By the Treaty in 1670.[132] Article 8: they are not to Trade in the Places Possessed by each other in America: and ships may be seized if they enter one anothers Ports – except in Cases of Storm, Pirates, or Enemies, by Article 10th. – and of Shipwreck by Article 11th. – But they are in no Case prohibited to sail within any distance from them: and indeed they are obliged to pass near each others Coasts in all their Voyages.

By Article 2d. the English are to keep possession of what they had in Charles the 2ds. time – And they had then Hutts<?> in Campechy[133] to cut Logwood. – And that Treaty was confirmed by the Treaty of Utrect. – And it was the opinion of the Board of Trade in 1717 and 1732 that we might cut Logwood there.

By the Treaty in 1715[134] we have a Right to gather Salt on the Isle of Tortugas.[135]

---

129 This section of the journal, which relates to the session of 1738, appears at the end of vol. 4 of the manuscript.

130 The proceedings reported here by WH took place not on 16 Feb., but on either Tuesday 28 Mar. or Thursday 30 Mar. On 28 Mar. a committee of the whole house considered the petition of the merchants trading to America, during which they 'heard evidence and counsel'. On 30 Mar., when the report of the committee was debated, Murray made a speech at the bar. (Cobbett, X, 643; C.J., XXIII, 130, 133–4.) Cobbett, X, 643–728, contains an account of the ensuing debate, but not of Murray's speech. See also Harley journal, above p. 34.

131 Signed at Madrid on 23 May 1667. For the text see *The Consolidated Treaty Series*, ed. C. Parry (231 vols., Dobbs Ferry, N.Y., 1969–86), X, 115–31.

132 Signed at Westminster on 8 July 1670. For the text see *ibid.*, XI, 395–401.

133 The city of Campeche in the south west of the Yucatan peninsula, Mexico.

134 Signed at Madrid on 14 Dec. 1715. For the text see *The Consolidated Treaty Series*, XXIX, 371–4.

135 Tortuga island north west of Haiti.

3. None of our Ships are to be stopped or searched on those Seas, on any pretence whatsoever. – The Spaniards have no such Right by any Treaty, and consequently cannot have it at all.

By the Treaty of 1667 they may examine if Contraband Goods are on Board, but that must be by sending for Papers only.

Contraband Goods are of two sorts; the One by the Law of Nations, as Arms and carrying to the Enemy, which for the sake of self defence may be seized; but then, those only (and no other Goods) are to be seized, and only in time of War.

The second sort are such as are prohibited by Treaty, but no such can be by the Spaniard supposed to be in our Ships, because all commerce is prohibited. – There are three species which the Spaniards pretend are Contraband, Logwood, Cocoa, and Peices of eight: but without just pretence; for Logwood grows in the Isle of Providence, and for several years past has been planted in Jamaica so as to make their Hedges of it: Cocoa in many of our Plantations, formerly in great quantities in Jamaca, and since the decline of their Sugar trade, has been recultivated with Care: And as to Peices of Eight there is less pretence since the Spaniards pay them in Jamaica to the S<outh> S<ea> Company for Negroes.

Since the Treaty of Utrecht the Spaniards have taken 160 of our Ships: 52 of them since 1728 or the Treaty of Seville. – From March 1734 to March 1736 he observed there was not one Capture; which he imputed to the Apprehensions of the Spaniards, that the English on such continued provocations might interupt their Conquest of Naples and Sicily: and from whence he justly inferred that the Spaniards had their Governours in the West Indies so much under Command as at any time to be able to prevent such Depredations.

Session the Sixth

I come now to the sixth Session of this Parliament: which met the 15th. of November 1739. This was earlier than Parliaments had met for many years: and was Occasioned by the Declaration of a War against Spain. Before I take notice of the proceedings in this Session; it will be necessary to take Notice of one thing which was the principal Consideration of the last. I mean the Convention concluded with Spain on the 14th. of January last year:[136] by which Spain stipulated to pay a certain Sum within four Months, as a reparation for pas<t> Injuries and Depredations: And all other Differences were reffered to a Treaty to be concluded within eight Months. The Opposers of the Ministry endeavoured to inflame the Nation on this Convention; representing it both in and out of the House, as an infamous betraying the rights of the Kingdom. They said the sum to be paid was not a reparation adequate to the Losses and Injuries received: and that no Convention should have been entered into, unless Spain had first expressly renounced her Pretentions of Searching our Ships in the American Seas; which was against the Law of Nations; and had been so declared the preceeding Session by both Houses. And if Spain had refused to comply; they should have declared War: and Foreseeing the great Expence it must inevitably bring on the Publick; the Loss and Interuption it must be to the Trade; and the difficulties it must lay them under; since any ill success would be imputed to their Conduct. Both Houses judged in the same manner; and therefore Voted thanks to the King for the Convention; As what might be the ground-Work of a safe and honourable Treaty. On passing this Vote in the House of Commons the Opposers exerted their utmost effort. And since they could not carry it there; endeavoured to divide the Nation uppon it. His Royal Highness countenanced the Opposition by his Presence in both Houses: And intended in the House of Peers (if he could have prevailed on himself to have spoken in Publick) to have declared himself against it. Sir William Wyndham (in the most solemn Speech I ever heard in Parliament) took a formal leave of the House, declaring he thought it dishonourable where the sentiments of the Majority were against the Sentiments of every other man in the Nation, who must conclude that Majority to be a Faction under an undue Influence. Accordingly he and the other Leaders, and about fourscore of the most violent Opposers appeared no more that Session in the House.[137] But he was doubly disapointed: First, in not being sent to the Tower for his Speech: and then in its not having the effect he expected: for above a hundered Gentlemen who had Voted against the Convention, still attended their Duty in Parliament: and were Men of as good figure and fortune as those who Absented. So that the Seceeders (as they have been since called) instead of becoming formidable, grew into Contempt. They durst not too strongly justify their own Conduct, for fear of Arraigning that of their Friends who remained in the House; whilst the sober part of Mankind condemned theirs as a rash and illegal step; which tended only to civil commotion. So that they were forced all to return this Session with shame into the House: and when in Debates they were sometimes reproached with that Conduct, scarce durst open their Mouths in their own Vindication.

The Ministry kept the Fleet all the last year in the Mediterranean, to be in readiness if Spain complied not with the Convention. Spain made this a pretence for breaking it; Alledging a Promise that the Fleet should be recalled: but probably she foresaw that as the Nation was universally inclined to the War, the Ministry would be forced into it:

---

[136] The convention of El Pardo. See Harley journal, above, pp. 36–7.
[137] For the 'Seceders' see *ibid.*, above, p. 37.

And therefore were unwilling to pay the Money to those who would so soon be their enemies. On failure of payment, Admiral Vernon[138] was sent with a Squadron to intercept the Assogues ships, and letters of Reprisal were soon after granted to all that desired them: Vernon had probably succeeded in the design, had he not been twice driven back by contrary Winds: At the end of the eight Months War was declared: and Vernons ill success was in some measure made up, by the Caraccas Ships falling into the hands of Haddocks Squadron:[139] which gave new Spirits to the Ministry at the Meeting of the Parliament.

When the Parliament met the Leaders of the Opposition seemed much divided. Wyndham, who had joyned himself of late to the Prince's Party, and was the Conductor of his Servants, had rendered himself Obnoxious to the Avowed Enemies of the Government, of which Shippen was the Head, but who were yet willing to joyn in any Opposition, in hopes of a total subversion. He was likewise looked upon with a jealous Eye by Pulteney: who liked not such a Rival in Popularity; nor to see him set himself at the head of a Party which he thought should be conducted by himself. In order therefore to show his own Consequence and that no Opposition could be carried on successfully without him, he made a Speech the first Day of the Session much to his own honour, and the Publick Utility. For when thanks were moved for the Speech from the throne, he joyned in heartily with the Motion: expressing his Zeal for the Royal Family: declaring the War to be a just measure: and by whomsoever conducted he would joyn in supporting it: to convince all the World, that however we differed in other Matters, yet when the whole was at stake we were unanimous. This Speech had a great effect. Not a word more was said. And I never observed greater unanimity in the House. After this things went on with so much ease that the Land and Malt Tax were both passed before Xmas.

Sir W. Wyndham made a Motion which was immediately and unanimously complied with: It occasion'd a conference with the Lords, and a joint Address to the King;[140] that he would not enter into any Treaty with Spain; unless our free Navigation to the American Seas was a preliminary.[141] Sir W<illiam> lost the Credit he expected from this Motion. It was said it was unnecessary; because every body Agreed in it before: It was expressed in the Addresses of both Houses last year,[142] and implied in the Convention.

There was scarce any Opposition 'till the Recess: except that Lord Polwarth and Sandys objected to the method of forming the Corps of the Marines to be raised: which was a thing little regarded.

A Call was moved for by the Opposers, and denied, (though it is unusual to deny such a Motion) it being said it was unreasonable in those Gentlemen to desire to force others to attend, who last Session so long neglected it themselves.[143]

When the Parliament met after the Recess, the Opposers determined to make many plausible Proposals; to regain their own credit, and to render the Majority Odious to the People.

---

[138] See Appendix.
[139] Nicholas Haddock (1686–1746), admiral c. in c. in the Mediterranean 1738–42, had blockaded the Spanish coast and taken valuable prizes.
[140] The joint conferences were held on 21 and 22 Nov., the address was presented to the king on the 23rd, and his answer was delivered on the 29th. *L.J.*, XXV, 431–5.
[141] See Harley journal, above p. 40.
[142] On 2 Feb. 1739. *C.J.*, XXIII, 209–10.
[143] See Harley journal (18 Dec. 1739), above p. 40.

The Thing they began with, and which had raised the greatest expectation, was a Bill to restrain the Number of Officers in the House,[144] which they said amounted to Above two hundered; who held their Places at the Will and Pleasure of one Member; and was an Influence not to be suffered in an Assembly, which should be free; and might carry any thing in favour of the Minister.

A Bill of this Nature had often been proposed and rejected; and twice before in this Parliament. Sandys now moved it; and (that the Tories and Patriots might appear united on the Question) was seconded by Watkyn Williams.[145] Sandys in opening the Bill said the intention was to exclude all Officers; except Lords of the Treasury, and Admiralty; Admirals; Generals and Colonels of Regiments; the Paymaster, and Secretary at War; the Attorney and Solicitor General; and Treasurer of the Navy.

As Sir W. Wyndham had always opposed Place Bills in the Tory Administration; he was forced to make a distinction to justify his Conduct now; he said he was against them in the ridiculous and unlimited way they were formerly brought in, of Excluding all Officers in general; but should always be for a Bill qualified in the manner this was intended.

I was the first who spoke against it, and as what I said gained me some Applause Amongst my Friends; and drew on me some displeasure from the Opposers; I shall set it down as near as Possible in the terms I made use of.

Mr. Speaker.

It seems strange to me, that a Bill should now be moved for, which has been so often and so justly rejected; and more than once in this very Parliament. I think the first time that ever I troubled you in this Place was in Opposition to a Bill of this Nature: for I have ever been of opinion that it is unnecessary; and if it should pass into a Law would be injurious to the Constitution.

It is unnecessary; because the Laws have already made sufficient Provision in the Case. The Gentleman who proposed the Bill does not contend for a total Exclusion: there must be some Limitation of who are and who are not to sit here: that limitation is already made by the Wisdom of our Predecessors, and in a Manner I believe we cannot improve. They went as far as they saw convenient to restrain the Influence of the Crown; they thought to go farther might too much restrain the Freedom of the People in the choice of their Representatives. They left us one Provision which will be sufficient at all times; which answers all future Exigences; and makes all Bills of this kind absolutely unnecessary: which is: that if any Member of this House accepts an Employment, he is subject to a re-election. He is sent back to his Constituents to see if they have any objection to him. If they conceive no ill opinion of him we ought not. We should not dictate to them whom they are, or are not to chuse; but leave them to the free choice of their own Representatives.

But Admitting for Arguments sake, what I can never admit in reality; that such a Bill could at any time be necessary; I ask what Necessity there is for it at the present Juncture? What has this, or what have late Parliaments done, to call for this extraordinary Caution? You shall know a Tree by its Fruits; and what Fruit have they produced? have they invaded the Rights of the People? No; Sir they have loyally and steadily supported this Family on the Throne; and this Family have supported Law and Justice. The Nation has flourished under their Care, and sure that is no Injury done to the Nation.

---

[144] See *ibid.* (29 Jan. 1740), p. 41, and *C.J.*, XXIII, 438.
[145] The debate was on 29 Jan., and the motion to bring in a Place Bill was rejected by 206 to 222, Harley being one of the tellers for the minority.

But what say our modern Libellers? should we believe them, there is no honesty within these Walls. Nor do they confine the Compliment to us only; they extend it to every Branch of the Legislature. Should we believe them, we must look on the Prince on the Throne as a Merciless and cruel Tyrant, ever seeking the distress and distruction of his Subjects: we must look on both Houses of Parliament, as a me<r>cenary Set of Banditti, ever ready to joyn in any enterprise of that Nature. Should we believe them, we must believe every Member of this House, to be either a very indigent Person or else to want common Sense or common honesty. But before we can believe them, we must disbelieve our Eyes. Look Sir to your Right and to your Left you will see Gentlemen of as good Figure, Fortune, Capacity, and Worth, as any in the Kingdom.

But these Libellers say we are all under an unjust Influence. Some, they say, always support the present measures because they are paid: others, they say, always oppose them because they are Angry. Those they say are actuated only by a prospect of Interest or Preferment; These only by a Spirit of Pride, Envy, Ambition, or Revenge. Base and false Insinuations; and the last I think the Worst; for if a Man does wrong, he is more excusable, when he does it on Temptation, than when he is prompted to it meerly by his own corrupt affections. But, Sir, however the Honour of this House may be Attacked without doors, let us preserve it inviolably within. If others think unjustly of us, let us think honourably, at least charitably of one Another. Don't let us countenance these Reports by a Bill of this Nature. It is almost joyning in the Calumny; It is almost confessing we are the Persons we are represented; No longer fit to be trusted, no longer fit to sit in this Place. What is this but to submit the Legislature to these Libellers, and to receive directions from them. This is Slavery indeed! I abhor Slavery in all shapes, but sure the worst is being Slaves to such Miscreants and to an ignorant Mob whom they endeavour to seduce.

Besides how is it possible to satisfy these People? Will a Bill of this nature do it? No. If some Gentlemen are to be excluded because they constantly adhere to the present measures, they will expect, that Others should likewise be excluded, who for years together have constantly opposed them. It is equaly as reasonable. Nor will this Bill be equitable or impartial without a Clause of that Nature. The Gentlemen who moved for the Bill mention'd no such Clause: but if the Bill comes in without it, it must be added in the Committee. But in my opinion, a short Bill would do better; setting forth in the Preamble, that we are altogether Corrupt, and become Abominable, that there is none that doth good no not one, and then enacting, that no Person, who now sits here should ever sit here again.

As a Bill of this sort is unneccesary so I think I can shew it is unreasonable. It is Injurious, not only to every Freholder but to every Voter in the Kingdom; by Abridging them in their Choice; and prehaps often preventing them from sending those Persons hither, whom they best like; and could most confide in. I know not, what other Gentlemen may think, but for my own part, I do not intend to be so ungratefull to my Constituents, as to tell them that because they have sent me here now they shall never have it in their power to do so Again.

It is Injurious to every Gentleman in the Kingdom, who is qualified to sit in this House; by depriving him of that Capacity to which he was born: a Capacity of Advising in making the Laws of his Country; and a Capacity of sharing at the same time in the Execution of them. Exclusion from the Senate has ever been esteemed a Punishment and one would imagine Gentlemen were guilty of some great Crime to deserve it. Is there a Man here who leads an immoral Life, or that makes this place an Asylum from his just Creditors, I wish there was a Censor rigid and severe as Cato himself to remove him from hence. Is there a Man here of whom it may be said

Vendidit hic Auro Patriam, Dominumque potentem Imposuit, fixit leges pretio
Atque refixit.[146]

I think he deserves to be stigmatized in this World, and in the next deserves the place
that the Poet asigns him. But in no other State was it ever dreamt of, that a Man should
be excluded from the Senate, for no other crime, but because he is a Servant to his
Prince. Is the Interest different? Is the service incompatible? Unhappy is the Nation
where such Maxims are advanced: they tend to discontent, they must end in Sedition.

It is Injurious to the Crown: as it would deprive the King either of the Heads or the
Hands of many (and prehaps very able) Subjects: if Advice in making the Laws was
to hinder the same Persons from Acting in the execution. It would also confine the
Crown in bestowing of Rewards, and I would ask Gentlemen where the favours of the
Crown can more naturally decend, than on Those who are first recommended by the
choice of the People.

It is Injurious to all the Commons of this Kingdom by throwing more power into
the hands of the Lords; and by that means breaking the Ballance of the Constitution;
for if the favours of the Crown are excluded this House, they will flow in larger
Streams to the Other.

But why is this Bill so partial? Why is it not extended to the other House? Is that
House more to be trusted? Does Title improve a Mans sense or Honesty? or does
Want of Title imply want of both? No. Gentlemen were sensible such a Bill could
never pass the other House. If then the Lords are too wise to give up their native
Rights; let not us be so weak as to part with Ours.

I ask now what Improvement we might expect from this Bill? Will Parliaments be
Wiser? Far from it: for they will be deprived of many of their ablest Members. Will
they be Honester? Far from it: for supposing that evil disposition which <the> Bill
supposes, in Prince and Parliament, of corrupting and being corrupted, I fear the
corruption would be doubled; for if Members are not to have Places; will they have no
Friends or Relations to receive Favours, or be Trustees for them; I fear the Payment
instead of being to them only, would be to them and their Agents. Will Parliaments be
less Dependent? Far from it: the Dependance on the Crown will continue the same,
and a new Dependance will be created on the Lords and others in Power. Besides
what is this Dependance so much talked of? Is not every Member fortified Against it
by the Estate, which he must have to sit here? Or will a Man for the sake of an Employment, which is precarious, and may be taken from him the next moment, sacrifice
Rights which are permanent to him and his Posterity? Will Parliaments be more
respected? Far from it: from Want of Power they will grow into Contempt: and many
who have now a regard for Parliaments on Account of their Seats there, may, if excluded from thence on Account of their Posts, use the Power of those Posts to form a
distinct Interest; which in the end may be distructive to the Parliament itself: As the
Power of the Army was in the last Century.

Upon my Word, Sir, this is not the way to reform Parliaments. I will tell you, what
is the right Way: It is to make Men Moral and Honest. I will tell you the Way to do
that: It is by a better Education. I will tell you what I think a better Education; It is not
to let young Noblemen and Gentlemen be so soon their own Masters; and to travel
void of Experience into foreign Countries, to be captivated with the Vanities of them,
and to transplant them into their Own. What an immence Sum does this Nation

---

[146] Vendidit hic Auro Patriam, Dominumque potentem
Imposuit, fixit leges pretio atque refixit.

Vergil, *Aeneid*, VI, 621–2.

Annualy pay to France for the Manufacturing of Fops! A love of these Vanities creates imaginary Wants (for natural ones are few and easily contented) these imaginary Wants create real Necessity: and real Necessity (if any thing) must create real Dependance. Let the Gentlemen propose a Bill to restrain Luxury or improve Education, and I will readily concur in it as the best way to reform Parliaments. As to this Bill if men are good it is unnecessary; if they are otherwise, it can have no effect.

Another Argument Against this Bill is, that it is unseasonable. Unseasonable under his present Majesty; who is far from attempting on the Liberties either of Parliament or People: And whose Virtues and those of his Royal Progeny afford us a long prospect of security. Unseasonable as it may raise Jealousies in the People; at a Juncture when we should all be united against the common Enemy. Unseasonable, as a time of General Election is not far off; when we must render an Account of our Actions to our Constituents; who will then Judge, if we are fit to come here again: Nor should we do any thing to prejudice them in their Opinion. I dare say the Gentlemen who moved this Bill intended no such thing: If they had they would have reserved this Motion to the next Session of Parliament. I am sure they did not make this motion, purely to have it rejected; that is a bad Reason. I am sure they did not make it purely to raise a Clamour against the next General Election; that is a bad Reason. For my own part I can conceive no good Reason for this Bill. It is unreasonable: It can have no good effect; it may have many bad consequences: It tends to Aggrandize the Lords and to depress the Commons: It is prejudicial to the Crown, to the Gentry, to the Freholders and Voters of the Kingdom: It is rendered unnecessary by the Laws in being: and it carries with it an Insinuation, reflecting on the honour of his Majesty, and of the present Parliament. I therefore hope that the Gentlemen, who have moved this Bill will retract their Motion; that it may not appear on the Votes.

On a Division 108 were for the Motion and 224 Against it.[147]

So small a Majority Animated the Minority; who in order to keep their Friends together moved for a Call of the House on the 21st. of February, and that they might appear to have some View, and that they would make some notable Mismanagement appear, they call'd on the three Offices concerned in the management of the Naval Affairs (the Admiralty, Navy, and Victualling) for such accounts, as would carry the most appearance of an Insinuation of a misaplication of Publick Money. As what new employments had been created in each since his Majesties accession: What additional Salaries had been granted: and how the Money Issued under the Article of contingences to each had been applied.

These Papers took up some time in preparing: and one of the most Material Occurrences in the interim was a Question concerning Priviledge: which regarded Lisle Member for Hampshire, who it was said had been guilty of many scandalous and fraudulent practices against his Creditors; and was fled out of the Kingdom to avoid the vengance of the Law. Lord Baltimore therefore moved for a Committee, which was appointed to enquire how far Privilledge extended to Members absent in foreign Parts. The Committee could find no Precedent in Point:[148] but however they came to a Resolution, that Privilledge should not be allowed to Members in Foreign Parts to stop any suits against them. On the Report, several considerable Members (who pretended to be Masters of Order) were against reading the Resolution at the Table, because it would then be published in the Votes: and it was not Agreeable to the

---

[147] The voting figures should be 206 to 222. See Harley journal, above p. 41.
[148] See *ibid.*, above pp. 41–2. The committee was appointed 31 Jan. 1740 and reported 13 Feb. *C.J.*, XXIII, 440.

Wisdom of Parliament to suffer their Privilledges to be canvassed. A general declaration was unnecessary; since the House would do Justice on particular Complaints. If a Complaint well grounded was made against a Member Abroad, they would fix a Day for his Appearance in the House; and if he did not then appear would suspend his Priviledge. It was acknowledged that when a Member was present, there never was an Instance of compelling him to wave his Priviledge; though a Man of honour would be ashamed to insist on it. As I abhor all pretence to Privilledge of this kind I spoke with Zeal for reading the Resolution, in the following Terms

Mr. Speaker.

This House has always been tender of making a declaration of its own Privilleges, as I apprehend for two Reasons. One is least by declaring that not to be Priviledge which realy is so, they might injure themselves; the other is, lest by declaring that to be Privilledge, which is not so they might injure their fellow Subjects. This last has been found very fatal by experience: for in the last Age, when this House declared what they pleased to be Privilledge, Privilledge (as an noble Historian observes)[149] became an unfathomable Abyss, which swallowed up the Laws and Constitution. Unhappy is the situation when Law and Privilledge clash! But where is the danger of Agreeing to the Resolution now before us? To obstruct Justice is not a Privilledge of this House, and therefore to declare we will not do so, can be no Injury to our own Privilledges. What can be more for the honour of the House, than to make such a declaration to the World, that all the World may see we renounce such ill-grounded Pretentions. Privilledge as far as it regards the Person of a Member ought to be sacred. He should be free from Insult, from Arrest, from imprisonment, that he may at all times appear in this House and Act as a free Agent in it. But I think extending the Priviledge to his Possessions is carrying it too far. I own (I speak it with defference to the House, I speak it without intending to reflect on any particular Members of it:) I own it gives me some regret to hear Gentlemen complaining here of small trespasses committed on their Estates in the Country. Do they not injoy the Protection of the Law in that Case in common with the rest of the Kings Subjects? If they do why do they call to their Aid the Priviledge of this House. But Admitting they may do it to guard themselves from Injury; yet sure they ought not to do it to do an Injury to others, in Opposition to the Law of the Land, in opposition to that fundamental Law of all Justice; of making Restitution and rendering to every Man his Due. I wish the Resolution had been General, instead of being confined to the Case of Members Absent in Foreign Parts. But sure their Case ought not to be better for their Absense. Absense with leave from the House is but a Toleration; without leave it is a Breach of the Orders of the House. And shall a Man plead a breach of the orders of the House as an Excuse for a violation of the Law?

Let us take care, lest the World say we make Laws for others and not for ourselves; that we are Law-breakers, as well as Law-makers; that after we have put down the Mint and other Priviledged Places, we have Erected a Mint in this Place. I hope we shall read and Agree to this Resolution for this very Reason which makes many Gentlemen Against it, that it may appear in the Votes and be known to the World.

On a Division 73 were for reading the Resolution and 77 against it.

---

[149] Edward, earl of Clarendon, *The History of the Rebellion and Civil Wars in England*, ed. W. Dunn Macray (6 vols., Oxford, 1888), I, 531–4.

At the beginning of the Session, Mr. Poulteney, for the Credit of proposing a Popular thing, moved for a Bill for the encouragement of Seamen, the same as passed in the 6th. of the late Queen,[150] by dividing the Prizes amongst them which they should take from the Enemy. Nobody objected to this; but only the Ministers objected to the manner of it, as it prevented the Crown from doing an Act of Favour: for as the Prizes belonged by Law to the Crown, the King intended to have proposed it as an Act of Favour to the Parliament.

This Bill gave rise to another for the Registering of Seamen: for the present Juncture made it evident, that on the breaking out of a War, there were not Seamen enough to be got to Man the Fleet in due time, and to carry on the Trade: and therefore some method was to be found out, always to know where to find them on such an Exegency. Therefore that the Oposers might not have the Credit of it, Sir Charles Wager moved for such a Bill; and he and Sir John Norris were ordered to bring it in.[151]

February 5th.

The Bill was presented, and read a first time and ordered to be Printed.[152] The Purport of it was, that the Admiralty should divide his Majesties Dominions into Districts, fix a Place in each where the Register should be kept, and Appoint an Officer to keep it: that every Person getting his livelyhood on the Water, should be obliged to Regester himself in his District, and by subject to Penalties if he did not: Persons regestered were obliged to serve: and many encouragements were given to them for their service.

Sir John Barnard and Mr. Poulteney objected to the Bill as being compulsory; and said it would discourage people from getting their livelyhood on the Water.

Sir John Norris said France practised it with success and could immediately Man a Fleet when they pleased.

Sir W. Wyndham said that was no Precedent for a free Nation; That this Bill put people on a Worse foot than a Press. And that he was for tempting them to Register Voluntarily.

Sir R. Walpole said that a voluntary Register was much best, if it would do: but that any Way was to be taken on an Exegency to Man the Fleet for the Guard of the Nation.

Sir J. Barnard complained, that the Ships that were manned, were too full Manned, which made it impracticable to man the rest. And that the Admiralty did not grant Protections enough to the Marchants.

Sir R. Walpole said, that after the Embargo there were 25000 men on board the Fleet: and that then Protections had been granted to 24000, which number was evidently employed in the Trade, besides those who were out upon foreign Voyages. That above 50000 were employed in the last years of the War, and Protections were not granted in the present proportion. That Marchants were not so favourably dealt with in Holland, for there they suffered no Ships to go to sea, till their Fleet was manned.

February 19.

The Bill was read a second time: and then the Opposers came prepared to declaim against it, as a Project as destructive to Liberty as the excise scheme, and calculated to give the Admiralty more Power to influence Elections. But they could not raise the Flame they expected: and many lost the Opportunity to speak against it as they intended: For Sir Charles Wager (whom nobody suspected of Ill-Intention) declared he was ready to give up the Bill, if Gentlemen did not like it. And Sir Robert Walpole

---

[150] 6 Anne, c. 65: Act for the Better Securing of Trade (1706).

[151] The bill was rejected on 19 Feb. 1740 at the committee stage. *C.J.*, XXIII, 468; p. 162 below.

[152] See Lambert, VII, 415–30.

said he was not consulted in it before it was brought in, nor was he concerned in the success of it. So nobody speaking in defence of it, the Question for committment passed in the Negative.[153]

But this matter did not end here; for Sir R. Walpole said, since the Bill was rejected, he hoped Gentlemen would propose something in lieu of it; in an affair so necessary as Manning the Fleet. On this Sir W. Younge moved for the House to go into a Comittee to consider of Heads for a Bill to encourage Seamen to enter Voluntarily. On the Proposition being seemingly Acquiesced in, many Members went away, thinking the business of the House over, when the Opposers taking Advantage of the House opposed the Question; and were for having a Private Comittee to examine into the Orders given by the Admiralty, and the Grievances of the Seamen: for now they maintained there were men enough, but that many who were fit to serve, were refused by the regulating Captains, on pretence of their not being able Seamen; others did not care to enter because of the Ill-usage they received from many Captains. On a Division 71 were for Sir W. Younges proposition, and 63 were for the other; which was justly rejected; for it tended only, to cast a reflection on the Admiralty, to weaken the Authority of the Comanders at Sea and to raise a Spirit of Mutiny in the comon Sailors, at a time, when Dicipline was most necessary.

February 20.

The Papers being delivered into the House from the several Naval Offices, on reading one from the Victualling Office concerning new erected Employments and Allowances, Lord Polwarth observed, there was a salary of £200 per Annum to T. Corbett, as Secretary of the Court of Assistants for the Relief of poor Widows of Sea Officers. There were at this time about 700 of those Widows, which made the Post a very troublesome one; and the Salary was esteem'd but a small gratification to Corbett, who was deservedly esteemed for his Industry and Capacity as under Secretary to the Admiralty. And this £200 per Annum was granted him by the Kings sign Manual out of the old Stores and Provisions of the Victualing Office, that it might not be taken out of (and consequently diminish) the Fund for the Relief of the Widows.

Lord Polwarth moved for a Writ to Elect a Member in his room, suposing his Seat to be Vacated. For he said this Allowance must be looked on, either as Anexed to his Post of Secretary; which was a new erected Place under the Crown, and made him incapable of sitting: or else as a Pension during Pleasure, which likewise vacated his Seat and Subjected him to a Penalty of £20 a day.

Corbett said he had had the Opinion of the best Lawyers to the contrary; and the House on a Division were of the same Opinion:[154] For it was said it was not a Place under the Crown, because he was put in by the Court of Assistants; nor was the £200 a Pension but a Salary annexed to his Post, which salary he would loose if he displeased the Court of Assistants.

Immediately after that Question Sandys moved another, which was, What new Employments had been erected since 1705 and whether any greater number of Commissioners had been employed since that time than before. It was said, that though it might appear invidious, and a Task no Gentleman liked, to name particular Members disqualified by such Employments, yet a general inquiry was free from Objection. That Minorca and Gibraltar were Accessions to the Crown since that time, which must occasion many new Places: and the Salaries continued by his Majesty's bounty

[153] Cf. Harley journal, above p. 43.
[154] For the division see *ibid*.

to the late Queens Servants must be now looked on as Pensions: and that since no new Law could be obtained to restrain the Number of Place-men in the House, they ought to keep strictly up to the Spirit of the old one.

But this Question passed in the Negative but by a small Majority.[155]

February 21.

The Day for the Call being come, and all expectations raised, Mr. Poulteney in a full House made a long and florid Harangue; and concluded with a Motion to Address the King to lay all Papers and Instructions relating to the Convention before the House. He said his Intentions were, that they should be delivered Sealed up, and referred to a Secret Committee to be chosen by Ballot, that it might be known whether our Right to a free Navigation had been insisted on, as it should have been: and whether our Minister in Spain[156] had any Authority to Accept the King of Spains Declaration reserving to himself a Power to suspend the Asiento Contract,[157] the Acceptance of which was made a necessary Step towards signing the Convention. He said he followed exactly the Precedent in the first year of the late King, when Papers and In-structions relating to the Treaty of Utrecht were referred to such a secret Committee. That the Minister was of that Committee as well as himself, and therefore he thought he could not now refuse to meet out the same Measure to himself which he had before meeted to others. That he would not be of the Committee himself, but wished that the Examination might fall into the Hands of Sir R. Walpoles Opposers, for he thought it would redound most to his honour to be Acquitted by them, if his Measures appeared to be wisely taken.

It was Answered that neither the Treaty of Utrecht and Convention, nor the Makers of them were alike. That those who made the Treaty of Utrecht intended by making that Treaty afterwards to have the assistance of France to bring in the Pretender, but to the Makers of the Convention, if mistaken, no ill design could be imputed. That the Treaty of Utrecht and its ill effects still subsisted; but the Convention was absolutely at an end. That calling for these Papers was in some measure impeaching the Conven-tion; which was inconsistent, after both Houses had voted it a good ground-Work for a future Treaty. And that Spain by breaking it had shewn they thought it beneficial to this Kingdom.

On a Division 196 were for the Question, and 247 Against it.

The Minister said on this Occasion; That he looked on it as his day of Trial. He had served long, and he believed that was his greatest Crime. When he endeavoured to form Articles of Impeachment against himself, he could Accuse himself of Nothing but what was likewise an Impeachment of some Act of Parliament, of some Resolution of that House. That in great Variety and Multiplicity of business he must have been subject to many Errors and Mistakes, But for the whole of his Conduct, he Appealed to the Judgement of the House and Submitted to their Justice.

I heard him afterwards say in Conversation, that about a Month before this Debate there had been a Meeting of the Leaders of the Opposers, to consult in what manner to proceed against him. Some were for always using the word Minister in the singular Number in both Houses; and making it as familiar to name him there, as in Print or in

---

[155] See *ibid.*

[156] Benjamin Keene (1697–1757), minister plenipotentiary to Spain 1727–34, envoy extraordinary 1734–9, and ambassador 1746–57.

[157] The Asiento was a grant made by Spain, by the treaty of Utrecht in 1713, to the South Sea Company, to allow one ship a year to trade directly with the Spanish colonies. The South Sea Company refused to pay arrears to Spain, and the Asiento was suspended in May 1739. By Oct. Britain and Spain were at war.

private conversation, and after laying that Foundation to follow the Precedent of the Duke of Buckingham's Case in King Charles the 1st. reign; and Impeach him on common Fame. Pulteney opposed this, as unjust without some particular Charge; they therefore left it to him to proceed in his own Way, and he in order to regain his Credit with them, which he had impaired by having joyned so heartily in the supply throughout the session formed the Above mentioned Plan, which he communicated to few or none, before he opened it in the House.

February 25.

The House going into the Committee of Supply to consider of the Ordinary Estimate of the Navy, all the Papers from the Naval Offices were referred to the Committee, and the Lords Baltimore and Polwarth, who had moved for them, were now to make what use of them they thought proper. The first (who had a ship of his own, in which he had rambled to many parts of the World, and pretended from thence to great Knowledge in maritime affairs) took on him the province to examine into the State of the Navy, and Lord Polwarth that of observing from the Papers any new Expense that had been brought on the Publick. The Comptroller and Surveyor of the Navy who were ordered to attend were examined at the Bar, and the substance of Sir Jacob Ackworth[158] the Surveyors evidence was. That the Ships built on the new Dimensions (which he advised) were about 2 feet wider, but not longer; carried their Guns higher; and their Complements were encreased. – Being asked if they were as good sailors, he said he had heard no Complaint of them. – That some of them were damaged Abroad by the Weather, and must return home:

He said there were now fit for Service 4 first Rates: 10 Second: 12 eighty Gun Ships: 14 Seventy: 23 Sixty: 25 Fifty: (in all 88 Ships of the Line, of which I think there 124 in the whole Navy: the rest being fifth and sixth Rates which amount together to about 50) he said there were 18 twenty Gun Ships, and 7 fire Ships now in Commission. That 7 40-Gun Ships, and 13 twenty were now building in Marchants Yards; where none had been built since the last War; but that they were obliged to build there now, the Kings Yards being employed on the larger Ships.

The Stores (he said) had not been surveyed since 1728 nor was there an Annual Estimate made of what would be wanted. But there were weekly and quarterly Returns made of their State; so that they could always Acquaint the Admiralty with it. That on their Orders they bought new ones, which were paid for by Bills made out on delivery of them agreeable to Contract.

As to the Moarings, he said, they always lay in the Water, ready for the Ships, whether they are in Harbour or no: and must be repaired, or renewed as Occasion requires.

He said he wrote Annualy to the several Yards acquainting them with the Number of Ships, that might probably be Employed at Sea the ensuing year: on which they returned to him Computations of the Expence of Moarings, repairs of Ships in Ordinary, Wharfs, Docks, and Buildings would probably come to, out of which the Ordinary Estimate was annualy formed. That a distinct account was kept of the Ordinary and Extra Repairs; but that they were paid for promiscuously.

Lord Baltimore said, that the whole Navy was 163,337 Tuns; which a very Judicious person had computed at a medium at £8 per Tun: and allowing the Stores, Rigging, and Ordinance of a Ship to be near the same Value of the Ship, it must then be computed at £16 per Tun. Which makes the whole Navy to be worth about £2,600,000. That 27s. of the £4 per Month being allowed for wear and tear, we had Voted as much

---

[158] Sir Jacob Ackworth (d. 1749), assistant surveyor 1714–15, surveyor to the navy 1715–49.

this Year for Wear and Tear as a fifth part of the Value of the whole Value of the Navy. Which seemed to him very extraordinary. That 19s. per Month seemed to him a large allowance for Victualing; when he could Victual his own Ship for 8d. a Man per Day; which fell something short of it. And he thought publick Offices, who contracted for large quantities, might buy cheaper than private Persons.

Corbett said, the Navy was now in a good condition, and must be kept so, whether the Money given Annualy by Parliament was sufficient or no; for it if was once let drop, it would not easily be retrieved. – That the £4 per Month (of which 30s. is for Wages, 4s. for Ordinance; 27s. for Wear and Tear; and 19s. for Victualling.) is an Establishment as old as King Charles the 1st. or at least Olivers days; when every thing was much cheaper than now. And therefore it is now too little: The 27s. is never sufficient for the Wear and Tear; which makes Extra-expences necessary. Nor the 19s. for the Victualing; which commonly amounts to 21s. often to 22s. and sometimes to <2>3s. 6d. – That all the services go hand in hand; and supply each other as occasion requires: but altogether the Allowance is too small, which Occasions an Annual encrease of the Debt of the Navy.

Lord Baltimore said, he was informed some Ships were rotten when they were launched which Sir C. Wager absolutely denied.

Lord Polwarth said, that in 1733 £1,200,000 was granted towards the Debt of the Navy; which was again encreased near £600,000 since that time. He wished therefore that a select Comittee might be Appointed to inquire into the Causes of it: though there appeared plainly to be some:

1. That the Article of Continginces, which now amounted to £46000 was paid out of the wear and tear; when it was owned that the 27s. allowed for that was not sufficient: That for seven Years past those Continginces had amounted to £41000 more than in any seven years before. That some Articles of those Contingencies, if reasonable ought to be inserted in the Ordinary Estimate; as the Salary of £400 per Annum to the Solicitor of the Navy; and the like Salary to the Judge Advocate; and that other Articles were for ridiculous Expences, as £250 per Annum for Candles etc. to the Commissioners of the Navy; etc.

2. That Bounties had been granted out of the Money arrising from the Old and Decayed Stores of the Navy and Victualling Offices, which was Publick Money by Authority unknown to the Law: Such as the £200 per Annum above mention'd to Corbett: <£>2,000 per Annum to the first Commissioner of the Admiralty: The Allowance of Taxes on the Salaries of the Treasurer, and Commissioners of the Navy and Victualling; which ought to be taken out of those Salaries; and with which they are chargeable by Law. And if it was thought a necessary Addition to their Salaries; it ought not to be taken in that Secret manner, but should be inserted in the Ordinary of the Navy. And that it was improper that the Commissioners should be interested in the Decayed Stores, because they might be less carefull to preserve them good.

3. That the Ordinary for the next Year was £18,000 more than in 1727 though we now have 126 ships at Sea, and then had 87. Which was to be imputed to such Articles as these: – A Clerk of the Journals, a new Office with £400 per Annum Salary. – The Salary of the Extra-Instrument to the Surveyor increased from £150 per Annum to £300 per Annum. About £1200 for Annual Repairs and Wages to Servants and Officers to take care of the Buildings and Gardens of the Admiralty: a Pile which cost £16000 Erected without Authority, out of the Money granted for Wear and Tear. – £500 per Annum for Fire and Candles to the Lords of the Admiralty. – £1096 more than in 1727 on the Superannuation, the Numbers of superannuated Officers now being 82. – £5860 more for Repairs. – £3000 for Victuals. – £2000 on Salaries.

It was Answered

1. That the Articles of Contingencies might at all times be called for, and Seen, and then the House will judge whether they are proper to be Allowed.

2. That the Old Stores (which Winington said were once the Perquisites of the respective Commissioners) are now constantly accounted for, and the Money Applied to Naval services. That the House knew the occasion of granting the £200 per Annum to Corbett. – That the £2000 per Annum to first Commissioner of the Admiralty was first granted in 1709 to the Lord Orford, and had been continued ever since. – That the payment of the Taxes on the Salaries was no new thing, was generaly known, and had been practiced ever since the Land-Tax was established.

3. That the Ordinary was only an Estimate of Expenses to be incurred, and which must be Accounted for the next year. If more was Voted than was necessary the Publick would avail its self of the Overplus; if less it must make good the Deficency. Clutterbuck spoke particularly to two Articles; 1. the Allowance of Fire and Candle to some of the Commissioners of the Admiralty; which he said was an old Allowance; but he dared to say that none of the Gentlemen, who now enjoyed it were at all solicitous about it. 2. As to the Clerk of the Journals, he was the Person who desired such an Officer should be Appointed, which he thought very necessary to inspect the Captains Journals, and be a Check upon them, after several of them on the Irish Station had been very negligent of their Duty, and justly dismiss'd from the Service. Thus ended this Debate without any Question put upon it. And the Ordinary was Voted in the Committee without a Division.

February 26.

The Resolution of the Committee being agreed to by the House; Lord Polwarth, that a Point he had so much laboured might not go off without something done upon it, moved a Question; that to apply any more Money to any Head in the Ordinary Estimates than what was voted for that Head was a misapplication. This was justly rejected: for it is more for the Interest of the Publick to issue the Money promiscuously, that it may be Applied as each Service calls for it, that the Overplus upon one head may supply the defect upon another: Whereas particular Appropriations would cramp the Service so it would be impossible to cary it on. And all the Publick can desire is to have just accounts of the Whole: And that it should be applied to such services as are most necessary.

He imediately after moved another Question, which was; that the money arrising from the old Stores was Publick Money, and ought to be Annualy Accounted for to Parliament, intending by that to make it part of the sinking Fund. – They who approved of the present Application of it, amended the Question, by changing the Words (accounted for to Parliament) to these (Applied to naval Purposes) but rather than let the Question be put in these Words he withdrew his Motion.

This was the last day that Lord Appeared in the house: for the Earl of Marchmont, his Father, dying he became a Scotch Peer, and so was excluded both Houses. This was no small Mortification to himself, and all the Opposers, who said it was a National loss. And indeed he was superior to any of his own Age in the House. He had an indefatigable Industry, a quick Apprehension, and ready Expression. There was no One who gave, and was like to give, the Minister more trouble; nor with whose personal behaviour he was more disgusted.[159]

---

[159] End of MS L(c) 1734.

December 1. 1741.

On this Day began the first Session of the third Parliament of this reign; which was not of a Temper so Agreeable to the Court as the last. The number of new Members was very great: and more of them had been chosen in Cornwall and Scotland than usual in Opposition to the Ministry by the Influence of the Prince and Duke of Argyle. So that the ennemies to the Administration promised themselves great things from their Proceedings.

About ten in the Morning the Duke of Dorset Lord Steward of the Household came into the Court of Wards to Administer the Oaths of Allegence and Supremacy to the Members; and after some of them were sworn, signed a Commission to them to swear the rest: and before two Oclock 487[160] were sworn; and soon after 513: a greater Number than ever had been known.

About two the King sent for the Comons, and Ordered them to proceed to the choice of a Speaker to be presented to him on Friday. Mr. Pelham in a hansom Panegerick proposed Mr. Onslow, and was seconded by Mr. Clutterbuck: As he had filled the Chair with great Abilities the two preceeding Parliaments, and (though a firm Friend to the Ministry) by his Impartial behaviour rendered himself universally Agreeable, it was unanimously Agreed to: then they Adjourned to Friday.

December 4.

Mr. Onslow with the House being returned from the House of Peers, reported that the King had approved of him for Speaker: and that he in the name of the Commons had made the usual Petition to his Majesty for freedom from Arrest for themselves and servants, Freedom of Speech, and free Access to his Majesty; which he had granted in as Ample Manner, as it had ever been injoyed in the time of any of his Predecessors. He thanked the House for the great Honour done him, which he would endeavour to deserve by a Faithfull discharge of his Duty: to do which and to behave respectfully to every Member in particular should be the Pride of his Life. He recommended to them an early Attendance, so as to dedicate the best part of the Day to business; and to Avoid Personal Altercation in Debate. He said before they could enter on business they must take the Oaths required: which he first took and subscribed alone in the Chair and then calling over the Counties Alphabetically they began to swear the other Members.

December 8.

All the Members being sworn, to the Number of 517 (including 4 double returns) the usual Standing Orders at the beginning of every session were made.

When the Speaker read the order for taking Strangers into Custody, I addressed myself to him in the following terms.

Sir.

I hope the Order you have just read will not be regarded as a thing of Course: It is of moment: and I hope will be better observed for the Future. For what can be more Absurd, than to establish a standing Order of the House, and to have every day Ocular demonstration of its being broke. This Order has been violated to that degree, that we have sometimes seen almost as many Strangers as Members in the House. It is no longer a House of Commons but a Common House; Common to all degrees of Persons that please to seat themselves in it. It is a Coffee House for every Jolle Man to pass away an hour with a Friend. It is a Play-house for the Ladies; which they frequent

---

[160] Harley has 489. See above p. 54.

almost as regularly as any of the other Theaters. The other House hath begun a reformation in this:[161] Their Doors are shut against all Strangers; even against the Members of this House.

The Lesson is good: the Law of Retaliation is good: And I hope when any Peer comes to this Door, the Door-keeper will say, your Lordship has no business here.

There scarce ever were so many members in Town as at present; but yet the House is so well contrived, that, if it is cleared of Strangers, I believe all may be seated. It is otherwise impossible; it is impossible they should hear the Debates, or give their assistance in them. It is too invidious a Task for a Private Member to stand up in his Place, and desire the House to be cleared, or to point to a particular Person, and desire him to be taken into Custody. We must therefore seek for redress from that Place where the Authority of this House is justly intrusted: to that Person who gives out his Orders with Dignity, Courage, and Impartiality; this must be one Labour added to those which you have generously undertaken for the sake of this House, and of the Publick.

It will be for your Honour; it will be for the honour of this Parliament, before we enter on Debate, to shew a steady resolution of adhering to those Rules which are to promote decency and Order.

On this the Speaker said, he would take care the Order should be punctually observed, if the House would support him in it.

It hath been hitherto well observed; and hath saved many hours in Dividing. And may prevent ignorant or Malicious People from carrying away false or partial representations of Debates.

The Speaker afterwards reported the Kings Speech, requiring the Advice and Assistance of his Parliament, with regard to the War with Spain, and the Perillous situation of the Affairs of Europe: The Motion for the Address of Thanks (which was drawn by the Ministers themselves) was put into the hands of Mr. Herbert; who opened it in a handsome Speech, which was modestly and sensibly seconded by Mr. Trevor: both Gentlemen of fair Fortunes and independent of the Court.

It was conceived in so general Terms; that it was not easy to object to it. However Lord Noel Somerset proposed to add Words at the end: importing that we would assist the King provided we were led into no Expense on account of his foreign Dominions; and was seconded by Mr. Shippen: This shewed there had been no Concert between them and the heads of the Patriots. For though this was agreeable to the Act of Settlement: yet it was objected to by Pulteney: he and the Princes Party being as unwilling to express themselves Openly on that head, as the Ministers themselves: probably for fear of disobliging the Prince; who (it was said) had the preservation of those Dominions as much at heart as the King himself. Lord Noel Somerset was prevailed on to withdraw his Amendment, though much against Shippens inclination. The Debate afterwards turned on an Expression in the Motion for an Address; viz: to thank the King for his Care in prosecuting the War with Spain. This they said, was too strong an Approbation before they were acquainted with particulars: and it was by Consent left out. So that the motion passed at last unanimously.

---

[161] There is no reference to this in the *L.J.* However, 'at intervals during the century the Lords enforced a complete exclusion of strangers, for which there are no references in the official minutes of the House'. See Anita Rees, 'The Practice and Procedure of the House of Lords, 1714–1784', University of Wales (Aberystwyth), Ph.D., 1987, p. 312. The Lords discussed standing order no. 122 (of 25 Jan. 1720), for clearing the house when public business was to be proceeded with, on 14 Jan., 6 April, 4 and 13 May 1742 when a motion to vacate it in order to substitute another standing order was rejected. *L.J.*, XXVI, 32, 92, 113, 120. See also Cobbett, XII, 639–42: Bishop Secker's journal, 13 May 1742; and B.L., Add. MS 6043, f. 113: Secker's journal, 6 Apr. 1742.

In the course of the Debate Pulteney addressed himself in a florid Harangue to the New Parliament. Said, as his Majesty had declared us to be in a Perillous situation: 'twas our Duty to inquire how we came to be so. It was his opinion; it was by a long series of Mismanagement. That not only measures but Men must be changed: and that this Parliament (different from what Parliament had lately been) must save the Nation. That he would move for a Day to consider of the State of it: and would mention some of the Heads he would go upon. As what occasioned the Miscarriage at Carthegena?[162] Why the Spanish Troops designed for Italy were suffered to imbark at Barcelona, without Opposition from our Fleet? Why the Queen of Hungary[163] was not assisted, though at the close of the last Parliament £300000 had been voted for that Service? Why the Danes and Hessians in our Pay were unemployed? And what Applications had been made to other Powers to second us?

Sir R. Walpole replied: that the unhappy state of Europe was owing to Accidents not in the power of the Ministry to prevent. But if we were accountable for it, it was rather to be imputed to the Opposition than Administration. That a Lord in the Opposition had lately been received at Paris with unusual honours:[164] much greater than he should have been, though he (as they said) had been blundering twenty years in their service. He desired his Conduct might be examined in a British Parliament: that the whole truth might appear: which had too often been concealed to his disadvantage; nay; that he had sometimes been obliged out of prudence to conceal it even when the revealing it would turn to his Justification. He said he would second the Motion for a Day to inquire into the state of the Nation: which inquiry he hoped would continue de Die in Deim 'till they went through the whole: and that they would not ramble but examine and determine one Point before they entered on another. And not do as was done some years ago on a like occasion: When a Day, Appointed to consider the Treaty of Seville, whas wholly spent in debating the Affair of Dunkirk.[165]

The Day was Agreed to be the 21st. of January: which was moved for by Pulteney and seconded by Sir R. Walpole.

December 9.

This being the first day for receiving Petitions, the Westminster Petition was first presented by Mr. Pulteney: who said the matter complained of was not only an Injury to so great a City; but the severest Wound to the Constitution: the High Bailiff having Arbitrarily and illegally closed the Poll: And having sent for an Armed force to controul the Election.

This Petition having occasion'd much discourse throughout the Kingdom by different representations of the Case, was ordered to be heard at the Bar on Tuesday following. The next Petition was presented by Sir W. Yonge, from the Mayor of Bossiney, complaining of an undue return: the Sheriff having delivered his Precept, and taken a Return from the Mayor of the preceeding year: When the Petitioner was in Actual possession of his Office; was invested in it by the preceeding Mayor himself:

---

[162] The ineffective bombardment on 6 Mar. 1740 by Admiral Vernon of Carthagena on the Caribbean coast of South America.

[163] Maria Theresa (1717–80) had succeeded her father, the Emperor Charles VI, in 1740 to the hereditary Habsburg lands, including Hungary, where she was crowned in 1741.

[164] Probably Lord Chesterfield, who was in Paris in Aug., Oct. and Nov. 1741, where he met Bolingbroke. See *The Letters of Philip Dormer Stanhope, 4th Earl of Chesterfield*, ed. B. Dobrée (6 vols., 1932), I, 92; II, 471–2, 476–9.

[165] The treaty of Seville was signed 9 Nov. 1729 between England and Spain. The port of Dunkirk was to have been razed by the 1713 treaty of Utrecht, but the French had continued to use it as a naval base.

Appeared at the Election in the Seat, and with the Insignia of Office: demanded the Precept; took a Poll, and signed a Return with the Publick Seal, of two other Members; which he tendered to the Sheriff, and the Sheriff refused to accept. And the Petitioner attended at the Door with the said Return, and with Witnesses to prove the Facts.

On the Question that the Clerk of the Crown should attend on Friday with the Return, it was carried in the affirmative 222 against 215.

December 11.

The Clerk of the Crown attending, and the Witnesses having clearly proved the Facts, it was carried to take off the Return of the sitting Members, and Annex the other Return, by 224 against 218. By which two new Members were introduced;[166] and the sitting Members were left (if they pleased) to be Petitioners. For as the Question only concerned the legality of the Return, nothing appeared concerning the Merits of the Election.

This was the first struggle between the Parties: and a very agreeable Conquest to the Court, as it gained four Votes at a very critical Juncture. For this reason the Opposers stickled hard for the sitting Members; and especialy the Princes Party; by whose Influence they had been Return'd; and who thought themselves concerned to vindicate (if possible) the Sherriff from the Imputation of Partiality; as he was nominated by his Royal Highness. And Probably the Point had been lost but for the solicitation of a Peer,[167] who having received an Injury of a particular Nature from one of the Sitting Members, engaged some Persons against them; who on all other occasions oppose the Court.

December 16.

The Committee of Priviledges and Elections now mett for the first time, and both Parties had determined long before to exert their whole strength in the Choice of a Chairman: and the Candidates were known. Earl Chairman in the two last Parliaments was proposed by the Ministry, and Doctor Lee, a Civilian of good Capacity and Character and Brother to Cheif Justice,[168] by the Opposers. Lee was chosen by 242 Against 238.

This was matter of great triumph to the Opposers; who now expected to carry all before them: They began to talk openly of stopping the Supply 'till their Advice should be taken: and it was easy to foresee that Advice would be to remove the Minister; whom they began to treat with the utmost contempt: and who was like to pass his time ill in a House so disposed.

December 18.

They now began to call for Papers, to found their Inquiry upon. And intended to make four Motions. For the Corrispondence between our Court and that of Vienna, of Paris, of Berlin, and the States General.

Mr. Pultney moved the first, to which Sir Robert Walpole said he could see little objection. He said the Expression of all Letters from the King to the Queen of Hungary and vice versâ was too general and unprecedented; it might include Private Corrispondence, which it was disrespectfull to call for, though he knew of no such.

---

[166] Richard Liddell and Thomas Foster had been elected on 12 May 1741. On 11 Dec. John Sabine and Christopher Tower were returned on petition. Sedgwick, I, 206; *C.J.*, XXIV, 13, 18.

[167] Lord Abergavenny. See Sedgwick, II, 217.

[168] William Lee (1688–1754), M.P. for Chipping Wycombe 1727–30, was chief justice of the king's bench in 1737.

This was taken up more strongly by others and at last grew into a formal long debate, and on a Division it was carried to leave out the words by 237 against 227.

Dodington moved the 2d. Question for the Corrispondence with Paris; which being Ammended like the 1st. passed without Opposition.

The 3d. Question for the Corrispondence with Berlin was moved by Sir John Rushout, which Sir Robert said he wished might be postponed. For he said there was an engagement of secrecy with that Court 'till a certain Day, which was between this and the 21 of January and calling for such Papers before that Day might give great Offence to that Court. After that Day they should probably be at liberty to lay them before them and if called for after the recess, they would have them as soon as if called for now. This seemed reasonable to many of the Opposers and on a Division it was carried by a majority of near thirty not to put the Question.[169]

The Opposers were enraged at this disapointment. And Waller, who was to move the forth Question, said, he saw no likelyhood of any good from it, and so refused to move it.

To compleat their disapointment, the Westminster Petition, which was to proceed on that day was Adjourned to Monday.

Their Dejection was very visible on this Occasion: and they went as melancholy from the House as they came sanguine into it.

December 22.

The Westminster Petition was now determined; and the Election declared Void.[170] By the Evidence it appeared that the Injury was done by the Party that complained. The sitting Members were scandalously insulted, both going to and at the place of Polling, by the Mob. The two first Days, Parties coming to Poll for them were stopped, and dispersed: many of their Voters ill treated and inhumanly beat at the Place of Polling. The Candidates, High Bailiff, and those that took the Poll, drove from the Hustings, with Stones and Dirt. Notwithstanding which the Poll continued on to the sixth day, and without much Violence, when the Sitting Members had a Majority of 250 or 300, and every body seemed to have Poll'd that had a mind to come, scarce a Man dropping in, in an hour: and it was proposed to Mr. Edwin to fix some time for closing the Poll which he refused. At length there came a great number of Persons from Clerkenwell (who as it was acknowledged on all hands had no Right to vote) and in a very riotous and tumultuous manner took possession of the Polling Place, declaring nobody should Poll 'till their Votes were taken: The High Bailiff refused to take them, but said they might if they pleased deliver in their Names in Writing to shew their demand; and he would Abide any Action or complaint they should bring against him. The tumult continuing the High Bailiff declared he would close the Poll, unless those who had a right would come and Poll: and accordingly ordered three Proclamations at about 7 or 8 minutes distance from each other, for that purpose: and immediately after the third took up the Books, and carried them into the Vestry[171] to cast up the Numbers. Nobody at that Instant (as the Evidence for the sitting Members asserted) demanding to Poll: which was contradicted by the Evidence of the Petitioners; but out of the great numbers they pretended had not polled, they could name but three or four, who lived near the Place, had been there every Day consequently might have polled before, and

---

[169] The vote on the Westminster election on 18 Dec. was 218 to 197. *C.J.*, XXIV, 33–4.

[170] On 22 Dec. 1741 the election (on 8 May) of Sir Charles Wager and Lord Sundon as M.P.s for Westminster was declared void. At a by-election on 31 Dec. Lord Perceval and Charles Edwin were elected. Sedgwick, I, 285–6; see also Harley journal, above p. 54.

[171] Of St Paul's Church, Covent Garden.

probably reserved themselves for that purpose. Lord Sundon and the High Bailiff being retired into the Vestry, the Mob surrounded the place, and threatened to have their Blood when they came out. This made it necessary to think of some means of securing themselves. They first sent the High Constable to see if he could quell them, but he was assaulted by his under Constables, who joyned in the Roit. Then three Justices (Blackerby, Howard and Lediard)[172] signed a Letter to the Commanding Officer of the Guards, informing him the Poll was Closed, and desiring him to send some Assistance. Accordingly about 60 Soldiers came and planted themselves in Covent Garden Church Yard, and saw Lord Sundon safe to his Coach: which was imediately pursued above half a Mile by the Rabble with Stones and Dirt, and that Lord had a narrow escape from their Fury.

This being the state of the Case: the House resolved that the High Bailiff had Acted in an illegal and Arbitrary manner: of which their was not the least Evidence. Yet he was ordered into Custody.

They next resolved that a Body of armed Soldiers came near the Place where the Poll was taken, before the Election was ended. Which was False in Fact; the Poll having been closed two hours before they came.

Then they resolved, that the presence of a regular Body of armed Soldiers at an Election, was a violation of the Freedom of it, and a defiance of the Laws and Constitution. Which was true; but not applicable to the Case.

A Question was then moved that the Justices, who sent for the Soldiers, were guilty of a High Crime and Misdemeanour; which was grounded only on Blackerby's giving Evidence of the Fact. It was said it was very hard, that a Mans Evidence in an other Cause should be turned against himself; and that he should be convicted without being heard in his Defence. This was so unjust they were forced to stop it. And the Justices were ordered to attend at a future day.

On this Occasion much was said of the Power of the Civil Majestrate to send for Soldiers. It was argued against it, that the Law had given him the command of the Constables; a power of Creating them; of summoning the Posse to keep the Peace; and when it had invested them with such Powers, would admit of no Excuse. That when Soldiers came to his assistance, they came in their Military Capacity, were commanded by their own Officers, and subject to Martial Law if they disobeyed them. To trust the Execution of the Laws in such hands was unconstitutional. – It was said, on the other hand, that Mens being Soldiers did not exempt them from the duty of subjects; whose Duty it was to obey the summons of the Civil Majestrate to keep the Peace. When they came, though they were subject to their own Officers, yet those Officers were subject to the Civil Majestrate. If (as was agreed) he might summon the Posse and Arm them; Why might he not as well summon those who were already Armed. And Clark[173] (Council for the sitting Members) cited a Case in Pophams Reports, where it was resolved by all the Judges in Queen Elizabeths Reign, that a Justice of the Peace, Sheriff, or any Peace Officer might call the Militia to their Aid.[174] Mention was made of four Quaeries, proposed about five years since, by the House of Lords, to the Judges, for their Opinion concerning the Behaviour of Soldiers, when summoned by Justices to suppress roits; how far they might Act either defensively or

---

172 See below, p. 175.
173 Possibly either Charles Clarke (c.1702–50), M.P. for Huntingdonshire 1739–41, and Whitchurch 1743; or Thomas Clarke (1703–64), M.P. for Mitchell 1747–54, and Lostwithiel 1754–61. Both were distinguished lawyers.
174 Sir John Popham (?1531–1607), chief justice of the king's bench, was the author of *Reports and Cases Adjuged in the Time of Queen Elizabeth* (1656).

offensively: to which the Judges have not yet returned any Answer: fearing prehaps least their determination might injure the Power of the Civil Majestrate on one hand, or the Liberty of the Subject on the other.

The House came to a Division on voiding the Election about midnight, which was carried by 220 against 216. The Opposition taking Advantage of the small Majority pursued their Questions, and kept the House sitting 'till near five in the Morning. Which was the longest as well as most violent proceeding I remember.

This was matter of great Triumph to the Opposition. As soon as the Question for voiding the Election was carried, it was said, his R<oyal> H<ighness> and the Princess made a Visit at that late time of Night to Lady C. Edwin[175] to congratulate her on the success. And Bonfires and Illuminations were made next night through the City of Westminster. The King was not a little displeased, as he looked on it, as an un-natural triumph over him in the City of his own Residence. And when the new Election came on it was carried against the Court without Opposition: No Candidates being found hardy enough to expose themselves and Friends to the Insults of the Rabble; who had received such Countenance and Sanction for their Licenciousness.

December 24.

The House adjourned to the 18th. of January; which a longer recess than Ordinary; and was thought to be intended by All; that after such hard struggles things should be brought to some Issue before the House met again; that the Publick Business might go on. It was generaly expected, throughout the Nation, either that the Minister would be dismissed; or that he would come to some Agreement with some of the Heads of the Opposite Party. And those who meant best, wished there might be an Accomodation with the Prince. The King thought it below his dignity to propose this directly: but he gave authority to Lord Cholmodeley, to speak to the Bishop of Oxford to assure his R<oyal> H<ighness> that if he would return to St. James's, he and his Servants should be well received, he should have £100,000 per Annum and order should be taken for the Payment of his Debts. His R<oyal> H<ighness'>s Answer was, that if it had been a Message directly from his Majesty, he should have thought himself bound in Duty to have waited on him: as it was, he only regarded it as a proposal from Lord C<hol-mondeley> that he could never consent to an Accommodation as long as Sir R. Wal-pole was in Power. By whom he conceived himself greatly injured; that he thought, Sir Robert should desire, as well as for his own sake, as that of the Publick, to retire.

January 19.

The double Return for the Shire of Berwick between Hume Campbell, and Sir J. Sin-clair[176] was determined in favour of the first.

The Commissioners for Shires in Scotland are Elected by the Freeholders having such an Estate holden by Patent of the Crown. By Act of Parliament a Roll is to be made up of these Freeholders every Michaelmas: and by consent of the Majority then present, those who have lost their Right are to be struck off the Roll, those who have acquired a right are to be admitted. Which is likewise to be done at the Election of a Commissioner to Parliament. A Prceses and Clerk is to be chosen to hold such Election, and to make a Return of the Commissioners elected to the Sheriff. At the choice of Prceses and Clerk the last Commissioner (if present) is to preside, and to call the Roll last made up either at Michaelmas or the Election of a Commissioner:

---

[175] Lady Charlotte Edwin, daughter of the 4th duke of Hamilton, had married Charles Edwin in 1736.
[176] Probably Sir John Sinclair (d. 1764), 2nd bt. of Longformacus, Berwickshire.

and by the Persons on that Roll pursuant to the last Resolution of the House in the Case of Peebles, is the Prœses and Clerk to be chosen. And to prevent Partiality in the last Commissioner, it is intended they should be chosen by those only; and whethether they have their Freedom or not. But afterwards at the Election of the Comissioner (as is said before) those who have no Freehold shall be struck off; those that have shall be admitted.

Hume Campbell (who was the Member in the last Parliament) presided at the Choice of Prœses and Clerk; and called over the Roll made up the Michaelmas preceeding for that Purpose. One Person on the Roll that was present, when called, did not Vote, because he had parted with his Freehold; another Person not on the Roll, was admitted to Vote with a Quaere, because he had acquired a Freehold. But which Steps were irregular, because deviating from the Roll last made up. But striking off this last, and adding the other, there yet remained a Majority of two for Hume Campbell's Prœses and Clerk. Sir J. Sinclair, seing this deviation from the Roll, objected to eleven others on the Roll, as having parted with their Freeholds: which Objection not being allowed, he and his Friends withdrew, and chose another Prœses and Clerk, who took a Poll likewise, for him and made a Return: Which proceeding was Irregular, and Coram not <sic> Judice: that when the House determined (as they did without a Division) the first Prœses and Clerk duly Elected, there appeared no Poll for him and his Cause fell to the ground. And the under Sheriff was ordered into Custody for making a double Return. Which to my Apprehension was a hardship: for it seems cautious to take both Returns; and by the Law of Scotland in this very Case a double Return was Adjudged not to be a false Return: and the Case of an English and Scotch Sheriff is very different: the first takes the Poll, and forms the Indenture of Return himself; but the last is to receive it from Another: and when Returns are tendered to him by different Clerks, 'tis unreasonable to compel him to judge which was duly elected.

January 21.

This day was appointed to consider the state of the Nation, which consideration was Adjourned for a Fortnight. Mr. Pulteney observed that the House was not prepared, not having the necessary Information before them. The King he said had asked our Advice; it was necessary to give it; but impossible without knowing the whole State of our Affairs. Many Papers had been denied as improper to be communicated to so Numerous an Assembly: no doubt there were many such: even some of those delivered in were of that Nature. He thought therefore the only Way to avoid any Inconvenience to the State was to appoint a Secret Committee to examine all State Papers, and to make a Report on which to found our Advice.

He proposed the Committee to consist of 21 to be chosen by Ballot: He said 21 Gentlemen might be taken out of the House of as great Ability and Integrity as were any where to be found: and on them he would willingly pin his Faith.

It was Answered: That if all Papers were not proper to be communicated, it was better to leave it to the King and Council to judge what were proper than to a Committee of our own. That if such a Committee was appointed, we must Act by implicit Faith; and take their Report for granted, though ever so unjust, because we could have no recourse to many Papers, on which it ought to be founded. That the King had asked the Advice of Parliament, but this would be the Advice only of 21, which would be absolute, and be invested with the whole power of the Privy Council and Parliament, not unlike the Committee of Safety a Century ago, who occasioned great Confusion. And that Secret Committees had never been appointed to inquire only, without forming particular Accusations.

Sir R. Walpole spoke with great Firmness. He said, he looked on the Motion to be cheifly levelled against him. That he desired to <be> tried by the present Parliament: to be treated like a Gentleman in the House: and when he was tried, to have the common Justice due to every subject of having their his <sic> Crimes specified. That he had long been loaded with general Calumny and Invective; but that none had yet pointed out any Particular, and said This was his Crime.

On a Division, it was carried in the Negative by 253 Against 250, which with the 4 Tellers and Speaker, made 508. A fuller House than any one remembers.

If the Opposition had carried the Question, they probably would have Ballotted that Night, for Sandys said in the debate, he hoped he should know the 21 before the House rose. So that they would have adjourned a short time for the Members to have formed their Lists, and were prepared with their own to have delivered to their own Party: which the Court Party could not be, not having had any Notice of the Motion. And if the Opposition had gained this Point they must have gone on without controul.

In this Debate Pulteney declared very explicitly and peremptorily, that he never would accept of any share in any Administration: but would always employ his Influence in Parliament, to support the present Royal Family and Constitution.

I supose he might have two Views in this declaration. One to shew that his past Conduct proceeded from Publick Spirit only; The other, to pave his Way to a Peerage: for if he will accept neither Power nor Profit, Honour is the only gratification left. And which a Court may be ready to bestow on him to remove him out of the lower House; where they may think his Parts and Popularity render him too powerful.

January 23.

The three Justices, who sent for the Soldiers to quell the Roit at the Westminster Election were reprimanded by the Speaker in Terms; which all his own Friends thought too severe; but which gave great pleasure to the Opposers; who desired that Fact might be represented as very heinous. Sandys and Cotton therefore immediately moved the thanks of the House for his Speeech, and that it might be printed. His Friends sat silent. At last Mr. Walpole said he was for the thanks of the House, but it was unusual to print Speeches on such Occasions; and Mr. Campbell spoke to the same effect. I was affraid the Speaker would be affronted: and therefore said, that though I was convinced in my own private Opinion, that the Men were innocent, and deserved rather thanks than Censure, yet since the Facts had appeared differently to the House, I thought myself bound by their Resolution, and taking the Facts as stated in their Resolution, the House could not be consistent with it self, without expressing a dislike of them; which could not be better expressed than in the Speech we had just heard; and I thought it both for his honour and ours that it should be printed;[177] that the Nation might see how zealous we all were for the Freedom of Election. – This the Speaker took kindly of me; and esteemed it as an Act of Friendship.

February 2.

This was the second day for hearing the Chippenham Petition, between Hume and Frederick Petitioners and Sir Edmond Thomas and Baynton the Sitting Members.[178] It was reported that there had been so much money spent on both sides at the Election;

---

[177] The Speech of the Speaker of the House of Commons, when He Reprimanded Nathaniel Blackerby, George Howard, and Thomas Lediard Esquires, at the Bar of the Said House, upon Saturday the 23rd Day of January, 1741 (1742).

[178] Alexander Hume and John Frederick. Sedgwick, I, 343–4.

that they both Agreed not so much as to mention it. Chippenham is a Borough by Prescription,[179] and probably in Queen Mary's reign consisted of 128 Houses; for Lands were then granted them by Charter, establishing a Bailiff and 12 Burgesses, with power to Admitt the inhabitants of those Houses, and those only, Freemen, so as to intitle them to share in those Lands; and a List of such Freemen and inhabitants have been regularly kept ever since. In 1624 there probably was an Attempt to confine the Election of Members to Parliament to the Bailiff and 12 Burgesses; for there was then a Resolution (which is the last) that the right of Election is in the Burgesses and Freemen more than 12 and that the Charter altered not the Custom.[180] It was insisted on by the Petitioners that that the Words Burgesses and Freemen meant only In-habitants Householders of those Houses: and by the sitting Members that they meant the Possessors of those Houses, though they took Possession, and were Admitted Freemen but an hour before the Election; which they said had been the constant Usage. – On a Division it went for the sitting Members by 236 against 235, the first day; and by a Majority of 16 the second day:[181] on which a few hours after the Peti-tioners gave up their Cause. Sir R. Walpole went out of the House immediately after the Division; and never returned; plainly foreseeing he could never for the future carry any Question in that House.

February 3.

This day had been Appointed, the Monday before, for the further hearing the Merchants Petition. And also for the Supply. When Sir R. Walpole said, it might be debated which Order should take place: and then it would be known whether the Publick Business which had been so long postponed, was to go on; and whether the Land Forces were to be granted. But it now appeared, he said this only to Amuse, and that a Resolution was taken not to suffer things to come to so desperate a Crisis. For when the House now mett, Expecting to sit late, all, but those few in the Secret, were surprised to see the Speaker prepared to go to the House of Lords, where the King was expected to Adjourn the Parliament for a Fortnight. It was said Sir R. Walpole was created Earl of Orford: was to resign his Places: and that during the Recess a new Ministry was to be formed that the Publick Business might go on without interuption.

Accordingly Sir Robert was created Earl of Orford: and on thursday the next Week resigned his Employments. But just at the Close of his Power he did some things unbecoming his Wisdom and Experience; and which were an Abuse of the Kings favour. For he obtained a Warrant for a Grant of £4000 per Annum to himself for Life: and some reversionary Grants to his Friends; but these were stopped on the repre-sentation of those who wished him Well. He also Obtained a Warrant to the Earl Marshal for Precedence to his illegitimate Daughter[182] as to the Daughter of an Earl. Which (whether proceeding from Paternal Affection or Vanity) revived the remem-brance of his own shame; disgusted the Nobility, and brought more Odium on him than prehaps any Act of Power.

---

[179] Meaning that the right of the borough to return a member had been established by ancient custom without the granting of a charter. Chippenham had first returned an M.P. in 1295, but did not receive a charter until 1554. See J.S. Roskill, L. Clark and C. Rawcliffe, *The House of Commons, 1386–1421* (4 vols., 1992), I, 691.

[180] For the resolution on 9 Apr. 1624, see *C.J.*, I, 759.

[181] The first day was 28 Jan. 1742, and the vote on the second day (2 Feb.) was 241 to 225. *C.J.*, XXIV, 66, 80.

[182] Maria (b. 1725), daughter of Maria Skerrett, Walpole's mistress, who became his second wife in 1738.

It was imagined by many that he would willingly have retired long ago: but I have reason to think his Passion for Power, when he resigned it, was as prevalent as ever. I have heard from those who have seen him in his retirement at Richmond that he should say, they were uneasy 'till they got him there, that now they wanted him to go to Houghton, and if he were there, they would probably want him out of the Kingdom: but he was resolved to stay where he was; to attend the House of Peers on Days of great business, and face his Enemies. A resolution prehaps most becoming an innocent man, and most conducive to his safty. But it might be more for the Kings service to remove to such a distance from Court, as to take off all suspicion of having any influence on the Councils.

His Majesty in regard to him, shewed his Constancy and Goodness in supporting an Old Servant, of confessed Abilities, and against whom nothing Particular had been charged, as long as he could consistantly with the Constitution; afterwards dismissing him with Honour. And as he shewed his goodness in not dismissing him on popular Clamour only; so he shewed his Prudence in dismissing him on the tacit Advice of Parliament, before things came to extremity. And rather to suffer the Advice of Parliament to controul the Prerogative than the Prerogative to prevent such Advice.

Mr. Pelham was the Next Person in the Kings Confidence and notwithstanding he had always been a steady Friend to the Minister, he had always kept up a fair corrispondence with Mr. Pulteney, who had been his great Opposer. They seemed now to make use of that corrispondence with an intention to unite the Royal Family, and those who were its undoubted Friends. To this end they intended, to introduce into the Ministry some of the Patriots (as they were now called) whose regard for the Royal Family was as undoubted as their Aversion to the Minister: and to exclude the Tories who were averse to the Hanover Succession at First; and had shewn no regard to the Family since. 'Till lately some of their leaders disparing of preferment any other way, had joyned with such discontented Whigs as followed the Prince. As these men were very Popular, his Highness had shewn them a particular regard: and seemed averse to a Reconciliation unless they were taken into a share of the Administration. Accordingly it was given out that the Ministry must stand on a Wider bottom; and that all Party distinctions were to be at an end.

On the Day Lord Orford resigned, Lord Wilmington was placed at the heard <sic> of the Treasury; Sandys was made a Comissioner and Chancellor of the Exchequer, and Sir John Rushout, Gybbon, and Compton the other three Commissioners. It was offered to Waller to be a Commissioner; but he refused: some say unwilling to come in without Assurance that the Minister should be impeached; and Against whom, it was said he had long been preparing Articles in revenge for his Father-in-laws disgrace.[183] Others say, he refused, to make way for Compton, in hopes that on that consideration his Father-in-Laws Incapacity might be taken off. And the making way for Compton was prehaps necessary to please Lord Wilmington; who I am well assured was dissatisfied; and probably because he had not the whole of what his Predecessor had. Lord Carteret was at the same time appointed Secretary of State.

The next day the Lords and Commons in the Opposition to the Number of about 300 met at the Fountain Tavern.[184] Where the Duke of Argyle spoke for taking in all

---

[183] John Aislabie (1670–1742), who was both Waller's father-in-law and stepfather, had been chancellor of the exchequer at the time of the South Sea Bubble and was disgraced. Sedgwick, I, 409–11; II, 505.

[184] The meeting took place on 12 Feb. at the Fountain tavern on the Strand. J.B. Owen, *The Rise of the Pelhams* (1957), pp. 97–8 gives the attendance as 'over 200 members of the Commons and 35 of the Lords'.

Denominations of Men; and for bringing Persons to Justice. Poulteney shewed great Moderation; being certainly averse to the first; and probably to the last. Sandys was attacked for taking a Place without their Privity. He said the business of the Publick must go on; the King had removed the Chancellor of the Exchequer: and if somebody did not accept the Office, his Majesty must employ the same person again; which he suposed they would not chuse. And that they ought not to think ill of him; 'till he had done something amiss.

The time between this and the meeting of the Parliament Pulteney employed in soliciting the Prince to return to Court, now the object of his displeasure was removed. But his Highness shewed an Aversion unless the Tories were taken in: which, it was said, gave Pultney much uneasiness. The Tuesday before the Parliament met, Pultney carried many Messages, between the heads of the Opposition assembled at Carleton House,[185] and the Ministers assembled at Lord Wilmington's About his Highnesses return to Court. Nor were the Terms settled 'till two in the Morning: When a Letter was sent to the King (then in Bed) that the Prince would wait on him the next day. Accordingly his Highness came the next day attended only by his own servants. The King only asked him how the Princess and Childeren did. After a short stay the Prince returned to Carleton House: and was immediately followed by the great Officers of the Court and all Persons then present. And Guards were sent to attend him. So there was to Appearance a reconciliation; which gave general Satisfaction.

The Heads of the Tories fearing to be left in the lurch met that Evening at Dodding-tons[186] to consult what to do. And came to a resolution to go all in a body to Court the next Day. Accordingly the next day (all except Shippen, and a very few more) followed the discontented Whigs to a place where few of them had ever been before. And prehaps it was not ill Pollicy: for by it they endeavoured to whipe off the imputation of dissaffection to the Family: they made it difficult for the discontented Whigs who had acted with them in concert so long to quit them: they showed the King their attachment to the Prince; and their power by that means to oppose him: And they shewed the Prince that if he Abandoned them they could seek their protection from the King. The King received them very graciously: and would sometimes afterwards in pleasantry ask, if any of his new acquaintance were at Court. His Majesty appeared gayer than usual through<ou>t this whole affair; but must be inwardly dissatisfied: and I have heard he should say; 'though they force my Ministers from me, I hope they will leave me my old acquaintance to play at Cards with'.

The Tories were after this very overbearing in the House; frequently throwing out hints of a total Change in the Ministry, and of bringing Offenders to Justice: the Prince's party either approving, or not daring to Oppose their proceedings. So Elections were all determined as they pleased. Nor was any Person heard with Patience that offered to contradict them in any thing.

One very good effect was that the Supply now went on with Ease: And when the same number of land Forces were moved for as last year Mr. Pulteney seconded the Motion. He said he was against soldiers when they were unnecessary, but they were now necessary. He laid it down as a Maxim that this Nation was to hold the Ballance

---

[185] Frederick, prince of Wales, owned Carlton House in Pall Mall. In late 1742 he rented and moved into Leicester House, but continued to use Carlton House for private parties. *Survey of London*, XXXIV, 447–8.

[186] According to Lord Egmont, the opposition meeting on 17 Feb. at the house of George Bubb Dodington consisted of 'above 100 Lords and Members of the House of Commons'. H.M.C., *Egmont Diary*, III, 254.

in Europe. There was no supporting it but by a Power on the Continent able to oppose France: That Power was the Queen of Hungary. That we were to proceed in supporting her neither with timidity nor rashness: not so as to engage us in an unnecessary War with France; Yet to shew France we were prepared: That Flanders was a Barrier to us, as well as to Holland: therefore that we should send Forces thither with such a Man at their head, as would convince the World we were in earnest: This, if it had no other effect, would occasion a powerfull diversion in favour of the Queen of Hungary: If things were gone so far already, that we could not support the Ballance on the Continent, we must then as an Island collect ourselves within ourselves, and stand on the defensive. He said none could suspect him of design in what he said, who had renounced all pretentions to Place or Power. – Shippen said he had never courted any past Ministry, nor would he any that was to come: that he was against this number of Forces now, for the same Reasons he was last year. That as the number was the same as last year, and the Arguments for them exactly the same; if we were to pursue still exactly the same Measures; he did not see why we might not still as well have the same man to conduct them. Vyner and Cholmodely said something to the same effect. Lord Cornbury made a fine speech to compliment Mr. Pulteney, and congratulate the Nation on the Kings taking the tacit Advice of his Parliament and the good effects like to follow.

March 9.

The Opposers, now thinking themselves secure, renewed their Attempt for a secret Comittee: and Lord Limerick made a Motion (which was seconded by Sir J. St. Aubin) that a Committee should be appointed to Enquire into the Conduct of our affairs both at home and abroad for the last Twenty years; which was the Aera of the late Ministers Power. It was understood, that there was to be another Question, that it was to be a Secret Committee of 21 and thinking themselves sure of success; they intended not (as I was told by one of them) to trust the Nomination to a Ballot; but to propose 21 Names Openly and put them to the Vote: But they were much disappointed, when on a Division by 244 Against 242. Pulteney was Absent, his Daughter dying during the debate: and Sandys was not yet reelected. The other three new Lords of the Treasury voted with their old Friends for the Enquiry. Some of the Prince's Servants were Absent: (Whether with his Approbation was unknown) and 4 or 5 Scotch Members who depended on Lord Tweedale, lately made secretary of State for Scotland: which Post had long been sunk, and was now revived to gain him.

The next day the Duke of Argyle resigned; and the Posts, which he had injoyed but a fortnight, imediately restored to those from whom they had been taken to Accommodate him. The Earl of Stair[187] was called from his Retirement, and Appointed General, and Ambassador to Holland in his room. It was said the Prince came to Court on a Promise (which was the only Condition) that the Duke of Argyle should be taken in: and that he now resigned to keep his own promise with the Tories, that he would not continue in, if he could not assist them. And it was given out that the new Lords of the Treasury would soon do the same. But when that was found not to be so; and that the Admiralty was filled up without one Tory in the Comission; they grew very angry, and seemed resolved to push things to extremity. Therefore they gave out amongst the Populace; that Lord Orford still governed the Councils: And that he

---

[187] John Dalrymple (1673–1747), 2nd earl of Stair, was appointed ambassador to the Hague, Mar. 1742–Nov. 1743, field marshall (18 Mar. 1742), governor of Minorca (14 Apr.), and c. in c. of the allied forces in Flanders (21 Apr.). He had been dismissed from his previous posts for opposition to Walpole in 1733.

came secretly by Night to Court from New Park:[188] which made his best Friends desirous he should remove from thence, to Obviate any pretence for such Calumny. They also stired up an Opposition where they could, to the New Lords of the Admiralty, in their re-elections. Lord Baltimore was strongly Opposed in Surry. And Doctor Lee (who was lately a great favorite) was now rejected where he was before Chose: Though he Accepted his Post, with the Approbation of the Duke of Bridgwater who brought him in; and had (as was said) his promis to be re-elected. He continued out of the House 'till the end of the Session, when the Government made a Vacancy for him in Another Borough.[189]

March 12.

The new Chancellor of the Exchequer was again introduced into the House: and immediately moved the 4s. Land Tax. For which he was reproached in the House by some of the Tories: who said, they had been deluded with a promis, that it should be kept for the last Ways and Means, to see if a shilling might not be taken off. He said it was Evident the Service could not be supply'd without it: and denied he had ever given any such assurance: Which was true: for the thing had only been mention'd by Lord Orford and Mr. Pulteney in a former Debate to court popularity.

March 15.

The Chancellor of the Exchequer moved to close the Committee for Elections for this Session: which had been usual, and he said was now necessary to give Gentlemen ease: and to allow more time for the Publick business: This was strennously opposed by his old Friends (who found they gained by hearing elections, by having him and others go with him by reason of old Engagements) but he carried his point on a division by a Majority of above 20.[190] It made them Almost as angry with the new Chancellor of the Exchequer as with the old one.

Much time was taken up this Session in hearing the Petitions of the Merchants, of which that from several Merchants of London, was the cheif. Sir Robert Godschal, Lord Mayor and one of their own Members, was put into the Chair of the Committee. And the Management at the Bar was left solely to Glover,[191] a young Hamburgh Merchant who was distinguished by his Poetry; but more by his Favour with the Prince: and who was employed to promote all popular schemes in the City against the Court: and who was very desirous of shewing himself on this Occasion. But he did not Answer the Expectations conceived of him, proceeding heavily and without Method. A List of the Captures (Amounting to above 300) was delivered at the Door, with a Chart of the Channel and neighbouring Coasts. The cheif heads of complaint were; Neglect in Appointing Convoys; in stationing Cruisers; Neglect of Commanders; not settling a Cartel for exchange of Prisoners; impressing Seamen out of Merchant Ships; disregard of those complaints by the Admiralty and Regency. On hearing the Evidence the Committee came to a Resolution; that there had not been necessary care taken in stationing Cruisers in and near the Chanel and soundings. Which was generaly thought true. Though the Admiralty excused it, by saying they

---

[188] Walpole's home at Richmond, which he had occupied as deputy ranger of Richmond Park since 1726 (his eldest son was ranger). See J.H. Plumb, *Sir Robert Walpole* (2 vols., 1956–60), II, 90 n. 40.

[189] Baltimore and Lee had to face re-election to the Commons having accepted positions of profit under the crown. Lee, opposed by his patron, Bridgwater, was not re-elected. He was returned for Devizes on 23 July 1742. Sedgwick, II, 244.

[190] 211 to 190. *C.J.*, XXIV, 129.

[191] Richard Glover (1712–85), poet and Hamburg merchant in London.

were a Board of Execution, and having been ordered by Government to get Ships ready for other services; that they had it not in their power to send so many as they might otherwise on this; especialy considering the difficulty of Maning the Fleet. And there had been always cruisers out, though not so many as might be wished.

The next Resolution was, that the refusal of Protections, and delays of Convoys to the Portugal Fleet had given the French an Opportunity to introduce new species of Wollen Goods there.

This was grounded on no Proof, but an incidental expression in a Letter from the British Consul at Lisbon. And if such Introduction was Fact, it was to be assigned, to another Cause, viz, the running Irish Wool into France. The Evidence was summed up by Glover in an inflaming speech of two hours. His Manner was theatrical and ridiculous. His Argument most Malicious. For he laid it down as a certain principle (what had long been inculcated in Print, but what was incredible to common sense) that there had long been a formed design to Affront and depress the Merchants; and to ruin the Trade of the Nation: and he wrested every the most trivial fact or Accidental expression to prove it. They ordered the Resolutions to be laid before the King, to introduce a change in the Admiralty; which it occasioned: but the change (as I said before) was not to such hands as the Opposers wished.

I believe there is no one Cause, to which the fall of the Minister is to be more ascribed, than to the hatred of the City of London. Which grew very inveterate after the Excise Scheme: by which particular Traders thought their Interests might be Affected. And therefore endeavoured to render him Odious. This naturaly raised his resentment; so that he held them in defiance and contempt, thinking himself secure in a Majority in Parliament. When I say he was Obnoxious to the City, I mean the inferior sort, of whom the Common Council was composed: for he ever retained much Credit with the monied men, especialy the Directors of the three Great Companies; who were always ready to favour his Schemes for raising the Supply. But the most Active and clamorous Citizens were generaly chosen Members of the Common Council, whose Acts were regarded as the Acts of the whole City. The Common Council was guided by particular Clubs and Cabals; and these were dictated to by a few Boutefeus. These had their Directions from some Leaders in both Houses of Parliament, who found them to be usefull Engines of Opposition. For they could by their means at any time obtain, such Addresses to the Crown, Petitions to the Houses or Instructions to their Members as they liked: Which were commonly no better than so many Libels on the Administration. These were studiously dispersed by means of the Newes Papers, and the Example of the Metropolis was recommended to other Cities and Corporations. So that the City was the Bell-weather of Sedition; and the source from whence the Waters of Bitterness and Discontent flowed through the Nation. This should be a caution to any Government not to establish populous Corporations, which generaly grow ungovernable; and turn the Privilidges they injoy above their Fellow Subjects to the Prejudice of that Power who granted it. But when they are once established, it is the Interest of a Minister to gain them to his Party.

March 23.

The Motion for a secret Committee was revived, Pulteney being returned to the House. This was unparliamentary; As it had before been twice rejected this Session. But to palliate it the Terms were a little Varied: and now it was a Committee to inquire into the Conduct of the Earl of Orford during the ten last years of his being Chancellor of the Exchequer: leaving it dubious whether it was to relate to his behaviour in that Office, or to his Conduct in General. The first was much pretended in the Debate, to engage the concurrence of the House, though the Words admitted of, and were afterwards taken in a larger sense. This being now carried by a very small Majority,[192] and the Committee being to consist of 21 Persons chosen by Ballot;[193] Lists were delivered by both Parties to their Friends; which few on either side altered, for such Alterations would render the Schemes on either side Abortive: but in such Numbers some few alterations there were, and always must be. In the Court List, six or seven of the most Moderate in the other List were inserted; which might induce some of the other side to put some of the most moderate of the Court List into their Own; by which means some of the most violent in that List, as Sir Watkin Williams, Sir John Cotton, Doddington, and Littleton were rejected, which shewed them the secret ill Opinion the House entertained of them; and five or six of the Court List were elected; who were a Check to any violence in the Committee And gave private intimations from time to time of their proceedings.

The Committee having power to send for Papers and Records, send Queries to most of the Offices concerned in the Revenue; but received general and unsatisfactory Answers. And having power to examine in the most solemn manner, they called a Midlesex Justice to their Assistance to Administer a general Oath to the Persons summoned to attend, to answer all such Questions as should be proposed. The first interruption to their proceedings was from Paxton Sollicitor to the Treasury;[194] who refused to answer a Question, saying it might affect himself. This was complained of by Lord Limerick their Chairman to the House; who committed him to Newgate,[195] where he remained a close Prisoner 'till the end of the Session. And this was done without the House being informed of the Question proposed to him. Which seems to me a very precipitate step; for if the Question be unknown, it cannot be known, whether his Objection was not legal; and if it was legal, his Imprisonment was unjust. This implicit defference of the House to the Committee, rendered their Authority terrible to the Subject; who saw he held his liberty but at their pleasure.

Finding they could make no important discoveries, they made a Report:[196] which was no more than a Complaint, of the Interruption of their Proceedings by the Obstinancy of Paxton, and the impossibility of going on without the Assistance of the Legislature. On this a Bill was brought in to indemnify all Persons who could give any information relative to the Earl of Orford; which was intended to be followed by another of Pains and Penalties, if they then refused to Answer. The Indemnifying Bill (as it was called) met with strong Opposition in the House, where it passed by a very small Majority: and was rejected by the Lords on the first reading.[197] Upon this the most violent in the House of Commons moved for a Committee (which was Appointed) to inspect the Lords Journals to know, what was become of the Bill: And their Report the next Day that the Lords had rejected it, a Motion was made by Lord Strange and seconded by Lord Barrington, that the Lords rejecting that Bill was an interruption of the Publick Justice of the Nation.[198] This was spoke against by the most serious and Moderate of the Opposers: as it tended directly to a breach with the other

---

[192] By 252 to 245. *C.J.*, XXIV, 146.

[193] Which took place on 26 Mar. *Ibid.*, pp. 151–2.

[194] Nicholas Paxton, solicitor to the treasury, 1730–27 July 1742.

[195] The complaint was on 13 April and the committal to Newgate on the 15th. *Ibid.*, pp. 180–1, 184.

[196] On 13 May. *Ibid.*, pp. 225–8.

[197] The bill was brought in on 15 May and passed 214 to 186 on the 19th; it was rejected by the Lords on the 25th (on its 2nd reading); the committee was appointed on the 26th by 164 to 159, and gave its report on the 27th. *Ibid.*, pp. 230, 245, 258–60.

[198] The motion was rejected by 245 to 193 on 27 May. *Ibid.*, p. 260.

House: and as it was unjust, for any branch of the Legislature to pretend to dictate to the other or censure their proceedings.

Though the Committee had declared they could not proceed without the Indemnifying Bill; yet they continued to meet and about the begining of July produced another Report:[199] consisting cheifly of these Articles. 1st. That the Treasury had made a disadvantageous Bargain in the rate of the Exchange for money to be remitted to Jamaca to pay the Troops. 2. That Lord Orford had interfered in the Wendover Election against Lord Limerick; and at Weymouth against Doddington. 3. That much greater sums than usual had been issued to Scroope the Secretary of the Treasury,[200] they summoned him before, after having obtained leave of the House of which he was a Member. He said as several of those Sums were paid him to the Kings private Order he could not answer without permission. That he thought the Oath illegal, which he could not take in such general terms as to Answer all Questions: but if they would propose any Question to him, if he could answer it, he would then take the Oath to do it. It was thought they would have complained of this to the House: but they had too much complaisance for the Court; where some of them already had, and others expected soon to make their Market.

When the Report was read, it was ordered to lie on the Table; no one offering to make any Motion on it. Nor was it afterwards resumed. At the Close of it, the Committee said they had before them several Matters relating to the Convention;[201] to which they would give all convenient dispatch. This put the Ministry under the Necessity of keeping the Houses sitting, that there might be no pretence to say they were cut short in their enquiry; though it was now late in the summer and few Members were left in Town.[202]

---

[199] Delivered on 30 June. *Ibid.*, pp. 289–331.
[200] John Scrope, M.P. See Appendix.
[201] Of El Pardo in 1739.
[202] The session ended on 15 July 1742.

November 16. 1742.

This was the first day of the second Session of this Parliament; which met after a short Prorogation of four Months. The Extraordinary ferment of the last Session was now succeeded by as great a Calm. The King acquainted the Houses with the happy turn of affairs in favour of the Queen of Hungary. That in order to support her, he had sent some Hannoverian Troops into the Low Countries not doubting but the Parliament would assist him in such necessary measures; as also in Prosecuting the War with Spain.

This was answered by very satisfactory Addresses from both Houses. That of the upper House passed without a division: none but the Earls of Westmoreland and Chesterfield offering any thing against it. The last saying he had many Objections; but should not then Offer them; because he did not find the House disposed to hear them.

In the lower House, the Address was handsomly moved and seconded by Lord Hartington and Lord George Sackville. Waller first made the common Objection that it was too particular, and might preclude future debates: and that we ought to return to the old usage of short and general Addresses. The Chancellor of the Exchequer answered that such Addresses might be well in times of Peace: but as the present practice had continued for above forty years; it was an improper time to change it, when we ought to encourage our Allies by the Vigor of our proceedings. Shippen and others objected; that it implied a promis of paying the Hannoverian Troops, which they never hoped to see in British Pay. And Pitt insisted on them being employed by the Kings Prerogavitive <sic>, without previous knowledge or consent of Parliament: which he called taking a Vote of Credit. It was answered: Hannover was not concerned in the Quarrel; but those Troops were employed for us. The Parliament must judge whether the Service was necessary. If it was they would as soon pay Hannoverian Troops as others; since they were as usefull, if not more so, as being subject to the same Prince. And Sir John Barnard declared, he thought they had been usefull in diverting France from Aiding Against the King of Sardinia; or sending more Forces against the Queen of Hungary; whom it was Absolutely necessary to support, for our own preservation.

On a division 259 were for the address proposed and 150 against it: a greater Majority, than ever I remember at the begining of any Session. Which may be ascribed to several reasons. One: that the Patriots (taken in on the dismission of the Earl of Orford) now joyned with the Court: prehaps, from principle; prehaps, from indignation for being libelled by the Tories for leaving them, and thence perceiving they could not support themselves any other way. Another: that the Prince's servants, and others having expectations from him, were come over; except Pitt and Lyttleton, who did not obey his Orders. Another: that many had expectations from the new Ministry: or saw nothing blameable in their Conduct. And the reasons for supporting a War, entered into by Advice of Parliament, were so Strong, that the Supplies went on unanimously; Nobody daring to Oppose them. This was a great disapointment to a few Boutefeus: who had procured Instructions to Members from London, Worcester etc., not to grant Supplies; hoping the Example would be followed by other Places, and raise a flame in the Nation. But these Instructions were regarded by sober Persons as subversive of the Constitution. Were opposed by counter Instructions from Bristol, Notingham etc. and were the subject of much ridicule both in and out of the House.

November 30.

Waller moved to address for Copies of the Defensive Alliances, mentioned in the Kings Speech, with the Czarina, and King of Prussia. This was deny'd: because it was not explained what use was intended to be made of them: because it was unparliamentary, his Majesty having only communicated the Newes to the House, and not made any demand in consequence of them: and because they were not compleated; for though such Treaties were agreed on, as his Majesty had informed the House, yet Mr. Pelham said, he could take on him to affirm, that one of them was not yet ratified by the respective Princes; and he believed neither.

December 1.

Lyttleton moved to revive the secret Committee and was seconded by Sir Watkyn Williams. The Pretence was that they had made important discoveries; and would have proceeded further if they had not been cut short in their Enquiry: and Sir Watkyn said, the Parliament should not have been Prorogued, but continued by Adjournment, as was done in the case of the Committee appointed to examine Harley and Prior.[203] – It was Answered that last Session, their discoveries were not thought of great Moment, for Nobody moved to take the Report into Consideration. That so far were they from being cut short, that they sat 'till every Body was tired: longer than any such Committee ever did before: and might be said to die a natural Death. That it was not a time now to keep the Minds of the People in a ferment, when we should be unanimous in the common Cause of Europe. That our Allies could have no dependance on us; if they saw us quarrelling with one another. But might fear we should desert them as we did before. Lord Cornbury (who had been of the Committee) said, he should be Against trusting any Persons with the like Powers again, without the most Absolute Necessity. – On a Division 280 were against it and 160 for it.[204]

December 3.

The Chancellor of the Exchequer being very Odious to the Opposition, for having deserted them: the young men amongst them dedicated this day to him: resolving to divert themselves at his Expence. Lord Barrington moved for a Place-bill, precisely the same, that the Chancellor had brought in for many years together. And said, he was sure it must now pass; because he doubted not of his Assistance.

He was seconded by Lord Hilsborough and Sir Watkin Williams and others read passages out of speeches, the Chancellor had formerly made for the Bill. After being very much ridiculed, he said, he had found by long experience, that such a general Bill would not pass. That the Way was to gain a little at a time; in which they had rarely failed, as was evident from many Statutes; particularly that which passed last session,[205] which was then thought satisfactory: not that he should be hereafter against going farther on a proper Occasion. The Motion was rejected by above 20 Majority.[206]

December 6.

Sir William Yonge moved for the same number of Guards and Garrisons for this year, as were Employed the last. Amounting (exclusive of 11550 Marines) to 39,965 Men. Which he said were at present disposed of after this manner. About 16,000 in Flanders: 4000 in Scotland: 4000 in America: and the remainder were in England, of which there were 2300 Invalids in Garrison; and about 3500 Guards about London.

---

[203] Robert Harley, 1st earl of Oxford, and Matthew Prior in 1715.

[204] The vote was 186 for and 253 against. *C.J.*, XXIV, 348.

[205] The act to exclude certain officers from being members of the house of commons passed on 21 May and received the royal assent on 16 June 1742. *Ibid.*, pp. 248, 276–7.

[206] The vote was 221 to 196. *Ibid.*, p. 351.

So that exclusive of these there could not be assembled above 8000 men in England to march upon any Emergency.

There was no Objection, but to that Part of the Forces which were sent to Flanders. It was said, that instead of those Forces it would be better to give the Queen of Hungary the Money they would Cost, which would pay a double Number of her own Forces. That it was not the Intention the last Session, that they should be sent, unless there had been an assurance beforehand that the Dutch would joyn us: that now it was evident they would not, they should be recalled; since they could be of no service without them. That our Auxiliaries could not Act in the Empire against the Emperor: and that they apprehended was the reason that the Hessians and Hannoverians did not follow Maillebois[207] in his March towards Prague, where they might have Assisted the Queen of Hungary: but Marched towards Flanders where they could not. – It was Answered: that the Forces in Flanders were desired by the Queen of Hungary, who best knew her own Necessities. That they were evidently of service to her there; for by Garrisoning her Towns, they gave her an Opportunity of drawing her own Forces from them. That it was better for this Nation to send her Men than Money: for by sending the Money the whole is spent Abroad; but by sending the Men not Above a third part is so. That the Forces now there were ready for Action; which was better than to have Forces to raise. That the Dutch had not absolutely denied to come in: The Forces being in Flanders was an encouragement to them to do so; but if they were withdrawn they certainly would not. That the Hannoverians could not March 'till Mallebois departed from their Frontiers: the moment he did, they marched to that Place where their service was thought most necessary. And Mr. Pelham said, he could take upon him to assert, that they would Act in any Place either in or out of the Empire, whenever required.

December 10.

Sir William Yonge moved in the Committee to take 16000 Hannoverians into the British pay. This was the Point on which the Opposition resolved to make their principal Stand. The People were prepared to believe it a very ill thing. A Pamphlet was published, intitled the Case of the Hannover Forces:[208] said to be written by the French Minister, or at least at his direction; the tendency of which was to shew; that since the Accession of this Family to the Crown, the Interest of Hannover was always the ultimate view in all our Foreign transactions: that the Interest of this Nation had constantly been sacrificed to that View, contrary to the Act of Settlement:[209] and then the People were left to draw this Conclusion; that if that Act was broken through, they were absolved from their Allegence.

The Debate against the Proposition, consisted for the most part of general Declamation. When once we took these Troops into our pay we should never get rid of them. That it was making us a Province tributary to Hannover. That this was a step, no Englishman could aprove of; such a one as the late Minister durst never Attempt: and Lord Carteret, who was looked on as the Author of this Advice was inveighed against by all as a bold, rash, enterprizing Minister. And Sir J. Cotton went so far as to call him Infamous Minister: he said he thought he understood Foreign Affairs better than

---

[207] Jean Baptiste François Desmarets (1682–1762), marquis de Maillebois, French soldier.
[208] The anonymous *The Case of the Hanover Forces in the Pay of Great Britain, Impartially and Freely Examined: with some Seasonable Reflections on the Present Conjuncture of Affairs* was written by Chesterfield and Edmund Waller.
[209] Of 1701, which established the protestant succession in the house of Hanover.

any Man in the Kingdom; and if you talked with him, he would not scruple to tell you that he thought so. Sir J. St. Aubin said, that he had flattered his Masters Passions to secure his own power; and had taken Advantage of a Virtuous Quality in his Prince, a love for his Native Country to persuade him to a thing, which might be a prejudice both to that Country and this. But I heard no real Argument (and indeed it was difficult to find any) if Foreign Troops were to be hired; why these was not as proper as any other: for it was confessed they were as good; and exactly the same Price. The only things which bore any colour of Reason against it were 1. That these Troops could not act against the Emperor; because by an Article of the Treaty of Munster,[210] if any German Prince made War against the Emperor and Empire, his Dominions should be put under the Ban of the Empire. – 2. That if we should have ill success, and Hannover should be attacked for supplying these Troops, we might think ourselves bound in honour to support our Prince in defence of it contrary to the Act of Settlement. – To the first of these it was answered; that these Troops Acting as Auxiliaries to the Queen of Hungary, would not act against the Empire, since it was in defence of the Pragmatic Sanction;[211] which had been confirmed by the Diet, and made a Law of the Empire. To the second, that we were under no greater Obligation to these than to any other mercenary forces: and that we could not be engaged in defence of Hannover without consent of Parliament; and what was done with such consent could not be a Violation of the Act of Settlement. – Two reasons were urged to shew, that these Troops were to be prefered to any other. The one: That they were under the direction of the same Prince: the other: That whereas other foreign Troops were always hired for a certain term of years; these might be dismissed the moment the Service ceased.

---

[210] Of 1648, which ended the Thirty Years War.

[211] The Habsburg family law of 1713 was designed to establish the undivided succession of the heirs of the Emperor Charles VI throughout the Habsburg lands. When it became clear he would be succeeded by his daughter, Maria Theresa, Charles embarked on a diplomatic negotiation to secure the agreement of the major European powers. Britain agreed to the Pragmatic Sanction in 1731. On Charles's death in 1740, Prussia repudiated it and invaded Silesia, thus precipitating the war of the Austrian succession.

December 1. 1743.

This was the first Day of the third Session: when the Parliament met after a Campaign successfull on all sides beyond expectation. His Majesty<'s> great Personal Bravery in the Battle of Dettingen,[212] had contributed much to the success of the Day. The Newes was received with great applause at first; and had rendered him popular. This made the enemies of his Government redouble their Arts to sully his Glory, and rob him of the Affections of the People. And they prevailed so far, that it began to be doubted amongst the lower sort, whether his Majesty had been present at the Battle: But as this could not long be Maintain'd against Matter of Fact: others maliciously insisted on his partiality to the Hannoverians in the Camp: As his Wearing a yellow Sash on the Day of the Battle; and his shewing more countenance and leaning more to the Advice of the Hannoverian Officers than the English. And it is certain, that not only the Earl of Stair, and the Duke of Marleborough (who resigned their Commands) but many other Officers returned home very discontented.

When the King returned home, he was not received with those demonstrations of Joy as might have been reasonably expected. And the Common Council of London in their Address taught a lecture of Sedition to the rest of the Kingdom, by designedly omitting the least Mention of the Victory at Dettingen. But their example was not follow'd by Bristol and Shrewsbury, who gratefully commemorated it.

The Address of the House of Commons was moved by Coke (eldest son to Lord Lovel) and seconded by Mr. York (eldest son to the Chancellor). It was (as usual) a repetition of the Kings Speech. One objection to it was, that it seemed to Approve of a Treaty (now called the Treaty of Worms)[213] which the King said he had concluded with the Queen of Hungary, and the King of Sardinia, and which he would lay before the House, before it was laid before the House. <sic> To which it was Answered, it was not an Approbation of the Articles of the Treaty (which were hereafter to be considered) but only of an Alliance between those Powers. The Rest was all Declamation. Pitt, speaking of the Libels that were complained of, said, there was some Matter in those Writings to be Adopted by that House: some Jealousies which he adopted. He was glad the King escaped from Dettingen; but those were blameable that advised a scheme that brought him into such danger. The Cause (though great) was too mean to call for his presence. The Treaty of Worms was a new period in our Foreign affairs, tho it looked fair (it might like the Convention) be clogged with a Protest. And he feared we might be brought into a War of Acquisition under pretence of securing the liberties of Europe. For his own part, he would only be tied down to support the Queen of Hungary. The Dutch did not joyn us: for they came the latter end of September when the Campaign was over. He would avow the Spirit now in the Nation. Ten Millions dislike the Troops of Hannover. There was one Minister who seems to have renounced Great Britain. The Gallant part of the Nation were returned home discontented. And he wished a Negative to the Address, that the King might feel that this Nation is not at this hour a contented Nation. – Winnington said, that the Success of this year might lessen the fears that Gentlemen had the last; as it had falsified their Prophecies. That vigorous measures were yet necessary; and that you could not carry on the War with one Man less. If Europe is now in a better state, it was owing in some measure to the Councils at Home. Let the Actions of Ministers justify them: but some Refflections went so high, as they could mean but *One*. He had not heard of a sole Minister: but if

---

[212] Fought in Bavaria on 16/27 June 1743 when a mixed force of British, Hanoverian and Austrian troops defeated the French. It was the last battle in which a British king led his troops.

[213] Signed 2/13 Sept. 1743.

there was, the Gentleman who spoke before him, had contributed more to the making him, than he had. – Doddington (in justification of his prophecies last year) said, that he had foretold our Troops would not Act, yet he never dreamt, but that if they were Attacked they would defend themselves. If we had the Victory, why did we not pursue the Enemy? or why not save our Men, but leave the dead to bury the dead? Hannoverians were the only persons preserved. In this Modern Way of Address the lumping things together before they could be considered was of ill consequence. If the House was not precluded by it, it was deceiving the Crown; and if they were precluded; they might after such an Address return to their Estates as Tenants and Receivers to gratify the Receivers of their Noble Minister, both at home and Abroad. – Fox said, this way of Addressing was not unprecedented, for the Convention was so Approved by the Gentlemen who spoke before him. – Lord Cornbury said, The Country and City had called for and forced the Crown to a War; that the Parliament gave the Army to be employed Abroad, for it was not wanted at home, and that the good effects of their being so employed was visible in the glorious but exploded Victory of Dettingen. As no Amendment was proposed it is most probable the Opposers intended not to divide: but on the Question Sir Francis Dashwood forced them to it. And on a division 278 were for the Address and 149 Against it.[/]

January 18.[214]

In the Comittee of Supply it was debated whether the Hannoverian Troops should be continued in pay. This Question had been anticipated by a Motion before the Recess, to Address the King to dismiss them. And on the Question of the British Forces in Flanders it was a point on which the Opposition had raised the discontent and Jealousy of the People. As they had told it abroad, so they maintained in the debate, that it was giving up the Interests of this Country, and making it a Province to Hannover: that it was the scheme of one Infamous Flagitious Minister, intoxicated with Power, who got and maintained his Power by flattering the Passion of his Master in this Point.

Pitt called him a cruel Task-Master and Sir John St. Aubin, one that only gave us leave to register his Will. Pitt said, he was the only Person that supported these Troops, and they the only Persons that supported him. He said he acquitted the respectable part of the Ministry of any hand in the scheme (intending to compliment Mr. P<elham> between whom and Lord C<arteret> it was thought both in Town and Country there was a competition for Powers). And H<ume> C<ampbell>[215] addressing him told him he had now an Opportunity of making himself a truly popular Minister, and gaining for ever the Affections of the Nation. But he generously said in the Debate, if there could be one Man base enough to flatter his Master for the sake of Power, and an other so cowardly as to give up his Opinion for the sake of Popularity; however he might detest the first he thought the last the most contemptible. Nor did the Insinuations stop at Lord C<arteret> but went even to the K<ing> (whom young Stanley, rashly in direct terms affirmed guilty of Partiality to those Troops): and Sir J. St. Aubin said, he had lost the hearts of the brave British soldiers, who saved him from being lead captive through the streets of Paris. And many called not only the Troops, but the

---

[/] What follows was not wrote into the book from whence the former part was transcribed, but was on loose peices of paper – of my Fathers writing.

[214] This section of the journal appears at the end of vol. 4 of the manuscript.

[215] See Appendix. Three other M.P.s have the initials H.C., but Hume Campbell, being a friend of Pitt, is the most likely here.

People and Electorate of Hannover, base, beggarly and pusillanimous: and bestow'd every injurious Epithet they could think of: which as it was unprovoked, seemed a designed affront to the Royal Family. The youngest Grenville[216] wished the Electorate under the Sea, and Pit to see it given by consent of the Royal Family to a younger Branch. Murray, Solicitor General, said, that could not be done without Consent of the Diet, and doubted if with such Consent The Family could devest itself of it: and therefore if we were uneasy that it was governed by the same Prince, where can our Discontents end. And Aislabie said, it had been considered when the Succession was settled, and found impracticable. In debating against the Question two Propositions were maintained. Some averred no Troops at all were necessary; others that these particular Troops were improper. To support these Propositions various Arguments were offered: many of them contradictory to others. Some said we were an Island. And therefore should not concern ourselves in Wars on the Continent. The Ballance of Power Sir J. St. Aubin said was a Variable Thing; and the People were jealous it was only used as a pretence to open our Treasures for the Electorate: and that we must not ruin ourselves to support our Allies. – Others said the Ballance was no longer maintainable, France was too powerfull and the other Powers too Weak. Some said we were not to Attempt it unless the Dutch joyned us more heartily; who came too late last year for the Campaign, which shewed they thought our schemes impracticable, and only made a shew of joyning that they might not intirely break with us. Others thought we had gained our end, since the Queen of Hungary was in possession of her Dominions; we were strong enough without those Troops to act on the defensive. Those who argued against these Troops in particular, said, if we gave the Queen of Hungary Money she could hire other Troops cheaper; or that we might ourselves. Others would give a larger sum for other Troops, to Appease the jealousy of the People, who feared we should never get rid of them. They were accused of Cowardice and Disobedience: it was said they could never serve again with our Troops, who hated them, for the partiality shewn them, and for the Honours they had usurped of Guarding the Kings Quarters; and being generaly nearest them. And that if the King went Abroad it would be dangerous to venture himself in an Army so divided.

It was answered, this was not a Time to Disband, when every other Power in Europe was Augmenting. It was sacrificing our own Troops in Flanders; it was deserting our Allies as in 1712.[217] (And as Mr. York said) with double Infamy because without giving them Notice. The Queen of Hungary's affairs would relapse. It was giving up all to France; who would become Absolute on the Continent; which would be followed by the loss of our Trade and Naval Power. We must make Peace with Sword in hand: France was now exerting to make one great Push, and As she succeeded, we were to expect either a reasonable Peace, or a prolongation of the War. – The Queen of Hungary desired Troops rather than Money. You cannot change these for others. None can be had of the Swiss: Would you hire them of the Elector of Cologne? He is Brother to the Emperor.[218] Of the Elector of Saxony? He hath claims on the Queen of H<ungary>'s Dominions. These are good Troops: They are ready; and as to any Jealousy, that these Troops were hired for the sake of Hannover; it arose from misrepresentation; for it was the Cause of Great Britain, and not Hannover, whose Interest

---

[216] Richard Grenville. See Appendix.

[217] When the tory ministry issued the duke of Ormonde with the infamous restraining orders.

[218] Charles VII (1697–1745), elector of Bavaria since 1726, and elected emperor in 1742 in the absence of a male Habsburg heir to Charles VI. He was the only non-Habsburg emperor (besides Francis I, husband of Maria Theresa) between 1438 and the end of the Holy Roman Empire in 1806. His brother, Clemens August, was the electoral prince archbishop of Cologne.

it was to be Neuter; or rather against the House of Austria. That these Troops had misbehaved there was no Evidence, and General Campbel[219] said he was near some of them that behaved Well. That they disobeyed Orders there was no more appeared, but that it was said, that Orders were delivered by Lord Stairs Aid de Camp to a Lieutenant Colonel (who's name was unknown) for the Rear to pursue the Enemy; who said he must have Orders from his Superior Officer. And General Onslow[220] declared he never heard of it till he returned to England: And Murray said, the Noble Lord had forgot himself 'till reminded of it in England. As to guarding the Kings Quarters, they never did it after the Kings arrived at Aschamfenberg, and then complained that the English Guards did not come to relieve them. As to their being generaly nearest to the Kings Quarters, that was Accidental: For the English being always on the Right (as the Post of Honour) and the Hannoverians on the Left, and the Kings Quarters being in the best house of a Town, he was nearest one part of the Army or another as it happened. – And as to the Misunderstanding between them and the English Troops, it was said to be no more than what was common in Armies composed of different Nations; and Marshal Wade who was to Command them, declared he apprehended no ill consequence from it.

On a Division the Question was carried by 271 against 226. It was debated again the next Day on the Report: when Pitt saying he was informed of many Facts, and could produce Persons to prove them, of partiality to these Troops, if any Gentleman doubted of them: he therefore proposed that the House would not agree with the Committee, before they inquired into these Facts. On which Mr. P<elham> said he could not sit still without desiring Gentlemen to consider to what such an Enquiry tended: were it to blame any Minister, it was a thing of no Consequence: he said he would use the Expression of a Noble Lord formerly, he spoke to their discernment and not to their Ears. On which several of the most Moderate Opposers declared, that though they should be against the Forces, they would be Against such an Enquiry, which could only tend to reflect on the King. The Question being insisted on for the Enquiry, it was rejected by 226 against 178 and then the House agreed with the Committee.[221]

The Treaty of Worms being laid before the House, Sir W. Williams moved to Print it for the use of the Members.[222] It was objected to because it was a Treaty not executed, and because the Crown had made no demand upon it. Mr. P<elham> said, he was very willing it should be made publick, but wished it might be by order of Government, and promised they should have it soon.[223] On which Sir W<atkin> acquiesed and withdrew his Motion.

After it was published, Waller said, he infered from several Expressions, that there must be secert Articles which were kept behind. And therefore moved for all the Papers, Letters, Memorials and Articles relative to it.[224] Mr. P<elham> said if they expected all the Corrispondence previous to a Treaty to be laid before the House, they

---

[219] James Campbell (c.1680–1745), maj.-gen. 1739, lt.-gen. 1742; M.P. for Ayrshire 1727–41.

[220] Richard Onslow, M.P. See Appendix.

[221] This vote was on 19 Jan. 1744. *C.J.*, XXIV, 512.

[222] The treaty of Worms was laid before the Commons on 9 Jan. 1744, and was considered in the committee of the whole house on 1 Feb., which reported the following day, when the house agreed to the resolutions 167 to 125. *C.J.*, XXIV, 498–502, 539, 543–4.

[223] It was printed as *The Definitive Treaty of Peace ... Between the Crowns of Great Britain, Hungary, and Sardinia, Concluded at Worms on the 2/13 of September* (1743).

[224] On 25 Jan. 1744. *C.J.*, XXIV, 520.

had better declare at once like Men, that they would never have any more Treaties, for no Power would ever treat with them on those terms. But he assured them on the Word of a Gentleman, there was no secret Article now subsisting, on which any of the Contracting Powers had demands on the other. He had himself signed the Ratification of the Treaty, because he had certain information, if it had not been done the King of Sardinia would have gone over to the Enemy, and then the Spaniards must have prevailed in Italy. And I heard that the Duke of Newcastle said that Day in the other House, where the same Question was agitated, that it was as impossible to maintain a War in Italy without the King of Sardinia, as in Flanders without the Dutch. Pit observing the Expression that no secret Articles were now subsisting, inferred that some Audacious hand might have signed such Articles, unknown to the Valuable part of the Ministry, which they had refused to ratify. And if he could be informed of such, he would himself make it an Article of Impeachment. The most Moderate of the Opposers voted against this Question, which was rejected by about 50 Majority.[225]

January 27.

A Notion had prevailed that an Additional Duty on Suggar was to raise the Supplies of the year. On which a Petition from several Merchants in that Commodity was presented, complaining of the Heavy Duty and how burthensome it was to raise it by Way of Excise. Heathcote had shewn the Petition to Mr. P<elham> who complained of this Indirect way of Petitioning against a Tax to be raised for the Publick service, against the Rules of the House: and throwing in the Word Excise to make the thing Odious; though it was well known he was against that way. When the time came to propose the Ways and Means, he should offer his Proposal and give his Reasons for it; ready to hear, and to come into any better Proposal. And therefore he hoped the Gentlemen would not desire the Petition to be printed at large in the Votes with such invidious insinuations. On which Heathcote and Calvert (the two City Members then present) consented it should not. On which I told Heathcote I was glad they used a Minister well who treated them with Civility.

Soon after he opened his Proposal for a Fund to borrow £2,800,000 for the service of the year, which at 3 per Cent would require £84,000. One Million the East India Company (whose Directors were fast Friends to the Ministry) had offered at 3 per Cent on a Prolongation of their Charter for 14 years, after 23 which they had to come, and three years Notice. The other £1,800,000 was to be raised by subscription for Annuities. He said he had three Funds proposed to him, which he would open to them and leave to another Day for their Consideration. The first an additional Duty of a Farthing per pound on Muscavado Sugars Imported: Another an Additional Duty on Tobacco (which now pays 5¾d per Pound) and the third the Overplus of the Additional Duties laid last year upon Spirits. He said, he prefered the first, as it would fall on the Consumer here and not hinder the re-exportation because of the Drawback. And he opened his Proposal with that Candor, as was universaly pleasing, and every body seemingly Acquiesed. But before the time of going into the Committee the Merchants and Planters took or pretended to take the Alarm; declaring their opinion that the Duty would fall on the Planters, and would be such a load as would force them to abandon the Sugar Colonies, so beneficial to the Trade of the Nation. In the Committee Bladen (one of the Commissioners of Trade) made a set speech against it, and it passed but by a smal Majority. Mr. P<elham> was so fair, as to allow some days for the Report. In the Interim there was a Meeting in the City, to frustrate the Scheme,

---

[225] The vote was 207 to 149 on 25 Jan. *Ibid.*

by proposing a specious thing in lieu of it; which was an additional Duty on Foreign Linnen Imported, in order to encourage the Irish and Scotch Manufactures. This captivated the Scotch Members; so that on the Report: the Resolution of the Committee was rejected by a Majority of 8.[226] – The first time I remember the Ways and Means frustrated – and it was a slight Mr. Pelhams Friends resented as an ill return for his Open dealing.

When they went again into the Committee, Mr. P<elham> proposed the Duty on Spirits, which was what Sir J. Barnard prefered in the former debate, and was supported by him; who said he should be sorry the Ways and Means should be longer debated when a French Fleet was on our Coast. This prevented Lord Limerick moving the Duty on Linnens, who informed the Committee what he intended, with his reasons for it. It was said it was improper to take that for a Fund, before we knew whether it would be a proper regulation in Trade with regard to those Countrys the Linnens came from: which was an Extensive consideration. But if they pleased they might enter on it, in a Committee for that purpose. On which assurance the Duty on Spirits was agreed to both in the Committee and House without a Division.

[226] This vote on 20 Feb. 1744 was 176 to 168. *Ibid.*, pp. 576–7.

EDWARD HARLEY'S PAPERS CONCERNING PARLIAMENTARY AFFAIRS

1. TO LORD HARLEY, 31 JANUARY 1716.

B.L., Add. MS 70381, ff. 164–5.

… There have been a great deal of pains taken to turn out the Auditors, upon Friday last there was a Petition brought into the House of Commons[1] against them, pretending that they took fees for Lottery orders, contrary to an Act of Parliament, which they design'd to have referr'd to Committee to search into it, but it being so dangerous a Precedent for themselves, Part of the Whigs vot'd for the Auditors, so it pass'd in the negative;[2] which was beyond their expectations. Mr Walpole spoke for them and voted otherwise; Coni<ng>sby took care to throw all the dirt, that he could scrape together, but it happned none would stick, or have any effect. The Plump Serjants[3] voted against them, for which deed Con<ingsby> is to get him made a Welsh Judge, but I think the Fool is in a sad case, when he that is to preferr him is to <sic> scandalous to be employed…

2. FROM MARTIN BENSON,[1] LEICESTER FIELDS, 4 APRIL [1717].

Brampton Bryan MSS, Bundle X.

Dear Sir

I defer'd giving myself the pleasure of writing to you the longer that I might be able to acquaint you that I have seen your Father, Lord Oxford and Lord Harley, whom I found all well and all much pleas'd with the accounts which I was in justice oblig'd to give them of you. I received the bill which you drew upon Mr Auditor[2] and he was very generous in paying me for that attendance which sufficiently itself had paid me in the pleasure I received from your company and conversation. I gave your Brother[3] your and Mr Lyddell's[4] token, you have both of you many thanks from him, and there were many enquiries after you at Mr Berresford's. I did not forget to mention to your Father the sending you a horse, he seem'd neither very averse nor very inclinable to it, for the present however I find you must content yourself with an Oxford hack.

I can write you no agreeable news to the University. The Depositions were yesterday consider'd in the house of Lords.[5] I was carried in and hear'd the whole debate, which was very long and lasted til about 7 a clock. Lord Clarendon was put into the Chair and the depositions and other papers were all first read, After which there was a silence for about half an hour, 'til the Duke of Buckingham in his pleasant way mov'd that if they had nothing else to do they might read the papers over again. Then the Duke of Kingston spoke and after him the Bishop of Bristol who spoke several times as did the Bishop of Chester, the Archbishop of York was the only one besides who spoke on that bench. Canterbury was not there. Bishop of Rochester made a motion once or twice to speak but was prevented by some other Lord, so that he did not speak

Letter 1
[1] See *C.J.*, XVIII, 352–3 (27 Jan. 1716).
[2] By 119 to 105, see *ibid.*, p. 353.
[3] Possibly Coningsby's fellow whig Herefordshire M.P., John Birch. See Appendix.

Letter 2
[1] Martin Benson (d. 1752) was EH's tutor at Christ Church, who had gained his B.A. in 1712 and his M.A. in 1713. He went on to gain his D.D. in 1728 and in 1735 become bishop of Gloucester. See Appendix.
[2] Edward 'Auditor' Harley, EH's father. See Appendix.
[3] Robert, then attending Westminster School. See Appendix.
[4] Possibly Charles Lyddell (d. 1757), matric. Christ Church 1716, later rector of Ardingley, Sussex.
[5] Relating to the riots in Oxford on the prince of Wales's birthday, 30 Oct. 1716. *L.J.*, XX, 436–7; H.M.C., *Lords MSS*, XII, 359–64.

to the main business, but only towards the conclusion of the debate about a rule of the house and receiving a Petition from the Vicechancellor, heads of houses, and Mayor, which on a division was rejected.[6] Duke of Bucks, Lord Abingdon, Lord Trevor, Lord Harcourt, spoke often and very well, Lord Chancellor <Cowper>, Lord Privy seal <Kingston>, Lord Sunderland, Townshend, and Parker, were the cheif Seakers on the other side. Lord Conningsby and Lord North and Grey I need not mention spoke every now and then. The Tories press'd much to have the debate adjourn'd and insisted that witnesses should be sent for to have the affair fully laid open before them and said that it was impossible to form a judgment on the depositions before them, but the other side call'd for the question and carried it 65 to 33, that the Vicechancellor and heads of houses were guilty of a neglect in not celebrating the Princes birthday, that the Major was first affronted by the Stones thrown into the room where he was, and that he was justified in what he had done. Lord Carteret was teller for the Whigs and Lord Orrery for the Tories. Lord Carlton divided in every question for the University, as did 6 of the Bishops. York, London, Hereford, Rochester, Bristol, Chester. St Asaph was there and on the other side. Oxford I suppose is not come up. After the question, Lord Sunderland mov'd that the Printing the depositions had been irregular and tending to sedition, and Lord Privy Seal mov'd that the Depositions and proceedings of the house upon them should be printed by an order of the house.[7] I was much afraid that they were going to move for a bill, but after they have made these resolutions in so plain a case we can expect no other but that they will soon bring one in. I have left Oxford at a very convenient time, and were it not that I have left you and a few other friends behind me there, I should have very little reason to regret my going the<re?.> <MS damaged> The short time which I had the happiness of spending <with?> you was enough to make me desire the continuance <of?> your friendship and acquaintance, and the good temper I experienc'd in you makes me hope I may depend on that happiness. It was I assure you with concern I parted from you and 'twill be a pleasure at any time to receive the favour of a Letter from you. Pray give my service to Mr Palmer.[8] I sincerely wish you all the advantages under his care which he is capable to give and you to receive from him, and I wish you all that health and happiness at home which I am oblig'd to go in persuit of abroad, wherever I am I shall always desire to be Your affectionate most obedient Servant M. Benson

My service to Mr Thomas,[9] tell him I shall soon write to him.

Endorsed: From Mr Benson. R. April 5 1717.
Addressed: To Edward Harley at Christ Church, Oxford.

---

[6] There were two divisions on that date, see H.M.C., *Lords MSS*, XII, 364, and below.

[7] For the orders of the House see *L.J.*, XX, 437. *The Several Depositions Concerning the Late Riot in Oxford* (1716), printed by John Morphew, must have been the version described by Sunderland as 'irregular and tending to sedition'.

[8] Samuel Palmer, matric. Christ Church 1709 aged 18, B.A. 1713, M.A. 1716. He was a student of Christ Church between 1710 and 1722, and EH's tutor from 1717. In 1720 EH wrote to Oxford describing him as 'good natured and easy and inclinable to make every one near Him so. No one denys Him to be a very good Scholar, and All acknowledge Him to be what is much better an Honest man. His Dependance is entirely upon your Lordship and Family. His Pupils are most of them gone or taken their Degrees, so that He is reduced to a very few, and has no Expectation of any more from our Present Governor' (B.L., Add. MS 70237: 16 Aug. 1720). He became rector of Brampton Bryan in 1721, and vicar of Leintwardine, Herefordshire, in 1729.

[9] Probably Timothy Thomas (*c*.1694–1751), matric. Christ Church 1712, B.A. 1716, M.A. 1719, D.D. 1735, rector of Preteign, Radnorshire 1727–51. Thomas also acted as EH's tutor. B.L., Add. MS 70498: Auditor Harley to EH, 19 Jan. 1719.

3. FROM ABIGAIL HARLEY, 28 MAY 1717.[1]

B.L., Add. MS 70088, unfoliated.

Though I do not intend to plague you with letters every day <I> canot forbear scribling to night that you may know what I do. When the Message came yesterday to the Comons that the Lords had fixed on Thursday June 13 for Lord Ox<for>ds Tryal there was silence for near a quarter of an hour, then without any debate resolved to consider the Message on Thirsday next, to which day they adjourned,[2] It is much talked of that the Act of Grace wil be imediatly sent down.

Tis said Dr Snape[3] wil have a great Audience tomorrow.

Your father is a little out of order this afternoon. Your mother brother and sister well.

Adieu

Endorsed: R: May: 29: 1717:/ From Mrs A: Harley

4. FROM ABIGAIL HARLEY, 12 JUNE 1717.

B.L., Add. MS 70088, unfoliated.

The Lords have this day put off my Lord Oxfords Tryal til munday June 24.[1] It was carried by 19,[2] Lord Sunderland named thirsday fortnight, affirmed there would be no Prorogation before, the Duke of Devon<shire> was for the 24, sev<e>ral spoke, Duke of Bucks, Lord Trevor, Lord Harcourt, against giving any longer time, Coningsby in a most impudent maner spoke on tother side but was taken down to order and told 'twas a high degree of Insolence to be there as a Judg in a case he was accuser,[3] he made malicious reflections upon Lord O<xford> then denied he meant him upon which a great laughter followed.

There was very short speeches made in the House of Comons by Mr. Bromley, Hungerford and Shippen, and latter mauled Sir J. Jekyl. I hope all wil do wel at last, excuse hast

Adieu

Endorsed: R: June: 13: 1717:/ from Mrs A. Harley
Addressed: For/ Mr Harley/ at Christ Church/ Oxon/ Frank/ E Harley

5. TO ABIGAIL HARLEY, 18 JUNE 1717.

B.L., Add. MS 70145, unfoliated.

… The Great Folks with you may make as great an noise with their intention to proceed to Tryall as they did at first with their Vast discoveries, and yet their Clamours and Bravadoes now may come to no more than they did then, unless their new

Letter 3
[1] EH's aunt.
[2] *C.J.*, XVIII, 570.
[3] Andrew Snape (1675–1742) was appointed to preach before the Commons on 29 May 1717 as a result of co-operation between the tories and the dissident whigs under Walpole. His attacks on Bishop Hoadly led to his dismissal as a royal chaplain in Nov. 1717. P.R.O., LC 3/63, p. 177.

Letter 4
[1] For the background see Clyve Jones, 'The Impeachment of the Earl of Oxford and the Whig Schism of 1717: Four New Lists', *B.I.H.R.*, LV (1982), 66–87.
[2] 76 to 57, see H.M.C., *Lords MSS*, XXII, 199.
[3] As an M.P., Coningsby had been one of the managers of Oxford's impeachment.

Committee Man the Serjant[1] out of his deep wisdom and Knowledge of the Law should see farther into a millstone than his Brethren, I take him to be as fit a man for their purpose as they could have pitched upon, He having so many of their own good Qualities, His Conscience being of an exact lentgh with theirs and will stretch upon an occasion to serve a freind with the best of them, so that the lentgh of this may very well make up for his want of Judgement and commonsense. Then there is no fear of his losing the Reputation he has got at the Bar if He should not know what is High Treason and what is othywise, or if he should happen to make a false step in the Law it will be past over as coming from him, so that the man acts upon sure grounds. To set down all his Excellencies would require more time than I have to spare: but you shall have some more of my thoughts about the man any opportunity...

Addressed: For/ Mrs Abigail Harley

6. DIVISION LIST ON THE IMPEACHMENT OF THE EARL OF OXFORD, 24 JUNE 1717.[1]

Brampton Bryan MSS, Bundle 117.

June 24 1717: A List of the Lords that voted in the Tryall of the Earl of Oxford wether the Commons should begin with the Treason Articles first or proceed in order; with the names of those that were absent, those marked thus * were at the Question but went out.

Against the Question.	*For the Question.*
Duke of Somerset	Duke of Grafton
Duke of Richmond	Duke of Shrewsbury
Duke of St Albans	Duke of Devonshire
Duke of Bolton	Duke of Buckingham
Duke of Marlborough	Duke of Rutland
Duke of Kent	Duke of Ancaster
Duke of Newcastle	Earl of Derby
Duke of Kingston	Earl of Pembroke
Duke of Portland	Earl of Dorset
Duke of Montrose	Earl of Salisbury
Duke of Roxborough	Earl of Bridgwater
Marquess of Annendale	Earl of Northampton
Earl of Lincoln	Earl of Thanet
Earl of Westmorland	Earl of Scarsdale
Earl of Manchester	Earl of Clarendon
Earl of Stamford	Earl of Cardigan
Earl of Sunderland	Earl of Anglesey
Earl of Carlisle	Earl of Burlington
Earl of Radnor	Earl of Litchfield

Letter 5

[1] Possibly Sir Joseph Jekyll (see Appendix). Elected in 1715 to the secret committee of the Commons to prepare the impeachment of the leaders of the late tory ministry, he defended Oxford and Ormonde against charges of treason, saying the evidence only amounted to high crimes and misdemeanours. See Sedgwick, II, 174.

Letter 6

[1] In EH's hand. This list has been previously published in Jones, 'Impeachment of the Earl of Oxford', pp. 80–6. Only the peers and bishops mentioned elsewhere appear in the Appendix.

Against the Question.
Earl of Yarmouth
Earl of Berkley
Earl of Warrington
Earl of Bradford
Earl of Godolphin
Earl of Cholmonely
Earl of Southerland
Earl of Rothes
Earl of Buchan
Earl of Lowdon
Earl of Haddington
Earl of Orkney
Earl of Tankerville
Bishop of Coventry and Litchfield
Bishop of Salisbury
Bishop of Landaff
Bishop of Oxford
Bishop of Glocester
Bishop of Bangor
Bishop of Lincoln
Bishop of Exeter
Marquess of Winchester
Lord Fitzwalter
Lord Tenham
Lord Byron
Lord Culpeper
Lord Herbert
Lord Haversham
Lord Cowper
Lord Harborough
Lord Cobham
Lord Parker
Lord Conninsby
Lord Torrington
Lord Cadogan
Lord Newbury
Lord Ross

No: 56

Absent

Prince of Wales
*Duke of Cleveland
Duke of Schonbergh
*Duke of Montague

For the Question.
Earl of Nottingham
Earl of Rochester
Earl of Abingdon
Earl of Plymouth
Earl of Orford
Earl of Rochfort
Earl of Greenwick
Earl Pawlet
Earl of Strafford
Earl Ferrers
Earl of Dartmouth
Earl Delorraine
Earl of Ila
Earl of Uxbridge
Earl of Carnarvon
Earl of Bristol
Earl of Hallifax
Viscount Hereford
Viscount Say
Viscount Townsend
Viscount Longueville
Viscount Lonsdale
Viscount Tadcaster
Viscount Castleton
Archbishop of York
Bishop of London
Bishop of Hereford
Bishop of St Davids
Bishop of Bath and Wells
Bishop of Chester
Bishop of Rochester
Bishop of Bristol
Bishop of St Asaph
Lord Abergavenny
Marquess of Lindsey
Lord Delaware
Lord Willouby
Lord Effingham
Lord North
Lord Hunsdon
Lord St John
Lord Compton
Lord Bruce
Lord Leigh
Lord Berkley
Lord Cornwallis
Marquess of Carmarthen
Lord Lumley
Lord Carteret

Absent	*For the Question.*
Marquess of Lothian	Lord Stawell
Earl of Suffolk	Lord Guilford
Earl of Exeter	Lord Ashburnham
Earl of Leicester	Earl of Arran
Earl of Berkshire	Lord Gower
Earl of Chesterfield	Lord Conway
Earl of Sandneck <Sandwich>	Lord Belhaven
*Earl of Scarborough	Lord Harcourt
Earl of Jersey	Earl of Orrery
Earl of Grantham	Lord Dupplin
Earl of Coventry	Lord Windsor
*Earl of Rockingham	Lord Mansel
Earl of Aylesford	Lord Middleton
Viscount St Johns	Lord Trevor
*Archbishop of Canterbury	Lord Lansdown
Bishop of Durham	Lord Masham
*Bishop of Winchester	Lord Foley
Bishop of Worcester	Lord Bathurst
*Bishop of Carlile	Lord Bingley
Bishop of Ely	Lord Carleton
Bishop of Norwich	
Bishop of Chichester	No: 88
Lord Brooke	
Lord Maynard	
Lord Lexington	
Lord Bernard	
*Lord Onslow	
*Lord Rumney	

No: 32

Endorsed: A List of the Lords what voted: June: 24: 1717: in Lord O<xford's> Case. Copyed.

7. 'MEMORANDUMS ABOUT LORD O<XFORD'S> TRYALL. 1717.'[1]

B.L., Add. MS 70088, unfoliated.

Monday, June 24: 1717 about ten a clock in the morning the Earl of Oxford went out of the Tower to Westminster, the Day appointed by the House of Lords for his Tryall, about 7 in the Morning a Company of Granadiers marched into the Tower to attend him to Westminster, commanded by Captain Broskely<?>;[2] There was an order sent to Leiutenant of the Tower[3] to bring his Lordship by water, he went in the Governors Barge with my Lord Harley, Mr Thomas Harley,[4] Governor Doyley and Mr Serjant the Gentleman jayler, The Guards with 12 Warders in boats.

Letter 7

[1] In EH's hand.

[2] Unidentified. Not in the Auditor's account in H.M.C., *Portland MSS*, V, 641–69.

[3] Robert Doyley, deputy to the lt.-gov. 1715, was acting lt.-gov. at this time.

[4] Thomas Harley (c.1667–1738), cousin of Lord Oxford, and M.P. for Radnorshire 1698–1715.

His Lordship came not back to the Tower till twelve a clock at night, only my Lord Harley and the Governor in the Coach.

Tuesday June 25: about 10 in the morning my Lord Oxford went again to Westminster in the same manner as before attended by Lord Harley, Mr Thomas Harley, and his Nephew Edward Harley. About two a clock his Lordship returned back by water, the Lords having agreed to allow the House of Commons till thursday morning to search Precedents, etc.

Thursday June 27: between 10 and 11 in the morning my Lord Oxford went again to Westminster as on Tuesday, The Lords did not come into the Hall this Day, The Commons had a Conference with the Lords who had a Debate upon it, and adhering to their Resolution of June 24 the Court was adjourned to Saturday the 29.

Between 5 and 6 in the Evening his Lordship went back to the Tower.

Friday June 28: in the Evening an order came to the Leiutenant of the Tower not to bring the Earl of Oxford to Westminster till Monday morning July 1.

Munday July 1: about 11 a clock the Earl of Oxford went to Westminster as before.

About 8 at night the Lords came into the Hall and acquitted the Earl of Oxford of the High Treason and high Crimes etc. nemine contradicente 106 of the Lords being present.

His Lordship went not home to his own house but to his Brothers in Lincolns Inn feilds, Not only the people but all the Guards that were drawn up in Palace yard shouted upon his Lordships being acquitted and I am told there has not been known so universal a Joy and such great rejoycing throuout England since the Restoration as was upon the Earl of Oxford being accquitted.

The Earl of Oxford came to the Tower July 16 1715: was one week at Mr Tollets[5] then removed to the Governor House when he was very ill, and from that day was confined to two Rooms where he continued with a constant chearfulness depending upon Gods Providence to clear his Innocence to the Whole Christian world, never sinking under his Sufferings, nor by any base submission betraying his own Innocence.

8. TO ABIGAIL HARLEY [AT EYWOOD], CHRIST CHURCH, 6 FEBRUARY 1717[/18].

B.L., Add. MS 70034, unfoliated; printed H.M.C., *Portland MSS*, V, 554

… I fancy you have hitherto found my news to be pritty true, considering how many Second handed Lies we have from London, which have been Stale in every Coffee house there for a week before. I shall (as to my Intelligence) find a great loss in Mr Thomas, who goes to London on Munday, but He has promised me to let me hear from him and to send me all the news that is stirring, which I will be sure to communicate, though I beleive there will not be much when this Session is over, which they talk will be in a months time or less. The Court were hard pushed on Teusday,[1] there were between 4 and 500 members present, and they carried their Point but by 18.[2] Walpole spoke very warmly against them as did Mr Jefferies, for them Mr Lechmere, Crags,

---

[5] Possibly George Tollet, former extra commissioner to the navy board 1702–14. For this identification see H.M.C., *Portland MSS*, IV, 216, 414.

Letter 8

[1] In a debate on the Mutiny Bill, see Cobbett, VII, 536–7.

[2] This must have been in committee as no vote is recorded for the 4 Feb. *C.J.*, XVIII, 713.

and Sir Humfry Polesworth,[3] the last noble Colonel I fancy has something more than half Pay. If the members can be perswaded to stay in Town and keep together, tis thought the Court will not venture to bring in their Terrible Bills this Session[4]...

9. TO ABIGAIL HARLEY AT EYWOOD, CHRIST CHURCH, 18 FEBRUARY 1717/18.

B.L., Add. MS 70034, unfoliated; printed in part H.M.C., *Portland MSS*, V, 555.

... There has been lately a very strong report that the Chancellor will certainly lay down, and that Lechmere is to be made a Lord in order to Qualifie him to take the others place, some say King is to be Char:ellor others Parker.[1] The Mutiny Bill came on in the House of Lords last Teusday[2] when several Papers were called for, some of which were the Accounts of what officers had been turned out, and what offices had sold, for how much, and who came in their places since the King came. Lord Trevor and the D<uke of> Argyle opened the Debate very handsomely and very well. Sunderland answered Argyle and reflected on him for voting one Sessions that the Peace was safe and Honourable and the next that it was a Disadvantageous one. Several warm words past between them and so the debate was adjourned till that day sennight, when a tight battle is expected. The new Knight[3] has (to my great joy) been found out to have exported and melted down the Coin, for which tis to be hoped he will be made to pay Lauce. A Debate in one of the Courts began upon the matter but was adjourned for fourteen days. Mr Bromley lies very ill at Kensington...

February 20th. <Postscript> This should have gone last post but was sent to late. No news since last but that the great Debate was farther adjourned till this day.

Addressed: For/ Mrs Abigail Harley/ At Aywood/ near Presteigne/ Herefordshire.

10. TO ABIGAIL HARLEY AT EYWOOD, [CHRIST CHURCH], 27 FEBRUARY 1717/18.

B.L., Add. MS 70034, unfoliated; printed H.M.C., *Portland MSS*, V, 557.

... Lord O<xford> spoke very boldly, clearly and easily, was answered by Stanhope who cast several reflections on him, which my Lord did not think proper then to answer, though he is resolved not to be silent if they touch upon any of those Points. They carryed the Bill by 14[1] So although we are beaten the Conquerors have not much to brag off. The Lords have entered their Protest against the Bill.[2] Bishop of Winchester and Townshend were amongst the Protestors. Some of the Courts Lords

---

[3] A cant name for James Grahme, M.P. (see Appendix), used by Grahme's friends, including Lord Bolingbroke. See H.T. Dickinson, 'Letters of Lord Bolingbroke to James Grahme', *Transactions of the Cumberland and Westmorland Antiquarian and Archaeological Society*, new ser., LXVIII (1968), 123.

[4] The Universities Bill and the repeal of the Occasional Conformity and Schism Acts. The session ended on 21 Mar. 1718. *C.J.*, XVIII, 774.

Letter 9

[1] Parker succeeded Cowper (who resigned on 15 Apr.) as lord chancellor on 12 May 1718.

[2] The Mutiny Bill was first read in the Lords on Thursday 13 Feb., not Tuesday the 11th (*L.J.*, XX, 607). For details see H.M.C., *Lords MSS*, XII, 512–16.

[3] Sir George Caswall. See the Appendix.

Letter 10

[1] 91 to 77 (with proxies) on the Mutiny Bill. See H.M.C., *Lords MSS*, XII, 514.

[2] There were four protests. *L.J.*, XX, 617–19.

said they were for making several alterations in the Bill, but dare not trust it in the House of Commons again...

Addressed: For/ Mrs Abigail Harley/ at Aywood/ near Presteigne/ Herefordshire

11. TO ABIGAIL HARLEY AT EYWOOD, CHRIST CHURCH, 9 MARCH 1717/18.

B.L., Add. MS 70034, unfoliated; printed H.M.C., *Portland MSS*, V, 557–8.

... It is talked that the House will rise this week, the sooner the better for every Bill that they bring into the House they carry though it is but by a small majority. The Bill of forfeited Estates was lost but by 11 or 12:[1] this last week, when they carryed another for rebuilding St Giles Church instead of one of the fifty new ones.[2] This was brought in by the Duke of Newcastle, and it is thought that this bills passing will be a great means of frustrating the good design of building new churchs, for several old ones will now desire the same favor with as much right and a better pretence than St Giles. Bishop of Chester spoke very warmly and very well against it. Two of the Commissioners, Salisbury and Gloucester, were for it as was Exeter. When they came to mention in the bill that it was enacted in the year of Queen Ann[3] the House divided, whether they should add the words of Pious and ever blessed Memory, and they carried it that they should be left out...

Addressed: For/ Mrs Abigail Harley/ At Aywood/ near Presteigne/ Herefordshire

12. TO ABIGAIL HARLEY, 18 MARCH 1717/18.

B.L., Add. MS 70034, unfoliated; printed H.M.C., *Portland MSS*, V, 558.

The King sent a Message yesterday to the House of Commons to let them know that he should want more money and more men at sea, to which a Address of thanks was voted to his Majesty for his vigilance and great care of this nation, and that they would the beginning of next Sessions give him what money or men he should think fit, 8000 Sailors are to be pressed.[1] A War with Spain is very warmly talked off; Stocks fall every day upon this report, The Spanish Envoy delivered in last week a memorial to the King. Smith has refused to be Treasurer of the Navy so Hambden has the place, General Erle is out of every thing but some say has a Pension settled on him.[2] Cowper is to be made an Earl, Earl of Royston... Bangor does not go to Londonderry.[3] The House of Commons will not be up till Thurday or Fryday,[4] to day the Septenial takes

---

Letter 11

[1] On 28 Feb. there was a vote of 86 to 111 on a clause in the Forfeited Estates Bill, which was then *passed* and sent up to the Lords (*C.J.*, XVIII, 757). It passed there by 82 to 76 on 11 Mar.

[2] The Bill for rebuilding St Giles's Church passed the Commons and was sent to the Lords on 17 Feb. (*ibid.*, p. 736). It passed the Lords on 8 Mar.

[3] 10 Anne, c. 20.

Letter 12

[1] *C.J.*, XVIII, 767.

[2] The pension was £1,200 a year. The most important posts he resigned were governor of Portsmouth and lt.-gen. of the ordnance. Sedgwick, II, 12–13.

[3] Benjamin Hoadly (see Appendix). In fact, William Nicolson, bishop of Carlisle, was translated to Derry on 2 May 1718.

[4] Parliament was prorogued on 21 Mar. (*C.J.*, XVIII, 774).

place,[5] several members are resolved not to attend. My Duty to my mother Dear love to Nedy<?>. Adeiu

Addressed: For/ Mrs Abigail Harley/ At Aywood/ near Presteigne/ Herefordshire

13. TO ABIGAIL HARLEY AT EYWOOD, 2 DECEMBER 1718.
B.L., Add. MS 70034, unfoliated; printed H.M.C., *Portland MSS*, V, 573.

… The repeal of Lord Bolingbroke's Attainder[1] is very much talked of and dayly expected to be brought into the House as a thing desired by K<ing> G<eorge>, and is to be recommended to the house in a message from his Majesty… You will see by the Votes that the first design of building the rifty new Churchs is knockt in the head by their rebuilding old ones and 'tis said we shall be £30000 in debt for them.[2]

Addressed: For/ Mrs Abigail Harley/ at Aywood/ near Presteigne/ Herefordshire.

14. TO ABIGAIL HARLEY, 7 DECEMBER 1718.
B.L., Add. MS 70034, unfoliated; printed H.M.C., *Portland MSS*, V, 573–4.

… Bolingbrooks bill is deffered for some time tho' it is thought that it will certainly be brought in before this Session is over, I am in great hopes of seeing him again Secretary under his present Majestys most auspicious reign, And then will his faithfull Ministry be entirely compleated…

Addressed: For/ Mrs Abigail Harley/ at Aywood/ near Presteigne/ Herefordshire

15. LORD NOTTINGHAM'S CLAUSE, 22 DECEMBER 1718.[1]
Brampton Bryan MSS, Bundle 117.

And Be it further Enacted by the Authority aforesaid, That from and after the End of this present Session of Parliament, All and every person and persons who in respect of any Office or otherwise shall be Required by Law to take the Oathes of Allegiance and Supremacy and the Oath of Abjuration prescribed in An Act made in the First year of his present majesty's Reign immediatly after the taking the said Oathes, shall Publickly and audibly make Repeat and Subscribe the Profession of Christian Beleif Contained in An Act made in the First year of their late Majesties King William and Queen Mary, Entituled An Act for Exempting their Majesties Protestant Subjects Dissenting from the Church of England from the Penalties of certain Laws; In the words following. 'I A.B. Profess Faith in God the Father and in Jesus Christ his

---

[5] The first parliament of George I had first met on 17 Mar. 1715, and under the old Triennial Act it would have ended on 16 Mar. 1718. The Septennial Act of 1716, which extended the life of a parliament to seven years, thus first came into effect on 17 Mar. 1718.

Letter 13
[1] Henry St John (1678–1751), 1st Viscount Bolingbroke, had been attainted in 1715 along with others in the late tory ministry. He had fled to France to become the Pretender's chief minister, but quickly became disillusioned and applied to return to England. He was pardoned in 1723 and the attainder reversed in 1725, though he was not allowed to resume his seat in the Lords. For the possibility of a bill in 1718, see H.T. Dickinson, *Bolingbroke* (1970), p. 150.
[2] See *C.J.*, XIX, 27–9.

Letter 15
[1] This clause was offered to the Bill for Strengthening the Protestant Interest (i.e., the repeal of the Occasional Conformity and Schism Acts) on 22 Dec. and rejected on the 23rd. *L.J.*, XXI, 35, where it is printed.

Eternall Son the true God, And in the Holy Spirit One God Blessed for Evermore, And do acknowledge the Holy Scriptures of the Old and New Testament to be given by Divine Inspiration.' Which Profession being Entred on a Roll, made, Repeated and Subscribed as aforesaid shall be kept in the same manner as the said Oathes when taken are Required to be Entred and kept, And all and every such person and persons neglecting or omitting to make, Repeat and Subscribe the said Profession of his Beleif in manner aforesaid shall Forfeit and Incurr the same Penalties and Incapacities as he should have Forfeited and Incurr'd in Case he had neglected or omitted to take the said Oathes or any of them.[2]

Bishops For this Clause were

ArchBishop of Canterbury
ArchBishop of York

Bishops of

Dr Robinson	London
Sir Nat<haniel> Crew[3]	Durham
Dr Hooper	Bath and Wells
	Chichester
Dr Trelawney	Winchester
Dr Biss	Hereford
Dr Gastrell	Chester
Dr Smalridge	Bristol
Dr Atterbury	Rochester
Dr Ottely	St Davids
	Oxford By Proxy[4]
	St Asap[5]

Bishops Against this Clause

Dr Hough	Worcester
	Litchfield and Coventry
Dr Tyler	Landaff
Dr Gibson	Lincoln who had Exeters Proxy
	Gloucester
	Bangor
	Ely
	Sarum
	Norwich
	Exeter By Proxy
	Carlisle
	Peterborough

Endorsed:[6] A Copy of a Clause offered by Lord Nottingham in the House of Lords December 22, 1718. It was thrown out upon a Divison several of the Bishops against it. Copyed.

---

[2] The list of bishops is in EH's hand.

[3] Nathaniel Crew was neither a knight nor a baronet, but he was the 3rd Lord Crew of Stene in the English peerage, the only person at this time to be both a spiritual and temporal lord of parliament.

[4] Cast by the archbishop of Canterbury. H.L.R.O., Proxy book, VII.

[5] In the manuscript St Asaph is followed by 'Lichfield and Coventry', which has been crossed out.

[6] In EH's hand.

16. FROM EDWARD PRIDEAUX GWYN,[1] WHITEHALL, 23 DECEMBER 1718.

Brampton Bryan MSS, Bundle X.

Dear Sir

I give you this trouble more to shew I am not forgetfull of your Commands than that I have much News to send you. Dr. Stratford[2] must have had so full an Account of what has passed, that I am sure you expect the less from me. The Church-Bill consisted of three parts, when presented by Lord Stanhope, the first repealed the obligation of taking the Sacrament upon entring into an office, the second takes away that clause of the Occasional Bill, which made it penal for one in Station to appear at a Conventicle, the third repeals the whole Schism Bill.[3] Such warm Opposition was made the second day, that Lord Sunderland himself proposed waving the first part, and afterwards owned that it had never been part of the Bill, unless the Bishops of Glocester, Lincoln and Bangor had declared they would not appear for the Bill without it. Whatever suspicions may have been entertained of Father Francis,[4] they have all now vanished, and I believe his behaviour last week will be as satisfactory elsewhere, as it has been here to those, who were doubtfull. Lord Hatton is gone out of town, and has left his Proxy with Lord Carteret, Lord Stawell is away, and has none. You'll see by the news the King of Prussia has arrested several of his Ministers, but you'll excuse my trusting the Post with the reason which is generally given for this Step. It was moved this day in the House of Commons for adjourning till the 12th (the day before the Call) but carried in the Negative by a very gret Majority,[5] but Christmas day being so near it must be known to morrow, what recess the Court will allow of. I am sorry I answered more for Lord Essex than he made good for though he was very hearty in the late debate against the Spanish War,[6] yet he thought fitt to leave his new Relations[7] in this Church Bill, and I wish Haccam's Lunar Honesty don't prove too true. I congratulate you upon the Prince's appearing for the Church in a manner becoming one, that stands so fair for being defender of it and am dear Sir your most obedient humble Servant E P G

Letter 16

[1] Edward Prideaux Gwyn (?1698–1736), son of Francis Gwyn, M.P. for Christchurch at this time. He was to succeed his father in the seat in 1724 (until 1727, when he became M.P. for Wells, again succeeding his father, until 1729).

[2] William Stratford (*c.*1652–1729), B.A. 1692, chaplain to the house of commons and archdeacon of Richmond 1703, D.D. and canon of Christ Church, Oxford, 1705, rector of Little Shelford, Berks., 1707.

[3] For the background to this bill see G.M. Townend, 'Religious Radicalism and Conservatism in the Whig Party under George I: The Repeal of the Occasional Conformity and Schism Act', *Parliamentary History*, VII (1988), 24–44.

[4] Francis Gwyn. See Appendix.

[5] By 79 to 151. *C.J.*, XIX, 47.

[6] On 17 Dec. the Lords debated the king's message on declaring war on Spain (*L.J.*, XXI, 25). Britain (along with the allies of the Quadruple Alliance: France, Holland and Austria) hoped to counteract Philip V's attempt to overturn the terms of the treaty of Utrecht in Italy.

[7] On 27 Nov. Essex had married the daughter of the earl of Clarendon. Both Essex and Clarendon voted for the Church Bill (i.e., in favour of the repeal of the Occasional Conformity and the Schism Acts), but the earl of Rochester (Clarendon's first cousin) voted against (B.L., Add. MS 47028, ff. 264–5: division list of 19 Dec. 1718 on committing the bill. This is the only known surviving *division* list on this bill. However, there were three other votes on the bill).

My humble respects to Mr. Palmer, Mr. Wainwright,[8] the very worthy Professor,[9] and all other friends.

Pray desire Francis[10] I may soon hear how he does.

Endorsed: From Mr Gwyn R: Dec. 24. 1718. Occasional Bill repealed.

17. TO ABIGAIL HARLEY AT EYWOOD, 25 DECEMBER 1718.

B.L., Add. MS 70034, unfoliated; printed in part H.M.C., *Portland MSS*, V, 574–5.

... The Church Bill was read a third time on Munday or Teusday[1] I am not certain which; it was pass'd without a Division, it consisted of three Parts when presented by Lord Stanhope, the first repealed the Obligation of taking the Sacrament upon entring into an Office, the second takes away that clause of the Occasional Bill, which made it Penal for one in station to appear at a Conventicle, the third repeals the whole Schism Bill. Such warm opposition was made the second day that Lord Sunderland himself proposed the waiving the first Part, and afterwards owned that it had never been part of the Bill unless the Bishops of Gloucester, Lincoln and Bangor had declared they would not appear for the Bill without it. I have here enclosed a List of those Bishops who voted for and against the Bill. Upon the reading of the Bill A third Time Lord Nottingham offered a Clause to be added to it to prevent the Growth of Socinianism,[2] that no one should be admitted into any Place without subscribing to the Articles of Faith particularly that relating to the Divinity of our Saviour, and to profess his beleif of the Scriptures contained in the old and new Testament.[3] Lord Nottingham, Lord Oxford, Lord Anglesea and the two Arch Bishops spoke for this, Lord Stanhope, Sunderland, Ila<y> against it. All the Bishops that voted for the Church Bill voted against this clause and to these came over Litchfeild and Coventry so that they threw it out. Well may they strip the Church and her members of her Authority when they divest the head of both, of his Divinity. Lord Nottingham read a Letter from Exeter in the House which I have enclosed and to which I refer you. I hope it will be published and spread over the Kingdom that Peoples eyes may be open, and that no more poor souls may be deluded by these Ignorant Fanatical Infidels. It is reported in London that the King of Sweden is certainly killed,[4] I am affraid this report is too true...

---

[8] Possibly Thomas Wainwright (d. 1721), educated at Westminster School, student at Christ Church 1710–21, secretary to George Smalridge, bishop of Bristol and dean of Christ Church. See *Remarks and Collections of Thomas Hearne* (11 vols., Oxford, 1884–1914), VI, 73. His brother John was a regular correspondent of EH's cousin, Lord Harley (B.L., Add. MS 70400).

[9] Probably Thomas Terry (*c.*1678–1735), sub-dean of Christ Church 1712, regius professor of Greek 1712–35, and former tutor to Lord Harley, later 2nd earl of Oxford. E.G.W. Bill, *Education at Christ Church, Oxford, 1660–1800* (Oxford, 1988), p. 49. He was to become a royal chaplain and rector of Chalfont St Giles, Bucks., 1723–35.

[10] Francis Gwyn (?1699–1777), younger brother of Edward Prideaux, who was at Christ Church; he was later M.P. for Wells 1741–54. Sedgwick, II, 92–3.

Letter 17

[1] On Tuesday the 23rd. *L.J.*, XXI, 35.

[2] Strictly speaking, socinianism is the name given to the heresy which denied the essential divinity of Christ, after the two sixteenth-century Italian theologians Laelius and Faustus Socinus. In this context, however, it is probably being used as a term of obloquy. Socinianism was widely used by the high calvinist wing of the presbyterians and independents as a term of abuse against their more heterodox opponents. We are grateful to David Wykes for his comments on this point.

[3] See above pp. 206–7.

[4] Charles XII was shot at the siege of Friedrichshall on 11 Dec. in the Great Northern War.

<Postscript>[5] After the best enquiry I can make about the difference arisen among the Dissenters in and about Exeter concerning the Divinity of our blessed Saviour I find the Fact to be thus.[6]

About a year ago one Stogdon[7] a Dissenting Teacher preached a Sermon against the Divinity of Christ, this occasioned great disputes among them, and in their general Assembly at Exeter about Michaelmas last it was proposed that they should draw up a Confession of their Faith to which all might subscribe. But when they could not agree upon this, it was proposed that every one should subscribe a Paper either owning or denying our Saviours Divinity, and accordingly Sixteen subscribed against it, and thirty two for it. Among the former were Pearse,[8] Hallet[9] and Withers of Exeter[10] and Gilling of Newton Bushel.[11] Pearse is look't upon as the cheif of them and some of his Congregation having left him upon that account, those that are his Disciples are contriving to set up a new meeting House, wherein he may preach to them. He hath not yet quited his meeting, but whenever he preachs, He orders Clark[12] to omit the Gloria Patri.

<On reverse of postscript.>

Against Repealing the Occasional and Schism Bill etc.	For Repealing etc.
Arch Bishop of Canterbury	Worcester
Arch Bishop of York	Landaff
London	Lincoln
Durham	Gloucester
Bath and Wells	Bangor
Chichester	Ely
Hereford	Salisbury
Chester	Norwich
Bristol	Exeter
Rochester	Carlisle
St Davids	Peterborough
Oxford By Proxy	
St Asaph	
Litchfield and Coventry	
Winchester	

Addressed: For/ Mrs Abigail Harley/ At Aywood near Presteigne/ Herefordshire.

[5] This passage was probably not composed by EH, but copied by him from an account circulating in manuscript. An anonymous document containing the same account, not in EH's hand, is preserved among the Finch papers at the Leicestershire R.O., DG7/Box 4951/Bundle 25. We are grateful to David Wykes for bringing this document to our attention.

[6] On the controversy in Exeter, see Allan Brockett, *Nonconformity in Exeter, 1660–1875* (Manchester, 1962), pp. 74–95. On the wider controversy about the Trinity and subscription, see Roger Thomas, 'The Non-Subscription Controversy Amongst the Dissenters in 1719: The Salters' Hall Debate', *Journal of Ecclesiastical History*, IV (1953), 162–86.

[7] Hubert Stogdon (1692–1728), a candidate for the ministry at Exeter, was ordained at Shepton Mallet, Somerset, in 1718 and then became minister at Wookey.

[8] James Peirce (?1674–1726), independent minister at Cambridge, 1701–6; presbyterian minister at Newbury, 1706–13; minister of James's meeting, Exeter, 1713–19.

[9] Joseph Hallett (1656–1722), principal of the nonconformist academy at Exeter. His son, Joseph, who succeeded his father as minister of the Mint meeting in 1722, was also a non-subscriber.

[10] John Withers (1699–1729) became minister of the Bow meeting at Exeter in 1705.

[11] Isaac Gilling (?1662–1725), minister at Axminster, Silverton and Newton Abbot.

[12] This is not a name, but a reference to the clerk of the meeting. The copy in the Leicestershire R.O. reads 'the Clark'.

18. FROM EDWARD PRIDEAUX GWYN, WHITEHALL, 27 DECEMBER 1718.

Brampton Bryan MSS, Bundle X.

Dear Sir

I am by this to return you thanks for your last, though there is no News stirring, and little to be expected during the recess of Parliament. You'll see by the Gazette that the Court gives credit to the King of Sweden's death, but some expect further confirmation. The Prince's having given £500 to Westminster School[1] explains the reasons of the Bishop of Rochester's visit in Leicester fields this morining. I just now saw Censor White;[2] upon my telling him, I designed you a Letter by this Post, he desired his humble service, and having heard of Mr Berkeley's[3] being indisposed desires he may soon have a Letter from him, and that if he has any aprehensions of the small pox, he would remember the advice he gave him, to remove to Lasher's.[4] If I find Francis insists upon the Punctilio you mention, I'll break the Ice, rather than be deprived of the pleasure of his correspondence, but though an elder Brother must be kept at that distance, I am sorry he stands upon such Ceremony with his Father. You'll do me but justice in remembring me to all friends, as likewise in believing me to be Dear Sir your most obedient humble Servant E P G

The Bishops for the Bill were, Worcester, Sarum, Landaff, Norwich, Ely, Glocester, Lincoln (who had Exeter's Proxy) Bangor, Carlisle and Peterborough. I desire my humble respects to Dr Stratford.

Endorsed: From Mr Gwyn. R. Dec. 28 1718. Bishops who voted for repealing the Occasional Bill.

19. TO ABIGAIL HARLEY AT EYWOOD, 4 JANUARY 1718/19.

B.L., Add. MS 70034, unfoliated; printed H.M.C., *Portland MSS*, V, 575.

… My Father I hear has been out of order but is now pritty well again. He sent me down last Post a Copy of the Clause (which I have here sent you) against the Socinians enclosed in a most admirable Letter upon the same Subject, which he made Robin[1] write for him. Happy would it be for this Nation were there more in it like Him, of such strict Vertue of Such Exemplary Piety, then might we with reason hope for future Blessings, but at present the whole is so miserably corrupted, that we have nothing to expect but that Destruction which we are ripe for.

It is thought the Sessions will be over by the End of this month, the King goes very early to Hannover, The Cabinet Council are to be left Regents the Prince is to be

---

Letter 18

[1] The £500, along with £1,000 from the king, was for the rebuilding of the school dormitory. See Clyve Jones, 'Jacobites under the Beds: Francis Atterbury, the Earl of Sunderland and the Westminster School Dormitory Case of 1721', *British Library Journal*, (forthcoming).

[2] John White, censor of Christ Church, son of Robert of Westminster, M.A. 1707, proctor 1716.

[3] Probably William Berkeley (*c.*1700–33), son of 5th Baron Berkeley of Stratton, matric. Christ Church 1716 aged 16, later a captain in the royal navy. But it may be his elder brother John Berkeley (*c.*1697–1773), 'subscribed' Christ Church 1713, succ. 6th Baron Berkeley of Stratton 1741.

[4] Joshua Lasher (b. 1647), regius professor of medicine, Oxford, 1718–29.

Letter 19

[1] EH's younger brother Robert. See Appendix.

excluded from that power. Lord Sunderland stays a month after the Monarch and then goes to Hannover to him. Very High words passed between this Lord and the late Chancellor in the last Debate,[2] Accusing one another of Dishonesty and betraying their Country, several broken Sentences uttered, which, if any one had but gently blown the Flame, would have been filled up, and several Secrets revealed which have been long desired. The Lords have leave to Protest against the Late Bill at their next meeting[3]...

<Postscript> I will enquire how the Lord you mentioned voted...

Addressed: To/ Mrs Abigail Harley/ at Aywood near Presteigne/ Herefordshire.

20. FROM EDWARD PRIDEAUX GWYN, WHITEHALL, 8 JANUARY 1718/19.

Brampton Bryan MSS, Bundle X.

Dear Sir

The debate of yesterday was upon so extraordinary an Occasion, that I thought you would expect some Account from me, however imperfect it were. You'll hear from other hands, who spoke on both sides. Sir Thomas Hanmer, Mr Jeffreys, Mr Shippen, your Cousin Palmer,[1] Mr Snell, and Mr Strangeways with several others are allowed by every body to have distinguished themselves very handsomely against the Bill,[2] but Mr Walpole bore harder upon the Court than any Tory durst attempt to do. He begun with his reasons that made him against repealing the Bill, the passing of which he had formerly opposed. He said 'the Occasional Bill past, at a time when the ministry seemed to intend some hardships to them,[3] and that he thought that Act only a Prelude to the abrogating their Toleration. But that now this Bill had been brought into the other house by the chief of the Ministry, with a Clause in it that would in a Scandalous manner have evaded the Test Act, which though now dropped was a sufficient reason to discover their designs. That this would give a general Alarm to the Nation and a great handle to the disaffected, who would inculcate into the minds of the people, that many of the measures, which occasioned an unfortunate Prince's Abdication,[4] were now renewed. That whereas the Suspension of the Penal Laws and Test was laid to that King's Charge, he had mentiond before, how the Test Act had been lately struck at.[5] That whereas he was accused of seizing Charters, there had been lately a debate in Westminster-Hall for ten days together the result of which might have laid most of the

---

[2] Cowper was the late chancellor and the quarrel was presumably over the Church Bill.

[3] This is a reference to the dissent against rejecting Nottingham's rider to the Church Bill (see above, pp. 206–7) entered in the Journal for 23 Dec. 1718 at the next sitting of the house on 7 Jan. 1719. *L.J.*, XXI, 35.

Letter 20

[1] Thomas Palmer, M.P. for Bridgwater 1715–27 (see Appendix), described to Lord Harley by William Stratford as 'your cousin Palmer' (H.M.C., *Portland MSS*, VII, 300). According to Sedgwick (II, 322), his first speech in the Commons was made in June 1721. He is not listed in Cobbett, VII, 584, as speaking against the Church Bill.

[2] For the division list of 7 Jan. on the bill see Cobbett, VII, 585–8.

[3] The protestant dissenters.

[4] James II in 1688.

[5] The bill had originally contained the clause which made merely offering to receive the sacrament a qualification for office. This was widely seen as a proposal for 'evading entirely the Test Act'. H.L.R.O., Main papers, 13 Dec. 1718; B.L., Add. MS 47028, f. 264: Percival to Dering, Dec. 1718.

Corporations at their mercy.[6] That the Ecclesiastical Commission had been declared illegal, yet if fame might be credited, there was now a design of visiting the Universities. He desired them to remember, that a noble Lord, who presided in that King's Councils, and was excepted out of an Act of Grace for it, was afterwards at the head of King William's affairs,[7] and the reason assigned for this second Station was, that he had persuaded his former Master to those measures that ended in his ruin but he hoped no body sett him as a pattern now. That he thought there were people enough to fill all offices without capacitating any now disqualified and putt the case, suppose a secretary of state either wearied with business, or through restlesness of temper, desired to lay down, there was no occasion for sending abroad for one to succeed him, though he might be never so true a Penitent, but that there might be found at home, some man of abilities enough for that Station' (by which you'll easily percieve he glanced at Lord Bolingbroke, and does not favour his return) he concluded 'that to their comfort the heir of the Crown could see the ill Consequences of this, though the Ministry did not, and had openly protested against it'. The Tories made so brave a stand, that it's thought the victory is of little use to the Conquerors. You must have already heard how the division stood, and have remarked, that it was carried by the inauspicious number of 41.[8] Some of Walpole's party deserted him, but several others, not expected, joyned him, particularly Lords Castlecomer, and Hinchingbroke, Mr. Wallop, Mr. Smith, Sir Robert Worseley, Sir John Cope, Governor Pitt, and his eldest Son,[9] etc. Only four Scotch of the losing side. I should be very glad to hear what news is stirring at Oxford and am Dear Sir your very faithful humble Servant E P G

I desire my service to all friends.

When it was urged in the debate in relacon to the Schism Bill that it was unnatural to deprive Parents of the Educacon of their children, Shippen said 'Since it was now the case of the greatest Subject in England, he did not see why others should complain'.[10]

Endorsed: From Mr Gwyn: R. Jan. 9. 1718/19. Debate on the repealing the Occasional Bill.

21. TO ABIGAIL HARLEY AT EYWOOD, 8 JANUARY 1718/19.

B.L., Add. MS 70034, unfoliated; printed H.M.C., *Portland MSS*, V, 575.

Both Houses met yesterday. The Commons read the Church Bill a second time, upon which was a very warm and long Debate. Hanmer, Jefferes, Shippen etc. spoke admirably well against it as did several others. Upon a Division the Bill was carried by 41 (an ominous number), 202 against it, 243 for it. The Prince was in the Gallery. Several Whigs voted against it among which was Wallop of the Treasury. The Court are very angry at the Speaker,[1] they have something which is not yet known in

---

[6] Possibly *Rex* v. *Grant* tried in king's bench in the Michaelmas term, 5 Geo. I. It was a case to determine whether the obligation to make a declaration against the solemn league and covenant as prescribed in the Corporation Act of 1661 still remained. See *English Reports*, XCIII, 422–6.

[7] Robert, 2nd earl of Sunderland (d. 1702).

[8] The vote was 243 to 202 (*C.J.*, XIX, 48; and below). The number 41 was considered inauspicious as it was a reminder of 1641 and the outbreak of the Civil War.

[9] Robert Pitt. See Appendix.

[10] This refers to part of the quarrel in the royal family when George I took the prince of Wales's children away from their parents.

Letter 21

[1] Spencer Compton (see Appendix). As head of the prince of Wales's household at the time of the quarrel in the royal family, he had gone into opposition and co-operated with Walpole.

agitation against him, 'tis thought they will endeavour to remove him from the Chair by sending him to the House of Peers or by some other way that is worse. 'Tis talked that Cadogan will be out, and Argyle put in. Bolingbroke's business is again revived. Bishop of Rochester went to Court to complement the Monarch on new years day. The meaning of several steps this Prelate has lately taken are as yet a mystery, though people give shrewd Guesses...

Addressed: For/ Mrs Abigail Harley/ at Aywood near Presteigne/ Herefordshire

22. TO ABIGAIL HARLEY AT EYWOOD, 11 JANUARY 1718/19.

B.L., Add. MS 70034, unfoliated; printed H.M.C., *Portland MSS*, V, 575–6.

I have no other news but a further Account of the Debate in the House of Commons upon the Church Bill, to send my Dear Aunt by this Post. Sir Thomas Hanmer, Mr Jefferys, Mr Shippen, Cousin Tom Palmer, Mr Snell, and Mr Strangeways with several others are allowed by every body to have distinguish'd themselves very handsomely against the Bill; But Walpole bore harder upon the Court than any Tory durst attempt to do. He begun with his reasons that made him against repealing the Bill, the passing of which he had formerly opposed; he said, the Occasional Bill passed at a time when the Ministry seemed to intend some hardships to them and that he thought that Act only a prelude to the abrogating their Toleration; but that now this Bill had been brought into the other House by the Cheif of the Ministry with a Clause in it, that would in a scandalous manner have evaded the Test Act, which though it was dropp'd was a sufficient reason to discover their designs; That this would give a general Alarm to the Nation, and a great handle to the Disaffected, who would inculcate into the minds of the People, that many of the Measures which occasioned an unfortunate Princes Abdication were, now renewed. That whereas the Suspension of the Penal Laws and Test was laid to that Kings charge; He had mentioned before, how the Test Act had been lately struck at, That whereas He was accused of seizing Charters, there had been lately a Debate in Westminster Hall for ten days together, the Result of which might have laid most of the Corporations at their mercy; That the Ecclesiastical Commission had been declared illegal; That if Fame might be credited there was a Design of Visiting the Universities. He desired them to remember, that a noble Lord, who presided in that Kings Councils, and was excepted out of an Act of Grace for it, was afterwards at the head of K<ing> William's Affairs, and the reason assigned for this second station was, that he had perswaded his former Master to those measures that ended in his ruin; but he hoped nobody set him as a pattern now. That he thought there were people enough to fill all offices without capacitating any more disqualified, and put the Case, suppose a Secretary of State, either wearied with business, or through restlessness of temper, desired to lay down, there was no occasion of sending abroad for one to succeed him, though he might be never so true a Penitent, but that there might be found at home, some man of abilities enough for that station (by which you'll easily perceive he glanced at Bolingbroke and does not favour his return). He concluded That to their Comfort the Heir of the Crown could see the ill consequences of this, though the Minsitry did not, and had openly protested against it.

When it was urged in the Debate in relation to the Schism Bill that it was unnatural to deprive Parents of the Education of their Children, Shippen said, Since it was now the Case of the greatest Subject in England, he did not see why others should complain. The Tories made so brave a stand that it is thought the Victory is of little use to the Conquerors. The majority it was carried by I sent you in my last. Some of Walpole's party left him, though others, not expected, joyned him, particularly Lords Castlecomer and Hinchingbroke, Mr Wallop, Mr Smith, Sir Robert Worseley, Sir John Cope, Governour Pit and his eldest son, only four Scotch of the losing side. This Account I send you from a letter I received from London on Fryday...

Addressed: For/ Mrs Abigail Harley/ at Aywood near Presteigne/ Herefordshire

23. TO ABIGAIL HARLEY AT EYWOOD, 13 JANUARY 1718/19.

B.L., Add. MS 70034, unfoliated; printed H.M.C., *Portland MSS*, V, 576.

... Little news this post. All that I can send you is about the last Debate; and it may be what you will like to hear, that My Father spoke very handsomely against the bill, he laid open all the Exeter business (an Account of which I sent you some time ago) and in doing of it cleared the Dissenters; He seconded the motion made by Lord Guernsey for bringing in a Clause to prevent the Growth of Socinianism, which was rejected by a great Majority.[1] I hear my Father is much commended for what he said, and his Speech is extremely liked. The Lord[2] you enquired after, voted honestly in spight of Dutch principles. I hope at last he will be a thorough Convert...

Addressed: For/ Mrs Abigail Harley/ at Aywood near Presteigne/ Herefordshire

24. TO ABIGAIL HARLEY [AT EYWOOD], 18 JANUARY 1718/19.

B.L. Add. MS 70034, unfoliated; printed H.M.C., *Portland MSS*, V, 577.

... A Bill for the Regency is expected very soon in the House of Lords, but what the nature of it will be, whether the names will be certified in the Act, or left to the King's nomination is not yet certain.[1] On Wensday night Sir Edward Desboverie's Petition for Shaftsbury was heard at the Committee, where Benson was defeated, though, not only all the Germans, but the M<ona>rch himself solicited strenuosly for him.[2] The Princes Party and several of the other Court joyned the Torys upon this occasion, which shows that all sides were heartily weary of the sitting Member. Lechmere, Boscawen, Stanhope of the Treasury, etc., did not appear. About eleven Craggs moved for Adjourning, but losing it walked off with Asliabie and others; however, though the Cheifs were gone, the underlings were resolved to maintain their Post as long as they could, For Young, Erle of Bristol, Caswell, and some others of these second rated Members protracted the Debate with Speechs and Divisions till two in the Morning, when the Petitioner was voted duly elected by a Majority of 130 against 18.[3] The Torys have been of late so little used to triumphs, that you'll beleive this has elevated them. Benson is supposed to have exerted the utmost of his interest, so that 'tis not doubted but he will meet with the same Success, when the Committee make

---

Letter 23

[1] The vote was 234 to 136 on 9 Jan. See *C.J.*, XIX, 49; cf. Cobbett, VII, 589.
[2] All the peers of Dutch origin, descent, or connexion who voted (Schomberg, Portland, Rochford and Grantham), voted for committing the bill for the repeal of the Occasional Conformity and Schism Acts (B.L., Add. MS 47028, ff. 264–5).

Letter 24

[1] It appears never to have materialized, overtaken no doubt by the Peerage Bill.
[2] See Sedgwick, I, 236.
[3] This must have been in committee as no vote is recorded in *C.J.*

their Report to the House[4]... I have here inclosed a List of the Lords that Voted for and against the Church Bill[5]...

25. FROM EDWARD PRIDEAUX GWYN, WHITEHALL, 25 FEBRUARY 1719.

Brampton Bryan MSS, Bundle X.

Dear Sir

The two following pieces of News were so unexpected and surprising, that, when I heard them yesterday, I did not enough believe them, to trouble you with them last night. The first is in relation to the Chevalier,[1] who for several days has been reported to be taken by one of our Ships at Sea, but last night arived an express from Lord Stair, with a Letter, wrote from Genoa, which says, the Chevalier with Lords Mar and Melfort[2] Sett out from Rome on the 10th and that a few days after three Calathes,[3] and some attendants were seized by some German soldiers in the Milaneze, and the whole company were immediately carried to Milan and secured in the Castle there. I have forgott the day, on which they were apprehended, but it's agreed to square so well with the Chevalier's departure from Rome, that it was guessed him and his followers made up that company. However it's rumoured that a Letter of a fresher date from Genoa to Governor Pitt contradicts the whole story. So that till the next Mail full satisfaction cannot be expected. The House of Lords are adjourned to Friday, when they will remove into their old Apartment, it being now recovered by the report of the ablest Surveyors from the Terror, which Benson's Alarum[4] had putt them into. It's said a Bill is ready, and on that day will be brought into their House to encrease the number of Scotch Peers to 25, and to make them Hereditary, instead of Elective; and likewise to enact that the English Peerage for the future shall not exceed the number of 200, exclusive of Bishops, but that when any family is extinct, the King shall have the liberty of filling that Vacancy.[5] The advantage accruing by this Bill to the Lords is so apparent, that it will certainly pass with ease through their house, but if the Commons consent, they must surely be very forgetfull of themselves. This is so great an alteracon of the Constitution, that I believe the News of this Step will be as surprizing

---

4 William Benson (see Appendix) was unseated on 24 Jan. 1719, see Sedgwick, I, 455, and next letter.

5 Not found. A composite list giving the maximum strengths on both sides was published; a more specific one showing the vote on 19 Dec. 1718 on the committal of the bill was recorded by Lord Perceval. See *British Parliamentary Lists, 1660–1800: A Register*, ed. G.M. Ditchfield, David Hayton and Clyve Jones (1995), p. 45.

Letter 25

1 James Francis Edward, the Old Pretender, son of James II.

2 John Erskine (1675–1732), 6th earl of Mar, who had risen in 1715, fled to France and became one of the Pretender's chief advisers (until 1724), had been attainted in 1716; John Drummond (1682–1754), titular 2nd earl of Melfort, his father having been attainted in 1695, had been a maj.-gen. in the '15.

3 ? Calashes, a light carriage.

4 William Benson (see Appendix), as surveyor general of works, had reported that the house of lords was about to collapse and that members should transfer themselves to Westminster Hall. The house adjourned for a week and then received a report from the master-mason of works that the building was in good condition. Benson was eventually dismissed for his 'false and groundless' report. See Sedgwick, I, 455.

5 By the terms of the Peerage Bill (of which this letter is the first known specific account) the English and British peerages would have stood at 184 after the six extra allowed had been created. These, together with the 25 hereditary Scottish peers, gives a total of 209 (this ignores any princes of the blood, who were excluded from the terms of the bill). For the bill and its background see Clyve Jones, '"Venice Preserv'd; or A Plot Discovered": The Political and Social Context of the Peerage Bill of 1719', in *A Pillar of the Constitution: The House of Lords in British Politics, 1640–1784*, ed. Clyve Jones (1989), pp. 79–112.

to you, as it was here, but the truth of it is not disputed, which I cannot entirely say of the first part of my Letter. I should be glad to hear from you soon, how affairs go at Christ church and particularly whether Bromley[6] be returned to you, with my humble respects to Dr. Stratford I am your most obedient humble Servant E P G

Endorsed: From Mr Gwyn. R. Feb. 26 1718/19. Peerage Bill.

26. FROM EDWARD PRIDEAUX GWYN, WHITEHALL, 28 FEBRUARY 1718/19.

Brampton Bryan MSS, Bundle X.

Dear Sir

I could not deny myself the pleasure of acquainting you by the first opportunity that the melancholy story of my last has quite lost it's credit, and even those that wish it, profess not to believe it; The Informer's sending the Account immediately without waiting further Confirmation is owing to an eager desire of shewing his zeal, and it's said to appear by other Letters from the same place, that had he deferred his Intelligence for two days, he would have found it entirely contradicted. This day the House of Lords begun their grand affair; It was opened by the duke of Somerset, and seconded by the new Lord Steward <Argyll>; the former after declaring he thought Elective Peers were incongruous to the Constitucon of their House, and that they would be more at liberty in their votes if made Hereditary, insisted in the rest of his Speech upon preserving the dignity of that house, and thought limiting the number of those that were to sit there, one way towards it, and concluded with a motion that a day might be appointed to consider the State of the Peerage; the latter talked much of the grievances of the Peers of his own nation, in the Sovereign's being debarred the liberty of creating any of them English;[1] and said that any (who thought at all) must plainly see what an advantage Settling the number of Peers would be of, not only to the House, but to the nacon in general that by this method a Ministry would not have it in their power to turn the Scales by a new Creation whenever a Majority of the House should differ in opinion from the Court; and after Lord Oxford had made a short speech, the substance of which was that the Scotch peerage might be regulated, but that the Prerogative ought not to be invaded, it was agreed the State of the Peerage should be considered on Monday; when I hope to be there, and will send you the best Account, I can, of what pases. All the Whiggs, except the Leicester-fields party[2] espouse this Bill in the House of Lords, but I believe few Tories will joyn them. It's said the King will have liberty to create 10 English more, of which number it's said Lord Chief Justice King and Lechmere, and Boscawen will be three, and that Lord Castlemain with some of equal wealth with him (as Heathcott etc.)[3] wil be the rest.

---

6 William Bromley jr. (?1701–37), son of Speaker William Bromley (for whom see Appendix), was a student at Christ Church. He later became an M.P. See Sedgwick, I, 494–5.

Letter 26

1 The *English* peerage had been 'frozen' at the Anglo-Scottish Union of 1707; future creations were in the *British* peerage. In the Hamilton case of 1711, the Lords had resolved that anyone holding a Scottish peerage at the time of the Union and subsequently created a *British* peer could not sit in the Lords by virtue of their *British* peerage.

2 The 'Leicester-fields party' were supporters of the prince of Wales (the name taken from his residence Leicester House in Leicester Fields). He was personally opposed to the Peerage Bill as it would have curtailed his prerogative when he succeeded as king. Later his party in the Lords, led by Lord Lumley, supported the bill. See Jones, '"Venice Preserved"', p. 82; below, p. 222.

3 Castlemaine was a rich banker; Heathcote was a rich East India merchant. See Appendix for both.

The nine Scotch are as follow. Dukes of Hamilton, Buccleugh, Queensbury, Douglas, and Athol, Marquis of Tweedale, and Earls of Crawford, Findlater and Marchmont.[4] Were the House of Commons well attended, there might be some hopes of doing justice to this Bill in that House, but since not six of all the West Saxons[5] are in Town, I fear an Aristocracy will go down with them by a greater Majority than 41.[6] My respects to all friends particularly Mr. Bromley, whom I soon design to trouble with a Letter, I am Dear Sir Your very obedient humble Servant E P G

Endorsed: From Mr Gwyn. R. Mar. 1. 1718/19.

27. TO ABIGAIL HARLEY AT EYWOOD, [CHRIST CHURCH], 1 MARCH 1718/19.

B.L., Add. MS 70034, unfoliated; printed H.M.C., *Portland MSS*, V, 578.

… There is not business enough before the Parliament to keep them sitting a Week, but the Ministry themselves own the Sessions will not End till Easter, Every body from hence concludes that some extraordinary business is upon the Anvil, but of what nature I won't pretend to guess since opinions about it are so various… There is much talk in London of a Bill's being to be brought into the House of Lords to encrease the number of Scotch Peers to 25, and to make them Hereditary instead of Elective, and likewise to enact that the English Peerage for the future shall not exceed the number of 200, exclusive of Bishops, but that when any Family is extinct, the King shall have the liberty of filling that Vacancy. This is so great an Alteration of the English Constitution and Scotch union, that I beleive the news of it, will be as surprising to you as it is here. But the truth of it is not much Disputed…

Addressed: For/ Mrs Abigail Harley/ at Aywood near Presteigne/ Herefordshire

28. FROM EDWARD PRIDEAUX GWYN, WHITEHALL, 4 MARCH 1719.

Brampton Bryan MSS, Bundle X.

Dear Sir

Every body seems to agree, that the P<rinces>s Sobieski[1] has escaped, and that the Chevalier is not taken, but <it?> is doubted whether Lords Mar and Perth be not, the Jacobites give out *that the* bride and bridegroom are mett, and both are barqued for Spain. The House of Lords did not begin their debate till yesterday and satt so late,

---

[4] These nine peers were to be additional to the 16 elected representative peers already sitting.

[5] The term West Saxons applied to the west country M.P.s. It resulted from the extensive western interests and connexions built up since 1678 by Sir Edward Seymour M.P. (d. 1708), 'general of the West Saxons': 'A Dialogue Betwixt Whig and Tory' (1693), in *A Collection of State Tracts Publish'd in the Reign of William III* (3 vols., 1705–7), II, 309. This grouping had other names, such as 'Seymskeyes Western Empire' (H.M.C., *Portland MSS*, IV, 222). In 1705 Robert Harley was told that Francis Gwyn M.P. was 'Seymour's successor in his western Empire': Lord Poulett to Robert Harley, 2 May, quoted in Keith Feiling, *A History of the Tory Party, 1640–1714* (Oxford, 1924), p. 378. See also Lord Weymouth to James Grahme, 27 Sept. 1703, 'Sir Chuffer [Seymour] will be in town … and our West Saxons will come up quickly': Levens MSS quoted in W.A. Speck, *The Birth of Britain: A New Nation, 1700–1710* (1994), p. 56. See also, below p. 244 for a reference to the 'Saxon Corner' where west country M.P.s sat in the Commons.

[6] A reference to the majority that passed the Church Bill. See above, p. 213.

Letter 28

[1] Clementina Sobieski had been imprisoned at Salzburg by the emperor at the request of George I while on her way to Rome to marry the Pretender.

that I had not time to write last night. The Speakers were dukes of Bucks, Newcastle, Roxburgh and Montrose, Marquis of Anandale, Earls Sunderland, Peterborough, Carlisle, Nottingham, Poulet, Cowper and Islay, Archbishop of York, Bishops of Rochester, Glocester, and Peterborough, Lords Townshend, Carteret and Coningsby. Lord Sunderland begun the debate with an Historical deduction (as he called it) of the Steps that had been taken towards an Union from the time of King James the 1st, said that the constant obstruction to it had been fixing the number of Scotch peers and regulating their manner of sitting in the English house, that at the Union, when both sides had agreed upon the number, they were established upon a footing derogatory to the dignity of both Peerages, that he had the honour of being a Commissioner, and should never have agreed to this part of the Treaty had it not been for establishing the Succession in the House of Hannover, That he was in the late Queens service when the duke of Dover[2] was created and represented it to her, that that would be looked upon as an Invasion of the Union and that he doubted whether even that Lords services would procure him an easie Seat in the House of Lords. He then said that that Lord had been admitted quietly, yet in the next instance which was the duke of Brandon's they had passed a Resolucon which excluded for ever any Scotch Lords from the benefit of <an> English Peerage,[3] that if this were adhered to (as he believed it would be) they should lose the Company of the young duke of Dover, who notwithstanding his Father's merits and his being a youth of great hopes would not be allowed a Seat there.[4] He believed both nacons thought the Tenure by which Scotch Lords satt very improper, and then proceeded to open his Scheme of having 25 hereditary instead of the Elective, but that these sixteen might be allowed to sitt, till the end of the sessions, when the whole might be named. He then toke notice of the great increase of the English peerage in the late Reigns, and that his Majesty had graciously offered not to insist upon his prerogatvie if that stood in their way, and having talked a good deal of limiting the number, he said it might be however proper to come to some resolucon first in relation to the Scotch Lords and then concluded for putting the Question. 'Whether in lieu of the 16 elective there should be 25 Hereditary peers for the future to represent the peerage of Scotland'. Lord Cowper stood up next and said, that it must be very agreeable to him and everyone there to preserve the honour, dignity, and independancy of that house, which had subsisted for many ages with the greatest splendor without the limitacon now proposed, that therefore none could say it was absolutely necessary. That there had been in some reigns an abuse, or at least an excessive use, of the prerogatvie of the Crown, but he thought, the more ready his Majesty was to part with it, the more tender they should be of it, if any other way could be found to attain their end. That there was an old limitacon, which if always well observed, would have been sufficient, ministers advising the Crown to be sparing in conferring honours, and never doing it but to those whose transcendent merits called for them, and whose choice the whole world would approve; that he could not pretend to say whether they could be sure of that now, but left it to the ministry (who knew better) to answer whether that would be the case or not; that ministers had great honours and emoluments belonging to their Stacons, that they might ease the Crown

---

[2] The Scottish 2nd duke of Queensberry had been created duke of Dover in the British peerage in 1708. He had sat in the Lords by virtue of his new peerage until his death in 1711.

[3] The Lords' resolution of 1711 following the duke of Hamilton's case (he had been created duke of Brandon in the *British* peerage) did not prevent Scottish peers being created British peers, but only from sitting in the Lords by virtue of that peerage. By a vote in 1709 over the duke of Queensberry, Scottish peers holding British peerages also could not vote or stand in the elections for the representative peers.

[4] See below, pp. 225–7.

of part of the burthen, and that none could do their King or country better service, than by screening him from the importunities of those, who might press for honours, when they did not deserve them, that if it should be judged necessary to restrain the number, he thought they should do it to the present, for it would be very absurd to leave room for the Continuance of an abuse, which they apeared so zealous to prevent. That he believed they were all willing to change the Tenure of the Scotch peers, but that surely those who had the chusing the Elective ought to name the Hereditary ones, which were to represent them for ever. That in common justice no man's property was to be taken away without his own consent, that he thought therefore the peerage should be summoned to agree to this alteracon and to chuse their future Representatives, and having laboured for a good while to shew the injustice of the 25 being nominated by any but the whole peerage of Scotland, was answered by Lord Sunderland, 'that then they must summon a Scotch parliament for that the Commons as well as the Lords had passed the Act in that Kingdom, which made the Scotch peers Elective; that he did not think the consent of either necessary; that in the Septennial Bill,[5] (the merits of which he would not enter into) the Commons of Great Brittain had continued themselves for a longer time than they were chosen, without consulting their Principals'. To which Lord Cowper replyed 'that the Commons of Scotland had no concern in this alteracon, it being a matter entirely indifferent to them and only relating to the peerage, that the Septennial Act being only a Temporary continuance did not reach the present case, but believed no body would advance, that the Commons of England could pass an Act to make themselves Hereditary without having recourse to their constituents'. The Duke of Newcastle said, 'since the King had waved his prerogative, and that it was now flung among them, he hoped they would not lett it return'. His whole Speech was so heavy and consisted only of the common Arguments that it is not worth troubling you with. Lord Peterborough was for restraining the number of peers and said that what a noble Lord had menconed of advising a Ministry to do right would be ineffectual, though the great Tillotson[6] should preach to them from the pulpit. The Bishop of Rochester said it was a complicated Question and would have divided it into three, he said at the end of a parliament the Scotch peers must assemble to elect new representatives, that therefore they might as easily be summoned to chuse the 25 Hereditary. The ArchBishop of York was against increasing the Scotch, that it might be used as an Argument for increasing the English, that if two were added to the Sixteen, they would have the same proportion to English Lords, as the 45 in the other house had to the rest of the Commons. The drift of the Scotch speeches were to shew that it was impossible to have an Election in Scotland and that it was not necessary to ask the consent of the Scotch peerage, since it was plain they were bettered by it. To day the Committee will proceed upon the English peerage; whither I am just going, and therefore must conclude Yours most sincerely E P G

The Resolucon was carried without dividing[7] That in lieu of the 16 Elective there should be 25 Hereditary to be declared by his Majesty.

Endorsed: From Mr Gwyn. R. Mar. 5. 1718/19.

---

[5] The act of 1716 changed the maximum length of a parliament from three to seven years. It applied immediately so that the Commons elected in 1715 sat until 1722.

[6] John Tillotson, archbishop of Canterbury, 1691–4.

[7] There was a division of 86 to 30 in favour. This was the only one during the whole course of the Peerage Bill, both in Mar.–Apr. 1719 and Nov. 1719.

29. FROM EDWARD PRIDEAUX GWYN, WHITEHALL, 5 MARCH 1718/19.

Brampton Bryan MSS, Bundle X.

Dear Sir

Yesterday the Lords proceeded to take into Consideration the State of the English Peerage, the debate was opened by Lord Carlisle, who gave him self the trouble of a very long Speech, but spoke so very low that I believe scarce ten in the house heard him, so that unless his Lordship will please to print, I can give you no account of what he said; the motion that he concluded with was; 'That the proportion of the Peerage of Great Brittain for England should not exceed the present time number above six, but that upon any failure the King might Supply the vacancy out of Natural born Subjects of Great Brittain, and so toties quoties as often as it shall happen'. This was seconded by the Duke of Kingston 'who argued that it was very reasonable the nomination of at least six above the determined number should be left to the King, as a decent return for his gracious message'. Lord Stanhope thirded the mocon, who said 'that the Peerage had been increased 120 since the 1st. of James the 1st., that indeed from that time the Commons by reason of the increase of Trade had so increased in wealth and power, that creating of the most considerable among them Peers had from time to time (he thought) contributed towards supporting the dignity of that house; that it was a constant rule in Government to preserve an equal ballance and due equilibrium between the several parts of it, that one might not outweigh the other; that were he to form the Government de novo, he would not think of a less number of Peers than they were at present, but thought this might be a proper standard for the future. 'That the numerous creacons of late years had made more commoners think of peerages, than formerly used to do. That he did not speak without knowledge there had been great importunities of this kind, that though a King and ministry might withstand them, yet such uncommon virtue and steadiness was too great to be always expected in a Court. That by a Limitation the Crown would be eased of this Burthen, and be secured against any Arguments which Commoners of wealth and power should bring, when they pressed for <a> peerage; that, though they restrained themselves to the present number except six (as he hoped they would do) yet extinctions of honours would happen so often, that there would be always vacancies enough, to reward as much merit, as these ages were likely to produce. That though he had great regard to the peerage, and knew this Limitacon would much strengthen the honour and independency of it, yet he would never consent to it, were he not satisfied it was of equal advantatge to the Commons. For as the Ballance would be too much against the Lords if there were fewer peers of fortune, so it might hereafter turn too much for them, if this Latitude of creating without any restraint were continued. For if in time 150 of the wealthiest and most powerful Commoners should be created Peers, their Interest joyned to what was in the House already would have almost an entire sway in Elections, and reduce the Majority of those that would be chosen to little better than Bayliffs to the Peers. He then concluded with thirding the mocon. Lord Cowper was for reducing the number that was to be left to the King as low as possible, and said he had rather it sould be even 5 than six, and thought it proper they should not be made immediately but a vacancy or two always reserved by the Crown, that it might be sure of always having an opportunity to reward merit. Not one Lord opposed this Resolucon of restraining the number; but the rest of the day was spent in a mere point of Heraldry (viz. how far the Baronries succession of the Peers eldest sons, who were called by Writt did extend) the debate upon which Question was pleasanter to me, that am a dabbler in Heraldry to hear than it would be to you to read. However this lasted them till after six a Clock, the following Lords spoke either to this point, or to the wording some of the Resolucons. Dukes of Bucks and Argyll, Earls of Sunderland, Peterborough, Nottingham, Islay, and Strafford, Lords North, Lumley, Carteret, Harcourt, Trevor, Parker, and Bishop of Rochester. The rest of the Resolucons were these. That when the Father of any Peer called <by> writ to the House of Peers died, the King might create another in his room. 2dly. That for the future no Baron should be created by Writt; 3dly that no Patent granted for the future should extend further than to the Grantee and the Issue Male of his body. There appeared so little opposicon to the Bill in general, that it will probably be sent to the other house next week, where I hope there is greater prospect of it's being opposed, than at first thoughts one might expect. I have been so tedious already, that I won't pretend to trouble with any other news; but conclude with what I hope you won't think as news My assurances of being your most obedient humble servant

Endorsed: From Mr Gwyn. R: Mar: 6: 1718/19.

30. FROM EDWARD PRIDEAUX GWYN, 5 MARCH [1719].

Brampton Bryan MSS, Bundle X.

Dear Sir,

My other Letter, which I wrote this morning, being Sent to the Post-house before I came home, I give you the trouble of a Second to acquaint you with a surprizing piece of News, which I did not at first credit, till Lord Stanhope talked of it publickly in the House of Lords. That Lord Stair[1] had sent Intelligence of a great Imbarcation of Troops making at Cales and another port in Spain, that these Squadrons are to joyn, be under the Command of the Duke of Ormonde, and to land at Bristol. This is so much believed, that Routes are making at the War-office for the march of four Regiments of foot and two of Dragoons into the West. I forgott to mention in my former Letter the two last Resolucons of the Lords Committee last night,[2] the 1st. that the King should not be restrained from creating any Prince of the Blood a Peer of this Realm, the 2d. that any Patent of Peerage granted for the future contrary to any of these Resolucons should be null and void. To day the Report was made and agreed to by the Lords who likewise voted that if any of the 25 Scotch Peers died without issue male his Title and Seat in Parliament should be enjoyed by any who were within the entail of the Scotch honour, then the Lords ordered the judges to draw up a Bill pursuant to these Resolucons. You may be assured of the following piece of News that at a late meeting of the dissenting Teachers in Town 57 consented and 53 refused to Sign this article: I believe the Father, Son, and Holy-Ghost to be one God blessed for evermore.[3]

With respect to friends I am Yours most faithfully E P G

Endorsed: From Mr Gwyn R: Mar: 6: 1718/19.

Letter 30

[1] Lord Stair was ambassador in Paris at this time. See Appendix.

[2] Eleven resolutions were reported on 5 Mar. See *L.J.*, XXI, 89–90.

[3] The crucial meeting in the 'non-subscription controversy' had taken place in Salters' Hall on 24 Feb. 1719, when the ministers in London voted by 57 to 53 against the inclusion of a declaration on the Trinity in a paper of 'Advices'. Gwyn refers here to a further meeting, in Mar. 1719, where a group withdrew from the proceedings to sign a declaration of their belief in the Trinity, by subscribing to the 1st Article of the Church of England and the 5th and 6th Articles of the Assembly's catechism. A paper at Brampton Bryan records the names of 60 subscribers, plus one who signed later, and 53 non-subscribers. Brampton Bryan MSS, Bundle 117.

31. FROM EDWARD PRIDEAUX GWYN, WHITEHALL, 7 MARCH 1718/19.

Brampton Bryan MSS, Bundle X.

Dear Sir,

I am very much obliged to you for your last, and the Copy of the Inscription you sent me in it; your Letter, wherein you first mentioned the Statue came to my hands; and I ask pardon for not acknowledging the receipt of it sooner.[1] Lord Trevor's behaviour in the late debates has been but the same with almost every Peer, and it's undoubtedly for the advantage of that House that the Bill should pass, so that we may even allow Simon[2] himself to have no sinister end in appearing for it. As the Bill cannot come to the Commons this ten days, the Gentlemen in the Country have no reason to complain of want of time; there's yet no judging of it's fate in the lower House, since it so much depends upon the attendance of the Tories, and desertion from the Whiggs.[3] You must have heard with how much rudeness and insolence Lechmere treated Craggs upon the Iron Bill,[4] It was said this morning that the ministry finding him thus intractable had resolved to dismiss him immediately, but I have since heard that he has beged the Secretarie's pardon, and has obtained a promise of being one of the Six. Boscawen has had a Warrant for a viscount this twelve-month and is now to take out his Patent;[5] The Lord How of Ireland is likewise to be another of the six, and to marry Madam Kilmanseg's daughter.[6] It's again confidently reported the Chevalier is in the Castle of Milan, but since they, who revive this Story, would possess us with fears of an Invasion I don't well see, how both can be credited. The troops are preparing to march to the west, and are to be commanded by Wills and Gore.[7] I am very sorry to hear the Ague can find Palmer at Oxford as well as in Essex but I hope soon to hear a better Account of him, with service to him and all friends I am, your most obedient humble servant E P G

Endorsed: From Mr Gwyn. R. Mar. 8 1718/19.
Addressed: For Mr Harley at Christ church, Oxford.

32. FROM EDWARD PRIDEAUX GWYN, WHITEHALL, 26 MARCH 1719.

Brampton Bryan MSS, Bundle X.

Dear Sir

I am not only obliged to you for yours by the last post, but my Father owes it to you, that he received the like favour from Francis, which is almost as great a rarity, as the meteor he described. This day the Lords in a Committee proceeded on the Peerage

---

Letter 31

[1] Neither of these letters has been traced.

[2] Possibly a family cant name.

[3] For the two forecasts of the support and opposition in the Commons by James Craggs jr. and Lord Sunderland in late Feb. and mid Mar., which confirmed Gwyn's point, see Jones, '"Venice Preserved"', pp. 99–100.

[4] A bill to prevent the inconveniences arising from the seducing of artificers in iron and steel manufacturing into foreign parts had its 1st reading on 5 Feb. and passed the Commons on 5 Mar.; it was lost by the prorogation on 18 Apr. *C.J.*, XIX, 89, 120, 163–4.

[5] Boscawen was created Viscount Falmouth on 9 June 1720.

[6] On 8 Apr. 1719 Howe married the daughter of Baroness Kielmansegge (George I's half-sister), later countess of Darlington.

[7] For Wills see Appendix; Humphrey Gore (d. 1739), brig.-gen. taken prisoner at Brihuega in Spain in 1710; maj.-gen. 1727; lt.-gen. 1735.

Bill, and (having received a Clause from the Judges to enable the King to nominate the duchess of Buccleugh[1] one of the 25, that her son might have a seat in Parliament) went through the Bill and ordered it to be reported on Monday sevennight, then adjourned to Thursday, the Commons have done the same; you'll see by this that the patrons of this Bill are not so eager to send it down as they were a Week ago, hoping (I suppose) by these delays to make some of the Country Gentlemen weary of such an Attendance, but the Members are at present in so High mettle, that I don't find this art is like to avail; nay I hope it might invite some up, who might have despaired of being there in time, had the Bill come down sooner. There are already near 500 in town, and more dayly expected. The duchess of Munster is to be made an English duchess.[2] It was at first said, her title would be Canterbury, but now that it will be Kendale, which has been formerly enjoyed by some of the Royal Family.[3] You'll see by the prints that Lord Dundonald[4] (who joyned in the Scotch petition[5]) has orders to sell his Troop of Guards, and Lord Faulkland[6] who likewise signed it, has lost his pension. Bos<cawen> who has declared for the Bill, yet says if it passes, he shall not be one of the six. I cannot think of any thing else to trouble you with but that I am yours most assuredly

I believe you'll like the second plebeian better than the first I cannot say positively who is the Author, Sir R. Steele, and Walpole were at first named but most agree, that it's too good for the former, and too bad for the latter.[7]

Endorsed: From Mr Gwyn. R. March 27, 1719. Peerage Bill.

33. FROM EDWARD PRIDEAUX GWYN, WHITEHALL, 16 APRIL 1719.

Brampton Bryan MSS, Bundle X.

Dear Sir

The Scarcity of News both from abroad or at home will I hope excuse a long silence. This day the Lords with the White staves brought the House of Lords a message in answer to their Representation about Benson 'that His Majesty in compliance with their address had suspended Mr. Benson from the execution of his office, and had given Orders to the proper Officer to prosecute him immediately'. The Lords thereupon ordered an Address of Thanks, and the Whole Proceedings to be printed.[1] His being first thrown out of the House of Commons, and now discarded by the Court it's thought has effectually done his business, and notwithstanding his reversion of an Auditorship it's probable the next news we have of him will be that he has crossed the Seas. The Commons have no business before them, and all the Bills with the Lords

Letter 32
[1] The widow of the duke of Monmouth, she was a Scottish duchess in her own right and was succeeded by her son, the earl of Dalkeith.
[2] Melusine von der Schulenberg (1667–1743), mistress, and possible morganatic wife, of George I, was created duchess of Kendal in 1719.
[3] Previously the Kendal title had been held by Queen Anne's husband, Prince George of Denmark (earl of Kendal and duke of Cumberland), the second son of James II (duke of Kendal), and the third son of Henry IV (earl of Kendal and duke of Bedford).
[4] John Cockrane (1687–1720), 4th earl of Dundonald, was col. of the 4th horse guards 1715–19.
[5] Against the Peerage Bill.
[6] Lucius Henry Cary (1687–1730), 6th viscount of Falkland.
[7] Steele was the author of *The Plebean*, No. 2 published on 23 Mar. 1719, which opposed the Peerage Bill.

Letter 33
[1] See Torrington, vol. 1718–19 to 1724–5, pp. 3–7.

will be ready for the Royal Assent by Saterday and that in all probability the Parliament will then be prorogued.[2] Lord C.[3] is ordered to sett out for his embassy to Holland within two or three days *whether it be his own choice* or not, I can't say. Or whether he'll be one of the six Dukes before he goes. The rest are, Earl of Manchester, duke of Manchester, Earl of Carlisle, duke of Northumberland, Earl of Berkeley, duke of Berkeley, Earl of Carnarvon, duke of Chandos, and Earl Stanhope but by what title I don't know. There is much talk of a new Chancellor and some say it will be Lord H<arcour>t and that the duke of Somersett will soon be declared Master of the Horse. By the latter end of next week I hope to be with you, and with services to all our friends am your very humble servant E P G

Endorsed: From Mr Gwyn. R. April 17. 1719.

34. TO ABIGAIL HARLEY AT EYWOOD, 17 DECEMBER 1719.

B.L., Add. MS 70145, unfoliated.

... I hear very little News now the great noise about the Peerage Bill is over[1]... The House of Commons very thin most of the members being gone down again, and it is thought nothing but some extraordinary Bill or the Serjeant at Arms will fetch them up. The House of Lords as empty. Duke of Queensbury Case was brought before them a week ago but their adjourning it from time to time seems to intimate that they are not willing that his Grace should have any seat in that House.[2] The great appearance that was at Leicesterfeilds the night the Bill was thrown out cannot but nettle very much, and certainly adds more Fuel to the Flame. Among your receipts pray add this infallible one, To Quench a Fire, through Oil upon it...

Addressed: To/ Mrs Abigail Harley/ at Aywood near Presteigne/ Herefordshire.

35. FROM EDWARD PRIDEAUX GWYN, WHITEHALL, 14 JANUARY 1719/20.

Brampton Bryan MSS, Bundle 102.

I am very much obliged to Dear Mr Harley for his kind expressions in his last, and do assure him that I esteem the liberty of a Correspondence with him as a great happiness. The Lords according to their Adjournment this day resumed the Duke of Queensbury's affair, the King's Council for Scotland were first heard to the point, whether a Minor being before the Union created a Peer of Scotland, was at liberty upon coming of age to accept or refuse that Patent. They agreed in the Affirmative, and after they were withdrawn, Lord Carleton made a long speech to distinguish the duke of Queensbury's case from Duke <of> Hamilton's, and to prove that the Lords resolucon in the case of the latter, could not prejudice the right of the former, and though he thought the Father's sitting in the House might give a sufficient title to the Son, yet supposing the Father by being a Scotch Peer under an incapacity of being created an

[2] On 18 Apr. *L.J.*, XXI, 152.
[3] Cadogan, ambassador to The Hague 1714–16, 1716–20.

Letter 34
[1] Reintroduced on 25 Nov. 1719, the bill passed the Lords in five days, but was rejected by the Commons on 8 Dec. by 269 votes to 177.
[2] The 2nd duke of Dover (3rd duke of Queensberry) had come of age on 24 Nov. 1719 and had petitioned the Lords for a writ of summons notwithstanding the 1711 resolution which barred Scottish peers with British titles.

English one, yet since the Scotch Lawyers had declared that the Earldom of Sollway by being granted to him when a minor, was according to the law of Scotland at his refusal when of age, the present duke was a Commoner when the remainder in his Father's patent was limited to him, and consequently had a right to the writt which he now demanded. Lord Sunderland answered that he thought the Duke of Q<ueens-berry> came under the judgment which they had made upon <the> Duke <of> H<amilton>; and that if the Principal person in the Patent was under an incapacity of receiving it, the Patent must be void as to the Grantee in remainder; that unless this were allowed, a Foreigner might be created a Peer, and if he entailed it on a Natural born Subject, that person in remainder might claim his Seat; he concluded that he was sorry his judgment would not permitt him to be for the Duke, but he should very gladly embrace any other way, supposing an Act of Parliament to make him easie. Lord Cowper answered him in behalf of the duke, afterwards the dukes of Bucks and Argyll, Lords Cowper and Guilford spoke for the Writt, Lords Coningsby, North and Gray, and Trevor against it, the chief point in debate among them was the Scotch Peerage, but even those who were against the duke expressed their readiness to agree to a Bill in his favour. It's now six a Clock, but the House nott up, though it might easily be guessed from the debate, that the Majority were not inclined in his favour; however it's hoped they may agree to relieve him by the other method. This is all the publick news I think stirring; some say a general Peace is concluded, but won't tell us what terms are stipulated for England.[1] Benson made me a visit this morning, and enquired very kindly for you. I am just going to dinner so you'll excuse hast from yours etc. E P G

Endorsed: From Mr Gwyn: R: Jan. 15 1719/20.

36. TO ABIGAIL HARLEY AT EYWOOD, 17 JANUARY 1719/20.

B.L., Add. MS 70034, unfoliated; printed H.M.C., *Portland MSS*, V, 590–1.

The General talk for this week past has cheifly turned upon the <Duke> of Dover's Affair, which was on Thursday last determined against him, though with no small solemnity for the Kings Council for Scotland were first heard to the Point, whether a Minor being before the Union created a Peer of Scotland, was at liberty upon coming of Age to accept or refuse that Patent, they agreed in the Affirmative (for the present Duke was created Earl of Solway in Scotland during his minority, and before the patent passed for creating his Father Duke of Dover). After the Council were withdrawn, Lord Carleton made a long Speech to distinguish the Duke of Queensbury's case from D<uke of> Hamilton's and to prove that the Lords' resolution in the case of the latter could not prejudice the right of the former. Lord Sunderland answered That he thought the Duke of Queensbury came under the judgement which they had made upon D<uke of> Hamilton, and that if the Principal person in the Patent was under an incapacity of receiving it, the Patent must be void as to the Grantee in remainder; that unless this were allowed a Forreigner might be created a Peer, and if he entailed it on a natural born subject, that Person in remainder might claim his seat; He concluded that he was sorry his judgement would not permit him to be for the Duke, but he should gladly embrace any other way (supposing an Act of Parliament) to make him easy. Lord Cowper answered him in behalf of the Duke; afterwards the Dukes of

Letter 35
[1] The treaty of The Hague of 17 Feb. 1720 ended the war with Spain when that country joined the Quadruple Alliance of 1718. It was ratified by Britain on 31 Mar.

Bucks <and> Argyll, Lords Cowper and Guilford spoke for the Writt. Lords Trevor, Harcourt, North and Coningsby against it. The cheif point in Debate among them was the Scotch Peerage, but even those who were against the Duke expressed their readiness to agree to a Bill in his favour. After six at night the House divided: 61 against the Writt, 42 for it. No Bishops Voted for it but Arch Bishop of York and Bishop of Chester. Oxford and Lincoln went out. Ruffen[1] and the rest staid and voted against him. It is said Lord Harcourt has all his Arrears paid and is to have £3000 pension. Some say a General Peace is concluded, but do not tell us what terms are stipulated for England...

Addressed: To/ Mrs Abigail Harley/ at Aywood near Presteigne/ Herefordshire

37. TO ABIGAIL HARLEY, 3 MARCH 1719/20.

B.L., Add. MS 70145, unfoliated.

... I hear my Fathers Bill to prevent the corruption of Juries is ordered to be Engrossd,[1] intend when it passes to write to him upon it... Gibraltar is certainly to be delivered up,[2] it was at first intended that This should be laid before the Lords and Commons, but that is now droped and it is to be done without it. The Call was moved for by Walpole and the discontented Whigs[3] and it is thought that This will then be enquired into...

Addressed: To/ Mrs Abigail Harley/ at Bramton Castle near Presteigne/ Herefordshire

38. TO [THE EARL OF OXFORD], LONDON, 5 APRIL 1720.

B.L., Add. MS 70237, unfoliated.

... The South Sea Bill was committed to Day in the House of Lords,[1] Duke of Wharton, Lord Cooper, and others spoke against it. It is thought the Bill will pass this Week. I have had the good fortune to assist the Turkey Company upon a Debate,[2] and They are pleased to flatter me, that what I said had carryed the Question in their Favour; If I could do this, What might have been done in other matters?...

Letter 36
[1] The Harley family cant name for Francis Atterbury, bishop of Rochester, based on Roffen, the Latin title of the diocese; sometimes given as 'Abbot Ruffen'. See B.L., Add. MS 70237: EH to [Oxford], 20 May 1720.

Letter 37
[1] The bill was ordered to be engrossed on 1 Mar. and passed its 3rd reading on 8 Mar. *C.J.*, XIX, 288, 296.
[2] Possibly a rumour concerned with the recent treaty of The Hague, see above Letter 35, n. 1.
[3] The call of the House for 8 Mar. was ordered on 25 Feb. On the 8th it was postponed until the 17th, and continued to be postponed until the 7 Apr. when it disappears from the record. *C.J.*, XIX, 282, 296, 304, 318, 326, 332–5.

Letter 38
[1] The bill was to allow the South Sea Company to take over a large part of the unfunded national debt. For the debate on the 1st reading on 9 Apr. with the speeches of Wharton and Cowper, see Cobbett, VIII, 646–7.
[2] Proceedings on the Levant (Turkey) Company's charter and by-laws took place on 27 Feb., 2, 7 Mar. and 12 Apr. 1720. On the 1 Apr. there was an order for the 3rd reading in the Commons of an 'Act for the prohibiting the importation of raw silk and mohair yarn...', which passed on the 6th. *C.J.*, XIX, 284, 290, 294, 327, 332, 337, 356.

39. TO ABIGAIL HARLEY, LONDON, 7 APRIL 1720.

B.L., Add. MS 70145, unfoliated.

... South Sea Stock sinks though the Bill is passed, the Monarch made no speech, which shews Lord St<anho>pe has brought no News for the Ministry to brag off. If you will have Peace you must buy it...

Addressed: For/ Mrs Abigail Harley

40. TO ABIGAIL HARLEY, 2 AUGUST 1720.

B.L., Add. MS 70145, unfoliated.

... There is again a fresh talk of a New Parliament which has gained so much credit with some, that Intrest is already making in several places, I must own my Faith is not yet strong enough to beleive it. Duke Wharton is again turned Tory,[1] being disgusted at the Ministry for not making him Lord Lieutenant of Bucks: He has promised to be the Freind of the Church and University, says his Family have been too long Enemies to both, and that He will endeavour to make amends for what they did. This is his common talk in publick Company. He has already promised to give £600 to All Souls College and intends to come over to the University to have a Doctor of Laws Degree conferred on Him...

41. TO ABIGAIL HARLEY, 23 FEBRUARY 1720/21.

B.L., Add. MS 70145, unfoliated.

... I was told last night of some Alterations that were to be made. Methuen Secretary of State, Poultney Chancellor of the Exchequer and Carpenter in the War Office in the room of Treby. Some think Lord S<underland> will stand his Ground though the others get Strength dayly. Edgcomb is to be Comptroller.

The Jury Bill passed the House of Commons without opposition, I hope it will meet with Success in the Lords:[1] The Lords expect a great deal of mirth on Saturday, when Lord Coninsby is to be heard against the Chancellor, the 2nd part of his Works are printed but not yet distributed[2]...

Addressed: For/ Mrs Abigail Harley/ at Bramton Castle/ near Presteigne/ Herefordshire.

Letter 40
[1] Wharton, a follower of the prince of Wales, who had not accepted the double reconciliation between the prince and the king and between the whig dissidents and the ministry in April 1720, had joined Lord Cowper's new opposition group in the Lords which consisted of whigs and tories. He was to desert the opposition for the ministry in Dec. 1721. See Clyve Jones, 'The New Opposition in the House of Lords, 1720–3', *Historical Journal*, XXXVI (1993), 313–15. The duke of Bridgwater was ld. lt. of Buckinghamshire, 1714–28.

Letter 41
[1] It had passed the Commons on 21 Feb.; and had its 1st reading in the Lords on 15 Mar. 1721. The 2nd reading was ordered for 30 Mar., but the house did not sit on that day and the bill never reappeared in the Lords which sat until 29 July (*C.J.*, XIX, 454; *L.J.*, XXI, 474, 489–90, 583–4). A two page *Abstract of the Bill for Preventing the Corrupting of Juries* was published.
[2] 'The First Part of Earl of Coningsby's Case, relating to the Vicarage of Lempster in Herefordshire' was read on 25 Feb., and voted a scandalous libel on the Lord Chancellor on the 27th (*L.J.*, XXI, 448, 450). Coningsby was committed to the Tower for six months. See Sedgwick, I, 571. The *E.S.T.C.* does not record a second part.

were present, and only five for the Bill, Canterbury, London, Winchester, Chester and Litchfield and Coventry. All the rest Divided against it.[1] To what a Dismal condition are we reduced! When B<ishop>s Defend Blasphemy and Infidelity, and Betray Religion, J<ud>gs skreen Corruptions in the Law, and the M<inis>try Villanies in the State. I think since our Holy Religion and its Great Author is thus betrayed, We can expect nothing but Misery and Desolation.

To shew that our Credit is as much taken care of as our Religion, the 7 Millions is given up. Crags Estate is made liable as Mr Aislabie, only they have granted to his Heirs all the Estate real and Personal that he was possessed of in December, 1719: but all the rest is confiscated[2]...

Addressed: For/ Mrs Abigail Harley

51. TO ABIGAIL HARLEY, 9 MAY 1721.

B.L., Add. MS 70034, unfoliated; printed H.M.C., *Portland MSS*, V, 621.

<P.S.> Since I sealed this the Car<dinal>[1] (who presents his most humble service) told me that Tom Vernon was yesterday expelled the House for attempting to corrupt Ross.[2] He called Ross out of the Committee and told him Aslabie<'s> Bill[3] was to come on, and offered him a large sum which Ross refused, and then told the House. I am very sorry for him, for I think him an honest man.

Addressed: For/ Mrs Abigail Harley

52. TO ABIGAIL HARLEY, 21 MAY 1721.

B.L., Add. MS 70145, unfoliated.

... I have a pleasant story to tell you of Ruff. He sent for a Copy of the Blasphemy Bill. Then sent for the Clerk to expostulate with Him for sending Him a false Copy. The Clerk to justify himself brought the Original to Him, and desired Him to compare them. He then begged his Pardon, and said the Reason of His Suspicion was, that He did not think it had been possible for any one to offer so absurd a Bill to the Lords. He thought Lord Nottingham had had the cheif Hand in drawing it up, and designed this as an Affront to Him. But it happened Lord Trevor was the person cheifly concerned. Lord N<ottingham> told this story to Lord Trevor...

Addressed: For/ Mrs Abigail Harley

Letter 50
[1] There were 13 bishops present. *L.J.*, XXI, 510.
[2] See Sedgwick, I, 592.

Letter 51
[1] Almost certainly the Harley family cant name for William Stratford, canon of Christ Church, and a regular correspondent of Edward, Lord Harley. H.M.C., *Portland MSS*, VII, *passim*.
[2] See Sedgwick, I, 499.
[3] The 'Bill for restraining John Aislabie Esquire from going out of the Kingdom for the Space of One Year...', which had had its 1st reading in the Commons on 14 Mar. At its 2nd reading and committal on 21 Apr. the house ordered that the committee of the whole house amalgamate this bill with the 'Bill for the Sufferers of the South Sea Company'. The new bill was considered by the committee on 8 May, passed the Commons on 7 July, and returned from the Lords with amendments, which were agreed to by the Commons, on 25 July. The bill appears to have been lost by the prorogation on the 29th (*C.J.*, XIX, 479, 522, 542, 627, 637–8; *L.J.*, XXI, 584). See below, p. 235.

53. TO ABIGAIL HARLEY, 27 MAY 1721.

B.L., Add. MS 70145, unfoliated.

… I hear my Father intends to leave the Town very soon, Monday sen'night is the Call when Another Report is to be considered wherein all the Members of both Houses concerned in taking Stock are to be named.[1] It was moved that Blunt should be allowed but a shilling but upon a Division he got a £1000, none of the others have less than 5000[2]…

Addressed: For/ Mrs Abigail Harley

54. TO ABIGAIL HARLEY, 30 MAY 1721.

B.L., Add. MS 70034, unfoliated; printed H.M.C., *Portland MSS*, V, 622.

I was in hopes to have told you My Dear Aunt of my Fathers being here this Evening, but being disappointed of a place in the Coach He has put off his Journey till to morrow, His Company will be a great refreshment to my Mother and upon that Account as well as the benefit which I hope he will himself receive from the Country Air and Quiet, I wish He was with you, To stay till the End of the Session would be very tedious, for there is no talk yet or any appearance of their rising, and what their long sitting will signify you may easily guess. You will see in Saturdays Votes the wrath of the House against Mist and their Zeal for the Monarch,[1] yet I think the Libel lyes in the Application and not in the Paper itself. If the Journal should have miscarried on Saturday let me know and I will send you one.

Upon the Allowance to be made to Blunt,[2] a warm debate arose. The Court violent against Him. Laurence Carter moved that He should have but a shilling. Walpole said that He was the Projector of this banefull scheme, that His Informations were only whispers and Hearsays, and that as He had been the cheif Contriver and Manager He should have the greater punishment. To This Shippen said, That He was no Advocate for Blunt, who had been recommended to the Favour of the House by the Secret Committee for the Light he had given them, but that now He perceived that the Discoveries Sir John had made were his greatest Crimes and therefore He was to be made an Example to deterr the other Directors from telling what They knew. As to that Gentleman every one within Doors and without agree in their opinion of Him, and the part he has Acted in this Affair, but let me tell Him This Step will sink Him lower than ever He has yet fallen. And I desire to put Him in mind that The Projector

---

Letter 53

[1] See *C.J.*, XIX, 568–78 for the report on 5 June. The call of the House had occurred on 22 May. *Ibid.*, p. 556.

[2] Sir John Blunt (1665–1733), director of the South Sea Company 1711–21, had been arrested in Jan., and was subjected to various penalties (see next letter).

Letter 54

[1] The Commons voted that the paper *The Weekly Journal or Saturday's Post* of 27 May was 'a False, Malicious, Scandalous, Infamous, and Trayterous Libel, tending to alienate the Affections if His Majesty's Subjects …' (*C.J.*, XIX, 562–3). Nathaniel Mist, jacobite publisher of the paper, was committed to Newgate. The *Votes* were the published record of the votes of the Commons; no equivalent existed for the Lords.

[2] For details of the penalties meted out by parliament to the directors and officers of the South Sea Company, see John Carswell, *The South Sea Bubble* (rev. edn., Stroud, 1993), pp. 224–9.

of this Banefull Project was Knighted upon his being restored to Favour.[3] After a long Struggle a £1000 was allowed Blunt. The others have more. It is said the M<onarch> is determined to go abroad, to secure Bremen and Verden[4]...

Addressed: For/ Mrs Abigail Harley

55. TO ABIGAIL HARLEY, 13 JUNE 1721.

B.L., Add. MS 70145, unfoliated.

... The Malt Tax was to be brought in this Day,[1] when that is passed, it is thought the Session will soon be over.[2] Those who are concerned in the great Loans are still uneasy, for their affair is recommitted.[3] It is said Lechmere will be Chancellor.[4] I hear no other News...

56. TO ABIGAIL HARLEY, 18 JUNE 1721.

B.L., Add. MS 70034, unfoliated; printed H.M.C., *Portland MSS*, V, 622.

... A Prorogation is expected. W<alpole> told the House upon the Debate about the 7 Millions, that that Money had been applyed one way by this Session already, and that It could not be applyed to another in the same Session, therefore a short Prorogation was necessary. It is thought this will be before the Directors Bill passes[1] so that if they have not freinds enough already they will have time to make more. Sir George[2] is so sure of this that He made a great Entertainment for all his City Freinds. And Mrs. A<isla>bie wrote to a Lady in this County that They should suffer little Damages besides the confinement.

Carlton is to be at the Head of the Ministry but is to have affairs made a little easy for Him. It is talked that the Malt and Land Tax is to be granted for another year if not for two...

Addressed: For/ Mrs Abigail Harley

---

[3] ? Sir George Caswall. See Appendix.

[4] Hanover had occupied the two Swedish duchies of Bremen and Verden in the Great Northern War, and they were ceded to Hanover in 1719. George I was seeking imperial investiture for them.

Letter 55

[1] On 13 June the House resolved to consider the malt tax in a committee of the whole House on the 20th. *C.J.*, XIX, 589.

[2] The parliament was not prorogued until 10 Aug. *Ibid.*, p. 645.

[3] It was resolved on the 14th to go into a committee of the whole to consider further a 'Bill for the Relief of the unhappy Sufferers in the South Sea Company'. *Ibid.*, p. 590.

[4] Lechmere (see Appendix), who was very unpopular, was dismissed as attorney gen. in 1720, and was raised to the peerage in Sept. 1721. See Sedgwick, II, 203–4.

Letter 56

[1] The 'Act for raising money upon the estates of the late sub-governor, deputy governor, directors ... of the South Sea Company' passed the Commons on 7 July and the Lords on 25 July. *C.J.*, XIX, 627; *L.J.*, XXI, 560, 579–80.

[2] Caswall.

57. TO ABIGAIL HARLEY, 22 JUNE 1721.

B.L., Add. MS 70145, unfoliated.

... A warm Debate arose upon the Supply which was carryed 196 against 135.[1] Molesworth bore very hard upon the Court but let drop an Expression that no one understood, That He must tell them that there were more Kingdoms than One that were Elective.

It is thought Ruff will as openly espouse the Court, as They espoused Him. He receives frequent Visits from Sun<derland> and Tow<nsh>end. But last week the Chan<cello>r whom Ruff had abused, was sent to visit Him and stayed long with Him. It is said He will carry with Him some stragling T<or>ys. Sir W<illiam> W<yndham> is suspected, and it is observable that He moved The Malt Tax when the Court were affraid to do it...

Addressed: For/ Mrs A: Harley

58. TO LORD HARLEY, 28 JANUARY 1721/22.[1]

B.L., Add. MS 70381, f. 169.

My Lord

Your Lordships Letter received this morning gave me no less a Concern than that which I am sure affected your Lordship when you write it. But one Expression made a deeper Impression upon me than the rest which is this *That Some Reasons are given for Lord O<xford'>s stay which are greivous to Hear*, which I could wish was a little Explained for the Ease of my own Mind which has been upon the stretch to guess what they could be, but the more I think the farther I am from the right. Yet am I certain it cannot be any thing common, at which your <illegible> Tenderness is so much concerned. But I must take the Liberty which I hope your Lordship will excuse of <illegible> and far from it, The state of Lord O<xford's> Health <is far from being – deleted> <illegible> so <good – deleted> <illegible> as is represented in London; and when we write that He is *better* and *pretty well*, It is not to be understood that he is perfectly recovered and has the same strength and vigour as formerly, but that He is not so bad as He has been. I think this Inducement enough to all Relations to urge him to hasten his journey and I can assure you never have been backward in this Duty which is owing to the preservation of so valuable a person.

As to the Affair of the County, Lord O<xford> has all along given your Lordship an exact Account of the Foot upon which he has put it. And I beleive his cheif Aim in pressing a meeting of the Gentlemen was that they might name a more fit Partner for your Lordship than any of those who have presented themselves, but finding they are most engaged for one, which is Goodyear, They have still reserved themselves to serve your Lordship, And I do not in the least doubt of a great majority to carry<?> it against any other competitor.[2]

Letter 57
[1] This must have been in committee as there is no record in *C.J.*

Letter 58
[1] Draft copy.
[2] For the background to this letter and the 1722 election in Herefordshire, see Sedgwick, I, 257–8, and above, pp. lvi–lviii. Eventually the two tory candidates, Velters Cornewall (see Appendix) and Sir Edward Goodere (1657–1739), 1st bt., won. Goodere was M.P. for Evesham 1708–15, Herefordshire 1722–7.

59. TO LORD HARLEY, EYWOOD, 9 FEBRUARY 1721/22.[1]

B.L., Add. MS 70381, ff. 170–1.

My Lord

I return your Lordship my humble Thanks for the favour of yours received last post. I am still in the Dark *as* to the *Reasons*,[2] which I suppose related to publick Affairs to which I am a perfect Stranger. I cannot help repeating it that the State of Lord O<xford's> Health is inducement sufficient for a visit <to> Him in London, and is a constant Argument with every one of us to presse Him not to delay which He designs as soon as he is able.

As to the Election of this County I perceive by several Hints from some of this County that the mismanagement (as it is called) of this County is laid to the Charge of my F<ather> and is given out that He is pursuing Africanus[3] Interest. I should be very much wanting to the sincere Freindship which I bear to your Lordship and the very great duty which I owe to Him, if I did not Endeavour to set this matter in a clear light.

As to the proposal of the meeting of the Gentlemen that was Lord O<xford's> own thought which He judged to be the most Honorable Method of proceeding and what was always done in this County and though I must own my Father entirely consented to it. But as to his espousing Africanus Interest and Sacrificing the Interest of the Family to Him; your Lordship knows the Tenderness He has for his own relations would never suffer Him to Think of it. And I can assure your Lordship he has been so far from this, that He has to Every body that has talked with him upon this subject publickly declared his opposition to His Measures and that He will acept any Commission or any thing else from Him and I beleive upon any Occasion Africanus would not find a warmer Antagonist in the County. And when<?> Sir H<ungerford Hoskyns> sent to desire his Vote He absolutely denyed Him.

I can easily guess from whence this comes, and Hope your Lordship will forgive me if I am wrong in imagining Fetuan[4] to be the busy body, whether it springs from the great alarms he has in hearing and beleiving every idle Story that is blown into his Ears or whether out of play <?> he choose to throw the burden upon another which only belongs to Himself I cannot tell. But this I must say upon good grounds. That He was the first that gave out your Lordship would not stand upon which the Gentle<men> in his neighbourhood promised one Vote. It was<?> easy to see the backwardness with which He received Lord O<xford's> proposal, and for fear that this should take effect, He slunk the County that He would not appear at such a meeting which He knew could entirely overthrow Africanus's Interest whose Favour he courts. For it is certain by what He said there to me He will court his Favour or fear his Power: He I know says <illegible> that a meeting of the Gentlemen at Hereford <illegible> my F<ather> refused to come, in this He acted a very wi<c>ked part first not to give Him the least notice of it till it was over, and then to report He staid purposely away. This my Lord is not acting as a friend or relation.

Letter 59

[1] Draft copy.

[2] For the reasons for Oxford's staying in Herefordshire, see previous letter.

[3] Harley family cant name for the duke of Chandos, ld. lt. of Herefordshire. See Sedgwick, I, 257–8, for rivalry between Chandos and the Harleys in the county.

[4] Harley family cant name for Thomas Foley, M.P. for Hereford 1701–22, see Appendix. For this identification, see B.L., Add. MS 70383, ff. 80–1, 82, 90, 95: Oxford to Lord Harley, 19, 26 Jan., 18 Feb., 18 Mar. 1722, and the account of the Hereford election in Sedgwick, I, 258.

60. FROM FREDERICK CORNWALL,[1] BROMFIELD, 23 MARCH 1721/2.

B.L., Add. MS 70085, unfoliated.

Worthy Sir

I am so well assur'd of your readiness to do all the service you can to your injurd Countrey, that I need not make much Apology, when I sollicit your Vote and Interest for Mr. Baldwyn of Bockleton,[2] who hath, upon all occasions, exerted himself in defence of our Constitution. You will by this means assert your own right, as a Burgess of Ludlow,[3] and your appearance will be of singular use to this Gentleman. The Day of our Election is fixd for Wednesday next.[4] My Duty attends my Lord and your Father, and I am with great respect and sincerity, Sir Your most Obedient Servant Fred: Cornwall

Sir.

I take this freedom with you, which I cannot so well do with your Father. Mr Baldwyn cannot fail of success, if his Friends come in, as may be expected at this time.

Endorsed: Mr Fred: Cornwall. R. Mar: 26/ 1722:/ Ludlow Election
Addressed: To/ Edward Harley Esq.

61. TO THE EARL OF OXFORD, LEMSTER [LEOMINSTER], 27 MARCH 1722: past six.

B.L. Add. MS 70237, unfoliated.

My Lord

The Poll is just over and I have only time to tell your Lordship how it stood: Croft 250: Caswall 205: Harley 91: Clark 30: Raby 16:[1] My Father had great offers last night from Caswall to come in to his Measures and Bribery which your Lordship may be assured He refused. He is very chearfull with many of his Freinds here.

I am My Lord Your Lordships most dutifull and most obedient Nephew E Harley
The Dissenters were to a man against my Father which I rejoice at.

Addressed: To/ The Right Honble/ The Earl of Oxford.

Letter 60
[1] Frederick Cornewall (c. 1677–1748), vicar of Bromfield, Shropshire, born near Leominster.
[2] Acton Baldwyn, see Appendix.
[3] The Harleys had participated in the politics of Ludlow since at least the 1690s. From 1701 it was a tory stronghold, and in 1713 Francis Herbert (M.P. for Ludlow 1698–1705) had offered his interest to Lord Harley to stand for the borough, but Harley decided to stand elsewhere (HoP, draft constituency article, by David Hayton).
[4] Two tories, Baldwyn and Abel Ketelby, were elected on 28 Mar. 1722, defeating the sitting M.P. Humphrey Walcot (a whig who had often voted with the tories), who had stood on the Chandos interest. Sedgwick, I, 311; II, 189, 504.

Letter 61
[1] See Sedgwick, I, 259, which gives Harley 92.

62. ACCOUNT OF PROCEEDINGS ON LAYER'S TRIAL, JANUARY 1723.[1]

Brampton Bryan MSS, Bundle 117.

On <15>[2] January 1722/23 the House of Commons Ordered that a secret Committee be appointed to examine Layer to consist only of the Privy Council. On Saturday January 19, 1722/23 The Secret Committee meet and went to the Tower the Members were these Poultney who they made Chairman, Walpole, General Wills, Hambden, Smith, Sir Joseph Jekyll Master of the Rolls. When they began examining Mr Layer He told them that his last Examination was to his Condemnation He supposed this was to his Execution. W<alpole> asked who was meant by Mr Steele who had £50000 from England yearly. He told Him it was the Regent. W<alpole> fell in a great passion and gave Him the Lye and other vile treatment. On Tuesday January 29 1722/23 was a great Debate in the House of Lords upon the two Protests which had been entered January 21 upon the Delay of the Publication of Layers Tryal.[3] The Debate was opened by Lord Townshend who spoke with great Passion and little Reason, Seconded by Duke of Dorset who proposed the Question which was a Censure upon the Protest and the Protesting Lords. On this side Spoke Harcourt, Carteret, Scarborough. On the other Cowper, Anglesea, Trevor, Coningsby, Peterborough, Bathurst, Strafford: this Question was carried by <blank>.[4] NB Layers Tryal was published that morning.[5]

63. 'SOME MEMORANDUMS ABOUT THE PERSONS TAKEN UP FOR THE PLOT IN 1722 AND 1723.'[1]

Brampton Bryan MSS, Bundle 117.

Christopher Layer a Barrister at Law and a Norfolk Man was the first who was taken up in <blank>.[2] He was bred an Attorney, but was afterwards called to the Bar. Lord Londonderry having a Morgage on Lord Yarmouths Estate came acquainted with Mr Layer and finding Him a ready Man at Business, employed Him in his South Sea Contracts, and after that sent Him to Paris to adjust his Accounts with Mr Laws in relation to the Missisipi[3] and from thence Layer went to Rome.

He was committed Prisoner to the Tower and after many Examinations before the Council and Secretarys of State He was tried at the Kings Bench on Wednesday November 21, 1722 by an Essex Jury. The Reason for this Mr W<alpole> gave to Mr

---

Letter 62

[1] Christopher Layer was the chief minor plotter in the jacobite so-called Atterbury Plot of 1722. For the best account of the plot and the trial see G.V. Bennett, *The Tory Crisis in Church and State, 1688–1730: The Career of Francis Atterbury, Bishop of Rochester* (Oxford, 1975), pp. 223–75; for a less-convincing account see Eveline Cruickshanks, 'Lord North, Christopher Layer and the Atterbury Plot: 1720–23', in *The Jacobite Challenge*, ed. Eveline Cruickshanks and Jeremy Black (Edinburgh, 1988), pp. 92–106.

[2] Here EH left a gap. See *C.J.*, XX, 90.

[3] A further five protests were entered on 29 Jan. *L.J.*, XXII, 63, 72–4.

[4] There were two votes on 29 Jan.: on the protests on the trial, 62 to 35; on the printing of the trial, 58 to 32.

[5] *The Whole Proceedings upon the Arraignment, Tryal, Conviction and Attainder of Christopher Layer, Esq; for High Treason ...* ran to 152 pages. A 12-page abstract was published: *A Supplement to the London Journal, of February 2. 1722–23*

Letter 63

[1] In EH's hand.

[2] Layer was arrested on 18 Sept. 1722. Kelly, another minor plotter, had, however, been arrested on 28 July. Bennett, *Tory Crisis*, pp. 253, 260.

[3] John Law, a Scottish financier who established the Mississippi Company in France, an equivalent of the South Sea Company.

Parsons[4] the Sheriff of London telling Him if he had not had that Chain about his Neck They would have tryed Layer by a Midlesex Jury.

The Tryal was very long and held till five the next morning when the Jury brought Him in Guilty. A Sentence of Death was then pronounced upon Him, and accordingly a Rule of Court made for his Execution.

On <15>[5] January, 1722/23 The House Commons ordered that a Secrett Committee be appointed to examine Layer which was to consist only of the Privy Council. On Saturday January 19 The Secret Committee met and chose Mr William Poultney for their Chairman the other Members were these, Robert Walpole, Chancellor of the Exchequer, General Wills, Sir Joseph Jekyll Master of the Rolls, Hampden, Smith; who went with their Chairman on this day to the Tower to examine Layer, who told them that his last Examination was to his Condemnation He supposed this was to his Execution. And upon his not giving them the Answers they would have had from Him, and particularly telling them that Mr Steel in his Cyphers was the Regent who had £50000 from England. W<alpole> broke into a violent passion, calling him Names, and had struck Him if the Table had not been between them.

Layer having been often reprieved as <blank>[6] and so long a time having passed without the Tryal being published, Some of the Lords thought fit to take Notice of it, and having no Satisfactory Answer from the Ministry who notwithstanding carried their Question, several Lords protested January 21.

On Teusday January 29, 1722/23 upon a Motion of Lord Townshend The two Protests about the Delay of the Publication of Layers Tryal were taken into Consideration. Upon this a great Debate arose began by Lord Townshend who spoke after his usual manner with great passion and little Reason, He was Seconded by Duke of Dorset who concluded with a motion which was to censure the Protests. On this side spoke, Lord Harcourt, Carteret, Scarborough, on the other Cowper, Anglesea, Trevor, Coningsby, Lechmere, Bathurst, Strafford. NB: Layers Tryal was published this morning.

64. TO MR BROME,[1] LONDON, 18 APRIL 1723.[2]

B.L., Add. MS 70086, unfoliated.

Dear Sir

It has been thought a very distinguishing mark of Freindship to Do what is askt; but you have carryed yours a Degree higher, for your Kindness to your Freinds is exerted in their Behalf even before They make the Request; And among These I should be very unworthy to be reckoned of the Number, should I omit any opportunity of making my most thankfull Acknowledgments to You for the several testimonies you have given me of your steady Freindship particular<ly> for the last Instance, and therefore desire you would accept my hearty Thanks for it. After this I must trouble

---

[4] Alderman Humphrey Parson, M.P. for Harwich. See Appendix.

[5] Here EH left a gap.

[6] Layer's trial was held on 21–7 Nov. 1722, but he was not executed until 23 May 1723. Bennett, *Tory Crisis*, pp. 262–3, 272.

Letter 64

[1] Possibly William Brome, who wrote a letter to EH on 6 Sept. 1735 with condolences on his father's death. B.L., Add. MS 70498, ff. 2–3. The letter printed here refers to an approach made to EH to stand for Herefordshire at a time when Sir Edward Goodere was ill.

[2] Draft.

you in making my Complements to Those Gentlemen to whom I am so much obliged, and to express the great Sense I have of the Honour they design me, And that it will be with the greatest Chearfullness that I shall accept of their Service when ever the Occasion offers, and shall only regret that I have neither Power nor Abilities equall to my Inclination and Desire to do them Service. As this whole Affair is left to your Prudent Management, so if you think I should return my thanks to any Particular Person You will please to let me know. If not as only a General Application was made, so a general Acknowledgement may do at present.

65. TO ANON, 14 MAY 1723.

Brampton Bryan MSS, Bundle 117.

Reverend Sir

I return you many thanks for the favour of yours received yesterday. I was out too late on Saturday to send you an Account of the Bishops Defense[1] which I heard with the greater pleasure for it exceeded my expectation, and was glad to see Him exert so much Spirit when the occasion for it was so great. The Defense was clear Strong and well put together, It took in all the Heads of the Accusation against Him, but He was most particular upon those which his Counsel had not touched upon, And I think He gave a full, clear and Distinct Answer to them all, and with great fairness proved that He was not guilty of any of Those Facts which they had charged Him with. And I am certain an unprejudiced Person upon Hearing the Accusation and the Defense would have instantly pronounced Him not Guilty.

As to that part of his Speech which related to the Severity of his Punishment, He mentioned it in the most moving expressions, and which drew Tears from Many even from some of the most relentless, Yet these were soon wiped away, and the Violence of their Nature returned strong again, but none appeared so Hardned as his Brethren to whom He applyed Himself in a very severe as well as a moving manner, which at least might have awakened them, if it had not any other consequence. He bore very hard upon the Council against Him particularly Reeves[2] who was in the greatest Confusion while He was speaking. In the middle of his Defense (which lasted above two Hours) He desired the Preamble to Sir John Fenwicks Bill[3] might be read, that He might sit down and take a little refreshment, after this was read, He severely lashed his Freind the Attorney <Raymond>, saying, After He had showed the difference of that Bill and His, that He was surprised that Those who had spoke so very well against that Bill, should now be so strenuous for the passing of the Bill against Him, and should employ their Abilites and parts against their Knowledge and their Conscience. At the latter end of his Speech He drew a very fine Comparison between Lord Clarendons Case[4] and his own, in which He said He fell far short of a likeness to that Great Man but excepting two particulars which was His Innocence and the Severity of the Punishment, your Lordships may make a difference between us in this latter respect but you cannot take from me the resemblance I bear to Him in the former, But

---

Letter 65

[1] Atterbury's defence was delivered to the house of lords on 11 May 1723. It is printed in *The Epistolary Correspondence ... of ... Francis Atterbury* (2nd edn., 5 vols., 1789–98), V, 365–94.

[2] Thomas Reeve (d. 1737), counsel for the crown against Atterbury; K.C. 1718, serjeant at law 1723, judge of common pleas 1733–6, chief justice of common pleas 1736–7.

[3] The Bill of Attainder against Sir John Fenwick for his part in the plot to assassinate William III in 1696.

[4] Edward Hyde, 1st earl of Clarendon, had been impeached by the Commons in 1667.

if your Lordships shall determine that I must be a Sacrifice let it fall upon me alone, God forbid that it should be made a Precedent, and what ever becomes of me I beseech you for the sake of yourselves and your Posterity, That you will still preserve inviolable the Laws and Constitution of my Country and those Liberties which I could be deprived of and the only way to perpetuate them is to put a stop to such fatal Precedents.

66. LIST OF THOSE WHO SPOKE FOR AND AGAINST THE BILL AGAINST THE BISHOP OF ROCHESTER ON 16 MAY 1723.[1]

Brampton Bryan MSS, Bundle 117.

Wednesday May 16, 1723.
That the Bill against the Bishop of Rochester pass.
In the Debate there spoke.

Against the Bill	For the Bill
Lord Paulett	Bishop of Salisbury Willes
Bishop of Chester	Bishop of London Gibson
Duke of Wharton	Lord Finlatter
Lord Bathurst	Duke of Argyle
Lord Strafford	Lord Lechmere
Lord Foley	Lord Peterborough
Lord Trevor	Lord Cholmondeley
Lord Gower	
Lord Cowper	

67. FROM THE EARL OF OXFORD, DOVER STREET, 4 JULY 1727.

B.L., Add. MS 70498, ff. 68–9.

Sir

By your letter of last post you have, I think put the affair upon a very right foot and I think you must succeed[1] but yet give me leave to say nothing should be neglected by you that is reasonable for this is certain you come in upon an Interest that if well managed will carry you on through your life, I hope you have received my letter about the Venison and will dispose of it as you judge proper.

I have seen Velters[2] and I think I have knocked in the head all manner of Jealousie except some wise refiners put some more into his head which I think they can very hardly do. Lord Harry Bridges[3] is set up for Radnorshire by my cosen Harley[4] you have an account of that affair from other hands. – I spoke to Mr. Bromley[5] who is a

---

Letter 66
[1] In EH's hand.

Letter 67
[1] EH was elected M.P. for Herefordshire on 6 Sept. 1727, along with Velters Cornewall, without a contest.
[2] Velters Cornewall. See Appendix.
[3] Lord Henry Brydges had succeeded his elder brother in their father's courtesy title of marquess of Carnarvon on 27 Apr. 1727 (see Appendix). On 22 Aug. he was elected M.P. for Hereford. For the Chandos interest in Radnorshire see Sedgwick, I, 380 and D.R.Ll. Adams, 'The Parliamentary Representation of Radnorshire 1536–1832', University of Wales (Aberystwyth) M.A., 1969, ch. 4.
[4] ? Thomas Harley (c. 1667–1738), of Kinsham Court, Herefordshire, M.P. for Radnorshire 1698–1715. He was a first cousin of the 1st earl of Oxford.
[5] William Bromley, M.P. for Oxford University. See Appendix.

Trustee for Lord Weymouth for the Interest for you and Cornwall – My service to all. Do not take up your time in writing to me except you have any commands for me.

Addressed: To Edward Harley Esqr. at Eywood near Presteigne. Frank Oxford.
Endorsed: Ld Oxford July 4: 1727. County of Hereford.

68. TO WILLIAM BRYDGES[1] AT TIBBERTON, EYWOOD, 4 JULY 1727.

Hereford R.O., Brydges Papers, A81/IV/William Brydges, 1714–40.

Sir

I was in hopes to have had an opportunity of paying my respects to you at Tibberton before this, and to have applyed to you in person for the favour of your Vote and Interest at the next election for this County; but finding that I cannot yet be master of my own Time, I am forced to take this way which is not so agreeable to me as waiting upon you would be, and which I hope soon to do. The most humble services of all this Family attend you and your Lady. I am Sir your most humble Servant
E. Harley

69. TO AUDITOR HARLEY, EYWOOD, 11 MAY 1729.

B.L., Add. MS 70140, unfoliated.

… The unexpected Success of the Bill against Bribery[1] gives me the greatest Satisfaction, could one possibly have foreseen the turn which it has took, I should with a great deal of pleasure have rode post to have been at the Debate and to have given a most hearty Vote against Corruption. It is a bad Omen for a Commander in a seige to have a Breach made in that part where he placed the greatest security…

70. TO MARTHA HARLEY (AT EYWOOD), 5 FEBRUARY 1730.

B.L., Add. MS 70497, unfoliated.

… Yesterday was the Debate upon the Hessian troops, Whether these forreign forces should be still kept in English pay, the Debate began about one and lasted till between 8 and 9 and was carried on with more Spirit and viguour than any I have heard since I have been in the House. Sir R<obert> was often challenged but declined being engaged and spoke only to a matter of form. For the attack was begun while the Speaker was in the chair and the Question was Whether the Estimates for keeping up the Hessians should be referred to the Committee of Supply, which Gentlemen who thought them a burden and against the Act of Settlement were entirely for rejecting. Some of the old Whigs particularly Heathcote[1] Nephew to Sir Gilbert flamed upon this occasion, and was so free with his Majestys dominions abroad, and talked so much of the Compact between King and People upon revolution principles that had

---

Letter 68
[1] William Brydges (1681–1764) of Tyberton, Herefordshire, was a cousin of the duke of Chandos. See also below, p. 251.

Letter 69
[1] The 'Act for the more effectual preventing of Bribery and Corruption in the Election of Members to serve in Parliament' passed the Lords on 6 May and received the royal assent on the 14th. *L.J.*, XXII, 419, 437.

Letter 70
[1] George or William Heathcote. See Appendix.

any from the West Saxon Corner[2] spoke what he did, He had been sent to the tower, and I dare not write what He spoke though the Prince was in the Gallery. This Debate was mostly carried on by the young Gentlemen, Poultney and the old Speakers except Shippen who spoke extreamly well leaving the feild for them, and when I found it was so I did not decline taking my share, and though I could but weakly support my part, yet I had this satisfaction to make as publick a protest as I was able against making myself and those I represent tributary to any forreign state. Upon the Division the Minority were not Contemptible. Ayes 248. Noes 169.[3] I hear to day Lord Bingley is to succeed Methuen as Treasurer of the Household and to come into the Treasury...

Addressed: For/ Mrs Harley/ at Eywood/ near Presteigne/ Herefordshire.

71. TO MARTHA HARLEY, LONDON, 28 FEBRUARY 1730.

B.L., Add. MS 70497, unfoliated.

... The call is put off till Thursday sen'night, yesterday we finished the Dunkirk affairs,[1] when I was in the House from 10 in the morning till after three this morning, but I thank God I am very well after so great a fatigue, which I intend to make amends for to night, for though it is early, yet I intend going to bed as soon as I have finished this letter. Though I was so many hours without eating and in excessive heat the House being as full as ever it could hold, yet I thank God I have not the least Headach or disorder, and I was thus far pleased with the lentgh of the Day because it gave me an opportunity of publickly justifying my Lord Oxfords Memory and Administration in a direct answer to Sir Rob<ert> who had unjustly reflected upon both, I had so fair an opportunity for a full stroke that I assure you I did not spare to give it home according to the best of my capacity, though Lord O<xford's> Memory did not want so mean an Advocate...

Addressed: For/ Mrs Harley/ at Eywood/ near Presteigne/ Herefordshire.

72. TO MARTHA HARLEY, 26 MARCH 1730.

B.L., Add. MS 70497, unfoliated.

... I brought in the Jury Bil this morning,[1] and if it was not for the Recess which will be now at Easter I should hope to get it through the House in as short time as is possible for a Bill of this Nature, for I do not apprehend any opposition to it, and only

---

[2] The area of the Commons in which sat the west country M.P.s – the 'West Saxons' (see above, p. 218). The term had been in use since at least the 1690s. See *Letters Illustrative of the Reign of William III... by John Vernon* (3 vols., 1841), II, 345: Vernon to Shrewsbury, 17 Aug. 1699, where Vernon refers to 'the Saxon Corner'.

[3] *C.J.*, XX, 430–1. A division list for this vote has survived. See Chandler, VIII, Appendix.

Letter 71

[1] The port of Dunkirk had been ordered to be demolished by the treaty of Utrecht in 1713. The inhabitants had recently been repairing the port. The Commons resolved to address the king to apply to France for the demolition of the repairs. *C.J.*, XX, 469.

Letter 72

[1] The Bill for the Better Regulation of Juries was in committee on 3, 8 and 10 Apr., passed the Commons on the 20th, had its 1st reading in the Lords on 21 Apr. and passed on 12 May. The Commons agreed to the Lords' amendments on the 14th and it received the royal assent the following day (*C.J.*, XXI, 522, 532, 536, 547, 551; *L.J.*, XXIII, 544, 572, 576, 578). The bill is printed in Lambert, VII, 21–7.

fear it may be killed with kindness being over loaded with clauses by them who are over zealous to have it pass. But this Recess will fling me a week extraordinary behind Hand, and keep longer than I wish for, and nothing but what I hope will be of such publick good would keep me another day in Town. I hope after the Recess when the House meets again and the Bill had been read a 2d time I may be able to tell you when the Horses shall meet me...

73. TO MARTHA HARLEY, 28 MARCH 1730.

B.L., Add. MS 70497, unfoliated.

...for enclosed you will see that I have presented the Jury Bil and that the House meets again on Thursday and therefore hope to get it passed in a fortnight after ... therefore am resolved now not to lose a day but to push the Bill as fast as I can, for I every day grow more impatient to be with you my Dearest and the little ones...

74. TO MARTHA HARLEY, 2 APRIL 1730.

B.L., Add. MS 70497, unfoliated.

My Dearest

I left Brasted[1] very early this morning that I might come time enough to the House to get the Bill read a 2d time, and though I was disappointed in it to day, yet the Speaker has promised me it shall be read to morrow, and committed for Teusday, if I have the good fortune to get it that day through the Committee, the cheif Difficulty of it will then be over, and I should hope then to fix what time my Horses might meet me the week following, yet though I impatiently long for the day to come when I may leave this filthy town, and return to your Arms who I love beyond expression, I dare not flatter myself too much because ten thousand things may disappoint me...

75. TO MARTHA HARLEY, 11 APRIL 1730.

B.L., Add. MS 70497, unfoliated.

My Dearest

I can with great satisfaction acquaint you that the Jury Bill went this day through a Committee of the whole House when I had the Honour to be put in the Chair, both the Attorney and Sollicitor General[1] was so kind to attend it, and have given such countenance and made such amendments to the Bill, that I please myself that it will meet with as kind a reception in the House of Lords as it has done in the Commons. I am to report the Bill on Wednesday, and hope to carry it to the Lords before this day sen'night that nothing may prevent my coming out of town on Monday...

Letter 74
[1] Brasted Place, near Westerham, Kent, was the home of EH's sister Abigail and her husband, John Verney (1699–1741), M.P. for Downton 1722–34, 1741; 2nd justice of Brecknock circuit 1726–32; attorney-gen. to Queen Caroline 1729–37; master of the rolls 1738–41. They had married in 1724. See Sedgwick, II, 495–6; E. Foss, *Judges of England* (10 vols., 1848–64), VIII, 176–7.

Letter 75
[1] Sir Philip Yorke and Charles Talbot.

76. CLAUSE OF EDWARD HARLEY'S JURY BILL.

Brampton Bryan MSS, Bundle 117.

And It is farther Enacted That the Name of each Person summoned and impanelled, shall be written with his addition and Place of abode in distinct Peices of Parchment or Paper of equal Size and Bigness and shall be delivered to the Marshall of the Judge of Assize or Nisi Prius etc. by the Undersheriff or his Agent, and shall by Direction of such Marshall be rolled up all in the same manner as near as may be, and put in a box or Glass; and when a Cause is brought to be tried, some Indifferent Person, by Direction of the Court, shall in open Court draw out Twelve of the Parchments of Papers one after another; and if any of the Persons drawn shall not appear, or be challenged and set aside, then a further number till 12 be drawn who shall appear which shall be the Jury to try the Cause; and the names of the Persons so drawn and sworn shall be kept apart in some other box or Glass till the Jury have given in their Verdict and the same is recorded, or till the Jury shall by Consent of the Parties, or Leave of the Court be discharged and then they shall be rolled up again and returned to the former Box to be kept with the other Names as long as any Cause remains to be tried.

Every Person whose Name shall be drawn, and shall not appear after being called three times, upon Oath that He had been lawfully summoned, shall forfeit and pay for every Default not exceeding £5 nor less than 40s unless reasonable Cause of Absence be proved by Oath or Affidavit to the Satisfaction of the Judge who sits to try the Cause.

Any Person having an Estate in Land in his own Right of the yearly Value of £20 over and above the reserved Rent payable thereout, being held by Lease for the absolute term of 500 years or for 99 years or any other Term determinable on one or more Lives, such Persons shall be inserted in the Lists and in the Freeholders book, and the Persons appointed to make such Lists are hereby directed to insert them accordingly, and such Leaseholder may be summoned and impanelled to serve on Juries as Freeholders may, and subject to like Penalties for not appearing

The Courts at Westminster, upon motion made in behalf of his Majesty, or on the Motion of any Plantiff or Defendant in any Indictment or Information for any Misdemeanor or in any action or suit whatsoever are brought or prosecuted in any Court there, are authorised and required to order a Jury to be struck before the proper officer for the Trial of Issues joined and triable by a Jury of twelve Men as special Jurys are usually struck in those Courts. And the Jury so struck shall be the Jury returned for the trial of that Issue. The Person who shall apply for such Jury shall pay the Fees for striking it and shall have no Allowance for the same on Taxation of Costs.

Sheriffs shall not return any Person to serve on a Jury for Trial of any Capital offence, who would not be qualified in Civil Causes.

This act shall be openly read once in every year at the General Quarter Sessions to be holden for every Place in England and Wales next after the 24th of June.

77. PAPER ON THE JURY ACT OF 1730.[1]

Brampton Bryan MSS, Bundle 117.

As the Tryal by a Jury is the distinguishing Privilege of an Englishman, the best Security of his Life and his Property, And as the Parliament has now taken care to put

Letter 77
[1] In EH's hand.

a Stop to the notorious Corruption which had broke into it by passing this Act, so it is to be hoped that Every Man in his several station will use his best Endeavours to make this Law effectual.

The Justices of the Peace by taking care to inform the Constables and Freeholders within their Divisions of the Duty that is required of them, and by seeing that perfect Lists of the Pesons qualifyed to serve on Jurys are exactly made up and that the Freeholders book may be compleated by the Clerk of the Peace.

The Constables <Tything?> Men and Head boroughs are the Persons required by the 7 and 8th of King William 3 and the 3 and 4 of Queen Anns to make up these Lists. The Persons qualifyed to be inserted in these Lists are Freeholders and Copyholders, of £10 per annum in England and £6 in Wales, and Leaseholders for Lives of the yearly value of £20 being of the age of 21 and not above 70 years. And by this act the Petty Constables are only required to make up True Lists of the Persons qualifyed to serve which Lists they are to put on their own Parish Church Door two or more Sundays 21 days before Michel<mas> and to leave a Duplicate with the Church Warden or overseer of their Parish, and also to swear to the truth of such List before a Justice of Peace, and then deliver their List to the High Constable who is to carry it to the Quarter Sessions. And as they are excused from attending themselves with these Lists at the Michel<mas> Quarter Sessions so they ought to be the more carefull in observing their Duty required by this Act.

But as the Act almost entirely depends on the Freeholders attendance, so it is to be desired that Every Man will be ready and willing to do that common Justice to his neighbour as well as Service to his country in General, as constantly <and> punctually to attend when ever summoned. And since <only?> they cannot be summoned but once in two years (except in the Countys of York and Rutland) and are thereby freed from the oppression and Execution of Bailiffs and Under Sheriffs.

78. TO MARTHA HARLEY, 11 FEBRUARY 1731.

B.L., Add. MS 70497, unfoliated.

...I am forced to hurry down to the House though it is now but just ten, where we shall have a long day on the Pension Bill,[1] if they can prevail on their numbers to throw it out ... The Pension Bill is committed for Teusday without a division, which is no small triumph...

Addressed: For/ Mrs Harley/ at Eywood/ near Presteigne

79. TO MARTHA HARLEY, 18 FEBRUARY 1731.

B.L., Add. MS 70497, unfoliated.

... We had yesterday a very long and good Debate upon the third reading <of> the Pension Bill, if a Debate can be called such where so much Argument was urged on one side, and so little on the other. Sir R<obert> spoke 3 quarters of an hour against

Letter 78
[1] Pension and place bills were designed to stop M.P.s holding pensions and offices. They were a frequent feature of the Commons (there was one in 1730 and again in 1732), and, though they were opposed by the ministry, they were often allowed to pass the lower house as the ministry knew they would be thrown out by the Lords. The 1731 bill was read a 1st time in the Lords on 20 Feb. but was rejected on its 2nd reading on 2 Mar. *C.J.*, XXI, 622; *L.J.*, XXIII, 618, 628–9.

the Bill, yet his own people could not be worked up, and the Bill passed without a Division. The Bill is to be carryed to the Lords to day, and I am going down early to attend it, for I think one cannot bear too publick a testimony against Pensions and Corruption

... The Ministry are hurrying all their affairs in the House, and it is the general opinion that the Sessions will be short, which is the best News that I know I can send you, I impatiently wish it over, that I may return to My Dear Patty...

Addressed: For/ Mrs Harley/ at Eywood/ near Presteigne

80. TO MARTHA HARLEY, 23 FEBRUARY 1731, 'past 7'

B.L., Add. MS 70497, unfoliated.

My Dearest

I am just come from the House where I have been since ten, am perfectly well but very hungry... The Debate was whether an Address to the King desiring him to lay before the House a Declaration made by the Spanish Minister at Paris, that the King of Spain thought Himself free from any obligation of the Treaty of Seville. Ayes 121. Noes 243[1]...

Addressed: For/ Mrs Harley/ at Eywood/ near Presteigne

81. TO HERBERT AUBREY,[1] RED LYON SQUARE, 22 JANUARY 1731/32.

Hereford Record Office, Brydges Papers, A81/IV/William Brydges, 1714–60.

Sir

The Letter from you and the other Gentlemen coming yesterday to the House after it rose, I did not receive it till this morning. As the Clauses (except the last) are general and will extend to all Turnpike Bills,[2] I am not willing to depend upon my own Opinion how far they may be agreeable to the forms of the House, and therefore would consult other Members of better Capacity and longer Experience than my own; And as the House did not sit to day I must defer a fuller answer to the Gentlemens Letter till I can have made the best Enquiry I am able into this matter, upon which Account I hope both They and you will excuse the shortness of this from Sir Your most humble Servant E Harley

Addressed: For Herbert Aubrey Esqe at Clehonger near Hereford. Free E Harley
Endorsed: 1732 Harley to Mr. Aubrey

Letter 80

[1] *C.J.*, XXI, 642. By the treaty of Seville of Nov. 1729, Britain and France agreed to the Spanish succession in the Italian duchies.

Letter 81

[1] Probably Herbert Aubrey (c.1664–1744), of Clehonger, three miles south-west of Hereford, who voted for the winning tory candidates at Hereford in 1741 and for the winning whig candidates in 1747 (Hereford poll books). He was the son of Herbert Aubrey (c.1635–91), M.P. for Hereford, 1681–5, and the father of the recipient of Letter 110 below.

[2] This probably refers to the preliminaries to a turnpike bill to make effective an act of 1729 for punishing persons who destroy turnpikes, which was ordered to be brought into the Commons on 2 Mar. 1732 as a result of three petitions. On 22 Mar, the mayor, aldermen and citizens of Hereford petitioned in its favour as did the justices of the peace, gentlemen and freeholders of Herefordshire. It became law on 1 June. *C.J.*, XXI, 828, 866, 939.

82. DRAFT OF THE JURY BILL, 1733.[1]

Brampton Bryan MSS, Bundle X.

1733

Whereas an Act made in the third year of his present Majestys reign entituled an Act for the better regulation of Juries, and another act passed in the fourth year of his said Majestys reign Entituled an act to Explain and Amend an Act made in the third year of his Majestys Reign (intituled an act for the better regulation of Juries) so far as the same relates to the County of Middlesex have been found upon Experience to be very beneficial and usefull to the subject in better securing their Properties and Estates by preventing the Evil practices neglects and abuses that have been used in returning and corrupting of Jurors returned for the Trial of Issues joined to be tried before the Justices of Assize or Nisi Prius and the Judges of the Great Sessions in Wales and the Judge or Judges of the Sessions for the Counties Palatine of Lancaster Chester and Durham. Which said acts were to continue and be in force untill the first Day of September 1733 and from thence to the End of the then next Session of Parliament. Therefore for continuing the Same Be it Enacted by the Kings Most Excellent Majesty by and with the Consent of the Lords Spiritual and Temporal and the Commons in this present Parliament assembled and by the Authority of the same That the said Two recited acts shall be and are hereby continued and shall be in force and be made perpetual.

Endorsed: Draft of a Bill for making perpetuall the Act for the better regulation of Jurys. 1733.

83. FROM AUDITOR HARLEY, BATH, 9 FEBRUARY 1733/4.

B.L., Add. MS 70498, ff. 63–4.

I read Your Letter with a just Sense of that Tenderness and Regard with which You had Vindicated my Character.

I have been many Years in this Office and I cannot recollect that any one Revenue Account has been Pass'd without my Examination and Signing, except that of the Additional Duty upon Stamps which was granted to make good the Depredation of my Lord Chancellor Macclesfield.[1] I do not write to Bangham upon this Subject, but Desire you will talk fully with him upon it; and as you have opportunity you may mention this to Mr. P–[2] or any one Else as you see Occasion. I never once went out of Town without the leave of the Trea<su>ry, and as any Accounts requir'd Dispatch they were always sent to me in the Country to be Examin'd, and upon which I return'd

---

Letter 82

[1] EH's previous Jury Act of 1730 (see above, pp. xliv–xlvi) was due to expire at the end of the next session after 1 Sept. 1733 (3 Geo. II, c. 25, clause 22), and a bill was proposed that it (and six other acts) be made perpetual. It was first read in the Commons on 2 May 1733, passed on the 17th, returned from the Lords with amendments on the 29th, which were agreed to by the Commons on 1 June, and received the royal assent on 13 June. *C.J.*, XXII, 128, 136, 152, 165, 169–70, 203; *L.J.*, XXIV, 273, 278, 281–2, 284, 310.

Letter 83

[1] This possibly refers to the order by the Commons on 23 Jan. 1734 to lay before the house an account of the arrears in the land tax and the duties on houses which were outstanding at Christmas 1733, together with the names of the receivers in whose hands the arrears remained. The accounts were presented on 6 Feb. Further accounts for land tax in the Exchequer were ordered on 22 Feb. and were referred to the committee of ways and means on 11 Mar. *C.J.*, XXII, 211, 232, 251, 276–7.

[2] Possibly Henry Pelham (see Appendix), at this time paymaster general.

my Observacons where I found it necessary. As to my Deputy and Clerks I think I may venture to Say that there is no Office where the Deputy and Clerks are more faithfull in discharging their Duty.

I thank you for the Abstract of the Bill[3] with the Observations upon it; I think there is one Omission and that is, Explaining that the Conviction and Penalty of £500 is to be recovered, by the Verdict of Twelve ffreeholders which are Impannell'd in such a manner as they cannot be Corrupted, and therefore will not fail to do justice to themselves and their Country upon the Violation of this Law...

84. SPEECH ON THE MOTION TO REMOVE WALPOLE, 13 FEBRUARY 1741.

Bodl., MS Ballard 29, f. 130.[1]

Mr. Edward Harley (now Earl of Oxford)'s Speech in the House of Commons, upon the Motion to remove Sir Robert Walpole

Mr. Speaker,

I do not stand up at this time of Night either to accuse or flatter any Man. Since I have had the Honour to sit in Parliament,[2] I have opposed the Measures of the Administration, because I thought them wrong; and as long as they are so, I shall continue[3] as constant an Opposition to them. The State of the Nation by their[4] Conduct[5] is deplorable; a War is destroying us abroad, and Poverty and Corruption are devouring us at home.

But whatever I may think of Men, GOD forbid that my Private Opinion should be the only Rule of my Judgment. I should desire to have an Exterior Conviction from *Facts* and *Evidence*; and without these, I am so far from *condemning*, that I would not *censure*, any Man. I am fully satisfied in my own Mind, that there are those who give pernicious and destructive Counsels; and I hope a Time will come, when a proper, legal, and Parliamentary[6] Enquiry may be made, and when clear *Facts* and full *Evidence* will plainly discover who are the Enemies of their Country.

A noble Lord, to whom I have the Honour to be related,[7] has been often[8] mention'd in this Debate. He was *Impeach'd* and *Imprison'd*, and by that Imprisonment his Years

---

[3] Probably the bill to make more effectual the 1710 act (9 Anne, c. 5) for qualifying M.P.s. It was ordered on 25 Jan. 1734, but rejected on its 2nd reading on 19 Feb. Though ordered to be printed on 13 Feb., it does not appear in Lambert. *C.J.*, XXII, 212, 239, 245.

Letter 84

[1] For EH's version in his journal see above, pp. 50–1. Contemporary printed versions can be found in the *London Magazine*, XI (1742), 167–8, and the *Gentleman's Magazine*, XIII (1743), 173. It seems clear from the letter written by EH at Eywood on 1 June 1741 to his wife, who was at Bath, that he had probably sent a copy to the *London Magazine* for publication: 'If the *London Magazine* published this Day June *the first with the Debate on the Motion against Sir R[obert] Walpole* can be had at Leaks or any other shop in Bath pray bring it with you.' B.L., Add. MS 70497. The two published versions are slight textual variants on the manuscript copy printed here and the differences (except of spelling, punctuation and capitalization) are noted below. A version is also printed in Cobbett, XI, 1268–9, which is closest to the *L.M.* version.

[2] Here *G.M.* has 'the Senate'.

[3] Here in *L.M.* and *G.M.* is inserted the words 'to give'.

[4] 'their' replaced by 'the' in *L.M.* and *G.M.*

[5] Here in *L.M.* the words 'of our Ministers' are inserted.

[6] Here *G.M.* has 'Senatorial'.

[7] The 1st earl of Oxford.

[8] 'often' omitted in *G.M.*

were shortned; and the Prosecution was carried on by the Honourable Gentleman[9] who is now the Subject of your Question, though He knew at that very Time that there was no *Evidence* to support it. I am now, Sir, glad of this Opportunity to *return Good for Evil*, and to do that Honourable Gentleman and his Family that *Justice* which He denied to Mine.

85. TO WILLIAM BRYDGES,[1] LONDON, 21 FEBRUARY 1741.

Hereford Record Office, Brydges Papers, A81/IV/William Brydges, 1741–61.

Sir,

If I had not received the favour of your Letter yesterday, I should by this Post have returned my humble Thanks for the very obliging manner in which you were pleased to express yourself on my Account to Mr. Hopton,[2] but am more indebted to you for your endeavours to preserve the Quiet of the County, which I find by your Letter as well as from others that some Gentlemen are desirous to disturb. I should imagine that as soon as they perceive that this Measure is not so well relished by Gentlemen of Honour and disintrested Freeholders as it may be in a Borough, they will not be willing to expose themselves to the censure of making an opposition, only for the name of opposition. I shall be very glad to hear that affairs go on prosperously at Hereford, for if open and avowed Corruption cannot receive a check, it will be a jest for any Country Gentleman to pretend to an Interest even at his own Door, and it will be well if the Torrent at last does not Sweep away all that He has.

I had the Honour of a Visit this week from Duke Chandos, when I mentioned to Him Mr Williams illness, and how agreeable it would be to you that either Mr Symmonds or Mr Russel[3] might succeed in case of his Death, indeed I more particularly recommended Mr Symmonds as I was more particularly acquainted with Him than Mr Russel and as several other Gentlemen had mentioned Him to me. The Duke told me that He had already been applyed to, (I suppose for Mr Lane)[4] but had made no Promise as Mr Williams was living, but seemed inclined to serve either of the other Gentlemen. I afterwards took the Liberty to represent to his Grace how unfortunate His Resignation of the Leiutenancy and Custos would be at this time, and how desirous the Gentlemen of the County were that He should continue them in his Hands. I find that He had by Letter signified his Desire to resign these and those of Radnorshire; upon which Tom Lewis[5] obtained a promise of the Stewardship of Cantred Melenith, which the Duke had no intention to resign, and upon his Grace seeing in the Papers how worthily this was disposed of, He sent a second Letter that He did not think of parting with this unless it was taken from Him, which He had soon after assurances sent Him was not to be and no Person is now talked of for either of the Leiutenancys, though it was said that Mr H. Williams[6] was to be the Man.

---

[9] 'Gentleman' is replaced by 'Person' in *L.M.* and *G.M.*.

Letter 85

[1] William Brydges (see above, p. 243, n. 1) stood for Hereford in 1741, but came bottom of the poll. See Sedgwick, I, 258.

[2] Edward Hopton. See Appendix.

[3] Possibly James Symonds, a Hereford common councilman, and mayor in 1735 and 1749. It has not been possible to identify Russel.

[4] Possibly Thomas Lane, attorney and Hereford common councilman, and mayor in 1729.

[5] Thomas Lewis, M.P. for New Radnor Boroughs. See Appendix.

[6] Charles Hanbury Williams (see Appendix), became ld. lt. of Herefordshire on 16 July 1741.

Though I have already trespassed too much upon your time, yet you may perhaps be willing to hear the Event of the charge against Sir R. W<alpole> on Fryday was sen'night. The Question moved by Mr Sandys was to Address the King to remove Him from his Presence and Councils for Ever.[7] But the Accusation being general, and no particular facts proved either by written or viva voce Evidence I was one of those Gentlemen among a great number who withdrew and would not vote in the Question, We think we have acted consistent with our own Principles which so much abhor Bills of Pains and Penalties, that we avoided even the shadow of one, the censuring anyone upon common fame without Evidence. For the Question 106. Against 290. It was computed that near 500 Members were in the House, by which you may guess the numbers that withdrew. The same Question was proposed the same day in the House of Lords. The Numbers on the Division there were Contents 47: Proxies 12 }59. Not Contents: 89 Proxies 19 }108. It was afterwards moved

That any attempt to inflict any kind of Punishment on any Person without allowing Him an opportunity to make his Defense or without Proof of any Crime or Misdemeanor committed by Him is contrary to Natural Justice, the fundamental Laws of this Realm and the ancient established Usage of Parliament and is a High Infringement of the Liberty of the Subject.

The Previous Question being put whether this Question be *Now* put. The House Divided Contents 81. Not Contents 54. Then the Main Question passed in the Affirmative. The House of Lords sat till one in the morning and the Commons till three...

86. TO MARTHA HARLEY, EYWOOD, 7 MAY 1741.

B.L., Add. MS 70497, unfoliated.

... God be thanked we have had here the finest Gentlest rain since Teusday that could be wished, which has given this poor Countrey another face, and makes every one Chearfull in the midst of Poverty and Corruption. As the rain began while my Brother and I were walking the Town of Leominster, I could not help smiling to hear the reflections the Freeholders and Country Men who attended us made to the Townsmen. See here what our Members have brought with them, Rain is better riches, than all the Money that is given to corrupt you. I am just returning to Leominster the Election being to be to morrow, when I beleive my Brother will lose it with great Credit and Honour, being supported by the united Voice of the County and the substantial Inhabitants. But Money is powerfull. I shall keep open my Letter to tell you how it goes.

Leominster Fryday night.

We have had here a most honourable Defeat, Bribery was so flagrant that Several of the Voters returned the Money in the open Court. When the Poll closed the Numbers were. Harley 152. Hanbury 339. Caswall 330. Crowther 7.[1] I must leave the particulars of the Election till I see you. I thank God I am very well, and My Brother and I in more spirits that if we had a Victory...

Addressed: For/ Mrs Harley at Mrs Anne Philips/ in Bath

---

[7] *C.J.*, XXIII, 648 (13 Feb. 1741).

Letter 86
[1] Sedgwick, I, 259 reverses the figures for Hanbury and Caswall.

87. TO MARTHA HARLEY (AT BATH), EYWOOD, 10 MAY 1741.

B.L., Add. MS 70497, unfoliated.

… I came from Leominster last night with my Brother and I thank God am perfectly well, I am extreamly obliged to Dr Crank not only for the Zeal with which He espoused my Brothers cause, but for the particular care and civility He showed to me, in making his House the same to me as my own. He will be at Bath in a weeks time and intends to wait upon you with a particular account of the Election. I desire you will mention to Him the sense and regard I have for his Freindship and it will not be amiss to do the same to Dr Frewin<?>.[1] The Family is now rid of Leominster in the most honourable Manner, the Honest Men with whom we would always desire to live with as Neighbours, are fully distinguished from the Fawners and the Knaves. We intend to print the Poll that the whole Country shall see the one and the other.[2] The two New Members had no better sense than to suffer their two Footmen to be carried round the Town with Musick before them the morning after the Election in the same Chairs they had been in the night before. The Town took it as a High affront and said they supposed it was to tell them that as They had bought the Town to day, their footmen should be choose to morrow…

Mr Br<other> is in high spirits upon his Defeat…

88. TO MARTHA HARLEY, EYWOOD, 12 MAY 1741.

B.L., Add. MS 70497, unfoliated.

… I have to day finished my circuit of Elections (except my own) and am I thank God very well, though not a little tired of them. I am just come from Radnor where I have left them Polling and I think Gwynn[1] will loose it for want of management. I hope Hopton and Winford[2] will have success, for when I left them yesterday they were both a Head of the General[3] and Westphaling,[4] who were much cast down with the Voters bringing the Money into Court which had been given them, a 2d part of Leominster. I am in hopes our County Election will be tomorrow sen'night, they threaten that a Poll will be demanded for Clark.[5] I publickly declared at Leominster and Hereford That I had so just an opinion of the Integrity of the Freeholders and such a Contempt of the opposition, that I would not so much as ask a Vote, but would leave myself to their free choice which was not to be corrupted like the Voters of Leominster and Hereford. This very much pleased the Freeholders, and I hope will prevent the Folly talked of.

Letter 87

[1] It is unlikely that this is the same person as the Dr Frewin mentioned in John Harley's letter of 11 Jan. 1751. See below p. 267, n. 16.

[2] It was printed as a broadsheet. The only known copy is in the B.L. at 1881.c.6(13.).

Letter 88

[1] Roderick Gwynne lost at Radnorshire to Sir Humphrey Howarth by 519 votes to 496 on 12 May. Sedgwick, I, 380.

[2] They (for whom see the Appendix) did win at Hereford on 11 May. *Ibid.*, p. 258.

[3] Henry Cornewall (1685–1756), elder brother of Velters (see Appendix), had become a maj.-gen. in 1739; he was M.P. for Hereford 1747–54. *Ibid*, p. 579.

[4] Herbert Rudhale Westfaling (?1671–1743), M.P. for Hereford 1717–27.

[5] In the event EH and Velters Cornewall were returned unopposed on 27 May. Sedgwick, I, 257.

We have as cold Winds as in Winter which I am affraid will destroy our hopes of a plentifull year of Cyder which the very fine blow had given. But we have no reason to expect fruitfull seasons while so much Corruption and vile Perjury prevails...

Addressed: For/ Mrs Harley/ at Mrs Anne Philips House/ in Bath

89. TO MARTHA HARLEY (AT BATH), NEWPORT, 15 MAY 1741.

B.L., Add. MS 70497, unfoliated.

My Dearest

I am just come here to Dinner from the Weobley Election, and write for fear I should be too late for the Post at Home, for I am not willing to lose any opportunity of conversing with one I so entirely Love. The Election at Weobley has ended very happily. Lord Weymouth, Lord Chedworth lately Jack How, Sir W. Corbet, Herbert, Hanbury, Winington, Westfailing, etc. appeared on one Side, and Sir J. Morgan and a body of Country Gentlemen on the other and Happy for the former that they did appear, for the Spirits of the People were so high that there was a great deal of Difficulty to prevent their being unruly. In short a Compromise was agreed on. Sir J. Buckworth quitted on our side and Mansel Powell was turned out on theirs which was insisted on as the first preliminary, so that Lord Carpenter and Lord Palmerston were chose without opposition. The Joy of the Country on Powells defeat is very great and Winington told me that He is not to be brought in any where else. Had Powell stood and the Constables returned Him, I am affraid it would have been impossible to have prevented the peoples tearing them to peices.

Radnorshire Election ended at one a clock this morning. Howarth 519. Gwynn 496. Do not imagine I was there at that time, I assure you I was fast asleep in my own bed. Most vile practices used to secure a Majority, the Particulars I will leave to Mr Gwyn who returns soon to Bath. They now begin to see what the Spirit of Whigism is, by what they feel.

I thought my Election would be the 20th but it is not till the 27th...

90. TO MARTHA HARLEY, EYWOOD, 17 MAY 1741.

B.L., Add. MS 70497, unfoliated.

... He <brother Robert> leaves me on Teusday being obliged to go to attend the Duke of Portlands Cause for which He is under great concern. He is not a little pleased with his Defeat <at> Leominster, for all the Men of substance and Virtue were for Him, and the Country make his Cause their own, and think themselves sold with Him, and are so enraged that they are determined not to deal with any in the Town who voted against Him, I fancy this will humble the Gentlemen very sufficiently. Phil. Hooper gave both his Votes against My Brother. Kinnersley[1] was more cunning and gave his first vote for Him. Mr Coates the Bailif acted in the most upright impartial manner through out the whole Poll and at the end of it as He was to give his Vote the last, to show his respect to my Brother though He saw He had lost it by so great numbers, He gave Him a single Vote for which I shall always value him.

Letter 90

[1] Probably Francis Kinnersley, 'Peruke-maker', who voted for Harley and Caswall. *Leominster Borough. An Exact Copy of the Poll, taken ... the Eighth Day of May, 1741, before John Coates, Esq; Bailiff* (n.d.).

The County Election is the 27th, when I am threatned with an opposition, for which I have shewn such a Contempt, that I have told the Freeholders publickly that I would not affront them so much as to sollicit their Votes. If those who have been spreading corruption in Hereford and Leominster should appear that day, I am apt to think they will have a reception from the Freeholders that will not please them. The Courtiers have appeared in very fine Laced Cloaths at their Elections, which makes me as a Country Gentleman be pleased with my plain Frock, though I intended a bit of Finery in my Wastecoat, but cannot find that it is come from London, unless Nem put it in yours or her own box. I wish she would write me word by the return of the post it should be so, and how I may get at it...

Addressed: For/ Mrs Harley/ at Mrs Anne Philips/ in Bath

91. TO MARTHA HARLEY, EYWOOD, 22 MAY 1741.

B.L., Add. MS 70497, unfoliated.

...The following Lines sent me by an Unknown Hand will divert you.

On the Two Footmen who were carried in the Chair at Leominster

Soon as the Horrid Scene was 'oer
And all the Guilty Crew had Swore
(Whither in Earnest or in Joke)
But thus ('tis said) the Members Spoke.
Ye Burgesses of Lemster Wait
And View our Livery Men in State
We'll give you Reasons plain and Clear
For this their Triumph in our Chair.
We Know you so corrupt and base
That thus we tell you to your Face
To Represent such wretched Elves
Our Skips are fitter than Ourselves...

Addressed: For/ Mrs Harley/ at Mrs Anne Philips/ in Bath

92. TO MARTHA HARLEY, HEREFORD, 26 MAY 1741.

B.L., Add. MS 70497, unfoliated.

My Dearest
I came here yesterday as there was so much talk of an Opposition, that I might judge myself of the reallity of it; and I think it must dwindle to nothing, for the nearer the time of trial approaches, the appearance of a contest fade, and If the Post did not go out before We go into Widemarsh to morrow I should send you an Account of our Success without trouble...

May 27:
We are to go to Court in an hour, and I see yet no appearance of any opposition. Ag<ain> I shall have the Honour to be chose In the freeest Manner for I have not asked a Vote. And if a Poll should be demanded the Zeal of the Freeholders for me would be very great. Many of the Common ones having offered to come at their own Expence. I pray God bless you and give us a joyfull Meeting...

93. TO MARTHA HARLEY, HEREFORD, 29 MAY 1741.

B.L., Add. MS 70497, unfoliated.

My Dearest
    The Elections are now over, and I thank God that I am so perfectly well after the fatigue and hurry of them, I had little trouble in my own where there was no Opposition, the appearance of Gentlemen and Freeholders very great...
    Mr Vaughan[1] has desisted for Breconshire, which I am glad of as He has saved the expence of a Poll...

Addressed: For/ Mrs Abigail Harley/ at Mr Philips in/ Bath/ E Free Harley

94. FROM DR TIMOTHY THOMAS,[1] WREXHAM, 5 JUNE 1741.
'Fryday morning'.

B.L., Add. MS 70085, unfoliated.

Sir,
    The Account that was brought to this place from Denbigh last night runs thus.[2] They polled by Tallies of 20 men at a time. On Wednesday Mr. Middleton[3] could not make up one Tally, and Sir W.[4] polled some scores. Yesterday Mr. Middleton polled but two, and made an offer of yielding and throwing up the Poll, but the High Sheriff[5] (who is it seems a most thorow paced person, and from whom any Vile behaviour may be expected,) would not suffer him to give up. Sir W. is said to be above 300 before them last night, and there can be no doubt of his carrying it by a very great Majority, but still I find people are suspicious of some Villany from the Sheriff in making the Return. If I hear any more before I send my Servant homewards (who brings this letter) you shall know of it. If there be any foul play in the Return, I find the universall disposition of all sorts in favor of Sir W– to be so sanguine, that it is dreadfull to think what the consequence may be: Soldiers are quarterd all about at convenient distances, against any Event: But I am told that both Sir W and his friends behave with great prudence and Temper in preventing all Tendencies to Tumult, though they have great provocations. It is computed that Sir W–'s Expence at the Town of Denbigh only has been at least £600 a day ever since the Election begun on Tuesday was seennight, besides a monstrous Expence at Ruthen and other places all the time.
    Rhuabon, just by Sir Watkin's,[6] 8, o'clock, Evening. Fryday, June 5th. One of Sir W–'s servants is just now arrived Express from Denbigh, with the following account to Lady Williams; viz. That the Books were closed about 3 o'clock this afternoon

---

Letter 93
[1] Probably William Gwyn Vaughan (?1681–1753), of Trebarried, Breconshire, who had been M.P. for that county 1721–34. Sedgwick, II, 493–4.

Letter 94
[1] Timothy Thomas. See above p. 198, n. 9.
[2] For a detailed account of the 1741 Denbighshire election see Peter D.G. Thomas, 'Wynnstay Versus Chirk Castle: Parliamentary Elections in Denbighshire, 1716–1741', *National Library of Wales Journal*, XI (1959), 113–21.
[3] John Myddelton, M.P. for Denbigh Boroughs 1733–41 (see Appendix), who, though a tory, had formed an electoral alliance with the government to recover the county seat. See Sedgwick, II, 287–8.
[4] Sir Watkin Williams Wynn. See Appendix.
[5] William Myddelton, a relation of John Myddelton. Thomas, 'Wynnstay Versus Chirk Castle', pp. 113, 117, 119.
[6] William Wynn's seat was at Wynnstay, Denbighshire, near Ruabon, five miles south of Wrexham.

with a mutuall consent, That the Sheriff declared there was a Majority of 419 for Sir W – and he accordingly declared Sir Watkyn duly chosen, and he solemnly engaged to make a Return accordingly on Wednesday next, and gave such reasons for this Delay of the return as fully satisfyed Sir Watkyn and his friends, who are not suspicious of any foul play intended.[7] But were I concerned I should be thinking of – timeo Danaos – Sir W– is expected at home at Wynstay by dinner time. I am so distressed in time that I cannot stay, to have a look at him. I am your very Faithfull humble Servant Timo thomas.

I wrote to Street by the Cross-post on Thursday, but perhaps this may come to Eywood before that reaches Him; And no doubt, but he would be glad to know the Contents of this: What I wrote to him being before the Conclusion of the affair.

Endorsed: Dr Thomas./ Election for the County of/ Denbigh.
Addressed: For/ The Honble. Edw: Harley Esqr/ at Eywood.

95. TO LORD HARDWICKE, EYWOOD, 26 JUNE 1741.

B.L., Add. MS 35586, ff. 368–9.

My Lord
    Since it has pleased God to determine my Lord Oxfords Life, and as his Lordship Died without issue Male,[1] I have taken the liberty to acquaint your Lordship that his Titles descend to me as Great Grandson to Sir Robert Harley to whose Heirs Male the Patent of Creation is granted, and therefore beg leave humbly to apply to your Lordship that you would be pleased to give Orders for the issuing of the Writ of Summons. I am with great Respect My Lord Your Lordships most obedient humble Servant Oxford

Endorsed: Eywood June 26, 1741/ From the Earl of Oxford/ for his writ.

96. TO THOMAS FOLEY,[1] EYWOOD, 26 JUNE 1741.

Brampton Bryan MSS, Bundle 117.

Sir
    I had a Letter this morning from my Brother that He would not at this time stand for the Country. I hope you will meet with the greatest success, and if I can in the least promote it you may Command all the Service in my power. Be pleased to make my Wifes and my most humble Service acceptable to the Ladies and Mr Foley. I am Sir Your most humble Servant Oxford

---

[7] At the election on 26 May Wynn won by 1352 to 933 after 'a costly campaign', marked by the mass creation of new voters on both sides. Myddelton, however, was returned by the sheriff, who disallowed nearly 600 of Wynn's voters, so that the final poll was 847 to Myddelton and 758 to Wynn. On a petition to the Commons after Walpole's fall, Wynn was returned. Sedgwick, I, 375; II, 287–8; Thomas, 'Wynn-stay Versus Chirk Castle', pp. 113–21.

Letter 95
[1] The 2nd earl of Oxford had died on 16 June. The patent of creation of the earldom stated that after the failure of the male heirs of the 1st earl, the title should pass to the next male heir of Sir Robert Harley (1579–1656), the 1st earl's grandfather.

Letter 96
[1] Thomas Foley (see Appendix) was returned unopposed for Herefordshire on 6 Jan. 1742. Robert Harley wrote to him on 3 Sept. 1741 confirming that he would not be standing 'in order to preserve the friendship between the two families and the Unity of the County'. Brampton Bryan MSS, bundle 117, draft.

97. TO LORD HARDWICKE, EYWOOD, 22 JULY 1746.

B.L., Add. MS 35588, ff. 264–5.

My Lord

I hope your Lordship will pardon my giving you this trouble which I was in hopes I should not have had any Occasion to have done, for I fully intended to have set out to morrow morning (having prepared every thing for my journey) that I might obey their Lordships Summons.[1] But I have received an Account that one of my Children is taken ill of the Small Pox at my House in London, This News has greatly affected my Wife, who has been very lately extreamly ill, but was so much recovered that I thought I might leave her with safety, but I now fear a return of her illness, especially if it should please God that any thing amiss should happen to my Son, and in such a Case it would add to my Greif to be absent from Her.

I would humbly offer it to your Lordships Consideration, that supposing I was now in town, whether the present Circumstances of my Family would not be a just excuse for my absence; as my Son is in my own House where I should every day see and be with Him, (for I am sure no one would think it reasonable that I should debar myself that Satisfaction) and as the Distemper would be at the Heighth and the Infection the strongest about the time of the Trials, I think it would be very indecent in me and it might be very unsafe for others, if I was to presume to appear in Publick, where I might give just offense to many Lords and Others who have not had this Distemper.

I have thus naturally and plainly laid my Case before your Lordship, and as my absence is occasioned only by this Accident which I could neither foresee nor avoid, and proceeds more out of Respect to their Lordships than any Disobedience to their Orders, I hope your Lordship will favourably represent me to their Lordships and that they will be so compassionately indulgent as to excuse my Attendance, and that your Lordship will be pleased to forgive this great trouble which I have given you, which will greatly oblige My Lord Your Lordships most obedient humble Servant Oxford

Endorsed: Eywood July 23d. <sic>/ 1746./ From the Earl of/ Oxford.

98. TO THE DUKE OF NEWCASTLE,[1] EYWOOD, 22 JULY 1746.

B.L., Add. MS 32707, ff. 486–7.

My Lord

I hope your Grace will pardon my giving you this trouble, which I was in hopes I should not have had any Occasion to have done, for I fully intended to have set out to morrow morning (having prepared every thing for my journey) that I might obey their Lordships Summons. But I have received an Account that one of my Children is taken ill of the Small Pox at my House in London, This News has greatly affected my Wife, who has been very lately extreamly ill, but was so much recovered that I thought I might leave her with Safety; but now I fear a return of her illness, especially if it should

---

Letter 97

[1] On 27 June the lord chancellor was ordered by the house to write to all peers requiring their appearance and attendance at the trial of the jacobite peers, Lords Kilmarnock, Cromartie and Balmerino, set for 28 July. *L.J.*, XXVI, 599.

Letter 98

[1] Sent via the duke of Portland (for whom see Appendix), see next letter. Portland was related to Newcastle through his wife Margaret, who was the only child of Henrietta Cavendish (wife of the 2nd earl of Oxford), Newcastle's first cousin.

please God that any thing amiss should happen to my Son, and in such a Case it would add to my Greif to be absent from Her. I would humbly offer it to your Graces Consideration, that supposing I was now in town, whether the present Circumstances of my Family, would not be a just excuse for my absence; as my son is in my own House, where I should every day see and be with Him, (for I am sure no one would think it reasonable that I should debar myself that Satisfaction) and as the Distemper would be at the Heighth and the Infection the strongest about the time of the Trials, I should think it would be very indecent in me, and it might be very prejudicial to others, if I was to presume to appear in Publick, where I might give just offense to many Lords and others who have not had this Distemper.

I have thus naturally and plainly laid my Case before your Grace, and as my Absence is occasioned only by this Accident which I could neither foresee nor avoid, and proceeds more out of Respect to their Lordships, than any Disobedience to their Orders, I hope your Grace will favourably represent me to their Lordships if there be any occasion, and that they will be so compassionately indulgent as to excuse my Attendance, and that your Grace will be pleased to forgive this great trouble which I have given you, which will greatly oblige My Lord your Graces most obedient humble Servant Oxford

Endorsed: Ld Oxford./ Eywood. July 22 1746

99. FROM THE DUKE OF NEWCASTLE, NEWCASTLE HOUSE, 26 JULY 1746.[1]

B.L., Add. MS 32707, ff. 482–3.

My Lord

I had this day the honor of your Lordship's letter from the Duke of Portland,[2] and am extreamly sorry for the Indisposition of your Family, and I shall not fail to acquaint the House with your Lordships Intention to have attended according to their orders had not your Lordship been prevented by <the illness?> mentioned in your letter.[3] I am very glad of any opportunity of assuring your Lordship of the <illegible> respect with which I am.

Endorsed: To Lord Oxford./ July 26 1746

100. TO THE DUKE OF NEWCASTLE, EYWOOD, 29 JULY 1746.

B.L., Add. MS 32707, ff. 499–500.

My Lord

I cannot be too early in my acknowledgment of the Honour of your Graces Letter which I received this Morning, and in returning my humble Thanks to your Grace for your great Civility to me and my Family in representing my absence in a favourable manner to the House of Lords. I am with great Respect My Lord Your Graces most obedient humble Servant Oxford

Endorsed: Eywood. July 29. 1746/ Earl of Oxford

Letter 99
[1] Draft.
[2] Portland was married to the Margaret Harley, the daughter of EH's first cousin, the 2nd earl of Oxford.
[3] On 28 July the house was called over and the 49 absent peers noted in the Journal. On the 4 Aug., after the trial, the house considered the list of absent peers, and witnesses 'were examined, with relation to the Non-attendance' of nine of them, including Oxford, 'who were thereupon severally excused'. *L.J.*, XXVI, 616–17, 631; see also below, pp. 260, 262.

101. TO LORD HARDWICKE, EYWOOD, 29 JULY 1746.

B.L., Add. MS 35588, f. 284.

My Lord

I received the favour of Mr Perkins[1] Letter this Morning and am very much obliged to your Lordship for the kind Notice you are pleased to take of my Case which occasions my absence. I am very sorry to find that your Lordship has been out of Order, and wish the great fatigue your Lordship must undergo may not add to it.

That your Lordship and your Family may enjoy perfect Health and Happyness is the hearty wish of Your Lordships most obedient humble Servant Oxford

102. FROM JOHN HARLEY,[1] 29 JULY 1746.

P.R.O., 30/20/24/2, pp. 101–4.

Dear Papa

I thank you for your Letter which I receiv'd Last night, I am Glad to hear that my Mamma is so much better, and hope that by this time her disorder has quite left her. I have now the pleasure to acquaint you that Billy[2] is out of all manner of Danger, he got up yesterday and has taken Physick to Day, and sat up to Eat his dinner, which he bore very well. Dr Mead[3] has done coming to him. As Billy will want his Wigs now he has began to get up; I should be glad if you would Let us know what Colour you would have them made of, as soon as you can.

The Trials came on in Westminster Hall on monday,[4] Thommy[5] and I were there, I have sent you as particular an account of it as I could remember. The Procession was as follows: The Lords came down in order and all in their Robes; The Judges walked first, then the Minor Lords, and then the Peers beggining with the Lowest Baron: As soon as Lord Chancellor was made high steward and took the Chair, he open'd the Patent and made a speech to the Lords on the occasion of their being assembled; The Warrants were then read and the three Lords brought to the Bar; Upon the Indictments being read Lord Kilmarnock[6] (who I think is as Handsome a Person of a man as ever I saw) and Lord Cromertie[7] both pleaded Guilty. Lord Balmerino[8] upon his Indictment

---

Letter 101
[1] Hutton Perkins, secretary to Lord Chancellor Hardwicke.

Letter 102
[1] John Harley (c.1728–88), 3rd son of EH, at Westminster School 1736–46, matric. Christ Church 1747, B.A. 1749, M.A. 1752, D.D. and dean of Windsor 1778, bishop of Hereford 1787–8.
[2] William Harley (1733–68), 6th child but 5th son of EH, at Westminster School 1743–9, matric. Christ Church 22 Dec. 1749, B.A. 1753, M.A. 1756, prebendary of York 1762 and of Worcester 1764.
[3] Richard Mead, M.D. (1673–1754), who had been appointed physician to George II in 1727. His clients included Walpole and Isaac Newton. *D.N.B.*
[4] The trial of three jacobite peers who had risen in the '45: Balmerino, Cromartie and Kilmarnock. For details see *L.J.*, XXVI, 615–24 (28 July).
[5] Thomas Harley (1730–1804), 4th son of EH, at Westminster School 1738–48, a merchant, M.P. for London 1761–74, Herefordshire 1776–1802, and lord mayor of London 1768.
[6] William Boyd (1705–46), 4th earl of Kilmarnock, taken prisoner at Culloden, convicted of treason and executed 18 Aug. 1746.
[7] George Mackenzie (c.1703–66), 3rd earl of Cromartie, taken prisoner at Dunrobin, convicted of high treason, lost his titles and estates, but received a conditional pardon.
[8] Arthur Elphinstone (1688–1746), 6th Lord Balmerino, taken prisoner at Culloden, convicted of treason and executed 18 Aug. 1746.

being read, made an objection to it, and denied his being at the taking of Carlisle, as was said in the Indictment, and desir'd they would acquaint him wither a flaw being in the Indictment would be of any service to him, in the case of Treason, as it is in other common indictments; which Question Lord Chancellor refused to answer; and told him that he must either Plead Guilty, or not Guilty, and then should make what defence or alledge what he please in Behalf of himselfe. Upon which he pleaded not Guilty. Four of the kings Council spoke against him. Serjant Skinner[9] who was one spoke neer three Quarters of an hour the meerest Nonsense that ever was heard; He gave a definition of Treason (that was pretty strange) that it was the *sin of Witchcraft* and such stuff; and then went through the whole series of the Rebellion, and compared the Highland *army to a swarm of Locusts* Destroying the fruit of the Land; and said that the success of the battle of Falkirk was only because *Victory staid for that glorious Hero the Duke*[10] whose very appearance struck Rebellion *with Paleness*, and much more such after <sic> nonsense as it not worth transcribing.

The Witnesses were examin'd, the Lords Adjourned to the house of Lords, where they had a long Debate whether Lord Balmerinos Plea had any weight or not, they likewise desired to have the Judges opinion of it, who gave it that it was no objection in the Case of Treason; Though it was in common Law; Upon which the Lords returned to Westminster Hall; Lord Balmeriono being ordered from the Bar, Lord Chancellor put it to the Vote beginning with the Lowest Baron, They all found him Guilty. Lord Foley who was there at the beginning, went out and would not vote, which makes great noise. The House was then Adjourn'd 'till Wensday Morning: and the Lords ordered back again to the Tower. They all three behaved with vast decency and shewed great courage. 'Tis said Lord Kilmarnock will make a speech in his defence too Morrow.

The Duke of Newcastle and Mr Pelham were examining Murray the Pretenders Secretary[11] from 5 O Clocks at night till Past six next morning, they have taken fourteen sheets of Paper of his definition, He has impeached of a great many people in England who sent Money and held correspondence with the Pretender when in England: One Dr Barry[12] a near relation of Lord Barrimore was therefore taken up on Sunday night, and a great many Messengers sent down into the North to take people up whose Names I have not yet heard, So that God knows who may see the End of bloodshed.

I beleive your excuse will be admitted of, but they have put it off 'till these Trials are over, then they are to take it in consideration.[13]

My Brother and I Join in Duty to you and My Mamma and Love to Patty and my Brothers and Service to Mrs Gower and all at Eywood.

I am your most Dutyful son John Harley

Endorsed: J: Harley/ July 1746./ Upon the Tryals of the Lords

---

[9] Matthew Skinner (1689–1749), prime serjeant 1734, M.P. for Oxford 1734–8, chief justice Chester 1738–49; counsel for the prosecution of the '45 rebels on the northern circuit, and against Lord Balmerino where, according to Horace Walpole, he made 'the most absurd speech imaginable'. Sedgwick, II, 425.

[10] H.R.H. Prince William Augustus (1721–65), duke of Cumberland.

[11] John Murray (1715–77) of Boughton, secretary to the Young Pretender, pardoned in 1748.

[12] Dr Peter Barry, London physician and cousin of Lord Barrymore.

[13] On 4 Aug. the nine peers (including EH) absent from the trial of the jacobite peers were excused. *L.J.*, XXVI, 631.

103. TO THE DUKE OF NEWCASTLE, EYWOOD, 8 AUGUST 1746.

B.L., Add. MS 32708, ff. 39–40.

My Lord

Be pleased to accept of my humble Thanks for the Honour your Grace has done me by making my excuse to the House, and am very much obliged to their Lordships and your Grace in allowing of my absence. I am with great Respect My Lord your Graces most obedient humble Servant Oxford

Endorsed: Aug. 8. 1746./ E. of Oxford

104. FROM ROBERT GWILLYM,[1] CHELTENHAM, 19 JUNE 1747.

B.L., Add. MS 70085, unfoliated.

My Lord

Your Lordship dos me a great deal of Honour in acquainting me with your Intentions of setting up my Lord Harley for the County, He is in mine and I believe in the Opinion of every Gentleman in it the properest person to represent it. I was never worth much Notice, but of less now than ever, therefore am the more oblig'd to you for the Notice you have taken of me. My Lord Harley may depend on any Service I can do him, and I dare say the Country are so unanimous in their Opinion of him, that he won't meet with the least Trouble.[2] I am with great Respect, Your Lordships most obedient and most oblig'd humble Servant Robt. Gwillym

Endorsed: Mr Gwillym June 19. 1747
Addressed: To/ The Right Honble the Earl of Oxford/ at/ Eywood/ near/ Presteigne

105. FROM THOMAS, LORD FOLEY, 25 JUNE 1747.

B.L., Add. MS 70498, ff. 37–8.

My Lord

I must begin with asking pardon of your Lordship for interfering in a matter which I have nothing to do with, but as it is out of a Sincere Regard to your Lordship and your family I hope that will plead my Excuse.

I see by the Papers that my Lord Harley has advertis'd standing for your County; as he is under Age[1] I am in great pain least some trick should be play'd him on the Day of Election, as I am inform'd that you cannot Entirely depend on your Sheriff.[2] You know it is in his <breast?> to object to my Lord's age if he thinks fit, and in that Case any one man that can poll but two Votes has a right to be return'd; which if it should happen I think would be of the most evil Consequence to your Family as well

---

Letter 104

[1] A Robert Gwillym voted in the Hereford election of 1747 for Henry Cornewall (a government supporter) and Daniel Leighton (a Leicester House whig). *An Alphabetical Copy of the Poll taken at the City of Hereford ... 1747* (Hereford, 1747), p. 9.

[2] He was elected unopposed, along with Velters Cornewall, on 15 July.

Letter 105

[1] Lord Harley (for whom see Appendix) was born on 2 Sept. 1726. He did stand and was returned unopposed.

[2] Bensalem Edwards of Bodenham, sheriff of Herefordshire 1747–8.

as to the Interest of the County. Now, with great Submission, I would suggest a thing which I think would obviate this Difficulty. My Cousin Foley's Election at Wyche[3] will be over before that of your County can come on. If he is chose there, suppose he was nominated for the County of Hereford, and at the meeting of the Parliament should promise he would make his Election for Wyche, and so open the County to my Lord Harley, who would then be at Age? I don't see any objection to this, which would effectualy secure my Lord Harley's Election. However I submitt it to your better judgement, but could not forbear mentioning it to you.

If Mr Rob<er>t Harley is with you at Hereford, I should be glad he would let me know by the Bearer, what Day is fixt for the Lemster Election,[4] for our Writs are not yet come Down, and if I can, I would contrive the Wyche Election not to interfere with this.

We have this Day settl'd our County Election amicably. Lechmere[5] has declin'd and Lord Deerhurst and Mr Pytts[6] were Unanimously agreed to. I am extremely pleas'd with the thing, for Reasons I will tell you when I see you.

If you know what is to be done at Hereford, you will oblige us in communicating it. I Believe Mr Winford will this Night, or to morrow morning declare for Worcester.[7]

I am Your Lordships most affectionate and Obedient humble Servant Foley

I should be glad of a Line by the Bearer.

Endorsed: Lord Foley/ June 25. 1747.

106. FROM SIR HUNGERFORD HOSKYNS,[1] HAREWOOD, 26 JUNE 1747.

B.L., Add. MS 70085, unfoliated.

My Lord

I have received the honour of a letter from your Lordship as to my approbation of Lord Harley's being one of the keepers of the rights and priviledges of the Commons of Great Britain in the ensuing parliaments.

My Lord, I've not the honour of being known to Lord Harley, but hope and indeed have no reason to doubt that he inherits the virtues of his father, so I think no person more proper. Wishing him success I am My Lord Your most Dutyfull and obedient Servant Hung: Hoskyns

Endorsed: Sr Hung: Hoskins/ June 27. 1747.

---

[3] Thomas Foley (1716–77) of Stoke Edith, Herefordshire, was elected at Droitwich (Worcestershire) on 1 July 1747 (but was unseated on petition on 16 Dec.). He sat for Droitwich 1741–7, 1754–68, and Herefordshire 1768–76. The Herefordshire election was on 17 July 1747. Sedgwick, I, 257, 355; II, 41.

[4] It was held on 30 June 1747. *Ibid.*, I, 259.

[5] Edmund Lechmere (1710–1805), M.P. for Worcestershire 1734–47.

[6] Viscount Deerhurst, an opposition whig, and Edmund Pytts, a tory (see Appendix for both), were returned unopposed for Worcestershire on 8 July 1747. Sedgwick, I, 353–4, 588; II, 202, 377.

[7] Thomas Geers Winford (see Appendix), a tory, was returned for Worcester on 1 July 1747 with the support of the corporation, which had created over 100 honorary freemen. On petition these votes were disallowed and he lost his seat on 11 Feb. 1748. Sedgwick, I, 356; II, 61.

Letter 106

[1] Sir Hungerford Hoskyns (*c.*1677–1767), 4th bt. of Harewood, Herefordshire (five miles north west of Ross-on-Wye), M.P. for Herefordshire 1717–22. Sedgwick, I, 257; II, 150–1.

107. FROM WALLWYN SHEPHEARD,[1] DORMINGTON, 12 JULY 1747.

B.L., Add. MS 70085, unfoliated.

My Lord

Being apprehensive that Young Mr Skipp had declared that the Hereford Election should be Retaliated by giving an Opposition for the County, I took the oportunity of calling at Ledbury on my Return from Worcester to be further satisfyed in that Point; and talking the Affair of Elections over, Mr Skipp the Elder in the presence of his Son, said, that he hoped there would be no opposition for the County, and that he thought Lord Harley and Mr Cornewall very proper persons to Represent it, or to that Effect: so that I beleive you'll find no disturbance from that Quarter: Neither do I find that any Interest hath been forming on this side the County; I have been at Marche with Mr Elkton, Mr Barnes[2] and others within these two days, who would have told me if any of Mr Westfaling's[3] Agents had been amongst the Freeholders, who are very numerous in that Neighbourhood. I am My Lord Your Lordship's most obedient and most humble Servant Wallwyn Shepheard

Endorsed: Mr. Shepherd. / July. 12. 1747.
Addressed: To The Right Honble. / the Earl of Oxford at / Eywood

108. FROM LORD HARLEY, LONDON, 23 JANUARY 1749/50.

P.R.O., 30/20/24/2, pp. 97–100.

Dear Pappa

I am very glad to find that you propose leaving Eywood next week, and that I am to have the Pleasure of seeing you so soon in Town. All your Friends are very glad that you are so much recovered, and are very desirous of seeing you in London, particularly Lord Shaftsbury who is so impatient that he has sent to me twice or thrice to know if the Day is fixed for your setting out. Mrs Foley was brought to bed of a Girl the latter end of last week, I did not know it when I wrote last Post, I have sent every day, and she and the child are as well as can be expected. Her Sister the Maid of Honour is dying of a Consumption.

As I was prevented last post sending you an Account of the Debate on Fryday <on the Mutiny Bill>[1] by Billy's[2] coming to Town, I will endeavour to put down the few particulars I can recollect of Lord Eg<mon>t's Speech.

Letter 107
[1] Two Walwyn Sheppards (senior and junior) voted at the 1741 Hereford election for the tory candidates Edward Cope Hopton and Thomas Geers Winford, while only Sheppard senior voted in 1747 for Cornewall and Leighton. *An Alphabetical Copy of the Poll taken at the City of Hereford ... 1741* (Gloucester, [1741]), p. 20; *Alphabetical Copy of the Poll ... 1747*, p. 18. A Walwyn Sheppard of Dormington (five miles east of Hereford) voted for Harley and Cornewall at the 1754 election. See *A Copy of the Poll ... for the County of Hereford ...* (Gloucester, 1754), p. 19.
[2] Possibly John Elton and William Barnes, cleric, both of Much Marche, near Ledbury, and both of whom voted for Harley and Cornewall in 1754. *A Copy of the Poll ... for the County of Hereford*, pp. 18–19.
[3] Herbert Rudhale Westfaling jr., who came third in the poll for Hereford on 3 July 1747. He had also stood unsuccessfully in 1734 and 1741. Sedgwick, I, 258.

Letter 108
[1] In the Commons on 19 Jan. 1750. *C.J.*, XXV, 944.
[2] William Harley. See letter 102, n. 2.

His Lordship said that he had looked into all the Regulations, ancient as well as Modern, that had ever been made for the Government of Armies, that there was no Instance of an Oath of Secrecy, excepting in the Articles of war in this Country, and those of Germany. That he hoped the Committee would recollect the Flame, which the taking the Hanover Troops into British Pay raised in the Nation;[3] that if such a measure in time of war and necessity could inflame the minds of mankind to so great a degree, that Gentlemen should consider what might be the consequence, if the People of England knew that German Military Government was adopted in this Country in time of Peace.

That he disliked a Captain General, that it was a Post in time of Peace, which was Anti-Constitutional, that besides it was Dangerous as well as expensive, and that as long as there was such a Command England can never hope to get rid of her Army, because it will annually be voted to support the Authority of the General.

That the Oath of Secrecy shut up the Doors of the House of Commons against enquiries, that it would be infamous in the Members to resign their Priviledges to the Army, which owed its existence to the House, and was a Creature of Parliament, that every Suspicion, which the Constituents had entertained of their Representatives, would be confirmed, that People had often wished without doors that Parliaments were laid aside, and that Mankind, it was to be feared, would resign their Liberties to some kind and benign Master, rather than trust any longer in the hands of their Representatives, who in former Parliaments, as often as they were entrusted by them, as constantly betrayed them.

My Lord Spoke an hour, but these were the most Remarkable things in his Speech. We are to have a long day, upon the Revision of the Sentences of Court Martials.[4]

Be pleased to give my Duty to my Mamma, my love to my Brothers and Patty, and Service to Mrs Gower.

I am, my Lord, Your Most Dutyful Son Harley

Endorsed: Ld Harley Jan: 23/ 1749/50/ Debate on the Mutiny Bill

109. FROM JOHN HARLEY, CHRIST CHURCH, 11 JANUARY 1750/51.

B.L., Add. MS 70498, ff. 75–6.

Dear Papa

I hope you received mine of yesterday, I fear you could make little out of it as I was obliged to conclude it so abruptly. The Face of things are quite altered;[1] The Statute[2]

---

[3] In 1742, 1744 and 1746.

[4] The Mutiny Bill was considered further on 23, 25, 29 Jan. (including an amended clause on courts martial) and 7 Feb., when it passed the Commons. *C.J.*, XXV, 946, 950, 968–9, 981.

Letter 109

[1] The fullest modern account of the Oxford University by-election is W.R. Ward, *Georgian Oxford. University Politics in the Eighteenth Century* (Oxford, 1958), pp. 188–91. See also Paul Langford, 'Tories and Jacobites, 1714–1751', in *The History of Oxford University. Volume V. The Eighteenth Century*, ed. L.S. Sutherland and L.G. Mitchell (Oxford, 1986), pp. 125–6, and the introduction, p. liv above.

[2] The statute of the university in question, 'De Privilegiis Universitatis et Civitatis simul non fruendis', is printed in *A True Copy of the Poll taken at Oxford, January 31, 1750[/1]. With several papers sent to The Common Rooms of the respective Colleges, Relating to the Election of a Member of Parliament for the University* [1751], p. 3. It stated that a candidate for the university seat must be a member of the university (i.e., a holder of an M.A. degree or above), but not be a member of the city corporation.

(which I find Sandford[3] has enclosed to you yesterday) is so extreamly strong that it is impossible for Sir Edward[4] ever to get over, though I do not hear that He himself as yet has publickly resigned, but the words are so very strong that none of his Freinds can think of supporting him; for it is not only accepting of any place in the Corporation, but the serio ambiisse, the even desiring or solliciting, that for ever Excludes the person, *in perpetuum excludatur*; so that resignation which has been thought of, will be of no Effect.[5] By this the whole state of Affairs are altered; what we at first proposed was lying by for Sir Rogers[6] Freinds to Join us, when upon a calculation they should find that they could not serve him; but this is now Entirely at an End. Upon the Statute being found yesterday Morning; Sandford waited upon the Rector of Lincoln[7] in order to sound him what Part He and the rest of Sir Edward Turners Freinds would act, and whether they would acquiesce in Sir Roger: to which the Rector said that He thought Mr Harley was a much more proper person than Sir Roger, and that He imagined that upon Sir Edwards giving up All his Freinds would be glad to Join my Brother:[8] but this is as yet kept private.

Now the Case is this, the All Souls people who wrote to Sir Roger are at present determin'd to push him to the utmost,[9] and have behaved very ungenerously to my Brother, after the civil treatment they have met with from His Freinds; By which means we are thrown into this Dilemma, that we must either immediately drop all thoughts of my Brother, or resolve to stand a Poll which would be very clear in our Favour: for could a standard be fixt between Whig and Torie, I am sure by the calculation that we have made the Majority of Tories are inclined to my Brother.[10] This I should be glad to have your opinion of as soon as possible: I find by All hands my Unckle Harley[11] if you approve of it must be the Person, for my Brothers not being called to the Bar,[12] is an objection that many who are extreamly attached to the Family do not care to get over. But this in fact will be the same thing, and for what I know perhaps better for my Brother, as my Unckle may resign without disobliging whenever He thinks proper.

As to the dividing the Intrest, It is thought by the sensible and moderate people, that this can be the only means of preserving the Peace and Quiet of the place: for if you should not care to have any of your Family involved in a Contest, (of which there

---

[3] A Mr Sandford of Balliol College voted for Harley (*ibid.*). Robert Sandford of Stratton, Glocs. matriculated in 1741 at Balliol College. He does not appear to have obtained an M.A., the minimum qualification for a vote in a parliamentary election. His younger brother John did in 1749 from All Souls (B.A. 1745, Oriel College).

[4] Sir Edward Turner (1719–61), 2nd bt., M.P. for Great Bedwyn 1741–7, Oxfordshire 1755–61, and Penryn 1761–6, polled only 67 votes at the election. Sedgwick, I, 306; II, 487–8.

[5] The controversy was over whether Turner, who was to resign his freedom of the city (acquired in 1742), could stand by virtue of his resignation and his honorary M.A. (1738) and D.C.L. (1744). The arguments can be followed in *A True Copy of the Poll taken at Oxford, January 31, 1750[/51]*. Newdigate also had an honorary M.A. (1738) and D.C.L. (1749), while Robert Harley had gained his M.A. in 1748.

[6] Sir Roger Newdigate (see Appendix), was elected for Oxford University on 31 Jan., with 184 votes. Sedgwick, I, 306.

[7] Euseby Isham (*c.*1698–1755), rector of Lincoln College 1731–55, voted for Turner.

[8] Robert Harley polled 126 votes. *A True Copy of the Poll taken at Oxford, January 31, 1750[/51]*.

[9] Of the 21 votes from All Souls, 18 voted for Newdigate. *Ibid.*

[10] In fact, most of Robert Harley's support came from the Oxford whigs, and he gained almost all the votes cast in the whig strongholds of Christ Church, Exeter and Merton. *Ibid.*

[11] Robert Harley, EH's younger brother and formerly M.P. for Leominster. See Appendix.

[12] Robert Harley was called to the bar on 21 Nov. 1751. *The Records of the Honourable Society of Lincoln's Inn. The Black Books* (5 vols., 1897–1968), III, 349.

can be no danger of Victory) the breach between the Heads of Houses and some of Sir Rogers freinds is so great that it is said that they are determind to sett up some other person who perhaps may not be so proper. This is the opinion of many sensible people, and was mention'd to Sandford by the person who met my Unckle in Somersetshire this summer, who likewise begged that my Brother might not be dropt. D–ke[13] of the same College is of the same opinion, and 'tis very probable they will Join if you should approve, though they do not care to declare openly yet.

Upon talking to the All Souls people a Compromise has been mention<ed>, that if we should for the sake of the Peace of the place give up this Election, whether or no they would promise for another time; but this they have refused, and declare they will make no such promise.

It has been proposed by them that is All Souls, that my Brothers name should be made use of to prevent any other Person being sett up, to this I made answer that we could never think of using my Brothers Freinds in that manner who had behaved in so handsome a Manner to him, and that I had no notion that my Brother should be made a Tool of upon any account.

We have had great difficulty in keeping this College quiet, I heard yesterday that the Cannons seemd to think it odd that they had never been spoke to; upon which I went to them, and told them that as my Brother had the honour of being mention'd in the University, I thought it decent to acquaint them with it, and how much you were obliged to, All his Freinds for it: I likewise shewed some of them your Letter, with which they were very much pleased. Dr Lewis[14] sett out of London this morn<ing> with the Master of Baliol,[15] who it is said is gone up to endeavour to persuade you to withdraw my Brother; but for many reasons, which I cannot explain now, I should think you had better not see him; for his behaviour in regard to my Brother is infamous; if you think you cannot avoid seeing of him, I hope you will not mind one word He says; perhaps you may think this very odd but I beleive I shall be able to satisfy you another time.

This Affair is so perplexing that I wish I may have been able to make you understand it clearly.

I have this moment received yours; and will give you a full answer to it too morrow.

Dr Frewin[16] is strongly for my Brother.

I will enquire into what you mention about Lord Cornbury.[17] I should think it would be of great service.

The Clock has struck five.

I am your most Dutyful son John Harley.

My Brother Joins with me in Duty.

Endorsed: J: Harley Jan 11: 1750–1

---

[13] Possibly George Drake, a fellow of Sandford's college, Balliol, but he supported Newdigate in the election.

[14] ? William Lewis (1714–72), a chemist of Christ Church, who delivered the oration at the opening of the Radcliffe Library in 1749. He voted for Harley.

[15] Theophilus Leigh (1693–1785), master of Balliol 1726–85, voted for Turner, his brother-in-law.

[16] Richard Frewin (c.1681–1761), Camden professor of ancient history 1727–61, and a physician (D.Med. 1711). He voted for Harley, along with 45 others from Christ Church; only six voted for Newdigate and Turner.

[17] M.P. for Oxford University 1732–51 (see Appendix). The by-election at the university was caused by his elevation to the peerage in his father's barony of Lord Hyde of Hindon, on 23 Jan. 1751.

110. TO MR [HERBERT] AUBREY,[1] 21 FEBRUARY 1750/1.[2]

B.L., Add. MS 70085, unfoliated.

Sir

I received the favour of yours last night,[3] and which gives me a fresh testimony of your friendship therefore cannot omit the first opportunity of acknowledging it. The greatest part of what you have heard of the U<niversity> E<lection> is without foundation which I will explain when I have the pleasure to see you and will only say that Christ Church did not set Him up but only supported Him as He was a Member of that College.[4] The Opposition was put upon a higher cause which had nothing to do with the Election, and the D<uke> of B: and myself were made the Principles in the Contest, I hope without the Knowledge or Consent of either, I can declare it was without mine as it was beyond my thought and that this Election was to determine who was to be Chancellor upon a Vacancy. And accordingly Letters were wrote, and persons sent to from all parts to appear, {and upon this Summons Mr Payne[6] and the other Chaplain from Badminton came and voted against my Son, whether by his G<race's> consent or privity I will not take upon me to say.}[7] It is well known by my freinds in the University that whenever the least mention was made to me in relation to the Chancellorship (which was improper to be talked of, as the present most worthy one was not only living but well, and I hope {in God} will long continue so) I always discouraged it, and as constantly to the utmost of my power promoted the D<uke's> Interest as the most proper person from his Quality, the greatness of his fortune, the uprightness of his Character and his near alliance to the Family which have for so many years[8] presided at the Head of that learned Body with so much Honour.[8] I was therefore amazed when I heard the Election was put on this footing, {and I had the satisfaction to find that the all our} the best freinds to the U<niveristy> here were as much surprised. – As to myself I am entirely satisfied with the Event, and am only anxious for the good of that Place for which I have so faithfull a regard, and which I hope always to preserve, and therefore am desirous that all Warmth all Seeds of Disunion should be extinguished, and that the Peace the Unanimity and Welfare of that Learned Body may always be promoted and flourish.

Letter 110

[1] Probably Herbert Aubrey (1693–1758), of Clehonger, near Hereford, son of the recipient of Letter 81 above.

[2] Draft.

[3] Not found.

[4] This refers to Robert Harley's candidacy at the Oxford University by-election. See previous letter.

[5] Duke of Beaufort. See Appendix.

[6] Probably Thomas Payne (*c.*1718–97) of Hereford, M.A. Brasenose College 1724, later a canon of Wells.

[7] This passage, and the following ones in this letter, which are contained in { }, are crossed out in the original.

[8] The earl of Arran was chancellor of the university 1715–58. He was younger brother to the 2nd duke of Ormonde (d. 1745), who had been chancellor 1688–1715, succeeding his grandfather, the 1st duke of Ormonde, chancellor 1669–88. The 2nd duke of Ormonde had married Mary Somerset (d. 1733), eldest surviving daughter of the 1st duke of Beaufort. She was thus a great aunt to the 4th duke of Beaufort.

111. FROM THE MARQUESS OF CARNARVON, GROSVENOR STREET, 27 MAY 1753.

B.L., Add. MS 70498, ff. 5–6.

My Lord

I recieved the Honour of your Letter, and the Petition inclosed;[1] I am greatly obliged to your Lordship for acquainting me with the Affair, and will not fail taking proper Notice of it, immediately. – I proposed myself, both yesterday, and to Day, the Honour of paying My Respects to your Lordship, before your leaving London, but have been prevented by Lady Carnarvons having been ill, which has confind me at Home. I therefore beg Leave in this Manner, to assure your Lordship, how heartilly I wish You, Lady Oxford and your whole Family all Health and Happiness. – If upon further Enquiry, I should find any Chance of Making any Thing of the Affair I mentiond to your Lordship concerning Radnorshire, I will beg Leave to trouble you upon that Head, by a few Lines: at present, I can only say, I shou'd be proud of representing that County, if I find it a Thing agreable to the Gentlemen of that County, and in particular to your Lordship; but will not take up any more of your Lordships Time at present than to assure you, that I have the highest Regard for your Lordship, and every One of your Family...

Endorsed: Ld Carnarvan May 27/ 1753.

112. FROM THE MARQUESS OF CARNARVON, MINCHENDON HOUSE, SOUTHGATE,[1] 9 JUNE 1753.

B.L., Add. MS 70498, ff. 7–8.

My Lord

Since your Lordship left London I have had a meeting with Sir Humphrey Howarth, who has assured me, that He does not propose offering Himself a Candidate for the County of Radnor, on Account of his Age and Infirmities, and if I offer Myself, will assist me with his Interest: therefore if your Lordship does me the Honour of your Protection, I flatter myself I shall not fail in this my first Effort. I hope your Lordship and Family got safe down to Eywood, and continue perfectly well. We left London last Week, and propose staying here, 'til the End of the Month, when we shall go into Hampshire...

Endorsed: Ld Carnarvan June 9/ 1753./ answered June 15

Letter 111
[1] Not found.

Letter 112
[1] The main seat of the Brydges family after the demolition of Canons, Minchendon House, Southgate, Middlesex had belonged to Carnarvon's wife, Margaret Nicholl. Built after 1664, it was demolished in 1853. V.C.H., *Middlesex*, V, 22, 143, 159–60.

113. TO THE MARQUESS OF CARNARVON, 16 JUNE 1753.[1]

B.L., Add. MS 70498, f. 9.

My Lord

I received the Honour of your Lordships Letter last post, and am extremely glad to find that your Lordship intends to stand for the County of Radnor at the next Election, and hope it will be made perfectly easy to you by Sir H<umphrey's> Resignation.[2] The Interest which my Family had formerly there has been disused for many years but what ever part of it is left shall with pleasure be employed in your Lordship<'s> Service, for I think it will not only be an Honour but a most lasting Service to that poor County to have your Lordship their Represrntative, and your being at the Head of it will be a means of delivering it in time, from the Oppression and Exaction it labours under.

Your Lordship must determine when Sir H<umphrey's> Resignation and your Declaration should be made publick, and no one can better advise you in this than Mr Walcot, who is I beleive still in London. I have been told sometime ago, that Mr Howell Gwyn[3] claims a promise of Sir H<umphrey> made at the last Election to resign in favour of Him at This (how true this is I cannot say), but it cannot be amiss for your Lordship to get this some how or other explained by the Knight.

Permit me to give you one caution, to have as little to do with Tom Lewis as possible, and not to mix your Interest or Election with his, but to be on your guard in all transactions with Him.

Endorsed: To Ld Carnarvan/ June 15. <sic> 1753

114. FROM THE MARQUESS OF CARNARVON, RAMRIDGE,[1] 28 JUNE 1753.

B.L., Add. MS 70498, ff. 10–11.

My Lord

My Journey hither, and the transacting some private Affairs, prevented my sooner acknowledging the Honour of your Lordships Letter of the 15. I am greatly obliged by your Lordships Kindness to me, and by your Assistance, flatter Myself with a Prospect of Success. I have enquired very narrowly into the Affair your Lordship hinted to me, concerning a Promise made to Mr Gwynne, but am told, there is nothing in it: however I am the last, to get at the Truth of it, if it is so.

I thank your Lordship for the List, and will take Care to apply to the People therein mention'd. I shall follow your Lordships Direction as near as possible, relating to Mr – whose Character I well know, though I am forced to keep him quiet. I did not observe any Fraction, in your Lordships Seal, but I shall wafer this, which I believe is the safest Way, and not inclose it as you will then see if it has been open'd...

P.S. I find the writing will be seen through the Paper therefore will inclose it.

Endorsed: Ld Carnarvon. June 28/ R. July 6: 1753/ answered July 13.

Letter 113
[1] Draft.
[2] Howarth remained M.P. until his death in 1755.
[3] Howell Gwynne (1718–80), M.P. for Radnorshire 1755–61, Old Sarum 1761–8.

Letter 114
[1] Ramridge House near Andover, Hampshire.

115. TO MARQUESS OF CARNARVON, EYWOOD, 13 JULY 1753.[1]

B.L., Add. MS 70498, ff. 14–15.[2]

My Lord.

Your Lordships Letter which I received on the 6th found me confined to my Chamber by a severe fit of the Gravel which prevented my acknowledging the Honour of it sooner. I thank God I am now able to get a little abroad.

I was much surprized to see a Meeting Advertised in the London Papers to be on Monday last at Knighton,[3] when no notice had been given of it in the Country. So few Persons met that it ended in the Nomination of no one, but as Sir Humphry and Mr Howel Gwyn the latter claimed the Promise of his Resignation and Interest which the old Knight denyed to have made, which produced Squabbles and abuse between them.[4]

A Report has prevailed that Your Lordship is set up by Lewis and that his Intrest is to bring you in, and I am informed that some Letters of Your Steward Meredith has given encouragement to this Report. This has extreamly exasperated not only the Gentlemen but the Common freeholders, who declare if this is true they will raise an Opposition, for these 2 Persons are so thoroughly detested and dispised that they are determined not to be dictated by them. For a Confirmation of this I herewith enclose a Copy of a Letter to Me with my Answer rece<iv>ed on Tuesday from 4 Principal Gentlemen of the County[5] and of as good Character who are My friends and would be Your Lordships were they satisfied in this point. My Answer has so far had its effect as at Present to Silence the Clamour and Jealousie it raised, though I fear its breaking out again unless an effectual stop be put to it by Your Lordship otherwise it will not be in My Power to engage them and several others.

As I have not only Your Lordships Interest but Honour at Heart you will give me leave to write with that freedom by which I can only Properly serve You, and which becomes one who would use his best endeavours to pave the way for Your Lordship to a quiet and honourable Election, which I believe you would Certainly have were the Gentlemen and Freeholders satisfied in this Particular, for they seem generally to approve of your Lordship. But I will not answer for the consequences if Your Lordship submits to be directed by Lewis or enter into any of his Schemes. – It cannot be supposed that you are to refuse his Vote and Interest but to avoid being any way his Nomination, which would do You ten times more hurt than all the Interest he can make can do you good. Your Lordship having some particular Agent is certainly necessary but give me leave to say not out of prejudice to the Man, but for your Intrest, Meredith would be the most Improper one, as he is so Obnoxious to the County being a tool of Lewis.

Letter 115

[1] Copy not in EH's hand.

[2] An earlier draft, in EH's hand, is to be found at ff. 12–13.

[3] The *London Evening Post*, no. 3999, 3–5 July 1753, carried the following advertisement:

'The Gentlemen, Clergy, and Freeholders of the County of Radnor, are desired to meet at the Chandos Arms in Knighton on Monday the 9th of July to think of a proper Person to represent the County at the next General Election.

'N.B. They are earnestly desir'd to keep themselves disengaged 'till the Meeting is over'.

[4] In the earlier draft the end of this paragraph is as follows: '... but so few met that it ended in nothing, and no person was nominated. Mr Gwyn being there claimed Sir Humphrey's promise of his Resignation and Interest, which the old Knight denyed to have made, upon which there were squabbles and abuse between them.'

[5] Not found.

If your Lordship should have been told by any one, that Party prevails in the C<ounty> of Radnor, He greatly misrepresents it. For the Distinctions there have not been Whig or Tory, Court and Country, but their opposition has been to the Oppression of their Members, and their struggle and endeavours have been to get Rid of them, which would have been successful had they had a impartial returning officer and a legal Election.

It is said another Meeting will be appointed for the Assize week when it would be very proper for Your Lordship to be Present when you would see many Gentlemen and Freeholders and save you a great deal of Trouble, and I hope your Lordship will do me the Honour to make My House your Home as I am within an hours ride of Presteigne.

In the mean time for quieting the Minds of the Country I would submit it to Your Lordship whether it might not be proper to Publish in the Gloucester Journal 3 or 4 times an Advertisment something to the effect of the enclosed,[6] and if you should not approve of that, If it is directed to Mr Raikes Printer in Glocester it will be sufficient, or sent to Me.[7]

I must by this time have fully tired You, and I will release You after having begged your Pardon for this Freedom, which is occasioned only by that sincere concern and Regard I have for Your Honour and Intrest. I am Your Lordships most faithfull humble Servant Oxford

Since I wrote this I hear a meeting was held yesterday for Breconshire when My Br<other-in-law> Morgan[8] was I may say unanimously declared the Candidate, there being only Mr Howel Gwyn and 3 Attornies who opposed it.

Enclosed is a list of some other Persons[9] who should be wrote to.

I should be obliged to Your Lordship for an Answer as soon as Conveniently you can for no time is to be lost, and be pleased to let Me know where you are in the Country if there should be any Occasion for a Special Messenger.

Endorsed: Copy to/ Ld. Carnarvon/ July 13. 1753

116. FROM THE MARQUESS OF CARNARVON, RAMRIDGE, 19 JULY 1753.

B.L., Add. MS 70498, ff. 16–17.

My Lord

Your kind and Friendly Letter of the 13th. gave me great Concern, to find by it, you had been so much indisposed, but hope in God, your Disorder is intirely removed by this Time.

---

[6] Not found. However, the following advertisement appeared in the *Gloucester Journal* on 13 July 1753:
    'TO THE GENTLEMEN, CLERGY, AND FREEHOLDERS, of the County of *Radnor*.
    If I should be so happy as to meet with your Encouragement, I intend to offer myself a CANDIDATE *at the next* ELECTION *for the County of Radnor: And, as I shall think myself greatly obliged to every freeholder who will favour me with his* VOTE, *I therefore make this Public Address, till I can have an Opportunity of doing it in Person, as it is my Ambition to be the Choice of the Freeholders in* general, *and not of any par-ticular Set of Men, as hath been falsly represented.*   CARNARVAN'.

[7] In the earlier draft, the end of this paragraph is: 'In the mean time for quieting their Minds if your Lordship puts in the Glocester Journal 3 or 4 times, an Advertisement some thing to the effect if you do not approve the enclosed one.'

[8] Thomas Morgan (see Appendix) was the brother of EH's wife, Martha.

[9] Not found.

Your Lordships Letter is filled with such kind and generous Expressions, that I declare I am at a Loss to answer it, on Paper. I can only say, Whatever a gratefull Heart can think, I wou'd express, if I had Words sufficient, and thought I shou'd not intrude too much upon your Time. That I may release your Lordship as soon as possible, I will proceed forthwith, to our present Topick. – I confess I was greatly astonish'd at the Advertizement in the Papers, and was thoroughly concern'd at appearing in so bad a Light, both to the Gentlemen of the County, and to the common Freeholders; and had I not recieved your Lordships Letter last night, I fully proposed to have given over all Thoughts of that County, rather than have made so many Enemies in a Part of the World, where I own I had flatter'd Myself, I shou'd have met with no Opposition. For I declare upon My Honour, I had no other motive for standing for that County, than that I thought to pay a Compliment to it, by giving it the Preference to any other Place; when finding I was mistaken, I had resolved, to have put an End to a disagreeable Contest, by declining to stand: but upon Receipt of your Lordships Letter, I see plainly what has kindled this Flame, and protest I have no other Dealings with Mr. Lewis, than having desired his Interest, which He promised to give me: what He or Meredith may have spread about the County, for their own Ends, I know not, nor was it possible for me, to know the Tempers of the Gentlemen and Freeholders of the County: his Character I know, and have never seen him, since your Lordship wrote first to me about Him, not having been in London since. Sir H. Howarth I knew a great while ago, and upon being told He intended to decline standing, on Account of his Age, I desired Him to make his Interest over to me, if He was not pre-engaged, which after thinking upon it, some Time He accordingly promised; this my Lord is the true State of the Case, and my sole endeavour has been as farr as I was able, to steer clear of Party, that I might not give offence to any. I approve much of the Advertisement your Lordship has done me the Honour to send me, and will have it inserted in the Glocester Journal. I will likewise take Care, and apply to the Gentlemen your Lordship has mention'd, and shou'd be very glad to have your Recommendation for an Agent, one Watkyn[1] was formerly mention'd to me, and indeed I had Thoughts of employing Him, but thought it might be better to stay til after the Election, for Fear of making any Bustle. I shall not fail setting out for Radnorshire as soon as I am summoned, and am greatly obliged by your Lordships kind offer...

P.S. I shall continue here, all the Summer, My Direction is Ramridge near Andover.

P.S. I don't return the Copies of the Letters your Lordship sent me, for Fear of Accidents.

117. TO THE MARQUESS OF CARNARVON, 27 JULY 1753.[1]

B.L., Add. MS 70498, ff. 18–19.

My Lord

Your Lordships of the 19th gave me the greatest pleasure and satisfaction by finding that your Lordship received my Letter in that Sense and with that Freindship with which it was wrote, intended only for the promoting your Honour as well as Intrest which was only a 2d consideration with me compared with the first. Your Letter as well as the advertisement in the Glocester Journal came very opportunely, for I had that day invited the 4 Gentlemen and Mr Crowther to dine with me. To whom I shewed the advertisement with which they were much pleased and I likewise acquainted them

Letter 117
[1] Draft.

with part of your Lordship<'s> Letter which gave them greater Satisfaction and I asked them whether they would allow me to tell your Lordship so, to which they consented. By which and the Conversation I had with them as to the real Intrest and quiet of the County I think that all opposition is over, from that Quarter, or if any should appear from another it will be so weak a one that it would easily be crushed. I must acquaint you that they told me when the old Knight was at Knighton, He said That He would not stand unless the County would chuse Him without opposition but He would not undergo a Contest, I am told He has said the same in other places. I shall now make you laugh that the old K<night>[2] threatens Lewis his nephew and some others with an Action, for saying that your Lordship gave Him Money to resign, and that He has sold the County. This has been told me by Several. – I could likewise divert you by stories that you were to come to Harpton in Lewis<'s> coach, who has come down last week, and such other stuff given out only to embroil the County, and hurt your Interest. I have not yet Heard how L<ewis> relishes the advertisement, but when I can write with any Certainty you shall know. It has not yet got among the Common Freeholders who I dare say will be as well satisfied as the Gentlemen were. But whatever turn this takes I will send your Lordship the Truth.

I told the Gentlemen I thought there was no need of advertising any Meeting at the Assizes, for that was only to give a Handle for Disturbance, for as your Lordship had Declared yourself a Candidate, if any other person had a mind to do the same, let It come from Him, if not it was a publick sign that all would be quiet, to this they readily agreed, and some of them thought your appearance would be sufficient a little time before the Election. But I must submit it to your Lordship whether your appearing at the Assizes to which if you will give me leave I will wait upon you which I hear is to begin at Presteigne the 25th of August might not entirely quiet the County, when you would see most of the Gentlemen, and if there should be an occasion of visiting any of them, you would have good Weather, when by leaving it to the Spring you might meet with bad and perhaps I might be then in London.

What I meant relating to an Agent was if some Man of Character could be found who is well acquainted with the County and the Freeholders to go among them. And Here I am at present at a loss. As to your private Agent if you intend any alteration, I think you judge right to make none till after the Election, unless when you come down, you should see a necessity for it.

Endorsed: To Ld Carnarvan/ June <sic> 27.

118. FROM THE MARQUESS OF CARNARVON, RAMRIDGE, 6 AUGUST 1753.

B.L., Add. MS 70498, ff. 20–2.

My Lord
    The very particular Friendship your Lordship has honour'd me with, during my whole Life, and in this late Affair in Radnorshire, encourages me to open my Mind very freely to you on that Head, as I am thoroughly convinced what I shall here mention to your Lordship, will be kept an intire Secret, and flatter myself you will both pardon my Impertinence, and assist me with your Advice, I will beg Leave to detain your Lordship for a few Minutes.

---

2 ? Sir Humphrey Howarth.

I have been sometime weighing this Affair, in my Head, and after much Consideration, together with what your Lordship hinted to me in London, concerning a Sherif, the Whole appears to me in this Light: that though I shou'd be honour'd with your Lordships Interest, together with *That* of the principal Gentlemen and Freeholders in the County, yet my Election, wou'd greatly depend upon the Return of the Sherif, who I am apt to fear, is to be chose, not by the proper Persons, but by Mr Lewis. To confirm me in this Suspicion, I had last Post, a Letter from Meredith, who says He is going over to Harpton to consult with Mr Lewis, about settling the grand Jury, and appointing a Sherif (whose Letter I have inclos'd[1]); now *This* I comprehend perfectly well, and appears to me, in so scandalous a Light, that I cannot upon any Account, impose upon my own Conscience, or the good Will of the Gentlemen (who have favour'd me, with their Interest) so much, as to take any such methods, or contribute towards depriving a County, of freely choosing its own Member: on the other Hand, was I to make any stir about this Affair, I might bring a very disagreable Part upon Myself and Friends, be brought to fending and proving, and disoblige Many, without doing any good: This my Lord, togeather with one Reason more, which I will presently mention, makes me desirous of declining my Pretentions, to the County of Radnor: but this I cou'd not think of doing, without first consulting your Lordship (who have been my chief Prop), in what Manner I can retreat, without disobliging my Friends, or declaring the Reasons I have given your Lordship above, which I beg may never be mention'd, and I give you my Word and Honour, no One knows I have any such Intention, but My Father. The other Reason I have to present your Lordship, is, that if I do not represent the Citty of Winchester, I shall infallibly loose all my Interest there, which wou'd be a very disagreable Circumstance, as it is within four Miles of Avington,[2] which after Mrs Brydges's Decease, must be my capital Seat: I need not remark to your Lordship, the Satisfaction one has, in a little Command, so near ones House.

I have now my Lord disclosed my Mind intirely to you, and beg your Advice; and with the greatest Gratitude, thank You, for your great Goodness to me already; and hope, if in this Affair, I have express'd myself too freely, that you will impute it to the Desire I have to convince your Lordship of the true Motives, for this Resolution. I chose rather to send this by My own Servant, for Fear of Accidents. I must entreat your Lordship to take no Notice of my Intention to any One 'til I have had another Opportunity, of writing again to your Lordship. I am honour'd with two Letters from your Lordship of the 27th and 31 July, for which and every other Mark of your Esteem I am truly thankfull. I shall be very anxious for the Return of the Messenger, as I am in great Pain, for Fear I may not meet with your Lordships Approbation, as there is nothing I more earnestly wish for, though <I> am so little worthy of it...

Endorsed: Ld Carnarvan Aug 6: 1753/ R<eceived> from his servant: Aug 10/ answered the same night

Letter 118
[1] Not found.
[2] Four miles north-east of Winchester, Avington was inherited by the 2nd duke of Chandos in 1751.

119. TO THE MARQUESS OF CARNARVON, 10 AUGUST 1753.[1]

B.L., Add. MS 70498, f. 23.

My Lord

I have just received the Honour of your Lordship<'s> Letter by your Servant. I will not trouble you with expressing my Concern which the Contents of it gives me. I do assure you I had no other view in concerning myself in Radnorshire but as I thought the Representing that County would be agreeable to your Lordship as you have so great a property in it, and the Hopes I had of Seeing it in the Hands of a Person of Quality and Honour and rescued from the present Tyrrany and Oppression it labours under from low Mean Men. And I think I may without Vanity say that I had as far as lay in my poor power paved the way for your Lordships having a sure Majority of the Freeholders, what obstruction power or the Tools of Power might give <I could?> not answer for. I heartily wish that the Subject of your Lordships Letter had been considered before you had engaged so far: – If your Lordship had thought fit to have proceeded in this Affair, I would have endeavoured not to have given you wrong advice. As to your retreat no one can be a judge but yourself who have all the Circumstances of Winchester and Radnorshire before you and to determine which is most eligible for your Honour and Intrest. In this I cannot pretend to advice. But thus far I will venture to say, that anything is more Honourable than to be engrossed by Lewis and Howarth.

I return your Lordship Merediths Letter who if He was worthy of Notice I dare say might be disproved in it for I do not know a Gentleman that He dares speak to except the two He mentions.

When your Lordship is come to a final Resolution Be pleased to give me the earliest notice, that I may act consistent with my own Honour to the Gentlemen I had engaged that if your Lordship declines standing they may have time to act as they shall think most proper for the Intrest of their Country. And I assure your Lordship that the same Freindship which occasioned my espousing your Lordship<'s> Intrest at first will make me acquiess in whatever you determine.

Endorsed: Answer to Lord/ Carnarvan/ Aug 10: 1753

120. FROM THE MARQUESS OF CARNARVON, RAMRIDGE, 18 AUGUST 1753.

B.L., Add. MS 70498, ff. 24–5.

My Lord

I am honour'd with your Lordships Letter, by the Return of My Servant. – I assure your Lordship my giving up my Intentions for standing for Radnorshire, gives me the deepest Concern, nor cou'd I ever have entertain'd such a Thought, had it not appear'd to me, for the best, in every Respect, and doubt not but the Gentlemen of the County, may easily pick out a more worthy Person to represent Them, and One of a more active Disposition, by which means, He may do Them, much more real Service, than ever I shou'd have been able to have done Them, however good my Intentions might have been. – Your Lordships Friendly and Candid Behaviour to me, is the Thing that lays me under the greatest Concern, least by the Light this step of mine may appear to your Lordship in, I may forfeit that Place in your Esteem, which I value so much, and

Letter 119
[1] Draft.

consequently shou'd lament the being deprived of. I think it is incumbent upon me to give your Lordship the earliest Notice, of my Determination to decline standing for the County of Radnor, and can assure you no One knows it, as yet. – Next Post I will trouble your Lordship with an Advertisement, I intend putting in the Papers, which I hope will meet with your Lordships Approbation...

Endorsed: Ld. Carnarvan/ Aug 18: 1753

121. FROM THE MARQUESS OF CARNARVON, RAMRIDGE, 23 AUGUST 1753.

B.L., Add. MS 70498, ff. 26–8.

My Lord

I have taken the Liberty to inclose an Advertisement for your Lordships Perusal, which if I find, you approve of, I will insert in the Glocester Journal; but beg of your Lordship, to make any alteration in it, as shall appear right to you.

I shall this Post write to Sir H<umphrey> H<owarth> to acquaint Him with my Design: I am aprehensive this Affair may make much Noise in the County, and doubtless will disoblige many; but having acted to the best of my Knowledge in it, gives me some Satisfaction; and the Resolution I have taken, I meant well...

<Enclosed:>

To the Gentlemen, Clergy, and Freeholders of the County of Radnor.

Gentlemen

I beg Leave to take this Method, of returning you my sincere and hearty Thanks, for the Honour you have done me, in supporting my Interest hitherto, and to assure you, how concern'd I am, that I cannot have the Honour of representing you in the ensuing Parliament as I had flatter'd myself, but that I shall ever retain a thorough Sense of your Goodness to me, and a perfect Regard for the Interest of the County in general; and shall be always pleas'd in acknowledging myself, to be Gentlemen

Your most obliged
Humble Servant Carnarvon   23 August 1753.[1]

Endorsed: Ld Carnarvan Aug 23/ 1753/ answered Aug 31

Letter 121
[1] This advertisement appears not to have been printed in the *Gloucester Journal.*

WILLIAM HAY'S PAPERS ON
PARLIAMENTARY AFFAIRS

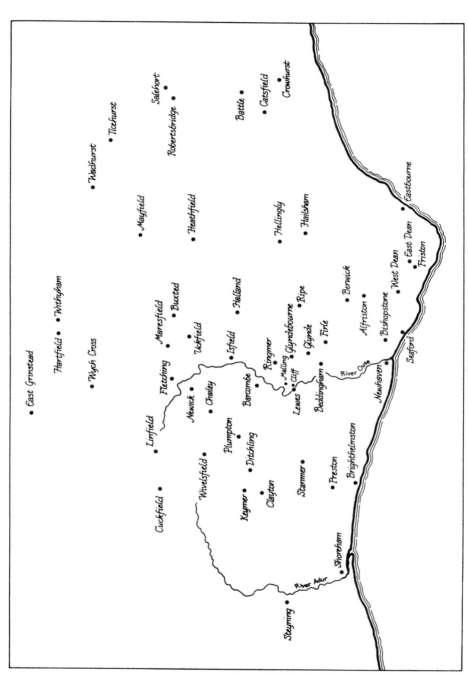

Map of Sussex illustrating places mentioned in Hay's papers

Tuesday next in their progress to Steyning. Wishing Your Grace health and success I remain, My Lord, Your Grace's, most devoted Servant W. Hay.

Endorsed: Lewes. Aug. 11. 1733./ Mr Haye

3. TO THE DUKE OF NEWCASTLE, GLYNDEBOURNE, 14 AUGUST 1733.

B.L., Add. MS 32688, ff. 98–9.

My Lord,

I should not have troubled Your Grace at this time, but for a Letter I received Yesterday from Mr. Tutte. He was on Friday last with Mr. Piggot, and found him in the common Cry against the Excise, but engaged him not to promise any body Yet, which he assured him he would not. Mr. Fane was hourly expected at his house to stay the setting Season: so that a Letter directed to Francis Fane Esqr. at Mr Piggot's at Stedham near Midhurst at any time within these ten days will probably find Mr. Fane there; and his Interest with Piggot will probably fix him right. I hear nothing new in this Quarter. Mr. Burnet[1] called on me this morning in his way to Lewes; and I acquainted him with the disposition of the several Voters in the Cliff. He tells me, that Ticehurst and Wadhurst are very much influenced by Mr. Courthope;[2] and that Mr. Fuller[3] of the Gatehouse makes interest in Mayfield for Mr. Pelham and Mr. Fuller. And that Sir T. Dyke[4] has been very busy in riding about the Country. Mr. Pelham's Tenant from Hellingly was with me this morning about business; he told me Jack Fuller had been riding round that neighbourhood: I asked him how his Neighbours were disposed: he said that he believed most in Hellingly and Haylsham would go the other way. That they liked Your Grace very well, but were very much dissatisfied with what had lately happened; for that he and his neighbours had heard, that Bread and Meat would have been taxed if it had not been for a Petition from Bristol. I assured him it was entirely false; and that such stories were spread abroad only to make him and other honest people uneasy: that what was done in relation to wine and Tobacco was with a very good Intention, and with no other View than to ease the People of the Land Tax: but since the thing was misrepresented, and they were dissatisfied about it, it was dropt, and would never be resumed. I am sorry, My Lord, that these things make so deep an impression; but trust that Cause must fail, that is supported only by Lies. I shall dine to morrow with Mr. Poole at Hook,[5] and design to call on some of the Isfield Freeholders in my Way. I had the honour of Your Grace's letter, and shall in every thing serve Your Grace to the best of my Abilities. I am, My Lord, Your Grace's most obedient Servant W. Hay.

Endorsed: Glynbourn. Aug. 14th. 1733./ Mr. Hay.

Letter 3

[1] Robert Burnett, steward of the household to Newcastle between 1715 and 1741 and his principal agent in Sussex, who sent many reports to the duke. However, only three canvassing lists by Burnett have survived in the Newcastle papers: lists of the freeholders of Burwash (9 July), Rotherfield (6 Oct.), and Mayfield (13 Oct. 1733). See ff. 19–20, 468–9, 498–50.

[2] Courthope of Whiligh in Ticehurst. His influence over the village is confirmed by Dr James Hargreaves on 20 Aug. (f. 148).

[3] Thomas Fuller of the Gatehouse in Mayfield.

[4] Sir Thomas Dyke (c.1700–56), 2nd bt. of Horeham in Waldron, Suss., and Lullingston Castle, Kent, son of the M.P. for Sussex in 1685–7 and East Grinstead in 1689–98. He was in opposition in Lewes and the county and voted for Bishopp and Fuller as a freeholder of Waldron.

[5] William Poole (1696–1779) of the Hook in Chailey. His wife was a daughter of Henry Pelham of Stanmer (see genealogical table).

4. TO THE DUKE OF NEWCASTLE, GLYNDEBOURNE, 16 AUGUST 1733.

B.L., Add. MS 32688, ff. 121–2.

My Lord.

I yesterday morning spoke with the following Persons, who (as I am informed) are all the freeholders in Isfield.

1. Dr Scot, who promised, if he was well enough, to go to the Election.
2. Mercer,[1] the Anabaptist Preacher, whom I talked to of the Schism bill: he said, he would make it his cheif business to influence his own Sect, and to undeceive his Neighbours in relation to the Excise. He said he was doubtfull whether his own Vote was good, and would not for his own reputation venture to give it, till he was assured that it was. His Father has the Estate for Life, and he the reversion, but his Father now pays him £26 per Annum Rent charge out of it during his life: Tis certain that in Law he has a freehold in the Rent, and I believe such a one as intitles him to a vote, especially as tis a Rent issuing out of Land; for I have since consulted the Statute 12. Annae. c. 5.[2] where Rents are mentioned; and, like Tythes, come under the notion of incorporeal Inheritances. I submit it to Your Grace's consideration: 'tis a point worth knowing; for many Votes may depend on the same construction.
3. Hammond. Who did not like that an Excise man should take an account of his Pork.
4. Moon. Who had always been for Your Grace, but believed he should never be so again, because You were for taxing his Victuals.
5. Foord.[3] Who said he would kill any Excise man that offered to come into his house.

I spent a great deal of time in discourse with them. Assured them that the Excise on Wine and Tobacco was intended for their benefit, and that if it had taken effect we should have had no land-Tax: but since it was not rightly understood, it was laid aside, and would never be revived. They said they did not value a tax on Wine and Tobacco, but did not like their Victuals should be taxed: I assured them there never was any such design, that I spoke of it of my own knowledge, and I hoped I had Credit enough with them to be believed: that those who told them these Stories knew them to be false; and did it to make them and other honest people uneasy, in order to cheat them of their Votes, and I believed with a very ill design; some of making themselves great, and others of bringing in the Pretender; that they ought to resent such Usage, and vote against them for endeavouring to impose upon them. They were so far mollified by what I said, that Hammond as good as promised to go right. Moon said if he did not vote for Your Grace, he would not vote against You. And Foord that he would talk again to old Mr. Newnham;[4] I am told he owes Mr. Newnham money, so that he will probably make him go right.

Letter 4

[1] Dr Thomas Mercer (1716–79) practised as a surgeon at Lewes. His father Robert, also a general baptist, farmed lands at Isfield and Sedlescombe. Sir William Collins, 'Some Memorials of the Mercer Family', *Transactions of the Baptist Historical Society*, VII (1920–1).

[2] Of 1712, which explained clause 1 in the 'Act [of the previous session] for the more effectual preventing Conveyance in order to multiply Votes for electing Knights of the Shires to serve in Parliament as far as the same related to the ascertaining the Value of Freeholds of Forty Shillings Per Annum'.

[3] Either Thomas or William Ford, both of Isfield and both of whom voted for Bishopp and Fuller as freeholders of Ringmer.

[4] ? John Newnham of London, who attended the opposition meeting in Lewes on 1 Sept. (f. 236).

I dined afterwards with Mr. Poole, who invited Erle[5] and Vinal[6] to meet me; they are two of the leading men in Chailey, and always used to be wrong; but we prevailed on them to promise not to go against us. I understood by them that a Story had prevailed in that neighbourhood, that your Grace had persuaded the man that I bound over to prosecute Halsted[7] at the Assises not to appear against him, because his Brother was a Voter at Hastings, and his father at Lewes: I assured them it was entirely false; and told them they might judge by that of the malice of Your Grace's enemies.

I am told, Mr. Mansel[8] has secured all the Votes in Fletching but two: he tells all his Neighbours, he will bear the expence of their going to the Election. He exclaims bitterly against Place-men and Pensioners; and tells them that my Lord Abergavenny has a Pension. I wish my Lord would exert himself in those parts; for Mr. Poole tells me he does not hear that he has sent about to the people of his Neighbourhood where he is Lord of the mannor. I know not whether I am to congratulate Your Grace on Sir Cecil's declaring for the County,[9] since he is a Person so little known. I am, My Lord, Your Grace's, most obedient Servant W. Hay.

Endorsed: Glynbourne. Aug. 16./ Mr Hay

5. TO THE DUKE OF NEWCASTLE, GLYNDEBOURNE, 21 AUGUST 1733.

B.L., Add. MS 32688, ff. 161–2.

My Lord.

I take the liberty to send Your Grace a letter, which I received yesterday from Mr. Tutte concerning the State of Affairs in and about Chichester. The Case of the Tenants of Bosham Mannor is particular, and might be turned to advantage in time of need.

I have received the honour of Your Grace's letters; and yesterday morning I waited on Mr. Springet, who told me he had secured 35 Votes in his Neighbourhood; and that he had sent an Account of them, together with lists of the Freeholders in the adjacent Parishes to Mr. Forbes.

I afterwards dined at Stanmer, where Mr. Pelham[1] shewed me lists of all the Freeholders in Keymer, Clayton, Ditcheling, and Wivelsfield; I think their whole number amounted to 32. And he said they would all go right, except the two Parsons,[2] Turner of Keymer,[3] and the two Middletons of Wivelsfield. He said, Mr. Campion was at Brighthelmston last Thursday solliciting Votes; but with very bad success; for out of 42 he could prevail upon but two. I heard that Mr. Western was to be at Preston last night: and desired Mr. Pelham by all means to be early in his Compliments, and wait

---

[5] ? Nicholas Earl, tallow chandler, overseer of the poor for the parish of St John's, and constable of Lewes in 1732–3 and 1739–40, who voted for the Pelhams at Lewes.

[6] Either Nicholas, who voted for Bishopp and Fuller, or John Vinall, who voted for Pelham and Fuller (a split vote) for Sussex.

[7] ? James Halstead, a grocer, who voted for Garland and Sergison for Lewes, or Richard, victualler, who voted for the Pelhams.

[8] The Hon. Christopher Mansel (d. 1744) of Newick Place (which, as second son of the 1st Baron Mansel, he inherited from his mother) appears to have been the chief agent for Sergison (ff. 198, 236, 331, 461). He was the elder brother of the Hon. Bussy Mansel, M.P. for Cardiff Boroughs (see Appendix). In 1744 he succeeded his nephew as 3rd Baron Mansel.

[9] Sir Cecil Bishopp, currently M.P. for Penryn, contesting Sussex. See Appendix.

Letter 5

[1] Thomas Pelham of Stanmer, M.P. for Lewes. See Appendix.

[2] William Lamb of Ditchling and Wivelsfield and Laurence Price of Clayton and Keymer. George Hennessy, *Chichester Diocesan Clergy Lists* (1900), pp. 51, 59.

[3] Richard Turner, gentleman of Keymer, voted for Bishopp and Fuller for Sussex.

upon him this morning; for without doubt, great Court will be made to a young Gentleman of his fortune.

I have often spoke to Mrs. Trevor about Paine the butcher; who has been very much pressed by the whole family; but he will not absolutely promise for fear of disobliging Mr. Bridger and Mr. Spence of Malling.

Mr. Hawes tells me that there is but one Freeholder in Berwick besides his Father: he is a Workman to Sir T. Dyke, and engaged to him; but he thinks he is not taxed at 40s. per Annum; so that his Vote may be justly objected to.[4] The rest of the Voters in that neighbourhood have been sent to by Sir W. Gage and Mr. Dobell.

There is a Young Gentleman, who has an Estate at Beddingham, who was about a month ago at Lewes and lodged at the White Hart, and Dick Verral[5] says he believes he will be soon again in the Country to look after his Affairs. I know him by sight; his name is Paget, he is a Barrister at Law; and Mr. Friend (who has remitted money to him) tells me, he lives in Bartlets Buildings in Holborn. I believe nobody has yet thought of him; nor does any body here know his Inclinations. But it is very probable a letter or message from Your Grace may secure him, and his Tenant too, whose name is Merchant, and who, Mr. Watts tells me, is a Freeholder.

Mr. Blackman[6] the Minister of Barcombe gave me the following list of Freeholders in his Parish

Edward Medley.	
John Goring.	
Thomas Attree.	
James Attree.	all wrong. Unless the Bretts of Lewes[7] can do
Francis Heasman.	any thing with Neal, who married their Niece.
John Carpenter	
John Lucas	
Edward Lucas	
Nicholas Neal.	

Mr. William Earl   he believes will be wrong, but are more likely
William Earl   to be prevailed upon than the rest.

John Jenner – used to be right, but is very doubtfull.
John Norris – he believes will be influenced by Mr. Newnham.
Robert Smith – by Mr. Fuller of Lewes, who has a Mortgage on his Estate.

Mr. Apsley[8] tells me, that Mr. Fuller dined with him in his return from Steyning; and that he declared that he did not join with Sir Cecil, but would stand on his own Interest; and I believe he is right in such a Declaration; for there are many in the East, that will be for Mr. Pelham and him, that would not be for him at all, if he was to insist

---

[4] John Hawes, vicar of Glynde 1725–50, rector of Berwick, Suss., 1743, voted for Pelham and Butler for Sussex. His father John Hawes (c.1669–1743), was rector of Berwick, Suss. 1695, vicar of Alciston 1696–1743, and also voted for Pelham and Butler. The other freeholder of Berwick, Thomas Susan, voted for Bishopp and Fuller.

[5] Richard Verrall (d. 1737), innkeeper of the White Hart in Lewes, one of the venues for the whig election clubs, provided 'election entertainments' in Lewes and at Bishopstone. He was constable of Lewes in 1716–17, 1729–30 and 1734–5, and voted for the Pelhams for Lewes in 1734. *Sussex Archaeological Collections*, LVIII (1916), 92.

[6] John Blackman, M.A., minister of Barcombe, voted for Pelham and Butler for Lewes.

[7] ? Walter, grocer, and William Brett, apothecary and constable of Lewes in 1737–8, both voted for the Pelhams for Lewes.

[8] John Apsley of Thakeham (see f. 119), J.P., canvassed and voted for the Pelhams for Lewes.

on a second Vote for Sir Cecil. The Gentlemen at Steyning entered into a Subscription to bear Sir Cecil's charges; which shews, they design to push on their Opposition in good earnest. I am glad they have pitched upon Sir Cecil, because he is little known; but I am sorry they have set up any body at all: for I think his standing must strengthen Mr. Fuller, and prejudice the other Candidates; for he will take off the second Votes of Mr. Fuller's friends, many of which would otherwise fall on Mr. Pelham and Mr. Butler. And he will likewise take off the second Votes of several of Mr. Butler's friends in the West, which will be a prejudice to Mr. Pelham there, as Mr. Fuller's taking off the second Votes of several of Mr. Pelham's friends in the East is a prejudice to Mr. Butler here. As things stand, I think it is as certain that Mr. Pelham is secure, as that Sir Cecil will loose it, and that if there is any struggle, it will be between Mr. Butler and Mr. Fuller. For, My Lord, if it is not too tedious, I would beg leave to state the Case thus. The single Votes for each Candidate will probably be so very few, as also the Votes for Mr. Pelham and Sir Cecil, and for Mr. Butler and Mr. Fuller, that I will throw them entirely out of the Question. I will then imagine the remaining Votes to be 100, 40 of them for Mr. Pelham and Mr. Butler, and 20 of them for Sir Cecil and Mr. Fuller. If the remaining 40 are equally divided between Mr. Pelham and Mr. Fuller on one side, and Mr. Butler and Sir Cecil on the other, it goes as we could wish; but if 30 of them should be for Mr. Pelham and Mr. Fuller, and only 10 for Mr. Butler and Sir Cecil, Mr. Fuller will be on a Par with Mr. Butler: which is not impossible, since the Free-holders in the East are much the most numerous. Your Grace who knows the State and Temper of the Country, consequently knows, where the Errors of these Suppositions lie: and I know will pardon the freedom I take of communicating my thoughts on a Subject, which I have much at heart.

Mr. Fuller told Mr. Apsley that either Sir C. Goring[9] or Mr. Middleton would stand at Arundel.[10] I hear of no alteration at Lewes. I am with much devotion Your Grace's most obliged and obedient Servant W. Hay.

Endorsed: Glyn Bourne. Aug. 21./ Mr Haye

6. TO THE DUKE OF NEWCASTLE, HALLAND,[1] 24 AUGUST 1733.

B.L., Add. MS 32688, ff. 175–6.

My Lord,

I have just received the honour of Your Grace's: and came hither to wait on Dr. Hargraves,[2] who is gone to Uckfield bowling-green. I have the good fortune to find Mr. Burnet here, who is going to Lewes. He tells me Mr. Crew sets out immediately from hence, and I take this opportunity to satisfy Your Grace with relation to the Votes at Ringmer. This is the list of them.

---

[9] Sir Charles Goring (1706–69), 5th bt. of Highden, nr Steyning, Suss. (see also below, p. 334), voted for Bishopp and Fuller as a freeholder of Washington.

[10] Neither did. Arundel was uncontested. See Sedgwick, I, 332. Amongst others Thomas Hurdis and J. Butler reported this rumour to Newcastle. In Butler's case it was more than rumour – he reported what he had heard in conversation with Middleton: 'Yesterday Sir Charles Goring came to a Resolution to stand for Arundel, if he had refused Mr Middleton was to have been the man to oppose Sir John Shelly [Newcastle's brother-in-law]. I am of the opinion in case a Second Person will be of Service for that Town, Mr Middleton will not yet decline it' (ff. 110, 111: 16 Aug.).

Letter 6

[1] One of the three Pelham ancestral homes in Sussex.

[2] James Hargraves (d. 1741), D.D. Cambridge 1718, rector East Hoathly, Sussex, 1719–41, and of St Margaret's, Westminster, 1730–4, chaplain to the king 1724–39, dean of Chichester 1739–41.

Hurdis – Your Grace knows is right.

Berry – has promised and is certain.

Putland – has promised and I have an Influence on him.

Briant – is my Tenant.

Barnard – is Cosen and Servant to my Tenant Barnard and is certain.

Wellar – has promised and is workman to Sir W. Gage.

Hardes – has promised and works for Sir W. Gage.

Morris – Sir William's keeper.

Peckham – told me he reserved his Vote to be at my disposal.

Blunden – says Snooke[3] attempted his Wife, and is sure.

Boyce – is certain.

Stonehouse ⎫

Burt   ⎬   all three as sure Votes as my Own.

Burt   ⎭

Relfe – won't promise yet, but believes he shall be with us, Tenant to Mr. Watson.

Geer – has not promised any body, I believe he expects to be paid for his Vote.

Lawrence – will go for those he can get most by: I believe will be right.

Norton – lives cheifly at Hurst, will go his own Way; I believe in Principle wrong; if influenced, I believe by Mr. Campion.

Newenden – has Obligations to Sir T. Dyke; in inclination for us; and if not much pressed, will give one Vote for Mr. Pelham.

Pentecost – his Sister lives with Snooke; I am afraid will be wrong.

Snooke.

I hope, my Lord, they may be every where as much mistaken, as at Ringmer. I know not from whence their Confidence arises, but from expecting to deceive the People with Lies. I remain with sincere Attachment My Lord, Your Grace's, most obedient Servant W. Hay.

Addressed: To/ His Grace/ the Duke of Newcastle/ These.

Endorsed: Halland. Augt. 24./ Mr Haye.

7. TO THE DUKE OF NEWCASTLE, GLYNDEBOURNE, 30 AUGUST 1733.

B.L., Add. MS 32688, ff. 228–9.

My Lord,

Having received information that my Neighbour Snooke had asked the Freeholders of Ringmer to be at his House as Yesterday, I sent an Invitation to them to dine with me the same day, that I might be assured of their Inclinations. The following Persons were with me, and may be depended upon.

Hurdis.

Boyce.

Briant.

Stonehouse.

Burt.

Burt.

Morris.

---

[3] Henry Snooke, WH's political enemy in the parish of Ringmer where much of the Glyndebourne estate was situated, voted for Bishopp and Fuller for Sussex.

Wellar.
Lawrence.
Blunden.
Barnard.
Foord. }
Pocock. } who are new ones, that I was but lately informed of.

Hardes. he promised to dine with me, but was prevented by an Ague. he has absolutely promised.

Peckham. was prevented by business from dining with me; but is a sure man, if his Title to Vote is good, of which he has some scruple, that I am to clear up to him.

Berry. – is sure. has promised both Sir W. Gage and my self: but chose not to appear upon this Occasion, for fear of disobliging some of his Customers.

Putland. – he has promised me; but is stagger'd by his wife, who is afraid of loosing the advantage of teaching a Charity School; which old Snooke had the management of during his life, and with which I complimented his Son after his decease: and now he requites me very handsomely, by using it to compell the man to vote against his Inclination. This Charity is an annuity granted by my Aunt Stapely to the Parish of Ringmer for ever, and charged on my Cousin Dobell's Estate: Mr. Springet and others were the Original Trustees, the Survivors of whom had power by the Deed to nominate new Ones to succeed those deceased; and the Minister of the Parish is made inspector of the Charity: Several of the first Trustees dying, Mr. Springett appointed My Cousin Dobell and my self and (I think) Mr. Medley[1] by a new Deed; which I was such a fool as to leave in Snooke's hands after his Father's decease. I shall insist upon this Deed being delivered up to the Trustees or the Minister of the Parish; and if it is refused, I believe Mr. Springet and I shall endeavour to do our selves and Mr. Hurdis Justice.

Norton. is dying of the Stone, and will vote neither Way.
Finch. has promised to be neuter. but I fear may be seduced.

Pentecost. will go wrong, if not terrified by the Keeper of the Broyle, for trespassing upon it.

Relfe. who will go wrong. if not influenced by his Landlord Mr. Watson. And I wish Your Grace would write to Watson, to speak to him in strong Terms.

Geer. seduced by Relfe as I am told.
I did not know till lately that they were Freeholders.
Newenden. Sir Thomas Dyke's Man.
Snooke.

This is the exactest Account I can send Your Grace of the Voters at Ringmer. They have often been sollicited by Mr. Mansell; who has made several of them golden promises to make them Proselytes. I hope Your Grace's Accounts continue good from other parts of the County: I think there can be no doubt of success.

Letter 7
[1] ? Edward Medley of Coneysborough in Barcombe, barrister, who attended an opposition meeting in Lewes (ff. 236, 461).

Lewes.

My Lord.

I did not finish my Letter at Home because I intended to come to this place: the two Mr. Pelham[2] have just shewn me a list of the Town Voters; which gives me great pleasure, and I think must soon make Mr. Sergison and Mr. Garland ashamed of their Opposition.

Mr. Pelham tells me the Mr. Hill Comissioner of the Customs,[3] who is just going into Yorkshire, employs Watson (Relfe's Landlord) as an Attorney there, and has a great influence over him.

I have this moment received a letter from Jo: Taylor, telling me he was sorry he could not meet me in Town according to my appointment; that it is necessary Your Grace's dispute should be determined; that he will do all in his power to settle it without a Law suit: and desiring to know when I shall be in Town. I have no thoughts, My Lord, of going to Town till the meeting of the Parliament, unless Your Grace would have me; nor do I think it proper to answer his Letter, till I have received Your Grace's further Commands. I am, My Lord, Your Grace's, most obliged and devoted Servant William Hay.

Endorsed: GlynBourn. Aug. 30./ Mr Haye

8. TO THE DUKE OF NEWCASTLE, FIRLE, 6 SEPTEMBER 1733.

B.L., Add. MS 32688, ff. 273–4.

My Lord,

On Monday I attended Sir W. Gage to Buxted, where he entertained the Freeholders at Dinner; Mr. Clarke[1] told me their whole number is 24: we had 13 with us; Dick Gosling[2] was ill, and could not be there; but we called upon him, and he as good as promised Sir William not to be against us. Mr. Medley[3] sent a Servant round to them the same day, but what Success he met with I don't know; only that the Ringers laid hold of him, and made him drink Sir William's health. On Tuesday Sir William invited the Freeholders of Fletching to Maresfield; I think they are 28 in all; there were 11 with us; and Mr. Newnham[4] said if he had stirred early enough, he believed he could have secured almost all of them; Will has promised to exert himself, and as the thing now stands, it is not doubted, but by his Interest, My Lord Abergavenny's, and Sir T. Wilson's,[5] at least 20 of them will go right. Which entirely confutes the report I heard before, that Mr. Mansell had secured them all: and Indeed I cannot conceive where his great interest lies, for I am assured that half the Voters at Chailey, will either be neuter, or against him. There was amongst the Fletching Voters, that were with us, one that was Tenant to the old Lady Abergavenny, and who had been so formerly to Mr. Newnham: Mr. Newnham sent the man to the old Lady for leave to come to us; she told the man that he should be directed by Mr. Newnham; that he could not follow

---

[2] Thomas Pelham of Stanmer and Thomas Pelham of Lewes. See Appendix.
[3] John Hill, commissioner of the customs in London, 1723–44 (f. 247).

Letter 8
[1] William Clarke (c.1695–1771), rector of Buxted, Suss. 1724–68, prebendary of Chichester 1727, voted for Pelham and Butler for Sussex.
[2] A Richard Gosling of Buxted did not vote in the Sussex election in 1734.
[3] Thomas Medley (d. 1735) of Buxted.
[4] John Newnham of Maresfield Park.
[5] Sir Thomas Wilson (c.1682–1759), 4th bt. of Eastbourne, Suss., was resident at Fletching and voted for Pelham and Butler.

an honester Gentleman, or one that wished the good of his Country more; which gave the old Gentleman great pleasure, and shewed no ill disposition in her Ladyship. Sir T. Wilson was with us, and very hearty; and said, he would shew the Egels,[6] they were not the only Persons to be considered in Uckfield. Yesterday was our meeting here; but as there were no Appeals to the Land Tax, no people attended us upon that Account; we licenced the Alehouses, but had no Freeholders with us, but what were before our Friends: Sir W. Parker was not with us; but whilst we were together he returned with Mr. Chowne[7] and Mr. Fagg from their western expedition, and stopt at Mr. Chowne's tenant's here; and whilst we were busy, they were tampering with a Voter or two, that were his workmen: Sir W. Gage soon took the Alarm; and was so much on his mettle, that he immediately secured every voter in Firle within his own Walls, and talked to them so much last night over a bowl of Punch, that I believe £10000 would not purchase one of them. The Glynd Ladies have secured Paine: and I will soon get a letter sent to Mr. Wilson near Mestham, as Collonel Pelham[8] desired me, when I saw him on Tuesday at Maresfield. He told me that Mr. Smith of Withyam[9] informed him that day, that things stood very well there, and at Hartfield. Mr. Hawes tells me, that Mr. Leland Parson of East-Dean and Friston[10] is inclined to go wrong, but has declared he would not promise any body, till he heard from the Bishop of Bangor[11] to whom he has particular obligations; I wish Your Grace would get the Bishop of Bangor to write to him:[12] I informed Collonel Pelham of this at Maresfield; who has probably writ to Your Grace on the same Subject. I wish Your Grace would write very earnestly to Mr. Watson about his Tenant at the Broyle, who tries to do us all the mischief he can: Sir W. Gage and I design to write to him on the same subject. We have undeceived many People in relation to the Excise; and many of the Stories, the opposite Party tell on that Subject, are so very incredible, that the Country People are not terrified with them, but begin to treat them with contempt and ridicule. We are now going to Bourn Races. I wish Your Grace all happiness: and am, My Lord, Your Grace's, most obliged and devoted Servant W. Hay.

Endorsed: Firle. Sept. 6. 1733./ Mr Haye

9. TO THE DUKE OF NEWCASTLE, GLYNDEBOURNE, 12 SEPTEMBER 1733.[1]

B.L., Add. MS 32688, ff. 325–6.

Copy of Part of a Letter from Mr Haye to My Lord Duke of Newcastle.

My Lord

On Monday I waited on Mr Pelham and Mr Butler to My Lord Wilmingtons,[2] who had invited the Freeholders of Bourn to meet Them. I think His Lordship told me,

---

[6] A Justin Eagles of Uckfield voted for Bishopp and Fuller for Sussex, while a John and a George Egles (of Wadhurst) attended an opposition meeting in Lewes on 1 Sept. (ff. 236, 461).
[7] Thomas Chowne of Alfriston attended an opposition meeting at Lewes on 1 Sept. (ff. 236, 461).
[8] James Pelham of Crowhurst, Suss., M.P. for Newark, and Hay's uncle by marriage. See Appendix.
[9] ? John Smith of Withyham, voted for Pelham and Butler for Sussex.
[10] Thomas Leyland (1699–?1763), vicar of West Dean, Suss., 1728–63, rector of Singleton 1743–63.
[11] Thomas Sherlock. See Appendix.
[12] The duke must have already written to the bishop, for Sherlock wrote to Newcastle on 8 Sept. saying he had written to Leyland '[i]n obedience to your Grace's commands' (ff. 297–8).

Letter 9
[1] Copy, not in WH's hand.
[2] Compton Place, in Eastbourne, Suss., seat of Spencer Compton, earl of Wilmington.

Their whole Number was 45. Of which there was 37 at His House, whom He lookd on as secure. The next day, I dined at Fowington; and My Cousin Dobel told me, that the Number of Voters in Bourn was but 28, and that Sir Walter Parker assur'd Him, that 20 had actually promis'd Him, and given Him leave to write down Their Names. I did not contradict this Account, which is so inconsistent with the other; but Your Grace will easily judge, who is best acquainted with their Number, and Disposition. Mr Dobel told me, that He had met with very good success Himself at Hailsham: That of 32 Voters, 26 had engag'd for double Votes, and agreed that He should take down their Names in Writing. I told Him, I had heard a different Account from thence, and that the Number of Votes there would be near equal: He said, that Your Grace's Agents flatter'd you: That, They had met with ill Success in most Places: That People would not promise your Grace's Servants; but expected to be waited on by Persons of a Superior Rank: That on Their Side Gentlemen of Fashion had ask'd Votes in All Places throughout the County, and in many, two Months before any of the Candidates had declar'd: That They imparted their Accounts to Each Other at their Monthly Meetings: That He had Himself perus'd the Lists of almost all the Parishes throughout the County; And, That in Most of Them They had a Majority of Two to One: and He said, They should meet twice or thrice more to communicate Their Intelligence: He spoke all with a serious Air, and as a Person, that beleiv'd what He said: and I confess, that what came from a Person of His Veracity would have made an Impression on Me, had I not been sensible, how apt Gentlemen are to magnify their own Interest, and to give each Other more flattering Accounts, than Any Your Grace is like to receive from Your Own Agents. Your Grace, no doubt, has heard of the disorderly Behaviour of the Mob at Selmeston Fair,[3] which was set on foot, and encourag'd by some Gentlemen there; who were enrag'd that almost all the Freeholders were in a Booth, with Your Grace's and Sir Wm. Gage's Servants.

Endorsed: Copy from Mr Haye./ Glynbourn. Sept. 12./ 1733

10. TO THE DUKE OF NEWCASTLE, GLYNDEBOURNE, 24 SEPTEMBER 1733.

B.L., Add. MS 32688, ff. 379–80.

My Lord,

   I received another letter last post from J. Taylor, informing me that Mr. Gibbon had no Objection to Dr. Russell as a Referree. But he says he believes he shall have occasion the latter end of this week or the beginning of next to come into this part of the Country himself, and would take that Opportunity of going to see the Place, which he never yet did, and which it is proper he should do; and that if I would take the trouble of meeting him at Newhaven, we might perhaps accommodate the Matter upon the Spot. I have writ in Answer, that if he would give me notice of his coming, I would wait upon him there. I think it is Your Grace's pleasure that I should insist on every part of my first proposal, except Mr. Gibbon's payment of £50, which I shall punctually observe: but if Your Grace has any other Commands in relation to that Affair, I hope You will honour me with them by the next Post.

   I waited on Mr. Pelham at Robertsbridge and other Places in Hastings Rape; throughout which his Success even exceeded his expectations. I had the honour of his

---

[3] There are no reports of the fair at Selmeston, but Burnett gave Newcastle an account of mob behaviour at Robertsbridge fair on 14 Sept. where there were 'some Broken heads' (ff. 337–8: 15 Sept. 1733).

Company here on Friday as he went to Cliff Fair,[1] when he told me that he met with the worst encouragement the day before at Rotherfield, where he and Mr. Butler did not meet with above eight Voters that would declare in their Favour: but Counsellor Staples[2] (whom I saw at Halland on Saturday) told me he believed there would be a great turn there when My Lord Abergavenny appeared amongst them: that he had wrote to hasten his Lordships Journey, and that he believed he was upon the road. Mr. Pelham and Mr. Butler had an Opportunity of seeing a great many Freeholders at the Fair, and there was a pretty good appearance of them the next day at Halland. Ambrose Galloway distinguished himself on the day of the Fair, by causing several Pieces of Cannon to be fired in his Yard, and collecting a Mob on board a Barge in the River, which he had adorned with a Board on which was inscribed No New Excise. Mr. Kidder[3] tells me he has talked with Whitfeld, who gives himself the Airs of a great Patriot and Politician: but Your Grace is however obliged to him for declaring a pretty good Opinion of You; he says You set out in the World with good Principles, and have acted upon them till this last Affair: he says, that he and all considerable Merchants have great Obligations to those Gentlemen, that relieved them against a Scheme, which would have proved their Ruin: and that they ought to express their Gratitude to them: that he would shew that he had some Interest at Lewes; and he thought Mr. Garland a proper Person to represent it, because he understood Trade. I went Yesterday with Mr. Kidder to make a Visit to Wylbar the Grocer,[4] who as well as himself married one of Tom: Friends Sisters, and is one of the most considerable Tradesmen in Town: Kidder told me he believed he had conceived some Prejudice against the present Members for Voting for the Excise, and believed it was the only thing that made him not declare in their Favour; which made me resolve to talk to him on that Subject: He told me that if the Bill for excising Tobacco had passed, he would have given over that branch of his Trade, as he believed every prudent man would have done, rather than be subject to the trouble and penalties of that Law; that there was great difference between excising a liquid and a dry Commodity; that the first was easily done; but the trouble of unpacking and weighing the last, was an intollerable burden upon the Tradesman, which he believed those that proposed it, did not throughly understand or consider: I told him, whatever difficulty there might be in the execution of the Scheme, he could not imagine there was any ill intention, since it was of no Profit to any that proposed it; that there was no design of laying a hardship on him or any other man, but only of benefiting the Publick; if they were mistaken, it was only a mistake; and it was very unjust to conclude from thence that those that voted for it were betraying the liberties of their Country; or to raise reports of them that no man of common sense could believe: he assented to all that I said; and I believe may be gained if properly applied to: I have lately begun to deal with him, which I hope will add weight to my other Arguments. I am My Lord Your Grace's most obliged Servant W. Hay.

Endorsed: Glynbourn. Sept. 24./ 1733./ Mr Hay.

Letter 10
[1] Henry Pelham and James Butler, M.P.s for Sussex, were on a canvassing tour of the county. Pelham was at Robertsbridge on 14 Sept. and at 'Clift faire' on the 21st (ff. 337–8, 371: R. Burnett to Newcastle, 15 and 22 Sept.; f. 339: H. Pelham to Newcastle, 16 Sept.).
[2] Elfred Staples of East Grinstead, barrister, who corresponded with Newcastle (e.g., ff. 311–12). Burnett on 25 Sept. 1733 referred to him as one of 'your grace's friends' (f. 383).
[3] John Kidder of Glynde voted for Pelham and Butler for Sussex.
[4] John Wilbar voted for Garland and Sergison for Lewes.

11. TO THE DUKE OF NEWCASTLE, GLYNDEBOURNE, 9 OCTOBER 1733.

B.L., Add. MS 32688, ff. 480–1.

My Lord,

Last night died at Ringmer Old Mr. Hurdis,[1] in whom Your Grace has lost a Voter and Well-wisher. As the Living is Void by his Death, I hope Your Grace will have it in Your Power to recommend one to the Archbishop[2] to succeed, as zealously attached to Your Grace's Interest; which will be serviceable there, and which I, who am the chief Proprietor in the Parish, shall esteem the best Qualification. Your Grace, no doubt, has heard, that the opposite Party had their Monthly Meeting last thursday at the White Horse at Lewes; where, I was inform'd, about 37 were present. Some of them staid in Town the next day to honour Mr. Fuller with their Appearance at the Sessions: but every thing passed quietly; and they were observed to be less clamorous than usual; having lost some of their Spirit on the loss of the Constables. I am, My Lord, Your Grace's most obliged and devoted Servant W. Hay.

Endorsed: Glynbourn. Octr: 9th: 1733./ Mr. Hay.

12. TO THE DUKE OF NEWCASTLE, GLYNDEBOURNE, 11 OCTOBER 1733.

B.L., Add. MS 32688, ff. 482–3.

My Lord,

Though I came home late this Evening, and have but Just received the inclosed from the Younger Hurdis,[1] I cannot forbear sending it to Your Grace: by which you may perceive the Intrigues of my Neighbour Snooke; and how much the Parish of Ringmer depends on Your Grace to frustrate them. I believe he is gone to wait on the Archbishop with a false Account of the state of the Parish, and to compliment Dixon[2] (whom the Opposite Party call their Chaplain) with his recommendation. I am, My Lord, Your Grace's, most obliged and devoted Servant W. Hay.

Endorsed: GlynBourn. Oct. 11./ Mr Haye.

13. FROM JAMES HURDIS, 11 OCTOBER 1733.

B.L., Add. MS 32688, ff. 490–1.

Sir.

It having pleased God to take my poor Father out of this Life, and the Living being therefore vacant, some of the parishoners came and told me they were greatly affraid they shou'd have a minister that wou'd not be acceptable to 'em; upon asking the reason, they said, that as soon as Mr. Snooke heard of our misfortune, he immediately posted away to London. Mr. Dixon was seen by several at his house on Tweesday

Letter 11

[1] Rector of Ringmer, see above, p. 284, n. 2.

[2] William Wake. See Appendix.

Letter 12

[1] James Hurdis, collector of customs at Newhaven, 1710–69, was the second surviving son of Thomas Hurdis, the late rector of Ringmer. The enclosed is the next letter.

[2] Charles Dixon (Dickson), parson of St John's, Lewes, attended the opposition meeting on 1 Sept. (ff. 236, 461), and voted for Bishopp and Fuller for Sussex.

morning in deep Conference with him and at noon he set out on his Journey. What they apprehend, is, that as Mr. Snooke has always industriously destinguish'd himself an open Enemy to the Parish, (for which reason they have unanimously determin'd never to Chuse him into any office) if by his, or any other interest, he shou'd get a Person of the same Kidney as himself, it will involve 'em in the greatest uneasiness imaginable, that not only the Parish will be sufferers, but his Grace's interest will be also in great danger. To be the minister's Church-Warden is what he has wanted ever since his outward reconciliation to our family, declaring what great things he wou'd do if my Father wou'd chuse him; the parishoners were very uneasy till my Father satisfied 'em in the Matter.

Now Sir they desire to have your opinion whether or no a petition drawn-up and sign'd by yourself and the rest of the Parishoners (who all unanimously agree to set their hands to it) to the Duke of Newcastle wou'd not be an effectual Method to frustrate the designs of this busy man. They do not presume to dictate to his Grace who to send, but only desire that he wou'd use his interest with the ArchBishop, to send one who is entirely in the interest of the present Government and a man not to be easily influenc'd by Mr. Snooke. All this I was desired to tell you; they said, they shou'd be impatient to know your opinion of the Matter, well knowing that delays in an affair of this kind, are dangerous, and that a Letter from you wou'd greatly oblige them, as also Sir Your Most obedient humble Servant J. Hurdis.

P<o>st<script>: we heard there was a Letter sent the same day to Newick.[1]

Addressed: To/ William Hay Esqe/ at/ Glyndbourne.
Endorsed: Ringmer. Oct. 11. Mr. J. Hurdis to Mr. Haye.

14. TO THE DUKE OF NEWCASTLE, GLYNDEBOURNE, 15 OCTOBER 1733.

B.L., Add. MS 32688, ff. 504–5.

My Lord,

I am sorry I have no better subject to entertain Your Grace with than my Neighbour Snooke; who went to London with his Chaplain Dixon, on Tuesday last, and returned on Saturday. Tis currently reported at Lewes, and all over the Country, that he went to make a proposal to the Archbishop to augment the living with £50 per Annum at his Death,[1] if his Grace would present Dixon. I have not heard whether he saw the Archbishop, or what reception he or his proposal met with. It was not very likely to succeed; for it is not to be imagined that the Archbishop will relinquish his own Nomination (the only one likely to be in his time) for the sake of improving the living for his Successors. Nor was it very decent to try to bribe an Archbishop, and tempt the most reverend Father in God to commit Simony. However it shews my Neighbour Snooke to be a man of Spirit, who would not stick at some expence to gain his Point; and Dixon a designing Fellow, who knows when he has found a proper Tool to work with. If Your Grace has any Interest with the Archbishop, I hope You will employ it to keep a declared enemy from us, who might be troublesome, to Your Grace's Friends who have any Concern in the Parish. Your Grace knows best, how You intend to dispose of

Letter 13
[1] The place of residence of Christopher Mansel (see above, p. 287, n. 8), and also of Charles Payne (Paine), another attender at opposition meetings at the Star Inn, Lewes (ff. 331, 333).

Letter 14
[1] The living was worth £140 per annum (f. 493: Thomas Hurdis to Newcastle, 11 Oct. 1733).

Young Hurdis; but I know no body better than him, or any that is more likely to succeed on Your Grace's recommendation; since the Archbishop had a personal regard for his Father, and formerly promised to do something for him: and I think it no small recommendation that my Neighbour Snooke has taken an unreasonable Aversion to him. I am with the sincerest Attachment My Lord, Your Grace's, most obedient Servant W. Hay.

Endorsed: Glynbourn Octr: 15th: 1733./ Mr. Hay.

15. TO THE DUKE OF NEWCASTLE, GLYNDEBOURNE, 19 OCTOBER 1733.

B.L., Add. MS 32688, ff. 526–7.

My Lord,

I was honoured with your Grace's Yesterday with Dr. Lynch's inclosed,[1] which I communicated to Young Hurdis this morning, and to several of the Parishioners of Ringmer, who seemed well pleased to have a man of Mr. Hurdis's principles to succeed him.[2] Mr. Pelham[3] went to day to Stanmer to meet his brother,[4] who came from Hook to conferr with Him, but on what Subject I don't know. This prevented my waiting on him to day, which I intend to do to morrow morning; and will urge what Your Grace desires in the strongest terms I am able. But I fear he will have little regard to it, as he has to any representations of his Friends; for I never knew a man more wedded to his own Opinion, or so backward and reserved in communicating it to those that wish him well. When I have told him what I have heard of particular Persons falling off, he has not minded it; when I tell him he wants brisk Agents, he shakes his head, and says, his business is not to be done that Way. He says, he does not value being elected himself, but to support Your Grace's Interest he will spare no expence, and will make as bold a push as any man: when that is to be done or in what manner I can't tell; but I am persuaded it is much easier to prevent promises, than to bring people back after they have promised. As to Mr. Pelham of Stanmer, he never comes to Lewes but he gets drunk, and then talks in so imprudent and extravagant a manner, that he makes his friends very uneasy; and I never see him there but I wish for his absence. When I hear of people's going off, as I sometimes do, I impute it to the diligence of theirs and the negligence of Your Grace's Agents. I wish Mr. Pelham would move round the Town more himself; I wish Story[5] and some others like him were constantly on the Spot, to converse with the People, to learn the Sentiments of the inferior Sort, and to give intelligence of what passes. Another Cause of the Defection of our Friends is their ill Usage, for as soon as a man has promised, no more notice is taken of him; whilst those of the other Party are caressed and entertained: I hope the Mr. Pelhams will correct this for the future: and that Your Grace's presence in the Country will attone for it. Mr. Sergison invited the Voters to Cuckfield last Wednesday, I have

---

Letter 15

[1] John Lynch (c.1698–1760), prebendary of Canterbury 1723–34, chaplain to the king 1727–34, dean of Canterbury 1734–60, son-in-law of Archbishop Wake 1728. His enclosed letter is probably a copy of that at ff. 516–17.

[2] Robert Talbot (c.1695–1754), rector of Swalecliffe, Kent, 1727–33; vicar of Ringmer 1733–6; rector of Stone, Kent, 1736–54; headmaster of King's School, Canterbury, 1747–50; married to the sister of John Lynch.

[3] Thomas Pelham of Lewes, M.P. for Lewes.

[4] James Pelham of Crowhurst, M.P. for Newark. See Appendix.

[5] Lancelot Story, described below p. 302 as a captain. On 20 Oct. he was to deliver Newcastle's letter of 16 Oct. (copy at ff. 510–11) to most of the 15 Lewes voters to whom it was directed (f. 573).

not yet heard who was there, but My Lady Poole,[6] who is now here, tells me, there were some, who were reckoned our friends; and she heard that Head the writing Master[7] had entered himself of the Enemy's Club. Lawrence the Tailor,[8] who makes my Liveries was here the other day; he was looked upon as an Enemy, but he told me he had not promised, and would not till the Election; that as he was a tradesman he must follow his Interest; he complained that Mr. Pelham and Mr. Apsley had hindered him of the Place of Cryer to the Sessions; I told him it might be in my power to assist him in that hereafter: he said his Father was always in Your Grace's Interest, and that his father and himself used to work for Your Grace and the rest of the Family; but he had not taken a farthing from you these three years, and he never did any thing to disoblige You; I told him I would inform Your Grace and the Mr. Pelhams of it; and he said he should be obliged to me if I would. I design to give him hopes of making Mr. Trevor's Liveries; and I wish the Young Gentleman would make him a promise of it. If Your Grace could bring him into the Country with You, his appearance at Lewes, and the expectation of future favours from him might do much Good. Hoskin the Peruke-maker[9] is another who is esteemed an Ennemy: he has of late worked for me; and his Mother is Nurse to my Boy: he told me he had not promised nor would without acquainting me; he said he would give ten pounds there might be no Poll; that he esteemed Your Grace, and wished well to the Family; but all his Customers but my self were the other way, and he depended on them for his bread: I believe, My Lord, if it could be made worth his while to be for You he would not be against You.

I was at Plumpton on Wednesday. Mr. Springet has been very ill, but continues very zealous; he says he does not want money, and won't spare it in a good cause; and if I were to stand any where, he would if it was necessary spend five hundred pounds to support me. He intends soon to give an entertainment at Ditcheling to the neigbouring Parishes. And talks of giving money in Charity to the most indigent Voters at Lewes. I intend to wait on him soon again to promote these good resolutions.

I was Yesterday at Newhaven, as I have been twice before this Week to see them Work on the Harbour, which at Mr. Pelhams and my desire was opened on Monday last. The Ennemy have murmured at its not being opened, though all diligence has been used in that work. The man has been baffled in one or two attempts which he made before by bad Weather. And those who complain most are in great hopes that this will prove abortive, and are very angry with me that I take so much pains in the affair: but there is a good progress made in it, and I flatter my self, if the Weather continues good till the next Spring Tide, and the Man is well assisted with horses, that it will take effect. I have sent my own horses to Newhaven to attend the Work as long as they are wanted; and have taken the liberty to send to Mr. Bodle[10] and Sir W. Gage's Servants to lend their assistance; since I am sure if Your Grace and Sir W. had been in the Country, you would have given Orders to that purpose. I hope I shall oblige the Country, and do a kindness to many persons against their inclinations. If it does not succeed, there is some merit in the attempt. I remain My Lord, Your Grace's, most obedient Servant W. Hay.

Endorsed: GlynBourne/ Oct. 19th./ Mr. Haye.

[6] Frances, sister of Thomas Pelham of Stanmer, had married Sir Francis Poole (c. 1682–1763), 2nd bt. of the Friars in Lewes (from 1734), later M.P. for Lewes in 1743–63. See below, p. 316, n. 5. She was an aunt by marriage of WH's.

[7] John Head, schoolmaster, voted for Garland and Sergison for Lewes.

[8] Andrew Lawrence, tailor, voted for Garland and Sergison.

[9] Richard Hoskins, perukemaker, voted for Garland and Sergison.

[10] John Bodle of Bishopstone (Newcastle's seat near Seaford) voted for Pelham and Butler for Sussex.

16. TO THE DUKE OF NEWCASTLE, LEWES, 25 OCTOBER 1733.

B.L., Add. MS 32688, ff. 584–9.

My Lord,

I have urged to Mr. Pelham what Your Grace desired, who tells me he will do any thing his Friends desire; or any one of them in particular: though I confess he has since been backward in complying with some Proposals made to him. He has been desired to establish Clubs for the inferiour Voters at the Black and White Lyons, and to employ Lawrence the Jockey[1] as a publick Orator there: he approves of the thing, but tells me tis not yet to be done, nor is it proper for him to give me all his Reasons; but by what I can collect from him his main reason is, that he does not care to do any thing of that kind without consulting Your Grace: He was told the other day, that Dixon the Parson had sent to Morris the Shoemaker,[2] who is his tenant, (and has promised Your Grace,) that if he did not come to their Club at the White Horse, he would turn him out of his House; the Fellow went, but I believe made no promises: his Wife was concerned at his Going; and told Earl of it, who brought the Information to Mr. Pelham. I desired Mr. Pelham, to prevent any ill impression, to send for the Fellow, or by some other way to assure him that he should not be a sufferer by any threats of that kind: he said he did not think it proper, nor to give any reasons for his Opinion. Nor does he think it proper to go round himself to the People, nor to send for them to his own, or any body's House; as he might do very conveniently, and talk to half a dozen of them every Evening: nor do I find that any body goes round to the People from time to time to know the Alterations in their Tempers and Opinions. This has lost Ground; and Reeves the Constable,[3] and Morris the Mason[4] told me last night, that they thought if Mr. Pelham had stirred early, he might have saved half those that are gone over to the other side. Reeves told me that he hoped some favour might be shewn to Ridge[5] his Neighbour, who is both a Woolen Draper and Grocer, and that he should take it as done to himself. Ridge was the other day at Sergison's, but he told Reeves he did not promise, nor would: and Reeves says his inclinations are for us; but he told him, that he could not but resent, that though he had lived so long in Town, he never sold any thing to the family; nor ever had any notice taken of him, though he had been of Your Clubs: Reeves said the least favour would set him right: I asked him, if Sir W. Gage was to remove his Custom from Wilbar to him as a Grocer (in case Wilbar went wrong which tis very probable he will do) whether it would oblige him; and he said in the highest degree. Young the Collar-maker[6] has been sollicited by Mr. Kidder and Mr. Palmer,[7] and to day by Mr. Poole,[8] who has employed; and he promises

---

Letter 16

[1] William Lawrence, jockey, voted for the Pelhams for Lewes.

[2] Possibly Thomas Morris who voted for Garland and Sergison. But in the poll book he is identified as a fruiterer.

[3] James Reeve, currier and constable of Lewes in 1733–4, voted for the Pelhams.

[4] Arthur Morris, the leading builder in Lewes and constable in 1735–6 and 1740–1, voted for the Pelhams for Lewes, and Pelham and Butler for Sussex (Brent, pp. 209–10).

[5] ? Thomas Ridge, mercer and headborough (or petty constable) of Lewes in 1727–8, voted for Garland and Sergison for Lewes.

[6] William Young, collar maker and churchwarden for the parish of All Saints, voted for Garland and Thomas Pelham of Lewes (a split vote) for Lewes.

[7] ? Robert Palmer of Seaford, voted for Pelham and Butler for Sussex.

[8] William Poole, owner of the Hooke at Chailey, who had married Grace, sister to Sir Thomas Pelham of Stanmer and Frances, wife of William's cousin, Sir Francis Poole (see above p. 299, n. 6, and the genealogical table).

19. TO THE DUKE OF NEWCASTLE, GLYNDEBOURNE, 27 OCTOBER 1733.

B.L., Add. MS 32688, ff. 601–2.

My Lord,

I had scarce sent my Letter to day to the Post, when I received the honour of Your Grace's by the hands of Mr. Ward, with one directed to the Corporation of Seaford;[1] which I will deliver on Tuesday next according to Your Grace's directions. I went this afternoon to Chinton, and would have sent for Mr. Chambers thither,[2] but Mr. Palmer told me he was not at home; and Mr. Harrison[3] is with Sir W. Gage in France; so that I had nobody to consult with on the subject of Your Grace's Letter but Mr. Palmer. He thinks on my appearing there as a Candidate, it will be necessary to do something more than barely to give them Your Grace's annual entertainment; therefore he thinks it will be proper (as Your Grace intimates) to give a dinner to the Gentlemen, a double fee to the Ringers, and a double portion of Beer to the Populace. I asked, if all the Voters could be invited to dinner, but he says tis impossible, for their Wives and families, and all the Rabble would come with them, which would run the thing to a monstrous expence: but he thinks it very proper to assure the common Voters of the half Guinea: and indeed my Lord, I think it will be money well bestowed; for if they are not very well used now, they may resent it against the general Election; when 'tis apprehended the Opposite Party may endeavour to stir up an Opposition to Your Grace here as well as at other Places. The Method I propose is this; when I ask their Votes in the Evening, I will tell them that I was sorry the House where I dined was not large enough to receive all the Company; but since that could not be, I had Authority from Your Grace to assure them, that when You came to Bishopston,[4] there would be half a Guinea for each man to spend as he pleases. Mr. Palmer has provided Faggots for the Bonefire;[5] and will order the Dinner, and every thing necessary; and will send to Mr. Bodle to invite the Freeholders of Bletchington, Bishopston, Heigton, Tarring and Denton to be there, which I think are all that can be there, except Glynd; who I hope for the better appearance will go along with me. Sir W. Gage makes a Bonefire, and entertains the People of Firle and the Neighbourhood. And Mr. Palmer and I think it would be an affront to Mr. Batchelor[6] to invite the People of Alfriston, who designs to give them a Hogshead of beer that day. I gave Mr. Ward to day a list of the Cliff Voters, and desired him to get one of the Young Mitchels to go round with him to them. And he promised me to call on Young Hurdis, to invite the People of Ringmer to Halland. I am, My Lord, Your Grace's most obedient Humble Servant W. Hay.

Endorsed: Glyn Bourn. Oct. 27./ Mr Hay

Letter 19

[1] A copy of Newcastle's letter to the corporation of Seaford recommending WH as the candidate to replace Philip Yorke, created Baron Hardwicke, is at ff. 592–3.

[2] ? James or Thomas Chambers of Seaford, who both voted for Pelham and Butler for Sussex. Chington was the Pelham farm in Seaford.

[3] ? Charles Harrison of Seaford voted for Pelham and Butler.

[4] Another ancestral house of Newcastle's situated near Seaford.

[5] To celebrate George II's birthday on 30 Oct.

[6] William Batchelor, owner of the Star Inn in Alfriston. See above p. 282, n. 12.

20. TO THE DUKE OF NEWCASTLE, GLYNDEBOURNE, 31 OCTOBER 1733.

B.L., Add. MS 32688, ff. 616–17.

My Lord,

I came this Morning from Chinting, where I lay last night after having executed Your Grace's Orders at Seaford. I met with the best reception there imaginable, and had the promise of every Voter: every thing passed as well as could be wished, and there could not appear a greater unanimity and Zeal for your Grace's Interest. I wish every other Place where Your Grace is concerned would shew as much gratitude in following their Example. The only dissatisfied person was Wood[1] who keeps the Gun, because the dinner was at the other publick house: I told him to bring him into good humour, that he might assure himself he would have his turn in all publick entertainments; and that the Voters that did not dine with me would be at his house in the Evening. I spoke to them there in the Evening: and told them, that Your Grace had given me leave to assure them, that since I could not have their Company at dinner, there would be half a Guinea for every man to spend when Your Grace came to Bishopston. They were extremely pleased, and said they liked it better than any entertainment. I gave about five pounds my self to Ringers, Strowers, Gunners etc; and if the dinner and entertainment was too expensive, I believe your Grace will not think it money misapplied, since I left all the people in good humour. I am going to Lewes this Evening. I have not heard the particulars of what passed there Yesterday, but in General that the Ennemy were very noisy. Hollibone[2] waits for this; which makes me subscribe abruptly Your Grace's etc W. Hay.

Endorsed: Glyn Bourn. Octr. 31st./ Mr Hay.

21. TO THE DUKE OF NEWCASTLE, LEWES, 3 NOVEMBER 1733.

B.L., Add. MS 32689, ff. 7–8.

My Lord.

I send Your Grace a list very different from what I sent before, and which I believe is upon better information. I have been here three days to gain all the intelligence and to lend all the Assistance I am able: and have applied my self to all Persons that I have the least concern with. The opposite Party are very industrious, and I am sorry to say it gain ground every day. Several of the neighbouring Gentlemen appeared in Town on the birth day,[1] and with their Party exceeded us in Shew. On thursday they had their monthly meeting; and yesterday Sir Cecil and Mr. Fuller, as I am informed, went round the town to sollicite Votes both for the Town and County: last night they had a Ball and invited several of the Tradesmens Wives; and afterwards the Ladies dispersed themselves into lodgings in several tradesmen's houses where they thought

Letter 20
[1] John (headborough of Lewes 1731–2) or James Wood; both voted for Pelham and Butler for Sussex as freeholders of Seaford.
[2] Thomas Hollibone (Holybon), letter carrier to Newcastle, voted for the Pelhams for Lewes. His vote was challenged because 'he was a poor Man with a large Family living in a small House, in which his Wife has only her third for her Life, was never taxed, that he might not be an Inhabitant, but the Constables said he had a Right to vote, and should be poll'd'. He voted for Pelham and Butler of Sussex.

Letter 21
[1] 30 October had been George II's birthday.

it best to employ their Interest. It is with the greatest concern I tell Your Grace that things grow worse and worse; and if some speedy remedy is not found out the election will be in great danger: if it is lost, the loss of it must be imputed entirely to Mr. Pelham's[2] inactivity: who will not stir for all the frequent and earnest sollicitations of myself and all his Friends: He knows little of his Affairs; nothing but by report, though he has opportunities every hour of the day to satisfy himself of the truth. He has not been round the Town since he went with Your Grace, nor I believe asked a single man for his Vote: and I am firmly persuaded that half the Votes that have been lost have been lost by this unpardonable negligence: the people are affronted at it; and indeed he has no reason to expect their Votes if he does not think them worth asking; when the other side are perpetually courting them. I hope Your Grace will send him Your positive injunctions to alter his Conduct in this particular. I wish Your Grace would order Mr. Burnet to be here till your coming into the Country; for I fancy he might be more serviceable to you here than any where: and I hope Your Grace will come as soon as possible, with all the forces You can bring to oppose the torrent. And I beg of all things that you would bring Mr. Trevor with You; whose presence is very necessary: He has given me Authority by Miss Grace to use his Name; and where I have used it, it has had Good Effect, but his presence would be more effectual. Mr. Fuller tells me that Mr. Spence sometimes hints to him that he would be willing to change Sides, and says he has a great opinion of my Father Pelham,[3] whose speaking to him may do much: the gaining of him would be very material, for to my knowledge five or six Votes in Town would follow him absolutely, besides several for the County: Mr. Pelham is of the same Opinion; and wishes only for Your Grace's leave and directions to talk with him. – Some time ago the Ennemy gave out that Sir W. Gage was gone to France, because he would not intermeddle in the Election: I told Mr. Burnet of it, who informed Sir W. of it Yesterday as soon as he landed: he came to dine at the White Hart to day to vindicate himself. And He and I have stirred so much this afternoon, that we have done more than has been done a great while. We secured Turner the Cooper,[4] Turner the Clocksmith,[5] gained Read the Hatter,[6] made Wilbur[7] declare himself, have tempted Ridge with our Custom, and if he won't accept of it, intend to gain Burt[8] and Grover[9] with it: have sent to Newington of Ripe[10] to set his Nephew Willard right: have hindered Ridge the Tanner from letting a house to the adversary, and I hired another house for Mr. Pelham of Stafford;[11] I spoke to Brooke the Glazier[12] and have almost converted him, and I believe one Vote is sure: and promised Lawrence the Taylor Mr. Trevor's liveries if he went right. Your Grace will

---

[2] Thomas Pelham of Stanmer, M.P. for Lewes. See Appendix.

[3] Thomas Pelham of Lewes, M.P. for Lewes (see Appendix) and Hay's father-in-law.

[4] John Turner, cooper, voted for the Pelhams for Lewes.

[5] Richard Turner, clocksmith, voted for the Pelhams.

[6] ? John Read, draper and headborough of Lewes in 1734–5 and constable in 1739–40, who voted for the Pelhams for Lewes.

[7] John Wilbar, grocer, voted for Garland and Sergison for Lewes.

[8] ? Thomas Burt, grocer, split his vote and voted for Sergison and Pelham of Stanmer for Lewes, and for Bishopp and Fuller for Sussex, while Nicholas Burt, perfumer and headborough of Lewes in 1724–5, voted for Bishopp and Fuller.

[9] ? James Grover, grocer, voted for the Pelhams for Lewes.

[10] John Newington of Ripe voted for Pelham and Butler for Sussex.

[11] William Stafford, flaxdresser, voted for the Pelhams for Lewes and for Pelham and Butler for Sussex. The house was sublet by Pelham to William Bennett. See below, p. 330, n. 6.

[12] George Brooke, glazier and headborough of Lewes in 1732–3, voted for Garland and Sergison for Lewes.

be surprised at Mosely's defection, who says the other party have promised him more than any body else can give him; and at old Guipin,[13] who says he owes his bread to Whitfeld, and must go as he directs. It is very late, which makes me in haste to subscribe My Lord, Your Grace's, most obedient Servant W. Hay.

Endorsed: Lewes. Novr. 3d./ Mr Hay.

22. TO THE DUKE OF NEWCASTLE, LEWES, 8 NOVEMBER 1733.

B.L., Add. MS 32689, ff. 13–14.

My Lord,

I am to ask Your Grace's pardon for not acknowledging before this time the honour You did me in returning the Case with Sir P. York's[1] Opinion. My Time and thoughts have lately been so wholely taken up in this place, that I have been obliged to neglect my Friends at Ringmer more than I ought. The new Parson came thither last Tuesday, and having no Acquaintance in the place, was directed by his Clerk to my Neighbour Snooke's where he took up his Lodging for the first night: his name is Talbot; he married Dr. Lynch's Sister;[2] and is School-master at Stretham. I found him in this town yesterday; dined with him to day at Plumpton; and am to have his Company to morrow at my house. He told me he could not reside at Ringmer, and complimented me with recommending a Curate; I wrote this morning to Dr. Hargraves to meet him to morrow to pitch upon some person that may be serviceable to your Grace's Interest. Mr. Pelham has of late not been very well, which has made him unfit for business for some days. I believe he is very sensible of his Error in not going about and speaking to the People; and I believe resolves to correct it; but I doubt whether he will do it before your Grace comes into the Country: this remisness has made me stir more than otherwise I should think I had a pretence to do. Rowe, who keeps the Red Lyon has as good as promised me both Votes.[3] Grover promised me not to engage on the other side; and by the encouragement I gave him to hope for in his trade, and which may be easily given him now Wilbar has turned us all off, I believe he may be looked on as Ours. Balcombe the Carpenter[4] is gained by Sir W. Gage, who will employ him constantly in his own house. Brooke the Glazier I have dazled with prospect of Work at Glynd; I dare say he will give One Vote, and I question whether I sha'n't gain him entirely. Brown[5] has lately appeared with us; but he is a true Plebeian, and not to be thought of till the day of Election. Puxty[6] returned to his Colours last night at the White Hart: As did Buckwell the Salesman,[7] who will certainly be kept right by a Relation of the same name at Mayfield. The two Deans[8] I have endeavoured to set right, by insinuating that if the Son can't return to his old way of business, Your Grace is the only person that <c>an place him in another way of life. Harman the

---

[13] Isaac Guepin, clockmaker, voted for Garland and Sergison.

Letter 22

[1] To be created Lord Hardwicke on 23 Nov. See Appendix.

[2] Robert Talbot, vicar of Ringmer 1733–6, had married Anne Lynch.

[3] Erasmus Rowe, victualler, voted for the Pelhams for Lewes.

[4] Samuel Balcombe, joiner, voted for Garland and Sergison for Lewes.

[5] Nicholas Brown, gardener to Newcastle from the end of Nov. 1733, voted for the Pelhams for Lewes.

[6] Nicholas Puxty, tanner, voted for Garland and Sergison.

[7] ? John Buckwell, perukemaker, voted for the Pelhams.

[8] John Dean, butcher and constable of Lewes in 1721–2, and William Dean, shepherd, both voted for Garland and Sergison for Lewes and Bishopp and Fuller for Sussex.

Pipe-maker[9] <of >[10] St. Anns I desired not to be frigthned by his Landlord Spence; for if he turned him out of his House, I could promise him another in that neighbourhood. Whisket[11] told me he had promised Sergison one Vote; is a man of great Judgment, and very angry about the Excise; but I desired before he disposed of his other Vote, he would hear what your Grace could offer on the other side of the Question. Parson Bristed has agreed to let Philpot the Dancing Master come into his house at Lady day next, but I have pressed him very hard, and believe shall prevail with him not to quit possession till after the Election.[12] Nothing could be a greater pleasure to Your Grace's Friends than your presence here, which is become very necessary. I hope Your Grace will excuse the incorrectness of this Scrawl, for tis extreamly late. I am My Lord Your Grace's most obedient Servant W. Hay.

Endorsed: Lewes. Novr. 8. 1733./ Mr Hay.

23. TO THE DUKE OF NEWCASTLE, GLYNDEBOURNE, 10 NOVEMBER 1733.

B.L., Add. MS 32689, ff. 15–16.

My Lord,

Yesterday the new Minister of Ringmer dined here, and was met by Dr. Hargraves, who recommended Wellar of Battel,[1] who now has the Curacy of Heathfield, to be his Curate; and has sent to day to Wellar upon the Subject. Your Grace knows him to be firm to Your Interest, and I think he will do well in that Place. I left Lewes Yesterday morning, in a better situation since Sir W. Gage appeared there: most people in great Expectation of seing Your Grace, and very well disposed to receive You. In the Interim nothing is more necessary than for the Candidates to apply themselves to the People: Mr. Pelham now seems sensible of it, and lately told Mrs. Pelham that he thought of going round the Town next Monday. I am persuaded Your Grace would be glad constantly to know how affairs stand there; and therefore I shall take the liberty from time to time to send You an account of any particular Alterations that I either know or am informed of. In the list I sent Your Grace last I placed Howel[2] in the Class of those whose Votes I doubted of: Reeves has since informed me, that he certainly is a Voter, and will as certainly be a Friend; being a Person constantly employed under him. When I called on Mr. Bristed, he was confined to his house for fear of his Creditors; and on conversing with him I found him so honest a man, that I was resolved to do something to set him at Liberty: he told me Ashby[3] was the only Creditor that would not come to terms with him: I ordered a Letter of Licence to be drawn up for his other Creditors to sign; and have collected some money amongst my Friends and have paid Ashby. I sent for him Yesterday morning to the White Hart to pay him; and took that Opportunity of talking to him. I told him, that in paying him I did not only intend to do a kindness to Mr. Bristed, but to him too, in procuring him a Debt that might otherwise

---

[9] Thomas Harman, pipemaker, voted for the Pelhams.

[10] MS torn.

[11] ? Edward Whiskey, currier, voted for Garland and Sergison for Lewes and Bishopp and Fuller for Sussex.

[12] John Bristed, rector of St Peter's and St Mary's Westout (commonly called St Anne's) in Lewes, voted for Pelham and Butler for Sussex. See below, p. 336, n. 1.

Letter 23

[1] ? Francis Weller (d. 1741) ordained priest 1734, vicar of Hellingly, Suss., 1741.

[2] James Howell, currier and headborough of Lewes in 1733–4, voted for Garland and Sergison for Lewes.

[3] William Ashby, maltster, voted for the Pelhams for Lewes.

have been desperate: And that I did not believe the report that he intended to be against my Friends in the Election. He said he had never given any body any reason to think so; he said he had not promised any body, and assured me he would not; that he had often been invited to their entertainments, but always refused to go: and that he did not like their noisy doings. Whilst he was with me, Hopkins,[4] Manning,[5] and Michelborn, stood on the other side the Street watching his Motions; which observing out of the Window he said Yonder are the Spies; I shall not be gone five minutes, but some of them will be at me: I told him it would break their rest if they could not find out what passed between us, and therefore desired him to keep it a Secret, which he promised he would do: After a good deal of flattery and civil treatment, paying him his money, and promising to buy some Malt of him, I left him in very good humour, and well disposed to receive any favourable impression: so that he may be struck out of the Class of Ennemies, and placed among the Uncertain, if not in a better Rank.

I have just received the honour of Your Grace's: and am sorry that Your Grace will be detained so long in Town. I shall be ready to lend Mr. Burnett all the Assistance in my power; and am sure that nothing will be wanting on Sir W. Gage's Part. I will wait on him to morrow with Your Grace's Commands: and on Monday will go to Lewes, where I intend to be as much as at this Place. I will speak to Mr. Pelham with relation to Mr. Spence; who, as I am informed, told Mr. Apsley, that he was afraid that many of those, who opposed the Administration, intended to bring in the Pretender. Wishing Your Grace health and prosperity I subscribe my self with the sincerest devotion, My Lord, Your Grace's most obliged and obedient Servant William Hay.

Endorsed: Glynbourn Novr 10. 1733./ Mr Hay.

24. TO THE DUKE OF NEWCASTLE, LEWES, 12 NOVEMBER 1733.

B.L., Add. MS 32689, ff. 19–20.

My Lord,
I received the honour of Your Grace's letter, and shewed that part of it to Mr. Burnet, which concerned himself: he came late to the White Hart this Evening, and thought he could not get soon enough to Battel to be of any Service there. We had a large Company this Evening at the White Hart; and had some Fireworks and beer given to the Populace in commemoration of the Wedding;[1] but Mr. Pelham did not think it of Service to put Your Grace to the Expence of Orange-Coloured Favours. I spoke to Grover this Evening at Sir W. Gage's request, and told him I would endeavour to get him a Share of Sir W.s business, if he would promise; but he said he could not before the Election; but I believe 'tis an Offer he will not reject. Sir W. and Mr. Pelham sent for Tom Burt to come to them this Evening to the White Hart, but to preserve an exact neutrality he refused to come; but said he should be ready to wait upon them in another Place. Brooke the Glazier I will speak to again: and Lawrence I have tempted with Mr. Trevor's Liveries, but can get no satisfactory answer; he says he is not engaged,

---

4 Francis Hopkins, gentleman, voted for Garland and Sergison.
5 Henry Manning, surgeon, voted for Garland and Sergison.

Letter 24
1 The contract of marriage between Anne, the princess royal, and the prince of Orange had been signed by George II on 18 Oct. The prince arrived in London on 7 Nov. and the wedding was scheduled for the 12th, but it was postponed because he fell ill and he went to Bath to recover. The wedding finally took place on 14 Mar. 1734. *Gentleman's Magazine*, III (1733), 548, 606; H.M.C., *Egmont Diary*, I, 415, 424; II, 58–9.

and will follow his Interest. As to Smith the Butcher[2] he has promised Mr. Pelham of Stanmer to be right, though he sometimes drinks with the other Party. Adds the butcher[3] is in suspence between Mr. Pelhams Custom one way, and Mr. Medleys the other. Nick Burt (as Mr. Streke[4] says) is not engaged, but he is generally regarded as an Ennemy. Stredwick[5] and Guepin are declared such; but I will talk to the last as Your Grace desires. Head (as Mr. Welby tells me) is to have £20 per Annum to teach twenty poor Children, which Sergison and Garland are to cloath, and which are to go to School to him next Monday. Crow[6] they are to set up for a Writing-Master; and Taines the Baker for a Tallow-Chandler. Puxty has promised Sir W. Gage faithfully to be right. I called at Dean's but did not find him at home. The same at Whisket's; but Mr. Welby tells me he fears he has promis'd both Votes. Brett of St. Anne's I saw, who said he would vote for Pelham and Butler; but he had promised his Votes for the town about a Week since to the other side; he said the Mr. Pelhams had not asked him, nor taken any notice of him, and that the other Gentlemen had taken one of his Children, and would send him to their Charity School. Brooks the Bayliff[7] I sent for this Evening to the White Hart and he promised both the Mr. Pelhams there. Sir W. Gage and I begged of them to go round the Town to morrow; for they have lost many Votes for want of asking: but I very much doubt whether they will or no. Balcombe has absolutely promised Sir W. Gage. As Richardson has Mr. Springet; he had been seduced the other day by Whitfeld, if I had not writ to Mr. Springett to send for him to Plumpton. 'Tis very late. I am, My Lord, Your Grace's most devoted Servant W. Hay.

Endorsed: Lewes Novr. 12th 1733/ Mr. Hay.

25. TO THE DUKE OF NEWCASTLE, GLYNDEBOURNE, 15 NOVEMBER 1733.

B.L., Add. MS 32689, ff. 24–5.

My Lord,
    I came this Morning from Lewes; where Mr. Stonestreet[1] gave me the inclosed List: It was composed by himself and Mr. Earle; and shews Your Grace their Opinion of the Situation of Affairs. There are some things in it I think put to our disadvantage, but upon the Whole it Can't be far distant from the truth: And Your Grace may perceive by it how critical this Election will prove; and how much it will require every body's Attention. I wish Mr. Pelham had lent more to it; for the Ground the Ennemy

---

[2] William Smith, butcher, voted for Garland and Sergison for Lewes.

[3] John Adds, butcher, voted for the Pelhams for Lewes, and for Pelham and Butler for Sussex.

[4] John Streake, steward to Thomas Pelham of Stanmer and headborough of Lewes in 1736–7 and constable in 1740–1, voted for the Pelhams for Lewes.

[5] William Stredwick, 'inn-holder', overseer of the poor for St Anne's in 1732–3, headborough of Lewes in 1744–5 and constable in 1748–9, voted for Garland and Sergison, and Bishopp and Fuller.

[6] Edmund Crow, exciseman, voted for Garland and Sergison but his vote was disallowed. He had been under great pressure from both the constables, Friend and Reeves (the latter his landlord) to vote for the Pelhams. See p. 54 of the 3rd poll book. See above, p. lxxxiv, n. 147.

[7] ? James Brook, 'officer', voted for the Pelhams.

Letter 25

[1] Thomas Stonestreet, surgeon, voted for the Pelhams for Lewes and for Pelham and Butler of Sussex. See Judith Brent, 'The Pooles of Chailey and Lewes: The Establishment and Influence of a Gentry Family, 1732–1779', *Sussex Archaeological Collections*, CXIV (1976), 71, for his management of the 1739–41 Lewes election campaign with William Poole.

have gained is owing to his Inactivity, which has been much lamented by his Friends, and ridiculed by his Enemies: and many have made it an Excuse to Vote against him because he never asked for their Votes. This has thrown him into such a dejection of Spirits, that for a Week or ten days last past, he has lain a' bed all day, and lost all the time he should have employed in business. He was with great difficulty prevailed upon to go round the Town Yesterday with Mr. Burnet, which is the first time he has asked a Vote since Your Grace was in the Country. Had there been any Agent on Your Grace's part half so vigilant and active as Whitfeld, in getting the people together, and in bringing them to the Candidates, affairs would have worn another face at this time. I am very glad Mr. Burnet is come: he has already done good; and I dare say will stop any further mischief till your Grace comes into the Country. He last night made a Memorandum of such things as he and I could recollect to be most necessary to be immediatly done. Though I fear to be too tedious I shall trouble Your Grace with a few remarks on the inclosed list.

In St. Anne's.

Mr. Broomfield is likely to Vote for both S. and G. or not to Vote at all.[2]

Head was spoke to by Mr. Burnet. He said he was not actually engaged, but had almost resolved to be for S. and G.

Burt has promised Mr. P. of Stanmer, and is not engaged for his other Vote; will not promise it, but probably may give it for Sir W. Gage's Custom.

Old Dean I saw this Morning, and pressed very hard: he makes a Scruple of going from his Promise, though unwarily drawn into it: and all I can hope for is to hinder him from Voting, and getting one Vote from his Son.

John Harman Pipe-maker, brother to T. Harman of the same trade; tenant to Mr. Spence, and afraid of being turned out: I told his Brother last night that he should have any security to indemnify him for any loss on that Account: his Brother said he was well inclined, and that he had some power over him; and hoped to make him Vote right.[3]

Eager, the Baker, is to be tempted with the business that Figg and Faines have rejected.[4]

Rygate, Whisket, and Brett are three poor fellows and may possibly change their minds. The first is Tenant to Mr. Pelham's Servant; and has worked constantly at this house ever since March last; but was never asked for his Vote till yesterday.[5]

St. Michaels.

Mr. Burnet spoke to Guipin; who will Vote as Whitfeld directs.[6]

Cramp I hope may give both Votes.[7]

Brown will probably give both Votes.

Ob. Elliot tis to be hoped will do the same; being Cooper to Mr. P<elham> of Lewes and the Glynd family.[8]

---

[2] John Bromfield voted for Garland and Sergison for Lewes.

[3] John and Thomas Harman both voted for the Pelhams.

[4] Stephen Eager and Richard Figg (headborough 1728–9), both bakers, voted for Garland and Sergison. No Faines is recorded as voting.

[5] There is no record of a Rygate voting.

[6] Robert Burnett, see above p. 285, n. 1.

[7] Thomas Cramp, tailor, voted for the Pelhams.

[8] Obadiah Elliot, cooper and brewer (Brent, p. 32) and headborough of Lewes in 1738–9, and constable in 1754–5, voted for the Pelhams.

Brooke has been from home; that I have had no Opportunity of speaking to him since Your Grace's last letter.[9]

Old Court has been spoke to by Mr. Burnet, and at present does not think of deserting Your Grace's Interest.

Step. Apps is expected to be better than he appears on the List.[10]

St. John's.

John Sharp is expected to give one Vote.[11]

Hoskin may possibly do the same.

Morris is our friend, only afraid of being turned out of his house by Parson Dixon; Your Grace may promise him another if he is.[12]

The two Floods may change.[13]

All Saints.

Crow is Clerk to Whitfeld, but believe would be glad of a better Clerkship.

Barret may possibly give both Votes right.[14]

Lidgiter I hope will do so.[15]

Ch. Cooper I hope will do the same, being Smith to Mr. Pelham.[16]

Snashal Senior tis thought will Vote for Mr. P<elham> of Lewes.[17]

Marchant, the Musician, I believe is not fixed.[18]

And. Lawrence I am sure is not.

Ashby I am afraid is uncertain.

Bedle is to be turned out of Mrs. White's house, I believe.[19]

I am told, the Grovers who are tenants to Lord Abergavenny at Northease,[20] and Tom: Tourle who is likewise is <sic> Tenant,[21] talk loudly and make interest against his Lordships Inclinations: and I wish Your Grace would be so good as to inform him of it. I am, My Lord, Your Grace's, most obliged and devoted Servant W. Hay.

Endorsed: GlynBourn. Novr. 15./ Mr Haye.

---

[9] James Brook, officer, voted for the Pelhams, while George Brooke, glazier, voted for Garland and Sergison, and Samuel Brook, victualler, voted for Garland and Sergison, but was disallowed.

[10] No Stephen Apps is recorded as voting.

[11] John Sharp, bricklayer, split his vote for Garland and Pelham of Stanmer.

[12] Possibly Thomas Morris, see above p. 300, n. 2.

[13] William Flood, bricklayer, voted for Garland and Sergison.

[14] Thomas Barrett, clockmaker and constable of Lewes in 1714–15, split his vote for Garland and Pelham of Lewes.

[15] John Lidgitter, coffeeman and constable of Lewes in 1722–3, voted for Garland and Sergison. His coffee house, opposite the Star Inn, may have been patronized largely by the opposition. See above, p. 301, n. 11, for the whig coffee house.

[16] Charles Cooper, blacksmith, voted for the Pelhams.

[17] John Snashall senior, maltster, split his vote for Garland and Pelham of Lewes.

[18] John Machin, musician, voted for Garland and Sergison, but was disallowed. Having served at sea as a musician under Admiral Norris, he had lived several years in London as a clerk to his brother, a cider merchant, but in 1729 went to the East Indies as a musician under a Capt. Holding. His wife had then settled in Lewes, and Machin had joined her in 1731. See pp. 70–2 of 3rd poll book. See above, p. lxxxiv, n. 147.

[19] John Bedle, husbandman, voted for Garland and Sergison.

[20] James Grover, grocer, voted for the Pelhams.

[21] No person of this name voted at the Lewes election.

26. LIST ENCLOSED IN WILLIAM HAY'S LETTER OF 15 NOVEMBER 1733.

B.L., Add. MS 32689, ff. 26–7.

St. Anne's.

	P.	P.	S.	G.
R. Newdigate			–	–
R. Paine	–	–		
J. Broomfield			–	–
J. Apsley	–	–		
Jam. Grover	–	–		
Jos. Welby	–	–		
J. Head			–	–
T. Burt			–	–
Jos. Harman			–	–
Abr. Harman			–	–
Hen. Bean			–	–
W. Dean			–	–
W. Reynolds			–	–
W. Stredwick			–	–
John Harman			–	–
Ed. Rabson	–	–		
Nath. Adams	–	–		
Hen. Parker	–	–		
Step. Eager	–	–		
J. Bristed	–	–		
J. Rygate			–	–
Ed. Whiskett			–	–
Tho. Hollybone	–	–		
Geo. Brett			–	–
Ch. Cooper			–	–
	10	13	16	11

St. Michael's.

	P.	P.	S.	G.
T. Pelham	–	–		
R. Verral	–	–		
Ed Tasker	–	–		
Is. Guepin			–	–
Geo. Grantham	–	–		
Jos. Attersol	–	–		
Tho. Cramp	–		–	
John Wood	–	–		
W<alte>r Brett	–	–		
Wm. Brett	–	–		
Hen. Pope	–	–		
Wm. Attersol	–	–		
Wm. Wills	–	–		
Wm. Coombs	–	–		
Cater Rand	–	–		
Tho. Hollands			–	–
Jam. Daw Junr.	–	–		
Matt. Hunter	–	–		
Ri. Halsted	–	–		
Ab. Weston	–	–		
Hen. Manning			–	–
John Buckol	–	–		
John Kennard	–	–		
Tho. Kidger			–	–
Anth. Blundell			–	–
Jo. Edwards	–	–		
John Streeke	–	–		
T. Stonestreet	–	–		
J. Mitchel	–	–		
Wm. Stafford	–	–		
Wm. Bennet	–	–		
Eras. Rowe	–	–		
John Olive	–			–
Wm. Shelton	–	–		
Tho. Force	–	–		
Tho. Harman	–	–		
Jam. Halsted			–	–
Sam. Brooke			–	–
Ri. Plaw	–	–		
Step. Apps			–	–
Ja. Scott	–	–		
John Peckham	–	–		
Nic. Ansell	–	–		
Nic. Brown	–			–
Nat. Buckwell	–	–		
Gab. Ayres	–	–		
Ralph Cockle	–			–
Nic. Burt			–	–
Obed. Elliot			–	–
John Smallwell			–	–
Step. Avery	–	–		
John Holford			–	–
T. Friend	–	–		
J. Langford			–	–
John Gibson			–	–
T. Barnard			–	–
John Elliot			–	–
Step. Weller	–	–		
John Adds	–	–		
Geo. Brooke	–	–		
Ed. Verral	–	–		
Ab. Edwards			–	–
Ben. Court	–			–
Richardson				
	46	43	21	18

St. John's.

	P.	P.	S.	G.
Jo. Mosely			–	–
John Michelborne			–	–
John Read	–	–		
Wm. Grisbrooke	–	–		
Ed. Davey	–	–		
John Dean			–	–
Oliver Willard			–	–
Rob. Burstow	–	–		
Peter Fabre	–	–		
John Sharp			–	–
Hen. Apps	–	–		
Ben. Comber			–	–
Wm. Weston Senior	–	–		
Tho. Taylor	–	–		

St. John's.	P.	P.	S.	G.
Ri. Hoskin			–	–
Ri. Earle	–	–		
Tho. Morris			–	–
Mark Sharp			–	–
Sam. Brooke	–	–		
Ri. Flood			–	–
Wm. Flood			–	–
Jam. Daw Senior	–	–		
Ri. Turner	–	–		
Ri. Figg			–	–
Rob. Smith	–	–		
Ri. Puxty	–	–		
	14	13	13	12

All Saints.	P.	P.	S.	G.
P. Elphick			–	–
T. Brown	–	–		
Arth. Morris	–	–		
Sam. Balcombe	–	–		
Wm. Durrant			–	–
Ed. Trayton			–	–
Sam. Wheatly	–	–		
Nic. Stone	–	–		
Tho. Ridge			–	–
Jam. Reeves	–	–		
R. Crow			–	–
Tho. Novice	–	–		
Tho. Cheesman			–	–
John Cheesman			–	–
Sam. Isted			–	–
Tho. Barret		–		–
Wm. Lawrence	–	–		
John Denman	–	–		
Wm. Caldwald	–	–		
Ri. Harman			–	–
John Martin			–	–
John Lidgetter	–	–		
Jam. Howel	–	–		
Wm. Smith	–	–		
Ed. Rolfe	–	–		
Ri. Kidger			–	–
Ch. Cooper	–	–		
John Snashal Senior			–	–
John Snashal Junior			–	–
Tho. Snashal			–	–
Wm. Kemp			–	–
John Marchant			–	–
at late Reeds			–	–
Andr. Lawrence			–	–

All Saints.	P.	P.	S.	G.
Fr. Hopkins			–	–
Nic. Faines			–	–
Step. Heaver			–	–
John Turner	–	–		
John Scut			–	–
Wm. Ashby	–	–		
John Gele			–	–
John Wilbar			–	–
John Sawyers			–	–
Wm. Kester			–	–
John Wool			–	–
Ben Swane			–	–
Wm. Young	–			–
Wm. Grisbrooke			–	–
Amb. Galloway			–	–
Jam. Davis			–	–
Sam. Hutchins	–	–		
John Bedle			–	–
	17	20	34	33

	P.	P.	S.	G.
St. Annes	10	13	16	11
St. Michaels	46	43	21	18
St. Johns	14	13	13	12
All Saints	17	20	34	33
	87	89	84	74

Endorsed: List./ In Mr Haye's. Novr. 15

27. TO THE DUKE OF NEWCASTLE, LEWES, 18 DECEMBER 1733.

B.L., Add. MS 32689, ff. 86–7.

My Lord,

The Bad Weather prevented me from being here Yesterday: I have to day (according to Your Grace's directions) caused Tom: Balcombe[1] to send Notice in Writing to his Tenant Rygate to quit his House at Christmas. Morris[2] is not in Town to day, or I would have desired him to have done the same by his Tenant Balcombe. Mr. Pelham will speak to him to morrow. If he should be unwilling to do it; I should be glad to know, if it is Your Grace's pleasure, that Mrs. Vandyke should warn out her Tenant Elliot.[3] I spoke to Mr. Ayres for Rolfe[4] to defend himself; which perhaps he may legally till next Michaelmas, since he had no notice to quit before last: for, My Lord, I would propose this Question to Counsel.

Q. If a man hire a House at Michaelmas for a Year, and has no notice to quit before the Year is expired, and after the expiration of the Year continues in it without any new agreement; whether he is a Tenant for another Year, and may maintain the posession for that time; or whether he is barely a Tenant at Will, removeable at any time at the pleasure of the Landlord?

Sir Francis Poole[5] has been to day with the Mrs. Shorts to demand possession of his house at Xtmas; and is to have a positive answer next Fryday. I have delivered the Counterpart of Your Grace's Lease to Mr. Court, and left him in very good humour. I saw to day the Copy of a letter from my neighbour Snooke to Dicker;[6] advising him not to use the Duke of Dorset's name with the Freeholders of Ringmer, since it would force my Neighbour Snooke and his Friends to make reprisals in Kent, and for one Freeholder the Duke could make here for Pelham and Butler, they can make five there against my Lord Middlesex. Jack Mitchel says, that on talking with Harman[7] the Bailiff, and Harry Bean, he finds an alteration in them both for the better: and I hope the last will be improved by a letter from Lord Abergavenny.

After a very wet Journey I hope this will find Your Grace well in Town: and that You may ever continue so is the sincerest Wish of, My Lord, Your Grace's, most obliged and most Obedient Servant W. Hay.

P.S. Crips the Drawer of the Star, I am informed, has taken a lease of it, to make himself a Voter.[8]

Endorsed: Lewes. Decr. 18./ Mr Haye./ 1733.

Letter 27

[1] Thomas Balcombe of Lewes did not vote in the borough election, but voted for Pelham and Butler for Sussex.

[2] ? Arthur Morris, builder, voted for the Pelhams for Lewes and for Pelham and Butler for Sussex (see above, p. 300, n. 4); ? Thomas Morris, fruiterer, voted for Garland and Sergison for Lewes.

[3] John Elliot, perukemaker, voted for Garland and Sergison for Lewes.

[4] ? Edward Rolf, joiner, voted for the Pelhams.

[5] Sir Francis Poole had married in 1723 the daughter of Henry Pelham of Stanmer. See above, p. 299, n. 6. His vote at Lewes for the Pelhams was disallowed as not being a resident of the borough.

[6] ? Thomas Dicker of Salehurst, voted for Pelham and Butler for Sussex. For a copy of the letter see f. 83: Snooke to Dicker, 14 Dec. 1733. Henry Snooke had a freehold vote in Tenterden and voted for Dering and Vane for Kent in 1734. According to the *Poll for the Knights of the Shire to Represent the County of Kent...* (1734), pp. 240–2, there were 123 freeholders of Kent who lived in Sussex and who voted in 1734.

[7] Four Harmans voted in Lewes, but none are described as a bailiff. Two other Harmans voted in the Sussex election for Bishopp and Fuller, and one is listed as 'Serjeant Harman'.

[8] John Crips, the landlord of the Star, is not recorded as having voted at Lewes in 1734.

28. TO THE DUKE OF NEWCASTLE, GLYNDEBOURNE, 22 DECEMBER 1733.

B.L., Add. MS 32689, ff. 90–1.

My Lord,

I informed Your Grace in my last that T. Balcombe had sent notice in Writing to Rygate to quit his house. Morris went last Wednesday to Michell to have the like notice drawn up, to be served on his Tenant Balcombe; but Michell understanding that Balcombe's Year commenced last Michaelmas, thought he could not have notice to quit before next Michaelmas. The Case of Morris and Balcombe is exactly like that of Hopkins and Rolfe: and it is impossible to know what may legally be done in either, (or indeed in most cases that are likely to happen) till we know whether they are Termers for a Year, or barely Tenants at Will: which depends on the Resolution of the Question I sent Your Grace in my last; which it is absolutely necessary, should be immediately answered by Counsel, and the Answer sent into the Country: For if a Tenant has a right to stay in till next Michaelmas, nothing is to be done; If he has a Right till Lady-day, You can only give him notice to quit then: If he is barely Tenant at Will, an Ejectment may be brought against him immediately: And in Order to have it tried at the next Assises, (as I understand and am informed) the Declaration should be delivered before the Essoin day of next Term; which I believe is about the 19th. of <sic> 20th. of next month. And, My Lord, it would be very impolitick to wait the motion of the Ennemy in this Case; for if they do not deliver their Declarations till the last hour that is allowed by Law before the Essoin day, we may not have notice of their Intentions, and it will then be too late for us to do the same; and so they will gain an Advantage. I think therefore it is absolutely necessary (by a resolution of the Question I proposed) soon to know who we may proceed against, and to have Your Grace's directions, who You would have us proceed against. In looking over the list, the only persons of our Friends, who are legal Voters, that are liable to be removed, are, 1. Rolfe, who has had notice. 2. Ashby, tenant to Geale,[1] who has had notice from Ambrose Galloway to quit his Malthouse next Michaelmas. 3. Elliot the Cooper, tenant to old Kennard the hatter,[2] of whom I have heard nothing. – Kennard the turner (whose Vote is disputable)[3] had notice last Wednesday from the Widdow Attersol to quit his house at Christmas. – The Voters against us, who are liable to be removed, are. 1. Balcombe, tenant to Morris. 2. Crow, tenant to Reeves. 3. Harman, tenant to Ayres. 4. Dr. Comber,[4] tenant to Mrs. Corbridge; his house hired by Mr. Pelham. 5. Hoskin, undertenant to Earl. 6. W. Flood, tenant to Paw, who is tenant to Your Grace. 7. Guepin, tenant to Your Grace. 8. Edwards, tenant to Ri. Plaw.[5] 9. Elliot, tenant to Mrs. Vandyke: the house to be let from Xtmas to Collonel Pelham. I would have Mrs. Vandyke execute the Lease immediatly, and Collonel Pelham immediately after Xtmas send him Notice in writing to quit; for by looking Yesterday on a Memorandum made

Letter 28

[1] John Geale, gardener and brother-in-law of William Bennett (see below, p. 330, n. 6), who voted for Garland and Sergison.

[2] Two Kennards voted at Lewes, but neither is described as a hatter. Another Kennard (Daniel) of Lewes voted for Pelham and Butler for Sussex.

[3] John Kennard's vote was disputed as his landlady paid the taxes on the whole house, but the constables allowed the vote as Kennard paid part of the taxes to Mrs Attersoll. See below, p. 330, n. 8. He became headborough of Lewes in 1736–7.

[4] Benjamin Comber, M.D. Rheims, 'doctor of physick', voted for Garland and Sergison. Wallis, *Eighteenth-Century Medics*, p. 128.

[5] Richard Plaw, maltster and constable of Lewes in 1726–7, voted for the Pelhams.

between him and his Landlady about 3 years ago, I believe he is but a Tenant at Will. 10. Rygate, tenant to T. Balcombe. 11. Bean, tenant to Lord Abergavenny. 12. Cooper, tenant to Sir W. Gage's Tenant at Grinsted. – I forgot to mention Michell and Force,[6] who are tenants to Mr. Henshaw;[7] but will not probably be removed. – If my Brother Pelham[8] is not come this day to Lewes, I hope Your Grace will send him as soon as possible: for there are many things he could take care of on the Spot; which 'tis impossible for me (do what I can) at this distance to attend to.

The Shorts yesterday morning told Mr. Poole; they could not consent to let Sir Francis into Possession at Christmas.

I was at Plumpton on Thursday; when Mr. Springett communicated his design of establishing a Charity School at Lewes; for the benefit of the Town, and to promote Your Grace's Interest. He said, he soon expected Mr. Page[9] in the Country, who manages his Concerns in Town; and then he would send for me to meet him, and concert with him the proper method of doing it. He proposes to give £600 and to make Your Grace and all Your Family, and me, the Trustees. And I think for the sake of the Interest, the Powers to the Trustees, in nominating and displacing the Master and Boys, ought to be as general and extensive as may be. If Your Grace has any commands in relation to this Affair, I hope You will soon honour me with them. I am with the sincerest Attachment My Lord, Your Grace's, most obedient Servant W. Hay.

Endorsed: Glyn Bourn. Decr. 22d./ Mr Hay. 1733.

29. TO THE DUKE OF NEWCASTLE, GLYNDEBOURNE, 27 DECEMBER 1733.

B.L., Add. MS 32689, ff. 106–7.

My Lord,

I send Your Grace a List the most Complete that I have been Yet able to compose; which will give Your Grace a full prospect of the Town of Lewes, bring You acquainted with every Housekeeper, and inform Your Grace of almost every Particular: and I flatter my self that there are not many mistakes in it.

I make in it 69 Friends, 67 Enemies, and 13 One and One; and have given them all Advantages, for Reeves thinks Howel will at last be with us; J. Sharp,[1] will probably be one and one; and the same is to be hoped of Brooke; and Brett should be struck out of the number, and placed among the Certificate men; and Adds will probably give us both Votes: which would make 71 for us, 63 against us; and 14 One and One; which Your Grace can divide equally on our Side, and which their own Inclinations will divide pretty equally on theirs.

The Voters with this Mark (x) before them are such as are liable to be turned out of their Houses on each Side. And those with (L) subjoined to their Landlords Names have Leases.

---

6 Thomas Force (1709–42), minister of the presbyterian meeting in Watergate Lane, voted for the Pelhams (Brent, p. 152).

7 ? Philip Henshaw of Berkshire, who voted as a Lewes freeholder for Bishopp and Fuller for Sussex.

8 Thomas Pelham, M.P. for Hastings in 1728–41, WH's brother-in-law. See Appendix.

9 Probably John Page, M.P. for Great Grimsby in 1727–34, who stood unsuccessfully for Chichester in 1734. See Appendix.

Letter 29

1 John Sharp, bricklayer, did indeed split his vote for Lewes, voting Garland and Pelham of Stanmer, but voted for Bishopp and Fuller for Sussex.

I made Mrs. Vandyke execute her Lease of Elliots House to Collonel Pelham last Monday; so that he may now send him Notice to turn Out immediately. I saw My Brother Pelham soon after, who by Your Grace's Order sent Notice to Guepin. W. Flood is likewise Your Grace's Tenant. I wish Your Grace would send Positive Orders how many of them You would have proceeded against, that the time may not lapse. I understand tis P. Walters's Opinion, that they are but Tenants at Will; though he thinks they can't be ejected before the Election. But I should think it right to begin with some of them, that there may be room made for friends who are turned out. I think Reeves should warn out Crow to make Room for Ashby, who had notice last Saturday to quit his house:[2] and Morris might turn out Balcombe to make room for Rolfe. – I informed Your Grace that Kennard had notice in writing from the Wid<ow> Attersol, with an intent to make room for John Fryar,[3] whom they design to set up for an Iron-monger in that Shop. Last Monday they gave notice to several Poor people to quit their houses in order to fill them with new People: I desired My Brother Pelham to go to every one of them, to perswade them to keep possession, and to Assure them they should be indempnified; and to visit all the Women Housekeepers in town, to be con-vinced of their Inclinations.

Those Persons in the List with this mark (▲) are such, as besides the real Voters, wore Cockades, and walked in their Procession.

Amongst the Certificate men in the Poor Book, only J. Hoad and Rob. Gilbert[4] are likely to rent £10 per Annum. They have this Mark (x) before them. The last may be prevented by Pat. Hodge.[5]

Amongst the Persons not in the Poor Book, those with this Mark before them (x) are Certificate men. Those with this (xx) are Certificate men from one Parish of the Borough to another. Those with this (||) do not belong to the Parish. Those with this (=) are come into new houses since the making the Poor Book.

And now if Your Grace will give me leave, I will introduce the Mob to You one by one.

Persons not in the Poor Book.[6]

All Saints.

R. Jarvis – Joiner. Inmate with Balcombe. Of Ability to be put in the Poor Book.

J. Wool – formerly Servant to Dr. Tabor.[7]

J. Denman – A friend. Very poor. Lawrence might put another in his Room.

Hinkly – very poor. Has received Relief. Sawyers[8] may put an Ennemy in his place.

Cripps – very poor. Never paid to the poor. Certificate from St. Michaels.

Ja. Fryar – formerly Coachman to Mrs. Short. Lately brought in for a Voter.

---

[2] 'When "warned out" by the Coalition … the Duke found him [Ashby] a house in St Mary's Lane, and built him a malt house next door' (Brent, p. 175).

[3] John Fryer, gardener and shop assistant to Benjamin Court (for whom see above, p. 301, n. 11), voted for Garland and Sergison but was disallowed for being a yearly boarding servant.

[4] John Hoad, cowkeeper, and Robert Gilbert, glover (with another shop in Alfriston), both voted for Garland and Sergison, but the latter was disallowed.

[5] Patrick Hodge did not vote.

[6] Of the 63 persons listed as not in the Poor Book, only 13 voted or attempted to vote. Of the latter five suc-cessfully voted for the Pelhams (though two were unsuccessfully objected to – William Bennett and Edward Verrall, bookseller), the remaining eight voting for Garland and Sergison, but all were success-fully objected to: J. Wooll; James Fryer; John Feron, clocksmith; William Turle; Samuel Brooke, victual-ler; John Fryer, gardener and shop assistant; Richard Gates, victualler; and Benjamin Ellis, farmer.

[7] John Tabor, M.D., physician in Lewes. Wallis, *Eighteenth-Century Medics*, p. 583.

[8] ? John Sayers, who voted for Bishopp and Fuller for Sussex.

Martin – a Taylor. The house lately taken for him by P. Elphick.[9] But as he removed from another house in the same Parish, and was not in the P<oor> book before there is no reason to put him in now.

Bushnel – lives in Southover. Has only a room or two in the house.

Faines – lately taken the Widdow Pursers.

Stonestreet – keeps house. Mrs. Miller reserving but a small Part. She should agree that he should be put in the Poor book.

H. Lawrence – belongs to St. Johns. Extremely poor. Wat. Bret should put another in his Room. I believe he would consent.

E. Inskip – W. Lawrence should do the same.

West – Wilbar's man. They may put another in his place.

J. Merchant – whom I have placed among the Certificate men in the Poor book, because the house is Charged. Certificate from St. Anne's. Very poor.

St. Johns.

R. Boxel – Son in law to Taylor. Will give place to a Friend.

Ed. Blaber – receives £6 per Annum from Chelsea. A friend.

J. Apps – belongs to Bourn. Servant to Galloway. Tenant to Your Grace.

Jos. Rabson – to go into Wood's Wife's house. Taken by J. Cripps drawer at the Star of Dr. Ellis of Brighthelmston.

N.B. this was the first House hired since the Contest, as Dr. Russel can testify: though Whitfeld gives out that we begun the Practice. As he does that T. Balcombe was the first that warned out, when I saw Balcombe's Notice to Raggate copied from Hopkins's to Rolfe. If Rabson leaves his house, Your Grace may supply his place.

H. Morgan – an hundred and one.

R. Vaughan – Certificate man from Bourn. Very Poor.

Brown – Certificate man from Chailey.

N.B. Mrs. Hoyle Sister to Wat. Bretts Wife is their Landlady, and may let the Houses to Friends.

R. Apps – a poor man belonging to St. Michaels.

Rob. Greenfield – Cook at the White Hart.

Feroons – belong to All Saints.

St. Richardson – certificate man from Croydon. H. Apps his Son in Law.

Gates Senior – Poor. Long an Inhabitant. Never taxed.

Mansbridge – Certificate from All Saints. Gardner to Mrs. White.

Bolton – married Brown's daughter, not an Inhabitant.

T. Pockney – very poor. The house rebuilding. Taken by Sir W. Gage for Ja. Ouden.

J. Durrant – a friend. Not poor.

W. Tourle – has been long left out of the Poor Book for Poverty. Lodges with the Wid<ow> Verral his Tenant. He has warned her out.

J. Chate – Certificate from Godstone.

W. Henry – Cap. Story's man. Warned out last Monday by Michelborne.

St. Michael's.

Chr. Yokehurst – not lately taxed, nor very poor.

R. Gisbroke – very poor. Relieved.

J. Blaber – very poor. Cryer of the Town.

Fr. Smith – not very poor.

W. Bennet – taylor. Lately put into the house Mr. Pelham hired of Stafford.

T. Mantle – well inclined. Poor. But pays the Poor tax to his Landlady.

---

[9] Peak Ellphick, constable of Lewes in 1718–19, voted for Garland and Sergison, and for Bishopp and Fuller.

R. Collier – a friend. Not very poor.

Ja. Russel – Certificate from St. Anne's. Relieved from thence.

T. Cornford – never taxed, not ever relieved.

W. Attree – the same. A Friend.

T. Ellis – belongs to the Cliff. Inmate to Eliz. Rabson.

E. Verral – excused from the Tax at his own request.

H. Austen Junior – very poor.

Sam. Brooke – belongs to Beddingham. Not very poor.

Ja. Scott – the Gardiner. To be turned out to make room for St. Apps's Son.

T. Page – Certificate from Hamsey. Formerly Servant to Mr. Afford.

T. Weston – Certificate from Mayfield. Not very poor.

W. Cornford – from the Alms house.

R. Bennet – very poor. Under tenant to Rand.

Ben. Waite – inmate to Wills. Pays part of the tax to his Landlord.

H. Austen Senior – inmate to Gibson. Not lately taxed. Never relieved.

J. Fryar – Servant to Mr. Court: to be an Ironmonger in Kennards house.

J. Ridge – Mr. Pelhams tenant. Just taken his Mothers house of Wills.

St. Annes.

T. Adams – inmate to N. Adams his Brother. Belongs to St. Michaels. Should be put into a
House there and a friend succeed him in St. Anne's.

T. Winton – in part of Wid<ow> Stents. Belongs to All Saints. His Children in the Workhouse.

Gates – inmate to Dean. Belongs to St. Johns. To be put into Figs Hogsty.

Kimber ⎫
Jos. Blaber ⎬   All very poor. In H. Kennards house, which he is going into himself.
T. Morrey ⎭

Ben. Ellis – inmate to Wid<ow> Strong. And tis said has taken the house of her.

As to the Women, only those with this mark (x) are like to do us any prejudice, by having let their Houses already, or intending to do so. Su. Tourle tis said, will take in Dixon. Eliz. Rabson has already let hers to Whitfeld. He pretends he has hired the Wid<ow> Jones's, but she disputes the bargain and came to Mr. Pelham to complain of his Threats. He has hired a hole in the Wid<ow> Baker's, and put St. Eagers brother into it. The Wid<ow> Russel tis said has let her house to them. And the Wid<ow> Strong hers to Ben. Ellis. – But I see so many Friends amongst the Women, that I think we shall have a great Advantage against them.

As to the Empty Houses. Morris should finish his soon, and Mr. Lun might go into it. I am afraid Ayres's wont be ready soon enough. If Snashal goes into his we shall lose nothing by that. Sir W. Gage intends to put T. Jenners brother into his.[10] And Mr. Pelham may let his to T. Balcombe.

My Scheme in relation to the Women's houses I shall trouble Your Grace with another time.

I can't see that the Opposite Party have the Advantage in any particular. If we loose ground it must be by a Negligence that would be inexcusable: we should be as industrious to defend the place to the last extremity, as they are to carry on the Attack: We have almost as many good Motives for our Actions as they have bad ones for theirs.

I hope Your Grace will excuse the length of this from My Lord, Your Grace's, most obedient Servant W. Hay.

Endorsed: GlynBourn. Decr. 27./ Mr Hay.

[10] See below, p. 330, n. 9.

30. LIST OF VOTERS IN LEWES, ENCLOSED IN HAY TO NEWCASTLE, 27 DECEMBER 1733.

B.L., Add. MS 32689, ff. 108–9.

Occupiers	Landlords.
All Saints	
Browne	Browne.
Morris	Morris.
Wheatly	Wheatly.
Stone	Stone.
Reeves	Reeves.
Novice	Novice.
W. Lawrence	Bursto. L.
Caldwald	Brett.
Lidgiter	Mrs. Walters.
×Rolfe	Hopkins and Baker.
Turner	Turner.
×Ashby	Geale.
Hutchins	Mr. Fuller.
St. Johns	
Apps	Dr. Russell.
Puxty	Puxty.
Taylor	Mrs. Walters. L.
Earl	Tourle. L.
J. Brook	Newcastle and Daw.
Turner	Mrs. Hodge.
Smith	Newcastle.
Dawe	Dawe.
Read	Read.

Occupiers	Landlords.
St. Michaels.	
Shelton	Shelton.
×Force	Henshaw.
Harman	Kennard and Hopkins.
Plaw	Shelley.
Peckham	Peckham.
Brown	Brown.
Ayres	Ayres.
Turpin	Turpin.
×Elliot	H. Kennard.
Avery	Friend.
Friend	Friend.
Wellar	Wellar.
Verral	Lone.
Court	Court.
St. Annes.	
Paine	Paine.
Bristed	Bristed.
Apsley	Apsley.
Harman	Tonson.
Adams	Wid<ow> Studly.
Welby	Welby.
Parker	Edwards.
Grover	Bristed.

Occupiers	Landlords.
All Saints	
Davis	Kemp.
Ridge	Mrs. Dungate.
Howel	Mrs. Walters.
Smith	Baker and Hopkins.
St. Johns	
Mosely	Michelborne.
Michelborne	Michelborne.
Dean	Dean.
Willard	Vine.
×Comber	Mrs. Corbridge.
×Hoskin	Earl.
Morris	Dixon.
Sharp	Sharp.
×W. Flood	Newcastle and Daw.
Fig	Fig.
Sharp	Sharp.
St. Michaels	
×Guepin	Newcastle
Kennard	Kennard.
Hollands	Hollands.
Manning	Dr. Russel.
Blundel	Hiland.
Kidger	Hiland.

69.

St. Michaels

Pelham – Pelham.
Verral – Newcastle.
Tasker – Newcastle.
Attersol – Pelham.
Richardson – Richardson.
Cramp – Richardson.
Plummer – Watts.
Brett – Brett.
Brett – Brett.
Pope – Bristed.
Attersol – Attersol.
Wills – Wills.
Combs – Combs.
Rand – Warnet. L.
Dawe – Dawe.
Hunter – Maynard. L.
Batchelor – Steer's.
Weston – Weston.
Buckoll – Dr Russell.
Edwards – Pelham.
Streeke – Pelham.
Stonestreet – Stonestreet.
×Michel – Henshaw.
Stafford – Stafford.
Rowe – Rowe.

All Saints

Elphick – Elphick.
×Balcombe – Morris.
Durrant – Trayton.
×Crow – Reeves.
Trayton – Trayton.
Cheesman – Cheesman.
Cheesman – Cheesman.
Isted – Isted.
×Harman – Ayres.
Kidger – Hopkins and Baker.
Snashal – Snashal Senior.
Snashal – Snashal Senior.
Kemp – Kemp.
Lawrence – Hopkins.
Sacry – Sacry.
Heaver – Heaver.
Scutt – Galloway.
Geal – Geale.
Wilbar – Wilbar.
Sawyers – Wade.
Kester – R. Harman.
Grisbroke – Wid<ow> Grisbroke.
Galloway – Mrs. Court. L.

Halsted – Kennard and Hopkins.
Smalwel – Friend. L.
Holford – Mrs. Colgate.
Apps – Apps.
Buckwel – Buckwel.
Burt – H. Kennard.
Gibson – The School.
Barnard – Barnard.
×Elliot – Mrs. Vandyke.
×Edwards – Plaw.
Brooke – Brooke.

St. Annes

Brett – Brett.
×Raggate – Balcombe.
Stredwick – Stredwick.
Dean – Dean.
×Bean – Abergavenny.
Harman – Spence.
Harman – Harman.
Bromfield – Bromfield.
×Cooper – Edwards.
Newdigate – Newdigate.
Eager – Eager.
Head – Head.

67.

St. Johns

×St. Richardson	–	Dr. Russell.
▲Gates Senr.	–	⎫
××Mansbridge	–	⎬ Mr. Puxty.
‖Bolton	–	⎭
T. Pockney	–	J. Turner and Sir W. Gage.
J. Durrant	–	W. Tourle.
▲W. Tourle	–	W. Tourle.
P. Fabre	–	Willard.
W. Grisbrooke	–	Read.
×J. Chate	–	Read.
‖W. Henry	–	Michelborne.

St. Michaels.

Chr. Yokehurst	–	Mrs. Oliver.
▲R. Grisbroke	–	⎫
▲J. Blaber	–	⎬ Steers.
▲Fr. Smith	–	⎭
=W. Bennet	–	Pelham and Stafford.
T. Mantle	–	Wid<ow> Attersol.
R. Collier	–	
▲××Ja. Russel	–	Wat. Brett.
T. Cornford	–	
W. Attree	–	Wills.
‖T. Ellis	–	Eliz. Rabson.
E. Verral	–	Kennard and
▲H. Austen Junr	–	Hopkins.
▲‖Sam. Brooke	–	J. Plaw.
Ja. Scott	–	St. Apps.
▲×T. Page	–	
▲×T. Weston	–	Peckham.

St. Johns

| J. Blundel | – | Fig. |
| ▲×Rob. Gilbert | – | Mrs. Hodge. |

St. Michaels.

▲R. Stredwick	–	
N. Petow	–	⎫
▲T. Grover	–	⎬ Bean.
▲W. Jenner	–	
▲J. Clout	–	Wills.

St. Annes

| ▲W. Strong | – | T. Balcombe. |

12

Persons not in the Poor Book.

All Saints.

R. Jarvis	–	Morris.
▲J. Wool	–	Kester.
J. Denman	–	W. Lawrence.
Hinkly	–	Sawyers.
××Cripps	–	T. Balcombe.
▲=Ja. Fryar	–	Sawyers.
▲Martin	–	⎫
Bushnel	–	⎬ Mrs Walters.
▲=Faines	–	Wid<ow> Purser.
Stonestreet	–	Mrs. Miller.
▲‖H. Lawrence	–	Walt. Brett.
×E. Inskip	–	W. Lawrence.
▲×West	–	Mrs. Winton.

One and One.

Young	–	Young.
Swane	–	Swane.
Snashal	–	Snashal.
Cooper	–	Cooper, Minor.
Barret	–	Isted.
Olive	–	Olive.
Cockle	–	Cockle.
Adds	–	Adds.
Burt	–	Burt.
Rabson	–	Rabson.
Reynolds	–	Bean and Abergaven.
Bedle	–	Mr. Fuller.
Langford	–	Mrs. Yorton

13.

In the Poor Book, but not Charged

Hollibone	–	Hollibone.
▲Whiskey	–	Whiskey.
Weston	–	Weston.
Novice	–	Reeves.
▲R. Flood	–	Mrs. Hoyle.

5

Have served Parish offices, but not now in the Poor Book

| Burstow | – | Willard. |
| Halsted | – | Maynard. |

2

Renting £10 per Annum
not in the Poor Book.

Davis   –   Dean.
Grantham   –   Newcastle and Yorton.
Kennard   –   Wid<ow> Attersol.
Wood   –   Plumer and Watts.
Ansel   –   Peckham.
     5.

Certificate men in the Poor Book,
not renting £10 per Annum

    All Saints

▲Harwood   –   Isted.
▲Jos. Marling   –   T. Balcombe.
× J. Hoad   –   Kemp.
▲J. Merchant   –   Sawyers.

    St. Johns

||R. Boxel   –   Mrs. Hodge.
Ed. Blaber   –   Newcastle
▲||J. Apps   –   and
▲H. Morgan   –   Daw.
▲Jos. Rabson   –
▲×R. Vaughan   –   Mrs. Hoyle.
Brown   –
||Ri. Apps   –   Mrs. Web.
||Rob. Greenfield   –
J. Feroon   –   N. Burt.
▲J. Feroon   –

    St. Johns

▲W. Cornford   –   Weston and Pelham.
R. Bennet   –   Brooke.
B. Waite   –   Wills.
=Cat   –   Wid<ow> Strickland.
H. Austen Senr.   –   Wilh Gibson.
▲J. Fryar   –   Plummer and Wa<tts>
=J. Ridge   –   Wills.

    St. Annes.

▲Ben. Ellis   –   Wid<ow> Strong.

St. Michaels.

Wid<ow> Trower	—	Henshaw.
Wid<ow> Conley	—	Wid<ow> Conley.
Wid<ow> Jones	—	Henshaw.
Wid<ow> Strickland	—	Henshaw.
Wid<ow> Gumbril	—	Wid<ow> Gumbril.
×Eliz. Rabson	—	Eliz. Rabson.
Wid<ow> Press	—	St. Apps.
Wid<ow> Riggs	—	St. Apps.
Wid<ow> Best	—	St. Avery.
Mrs. Colgate	—	Mrs. Colgate.
Mrs. Oliver	—	Mrs. Oliver.
Mrs. Vandyke	—	Mrs. Vandyke.

St. Annes.

Mrs. Denham	—	Head.
Wid<ow> Beard	—	Wid<ow> Baker.
×Wid<ow> Baker	—	
×Wid<ow> Russel	—	Wid<ow> Russel.
Wid<ow> Stent	—	Wid<ow> Stent.
Mrs. Shelley	—	Mrs. Shelley.
×Wid<ow> Strong	—	Wid<ow> Strong.
Wid<ow> Studly	—	Wid<ow> Studly.

45

St. Annes

||T. Winton	—	Wid<ow> Stent.
××Kimber	—	
Jos. Blaber	—	Ed. Kennard.
T. Morrey	—	
▲||Gates Junr.	—	Dean.
T. Adams	—	Mrs. Studly.

66

Womens Houses.

All Saints.

Mrs. Alchorne	—	Mrs. Alchorne.
Mrs. Russel	—	Mrs. Uridge.
Mrs. Uridge	—	Mrs. Uridge.
Mrs. Tucker	—	Mrs. Oliver.
Mrs. Walters	—	Pellet. L.
Wid<ow> Miller	—	Wid<ow> Miller.
Mrs. White	—	Mrs. White.
×Wid<ow> Palmer	—	Sawyers.
×Wid<ow> Winton	—	Wid<ow> Winton.
Mrs. Shorts	—	Sir F. Poole.
Mrs. Puxty	—	Snashal Senior
Wid<ow> Carden	—	Cooper the Smith.
Wid<ow> Grover	—	Hopkins and Baker.

St. Johns.

×Mrs. Merchant	—	Plummer.
×Su. Tourle	—	Mrs. Web.
Mrs. Pilkinson	—	Will. Tourle.
Wid<ow> Verral	—	Dr. Ellis.
Woods Wife	—	Michelborne.
Wid<ow> West	—	Michelborne.
Wid<ow> Johnson	—	

St. Michaels.

Mrs. Yorton	—	Newcastle.
Eliz. Page	—	Mrs. Snooke.
Wid<ow> Sawyers	—	Wid<ow> Sawyers.
Wid<ow> Attersol	—	Snat L.
Mrs. Lardner	—	Mrs. Lardner.

Empty Houses

All Saints

—	Morris.
	Ayres.
	Snashal.

St Johns

St Michaels

Sir W. Gage's.
Mr. Pelhams.

St. Annes.

none.

5.

Endorsed: List./ In Mr Hay's. Decr. 27th.

31. TO THE DUKE OF NEWCASTLE, GLYNDEBOURNE, 29 DECEMBER 1733.

B.L., Add. MS 32689, ff. 110–11.

My Lord,

In the list I sent Your Grace I was guilty of a great oversight in omitting so eminent a person as Hopkins. My Brother Pelham tells me Reeves despairs of Howel, who is to be employed by a man in the Cliff, who is to give him £5 per Annum more than Reeves let Reeves offer him what he will; but I have desired my Brother Pelham to tell Reeves he should not suffer himself to be outbid; for this is a Year when worthless fellows are to be valued.

We dined to day with Sir W. Gage: and I left with him the following Memorandums.

To speak to the Wid<ow> Trower and Strickland to keep possession.

To fill the house he hired of Ridge with a good Friend.

To hire Parker's[1] house immediately, and eject Cooper.

To put Petit into the house he hired of J. Turner, to manage against Pixon and Michelborne.

To try to get one Vote at least of Edwards, Balcombe, and Grisbroke the Butcher (who begins to be dissatisfied) by doing him favours instead of Smith. (And we are set our Friends on Grisbroke who are his Customers.)

To confirm Cramp, and Puxty, who still talks of giving over Housekeeping at Lady day.

And now, my Lord I will trouble Your Grace with a Scheme of what I think we ought to do; and a computation of Alterations that may happen in each Parish to our Prejudice or Advantage.

We should deliver Declarations in Ejectment before the Essoin day of next Term, to Balcombe, Crow, Comber, Hoskin, W. Flood, Guepin, Elliot, Raggate, and Cooper.[2] To turn them out if possible before the Election, if not, to make room for our Friends after.

Ashby to succeed Crow, Rolfe Balcombe, Grover Guepin, Kennard Hoskin, Earle Elliot, Force Comber etc.[3]

We are to take care of good New Overseers. I will take that upon my self.

All our Friends to attend the Election of Churchwardens, and Bristed and Lun to favour us in their Nomination.

All our Friends to subscribe the Poor Books they approve.

None to be put into the new poor Books, that were before omitted; unless renting £10 per Annum, or of known Ability.

New Inhabitants since the making the last Books to be put in, if of ability.

Those that warn out their Tenants to give Notice to the Parish Officers, at the making of the new books, not to put them in. If it be thought adviseable; since the Ennemy may do the same; and they may well be taxed while they continue Occupiers, whether legally so, or not.

Letter 31

[1] ? Henry Parker, huntsman, voted for the Pelhams.

[2] All of these voted for Garland and Sergison, except Crow, whose vote was disallowed, and Cooper who voted for the Pelhams.

[3] All the proposed replacements voted for the Pelhams.

Michaelmas for a Year with Balcombe, so that nothing can be done against him. Plaw, (My Brother Pelham tells me) is unwilling to turn out Edwards, who is his Wife's Nephew, though H. Shelley has writ to him about it; but says, he will consult with Sir W. Gage how to get one Vote of him. Strong, T. Balcombe's tenant in St. Anne's (though no Voter) will have notice to morrow to quit to make room for one Stevens who is a friend. As J. Apps, and Old Morgan, Your Grace's Undertenants to Dawe,[2] are no Voters; 'tis scarce worth our while to trouble our selves with them. I think all our Friends have be spoke to to keep possession, and are resolved to do so. The only Voters, who are friends, that are liable to be turned out, are Ashby, Rolfe, Verral, and Kennard, who have had notice. Michel and Force, who are threaten'd by Whitfeld, who (tis said) has a letter, but not a letter of Attorney, impowering him to dispose of his houses. I don't reckon Elliot the Cooper whom they love too well to turn out, nor Earl who has a Lease till Michaelmas. These I think are all. Young Michel will be busy here a day or two in serving the Notices. When I said Elliot the Barber would have notice to morrow, I mean, if Collonel Pelham sends it time enough. He is to send a letter of Attorney to Young Michel to demand Possession for him. And if young Michel receives it time enough to execute it on Wednesday; he shall immediately after set out for town, to receive Your Grace's Instructions; which I should not have thought very necessary if Your Grace had not commanded it: for I suppose those instructions must relate to the framing the Declarations, and, the method of serving them on the Defendants; and we have already sent up a Declaration by young Scrase to Mr. Ward for his perusal and correction, and expect it soon back again for our Guide. Young Mitchel shall carry to town with him a Sketch of each Plaintiff and Defendant's title, that Counsel may better judge of each Case. I hope Your Grace will dispatch him back again as soon as possible, since the Declarations must be served before the 19th. of this month. – I am obliged to Your Grace for the Attorney's Opinion on my Queries. As to the Vestry at St. Michaels I knew nothing of it till it was over. I think our Friends have done nothing irregular there. But Michelborne himself I am told begins to be ashamed of their injustice at St. Johns. I believe they will not get their poor book signed: but if they do, and tis complained of at the Sessions, we shall endeavour to set it right. Mr. Pelham will stay till after the Sessions, and Sir W. Gage told me the other day that he would if it was Your Grace's pleasure. My Brother Pelham has writt to Sir W. Ashburnham this Evening. Sir W. Gage told me he would send to Board[3] and Fowle,[4] and I believe has done it. Mr. Hay[5] Your Grace says you intend to write to your self. I don't apprehend they will bring any body from the West: if we have notice of any such thing we must too. Ansel's being in the book does not take away Peckham's[6] Vote: their houses, Attersol tells me, are distinct. Ansel and Adds I am told are very Good Friends, and are like to prove so to us. Tom Friend is not now in Town; but has been with Mr. Pelham, and expressed his dislike of what was done in St. John's; and said, they had put in people that had no pretence to Vote.

---

[2] There were two James Daws, father and son, both bricklayers, and both voted for the Pelhams for Lewes, and one voted for Pelham and Butler for Sussex.

[3] John Board of Lindfield, J.P., voted for Pelham and Butler.

[4] Humphrey Fowle of Rotherfield, voted for Pelham and Butler.

[5] Richard Hay of Battle, voted for Pelham and Butler for Sussex.

[6] John Peckham, fuller, voted for the Pelhams, but was objected to as an inhabitant of Isfield, but the constables said he was taxed for the whole of his house in Lewes though it was claimed that 'he had only reserved one small Chamber with a Stove in it, to be there on Sundays, when he came to [a] Meeting'. Nicholas Ansill, a butcher of Firle, also polled for part of the same house and was objected to, but allowed because the constables 'said they were informed he had hired 10l. a Year'. He also voted for Pelham and Butler for Sussex.

I believe Your Grace need not trouble your self farther about Young Paine; I am told he and the Collonel are very ill together; insomuch that he sent orders to Michel to arrest the Collonel for a Debt; but My Brother Pelham persuaded Michel not to engage in it. I will desire Sir W. Gage to speak to the Collonel, but I am afraid it is speaking to a post. As to Puxty, I have no acquaintance with him, but my Brother Pelham will speak to him. As he will to Sam. Isted,[7] who we hear begins to be afraid of the Pretender. – I was last Friday at dinner in Sir W. Gage's Hall with 150 people: We drank Your Grace's health with such loud acclamations that You might have heard us at Newcastle House. I shall repeat the same health to morrow at my own house with my Seaford friends. It is a great pleasure to us all to hear Mr. Trevor has the small Pox so favourably. I am with the sincerest Attachment My Lord, Your Grace's, obliged and obedient Servant W. Hay.

Endorsed: Lewes. Jany. 7th./ Mr Hay./ 1733

34. TO THE DUKE OF NEWCASTLE, LEWES, 19 JANUARY 1733[–4].

B.L., Add. 32689, ff. 144–5.

My Lord,

It is now so late that I can't give Your Grace so particular a detail of our Transactions as you might expect, which would furnish out a Good Comedy with some Tragedy intermixed. There appeared yesterday on the bench Mr. Fuller, Sir W. Parker, Sir W. Gage, Sir W. Ashburnham,[1] Mr. Pelham, Mr. Board, Mr. Apsley, Mr. Hay, and my self.[2] We were honoured with the Company, of Mr. Sergison, Mr. Garland, Mr. Campion, Middleton, Dobell, two Faggs,[3] Sir C. Goring,[4] Mansel, Bridger, Bromfield, Alford, Short, Snooke, Turner, cum multis aliis. St. John's Poor Book, which we some time ago apprehended, did not appear: and I believe was signed since this Morning; for Mr. Apsley tells Michelborne[5] was to day at his house before he was stirring; and because he did not met with him, I suppose thought it a good excuse to get it signed by Sir W. Parker and Mr. Fuller. Mr. Fuller was scarce seated in the Chair, but he pulled a Paper out of his Pocket, which he said was just delivered to him, and was a rough draught of a Petition to Parliament to adjourn the Poll at the request of any One Candidate from Chichester to Lewes,[6] and desired to know of me whether he should recommend it in his Charge to the Grand Jury, and spoke loud enough to be heard by the Grand Jury and every body else. I gave as good an Answer as I could to so unexpected a motion, which was seconded by several Gentlemen who had nothing to do there and in discourse loud enough to be heard. I told Mr. Fuller that as it was forreign to the business of the Court I thought it improper to be proposed there; that I would not enter into the Consideration whether it was good or whether it was a bad thing; that probably I might approve of the thing my self, if I liked the manner of proposing it:

---

[7] Samuel Isted, gentleman, voted for Garland and Sergison.

Letter 34

[1] Sir William Ashburnham of Broomham in Guestling, M.P. for Hastings (see Appendix), and WH's uncle by marriage.

[2] See East Sussex R.O., QM 7, for the meeting of the quarter sessions of 17 and 18 Jan. 1734.

[3] Probably the Faggs mentioned below p. 336.

[4] Sir Charles Goring (see above, p. 289, n. 9) later married Robert Fagg's sister, who inherited the Fagg estates in 1740.

[5] John Michelborne, mercer and headborough of Lewes in 1723–4 and constable in 1736–7, voted for Garland and Sergison and Bishopp and Fuller.

[6] The poll for the Sussex county seats.

Mr. Sergison asked me, if I did not think it as proper, as for the Grand Jury at the Assises to propose Mr. Pelham and Mr. Butler to represent the County; I told him, that was done by the Grand Jury out of Court, and of their own Voluntary Motion. I was almost sorry, that I did not join in heartily with the Proposal, and recommend it in strong terms to the Country; but I thought it too adventurous a Step, without consulting my Friends. In the afternoon Mansel came from the Star to the White Hart to enquire for Board, and quarrel with him for not licensing an alehouse. Board returned his Compliments in kind, and a gentle Blow with a much harder, and would have thoroughly convinced him of his Error, if the Company had not interposed. Sir W. Gage and I happened to be engaged in business in another room during the whole dispute, but came in time enough to find the room in great Confusion; Mansel with a scratch on the nose, and Board with His Peruke off. As I found a breach of the Peace, I insisted on Security to keep the Peace; unless the Combatants promised it should go no farther; which at last they did. To day I was sent for by the Comissioners of the Pier to meet them at the White Hart; but I found it was with a design to bait me. When I came Mr. Newdigate[7] pulled out the Petition, engrossed, and subscribed by 13 of the Grand Jury, and the Gentlemen who appeared against us Yesterday, and some others of the Town; in all to the number of 75. He read it to me and said he should soon have a great number of hands, and desired me to subscribe it, I told him if he would alter some things in it which were false I would do it. I won't trouble Your Grace with the Incivilities that passed between Newdigate, Trayton, Bromfield and my self on this occasion. I suppose Your Grace may have heard of Col. Paynes death. All our Declarations were served Yesterday; which by Wrong Information from Mr. Ward Michel took to be the last day, which to day really was. This made them very busy in preparing Declarations to day, which they have delivered in the best manner they could at our Friends houses, (who have some of them kept out of the Way) by nailing them at their Doors and thrusting under their Doors. And I wish Your Grace would be informed whether such Service is good. I send Your Grace the enclosed paper for further entertainment, which was affixed to the Market House last thursday. Your Grace's etc. W. Hay.

Endorsed: Lewes. Janry. 19. 1733/4./ Mr Hay

35. ENCLOSURE IN HAY TO NEWCASTLE, 17 JANUARY 1734.[1]

B.L., Add. 32689, ff. 146–7.

Lewes 17th. January 1733.

At the Monthly meeting this day of the Gentlemen in the Interest of Sir Cicell Bishop and Mr: Fuller for the County Mr: Serjeson and Mr: Garland for the Town of Lewes Notice being taken that a report has been Spread that at a meeting at the Starr of the Gentlemen in that Interest a Health was proposed to a Speedy Journey to Hell to Mr Pelham of Stanmer and that the said Health was drank by the said Company one Gentlemen only Excepted, the Gentleman in the first place who is reported to have refused the said Health, and afterwards every Gentleman present most Solemnly declare that no such Health <h>ad ever been proposed in their Company that they Abhor'd all Healths of that Nature and Tendency and that the said Report is False and Scandalous.

---

[7] Richard Newdigate, a lawyer, voted for Garland and Sergison and Bishopp and Fuller.

Letter 35
[1] Not in WH's hand.

NB: the original paper that this is took from is in the hands of John Cripps at the Starr sign'd by the Gentlemen,

The persons that Sign'd were

Xpher Mansell	B. Comber	Fr. Hopkins
Cha: Goreing	Rob: Fagg	Ra: Beard
Ri: Newdigate	Hen: Goffe	Wm: Venall
Wm: Kemp	J: Fuller	Pk Elphick
J: Alford	Tho: Serjeson	Ed: Trayton
Hen: Campion	Hen: Snoke	John Davis
John Middleton	J. Thayer	
Hn: Fagg	J: Fuller Junior	
Wm: Dobell	Wm: Humphery	
Geo: Egle	Geo: Thayer	
Richd: Whitpaine	Wm: Hampton	
John Egles	Hen: Maning	
Nath: Garland	John Whitfield	

36. TO THE DUKE OF NEWCASTLE, GLYNDEBOURNE, 6 JUNE 1734.

B.L., Add. MS 32689, f. 263.

My Lord,

Ashby was here to day, and desired me to trouble Your Grace with a line, to inform You, that the building of the Malt-house has been at a stand these three weeks for want of materials; which he imputes to the neglect of Morris and Attersol, who were to carry on the Work. He is apprehensive that it will not be finished by the middle of September: and if it is not, he says he shall be a considerable Looser. I am sure it is not Your Grace's Intentions, that the Man should suffer any inconvenience; which I believe will be prevented, if Your Grace would be pleased to order Mr. Atkins sometimes to have an Eye to the work.

Bristed[1] has been with me too, to tell me, that Mr. Mansell has sent a Lawyer to him, to threaten him with a Chancery Suit, if he does not make reparation to Philpot the Dancing Master, for keeping him out of his house: he desired to know what to do in the thing. I advised him to offer to referr it; and if they would not accept of a reference; to employ some Lawyer to defend his Cause; and that his Friends would support him in it: I hear that Mr. Mansel gives out that he will ruin him: and that since his disappointment he is grown more violent than ever.

I am, My Lord, Your Grace's most obliged and devoted Servant W. Hay.

P.S. I forgot to tell Your Grace, that if You have any Commands, I shall be in Town next Saturday.

Endorsed: June/ 6

Letter 36

[1] John Bristed (see above, p. 309, n. 12) had voted for the Pelhams, but his vote had been challenged on the grounds that 'he was never taxed for his House, only for his glebe Land, that lay without the Burrough, and was so poor, that the parish excused his Taxes in 1732'. Friend, the constable, 'said he was taxed for Lands laying in the same Parish, and he should poll him'. For the details of letting his house to Stephen Phillpott, see pp. 25–6 of 3rd poll book. See above, p. lxxxiv, n. 147.

37. TO THE DUKE OF NEWCASTLE, GLYNDEBOURNE, 7 SEPTEMBER 1734.

B.L., Add. 32689, ff. 375–6.

My Lord,

The death of one of my Children, and the sickness of the other two, has confined me at home and prevented the enquiry I intended to have made in relation to the St. Michael's Poor Book. But since I had the honour to see Your Grace, Mr. Board has informed me, that the Sessions being adjourned to the White Hart on the Morning of the Election (on Boys's[1] account, who had omitted to take the Oaths the day before) he was one of the Justices there present; and that a Certiorari was then delivered to remove the Book, and that Mr. Mansell and either Barnard or Manning entered into a Recognisance to prosecute it with effect. The Clerk of the Peace told me, he had returned the Certiorari with a Copy of the Poor Book; but he mentioned nothing of the Recognisance; which (on recollection since) I believe should be returned likewise. I wish Your Grace would order Mr. Paxton to search whether any and what return has been made. If none has been made; to inquire how the Clerk of the Peace may be punished for his neglect. If the return has been regularly made; then to inquire what proceedings have been had upon it the two last Terms: And if none have been had (as I dare say none have, for no Notice has been given to any Body in the Country of any Motion) then to enquire what Method is to be taken to make the Sureties for Prosecution forfeit their Recognisance; and to enable the Parish Officers to collect the Poor Book: for I would fain falsify the Prophecy in their printed Poll; that the Book never will be gathered:[2] that that Pamphlet may be confuted in every Article. The Constables answer to it is very much approved of by Your Grace's Friends.[3]

I saw Pocock of Ringmer the other day, who assured me that he gave his Vote at Chichester, and was the third or fourth man who polled at the Waggon in the north Street: however he comes to be omitted in the Poll.[4] His Freehold is in Mayfield.

I have lately had a letter from Mr. Tutte, informing me that Mr. Miller is in a very ill state of health, and not expected to live long: and desiring me to be an humble Supplicant to Your Grace, that he may succeed him in the Place of Customer: and I hope if Your Grace has no Objection to him, that nobody else will. It is very irksome to me to be so troublesome to Your Grace on his Account; and I am sure Your Grace is so good as to think I would not be so; if it was not a Case of very great Necessity. I am with the sincerest attachment My Lord Your Grace's most obliged and obedient Servant W. Hay.

Endorsed: Glyn Bourn. Septr. 7th. 1734./ Mr. Hay.

Letter 37

[1] ? William Boyce of Lewes, who had voted as a freeholder of Ringmer for Pelham and Butler for Sussex.

[2] This is possibly a reference to certain comments in the opposition printed poll that the poor book 'had never yet been collected'. *A Poll Taken by Tho. Friend and James Reeve...*, p. 10.

[3] Printed as *An Exact State of the Poll Taken by Tho. Friend, and James Reeve, Constables of the Borough of Lewes, On the 27th Day of April, 1734. For the Election of Members to serve in this present Parliament. In Answer To a Pamphlet lately published relating to the said Election* (1734).

[4] He does not appear in the printed poll.

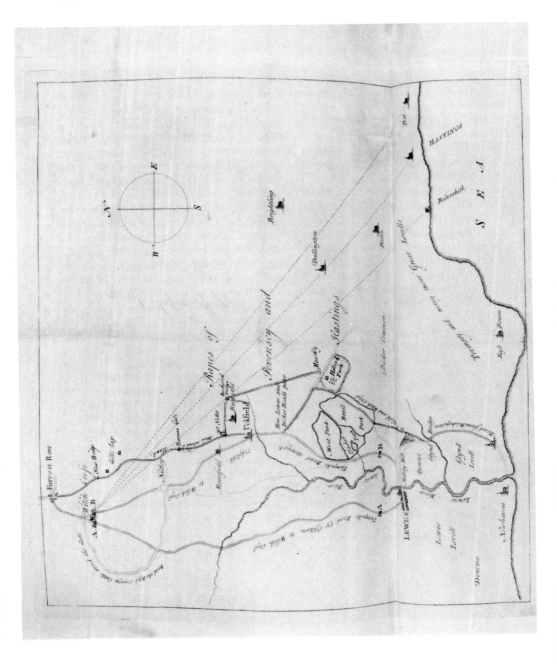

695

THE Letter A denotes *Offham* Pay-gate, Letter B *Uckfield* Pay-gate; and Payment at one Gate by Ticket carries through the other Gate on the same Road. *Note* also, Not one *Lewes* Carrier passes through the *Uckfield* Gate, unless occasionally; and that the *East* Country Carriers, ordinary and extraordinary, at moderate Computation, pay at *Witch-Cross*, though they leave the Turnpike-Road with the Road to the *Dicker*, or sooner,   40 *per* Year.

THOUGH the *East* Country Sheep and Cattle come into the Turnpike-Road with the *Dicker* common Road at sooneft, if the said Sheep and Cattle were to pass the Turnpike-Gate at *Witch-Cross*, they would pay to the same by Computation   30 *per* Year.

THAT all other Traffick, such as Horse-men, Carriages, Fish-Horses, and all other Sorts, arising from the Rapes of *Pevensey*, and *Hastings*, comprised between *Witch-Cross* and *Bishopston*, to *Hastings*, *Pett*, and from thence to *Witch-Cross*, are subject to pay at least four Times as much as the like Traffick from *Lewes*, at *Uckfield* Pay-Gate at *Witch-Cross*, so that the same may be counted as   40 *per* Year

so to Ten.

110 /10

Total : 120

AND if the Amount of the *Uckfield* Pay-Gate at *Witch-Cross* be computed at 120 *per* Year, at   3 *per Cent.* the same is worth 4000£

But   500 will mend the Road from *Witch-Cross* through *Uckfield*, till the *Lewes* and *Dicker* Roads part ; and   500 more will keep the same always in Repair ; so there will remain   3000 of the Money raised on the Rapes of *Pevensey* and *Hastings*, by the *Uckfield* Pay-Gate at *Witch-Cross*, to mend the dirty Road, about seven Miles in Length, between *Malling-Hill* and *Uckfield* Town, for the Benefit of no other Part of the Country, in passing to and from *Witch-Cross*, than to a narrow Tract thereof scarce two Miles in Breadth, as it is bounded on one Side by *Lewes* River, and on the other by the *Broil* and *Plasher* Parks. For the Road from *Bishopston* to *Witch-Cross*, and every Point that lies Eastward thereof, comes into the *Lewes* Turnpike-Road, through *Uckfield*, with the *Dicker* Road at sooneft. And whoever would travel from or to *Lewes* towards *Witch-Cross*, has a Turnpike Road by *Offham* : Therefore the Inhabitants of the Rapes of *Pevensey* and *Hastings* are sufficiently justified in acquiring to themselves, in a lawful Manner, a free and open Road, by the Parish of *Buxted*, to *Forest-Row*, missing the *Lewes* Turnpike-Road, as the same may be had by several Thousand Pounds less Expence.

Map illustrating the route of the proposed road from Uckfield to Langley, enclosed in Hay's letter to Newcastle, 20 Sept. 1753. B.L.. Add. MS 32732, ff. 964–5, by permission of The British Library.

38. TO THE DUKE OF NEWCASTLE, GLYNDEBOURNE, 20 SEPTEMBER 1753.

B.L., Add. 32732, ff. 692–3.

My Lord,

Last Tuesday I had a Visit from Mr. Fagge, who pressed me to write by this Post to Your Grace and Mr. Pelham[1] about his intended Road; as, he said, he would do himself. What he now proposes is to apply next Session for a Bill, to mend from Langley Bridge by Union Point to Witch Cross: to seperate by the Act (what is already done by Order of the Trustees) the Collection at Witch Cross from that at Malling Gate: and to apply it always in the first Place between Witch Cross and Union Point: and if at any time there is an Overplus, to apply it from Union Point towards Halland: To have a new and distinct Toll to be collected (I think) South of the Dicker, to be applied from Langley Bridge progressively to meet the Part mended by the Witch Cross Toll.[2]

That there may be no Objection from Persons, who have already lent Money, about changing their present Security into two separate Ones on each Toll at Malling Gate and Witch Cross; if they are unwilling to do it, he will engage to pay them off, and to find those that will.

The principal Objection (and which, he says, Mr. Rideout makes) is the diverting the Overplus of the Witch Cross Toll into a new Channel. This I should think very material; if I did not believe £200 per Annum collected at Malling Gate only a very ample Fund to mend from thence to Union Point.

Mr. Fagge seems to me at present to be in very good Humour with Your Grace and Mr. Pelham. He says, he will do nothing to breed any Uneasiness: and if You place any Confidence in him relating to this Affair, that he will not abuse it: and that he is persuaded, your Countenancing his Proposal will not only be beneficial to the Country, but a very popular Act.

Both he and Lord Northampton[3] have desired me to assist in carrying a Bill of this Sort thro' the House; which I have no Objection to, if it is agreable to my Friends.

To comply with Mr. Fagge's Importunity of writing both to Your Grace and Mr. Pelham, I have troubled Mr. Pelham by this Post in precisely the same Words.

I remain Your Grace's most obliged and devoted Servant W. Hay.

Endorsed: Glynbourn. Septr. 20th. 1753./ Mr. Hay./ R.

Enclosure: A printed map, giving the route of the proposed road and costings. See pp. 338–9.

Letter 38

[1] Henry Pelham, prime minister. See Appendix.

[2] A petition concerning the road from Union Point, near Uckfield, to Langley, in Sussex, was presented to the Commons on 5 Dec. 1753. WH was the chairman of the petition committee ordered to bring in a bill, and he steered the resulting bill through the Commons, carrying it to the Lords on 5 Feb. 1754. It passed the upper house on 13 Feb., and received the royal assent on 5 Mar., becoming 27 Geo. II, c. 24. *C.J.*, XXVI, 862–3, 873, 877, 940–1, 946, 962; *L.J.*, XXVIII, 197, 199, 202–3, 205, 230.

[3] In 1743 the 5th earl of Northampton had inherited the Sussex estate of Compton Place, Eastbourne, from his uncle, the earl of Wilmington.

BIOGRAPHICAL APPENDIX OF M.P.s
AND MEMBERS OF THE
HOUSE OF LORDS

This Appendix contains the names of all those M.P.s, peers and bishops who were sitting in parliament at the time they are mentioned in the text, or, in the case of M.P.s, were about to be elected. The details of other M.P.s and peers can be found in the footnotes when they are first mentioned. The constituencies of M.P.s given are only those occupied during the time covered by the text. For peerages: [E] = English (pre-1707 Union), [G.B.] = British (post-1707 Union), [I] = Irish, [S] = Scottish (pre-1707 Union). Fuller biographical details of M.P.s can be found in Sedgwick.

Abergavenny, William Nevill (d. 1744), 16th baron; succ. 1724; in 1730 he built a residence at Kidbrook in East Grinstead, Suss.

Abingdon, Montague Bertie (d. 1743), 2nd earl of; succ. 1699.

Ailesbury, Charles Bruce (1682–1747), 3rd earl of; succ. 1741.

Aislabie, John (1670–1742), M.P. for Ripon 1705–21; chancellor of the exchequer 1718–21.

Aislabie, William (*c.*1699–1781), M.P. for Ripon 1721–81.

Alington, Marmaduke (1671–1749), M.P. for Amersham 1728–34.

Ancaster and Kesteven, Peregrine Bertie (1714–78), 3rd duke of; succ. 1742.

Anglesey, Arthur Annesley (d. 1737), 5th earl of; succ. 1710.

Anglesey, Richard Annesley (*c.*1690–1761), 6th earl of; succ. 1737.

Annandale, William Johnston (1664–1721), 1st marquess of; cr. 1701; Scottish rep. peer 1709–13, 1715–21.

Annesley, Francis (1663–1750), M.P. for Westbury 1708–15, 1722–34; succ. under will to the personal and unentailed estate of his cousin, 5th earl of Anglesey, 1 Apr. 1737.

Anson, George (1697–1762), M.P. for Hedon 1744–7; lord of the admiralty 1744–51.

Anstruther, Philip (*c.*1680–1760), M.P. for Anstruther Easter Burghs 1715–41, 1747–54; lt.-gov. Minorca 1733–47; maj.-gen. 1739.

Archer, William (1677–1739), M.P. for Berkshire 1734–9.

Argyll, John Campbell (1680–1743), 2nd duke of [S]; succ. 1703; cr. earl of Greenwich [E] 1705; duke of Greenwich [G.B.] 1719.

Arundell, Hon. Richard (*c.*1696–1758), M.P. for Knaresborough 1720–58; master of the mint 1737–44; lord of the treasury 1744–6.

Ashburnham, Sir William (*c.*1677–1755), 2nd bt. of Broomham, nr. Hastings, Suss.; M.P. for Hastings 1722–41.

Ashley, Solomon (d. 1775), M.P. for Bridport 1734–41; governor of the York Building Co.

Aston, Sir Thomas (?1704–44), 4th bt., M.P. for Liverpool 1729–34, St Albans 1734–41.

Atterbury, Francis (1663–1732), bishop of Rochester and dean of Westminster 1713–23; deprived and exiled.

Aylesford, Heneage Finch (*c.*1683–1757), 2nd earl of; succ. 1719.

Bagot, Sir Walter Wagstaff (1702–68), 5th bt., M.P. for Staffordshire 1727–54.

Baldwyn, Acton (1681–1727), of Stokesay Castle, Shropshire, and (through his mother) Bockleton, Worcs., M.P. for Ludlow 1705–15, 1722–7.

Baltimore, Charles Calvert (1699–1751), 5th baron [I], M.P. for St Germans 1734–41, Surrey 1741–51.

Bangor, bishop of; *see*
  Hoadly, Benjamin (1716–21)
  Sherlock, Thomas (1728–34)

Barnard, Sir John (*c.*1685–1764), M.P. for London 1722–61.

Barrington, William Wildman (1717–93), 2nd viscount [I], M.P. for Berwick 1740–54; lord of the admiralty 1746–54.

Bath, William Pulteney (1684–1764), earl of; cr. 1742; M.P. for Hedon 1705–34, Middlesex 1734–42.

Bathurst, Allen (1684–1775), 1st baron; cr. 1712.

Bathurst, Benjamin (?1691–1767), M.P. for Gloucester 1728–54; brother of the above, and uncle of below.

Bathurst, Hon. Henry (1714–94), M.P. for Cirencester 14 Apr. 1735–54.

Bayntun Rolt, Edward (1710–1800), M.P. for Chippenham 1737–80.

Beauclerk, Lord Sidney (1703–44), M.P. for New Windsor 1733–44.

Beauclerk, Lord Vere (1699–1781), M.P. for New Windsor 1726–41, Plymouth 1741–50.

Beaufort, Charles Noel Somerset (1709–56), 4th duke of; succ. 1745; younger brother of below; M.P. for Monmouthshire 1731–4, Monmouth 1734–45.

Beaufort, Henry Somerset (1707–45), 3rd duke of; succ. 1714.

Beaumont, Sir George (?1664–1737), 4th bt., M.P. for Leicester 1702–9 Apr. 1737.

Bedford, John Russell (1710–71), 4th duke of; succ. 1732.

Bennet, Philip (d. 1761), M.P. for Shaftesbury 1734–5, Bath 1738–47.

Benson, Martin (1689–1752), bishop of Gloucester 1734–52.

Benson, William (1682–1754), M.P. for Shaftesbury 1715–19; surveyor-gen. of works 1718–19.

Berkeley, Hon. George (?1692–1746), M.P. for Hedon 1734–41, 1742–6.

Berkeley, James Berkeley (d. 1736), 3rd earl of; succ. 1710.

Berkeley, Hon. John (c.1697–1773), M.P. for Stockbridge 17 Feb. 1735–1741.

Berkeley of Stratton, John (c.1697–1773), 5th baron; succ. 1741.

Bingley, Robert Benson (d. 1731), 1st baron; cr. 1713; treasurer of the household 1730–1.

Birch, John (c.1666–1735), M.P. for Weobley 1701–2, 1705–32, 1734–6 Oct. 1735; attorney-gen. of Brecknock, Glamorgan and Radnor 1695–1712; serjeant-at-law 1705; queen's serjeant 1712; commissioner for forfeited estates 1716–25; cursitor baron of the exchequer 1729–35.

Bird, John (dates unknown), M.P. for Coventry 1734–7.

Bishopp, Sir Cecil (d. 1778), 6th bt. of Parham, Suss.; M.P. for Penryn 1727–34.

Bisse, Philip (1667–1721), bishop of Hereford 1713–21, previously of St David's.

Blackburne, Lancelot (1658–1743), bishop of Exeter 1717–24, archbishop of York 1724–43.

Bladen, Martin (?1680–1746), M.P. for Maldon 1734–41, Portsmouth 1741–6; col. 1709; lord of trade 1717–46.

Bolton, Charles Pawlet (1685–1754), 3rd duke of; succ 1722.

Bond, John (1678–1744), M.P. for Corfe Castle 1721–2, 1727–44.

Boone, Daniel (1710–70), M.P. for Ludgershall 1734–41, Grampound 1746–7, Stockbridge 1747–54; commissary gen. of muster 1742–6.

Bootle, Thomas (1685–1753), M.P. for Liverpool 1724–34, Midhurst 1734–53.

Boscawen, Hugh (c.1680–1734), M.P. for Penryn 1713–20; cr. Viscount Falmouth 9 June 1720.

Boteler, John (1684–1774), M.P. for Hertford 1715–22, Wendover 1734–17 Apr. 1735.

Bouverie, Sir Edward des (c.1690–1736), 2nd bt., M.P. for Shaftesbury 1719–34.

Bowles, William (1686–1748), M.P. for Bridport 1727–41, Bewdley 1741–8.

Boyle of Marston, Baron; *see* Orrery, 4th earl of.

Bramston, Thomas (c.1690–1765), M.P. for Essex 1734–47.

Brereton, Thomas (d. 1756), M.P. for Liverpool 1724–9, 1734–56.

Bridgwater, Scroop Egerton (1681–1745), 1st duke of; cr. 1720.

Bristol, bishop of; *see*
Smalridge, George (1714–19)

Bristol, John Hervey (1665–1751), 1st earl of; cr. 1714.

Bromley, Henry (1705–55), M.P. for Cambridgeshire 1727–41.

Bromley, William (?1663–1732), M.P. for Oxford University 1701–32; Speaker 1710–13; secretary of state 1713–14.

Bromley, William, jr. (?1701–37), M.P. for Warwick 1727–25 Feb. 1735, Oxford University 1737; son of the above.

Brooke, Francis Greville (1719–73), 8th baron; succ. 1727.

Bruce, Charles (1682–1747), baron; called to Lords in father's barony 1711; succ. as 3rd earl of Aylesbury 1741.

Brydges, Lord Henry; *see* Carnarvon, marquess of.

Buckingham, John Sheffield (1647–1721), 1st duke of; cr. 1703.
Buckworth, Sir John (1700–58), 2nd bt., M.P. for Weobley 1734–41.
Butler, James (c.1680–1741), of Warminghurst Park, Suss.; M.P. for Sussex 1715–22, 1728–41.

Cadogan, William (1672–1726), 1st earl; cr. 1718.
Caesar, Charles (1673–1741), M.P. for Hertfordshire 1727–32, 1736–41.
Calvert, William (?1703–61), M.P. for London July 1742–1754.
Campbell, John (1695–1777), M.P. for Pembrokeshire 1727–47.
Canterbury, archbishop of; see
    Herring, Thomas (1747–57)
    Wake, William (1715–37)
Carew, Thomas (1702–66), M.P. for Minehead 1739–47.
Carleton, Henry Boyle (d. 1725), baron; cr. 1714.
Carlisle, Charles Howard (1669–1738), 3rd earl of; succ. 1692.
Carnarvon, Henry Brydges (1708–71), styled marquess of, M.P. for Hereford 1727–34, Steyning 1734–41, Bishop's Castle 1741–4; succ. 2nd duke of Chandos 1744.
Carnarvon, James Brydges (1731–89), styled marquess of, M.P. for Winchester 1754–61, Radnorshire 1761–8; succ. 3rd duke of Chandos 1771; son of the above.
Carpenter, George (c.1695–1749), 2nd baron [I], M.P. for Morpeth 1717–27, Weobley 1741–7; succ. 1732.
Carter, Lawrence (1668–1745), M.P. for Leicester 1722–6.
Carteret, Baron; see Granville, 2nd earl.
Castlecomer, Christopher Wandesford (1684–1719), 2nd viscount [I], M.P. for Morpeth 1710–13, Ripon 1715–19; succ. 1707.
Castlemaine, Sir Richard Child (1680–1750), 1st viscount [I], M.P. for Essex 1710–22, 1727–34; cr. 1718; cr. Earl Tylney [I] 1731.
Caswall, Sir George (d. 1742), M.P. for Leominster 1717–21, 1722–41; banker, stockbroker and director of the South Sea Company 1711–18; knighted 10 Feb. 1718; connected financially with 1st earl of Oxford.
Caswall, John (?1701–42), M.P. for Leominster 1741–2.
Catherlough, Lord; see Westmorland, John Fane, 7th earl of
Chandler, Edward (?1668–1750), bishop of Lichfield and Coventry 1717–30, of Durham 1730–50.
Chandos, James Brydges (1674–1744), 1st duke of; cr. 1719.
Chedworth, John Howe (bef. 1690–1742), 1st baron, M.P. for Wiltshire 1729–41; cr. 1741.
Chester, bishop of; see
    Gastrell, Francis (1714–25)
Chesterfield, Philip Dormer Stanhope (1694–1773), 4th earl of; succ. 1726.
Chetwynd, William Richard (?1683–1770), M.P. for Stafford 1734–70; master of the mint 1744–69.
Child, Sir Francis (c.1684–1740), M.P. for Middlesex 1727–40.
Cholmondeley, George (1703–70), 3rd earl of; succ. 1733; Sir Robert Walpole's son-in-law.
Cholmondeley, Hon. James (1708–75), M.P. for Bossiney 1731–4, Camelford 1734–41, Montgomery 1741–7; lt.-col. 1731; brother of the above.
Clagett, Nicholas (d. 1746), bishop of Exeter 1742–6, previously of St David's.
Clarendon, Edward Hyde (1661–1723), 3rd earl of; succ. 1709; from c.1712 the main chairman of committees in the Lords.
Clayton, William; see Sundon, 1st baron.
Clutterbuck, Thomas (1697–1742), M.P. for Liskeard 1722–34, Plympton 1734–42.
Cobham, Richard Temple (1675–1749), 1st viscount; cr. 1718.
Cockburn, John (c.1679–1758), M.P. for Haddingtonshire 1708–41; lord of the admiralty 1717–32, 1742–4.
Coke, Edward (1719–53), styled viscount from 1744, M.P. for Norfolk 1741–7, Harwich 1747–53.

Compton, Hon. George (1692–1758), M.P. for Northampton 1727–54; lord of the treasury 1742–4.

Compton, Hon. Spencer; *see* Wilmington, earl of

Conduitt, John (1688–1737), M.P. for Whitchurch 1721–3 Apr. 1735, Southampton 3 Apr. 1735–1737.

Coningsby, Thomas (1656–1729), 1st earl of; cr. 1719; previously 1st baron, cr. 1716.

Conyers, Edward (?1693–1742), M.P. for East Grinstead 1725–7, 1734–41.

Cope, Sir John (1673–1749), 6th bt., M.P. for Tavistock 1708–27, Hampshire 1727–34, Lymington 1734–41.

Cope, John (1690–1760), M.P. for Oxford 1738–41; lt.-gen. 1743, c.-in-c. Scotland 1745.

Corbet, Sir William (1702–48), 5th bt., M.P. for Ludlow 1741–8.

Corbett, Thomas (c.1687–1751), M.P. for Saltash 1734–51.

Cornbury, Henry Hyde (1710–53), styled viscount, M.P. for Oxford University 1732–51; summoned to Lords in his father's barony as Lord Hyde of Hindon 1751.

Cornewall, James (1698–1744), M.P. for Weobley 1732–4, 1737–41; capt. Royal Navy 1724.

Cornewall, Velters (?1697–1768), M.P. for Herefordshire 1722–68.

Coster, Thomas (1684–1739), M.P. for Bristol 1734–9.

Cotton, Sir John Hynde (c.1688–1752), 3rd bt., M.P. for Cambridge 1722–41, Marlborough 1741–52.

Cowper, William (1665–1723), 1st earl; cr. 1718; previously 1st baron cr. 1706; lord chancellor 1707–10, 1714–18.

Craggs, James (1688–1721), M.P. for Tregony 1713–21.

Craven, Fulwar (d. 1764), 4th baron; succ. 1739.

Cressett, Edward (d. 1755), dean of Hereford 1736–49, bishop of Llandaff 1749–55.

Croft, Sir Archer (1683–1753), 2nd bt., M.P. for Leominster 1722–7.

Cumberland, William Augustus (1721–65), duke of; cr. 1726; 2nd son of George II.

Danvers, Joseph (1686–1753), M.P. for Bramber 1727–34, Totnes 1734–47.

Dashwood, Sir Francis (1708–81), 2nd bt., M.P. for New Romney 1741–61.

Dawes, Sir William (1671–1724), archbishop of York 1714–24, previously bishop of Exeter.

Deerhurst, George William Coventry (1722–1809), viscount; M.P. for Bridport 1744–7, Worcestershire 1747–51; succ. 6th earl of Coventry 1751.

Delawar, John West (1693–1766), 7th baron; succ. 1723.

Delme, Peter (1710–70), M.P. for Ludgershall 1734–41, Southampton 1741–54.

Denbigh, William Feilding (1697–1755), 5th earl of; succ. 1717.

Dering, Sir Edward (1705–62), 5th bt., M.P. for Kent 1733–54.

Desbouverie; *see* Bouverie, Sir Edward des

Devonshire, William Cavendish (c.1673–1729), 2nd duke of; succ. 1707.

Devonshire, William Cavendish (1698–1755), 3rd duke of; succ. 1729.

Digby, Hon. Edward (c.1693–1746), M.P. for Warwickshire 1726–46.

Dodington, George Bubb (?1691–1762), M.P. for Bridgwater 1722–54.

Doncaster, Francis Scott (1695–1751), earl of; restored to English title 1743; succ. 2nd duke of Buccleuch [S] 1732; Scottish rep. peer 1734–41.

Dorset, Lionel Cranfield Sackville (1687–1765), 1st duke of; cr. 1720; lord steward of the household 1725–30, 1737–45.

Douglas, Sir John (c.1708–78), 3rd bt., M.P. for Dumfriesshire 1741–7.

Drummond, John (1676–1742), M.P. for Perth Burghs 1720–42.

Ducie of Morton, Matthew (bef. 1700–63), 2nd baron; succ. 1735.

Dupplin, Thomas Hay (1710–87), styled viscount of [S], M.P. for Scarborough 16 Jan.–21 Apr. 1736, Cambridge 1741–58.

Earle, Giles (c.1678–1758), M.P. for Malmesbury 1722–47; chairman of committee of privileges and elections 1727–41.

Earle, Joseph (c.1658–1730), M.P. for Bristol 1710–27.

Earle, William Rawlinson (*c.*1703–74), M.P. for Malmesbury 1727–47, Cricklade 1747–61; son of the above.

Edgcumbe, Richard (1680–1758), 1st baron; cr. 20 Apr. 1742; M.P. for Plympton Erle 1702–34, 1741–2, Lostwithiel 1734–41.

Edwards, Thomas (?1673–1743), M.P. for Wells 1719–35.

Egmont, John Perceval (1711–70), 2nd earl of [I]; succ. 1748; M.P. for Weobley 1747–54, lord of the bedchamber and chief political adviser to the prince of Wales 1748–51.

Erle, Thomas (?1650–1720), M.P. for Wareham 1701–18; gen. of foot 1711; governor of Portsmouth 1694–1712, 1714–18; lt.-gen. of the ordnance 1705–12, 1714–18.

Erskine, Hon. James (*c.*1678–1754), M.P. for Clackmannanshire 1734–41, Stirling Burghs 1741–7.

Essex, William Capel (1697–1743), 3rd earl of; succ. 1710.

Eversfield, Charles (*c.*1682–1749), M.P. for Horsham 1713–15, 1721–42, Steyning 1741–7.

Exeter, bishop of; *see*
    Blackburne, Lancelot (1717–24)
    Clagett, Nicholas (1742–6)

Eyles, John (1683–1745), M.P. for London 1727–34; comm. for forfeited estates 1716–25.

Eyles, Joseph (*c.*1690–1740), M.P. for Devizes 1734–40.

Falmouth, Hugh Boscawen (1707–82), 2nd viscount; succ. 1734.

Fane, Francis (*c.*1698–1757), M.P. for Taunton 1727–41, Petersfield 1741–7, Ilchester 1747–54.

Fazakerley, Nicholas (?1685–1767), M.P. for Preston 1732–67.

Ferrers, Laurence Shirley (1720–60), 4th earl; succ. 1745.

Finch, Hon. William (1691–1766), M.P. for Cockermouth 1727–47, 1747–54.

Fitzwilliam, William (1720–56), 3rd earl [I]; succ. 1728; M.P. for Peterborough 1741–19 Apr. 1742; cr. Lord Fitzwilliam, Baron Milton [G.B.] 19 Apr. 1742, Earl Fitzwilliam [G.B.] 1746.

Foley, Thomas (?1670–1737), of Stoke Edith, Herefs., M.P. for Hereford 1701–22.

Foley, Thomas (?1695–1749), of Stoke Edith, Herefs., M.P. for Hereford 1734–41, Herefordshire 6 Jan. 1742–1747.

Foley, Thomas (*c.*1703–66), 2nd baron; succ. 1733.

Foley, Thomas (1716–77), son of Thomas Foley of Stoke Edith, Herefs. (above), M.P. for Droitwich 1741–7, 9–16 Dec. 1747, 1754–68, Herefordshire 1768–76.

Folkestone, Jacob des Bouverie (1694–1761), 1st viscount; cr. 1747.

Fox, Henry (1705–74), M.P. for Hindon 28 Feb. 1735–41, Windsor 1741–61.

Fox, Stephen; *see* Ilchester, 1st baron.

Furnese, Henry (aft. 1688–1756), M.P. for New Romney 1741–56.

Gage, Thomas (*c.*1695–1754), 1st viscount [I]; cr. 1720; M.P. for Tewkesbury 1721–54.

Gage, Sir William (1695–1744), 7th bt., M.P. for Seaford 1722–44.

Gastrell, Francis (1662–1725), bishop of Chester 1714–25.

Gibson, Edmund (1669–1748), bishop of Lincoln 1715–23, London 1723–48.

Gilbert, John (1693–1761), bishop of Llandaff 1740–8, Salisbury 1748–57, archbishop of York 1757–61.

Gilmour, Sir Charles (d. 1750), 2nd bt., M.P. for Edinburghshire 1737–50.

Glanville, William (*c.*1686–1766), M.P. for Hythe 1728–66.

Gloucester, bishop of; *see*
    Benson, Martin (1734–52)
    Willis, Richard (1715–21)

Godschall, Sir Robert (*c.*1692–1742), M.P. for London 1741–June 1742.

Gore, Charles (?1711–68), M.P. for Cricklade 1734–41, Hertfordshire 1741–61.

Gore, John (*c.*1689–1763), M.P. for Great Grimsby 1747–61; Hamburg merchant, leading government financier.

Gore, Thomas (?1694–1777), M.P. for Amersham 1735–46, Portsmouth 1746–7, Bedford 1747–54; muster-master gen. 1746–77.

Gore, William (*c.*1675–1739), M.P. for Cricklade 1734–9.

Gould, John (*c.*1695–1740), M.P. for New Shoreham 1729–34; director East India Company 1724–35.

Gower, John Leveson Gower (1694–1754), 2nd baron; succ. 1709; cr. Earl Gower 1746.

Grafton, Charles Fitzroy (1683–1757), 2nd duke of; succ. 1690.

Grahme, James (1650–1730), M.P. for Westmorland 1708–27.

Granard, George Forbes (1685–1765), 3rd earl of [I]; succ. 1734; M.P. for Ayr Burghs 1741–7.

Granby, John Manners (1721–70), styled marquess of; M.P. for Grantham 1741–54.

Granville, John Carteret (d. 1763), 2nd earl; succ. 1744; previously 2nd Baron Carteret since 1694; secretary of state 1721–4, 1742–4, 10–14 Feb. 1746; lord president 1751–63.

Grenville, George (1712–70), M.P. for Buckingham 1741–70; lord of the admiralty 1744–7.

Grenville, Richard (1711–79), M.P. for Buckingham 1734–41, 1747–52, Buckinghamshire 1741–7.

Guernsey, Heneage Finch, styled baron: *see* Aylesford, 2nd earl of.

Guernsey, Heneage Finch (1715–77), styled baron; M.P. for Maidstone 1741–7, 1754–7; succ. 3rd earl of Aylesford 1757.

Guilford, Francis North (1673–1729), 2nd baron; succ. 1685.

Gwyn, Francis (?1648–1734), M.P. for Christchurch 1717–22, Wells 1722–7.

Gybbon, Phillips (1678–1762), M.P. for Rye 1707–62; lord of the treasury 1742–4.

Halifax, George Montagu (1716–71), 2nd earl of; succ. 1739.

Hamilton, Lord Archibald (1673–1754), M.P. for Queenborough 1735–41, Dartmouth 1742–7; lord of the admiralty 1727–38, 1742–6; governor of Greenwich Hospital 1746–54.

Hamilton, Hon. George (*c.*1697–1775), M.P. for Wells 1734–5, 1747–54.

Hampden, Richard (aft. 1674–1728), M.P. for Wendover 1722–7, Buckinghamshire 1727–8; treasurer of the navy 1718–20.

Hanbury, Capel (1707–65), M.P. for Leominster 1741–7, Monmouthshire 1747–65.

Hanbury Williams, Charles (1708–59), M.P. for Monmouthshire 6 Mar. 1735–1747; ld. lt. Herefordshire 16 July 1741–1747.

Hanmer, Sir Thomas (1677–1746), 4th bt., M.P. for Suffolk 1708–27.

Harcourt, Simon (1661–1727), 1st baron; cr. 1711; cr. viscount 1721.

Harcourt, Simon (1714–77), 2nd viscount; succ. 1727; cr. earl 1749.

Hardwicke, Philip Yorke (1690–1764), 1st baron; cr. 1733; cr. earl 1754; M.P. for Seaford 1722–33; attorney-gen. 1724–33; lord chief justice 1733–7; lord chancellor 1737–56.

Hardy, Sir Charles (*c.*1680–1744), M.P. for Portsmouth 1743–44; lord of the admiralty 1743–4.

Harley, Edward (1664–1735), M.P. for Droitwich 1695–8, Leominster 1698–1700, 1701–22; joint auditor of the imprest for life 1702; brother of 1st, and father of 3rd earl of Oxford.

Harley, Edward, styled lord; *see* Oxford, 2nd earl of.

Harley, Edward; *see* Oxford, 3rd earl.

Harley, Edward (1726–90), styled lord, M.P. for Herefordshire 1747–55; succ. 4th earl of Oxford 1755; son of the above.

Harley, Robert (?1706–74), M.P. for Leominster 1734–41, 1742–7, Droitwich 1754–74; brother of 3rd earl of Oxford.

Harrington, William Stanhope (*c.*1683–1756), 1st earl; cr. 1742; cr. 1st baron 1730; secretary of state 1730–42, 1744–6.

Hartington, William Cavendish (*c.*1720–64), styled marquess of, M.P. for Derbyshire 1741–51; succ. 4th duke of Devonshire 1755.

Hatton, William (1690–1760), 2nd viscount; succ. 1706.

Hay, William (1695–1755), M.P. for Seaford 1734–55.

Heathcote, George (1700–68), M.P. for Hindon 1727–34, Southwark 1734–41, London 1741–7; alderman of London 1739–49; nephew of below.

Heathcote, Sir Gilbert (1652–1733), 1st bt., cr. 1733; M.P. for London 1701–10, Helston 1715–22, Lymington 1722–7, St Germans 1727–33; wealthy wine merchant.

Heathcote, Sir John (*c.*1689–1759), 2nd bt., M.P. for Bodmin 1733–41; son of above.

Heathcote, William (1693–1751), M.P. for Southampton 1729–41; nephew of Sir Gilbert.

Hedges, John (1688–1737), M.P. for Fowey 1734–7; treasurer to the prince of Wales 1729–37.

Henley, Anthony (?1704–48), M.P. for Southampton 1727–34.
Herbert, Henry Arthur; *see* Powis, 1st earl of.
Herbert of Chirbury, 1st baron; *see* Powis, 1st earl of.
Hereford, bishop of; *see*
  Bisse, Philip (1713–21)
Hereford, Price Devereux (1694–1748), 10th viscount; succ. 1740.
Herring, Thomas (1693–1757), archbishop of Canterbury 1747–57, previously bishop of Bangor and archbishop of York.
Hertford, Algernon Seymour (1684–1750), styled earl of; called to Lords in father's barony as Baron Percy 1722; succ. 7th duke of Somerset 1748.
Hervey, George William (1721–75), baron; succ. father (below) in barony 1743; succ. 2nd earl of Bristol 1751.
Hervey, John (1696–1743), baron; called to Lords in father's barony 1733; lord privy seal 1740–2.
Hillsborough, Wills Hill (1718–93), 2nd viscount [I], succ. May 1742; M.P. for Warwick 1741–56.
Hinchingbroke, Edward Richard Montagu (1692–1722), styled viscount, M.P. for Huntingdon 1713–22.
Hoadly, Benjamin (1676–1761), bishop of Bangor 1716–21, Hereford 1721–3, Salisbury 1723–34, Winchester 1734–61.
Hobart, Sir John (1693–1756), 5th bt., 1st baron; cr. 1728; cr. earl of Buckinghamshire 1746.
Hooper, Edward (?1701–95), M.P. for Christchurch 1734–48.
Hopton, Edward (1708–54), M.P. for Hereford 1741–7.
Howe, Emanuel Scrope (*c.*1699–1735), 2nd viscount [I], succ. 1713; M.P. for Nottinghamshire 1722–32.
Howe, John; *see* Chedworth, 1st baron.
Howarth, Sir Humphrey (*c.*1684–1755), M.P. for Radnorshire 1722–55.
Hucks, Robert (1699–1745), M.P. for Abingdon 1722–41.
Hume Campbell, Hon. Alexander (1708–60), M.P. for Berwickshire 1734–41, 1742–60; solicitor-gen. to prince of Wales 1741–6.
Hungerford, John (*c.*1658–1729), M.P. for Scarborough 1692–5, 1702–5, 1707–29.
Hutcheson, Archibald (*c.*1695–1740), M.P. for Hastings 1713–27.

Ilay, Archibald Campbell (1682–1761), earl of; cr. 1706; Scottish rep. peer 1707–13, 1715–61; succ. 3rd duke of Argyll 1743.
Ilchester, Stephen Fox (1704–76), 1st baron; cr. 11 May 1741; M.P. for Shaftesbury 1726–34, 1735–41, Hindon 1734–5; cr. earl of Ilchester 1756.
Irby, Sir William (1707–75), 2nd bt., M.P. for Launceston 24 Mar. 1735–1747, Bodmin 1747–61.

Jefferies, Edward (*c.*1670–1725), M.P. for Droitwich 1708–25.
Jekyll, Sir Joseph (*c.*1662–1738), M.P. for Lymington 1713–22, Reigate 1722–38; king's serjeant 1700; master of the rolls 1717–38.
Jenison, Ralph (1696–1758), M.P. for Northumberland 1724–41, Newport I.o.W. 1749–58.

Keene, Benjamin (*c.*1697–1757), M.P. for Maldon 1740–1, West Looe 1741–7; minister to Spain 1727–39; lord of trade 1741–4.
Kennett, White (1660–1728), bishop of Peterborough 1718–28.
King, John (1706–40), 2nd baron; succ. 1734; M.P. for Launceston 1727–34.
Kingston, Evelyn Pierrepont (*c.*1665–1726), 1st duke of; cr. 1715.

Laroche, John (*c.*1700–52), M.P. for Bodmin 1727–52.
Lawson, Sir Wilfred (1697–1737), 3rd bt., M.P. for Cockermouth 1722–37.
Lechmere, Nicholas (1675–1727), M.P. for Tewkesbury 1717–21; cr. baron 1721.
Lee, Dr George (?1700–58), M.P. for Brackley 1733–42, Devizes 1742–7, Liskeard 1747–54;

D.C.L. 1729; chairman committee of elections and privileges 1741–7.

Lewis, Thomas (1690–1777), M.P. for New Radnor Boroughs 1715–61.

Lichfield and Coventry, bishop of; *see*
 Chandler, Edward (1717–30)

Lichfield, George Henry Lee (1690–1743), 2nd earl of; succ. 1716.

Liddell, George (1678–1740), M.P. for Berwick-upon-Tweed 1727–40.

Liddell, Sir Henry; *see* Ravensworth, baron.

Limerick, James Hamilton (*c*.1691–1758), 1st viscount [I], cr. 1719; M.P. for Wendover 1727–34, 1735–41, Tavistock 1742–7, Morpeth 1747–54.

Lincoln, bishop of; *see*
 Gibson, Edmund (1715–23)

Lisle, Edward (1692–1753), M.P. for Marlborough 1727–34, Hampshire 1734–41.

Llandaff, bishop of; *see*
 Gilbert, John (1740–8)

London, bishop of; *see*
 Gibson, Edmund (1723–48)
 Robinson, John (1713–23)

Londonderry, Thomas Pitt (*c*.1688–1729), 1st earl of [I], cr. baron 1719, earl 1726; M.P. for Wilton 1713–27, Old Sarum 1727–8.

Lonsdale, Henry Lowther (1694–1751), 3rd viscount; succ. 1713.

Lovel, Thomas Coke (1697–1759), 1st baron; cr. 1728; cr. earl of Leicester 1744.

Lumley, Richard Lumley, baron; *see* Scarbrough, 2nd earl of.

Lyttelton, George (1709–73), M.P. for Okehampton 28 Mar. 1735–1756; secretary to the prince of Wales 1737–44.

Lyttelton, Sir Thomas (1686–1751), 4th bt., M.P. for Camelford 1734–41

Maddox, Isaac (1697–1759), bishop of Worcester 1743–59, previously bishop of St Asaph.

Manchester, Charles Montagu (*c*.1662–1722), 4th earl of; succ. 1683; cr. duke of Manchester 1719.

Mansel, Hon. Bussy (?1701–50), 4th baron; succ. 1744; M.P. for Cardiff Boroughs 1727–34, Glamorgan 1737–44; younger brother of Hon. Christopher Mansel.

Marlborough, Charles Spencer (1706–58), 3rd duke of; succ. 1733.

Marshall, Henry (1688–1754), M.P. for Amersham 1734–54.

Masham, Samuel (d. 1758), 1st baron; cr. 1712.

Maynard, Charles (*c*.1690–1766), 6th baron; succ. 1745.

Methuen, Paul (*c*.1672–1757), M.P. for Brackley 1713–14, 1715–47; treasurer of the household 1725–30.

Middlesex, Charles Sackville (1711–69), styled earl of, M.P. for East Grinstead 1734–42, 1761–5, Sussex 1742–7, Old Sarum 1747–54; succ. 2nd duke of Dorset 1765.

Milner, Sir William (*c*.1696–1745), 1st bt., M.P. for York 1722–34.

Molesworth, Robert (1656–1725), M.P. for Mitchell 1715–22.

Monson, John (?1692–1748), 1st baron; cr. 1728.

Montagu, John Montagu (1690–1749), 2nd duke of; succ. 1709.

Montjoy, Herbert Windsor (1707–58), 2nd baron; succ. 1738.

Montrose, James Graham (1682–1742), 1st duke of; cr. 1707; Scottish rep. peer 1707–10, 1715–34.

Moray, James Stuart (1708–67), 8th earl of; succ. 1739; Scottish rep. peer 1741–67.

Mordaunt, Sir Charles (?1697–1778), 6th bt., M.P. for Warwickshire 1734–74.

Mordaunt, John (1697–1780), M.P. for Whitchurch 1735–41, Cockermouth 1741–68; lt.-col. 1731.

More, Robert (1703–80), M.P. for Bishop's Castle 1727–41, Shrewsbury 1754–61.

Morgan, Sir John (1710–67), 4th bt., M.P. for Hereford 1734–41, Herefordshire 1755–67.

Morgan, Thomas (1702–69), M.P. for Breconshire 1747–69.

Morpeth, Henry Howard (?1693–1758), styled viscount, M.P. for Morpeth 1715–38; succ. 4th earl of Carlisle 1738.

Morton, James Douglas (*c*.1702–68), 14th earl of; succ. 1738; Scottish rep. peer 1739–68.
Murray, William (1705–93), M.P. for Boroughbridge 1742–56; cr. Baron Mansfield 1756; solicitor-gen. 1741–54.
Myddelton, John (1685–1747), M.P. for Denbigh Boroughs 1733–41, Denbighshire 1741–23 Feb. 1742.

Newcastle, Thomas Pelham-Holles (1693–1768), duke of; cr. 1715; secretary of state, southern department 1724–48, northern department 1748–54; 1st lord of the treasury 1754–6, 1757–62.
Newdigate, Sir Roger (1719–1806), 5th bt., M.P. for Middlesex 1742–7, Oxford University 31 Jan. 1751–1780.
Noel, Hon. James (1711–52), M.P. for Rutland 1734–52.
Noel, Thomas (*c*.1704–88), M.P. for Rutland 1728–41, 1753–88.
Noel, William (1695–1762), M.P. for Stamford 1722–47, West Looe 1747–57.
Norris, Sir John (*c*.1670–1749), M.P. for Portsmouth 1722–34, Rye 1734–49.
North and Grey, William North (1678–1734), 6th baron; succ. 1691.
Northampton, James Compton (1687–1754), 5th earl of; succ. 1727.
Nottingham, Daniel Finch (1647–1730), 2nd earl of; succ. 1682.

Oglethorpe, James Edward (1696–1785), M.P. for Haslemere 1722–54.
Onslow, Arthur (1691–1768), M.P. for Surrey 1727–61; Speaker 1728–61.
Onslow, Richard (*c*.1697–1760), brother of the above; M.P. for Guildford 1727–60; brig.-gen. 1742.
Ord, Robert (1700–78), M.P. for Mitchell 1734–41, Morpeth 1741–55.
Orford, Sir Robert Walpole (1676–1745), 1st earl of; cr. 1742; M.P. for King's Lynn 1702–12, 1713–42; 1st lord of the treasury 1715–17, 1721–42.
Orrery, Charles Boyle (1674–1731), 4th earl of [I]; succ 1703; cr. Baron Boyle of Marston [G.B.] 1711.
Osbaldeston, William (1688–1766), M.P. for Scarborough 21 Apr. 1736–1747, 1754–66.
Owen, John (?1698–1775), M.P. for West Looe 1735–41.
Owen, William (?1697–1781), M.P. for Pembroke Boroughs 1722–47, 1761–74, Pembrokeshire 1747–61.
Oxenden, Sir George (1694–1775), 5th bt., M.P. for Sandwich 1720–54.
Oxford, bishop of; *see*
    Potter, John (1715–37)
    Secker, Thomas (1737–58)
    Talbot, William (1699–1715)
Oxford, Edward Harley (1689–1741), 2nd earl of; succ. 1724; M.P. for New Radnor 1711–15, Cambridgeshire 1722–4.
Oxford, Edward Harley (1699–1755), 3rd earl of; succ. 1741; M.P. for Herefordshire 1727–16 June 1741.
Oxford, Robert Harley (1661–1724), 1st earl of; cr. 1711; uncle of the above.

Page, John (?1696–1779), of Chichester, M.P. for Great Grimsby 1727–34, Chichester 1741–68; he stood unsuccessfully for Chichester in 1734.
Palmer, Thomas (?1685–1735), M.P. for Bridgwater 1715–27, 1731–5.
Palmerston, Henry Temple (*c*.1673–1757), 1st viscount [I]; cr. 1723; M.P. for Weobley 1741–7.
Parker, Thomas (1667–1732), 1st baron; cr. 1716; lord chief justice 1710–18, lord chancellor 1718–25; cr. earl of Macclesfield 1721.
Parsons, Humphrey (*c*.1676–1741), M.P. for London 1727–41.
Pelham, Hon. Henry (1695–1754), of Esher Place, Surr.; brother of the duke of Newcastle; M.P. for Sussex 1722–54; paymaster-gen. 1730–43; 1st lord of the treasury and chancellor of the exchequer 1743–54.
Pelham, James (*c*.1683–1761), of Crowhurst, Suss.; M.P. for Newark 1722–41, Hastings 1741–61; lt.-col. 1st foot guards 1716; secretary to the prince of Wales 1728–37.

Pelham, Thomas (?1678–c.1760), of Lewes, Suss.; M.P. for Lewes 1705–41; father-in-law to William Hay.

Pelham, Thomas (c.1705–37), of Stanmer, Suss.; M.P. for Lewes 1727–37.

Pelham, Thomas (c.1705–43), jr., M.P. for Hastings 1728–41, Lewes 1741–3; brother-in-law to William Hay.

Pembroke, Henry Herbert (c.1689–1750), 9th earl of; succ. 1733.

Perry, Micajah (d. 1753), M.P. for London 1727–41.

Peterborough, bishop of; *see*
Kennett, White (1718–28)

Peterborough, Charles Mordaunt (c.1658–1735), 3rd earl of; succ. 1697.

Philipps, John (1700–64), M.P. for Carmarthen 1741–7.

Phillipson, John (1698–1756), M.P. for New Shoreham 1734–41, Harwich 1741–56; lord of the admiralty 1743–4.

Piers, William (1686–1755), M.P. for Wells 1716–22, 1729–34, 1735–41.

Pitt, John (?1706–87), M.P. for Wareham 1734–47, 1748–50, Dorchester 1751–61.

Pitt, Robert (?1680–1727), M.P. for Old Sarum 1713–22, Okehampton 1722–7; eldest son of Thomas (below).

Pitt, Thomas (1653–1726), M.P. for Old Sarum 1722–6; governor of the Fort of St George, Madras 1697–1709; father of above, M.P. for Okehampton 1722–7.

Pitt, Thomas (c.1705–61), M.P. for Okehampton 1727–54.

Pitt, William (1708–78), M.P. for Old Sarum 18 Feb. 1735–1747, Seaford 1747–54.

Plumer, Walter (?1682–1746), M.P. for Appleby 1730–41.

Plumptre, John (1679–1751), M.P. for Nottingham 1734–47, St Ives 1747–51.

Pollen, John, (?1702–75), M.P. for Andover 1734–54.

Polwarth, Hugh Hume Campbell (1708–94), styled lord, M.P. for Berwick 1734–40; succ. 3rd earl of Marchmont 1740.

Portland, William Bentinck (1709–62), 2nd duke of; succ. 1726.

Potter, John (?1674–1747), bishop of Oxford 1715–37, archbishop of Canterbury 1737–47.

Poulett, John (c.1668–1743), 1st earl; cr. 1706

Powell, Mansel (c.1696–1775), M.P. for Weobley 1747.

Powis, Henry Arthur Herbert (c.1703–72), 1st earl of; cr. 1748; cr. Baron Herbert of Chirbury 21 Dec. 1743; M.P. for Ludlow 1727–43; treasurer of the prince of Wales 1737–8.

Proby, John (c.1698–1762), M.P. for Stamford 1734–47.

Prowse, Thomas (c.1707–67), M.P. for Somerset 1740–67.

Pulteney, William; *see* Bath, earl of.

Pytts, Edmund (?1696–1753), M.P. for Worcestershire 1741–53.

Quarendon, George Henry Lee (1718–72), styled viscount, M.P. for Oxfordshire 1740–3; succ. 3rd earl of Lichfield 1743.

Ramsden, Sir John (1699–1769), 3rd bt., M.P. for Appleby 1727–54.

Ravensworth, Sir Henry Liddell (1708–84), 4th bt., 1st baron; cr. 1747; M.P. for Morpeth 1734–47.

Raymond, Sir Robert (1673–1733); M.P. for Ludlow 1719–22, Helston 1722–4; attorney-gen. 1720–4; lord chief justice 1725–33; cr. Baron Raymond 1731.

Robinson, John (1650–1723), bishop of London 1713–23, previously bishop of Bristol.

Rochester, bishop of; *see*
Atterbury, Francis (1713–23)

Romney, Robert Marsham (1712–93), 2nd baron; succ. 1724.

Ross, Charles (d. 1732), M.P. for Ross-shire 1709–22, 1727–32; gen. 1712.

Roxburghe, John Ker (c.1680–1741), 1st duke of; cr. 1707; Scottish rep. peer 1707–10, 1715–27.

Rushout, Sir John (1685–1775), 4th bt., M.P. for Evesham 1722–68; lord of the treasury 1742–3.

Rutland, John Manners (1696–1779), 3rd duke of; succ. 1721.

Ryder, Sir Dudley (1691–1756), M.P. for St Germans 1733–4, Tiverton 1734–54; solicitor-gen. 1733–7; attorney-gen. 1737–54.

Sackville, Lord George (1716–85), 3rd son of 1st duke of Dorset; M.P. for Dover 1741–61.
St Asaph, bishop of; *see*
    Wynne, John (1715–27)
St Aubyn, Sir John (?1702–44), 3rd bt., M.P. for Cornwall 1722–44.
St John of Bletso, John (d. 1757), 11th baron; succ. 1722.
Salisbury, bishop of; *see*
    Sherlock, Thomas (1734–48)
    Talbot, William (1715–21)
Sandwich, John Montagu (1718–92), 4th earl of; succ. 1729.
Sandys, Samuel (1695–1770), M.P. for Worcester 1718–43; cr. Baron Sandys 20 Dec. 1743; chancellor of the exchequer 1742–3.
Saunderson, Hon. Sir Thomas (c.1691–1752) (formerly called Lumley), M.P. for Lincolnshire 1727–40; succ. 3rd earl of Scarbrough 1740.
Say and Sele, Richard Fiennes (1716–81), 6th viscount; succ. 1742.
Scarbrough, Richard Lumley (c.1688–1740), 2nd earl of; succ. 1721.
Scrope, John (c.1662–1752), M.P. for Bristol 1727–34, Lyme Regis 1734–52; secretary to the treasury 1724–52.
Secker, Thomas (1693–1768), bishop of Oxford 1737–58, archbishop of Canterbury 1758–68, previously bishop of Bristol.
Selwyn, John (1688–1751), M.P. for Gloucester 1734–51.
Selwyn, John (c.1709–51), M.P. for Whitchurch 1734–51.
Seymour, Francis (1697–1761), M.P. for Great Bedwyn 1732–4, Marlborough 1734–41.
Shaftesbury, Anthony Ashley Cooper (1701–71), 4th earl of; succ. 1713.
Sherlock, Thomas (1678–1761), bishop of Bangor 1728–34, Salisbury 1734–48, London 1748–61.
Shippen, William (1673–1743), M.P. for Newton 1715–43.
Smalridge, George (1663–1719), bishop of Bristol 1714–19.
Smith, John (?1655–1723), M.P. for Andover 1695–1713, East Looe 1715–23; Speaker 1705–8.
Snell, John (1682–1726), M.P. for Gloucester 1713–26.
Somerset, Charles Seymour (1662–1748), 6th duke of; succ. 1678.
Somerset, Lord Charles Noel; *see* Beaufort, 4th duke of.
Speke, George (d. 1753), M.P. for Milborne Port 1722–7, Taunton 1727–34, Wells 1735–47.
Stair, John Dalrymple (1673–1747), 2nd earl of; succ. 1707; Scottish rep. peer 1707–8, 1715–34, 1744–7; ambassador extraordinary to France 1715–20; ambassador extraordinary to the Hague 1742–3; field marshal 1742.
Stanhope, Charles (1673–1760), M.P. for Milborne Port 1717–22, Aldborough 1722–34, Harwich 1734–41; secretary to the treasury 1717–21; brother to 1st earl of Harrington.
Stanhope, James (1673–1721), 1st viscount, cr. 1717; cr. earl 1718; secretary of state, southern department 1714–16, northern department 1716–17, 1718–21; 1st lord of the treasury and chancellor of the exchequer 1717–18.
Stanhope, Philip (1714–86), 2nd earl; succ. 1721.
Staplyton, Sir Miles (?1708–52), 4th bt., M.P. for Yorkshire 1734–50.
Stawell, William (c.1683–1742), 3rd baron; succ. 1692.
Steele, Sir Richard (1672–1729), M.P. for Stockbridge 1713–14, Boroughbridge 1715–22, Wendover 1722–7.
Stert, Arthur (d. 1755), M.P. for Plymouth 1727–54.
Strafford, Thomas Wentworth (1672–1739), 1st earl of; cr. 1711.
Strange, James Stanley (1717–71), styled lord; M.P. for Lancashire 1741–71.
Strange, John (c.1696–1754), M.P. for West Looe 1737–41, Totnes 1742–54; K.C. 1736; solicitor-gen. 1737–42.
Strangways, Thomas (?1683–1726), M.P. for Bridport 1705–13, Dorset 1713–26.

Suffolk, Henry Howard (1707–45), 10th earl of; succ. 1733.

Sunderland, Charles Spencer (1674–1722), 3rd earl of; succ. 1702; secretary of state 1717–18; 1st lord of the treasury 1718–21; groom of the stole 1719–22.

Sundon, William Clayton (1671–1752), 1st baron [I], cr. 1735; M.P. for Westminster 1727–22 Dec. 1741, Plympton 3 May 1742–1747, St Mawes 1747–52.

Sutherland, William Sutherland (1708–50), 17th earl of; succ. 1733; Scottish rep. peer 1734–47.

Talbot, Charles (1685–1737), 1st baron, cr. 1733; M.P. for Durham 1722–33; solicitor-gen. 1726–33; lord chancellor 1733–7.

Talbot, Hon. John (c.1712–56), M.P. for Brecon 1734–54.

Talbot, William (?1659–1730), bishop of Oxford 1699–1715, Salisbury 1715–21, Durham 1721–30.

Talbot, Hon. William (1710–82), M.P. for Glamorgan 1734–7; eldest son of 1st Baron Talbot; succ. 2nd baron 1737.

Thanet, Sackville Tufton (1688–1753), 7th earl of; succ. 1729.

Thomas, Sir Edmund (1712–67), 3rd bt., M.P. for Chippenham 1741–54.

Thompson, Edward (1696–1742), M.P. for York 1722–42; commissioner of Irish revenue 1725–42.

Torrington, Pattee Byng (1699–1747), 2nd viscount; succ. 1733.

Townshend, Charles (1675–1738), 2nd viscount; succ. 1687; secretary of state 1714–16, 1721–30; lord president 1720–1.

Tracy, Robert (?1706–67), M.P. for Tewkesbury 1734–41, Worcester 1748–54.

Trefusis, Robert (1708–42), M.P. for Truro 1734–41.

Trelawney, Charles (?1706–1764), M.P. for Liskeard 25 Mar. 1740–1754.

Trelawney, Sir Jonathan (1650–1721), 3rd bt., bishop of Winchester 1707–21, previously bishop of Exeter.

Trentham, Granville Leveson Gower (1721–1803), styled viscount, M.P. for Bishop's Castle 1744–7, Westminster 1747–54; lord of the admiralty 1749–51; succ. 2nd Earl Gower 1754.

Trevor, John (?1717–43), of Glynde, Suss., M.P. for Lewes 1738–43.

Trevor, Thomas (1658–1730), 1st baron; cr. 1712.

Turner, Cholmley (1685–1757), M.P. for Yorkshire 1727–41, 1742–7.

Tweeddale, John Hay (c.1695–1762), 4th marquess of; succ. 1715; Scottish rep. peer 1722–34, 1742–62.

Tyrconnel, Sir John Brownlow (1690–1754), 1st viscount [I]; cr. 1718; M.P. for Grantham 1722–41.

Vane, Hon. Henry (c.1705–58), M.P. for St. Mawes 1727–41, Ripon 1741–7, Durham Co. 1747–53.

Vere, Thomas (c.1681–1766), M.P. for Norwich 1735–47.

Vernon, Edward (1684–1757), M.P. for Penryn 1722–34, Portsmouth 21 Feb.–27 Apr. 1741, Ipswich 1741–57; vice-admiral 1739.

Vernon, Thomas (bef. 1683–1726), M.P. for Whitchurch 1710–8 May 1721, 1722–6.

Vyner, Robert (c.1685–1777), M.P. for Lincolnshire 1724–61.

Wade, George (1673–1748), M.P. for Bath 1722–48; lt.-gen. 1727, gen. of horse 1734, lt.-gen. of ordnance 1742, field marshal 1743.

Wager, Sir Charles (c.1666–1743), M.P. for Portsmouth 1715–34, Westminster 1734–41, West Looe 1741–3.

Wake, William (1657–1737), archbishop of Canterbury 1715–37, previously bishop of Lincoln.

Wales, Frederick (1707–51), prince of; cr. 1729.

Walker, Thomas (c.1664–1748), M.P. for Plympton Erle 1735–41, Helston 1741–7.

Waller, Edmund (c.1699–1771), M.P. for Great Marlow 1722–41, Chipping Wycombe 1741–54.

Wallop, John (1690–1762), M.P. for Hampshire 1715–20; cr. Viscount Lymington 1730, earl of Portsmouth 1743.

Walpole, Hon. Edward (1706–84), M.P. for Great Yarmouth 1734–68.

Walpole, Horatio (1678–1757), brother to prime minister Sir Robert Walpole; M.P. for Great Yarmouth 1722–34, Norwich 1734–56; ambassador to the Hague 1733–40.

Walpole, Hon. Horatio (1717–97), M.P. for Callington 1741–54.

Walpole, Robert (c.1701–51), 1st baron; cr. 1723; eldest son of Sir Robert (below); succ. as 2nd earl of Orford 1745.

Walpole, Sir Robert; see Orford, 1st earl of.

Ward, John (1704–74), 6th baron; succ. 1740; M.P. for Newcastle-under-Lyme 1727–34.

Warwick, Edmund Rich (1695–1759), 8th earl of; succ. 1721.

Watts, Thomas (d. 1742), M.P. for Mitchell 1734–41, Tregony 1741–2.

Wentworth, Edward Noel (1715–74), 9th baron; succ. 1745.

West, James (1703–72), M.P. for St Albans 1741–68.

Westmorland, John Fane (1686–1762), 7th earl of; succ. 1736; M.P. for Buckingham 1727–34; cr. Baron Catherlough [I] Oct. 1733.

Weymouth, Thomas Thynne (1710–51), 2nd viscount; succ. 1714.

Wharton, Philip Wharton (1699–1731), duke of; cr. 1718.

White, John (1699–1769), M.P. for East Retford 1733–68.

Whitmore, Thomas (1711–73), M.P. for Bridgnorth 1734–54.

Whitworth, Francis (1684–1742), M.P. for Minehead 1723–42.

Willes, John (1685–1761), M.P. for West Looe 1727–37; attorney-gen. 1736–7; lord chief justice common of pleas 1737–61.

Williams, Charles Hanbury; see Hanbury Williams, Charles

Williams, Sir Nicholas (1681–1745), 1st bt.; M.P. for Carmarthenshire 1724–45.

Williams (afterwards Williams Wynn), Sir Watkin (?1693–1749), 3rd bt., M.P. for Denbigh-shire 1716– 41, 1742–9, Montgomeryshire 1741–2.

Willimot, Robert (d. 1746), M.P. for London 1734–41.

Willis, Richard (1664–1734), bishop of Gloucester 1715–21, Salisbury 1721–3, Winchester 1723–34.

Willoughby de Broke, Richard Verney (1693–1752), 13th baron; succ. 1728.

Wills, Charles (1666–1741), M.P. for Totnes 1718–41; lt.-gen. 1715.

Wilmington, Spencer Compton (1674–1743), 1st earl of; cr. 1730; cr. baron 1728; M.P. for Sussex 1715–28; Speaker 1715–27.

Winchester, bishop of; see
    Trelawney, Sir Jonathan (1707–21)

Winchilsea, Daniel Finch (1689–1769), 8th earl of, 3rd earl of Nottingham; succ. 1730.

Winford, Thomas Geers (c.1697–1753), M.P. for Hereford 1727–34, 1741–7, Worcester 1747–8.

Winnington, Thomas (1696–1746), M.P. for Droitwich 1726–41, Worcester 1741–6.

Wodehouse, William (?1706–37), M.P. for Norfolk 1734–13 Mar. 1737.

Worcester, bishop of; see
    Maddox, Isaac (1743–59)

Worsley, Sir Robert (?1669–1747), 4th bt., M.P. for Newton I.o.W. 1715–22.

Wyndham, Sir William (?1668–1740), 3rd bt., M.P. for Somerset 1710–40.

Wynn, Sir Watkin Williams; see Williams, Sir Watkin.

Wynne, John (1667–1743), bishop of St Asaph 1715–27, Bath and Wells 1727–43.

Yonge, Sir William (c.1693–1755), 4th bt., M.P. for Honiton 1715–54, Tiverton 1754–5; secretary at war 1735–46.

York, archbishop of; see
    Dawes, Sir William (1714–24)

Yorke, Philip (1720–90), 1st son of Lord Chancellor Hardwicke; M.P. for Reigate 1741–7.

Younge, Hitch (?1688–1759), M.P. for Steyning 1740–59.

INDEX

In this index the first number cited is the page number; this may be followed by l., which means letter, and n., which means note. Thus, for example, 16, 286 l. 4 n. 2 means that there is a reference on page 16, and in note 2 to letter 4 on page 286.